Date: 9/30/21

GRA 741.5 CAR V.1
Cardcaptor Sakura.

PALM BEACH COUNTY
LIBRARY SYSTEM
3650 SUMMIT BLVD.
WEST PALM BEACH, FL 33406

Cardcaptor Sakura Collector's Edition volume 1 is a work of fiction. Names, characters, places, and incidents are the products of the author's imagination or are used fictitiously. Any resemblance to actual events, locales, or persons, living or dead, is entirely coincidental.

A Kodansha Comics Trade Paperback Original.

Cardcaptor Sakura Collector's Edition volume 1 copyright © 2015 CLAMP · Shigatsu Tsuitachi Co., Ltd. / Kodansha Ltd.
English translation copyright © 2019 CLAMP · Shigatsu Tsuitachi Co., Ltd. / Kodansha Ltd.

All rights reserved.

Published in the United States by Kodansha Comics, an imprint of Kodansha USA Publishing, LLC, New York.

Publication rights for this English edition arranged through Kodansha Ltd., Tokyo.

First published in Japan in 2015 by Kodansha Ltd., Tokyo, as *Nakayoshi 60 Shuunen Kinenban Kaadokyaputaa Sakura* volume 1.

ISBN 978-1-63236-751-8

Printed in China.

www.kodanshacomics.com

9 8 7 6 5 4 3 2 1

Translation: Mika Onishi and Anita Sengupta
Additional Translation: Karen McGillicuddy
Lettering: Aaron Alexovich
Editing: Paul Starr
Kodansha Comics edition cover design: Phil Balsman

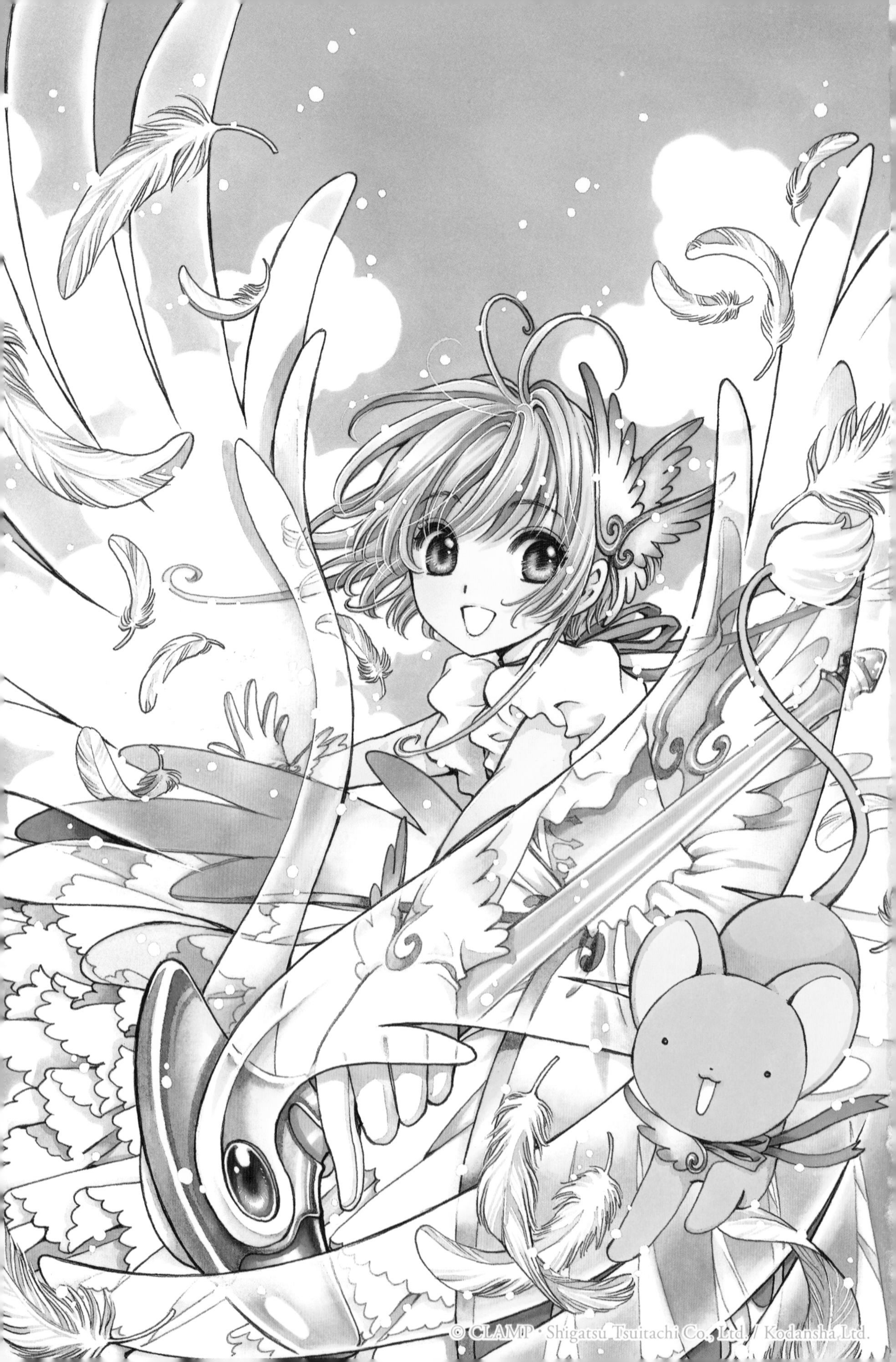

Collector's Edition

CARDCAPTOR SAKURA

Staff
Satsuki Igarashi
Nanase Ohkawa
Tsubaki Nekoi
Mokona

Planning
and presented by

CLAMP

HEREIN LIE THE CLOW CARDS...

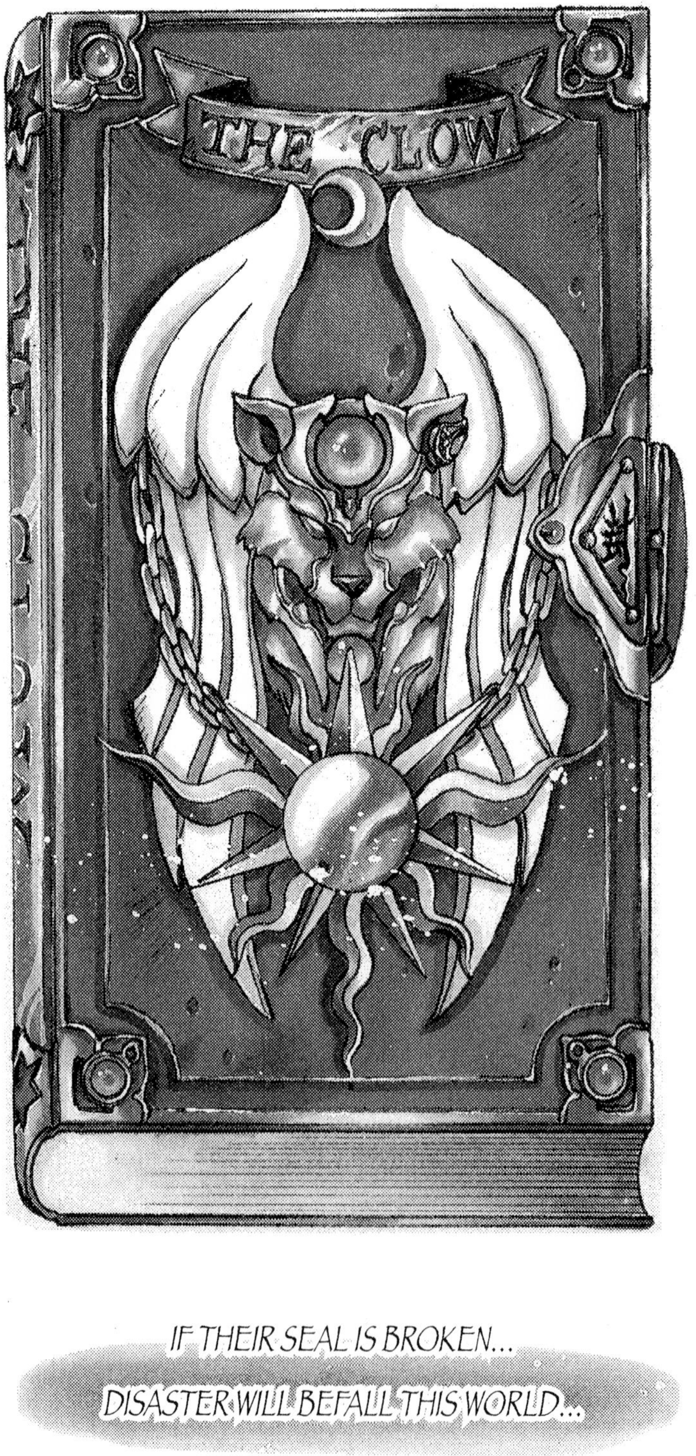
THE CLOW

IF THEIR SEAL IS BROKEN...

DISASTER WILL BEFALL THIS WORLD...

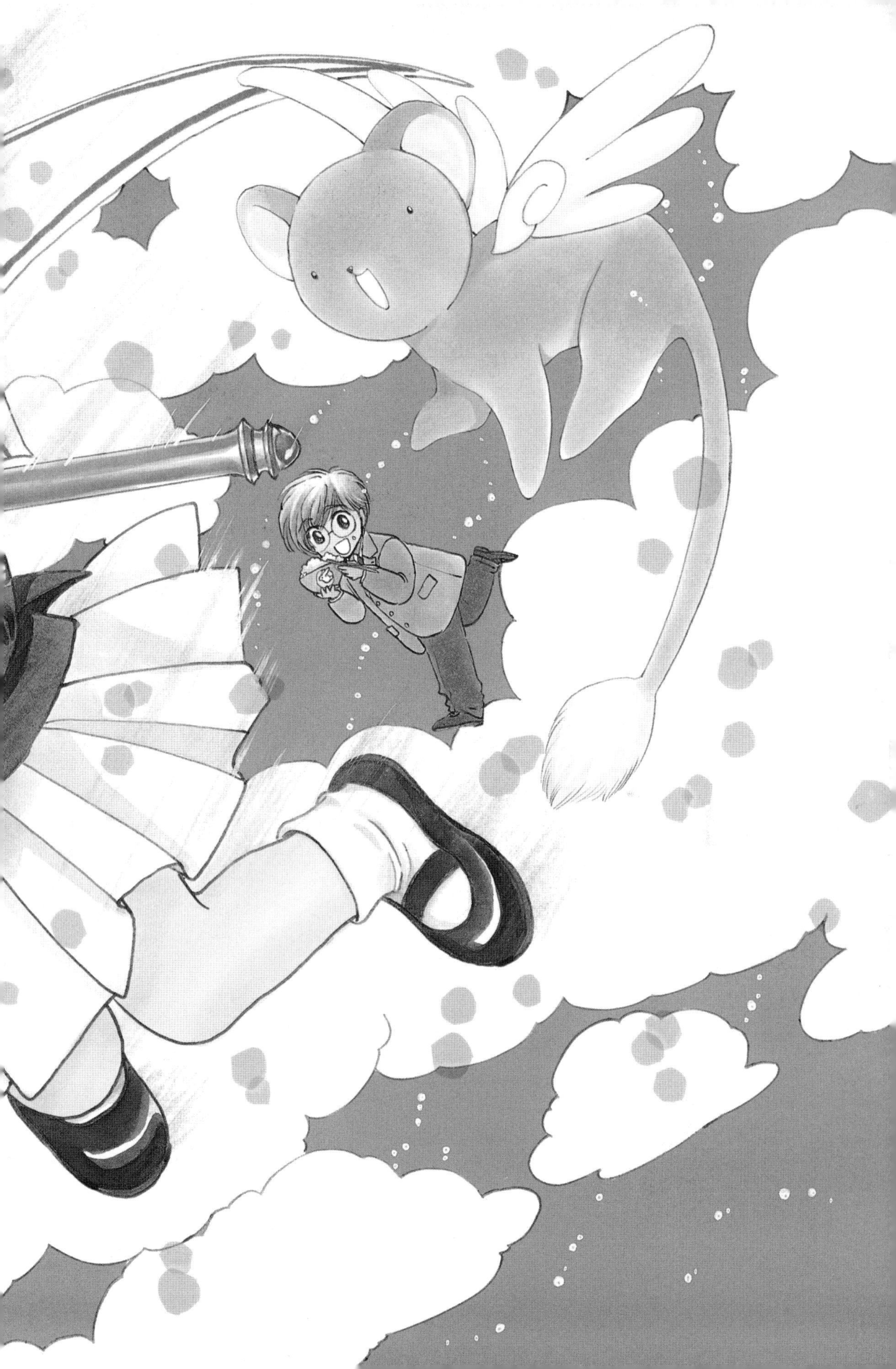

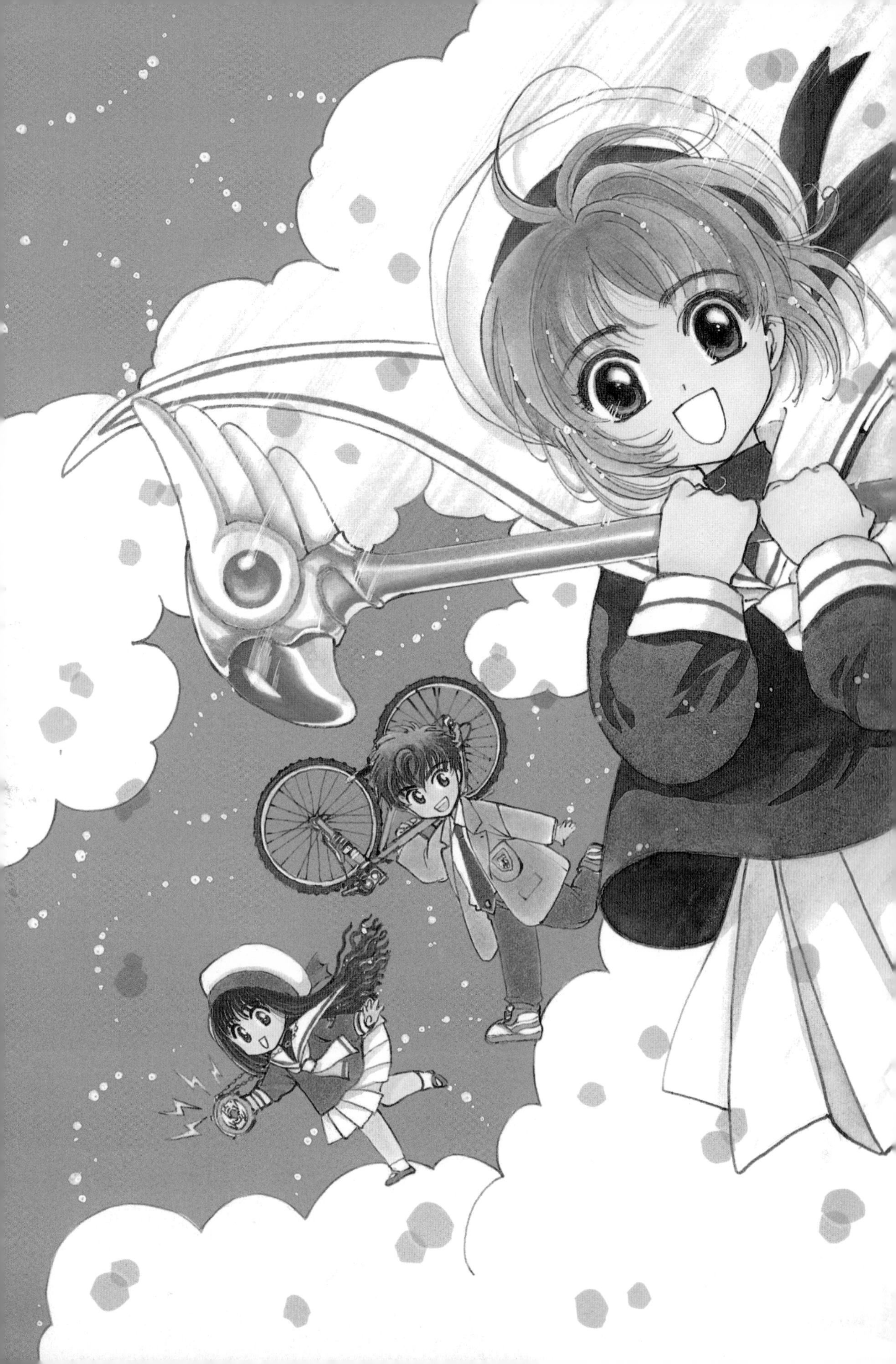

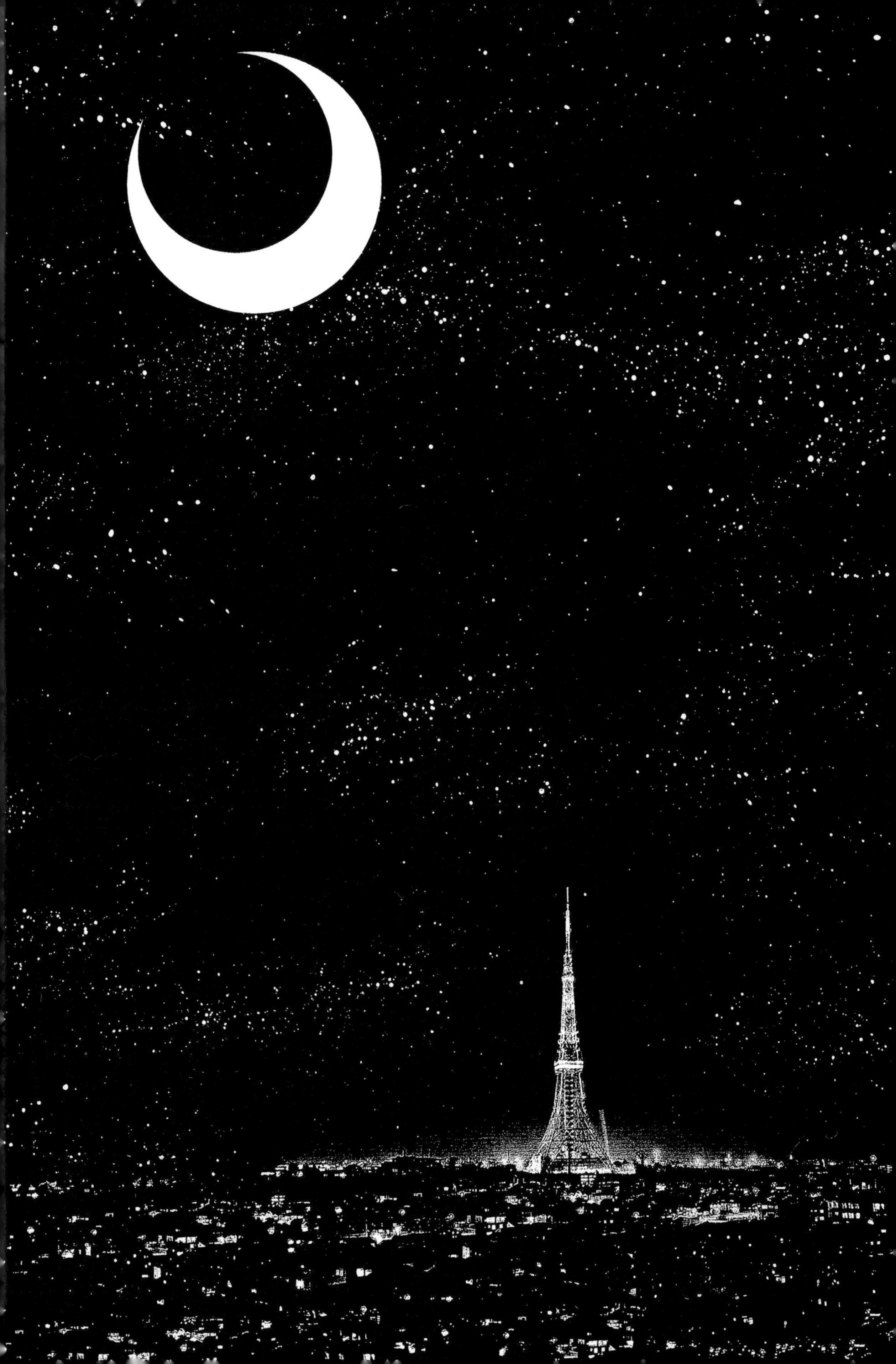

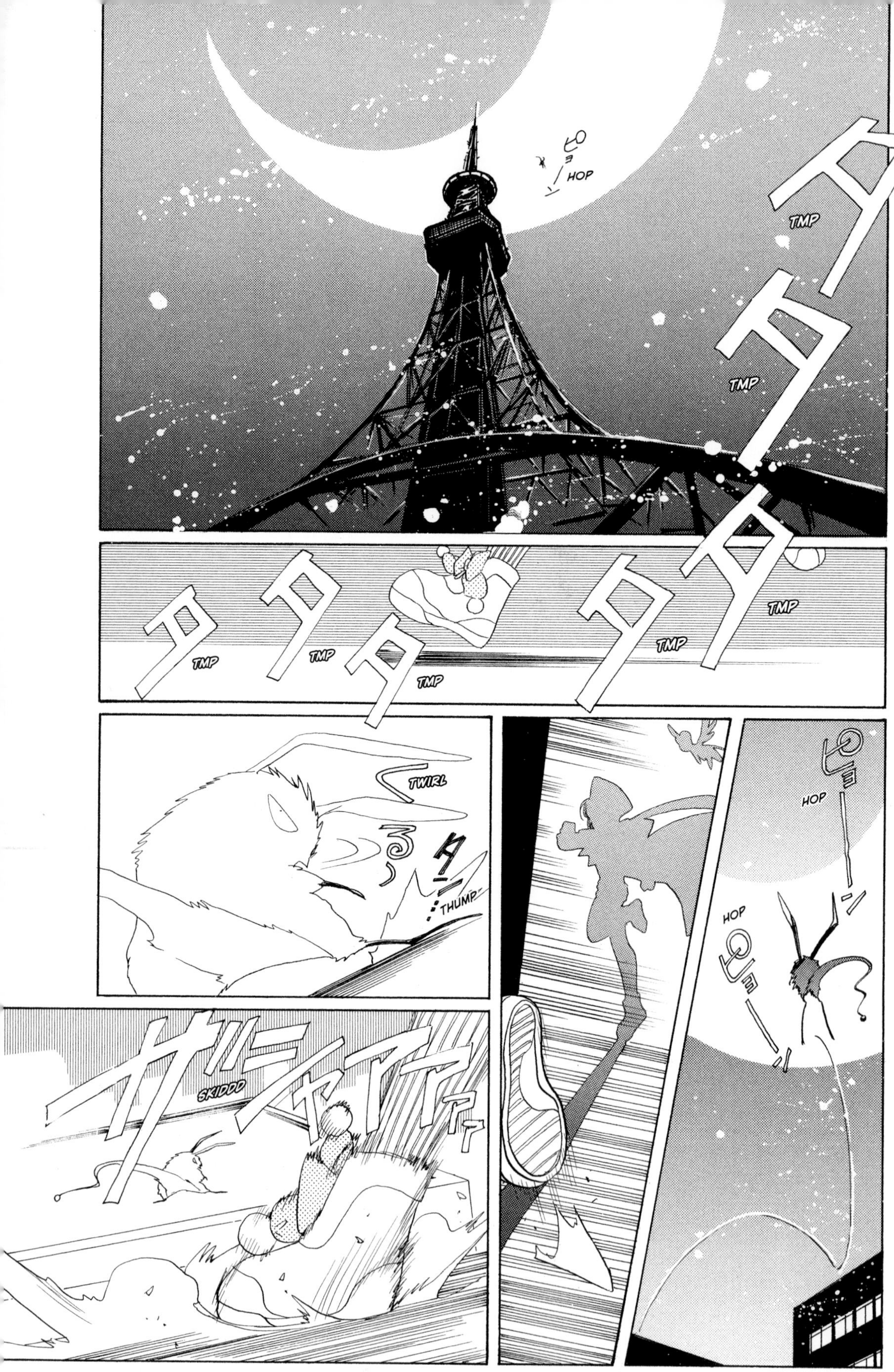

HOP
TMP
TMP
TMP
TMP
TMP
TMP
TMP
HOP
HOP
TWIRL
THUMP
SKIDDD

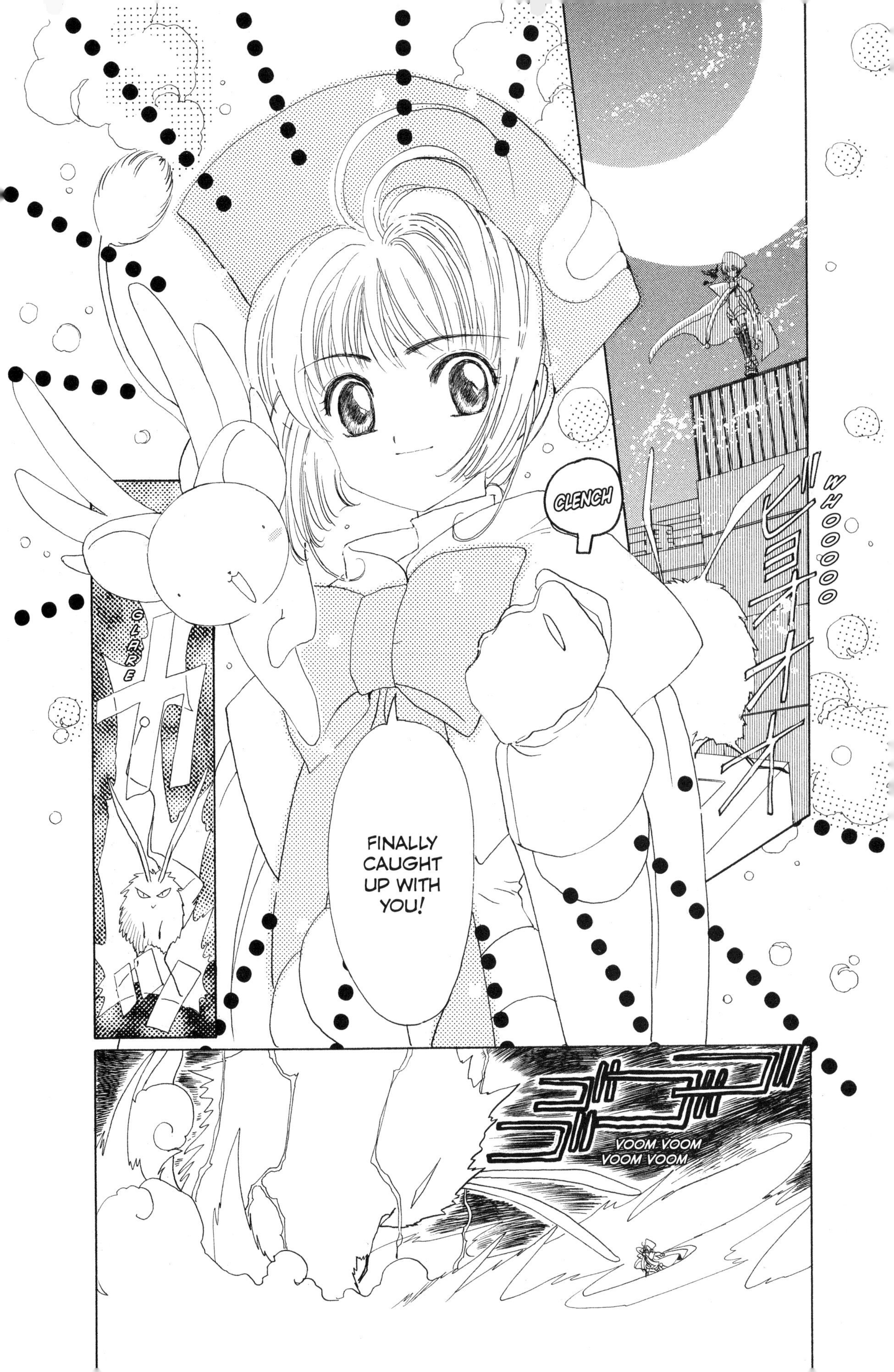
WHOOOOOO
CLENCH
FINALLY CAUGHT UP WITH YOU!
GLARE
VOOM VOOM VOOM VOOM

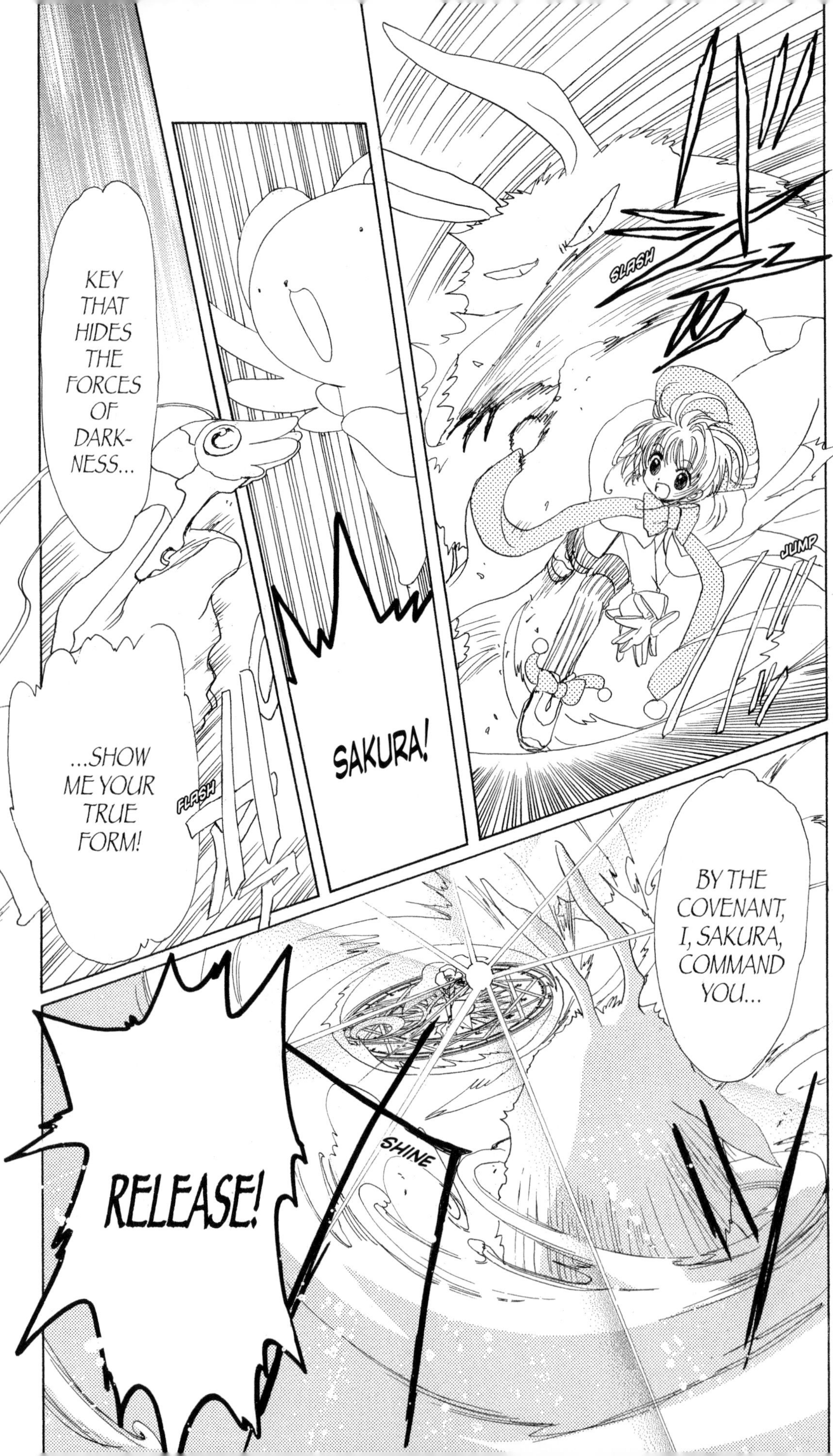
SLASH
JUMP
SAKURA!
KEY THAT HIDES THE FORCES OF DARKNESS...
...SHOW ME YOUR TRUE FORM!
FLASH
BY THE COVENANT, I, SAKURA, COMMAND YOU...
SHINE
RELEASE!

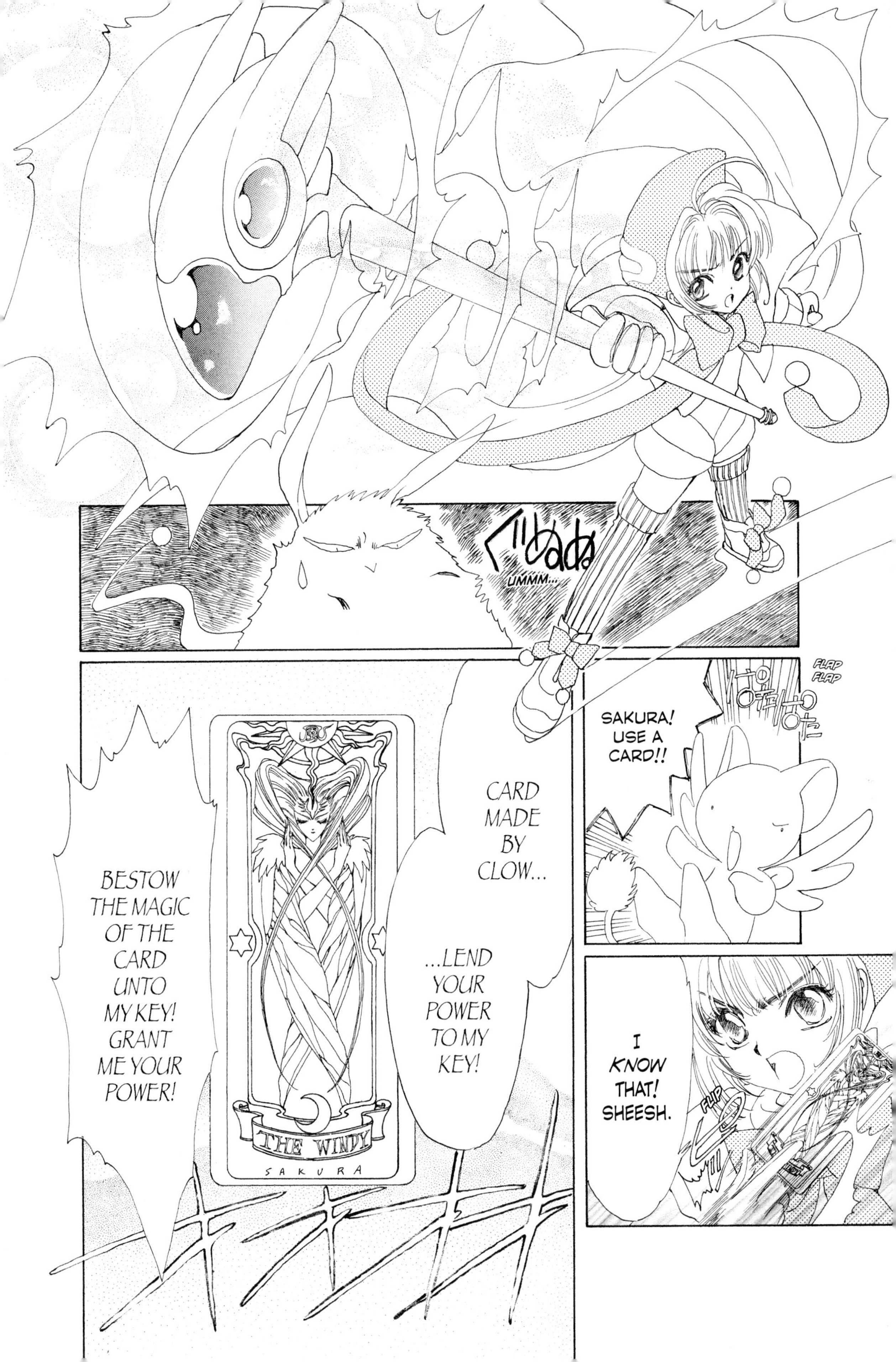
UMMM...
FLAP FLAP
SAKURA! USE A CARD!!
FLIP
I KNOW THAT! SHEESH.
CARD MADE BY CLOW...
...LEND YOUR POWER TO MY KEY!
THE WINDY
SAKURA
BESTOW THE MAGIC OF THE CARD UNTO MY KEY! GRANT ME YOUR POWER!

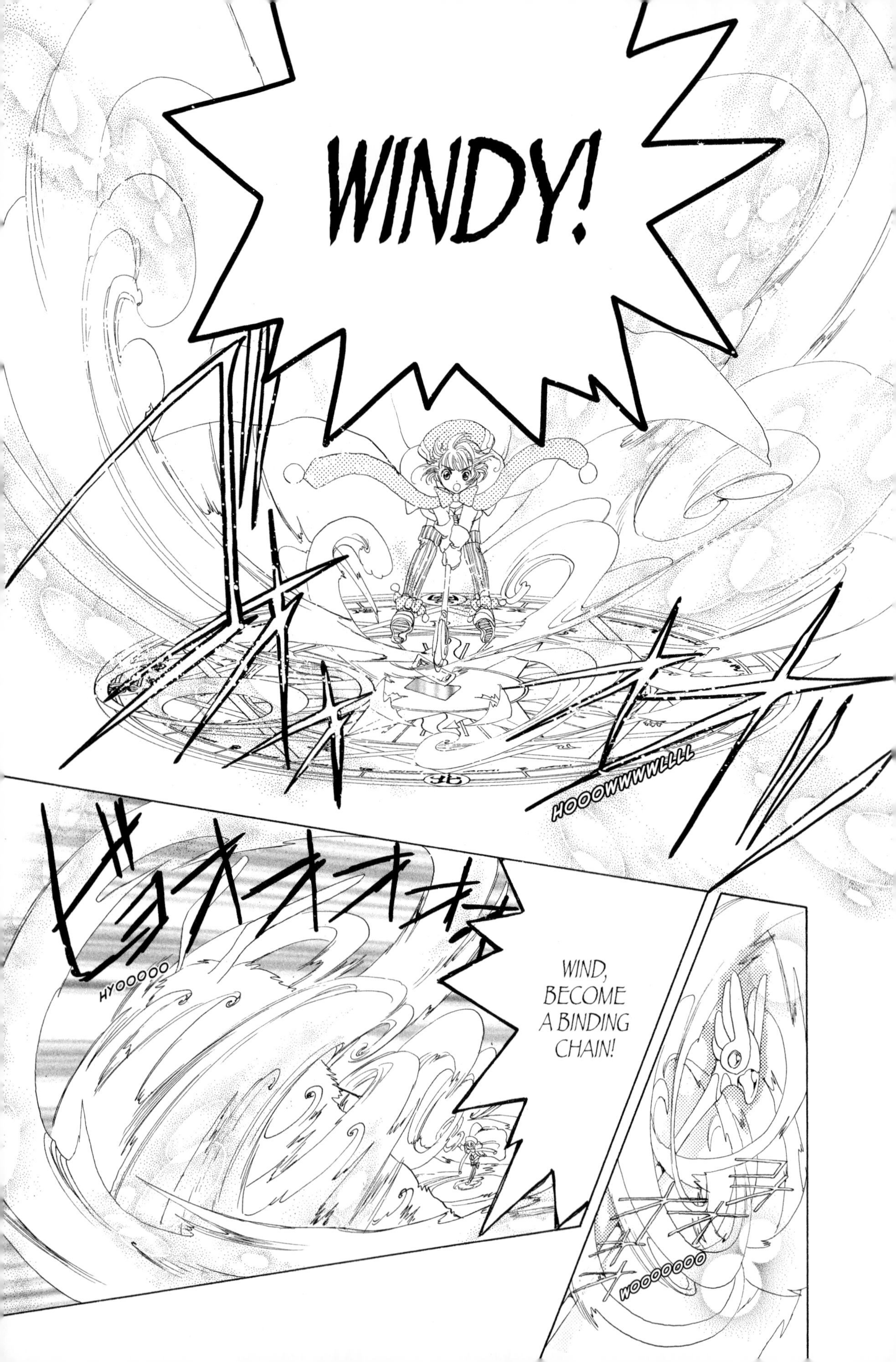
WINDY!
HOOOWWWWLLLL
WOOOOOOO
WIND, BECOME A BINDING CHAIN!
HYOOOOO

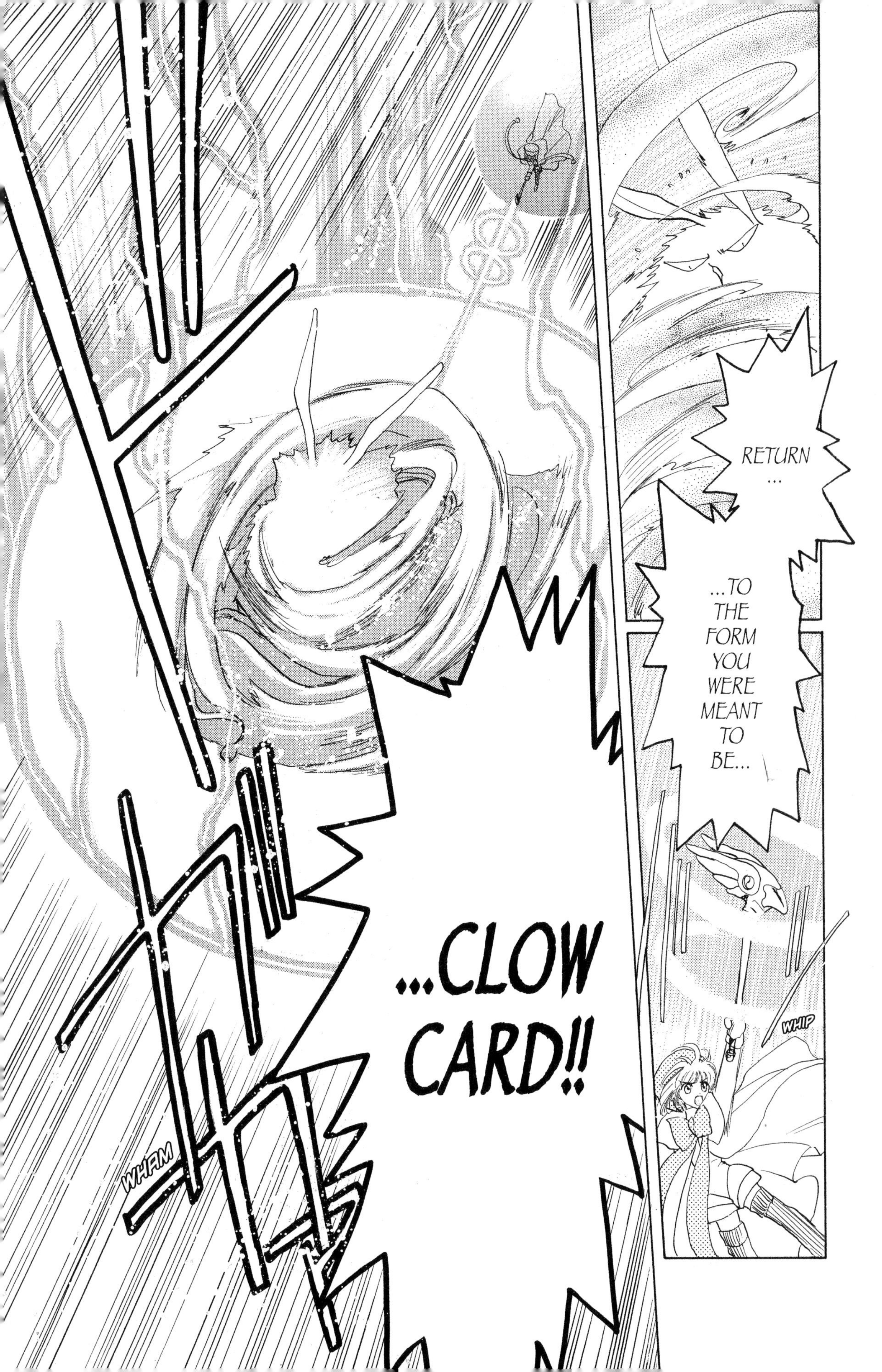
RETURN ...
...TO THE FORM YOU WERE MEANT TO BE...
WHIP
...CLOW CARD!!
WHAM

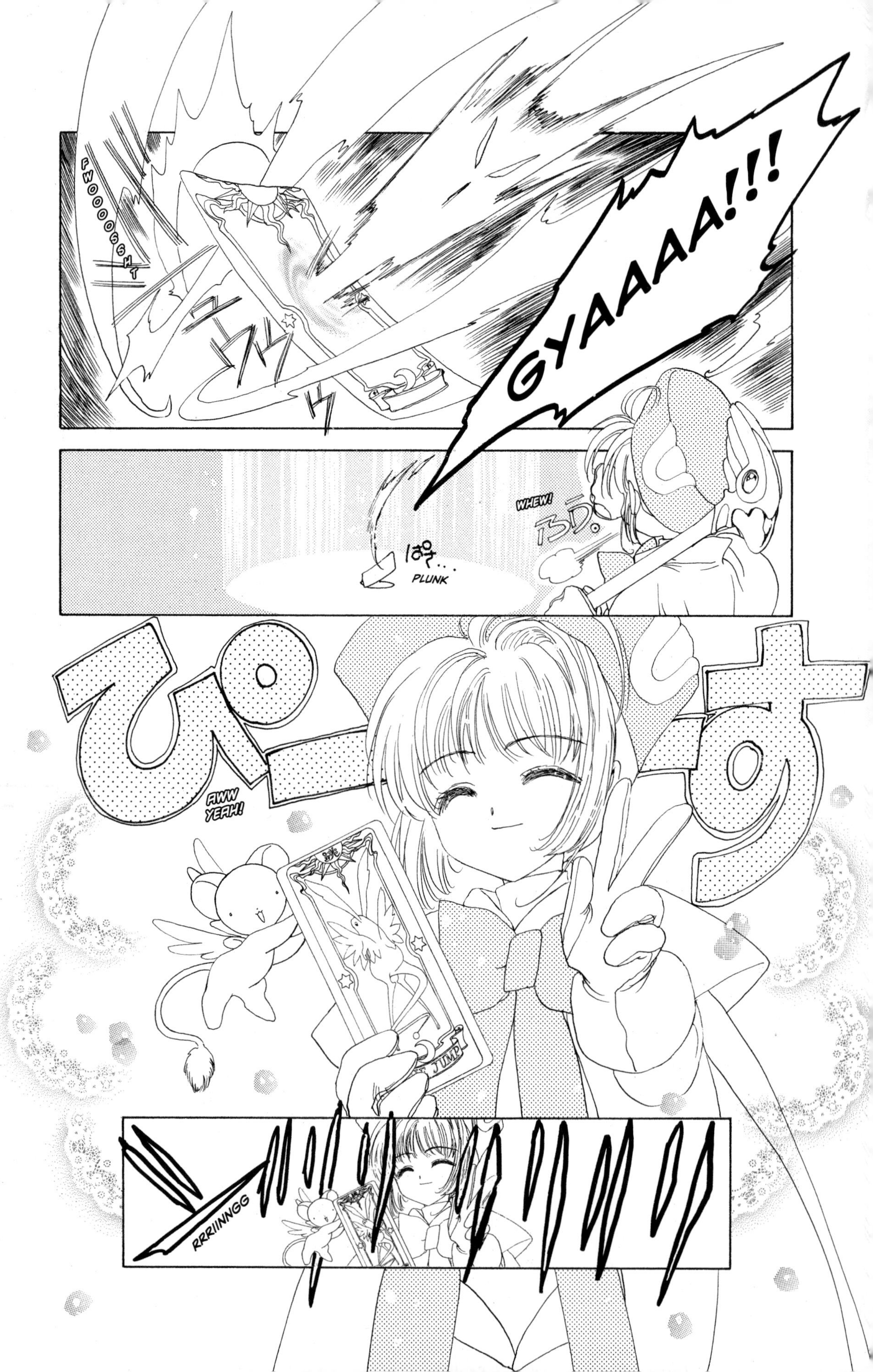
GYAAAA!!!
FWOOOOSSHT
WHEW!
PLUNK
ぴーす
AWW YEAH!
RRRIINNGG

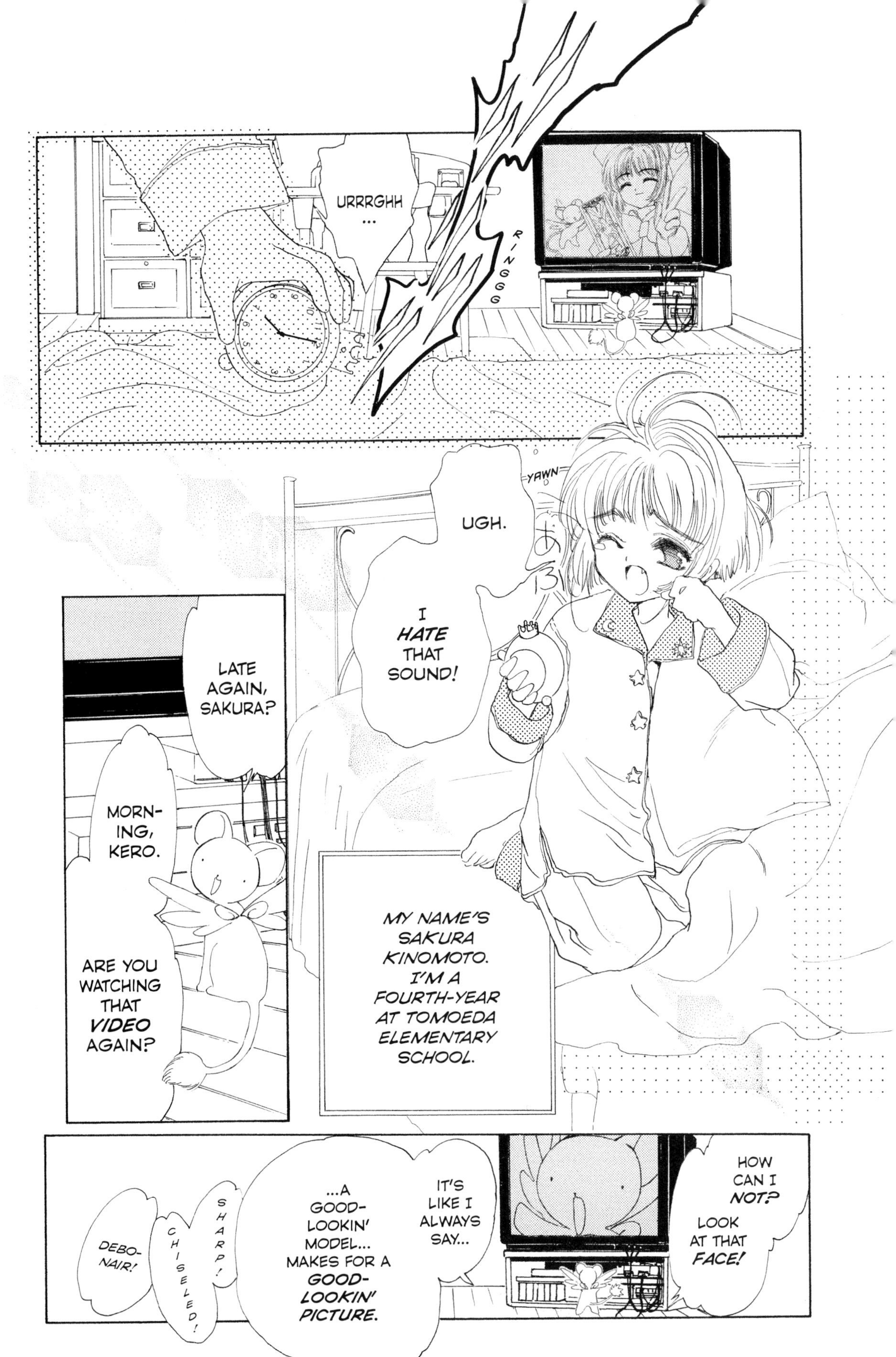

RINGGG
URRRGHH ...
YAWN
UGH.
I HATE THAT SOUND!
MY NAME'S SAKURA KINOMOTO. I'M A FOURTH-YEAR AT TOMOEDA ELEMENTARY SCHOOL.
LATE AGAIN, SAKURA?
MORN-ING, KERO.
ARE YOU WATCHING THAT VIDEO AGAIN?
HOW CAN I NOT?
LOOK AT THAT FACE!
IT'S LIKE I ALWAYS SAY...
...A GOOD-LOOKIN' MODEL... MAKES FOR A GOOD-LOOKIN' PICTURE.
SHARP!
CHISELED!
DEBO-NAIR!

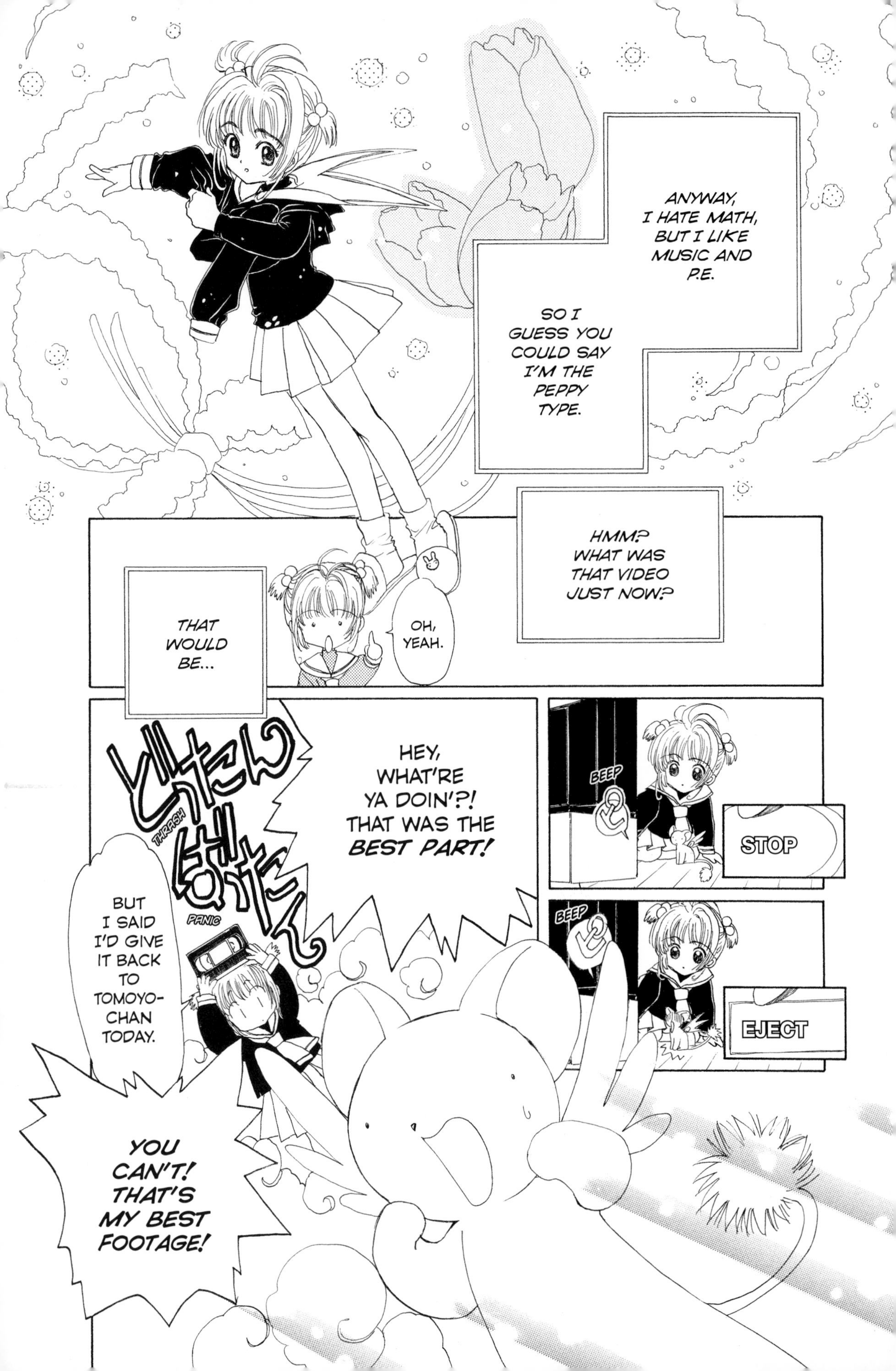
ANYWAY, I HATE MATH, BUT I LIKE MUSIC AND P.E.
SO I GUESS YOU COULD SAY I'M THE PEPPY TYPE.
HMM? WHAT WAS THAT VIDEO JUST NOW?
OH, YEAH.
THAT WOULD BE...
BEEP
STOP
BEEP
EJECT
HEY, WHAT'RE YA DOIN'?! THAT WAS THE *BEST PART!*
THRASH
PANIC
BUT I SAID I'D GIVE IT BACK TO TOMOYO-CHAN TODAY.
YOU CAN'T! THAT'S MY BEST FOOTAGE!

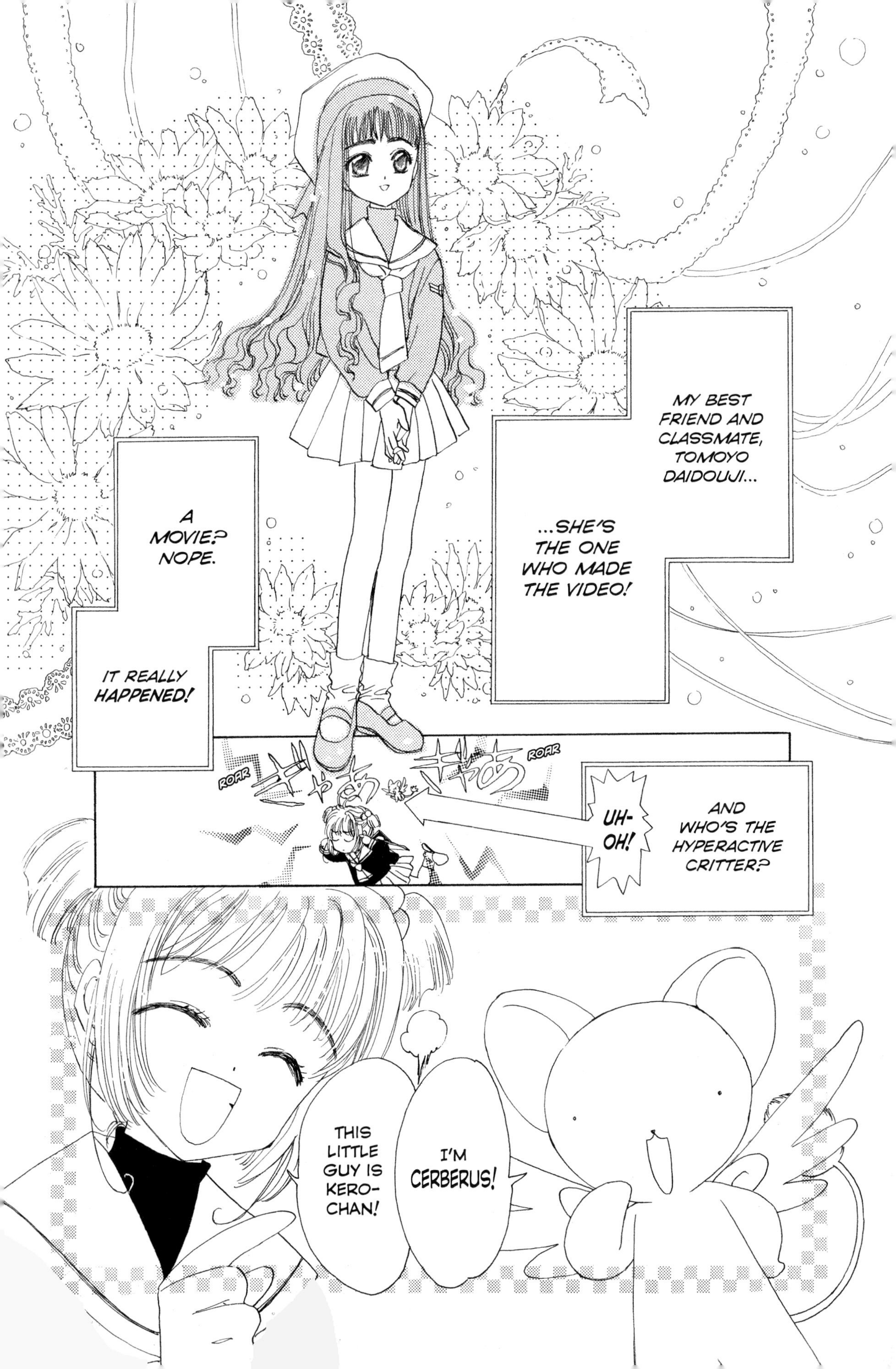
MY BEST FRIEND AND CLASSMATE, TOMOYO DAIDOUJI...
...SHE'S THE ONE WHO MADE THE VIDEO!
A MOVIE? NOPE.
IT REALLY HAPPENED!
AND WHO'S THE HYPERACTIVE CRITTER?
UH-OH!
ROAR
ROAR
I'M CERBERUS!
THIS LITTLE GUY IS KERO-CHAN!

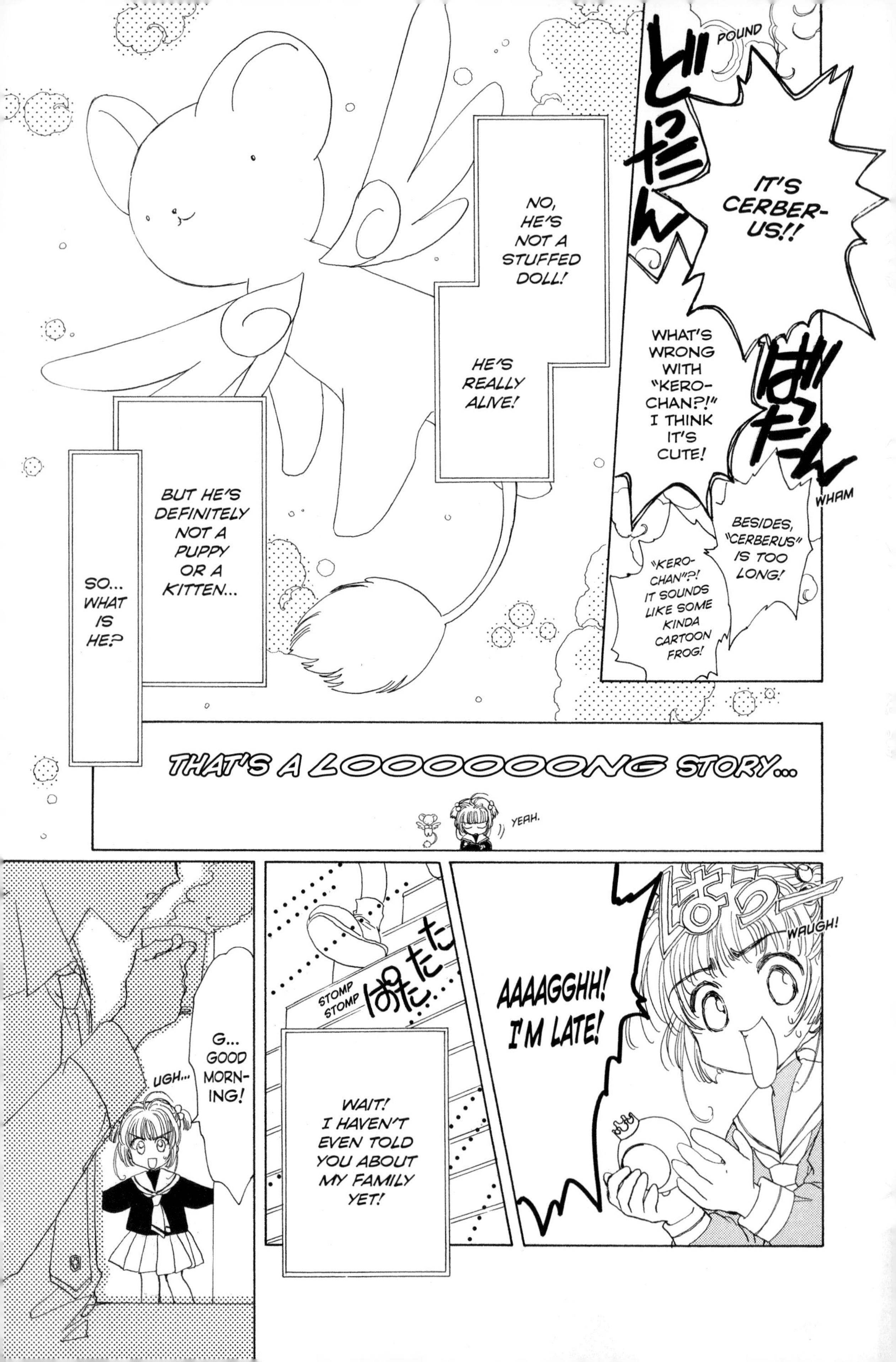
どったん
POUND
IT'S CERBER-US!!
WHAT'S WRONG WITH "KERO-CHAN?!" I THINK IT'S CUTE!
ばったん
WHAM
BESIDES, "CERBERUS" IS TOO LONG!
"KERO-CHAN"?! IT SOUNDS LIKE SOME KINDA CARTOON FROG!
NO, HE'S NOT A STUFFED DOLL!
HE'S REALLY ALIVE!
BUT HE'S DEFINITELY NOT A PUPPY OR A KITTEN...
SO... WHAT IS HE?
THAT'S A LOOOOOOONG STORY...
YEAH.
WAUGH!
AAAAGGHH! I'M LATE!
STOMP STOMP
WAIT! I HAVEN'T EVEN TOLD YOU ABOUT MY FAMILY YET!
G... GOOD MORN-ING!
UGH...

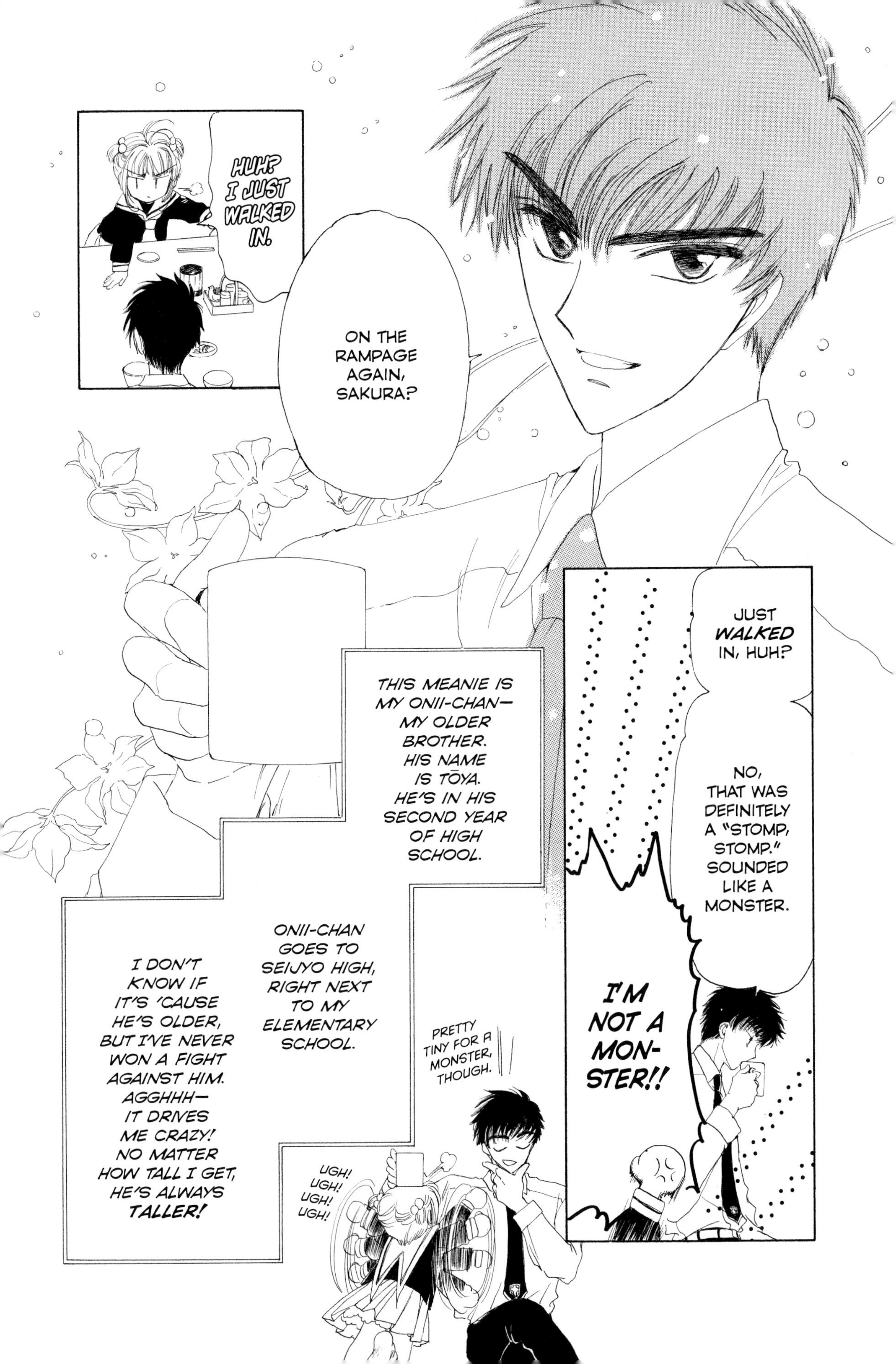
ON THE RAMPAGE AGAIN, SAKURA?
HUH? I JUST WALKED IN.
THIS MEANIE IS MY ONII-CHAN— MY OLDER BROTHER. HIS NAME IS TŌYA. HE'S IN HIS SECOND YEAR OF HIGH SCHOOL.
JUST WALKED IN, HUH?
NO, THAT WAS DEFINITELY A "STOMP, STOMP." SOUNDED LIKE A MONSTER.
I'M NOT A MON-STER!!
ONII-CHAN GOES TO SEIJYO HIGH, RIGHT NEXT TO MY ELEMENTARY SCHOOL.
I DON'T KNOW IF IT'S 'CAUSE HE'S OLDER, BUT I'VE NEVER WON A FIGHT AGAINST HIM. AGGHHH— IT DRIVES ME CRAZY! NO MATTER HOW TALL I GET, HE'S ALWAYS TALLER!
PRETTY TINY FOR A MONSTER, THOUGH.
UGH! UGH! UGH! UGH!

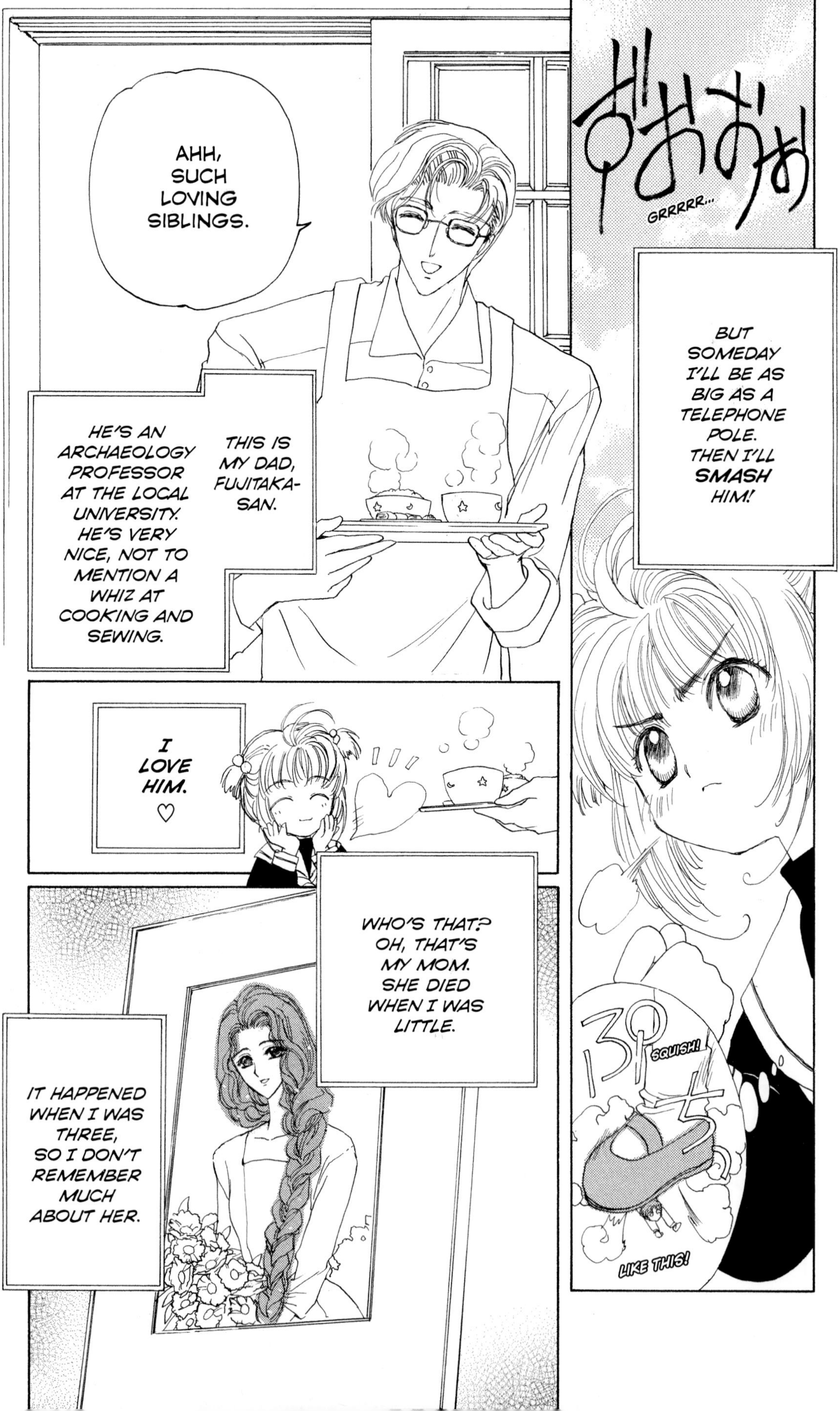
おおおお
GRRRRR...
BUT SOMEDAY I'LL BE AS BIG AS A TELEPHONE POLE. THEN I'LL **SMASH** HIM!
SQUISH!
LIKE THIS!
AHH, SUCH LOVING SIBLINGS.
THIS IS MY DAD, FUJITAKA-SAN.
HE'S AN ARCHAEOLOGY PROFESSOR AT THE LOCAL UNIVERSITY. HE'S VERY NICE, NOT TO MENTION A WHIZ AT COOKING AND SEWING.
I LOVE HIM. ♡
WHO'S THAT? OH, THAT'S MY MOM. SHE DIED WHEN I WAS LITTLE.
IT HAPPENED WHEN I WAS THREE, SO I DON'T REMEMBER MUCH ABOUT HER.

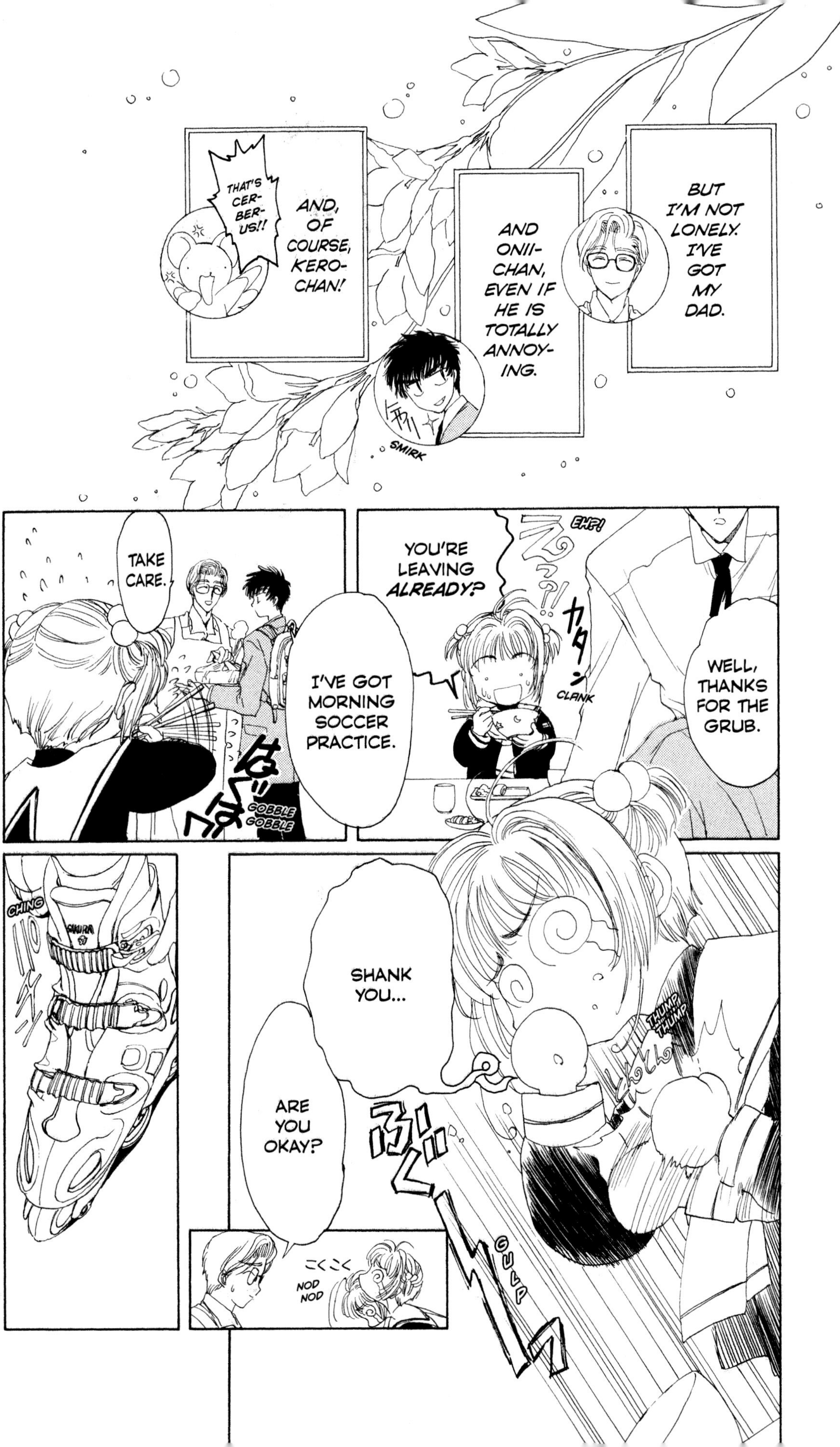
BUT I'M NOT LONELY. I'VE GOT MY DAD.
AND ONII-CHAN, EVEN IF HE IS TOTALLY ANNOYING.
SMIRK
AND, OF COURSE, KERO-CHAN!
THAT'S CER-BER-US!!
WELL, THANKS FOR THE GRUB.
EH?!
YOU'RE LEAVING ALREADY?
CLANK
I'VE GOT MORNING SOCCER PRACTICE.
GOBBLE GOBBLE
TAKE CARE.
THUMP THUMP
SHANK YOU...
GULP
ARE YOU OKAY?
NOD NOD
CHING

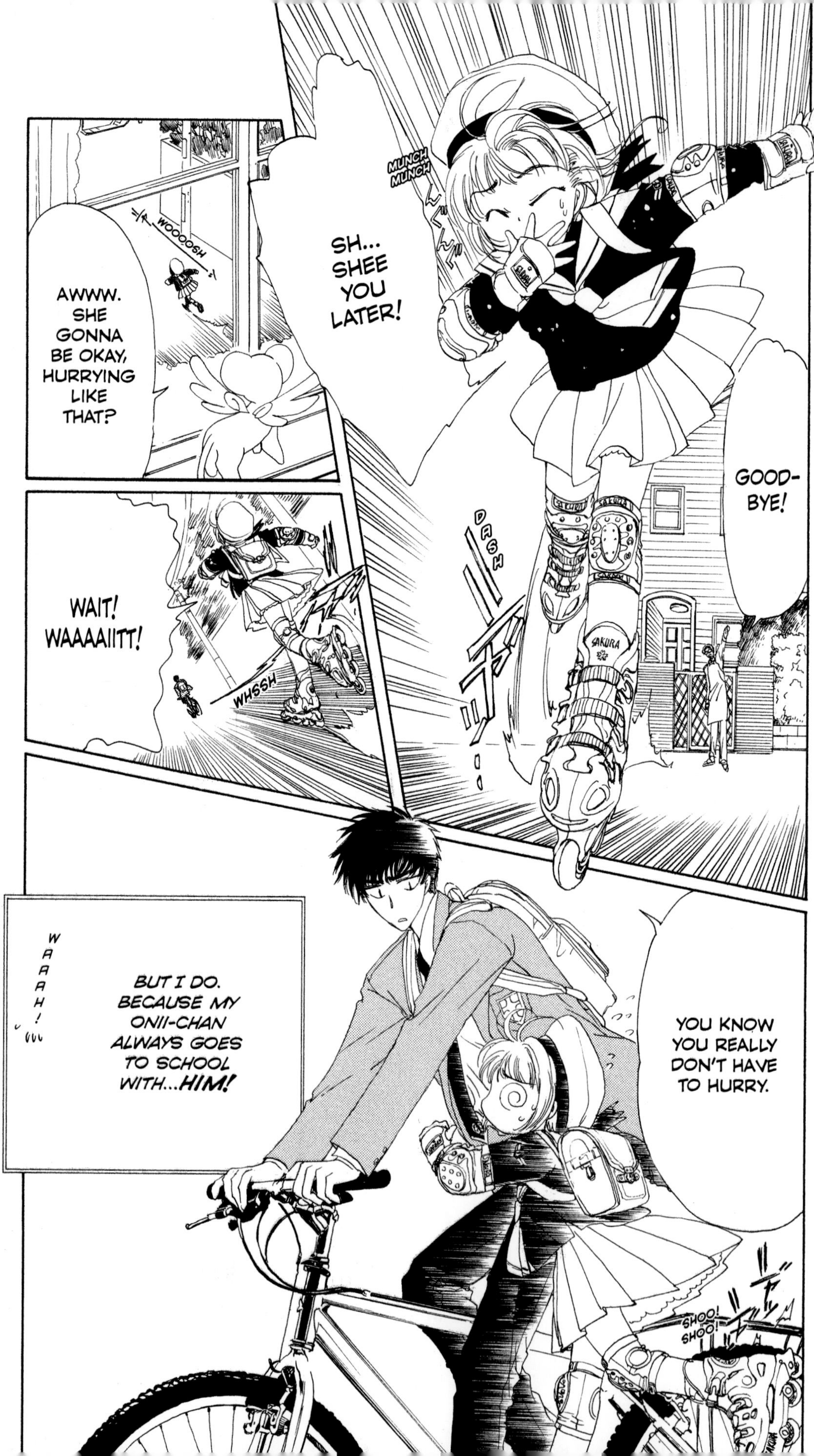
MUNCH MUNCH
SH... SHEE YOU LATER!
GOOD-BYE!
DASH
WOOOOSH
AWWW. SHE GONNA BE OKAY, HURRYING LIKE THAT?
WHSSH
WAIT! WAAAAIITT!
YOU KNOW YOU REALLY DON'T HAVE TO HURRY.
SHOO! SHOO!
BUT I DO. BECAUSE MY ONII-CHAN ALWAYS GOES TO SCHOOL WITH...HIM!
WAAAH!

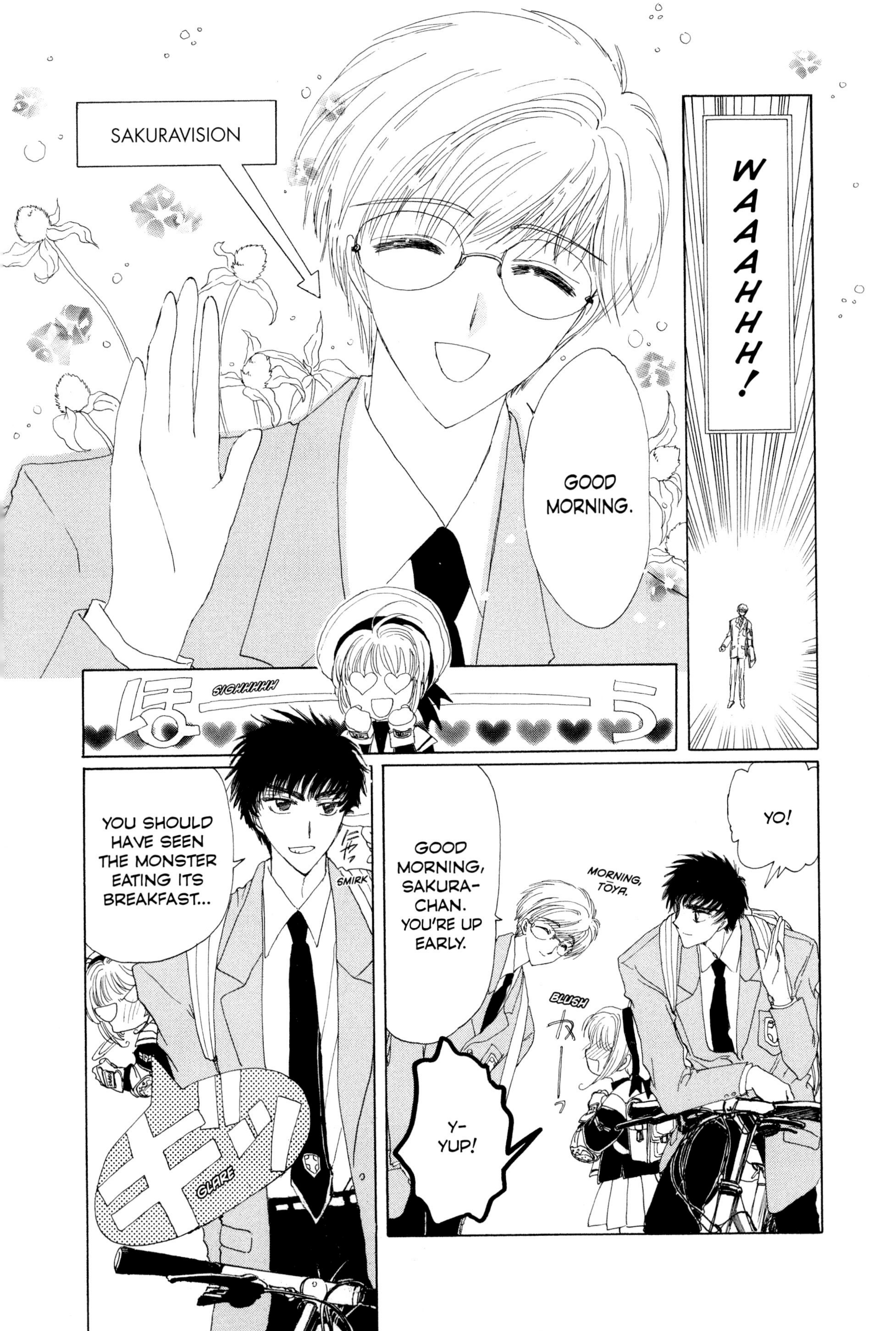
WAAAAHHH!
SAKURAVISION
GOOD MORNING.
ほーう
SIGHHHHH
YO!
MORNING, TŌYA.
GOOD MORNING, SAKURA-CHAN. YOU'RE UP EARLY.
BLUSH
Y-YUP!
YOU SHOULD HAVE SEEN THE MONSTER EATING ITS BREAKFAST...
SMIRK
GLARE

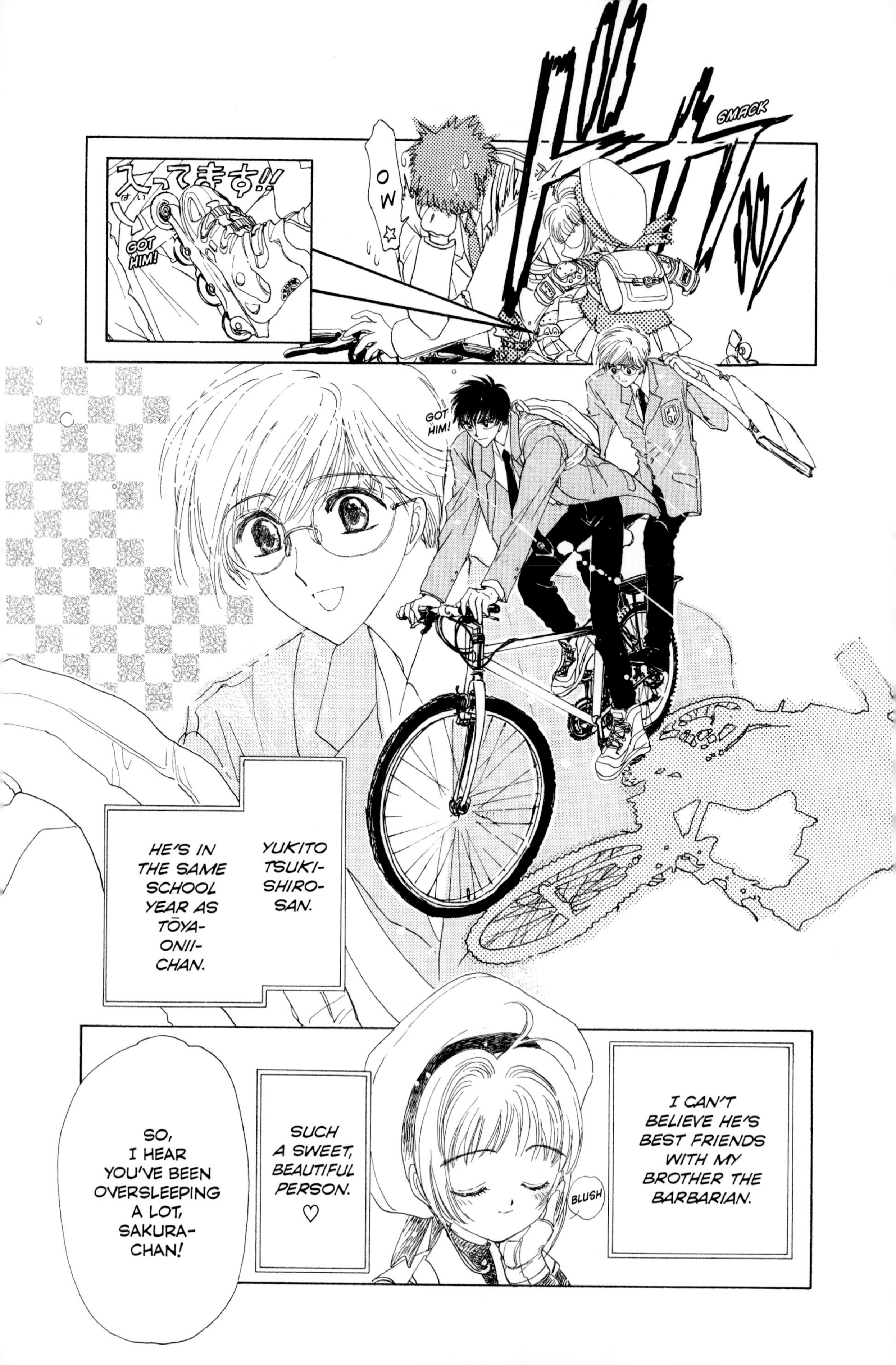
SMACK
OW
入ってきます!!
GOT HIM!
GOT HIM!
YUKITO TSUKISHIRO-SAN.
HE'S IN THE SAME SCHOOL YEAR AS TŌYA-ONII-CHAN.
I CAN'T BELIEVE HE'S BEST FRIENDS WITH MY BROTHER THE BARBARIAN.
BLUSH
SUCH A SWEET, BEAUTIFUL PERSON. ♡
SO, I HEAR YOU'VE BEEN OVERSLEEPING A LOT, SAKURA-CHAN!

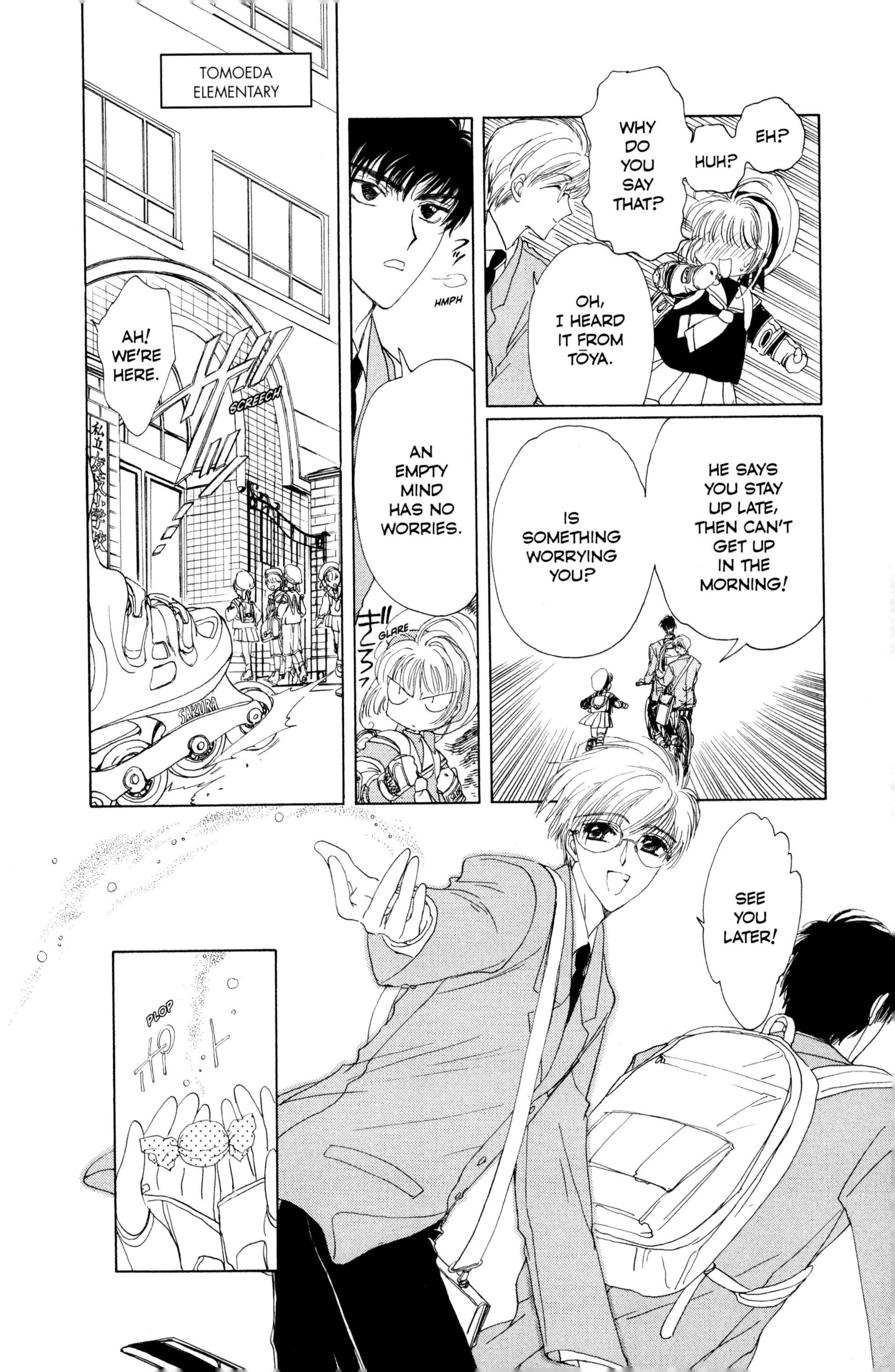
EH?
HUH?
WHY DO YOU SAY THAT?
OH, I HEARD IT FROM TŌYA.
HE SAYS YOU STAY UP LATE, THEN CAN'T GET UP IN THE MORNING!
IS SOMETHING WORRYING YOU?
HMPH
AN EMPTY MIND HAS NO WORRIES.
GLARE
TOMOEDA ELEMENTARY
SCREECH
AH! WE'RE HERE.
SAKURA
SEE YOU LATER!
PLOP

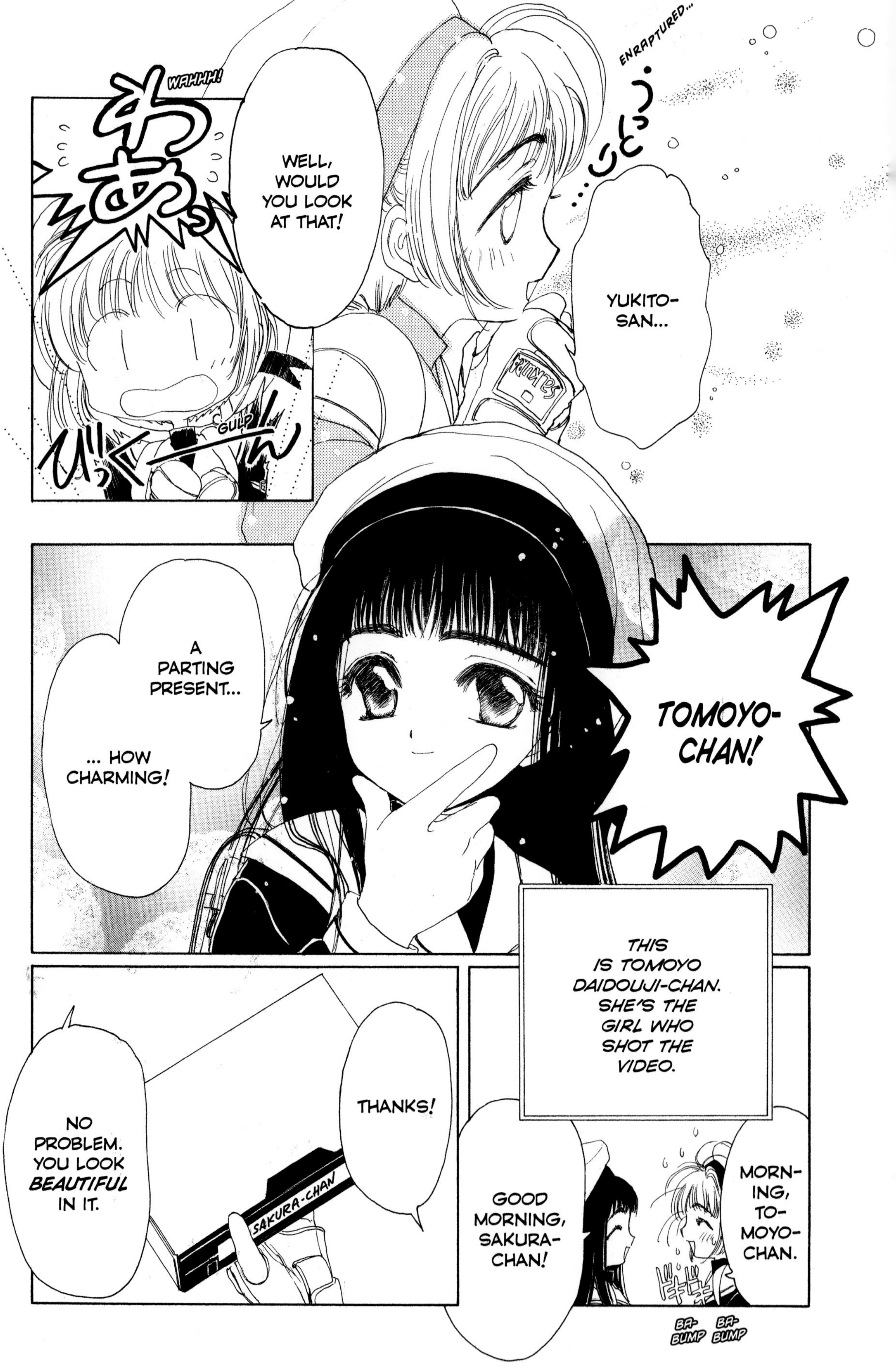
ENRAPTURED...
YUKITO-SAN...
WELL, WOULD YOU LOOK AT THAT!
WAHHH!
GULP
TOMOYO-CHAN!
A PARTING PRESENT...
... HOW CHARMING!
THIS IS TOMOYO DAIDOUJI-CHAN. SHE'S THE GIRL WHO SHOT THE VIDEO.
MORNING, TO-MOYO-CHAN.
GOOD MORNING, SAKURA-CHAN!
BA-BUMP BA-BUMP
THANKS!
NO PROBLEM. YOU LOOK *BEAUTIFUL* IN IT.
SAKURA-CHAN

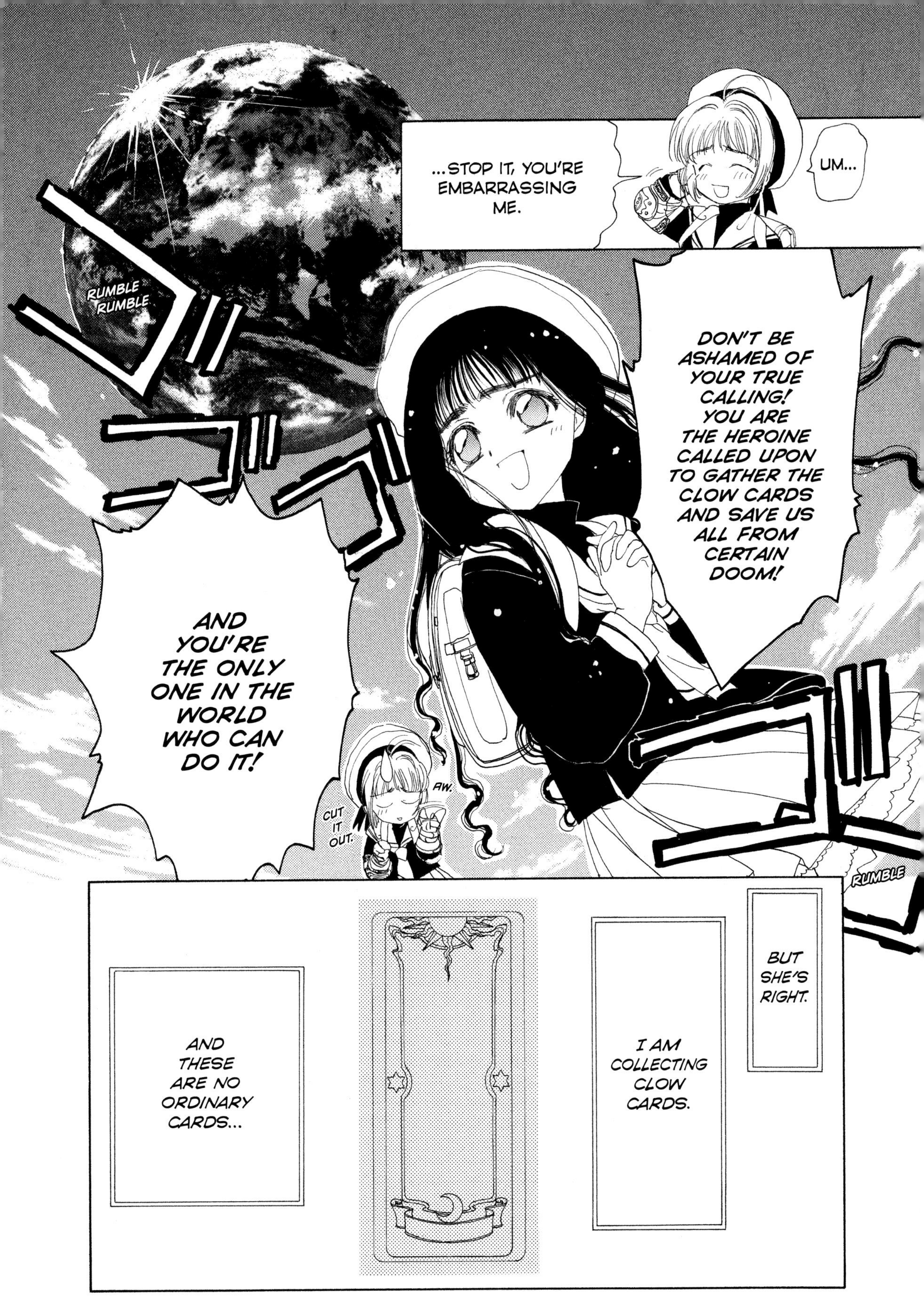
UM...
...STOP IT, YOU'RE EMBARRASSING ME.
RUMBLE RUMBLE
DON'T BE ASHAMED OF YOUR TRUE CALLING! YOU ARE THE HEROINE CALLED UPON TO GATHER THE CLOW CARDS AND SAVE US ALL FROM CERTAIN DOOM!
AND YOU'RE THE ONLY ONE IN THE WORLD WHO CAN DO IT!
AW.
CUT IT OUT.
RUMBLE
BUT SHE'S RIGHT.
I AM COLLECTING CLOW CARDS.
AND THESE ARE NO ORDINARY CARDS...

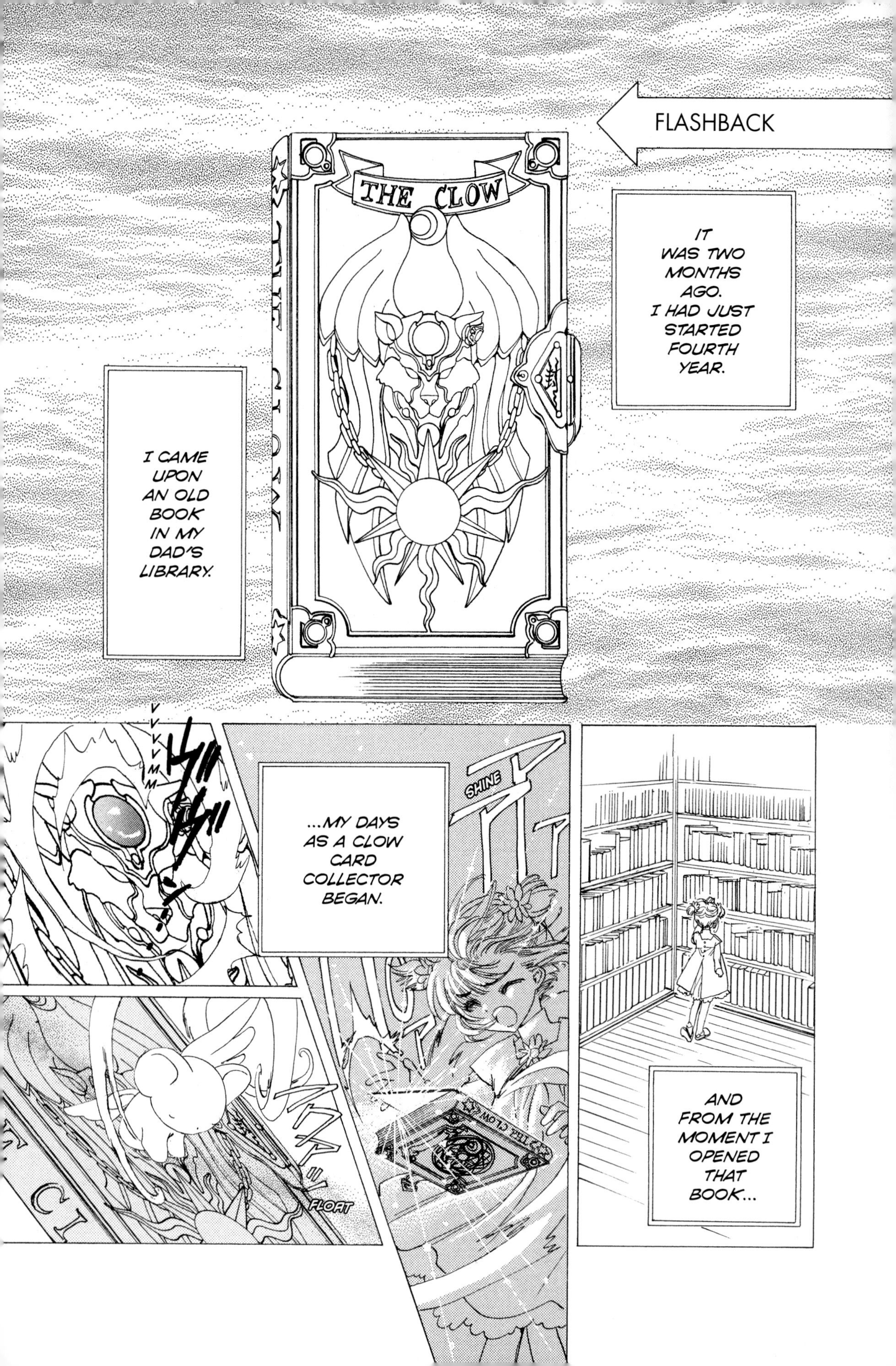
FLASHBACK
IT WAS TWO MONTHS AGO. I HAD JUST STARTED FOURTH YEAR.
THE CLOW
I CAME UPON AN OLD BOOK IN MY DAD'S LIBRARY.
AND FROM THE MOMENT I OPENED THAT BOOK...
SHINE
...MY DAYS AS A CLOW CARD COLLECTOR BEGAN.
VVVVVMM
FLOAT

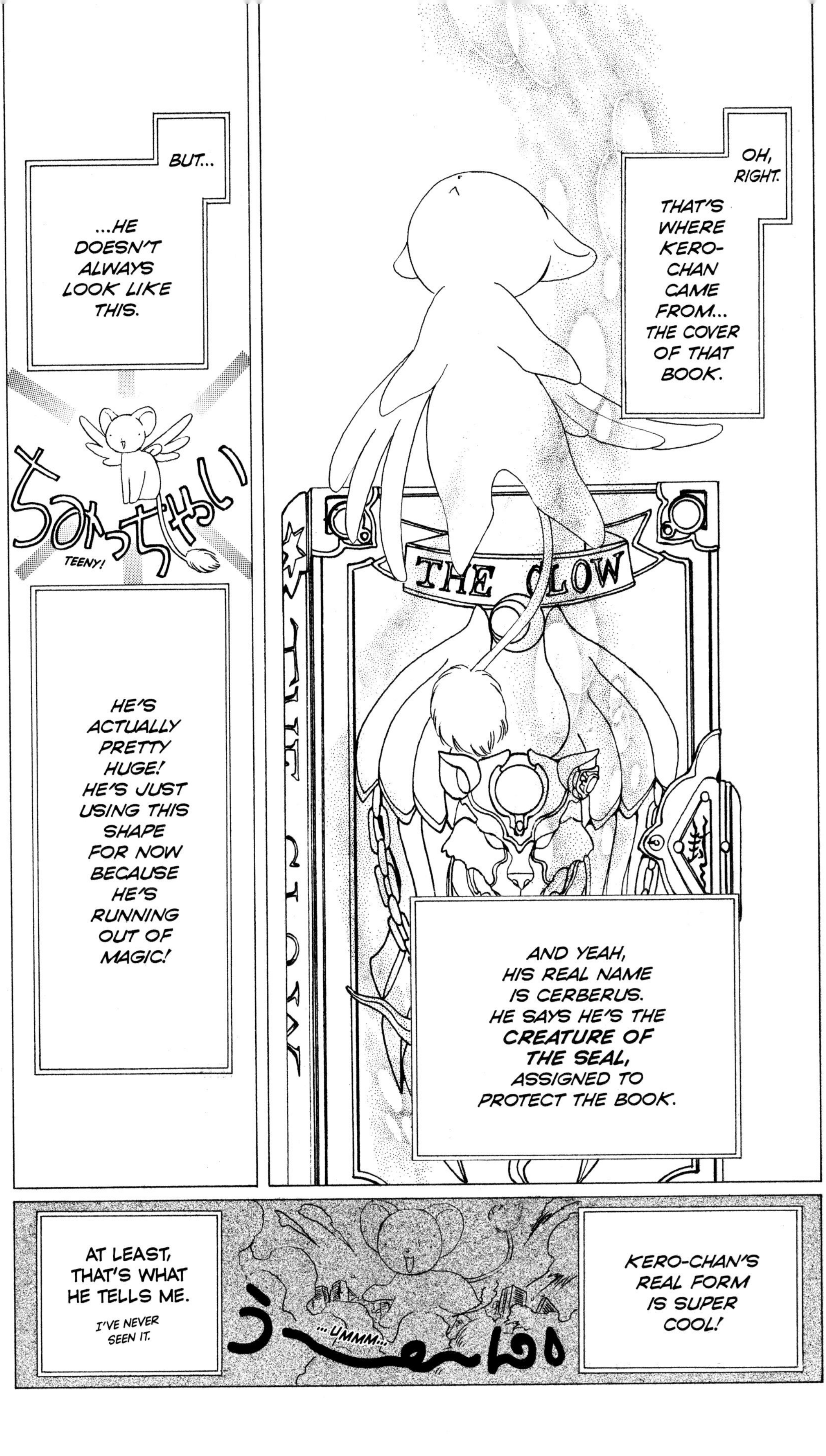
OH, RIGHT.
THAT'S WHERE KERO-CHAN CAME FROM... THE COVER OF THAT BOOK.
THE CLOW
AND YEAH, HIS REAL NAME IS CERBERUS. HE SAYS HE'S THE **CREATURE OF THE SEAL,** ASSIGNED TO PROTECT THE BOOK.
BUT...
...HE DOESN'T ALWAYS LOOK LIKE THIS.
TEENY!
HE'S ACTUALLY PRETTY HUGE! HE'S JUST USING THIS SHAPE FOR NOW BECAUSE HE'S RUNNING OUT OF MAGIC!
KERO-CHAN'S REAL FORM IS SUPER COOL!
...UMMM...
AT LEAST, THAT'S WHAT HE TELLS ME.
I'VE NEVER SEEN IT.

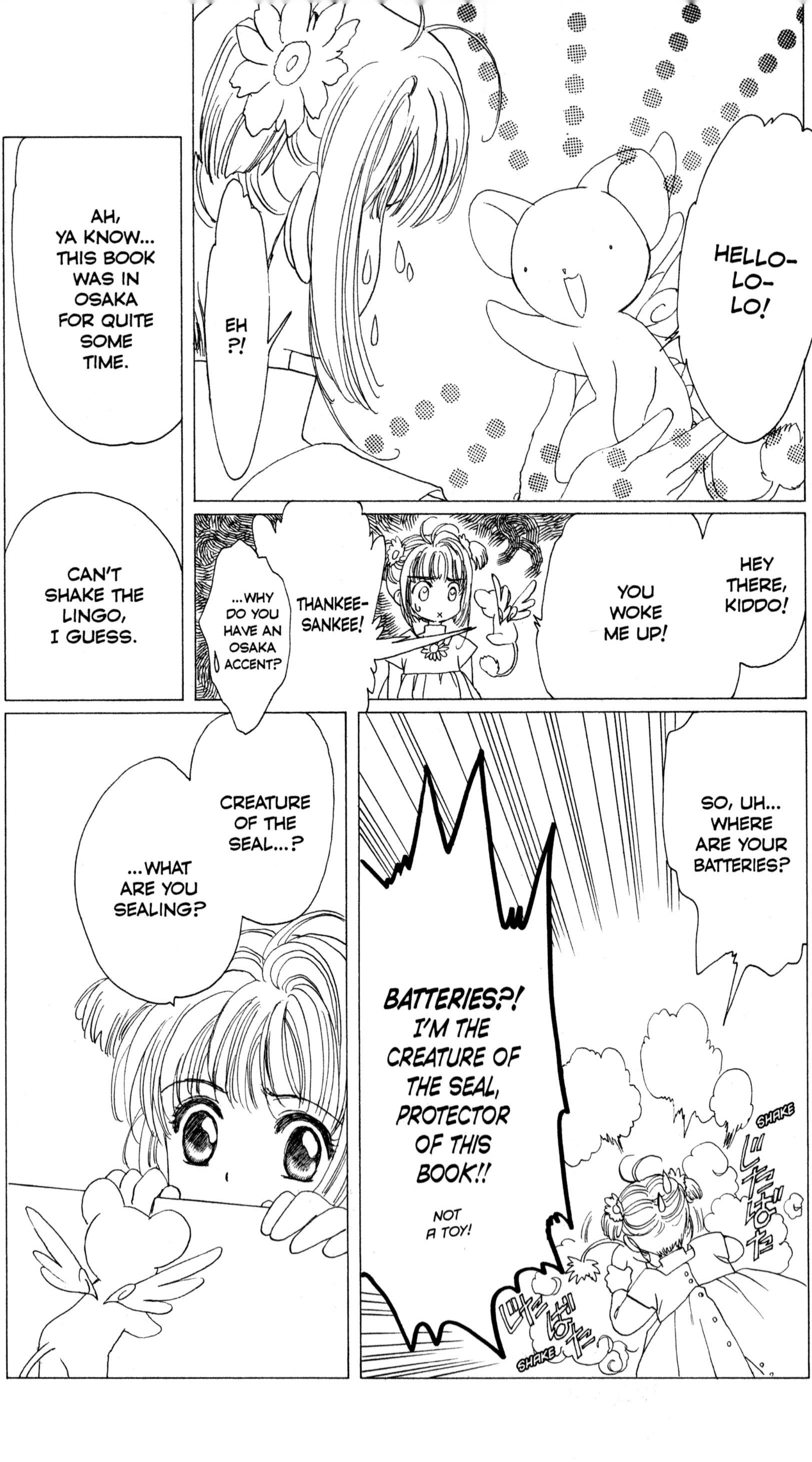
HELLO-LO-LO!
EH?!
HEY THERE, KIDDO!
YOU WOKE ME UP!
THANKEE-SANKEE!
...WHY DO YOU HAVE AN OSAKA ACCENT?
AH, YA KNOW... THIS BOOK WAS IN OSAKA FOR QUITE SOME TIME.
CAN'T SHAKE THE LINGO, I GUESS.
SO, UH... WHERE ARE YOUR BATTERIES?
BATTERIES?! I'M THE CREATURE OF THE SEAL, PROTECTOR OF THIS BOOK!!
NOT A TOY!
SHAKE
SHAKE
CREATURE OF THE SEAL...?
...WHAT ARE YOU SEALING?

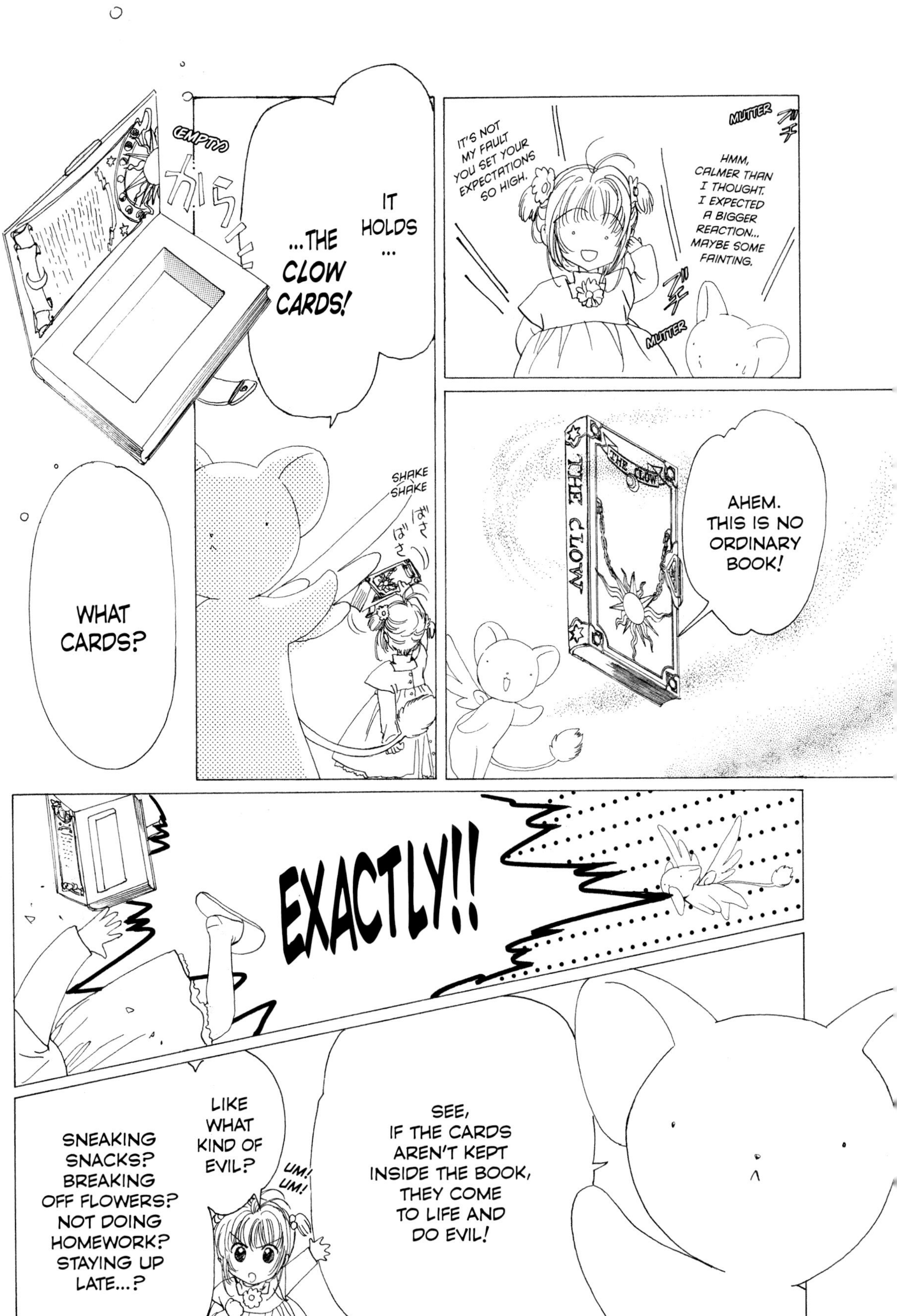
MUTTER
HMM, CALMER THAN I THOUGHT. I EXPECTED A BIGGER REACTION... MAYBE SOME FAINTING.
MUTTER
IT'S NOT MY FAULT YOU SET YOUR EXPECTATIONS SO HIGH.
AHEM. THIS IS NO ORDINARY BOOK!
IT HOLDS ...
...THE CLOW CARDS!
(EMPTY)
SHAKE SHAKE
WHAT CARDS?
EXACTLY!!
SEE, IF THE CARDS AREN'T KEPT INSIDE THE BOOK, THEY COME TO LIFE AND DO EVIL!
LIKE WHAT KIND OF EVIL?
UM! UM!
SNEAKING SNACKS? BREAKING OFF FLOWERS? NOT DOING HOMEWORK? STAYING UP LATE...?

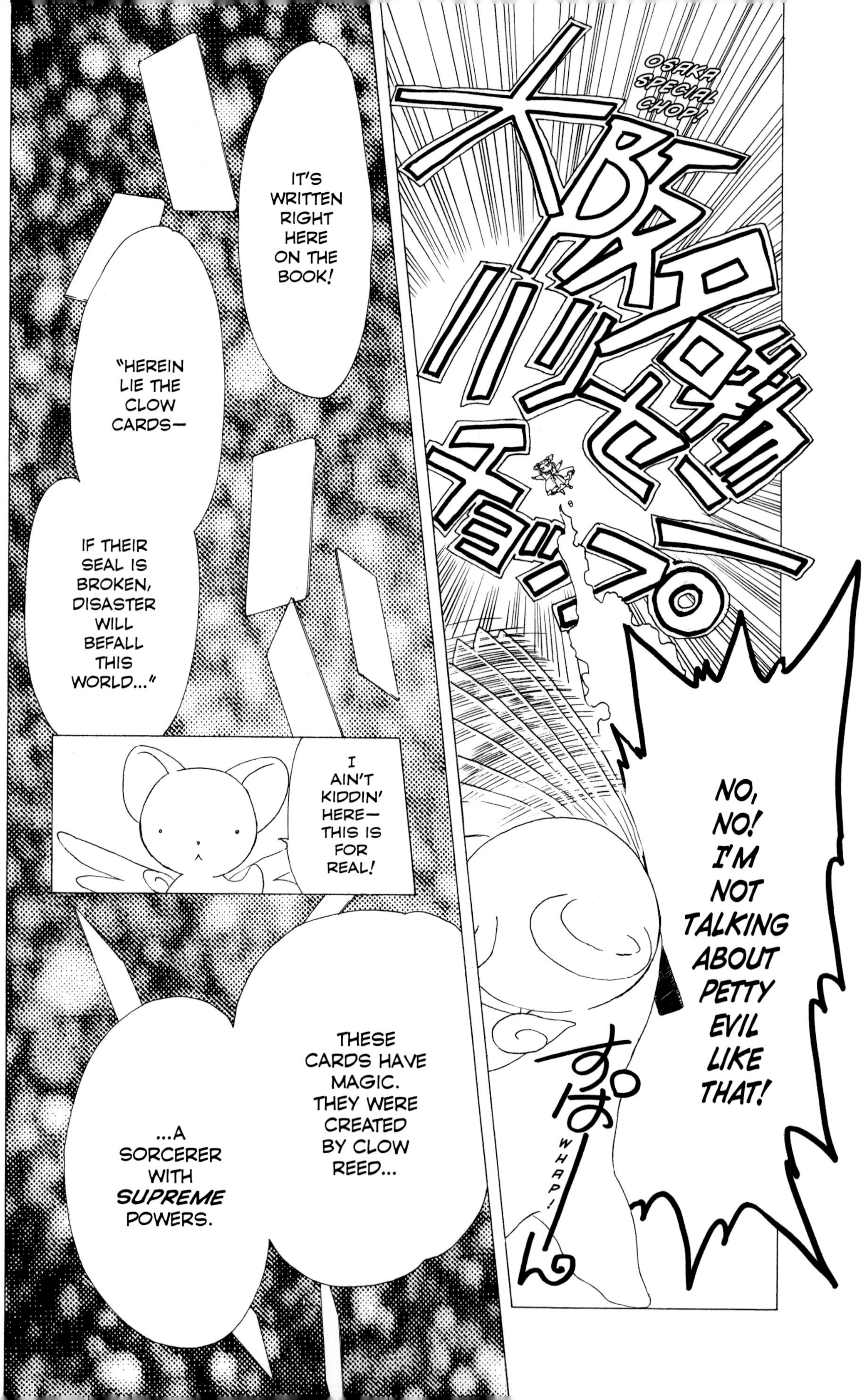
大阪スペシャルチョップ!
OSAKA SPECIAL CHOP!
すぱーん
WHAP!
NO, NO! I'M NOT TALKING ABOUT PETTY EVIL LIKE THAT!
IT'S WRITTEN RIGHT HERE ON THE BOOK!
"HEREIN LIE THE CLOW CARDS—
IF THEIR SEAL IS BROKEN, DISASTER WILL BEFALL THIS WORLD..."
I AIN'T KIDDIN' HERE—THIS IS FOR REAL!
THESE CARDS HAVE MAGIC. THEY WERE CREATED BY CLOW REED...
...A SORCERER WITH SUPREME POWERS.

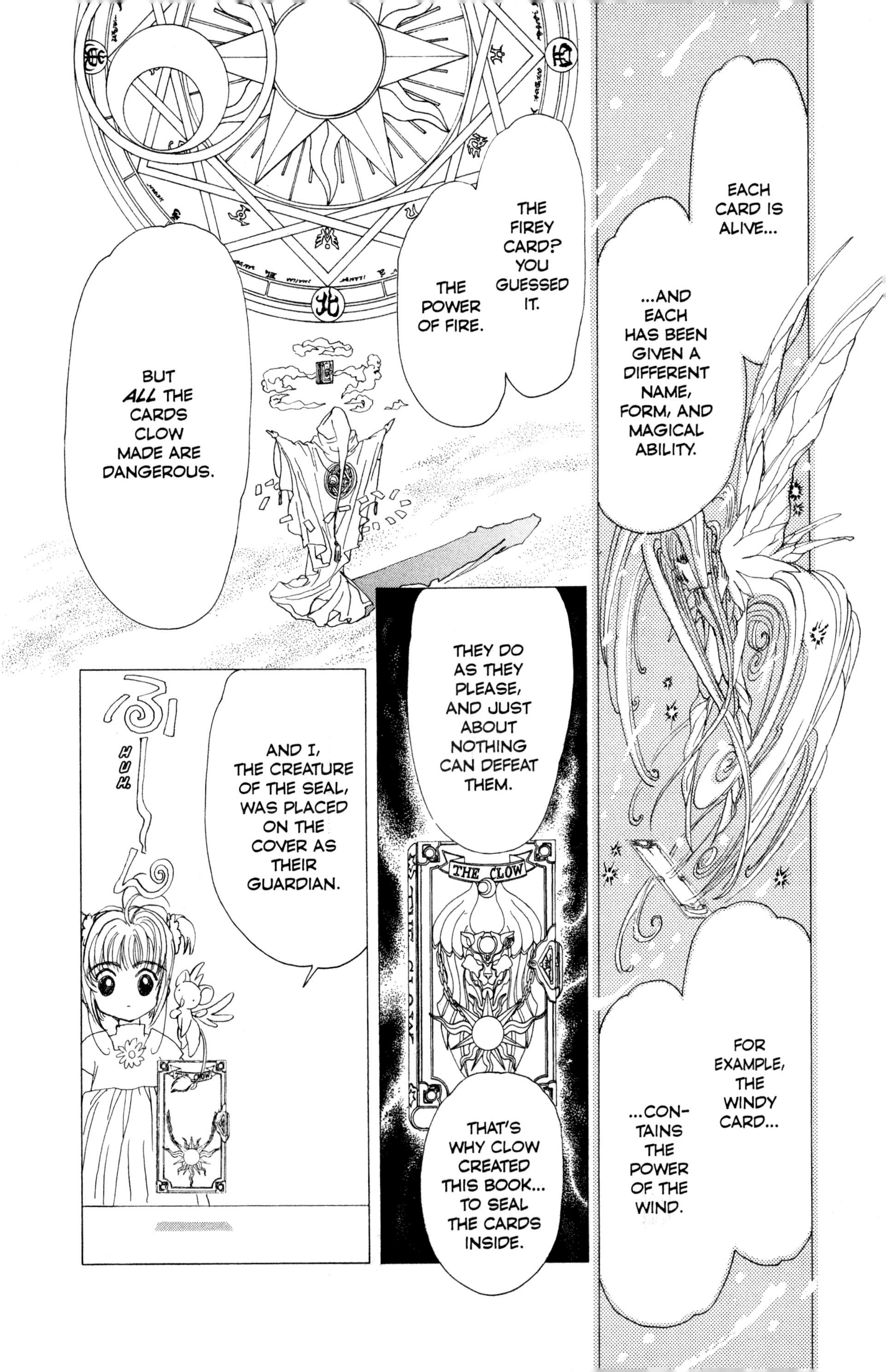
EACH CARD IS ALIVE...
...AND EACH HAS BEEN GIVEN A DIFFERENT NAME, FORM, AND MAGICAL ABILITY.
FOR EXAMPLE, THE WINDY CARD...
...CON-TAINS THE POWER OF THE WIND.
THE FIREY CARD? YOU GUESSED IT.
THE POWER OF FIRE.
BUT *ALL* THE CARDS CLOW MADE ARE DANGEROUS.
THEY DO AS THEY PLEASE, AND JUST ABOUT NOTHING CAN DEFEAT THEM.
THE CLOW
THAT'S WHY CLOW CREATED THIS BOOK... TO SEAL THE CARDS INSIDE.
AND I, THE CREATURE OF THE SEAL, WAS PLACED ON THE COVER AS THEIR GUARDIAN.
HUH.

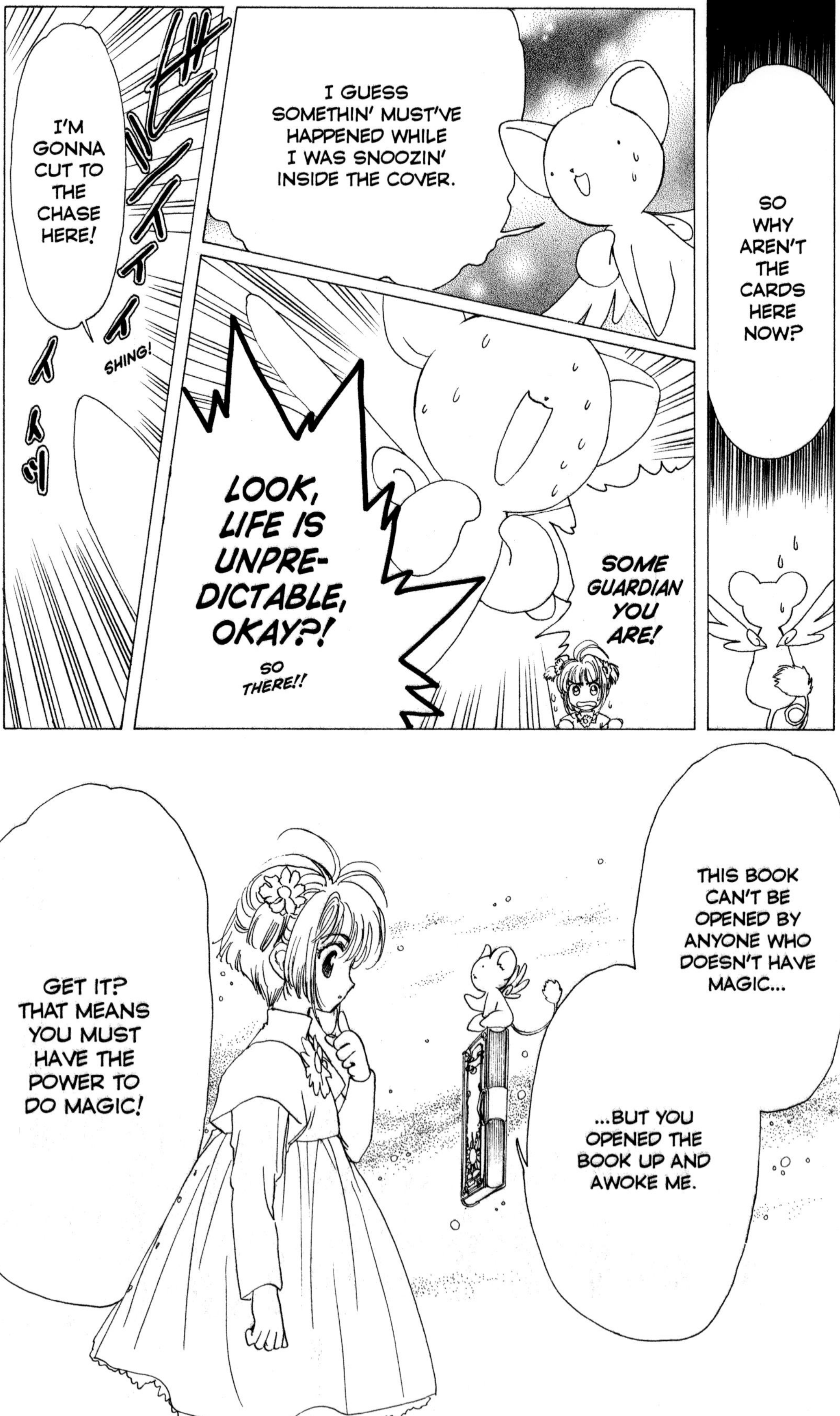
SO WHY AREN'T THE CARDS HERE NOW?
I GUESS SOMETHIN' MUST'VE HAPPENED WHILE I WAS SNOOZIN' INSIDE THE COVER.
SOME GUARDIAN YOU ARE!
LOOK, LIFE IS UNPRE-DICTABLE, OKAY?!
SO THERE!!
I'M GONNA CUT TO THE CHASE HERE!
SHING!
THIS BOOK CAN'T BE OPENED BY ANYONE WHO DOESN'T HAVE MAGIC...
...BUT YOU OPENED THE BOOK UP AND AWOKE ME.
GET IT? THAT MEANS YOU MUST HAVE THE POWER TO DO MAGIC!

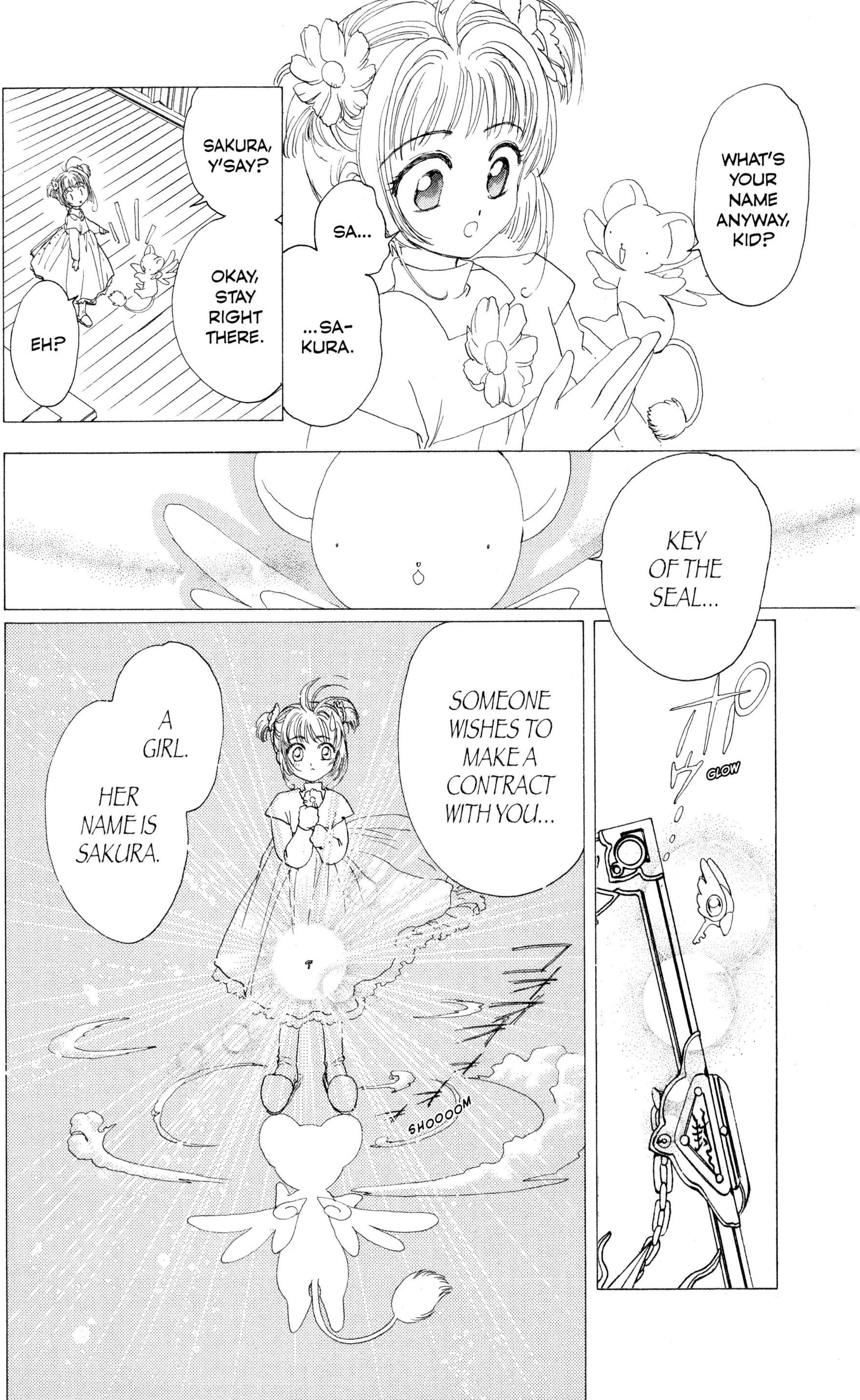
WHAT'S YOUR NAME ANYWAY, KID?
SA...
...SA-KURA.
SAKURA, Y'SAY?
OKAY, STAY RIGHT THERE.
EH?
KEY OF THE SEAL...
GLOW
SOMEONE WISHES TO MAKE A CONTRACT WITH YOU...
A GIRL.
HER NAME IS SAKURA.
SHOOOOM

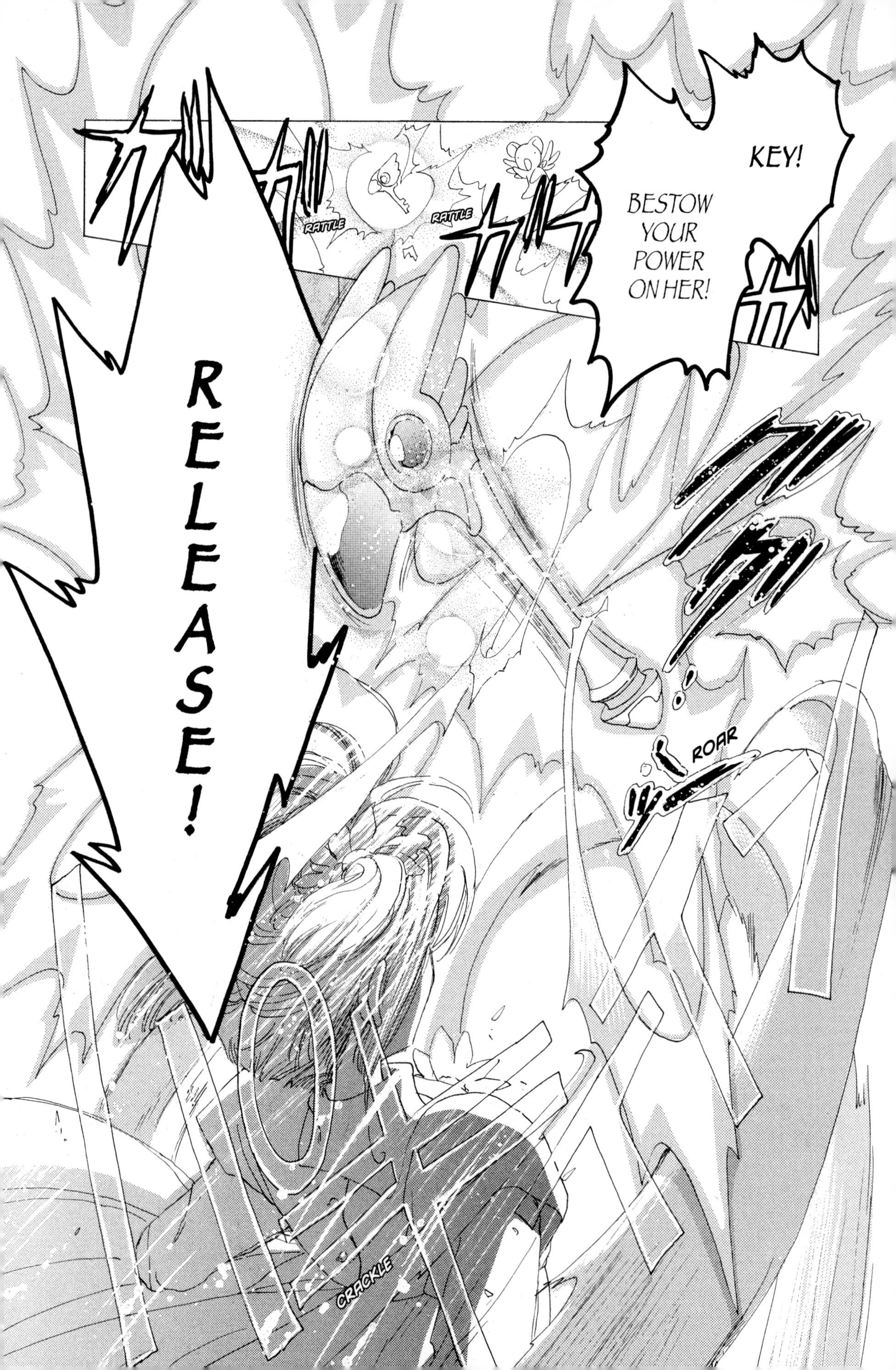
KEY!
BESTOW YOUR POWER ON HER!
RATTLE
RATTLE
RELEASE!
ROAR
CRACKLE

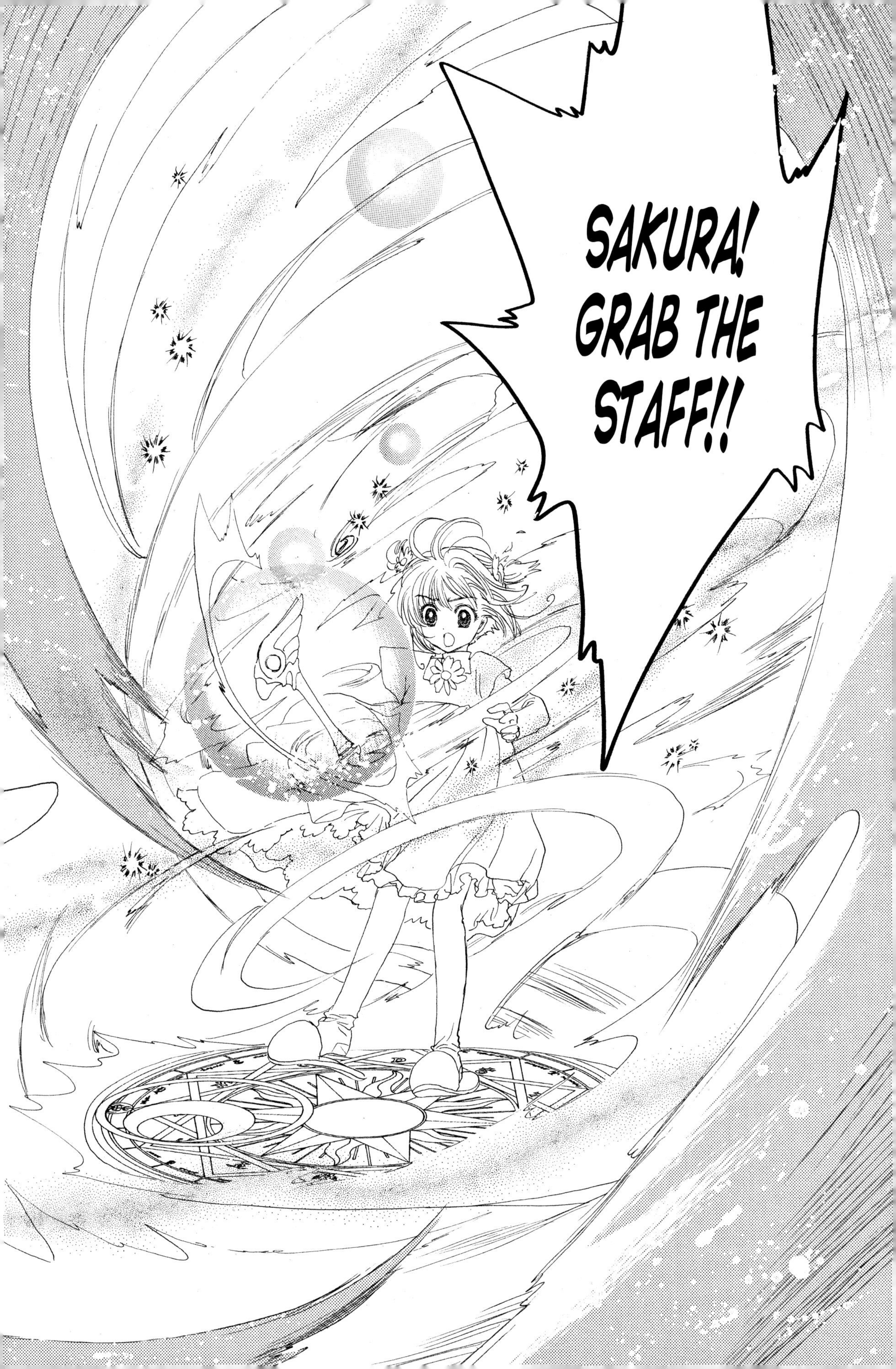
SAKURA! GRAB THE STAFF!!

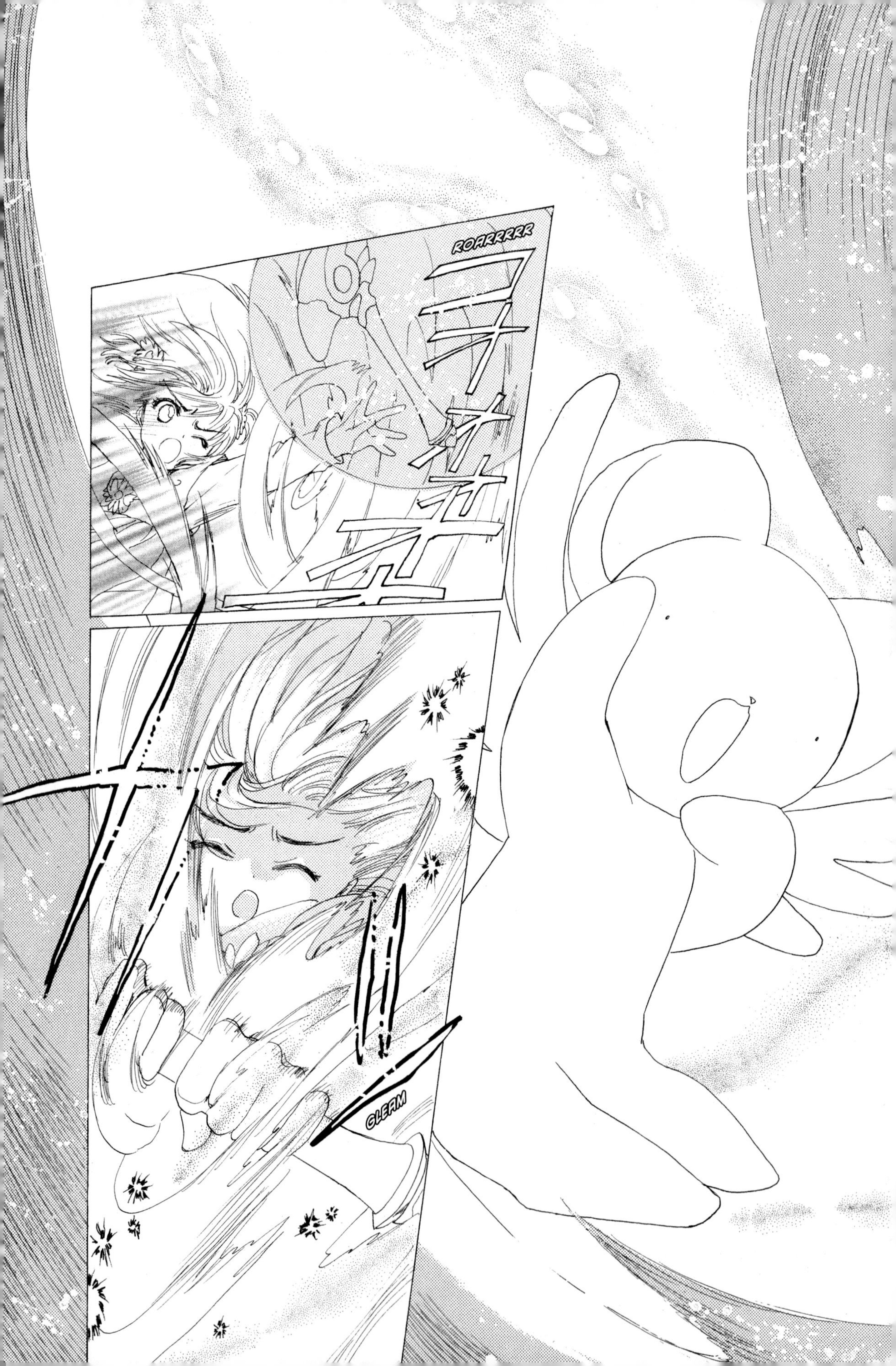
ROARRRRR
GLEAM

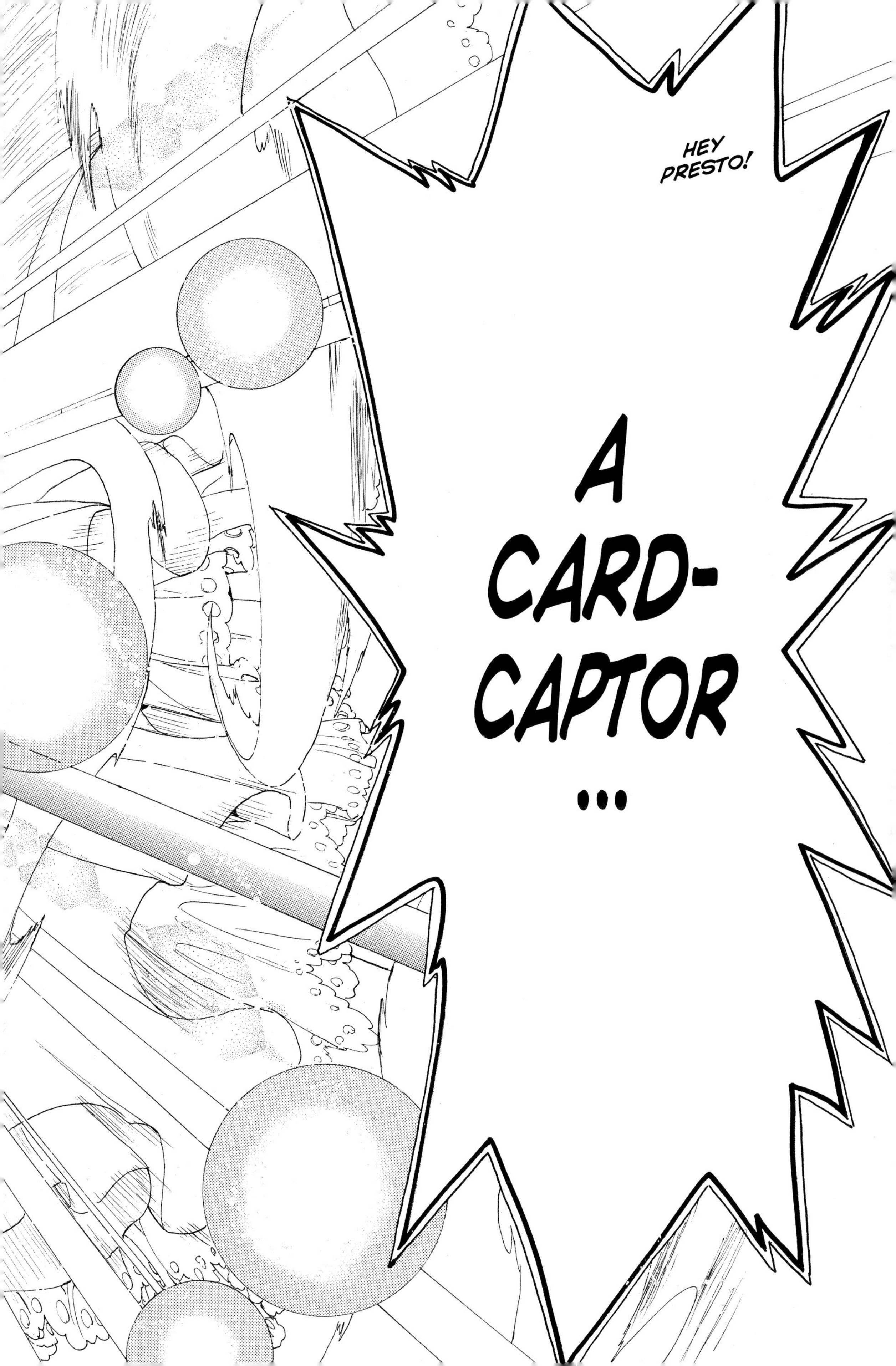
HEY PRESTO!
A CARD-CAPTOR ...

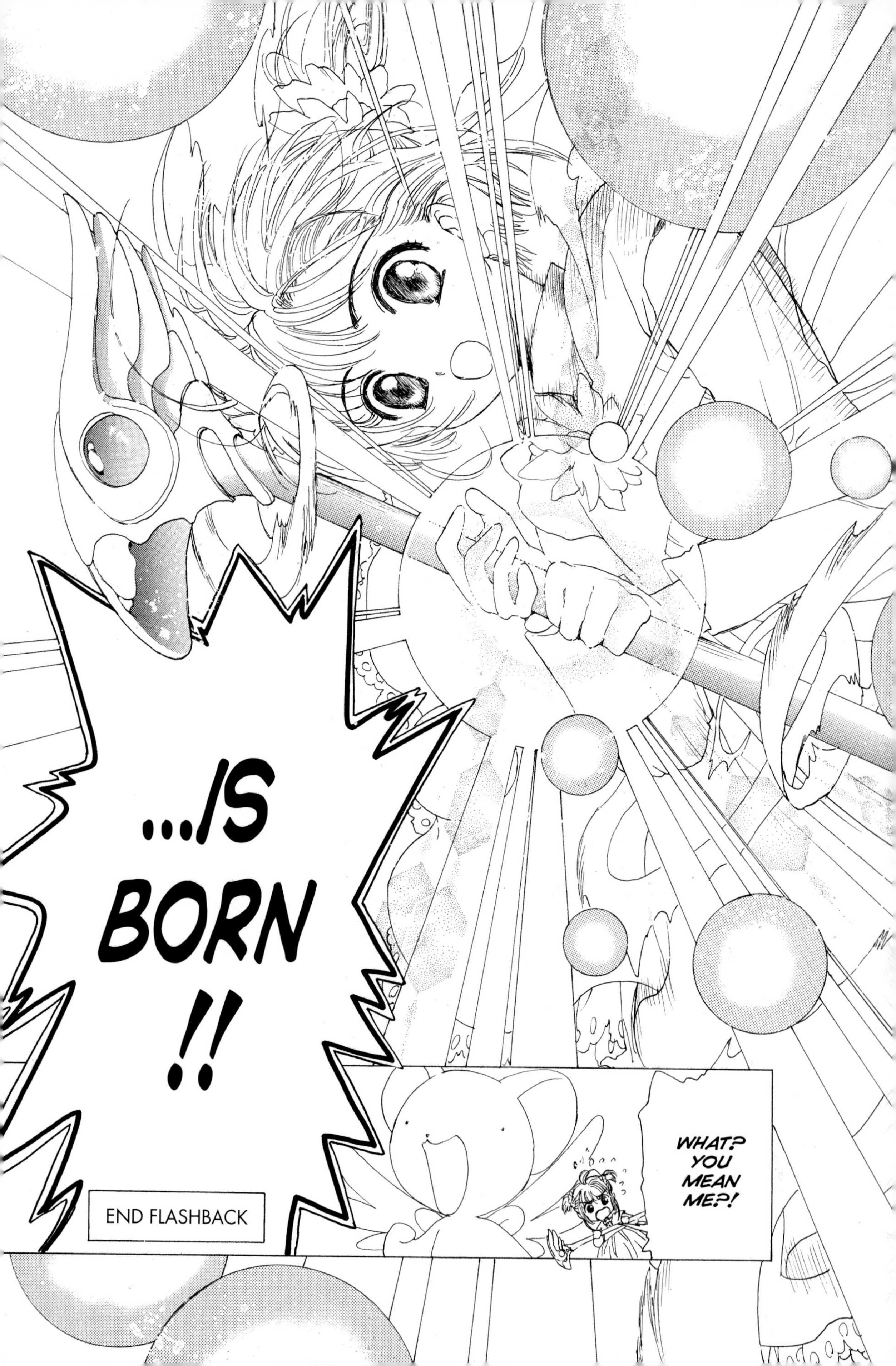
...IS BORN!!
END FLASHBACK
WHAT? YOU MEAN ME?!

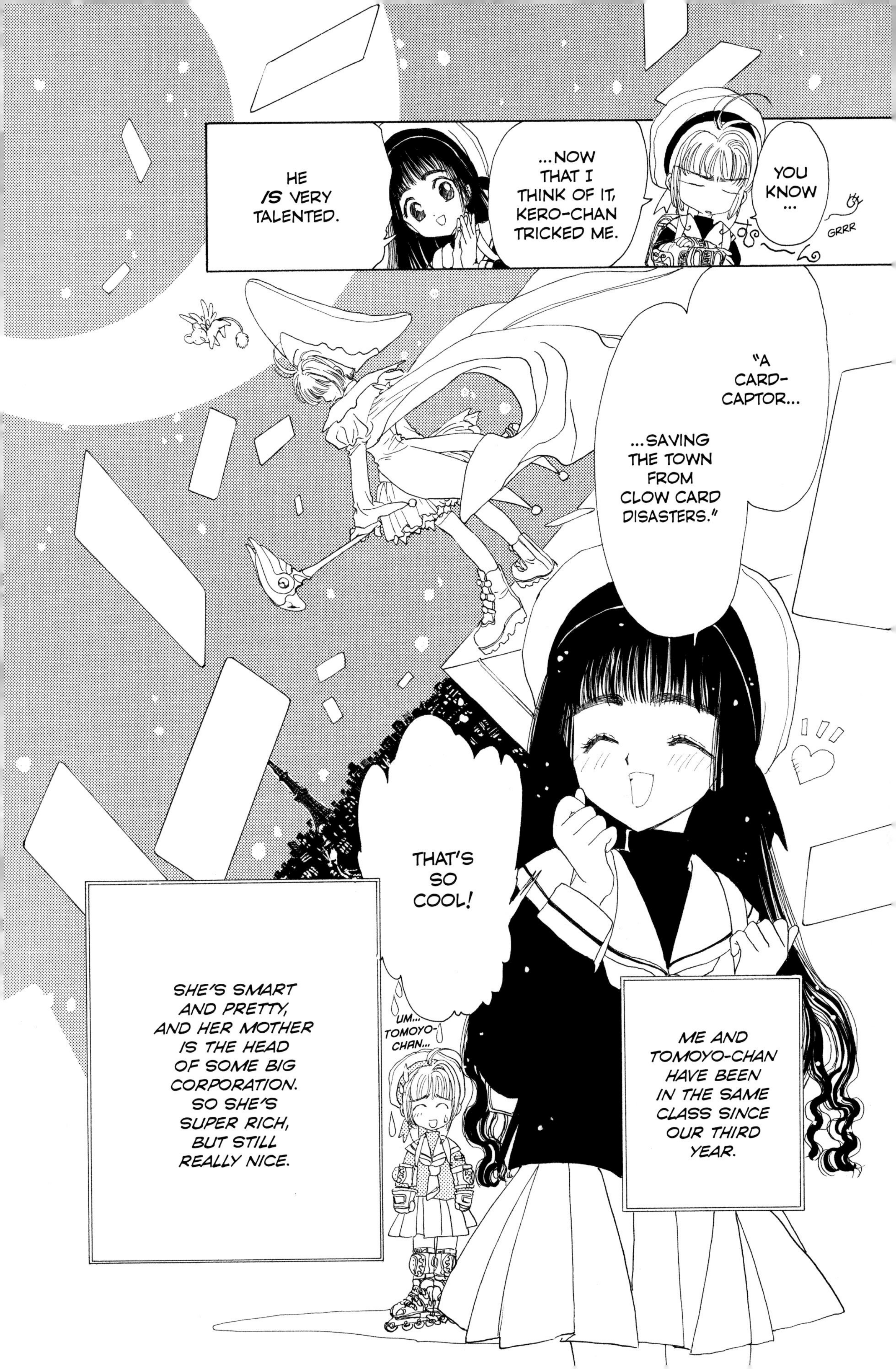
YOU KNOW...
GRRR
...NOW THAT I THINK OF IT, KERO-CHAN TRICKED ME.
HE *IS* VERY TALENTED.
"A CARD-CAPTOR...
...SAVING THE TOWN FROM CLOW CARD DISASTERS."
THAT'S SO COOL!
ME AND TOMOYO-CHAN HAVE BEEN IN THE SAME CLASS SINCE OUR THIRD YEAR.
UM... TOMOYO-CHAN...
SHE'S SMART AND PRETTY, AND HER MOTHER IS THE HEAD OF SOME BIG CORPORATION. SO SHE'S SUPER RICH, BUT STILL REALLY NICE.

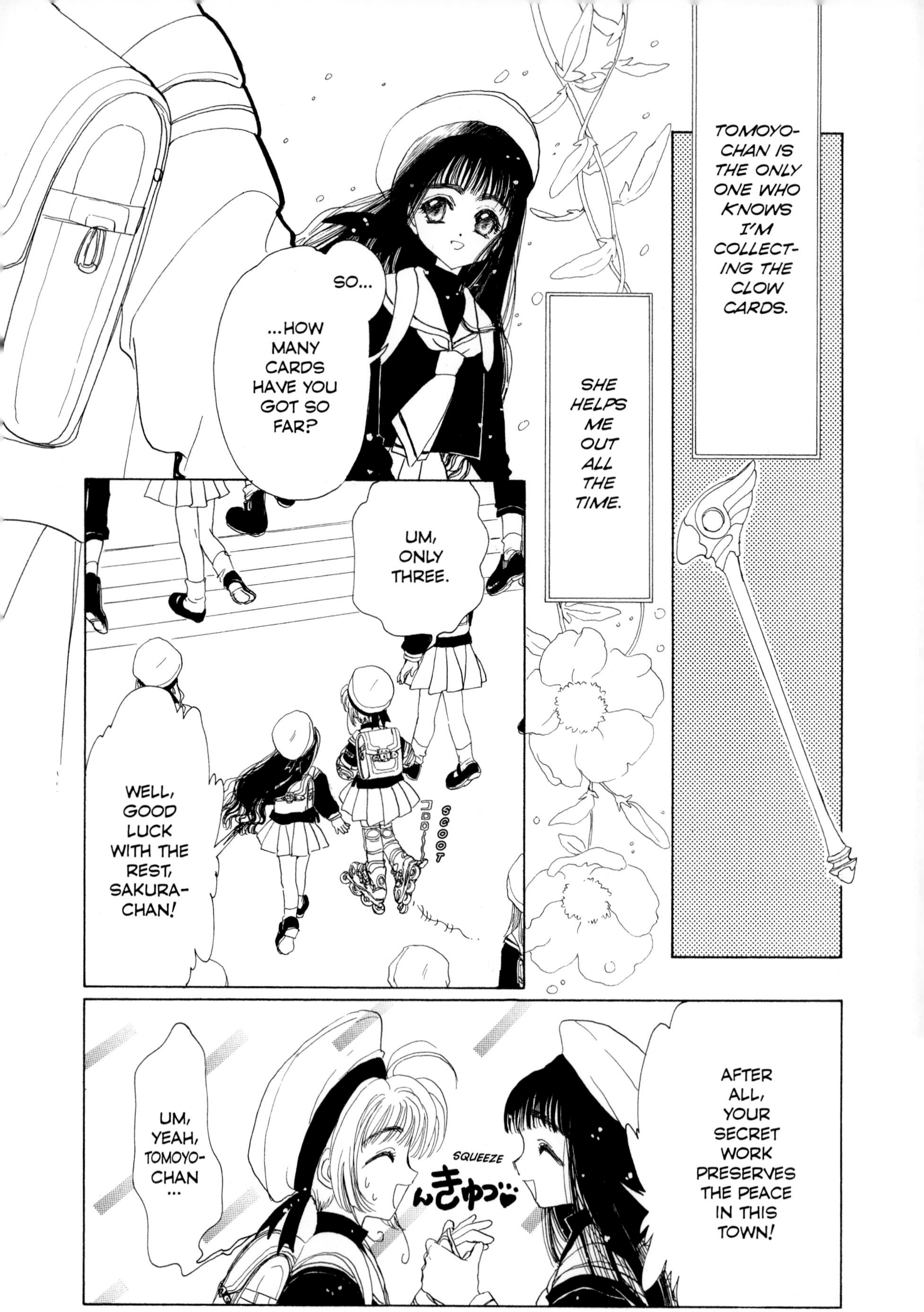
TOMOYO-CHAN IS THE ONLY ONE WHO KNOWS I'M COLLECTING THE CLOW CARDS.
SHE HELPS ME OUT ALL THE TIME.
SO...
...HOW MANY CARDS HAVE YOU GOT SO FAR?
UM, ONLY THREE.
SCOOOT
WELL, GOOD LUCK WITH THE REST, SAKURA-CHAN!
AFTER ALL, YOUR SECRET WORK PRESERVES THE PEACE IN THIS TOWN!
SQUEEZE
UM, YEAH, TOMOYO-CHAN...

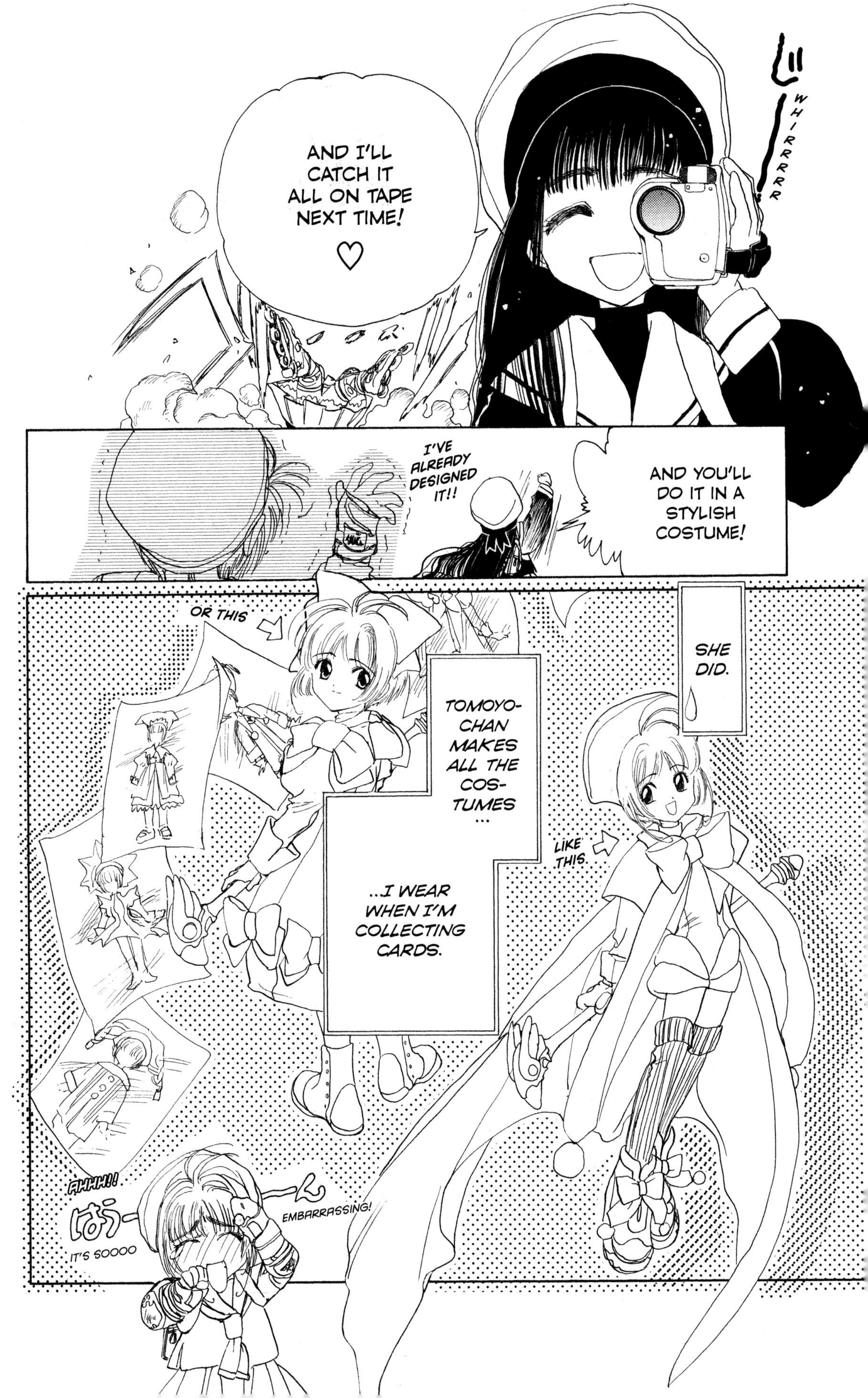
じ WHIRRRRR
AND I'LL CATCH IT ALL ON TAPE NEXT TIME! ♡
AND YOU'LL DO IT IN A STYLISH COSTUME!
I'VE ALREADY DESIGNED IT!!
SHE DID.
TOMOYO-CHAN MAKES ALL THE COS-TUMES...
...I WEAR WHEN I'M COLLECTING CARDS.
LIKE THIS.
OR THIS
はうーーん AHHH!!
IT'S SOOOO EMBARRASSING!

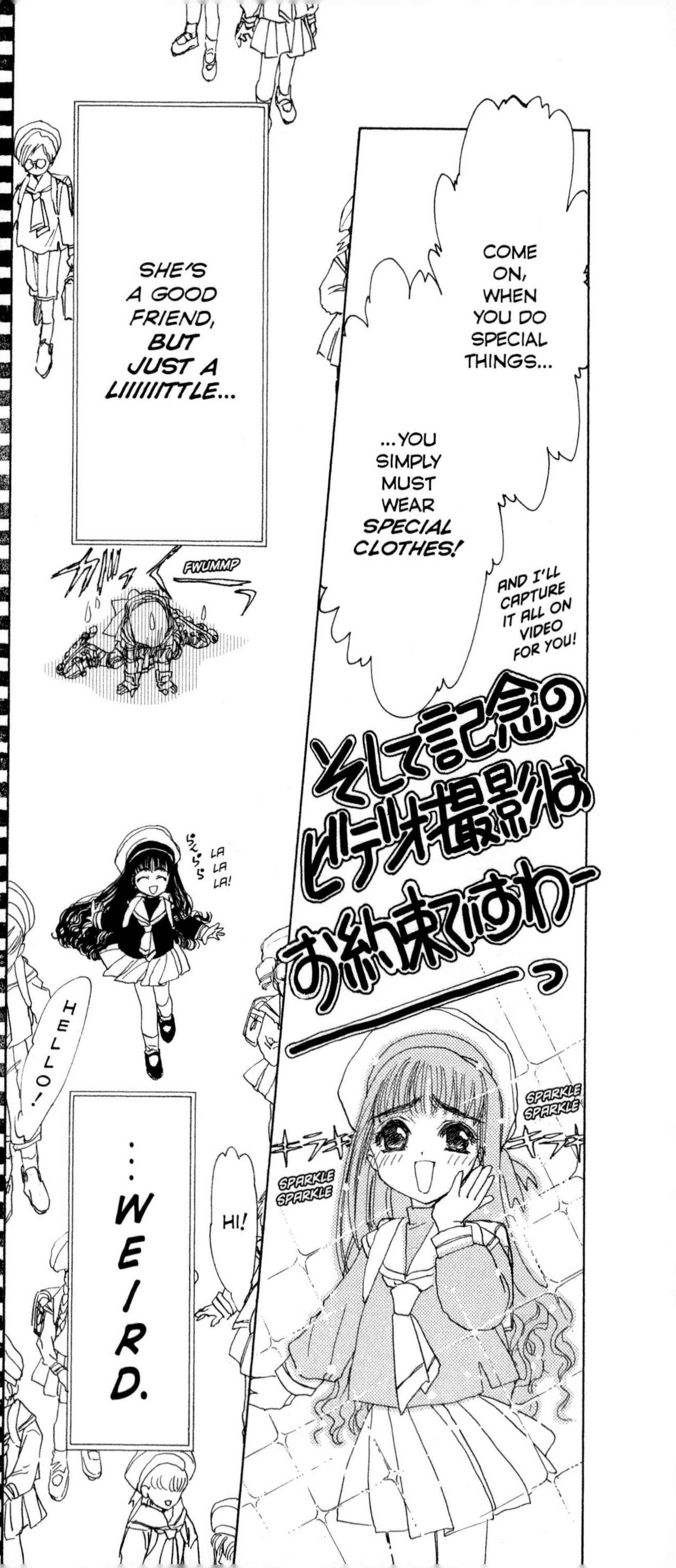
COME ON, WHEN YOU DO SPECIAL THINGS...
...YOU SIMPLY MUST WEAR SPECIAL CLOTHES!
AND I'LL CAPTURE IT ALL ON VIDEO FOR YOU!
そして記念のビデオ撮影はお約束ですわ——っ
SPARKLE SPARKLE
SPARKLE SPARKLE
SHE'S A GOOD FRIEND, BUT JUST A LIIIIIITTLE...
FWUMMP
LA LA LA!
HELLO!
...WEIRD.
HI!

1

SAKURA KINOMOTO

BIRTHDATE:
APRIL 1
BLOOD TYPE:
A
FAVORITE SUBJECTS:
P.E., MUSIC
LEAST FAVORITE SUBJECT:
MATH
CLUB:
CHEERLEADING
FAVORITE COLORS:
PINK, WHITE
FAVORITE FLOWER:
CHERRY BLOSSOM
FAVORITE FOODS:
RICE OMELETS, NOODLES
LEAST FAVORITE FOOD:
KONNYAKU
FAVORITE RECIPE:
PANCAKES
WISH LIST:
A NEW SCHOOL BAG

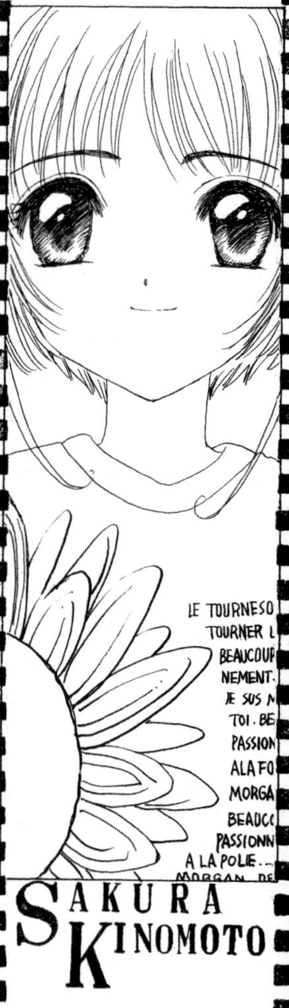
SAKURA KINOMOTO

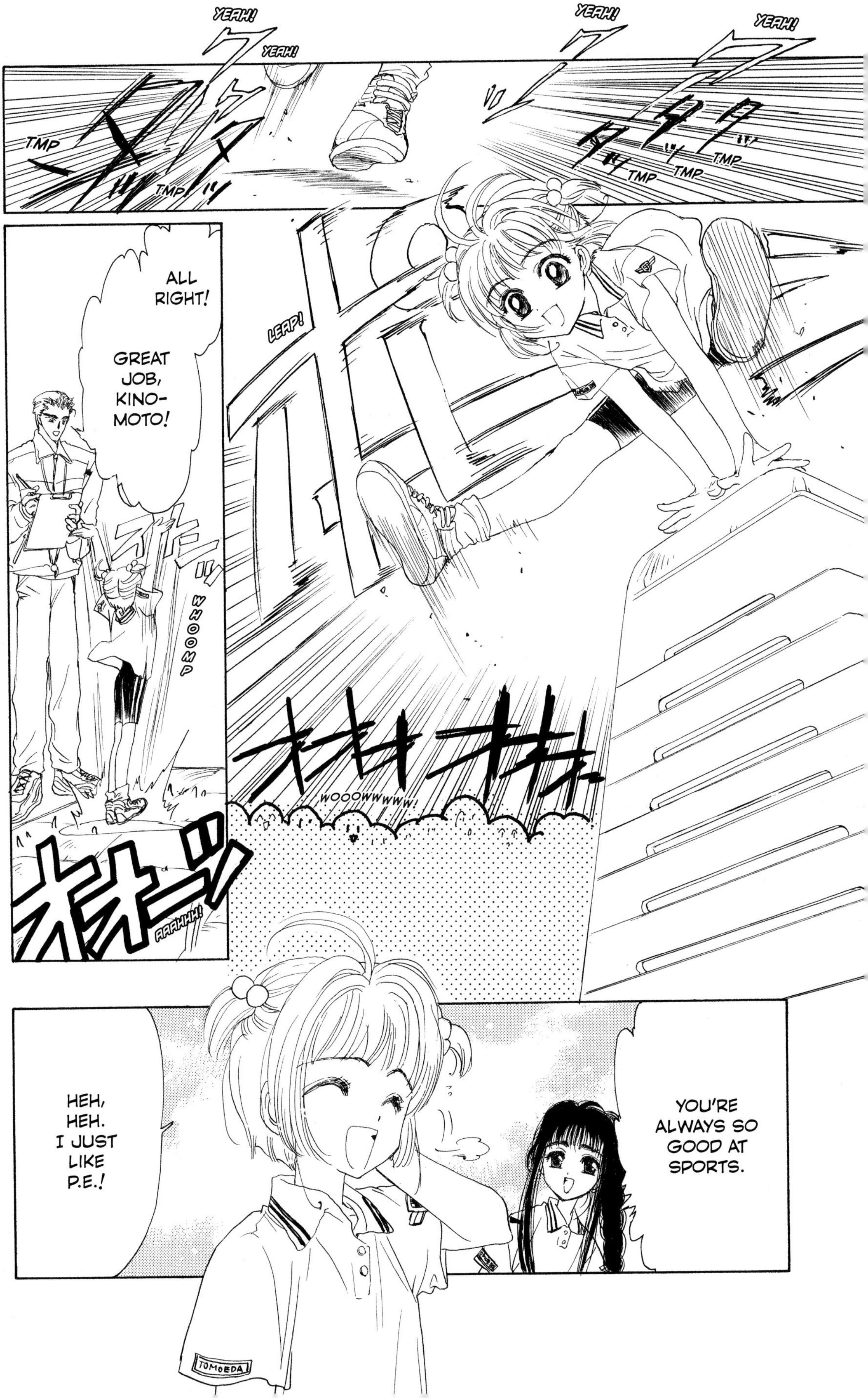
YEAH!
YEAH!
YEAH!
YEAH!
TMP
TMP
TMP
TMP
TMP
LEAP!
WOOOWWWWW!
ALL RIGHT!
GREAT JOB, KINO-MOTO!
WHOOOMP
AAAHHH!
YOU'RE ALWAYS SO GOOD AT SPORTS.
HEH, HEH. I JUST LIKE P.E.!
TOMOEDA

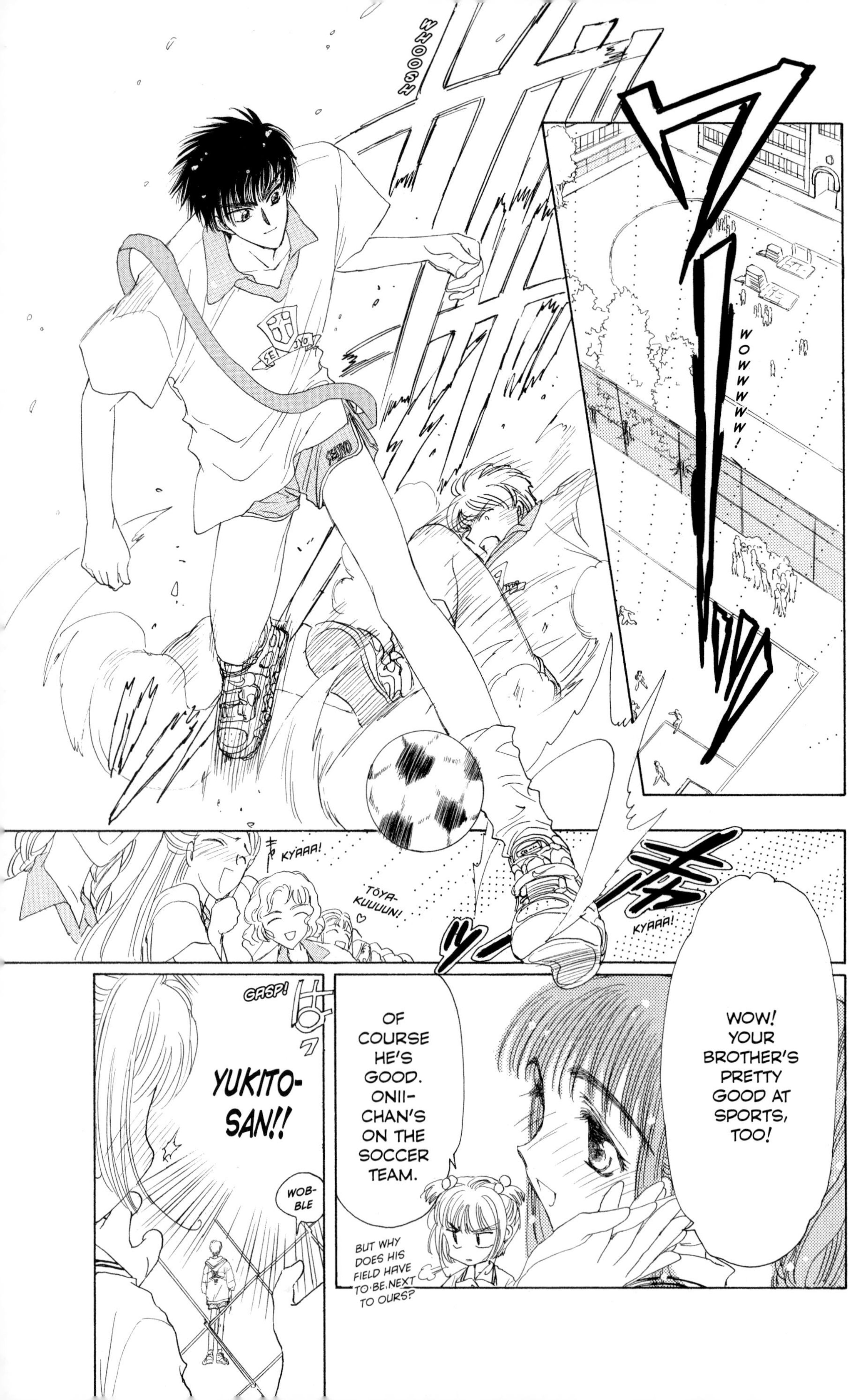
WOWWWWWWW!
WHOOSH
KYAAA!
TŌYA-KUUUUN!
KYAAA!
WOW! YOUR BROTHER'S PRETTY GOOD AT SPORTS, TOO!
OF COURSE HE'S GOOD. ONII-CHAN'S ON THE SOCCER TEAM.
BUT WHY DOES HIS FIELD HAVE TO BE NEXT TO OURS?
GASP!
YUKITO-SAN!!
WOB-BLE

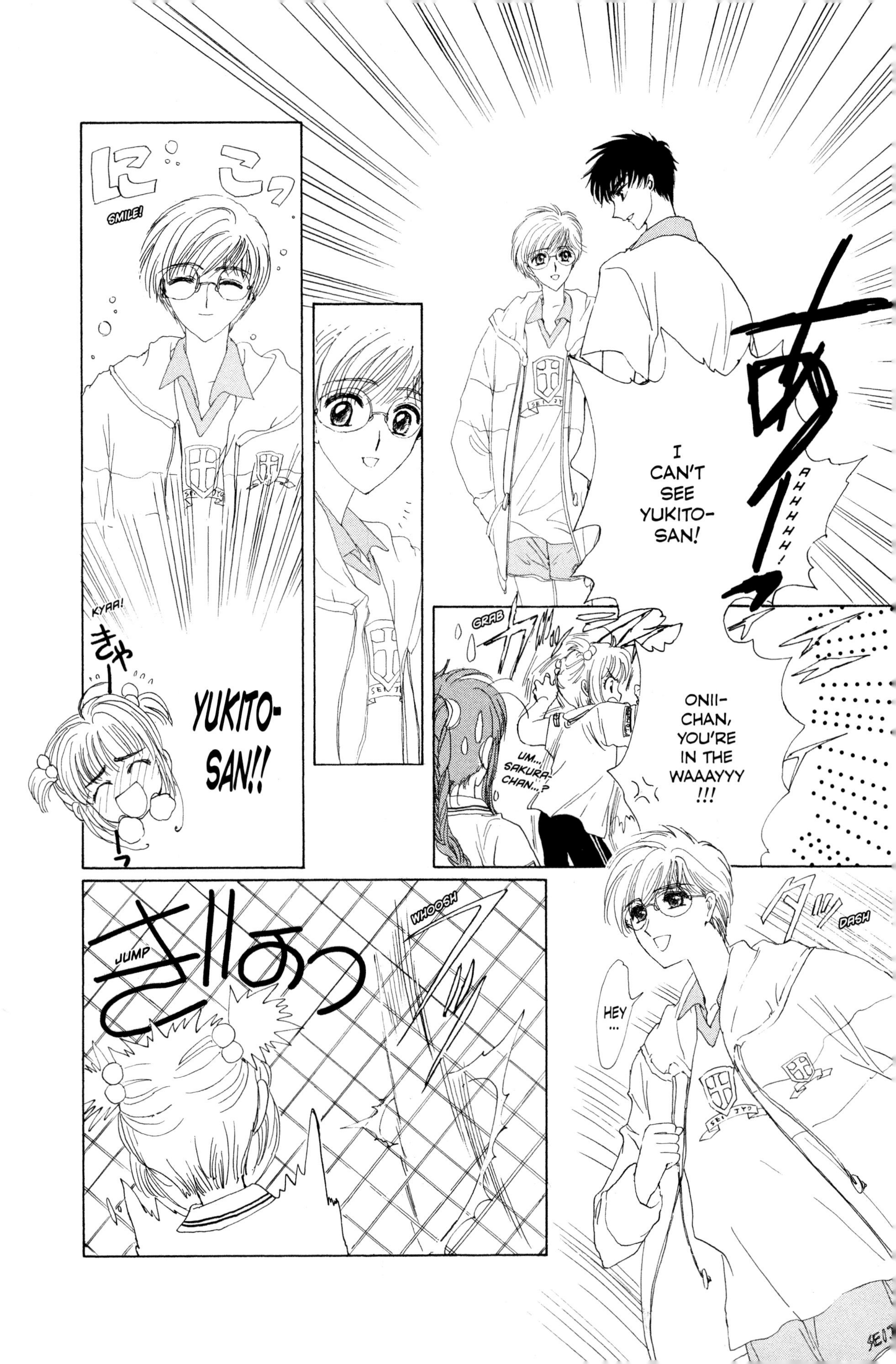
あーっ
AHHHHHH!
I CAN'T SEE YUKITO-SAN!
GRAB
UM... SAKURA-CHAN...?
ONII-CHAN, YOU'RE IN THE WAAAYYY!!!
にこっ
SMILE!
きゃーっ
KYAA!
YUKITO-SAN!!
タッ
DASH
HEY ...
WHOOSH
JUMP

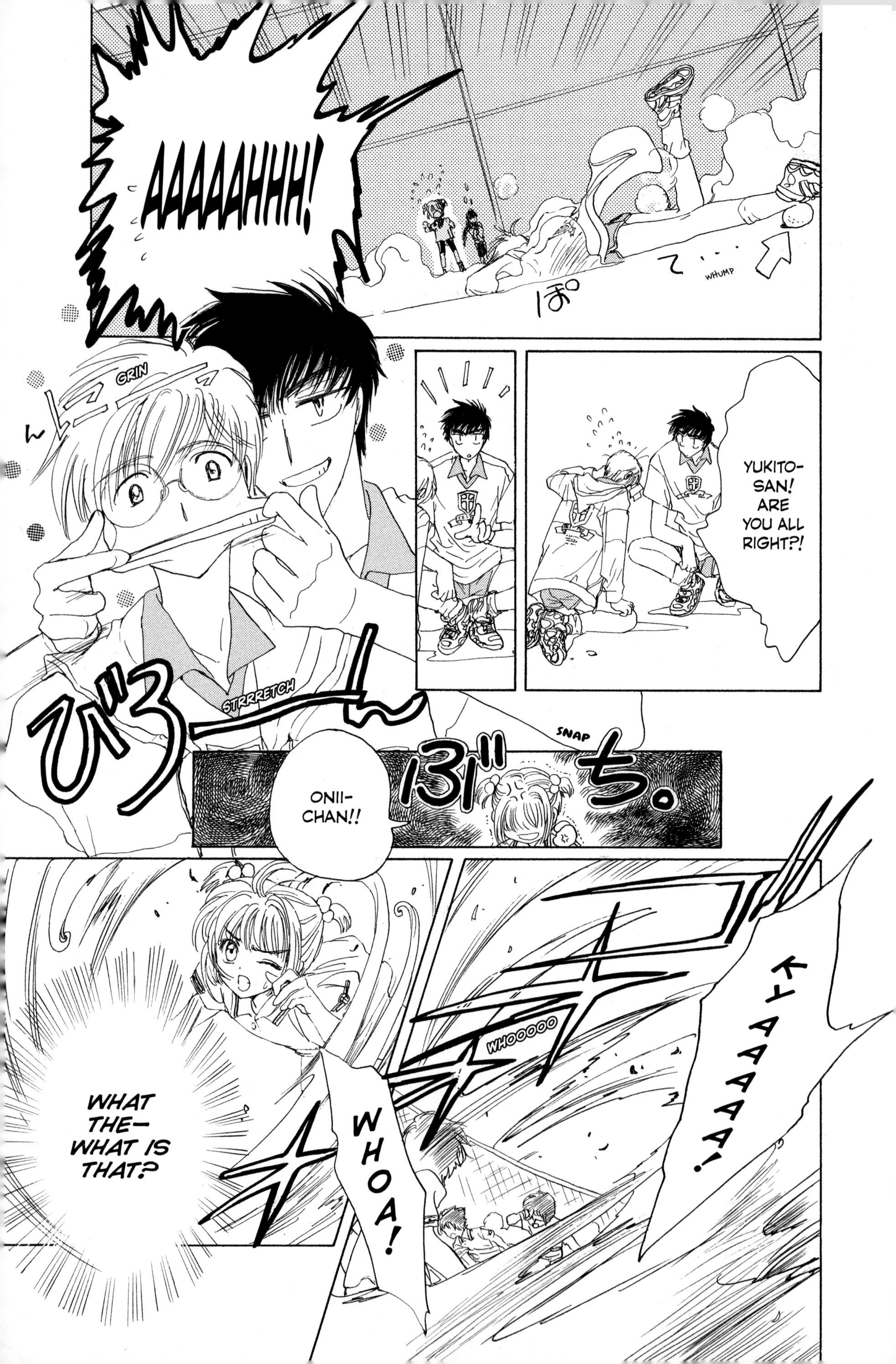

AAAAAHHH!
て...
ぽ
WHUMP
YUKITO-SAN! ARE YOU ALL RIGHT?!
ん
GRIN
びろーん
STRRRETCH
SNAP
ぶち。
ONII-CHAN!!
KYAAAAAAA!
WHOOOOO
WHOA!
WHAT THE—WHAT IS THAT?

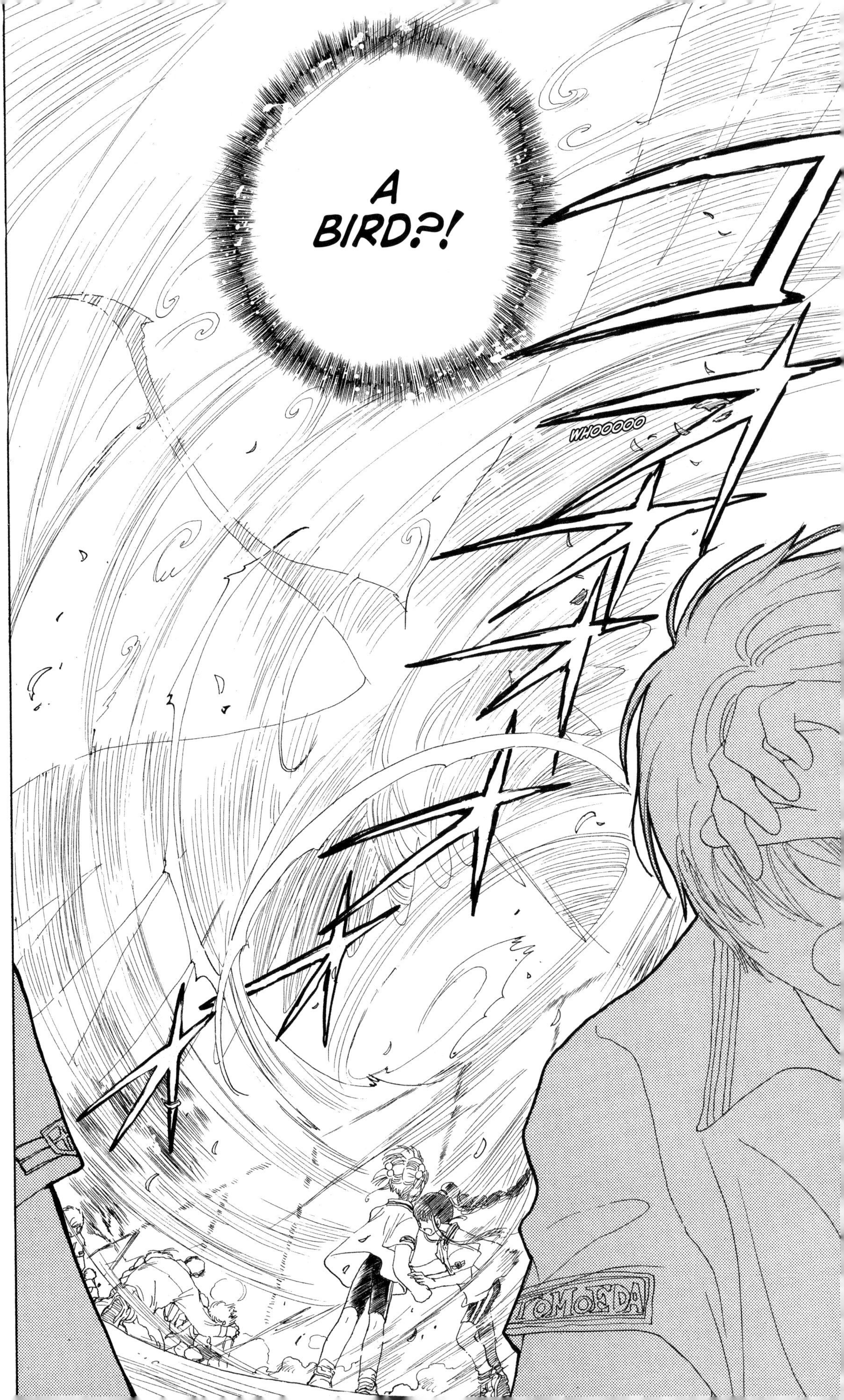
A BIRD?!
WHOOOOO
TOMOEDA

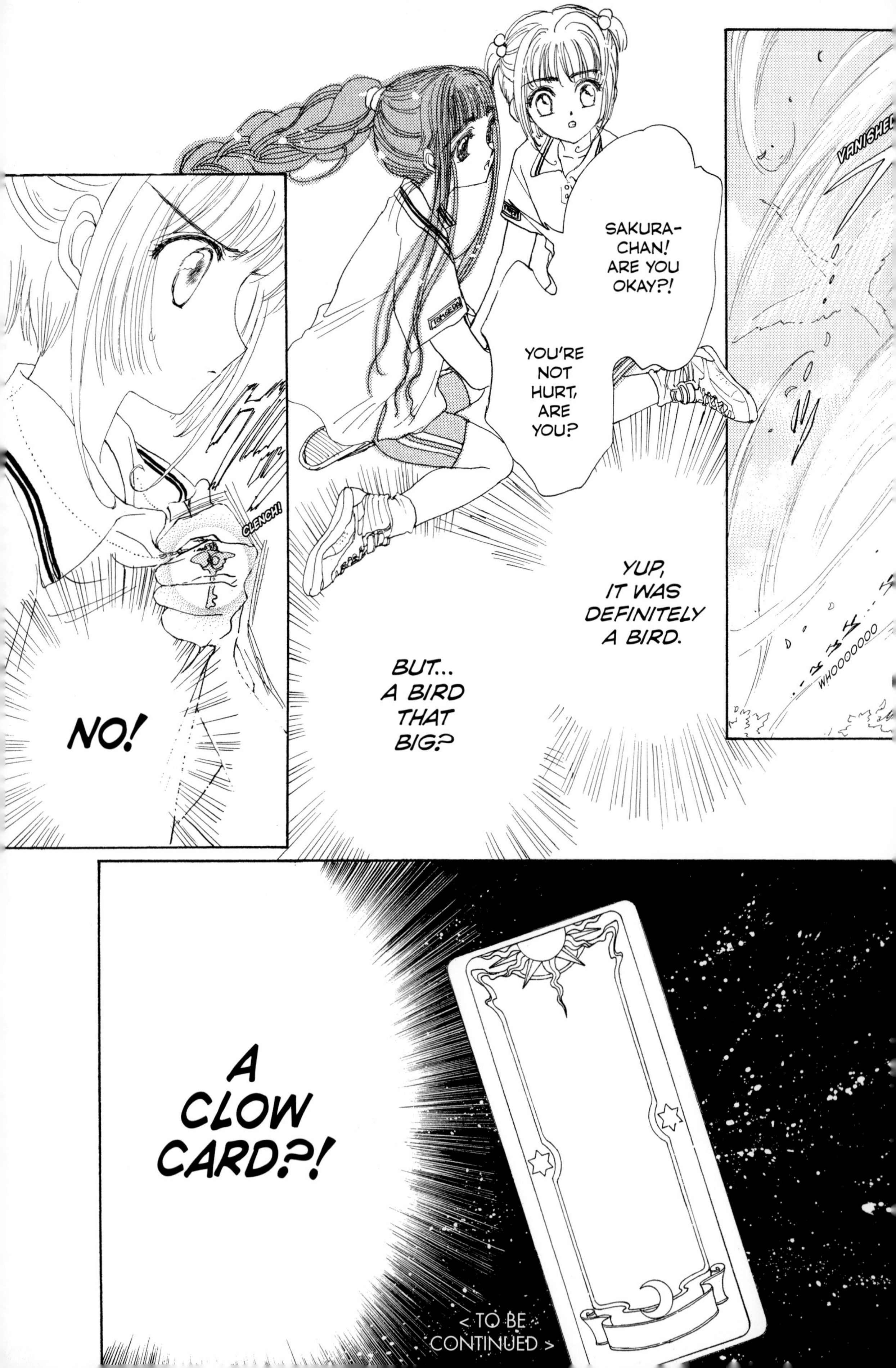
VANISHED
WHOOOOOOO
SAKURA-CHAN! ARE YOU OKAY?!
YOU'RE NOT HURT, ARE YOU?
YUP, IT WAS DEFINITELY A BIRD.
BUT... A BIRD THAT BIG?
CLENCH!
NO!
A CLOW CARD?!
< TO BE CONTINUED >

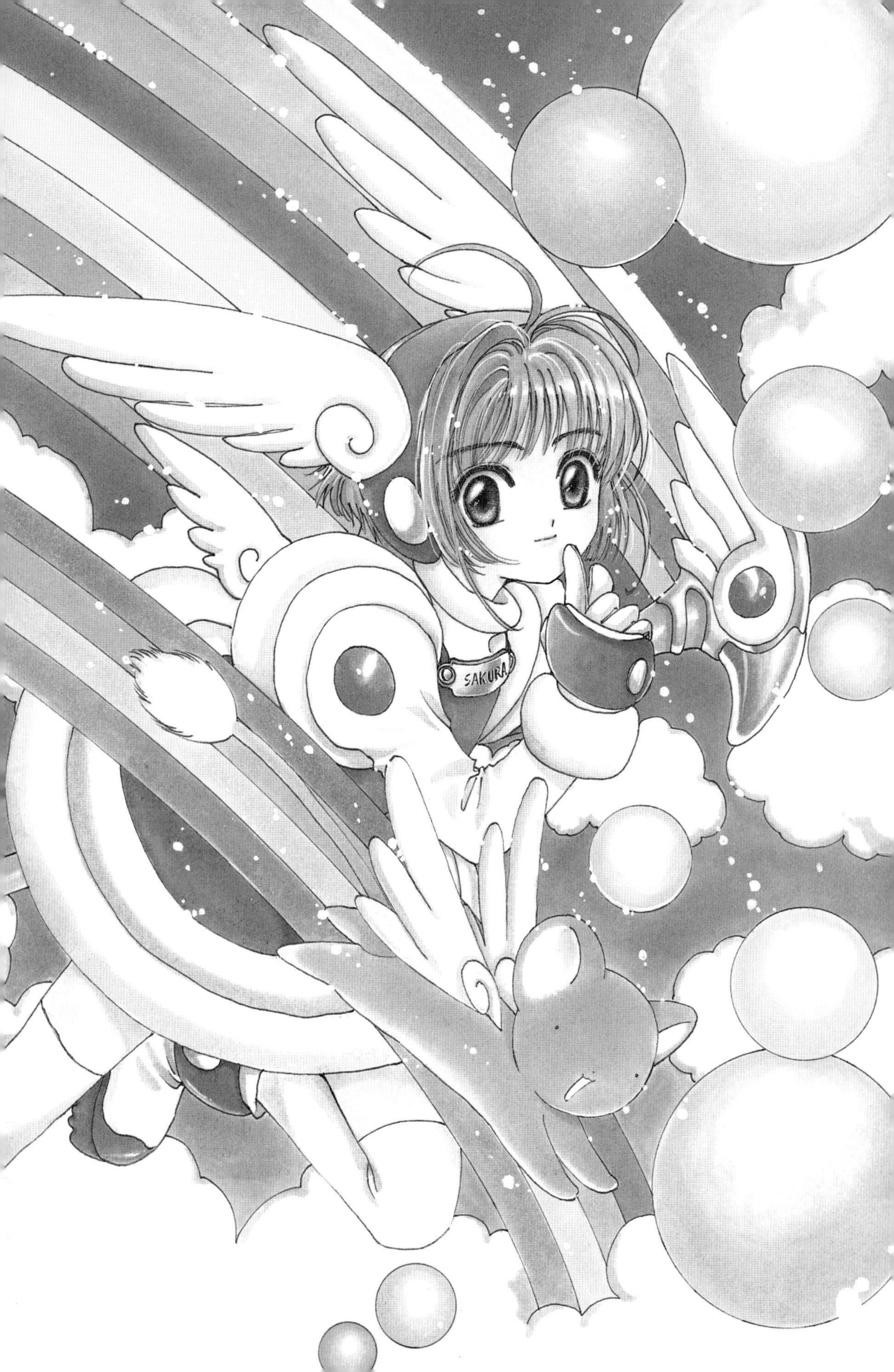
SAKURA

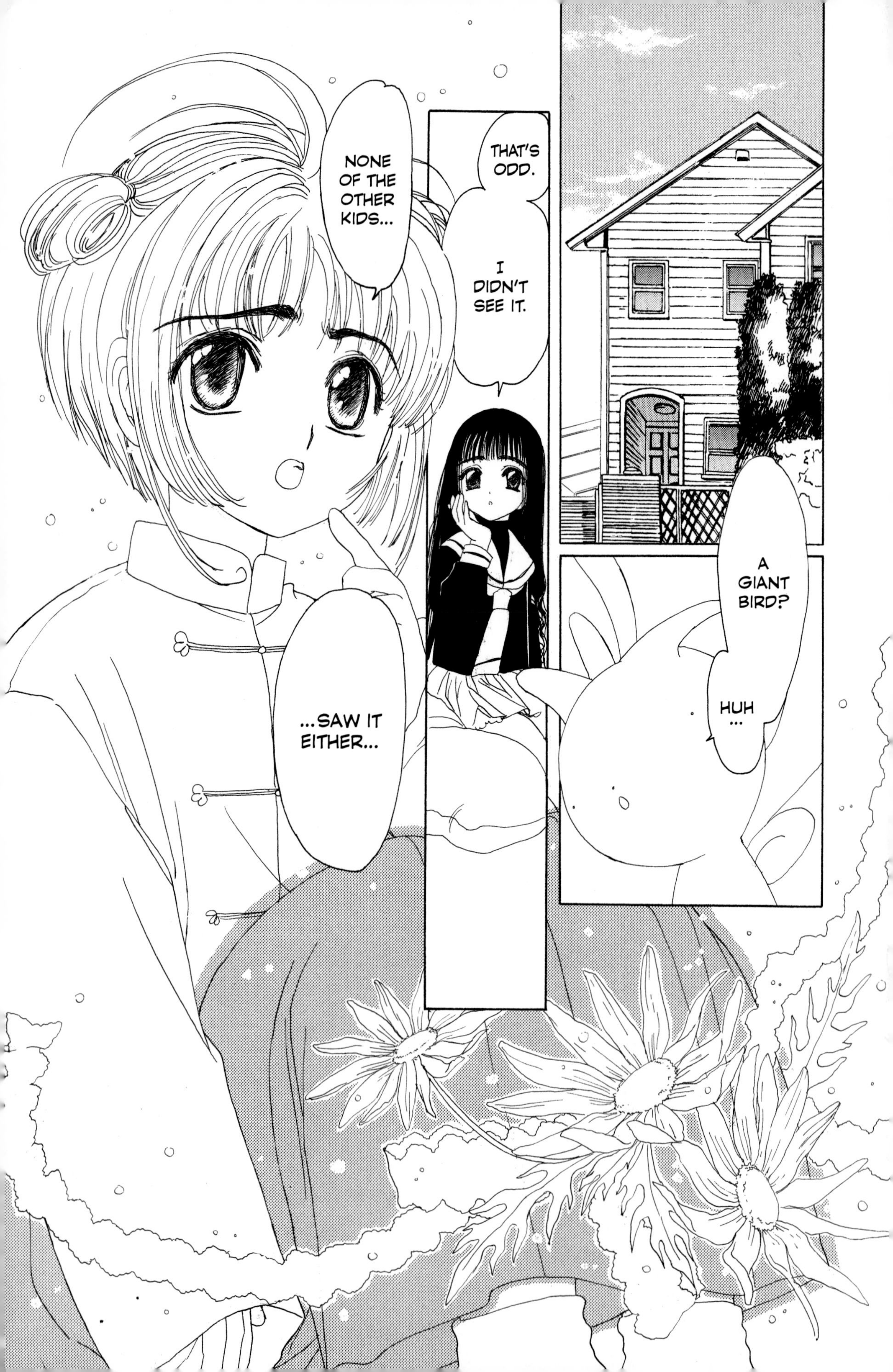
A GIANT BIRD?
HUH...
THAT'S ODD.
I DIDN'T SEE IT.
NONE OF THE OTHER KIDS...
...SAW IT EITHER...

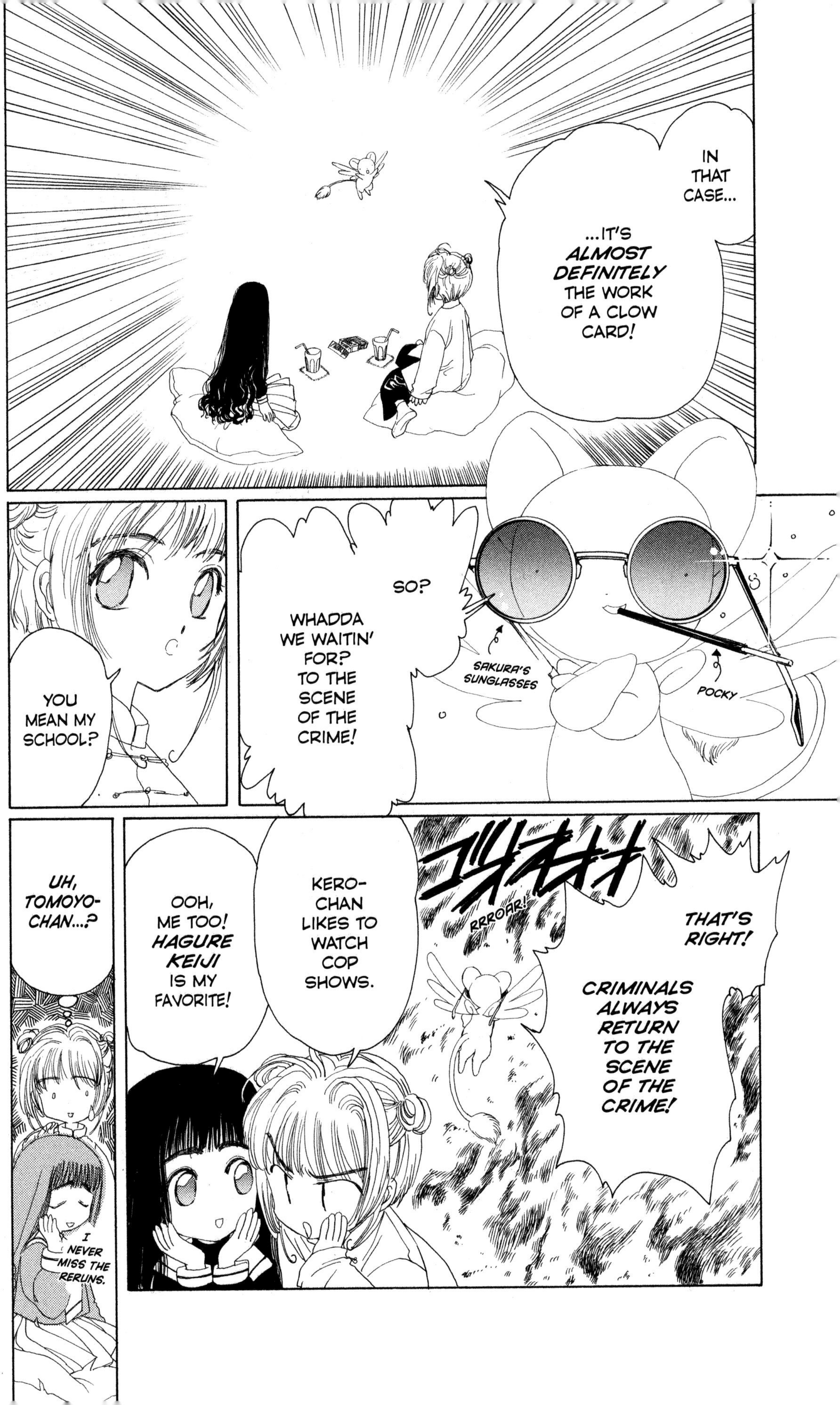
IN THAT CASE...
...IT'S ALMOST DEFINITELY THE WORK OF A CLOW CARD!
SO?
WHADDA WE WAITIN' FOR? TO THE SCENE OF THE CRIME!
SAKURA'S SUNGLASSES
POCKY
YOU MEAN MY SCHOOL?
THAT'S RIGHT!
CRIMINALS ALWAYS RETURN TO THE SCENE OF THE CRIME!
RRROAR!
KERO-CHAN LIKES TO WATCH COP SHOWS.
OOH, ME TOO! HAGURE KEIJI IS MY FAVORITE!
UH, TOMOYO-CHAN...?
I NEVER MISS THE RERUNS.

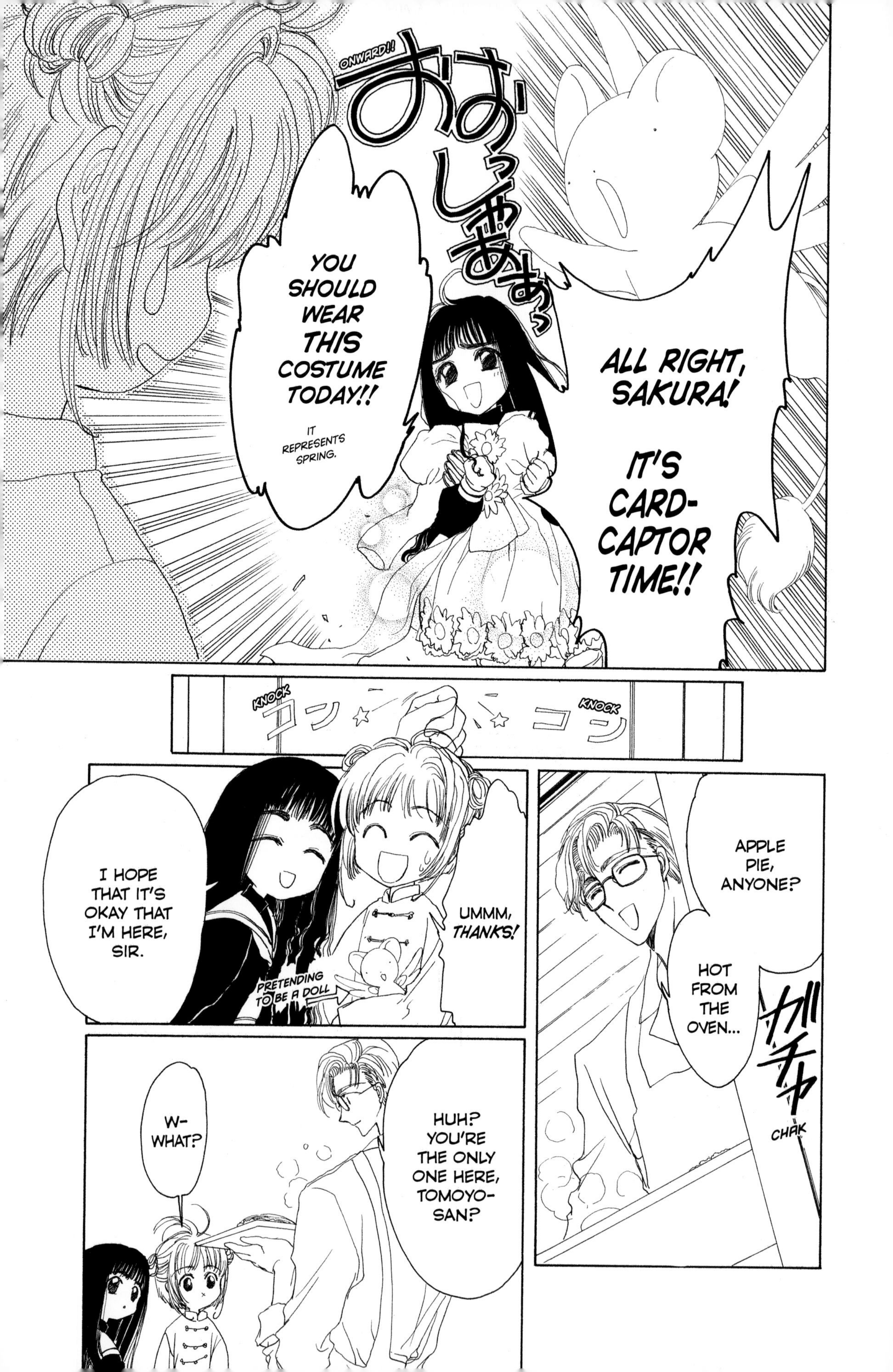
ALL RIGHT, SAKURA!
IT'S CARD-CAPTOR TIME!!
ONWARD!!
YOU SHOULD WEAR THIS COSTUME TODAY!!
IT REPRESENTS SPRING.
KNOCK
KNOCK
APPLE PIE, ANYONE?
HOT FROM THE OVEN...
CHAK
UMMM, THANKS!
PRETENDING TO BE A DOLL
I HOPE THAT IT'S OKAY THAT I'M HERE, SIR.
HUH? YOU'RE THE ONLY ONE HERE, TOMOYO-SAN?
W-WHAT?

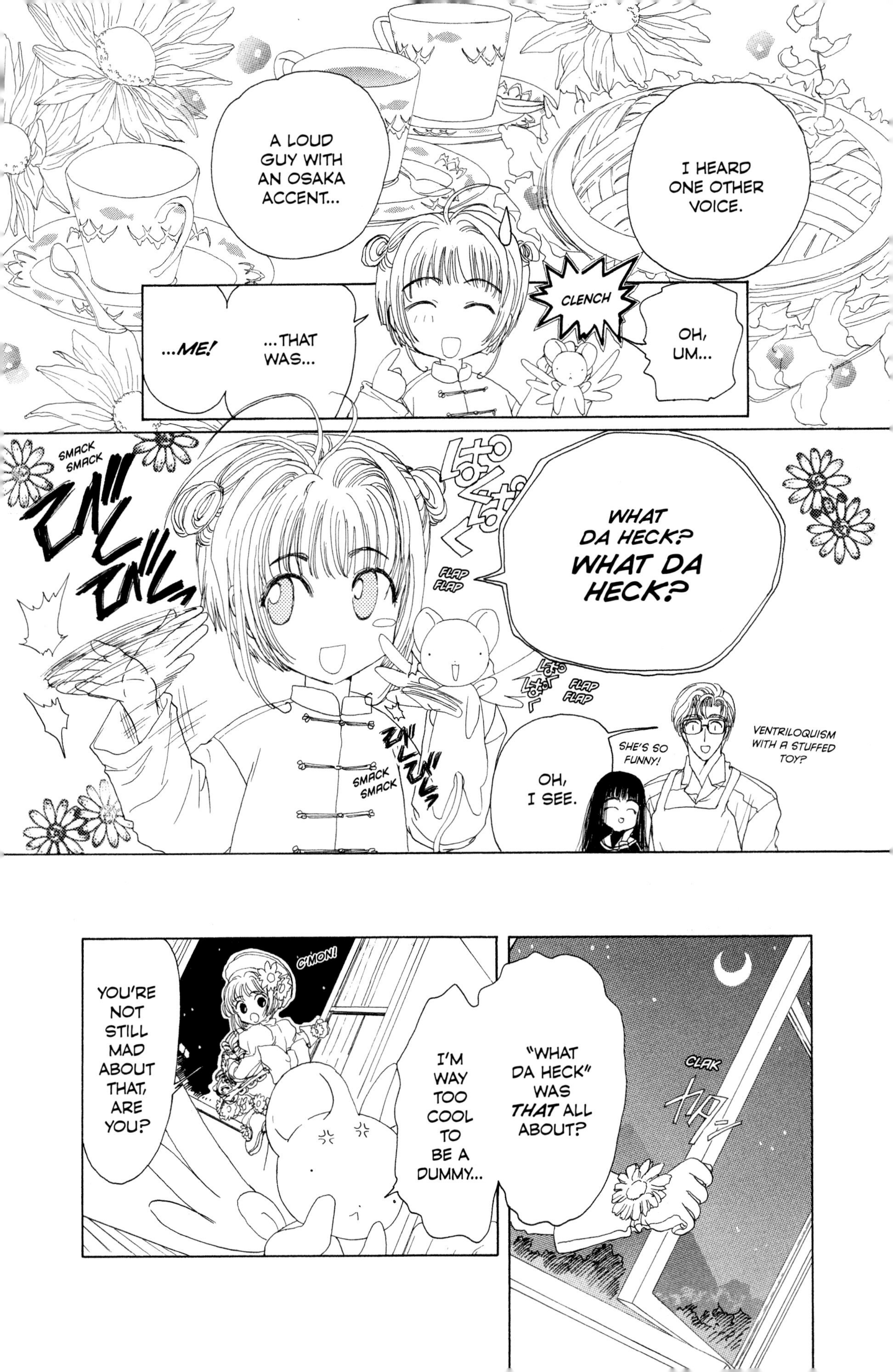
I HEARD ONE OTHER VOICE.
A LOUD GUY WITH AN OSAKA ACCENT...
OH, UM...
CLENCH
...THAT WAS...
...ME!
WHAT DA HECK? WHAT DA HECK?
FLAP FLAP
SMACK SMACK
FLAP FLAP
SMACK SMACK
VENTRILOQUISM WITH A STUFFED TOY?
SHE'S SO FUNNY!
OH, I SEE.
CLAK
"WHAT DA HECK" WAS THAT ALL ABOUT?
I'M WAY TOO COOL TO BE A DUMMY...
C'MON!
YOU'RE NOT STILL MAD ABOUT THAT, ARE YOU?

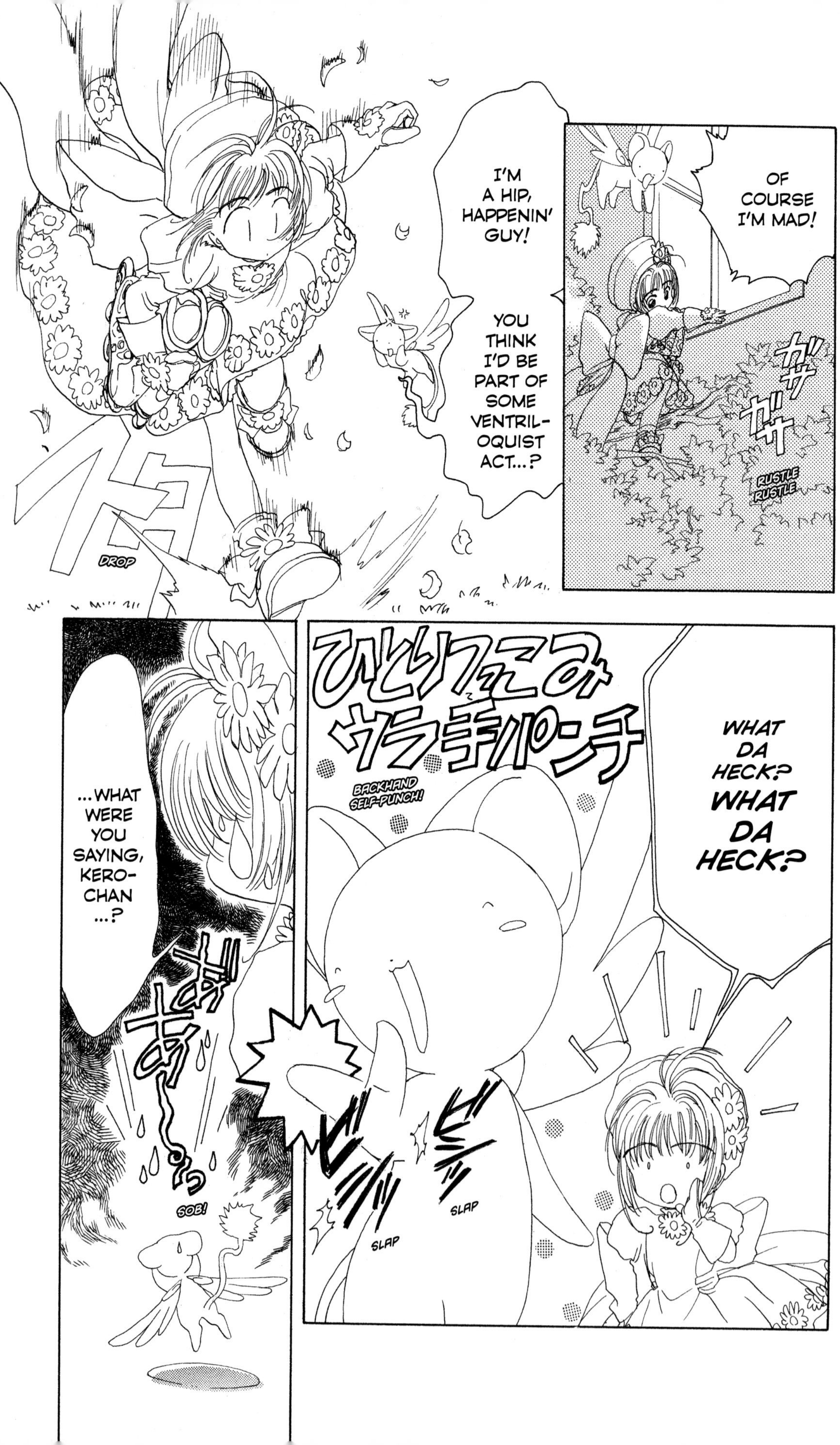
OF COURSE I'M MAD!
ガサ ガサ
RUSTLE RUSTLE
I'M A HIP, HAPPENIN' GUY!
YOU THINK I'D BE PART OF SOME VENTRIL-OQUIST ACT...?
DROP
ひとりつっこみウラ手パンチ
BACKHAND SELF-PUNCH!
WHAT DA HECK? WHAT DA HECK?
SLAP
SLAP
...WHAT WERE YOU SAYING, KERO-CHAN ...?
SOB!

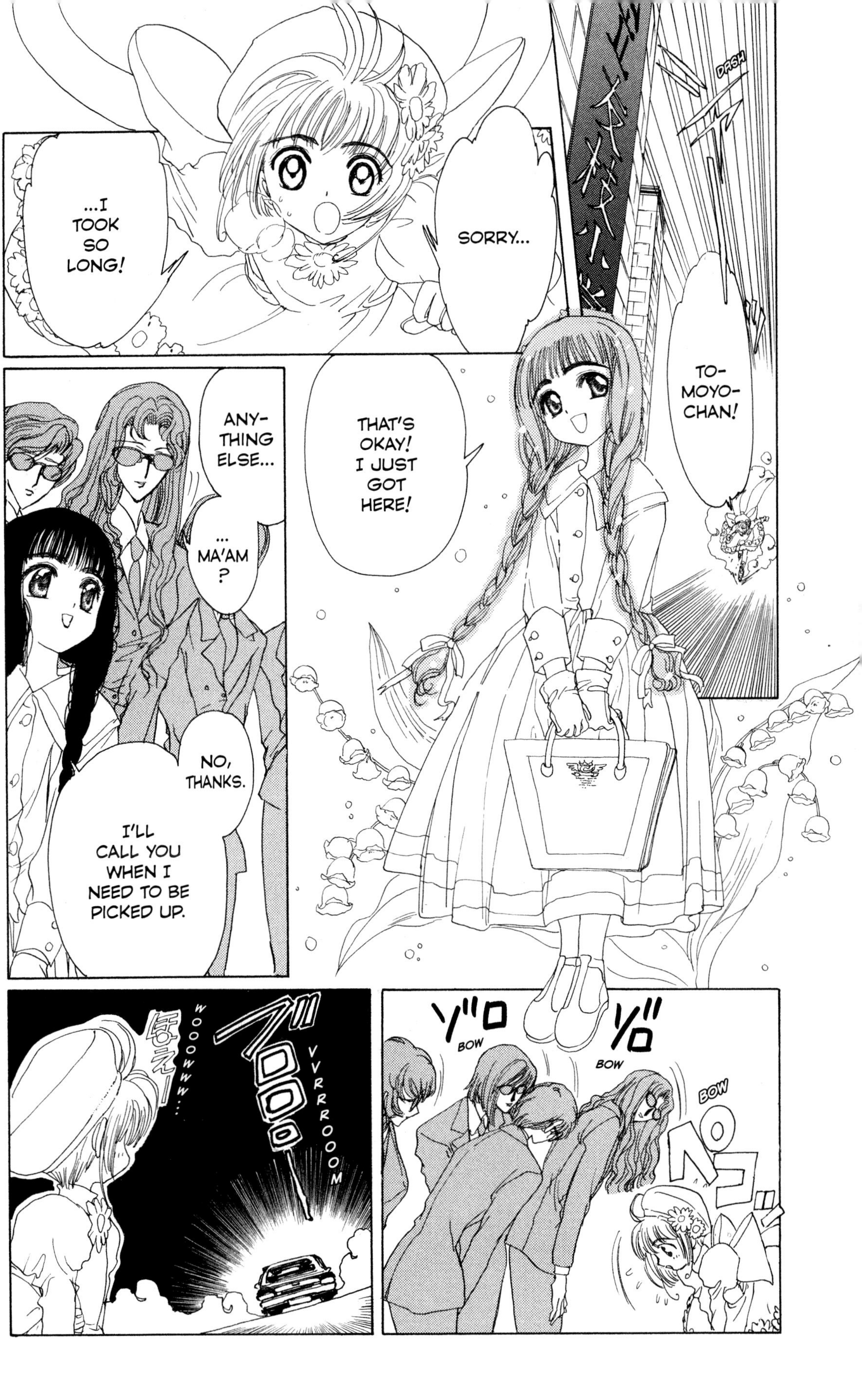
DASH
TO-MOYO-CHAN!
SORRY...
...I TOOK SO LONG!
THAT'S OKAY! I JUST GOT HERE!
ANYTHING ELSE...
...MA'AM?
NO, THANKS.
I'LL CALL YOU WHEN I NEED TO BE PICKED UP.
BOW
BOW
BOW
VVRRROOOM
WOOOWWW...

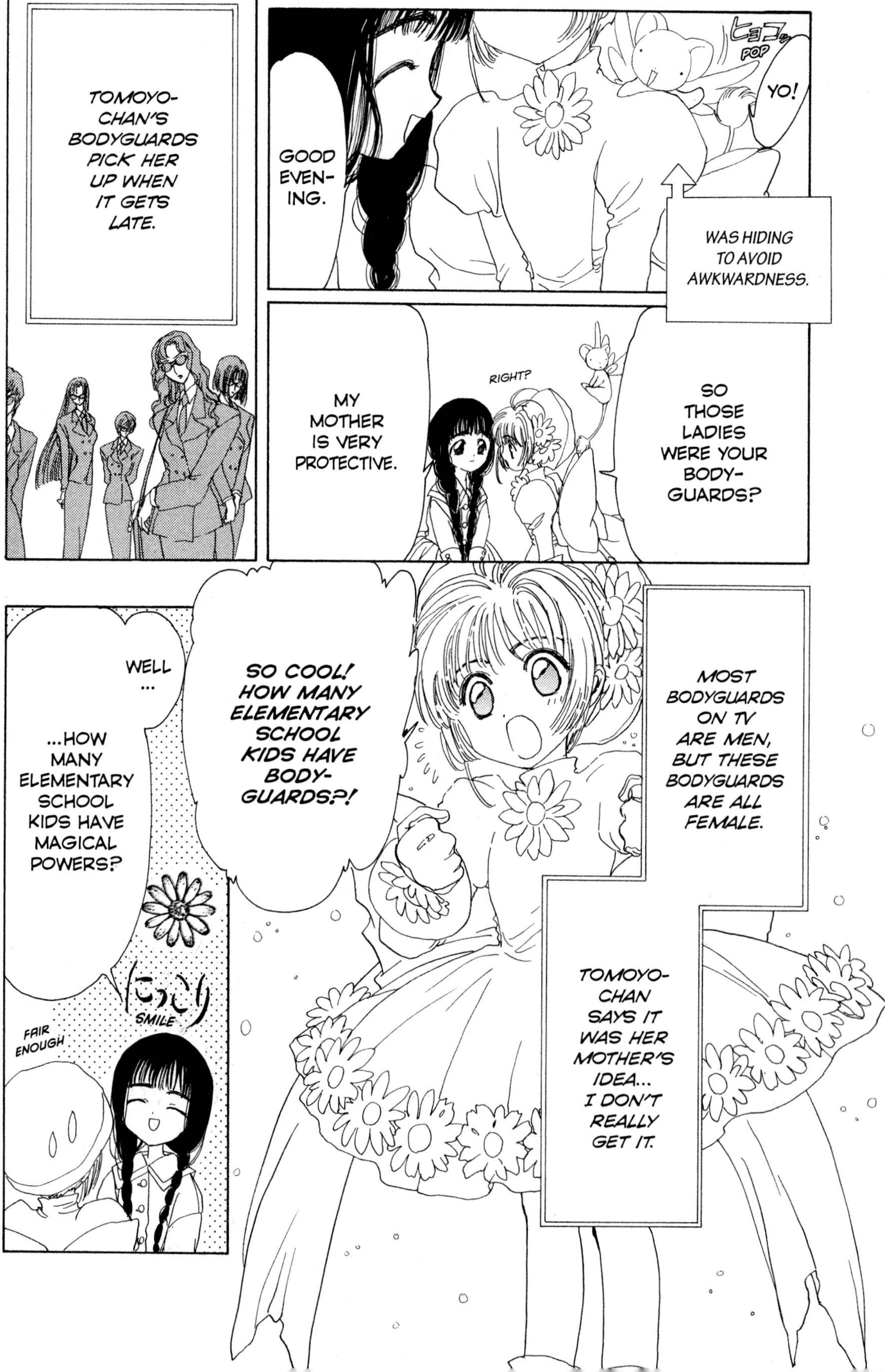
ヒョコッ
POP
YO!
WAS HIDING TO AVOID AWKWARDNESS.
GOOD EVENING.
SO THOSE LADIES WERE YOUR BODY-GUARDS?
RIGHT?
MY MOTHER IS VERY PROTECTIVE.
TOMOYO-CHAN'S BODYGUARDS PICK HER UP WHEN IT GETS LATE.
MOST BODYGUARDS ON TV ARE MEN, BUT THESE BODYGUARDS ARE ALL FEMALE.
SO COOL! HOW MANY ELEMENTARY SCHOOL KIDS HAVE BODY-GUARDS?!
TOMOYO-CHAN SAYS IT WAS HER MOTHER'S IDEA... I DON'T REALLY GET IT.
WELL ...
...HOW MANY ELEMENTARY SCHOOL KIDS HAVE MAGICAL POWERS?
にっこり
SMILE
FAIR ENOUGH

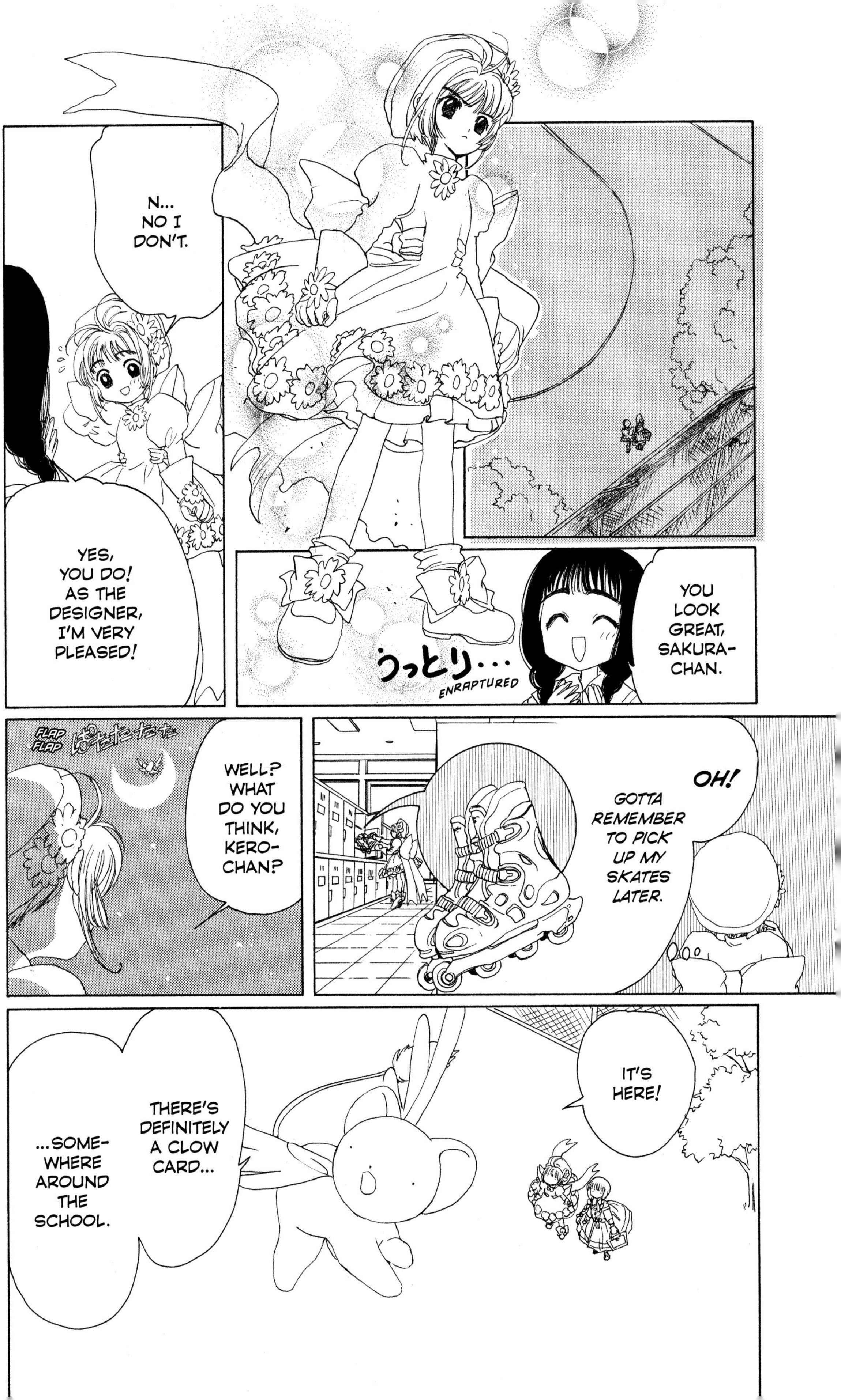
YOU LOOK GREAT, SAKURA-CHAN.
うっとり…
ENRAPTURED
N... NO I DON'T.
YES, YOU DO! AS THE DESIGNER, I'M VERY PLEASED!
OH!
GOTTA REMEMBER TO PICK UP MY SKATES LATER.
FLAP FLAP
ぱたたたた
WELL? WHAT DO YOU THINK, KERO-CHAN?
IT'S HERE!
THERE'S DEFINITELY A CLOW CARD...
...SOME-WHERE AROUND THE SCHOOL.

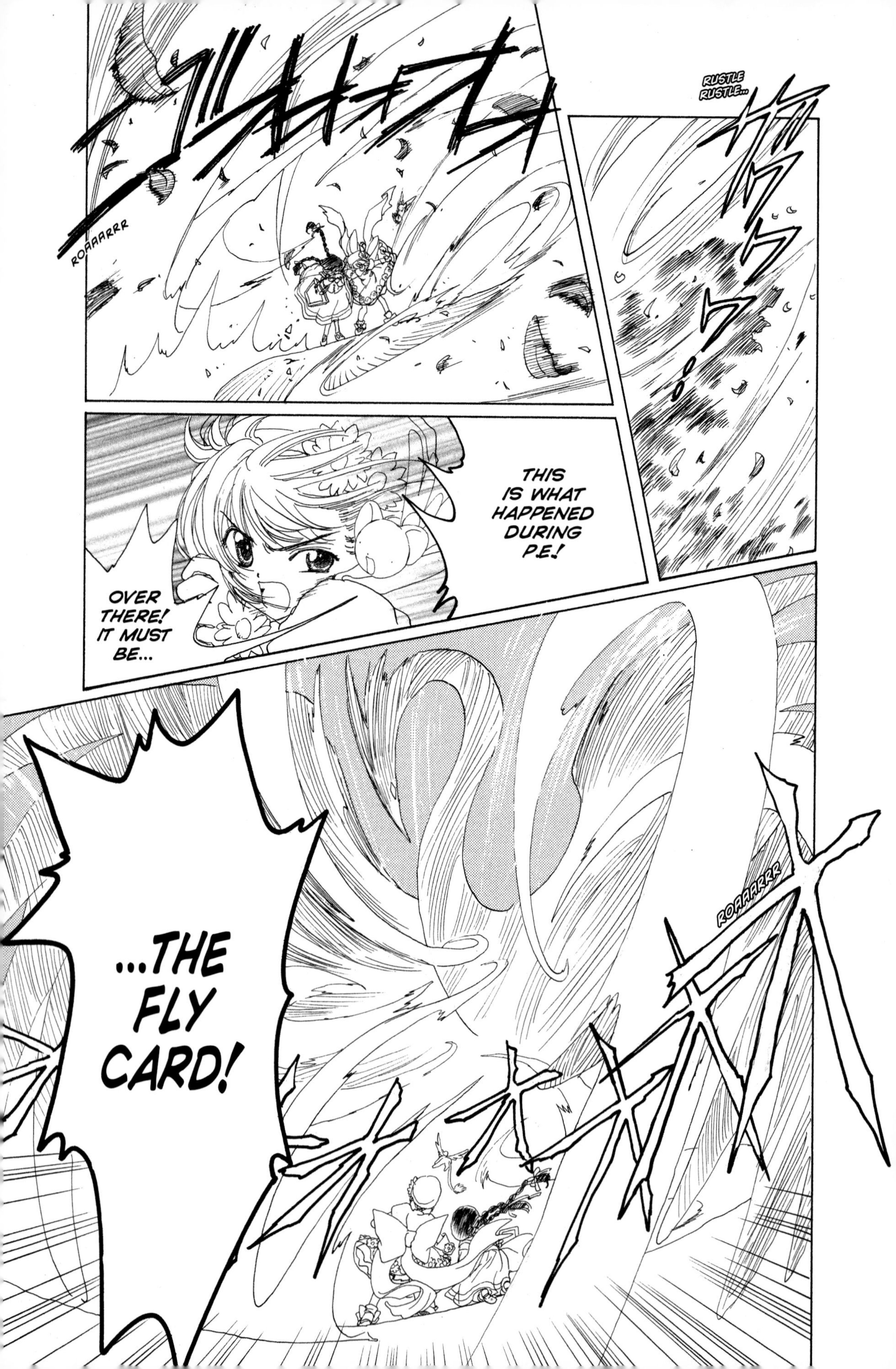
RUSTLE RUSTLE...
ROAAARRR
THIS IS WHAT HAPPENED DURING P.E.!
OVER THERE! IT MUST BE...
...THE FLY CARD!
ROAAARRR

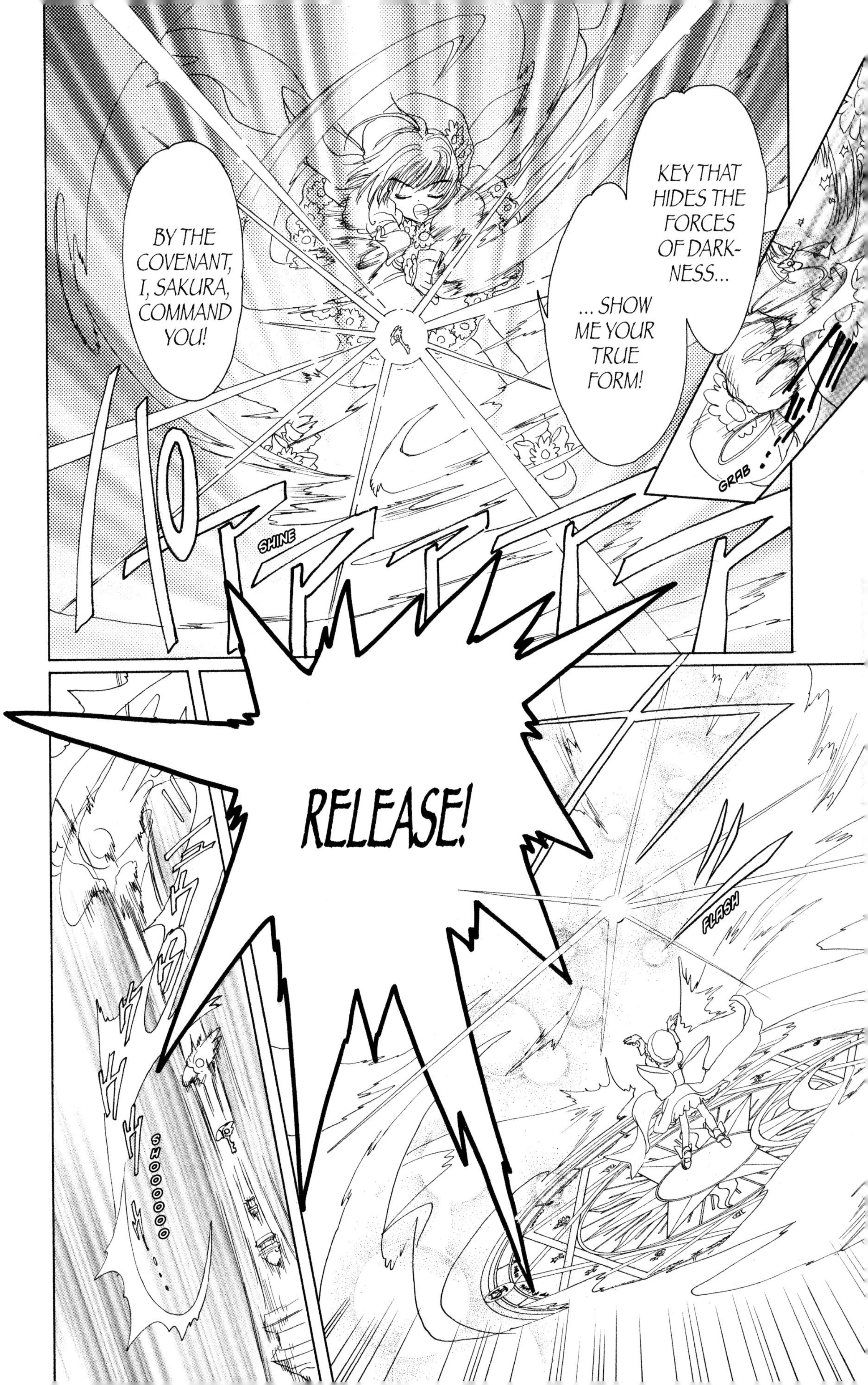
KEY THAT HIDES THE FORCES OF DARKNESS...
...SHOW ME YOUR TRUE FORM!
GRAB
BY THE COVENANT, I, SAKURA, COMMAND YOU!
SHINE
RELEASE!
FLASH
SHOOOOOOO...

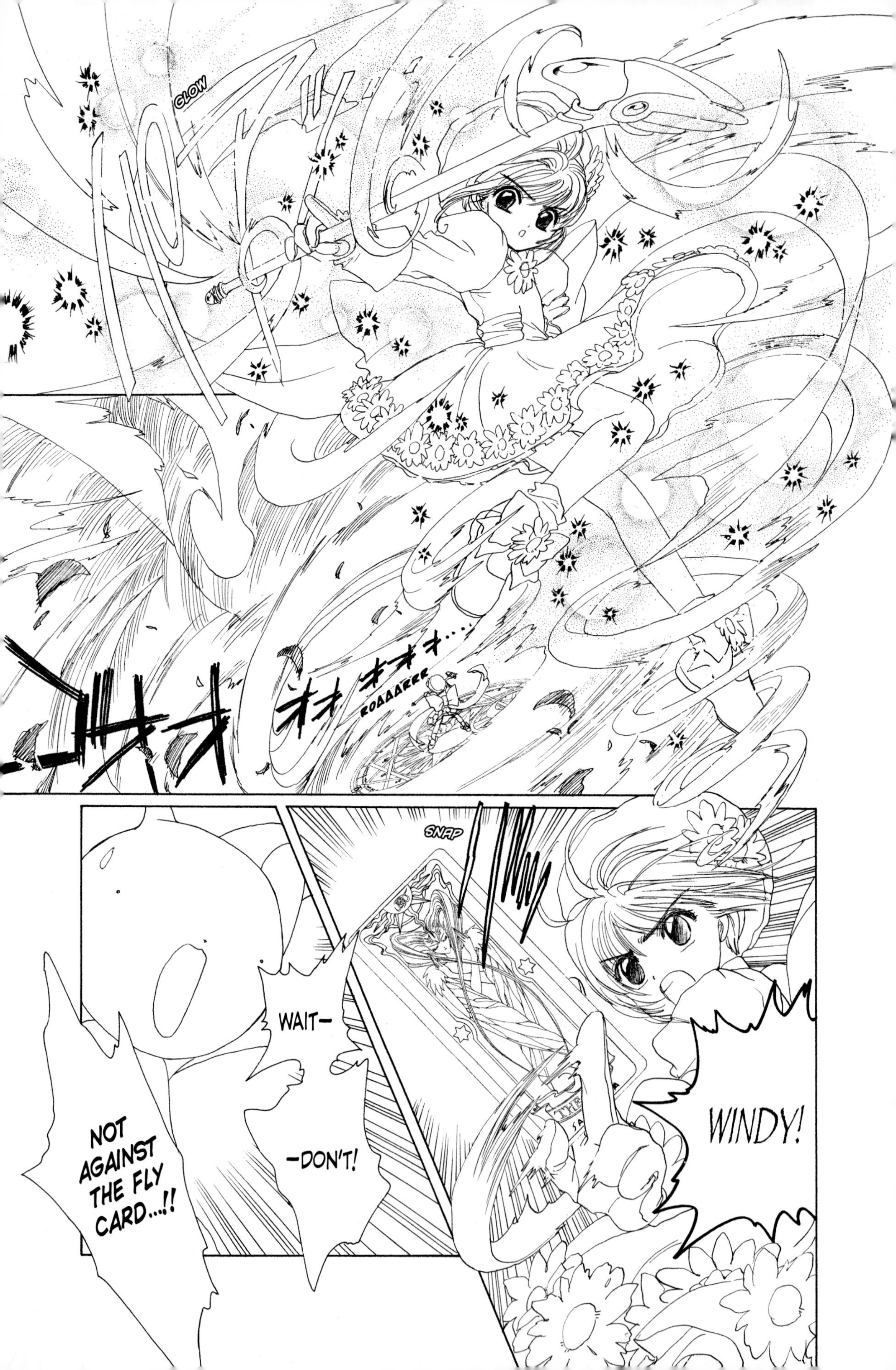
GLOW
ROAAARRR
SNAP
WINDY!
WAIT—
—DON'T!
NOT AGAINST THE FLY CARD...!!

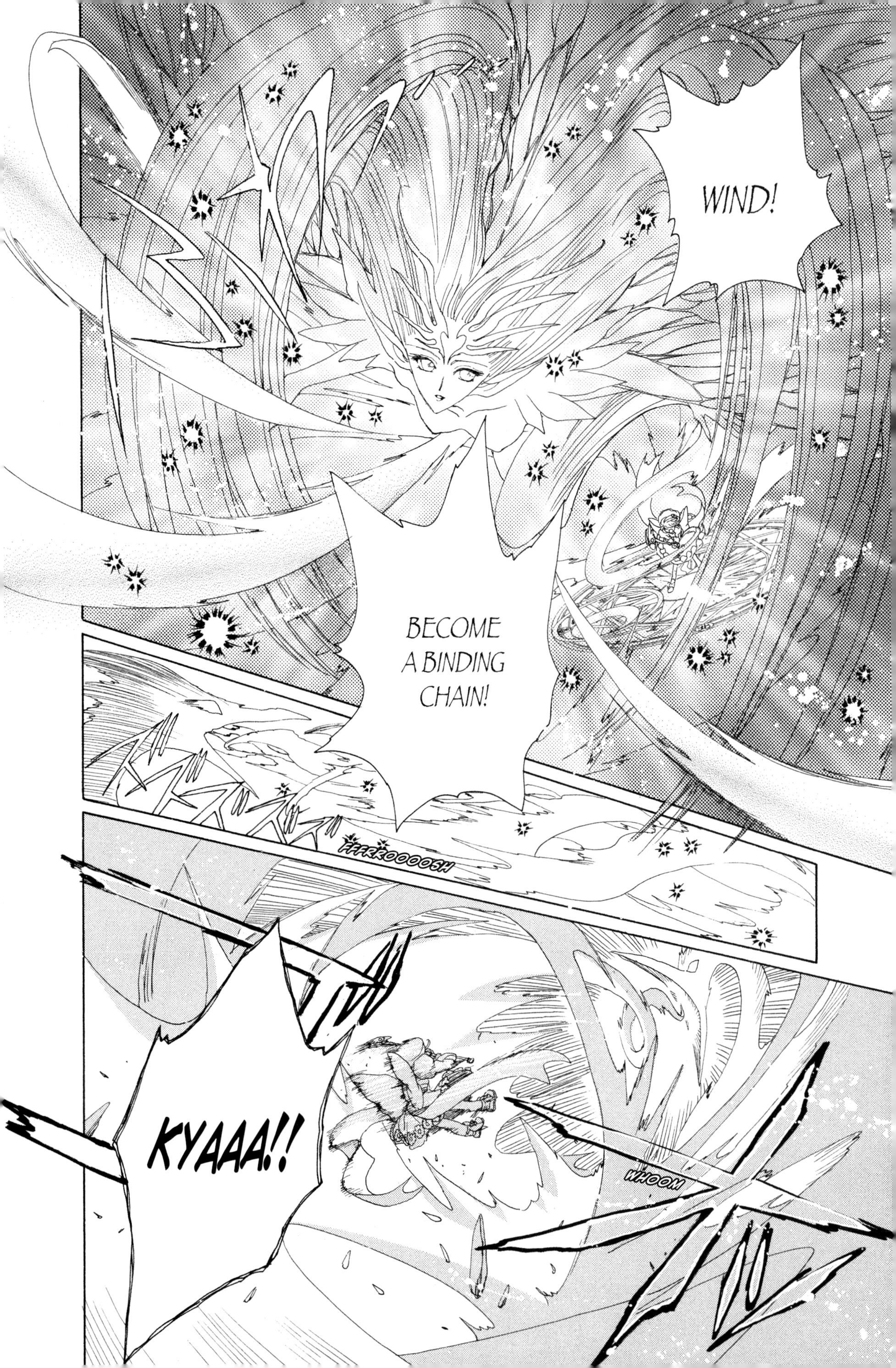
WIND!
BECOME A BINDING CHAIN!
FFFRROOOOOSH
WHOOM
KYAAA!!

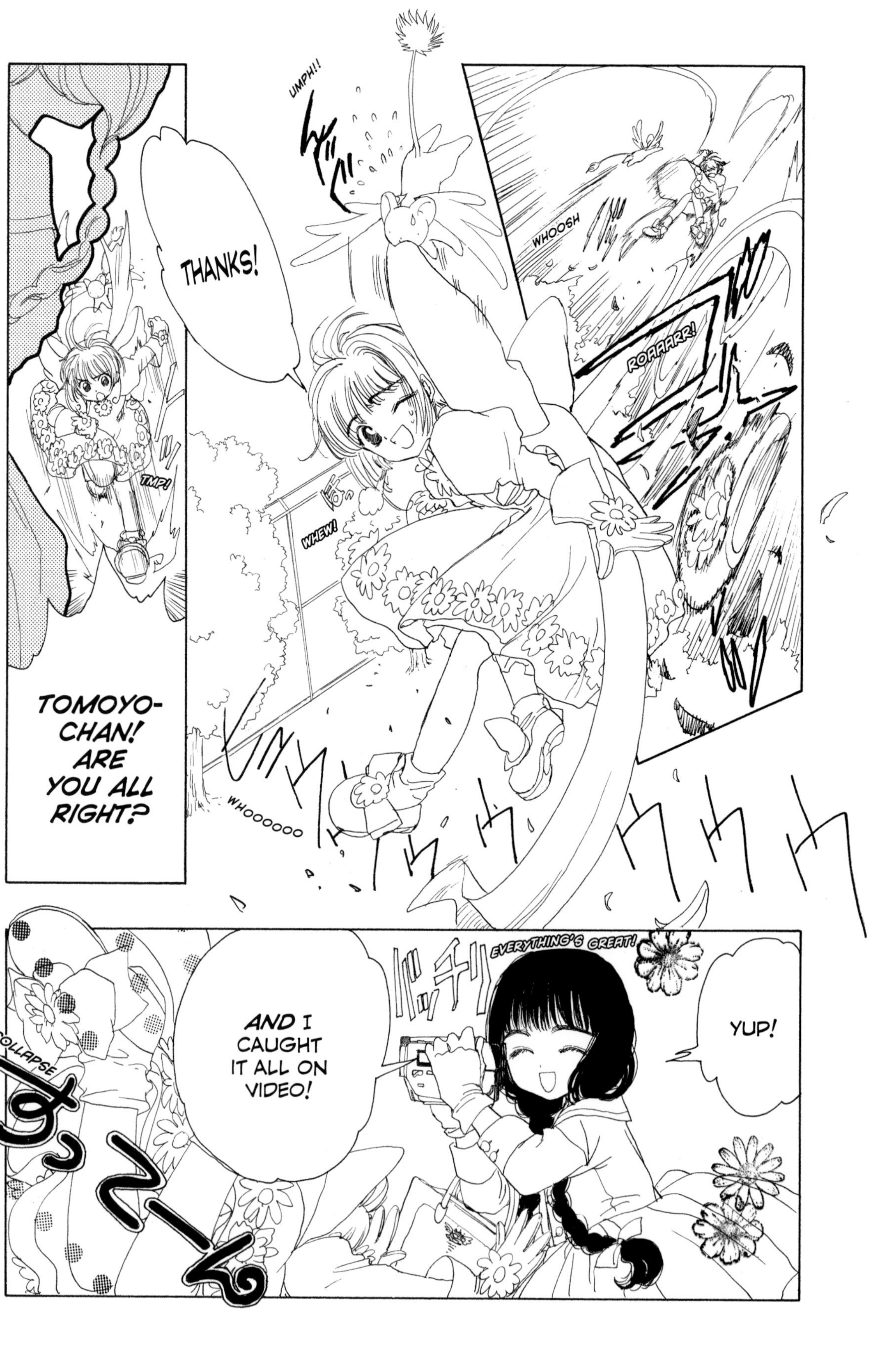

WHOOSH
ROAAARR!
UMPH!!
THANKS!
WHEW!
WHOOOOOO
TMP!
TOMOYO-CHAN! ARE YOU ALL RIGHT?
YUP!
EVERYTHING'S GREAT!
AND I CAUGHT IT ALL ON VIDEO!
COLLAPSE

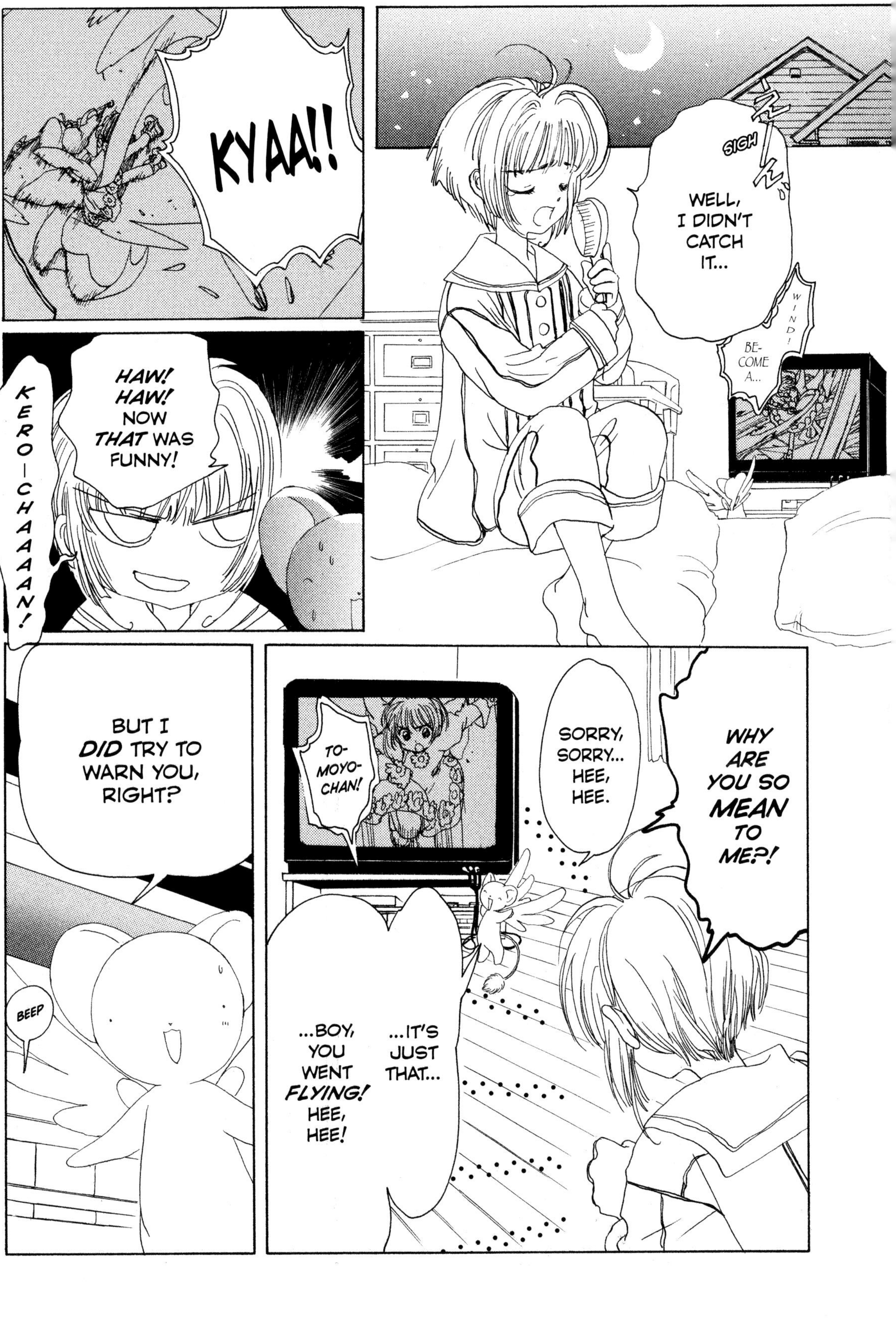
SIGH
WELL, I DIDN'T CATCH IT...
BE-COME A... WIND!
KYAA!!
HAW! HAW! NOW THAT WAS FUNNY!
KERO-CHAAAAAN!
WHY ARE YOU SO MEAN TO ME?!
SORRY, SORRY... HEE, HEE.
TO-MOYO-CHAN!
...IT'S JUST THAT...
...BOY, YOU WENT FLYING! HEE, HEE!
BUT I DID TRY TO WARN YOU, RIGHT?
BEEP

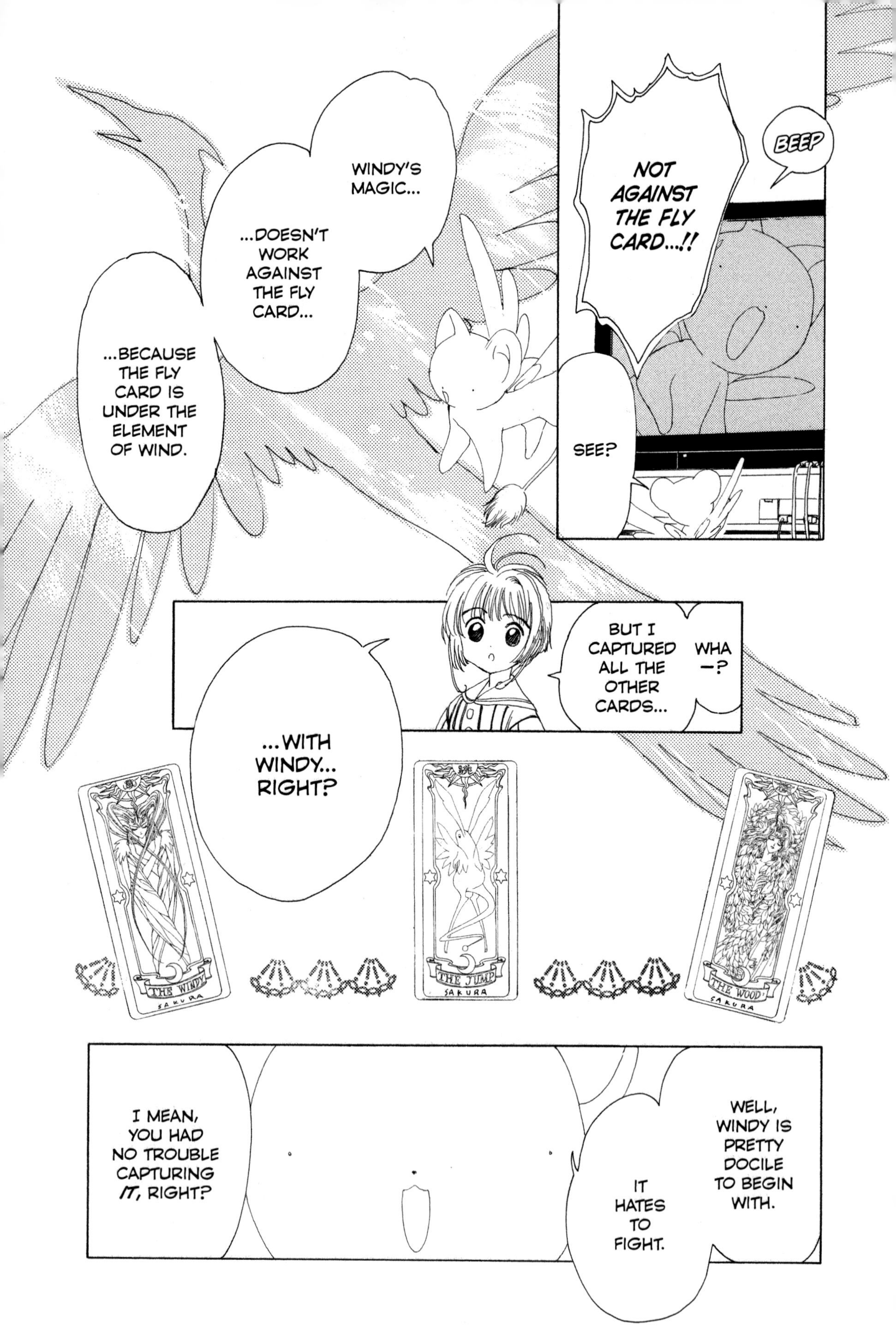

BEEP
NOT AGAINST THE FLY CARD...!!
SEE?
WINDY'S MAGIC...
...DOESN'T WORK AGAINST THE FLY CARD...
...BECAUSE THE FLY CARD IS UNDER THE ELEMENT OF WIND.
WHA—?
BUT I CAPTURED ALL THE OTHER CARDS...
...WITH WINDY... RIGHT?
THE WOOD
SAKURA
THE JUMP
SAKURA
THE WINDY
SAKURA
WELL, WINDY IS PRETTY DOCILE TO BEGIN WITH.
IT HATES TO FIGHT.
I MEAN, YOU HAD NO TROUBLE CAPTURING *IT*, RIGHT?

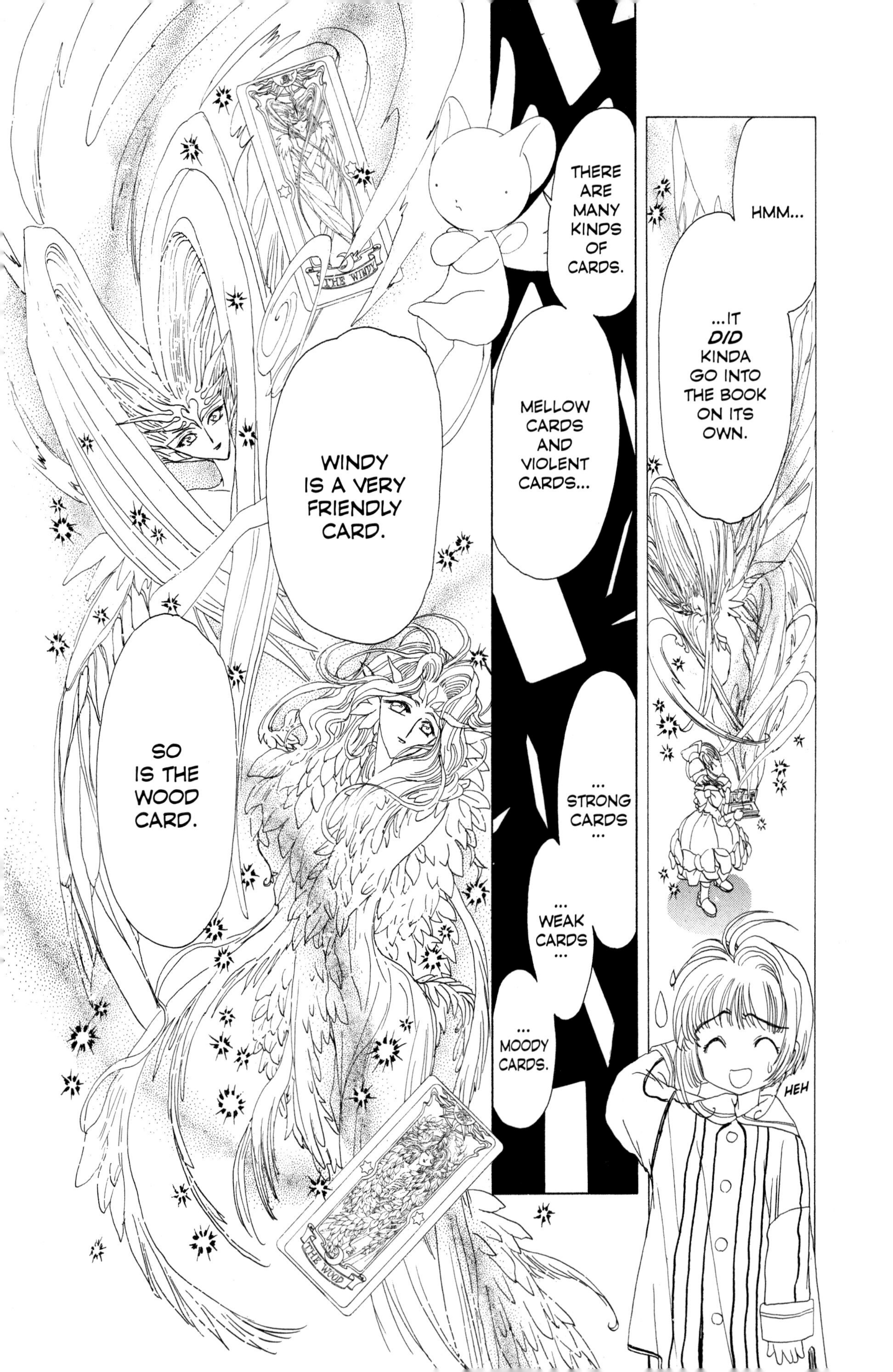
HMM...
...IT *DID* KINDA GO INTO THE BOOK ON ITS OWN.
HEH
THERE ARE MANY KINDS OF CARDS.
MELLOW CARDS AND VIOLENT CARDS...
...STRONG CARDS...
...WEAK CARDS...
...MOODY CARDS.
THE WINDY
WINDY IS A VERY FRIENDLY CARD.
SO IS THE WOOD CARD.
THE WOOD

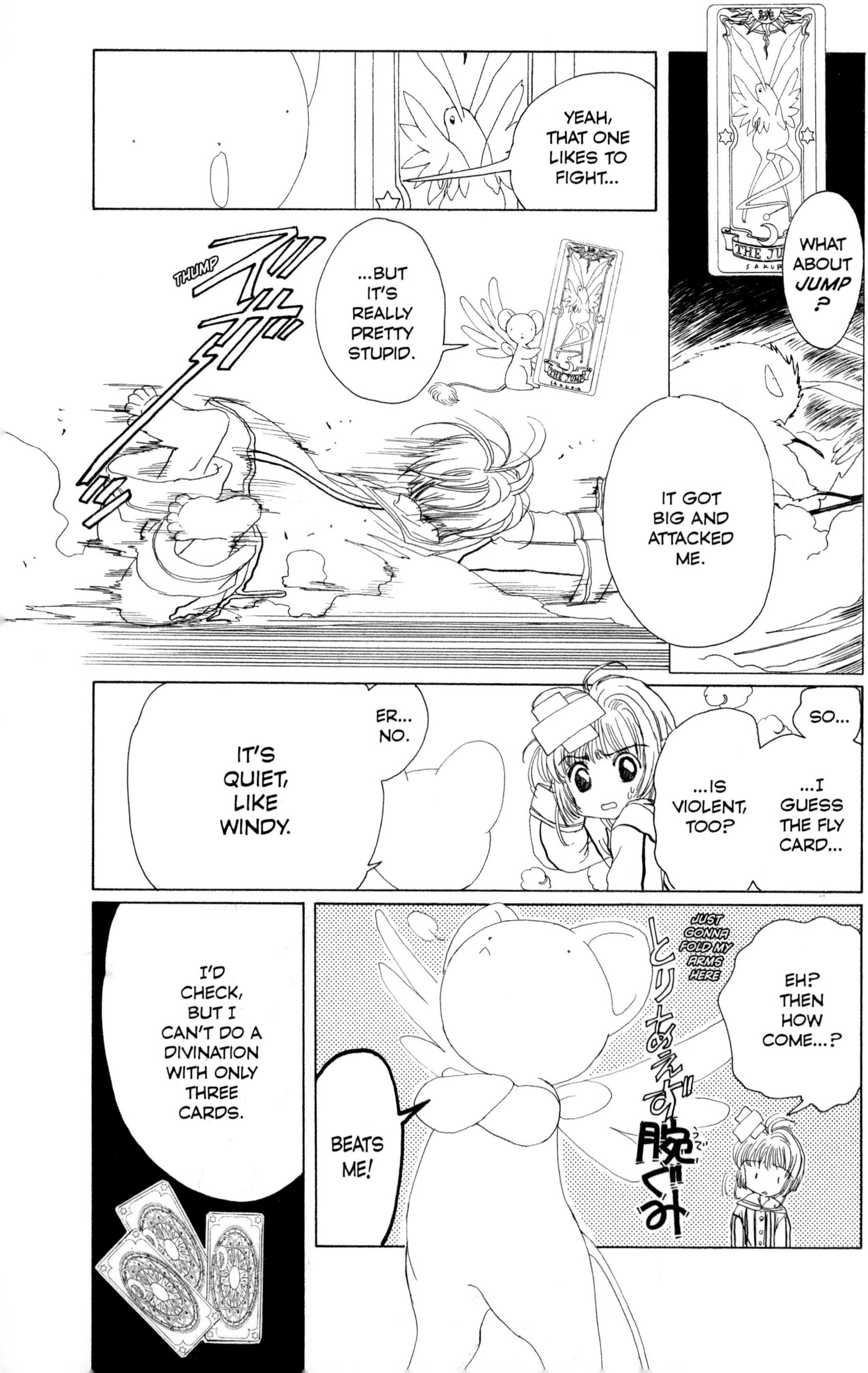
WHAT ABOUT JUMP?
YEAH, THAT ONE LIKES TO FIGHT...
...BUT IT'S REALLY PRETTY STUPID.
THUMP
IT GOT BIG AND ATTACKED ME.
SO...
...I GUESS THE FLY CARD...
...IS VIOLENT, TOO?
ER... NO.
IT'S QUIET, LIKE WINDY.
EH? THEN HOW COME...?
JUST GONNA FOLD MY ARMS HERE
とりあえず腕ぐみ
BEATS ME!
I'D CHECK, BUT I CAN'T DO A DIVINATION WITH ONLY THREE CARDS.

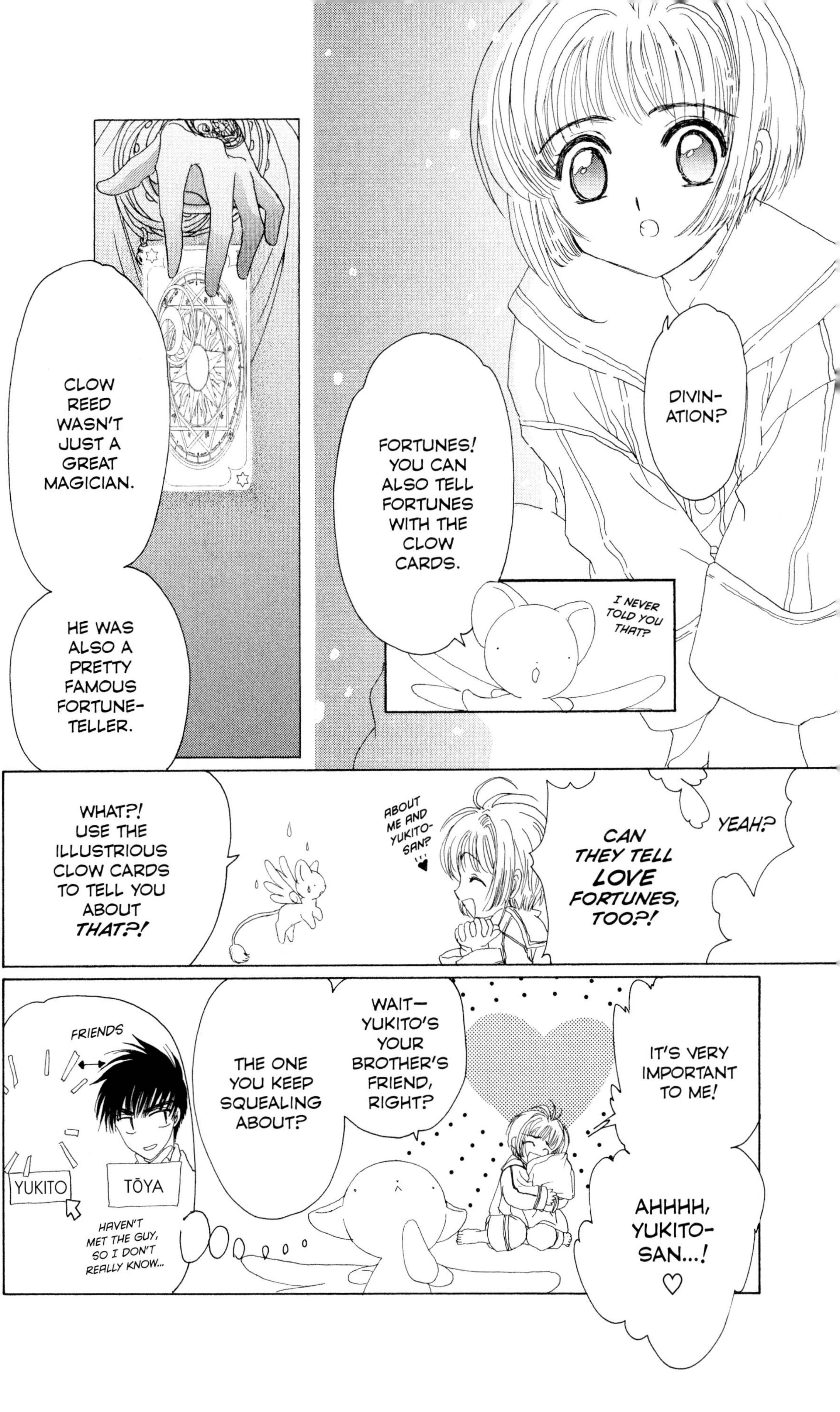

DIVINATION?
FORTUNES! YOU CAN ALSO TELL FORTUNES WITH THE CLOW CARDS.
I NEVER TOLD YOU THAT?
CLOW REED WASN'T JUST A GREAT MAGICIAN.
HE WAS ALSO A PRETTY FAMOUS FORTUNE-TELLER.
YEAH?
CAN THEY TELL LOVE FORTUNES, TOO?!
ABOUT ME AND YUKITO-SAN?
WHAT?! USE THE ILLUSTRIOUS CLOW CARDS TO TELL YOU ABOUT THAT?!
IT'S VERY IMPORTANT TO ME!
AHHHH, YUKITO-SAN...! ♡
WAIT— YUKITO'S YOUR BROTHER'S FRIEND, RIGHT?
THE ONE YOU KEEP SQUEALING ABOUT?
FRIENDS
YUKITO
TŌYA
HAVEN'T MET THE GUY, SO I DON'T REALLY KNOW...

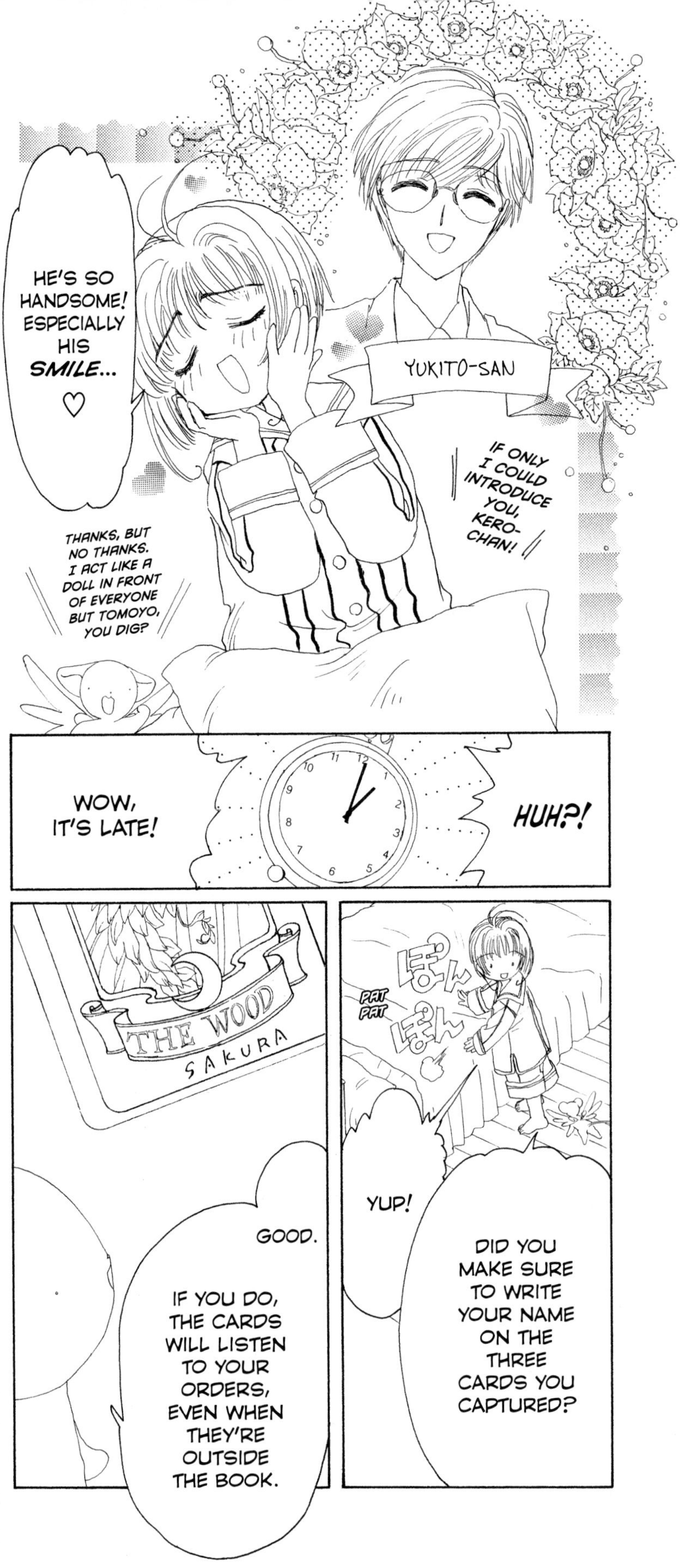
YUKITO-SAN
HE'S SO HANDSOME! ESPECIALLY HIS *SMILE*... ♡
IF ONLY I COULD INTRODUCE YOU, KERO-CHAN!
THANKS, BUT NO THANKS. I ACT LIKE A DOLL IN FRONT OF EVERYONE BUT TOMOYO, YOU DIG?
HUH?!
WOW, IT'S LATE!
PAT PAT
ぽんぽん
DID YOU MAKE SURE TO WRITE YOUR NAME ON THE THREE CARDS YOU CAPTURED?
YUP!
THE WOOD
SAKURA
GOOD.
IF YOU DO, THE CARDS WILL LISTEN TO YOUR ORDERS, EVEN WHEN THEY'RE OUTSIDE THE BOOK.

2

TOMOYO DAIDOUJI

BIRTHDATE:
SEPTEMBER 3
BLOOD TYPE:
A
FAVORITE SUBJECTS:
MUSIC, GRAMMAR
LEAST FAVORITE SUBJECT:
NONE
CLUB:
CHOIR
FAVORITE COLORS:
BEIGE, WHITE
FAVORITE FLOWERS:
MAGNOLIA, CHERRY BLOSSOM
FAVORITE FOODS:
SOBA, SUSHI
LEAST FAVORITE FOOD:
BELL PEPPERS
FAVORITE RECIPE:
ANYTHING ITALIAN
WISH LIST:
NEW VIDEO-EDITING EQUIPMENT

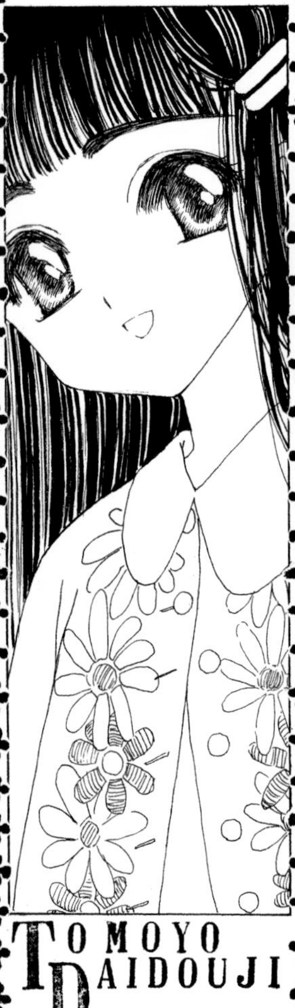

TOMOYO DAIDOUJI

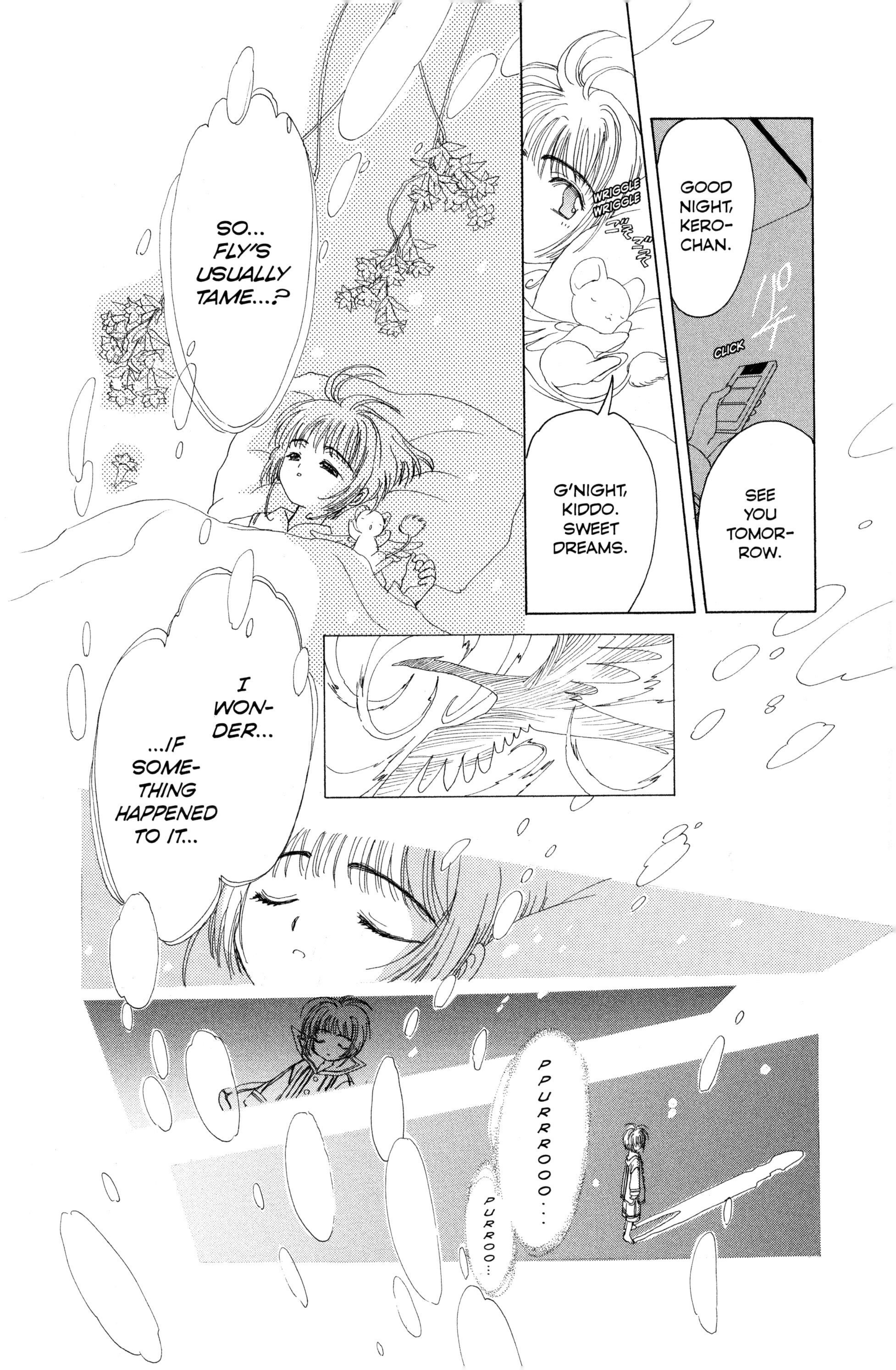
GOOD NIGHT, KERO-CHAN.
CLICK
SEE YOU TOMORROW.
WRIGGLE WRIGGLE
G'NIGHT, KIDDO. SWEET DREAMS.
SO... FLY'S USUALLY TAME...?
I WONDER...
...IF SOMETHING HAPPENED TO IT...
PPURRROOO...
PURROO...

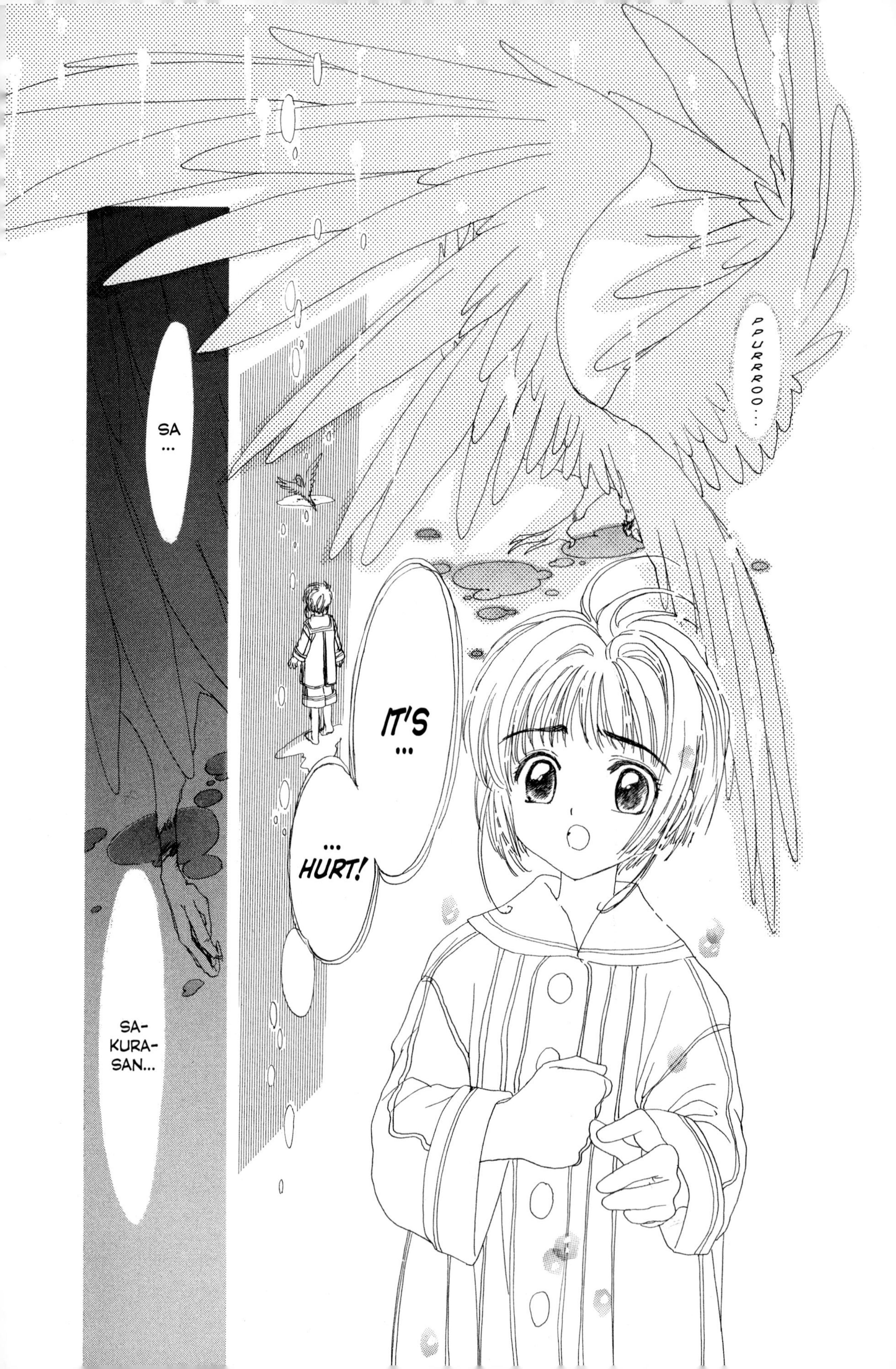
PPURRROO...
IT'S ...
... HURT!
SA ...
SA-KURA-SAN...

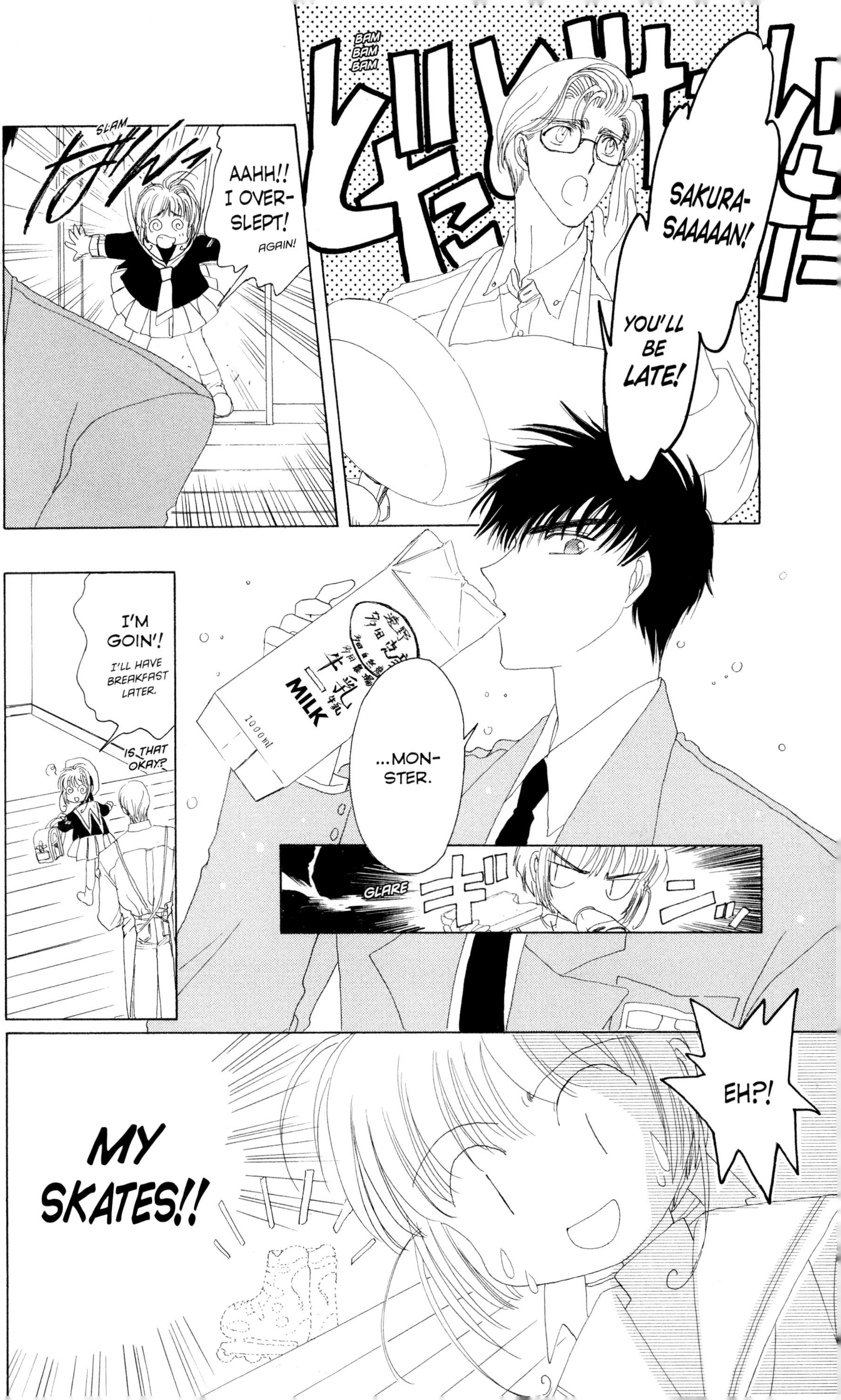
BAM BAM BAM
SAKURA-SAAAAAN!
YOU'LL BE LATE!
SLAM
AAHH!! I OVER-SLEPT!
AGAIN!
MILK
...MON-STER.
GLARE
I'M GOIN'!
I'LL HAVE BREAKFAST LATER.
IS THAT OKAY?
EH?!
MY SKATES!!

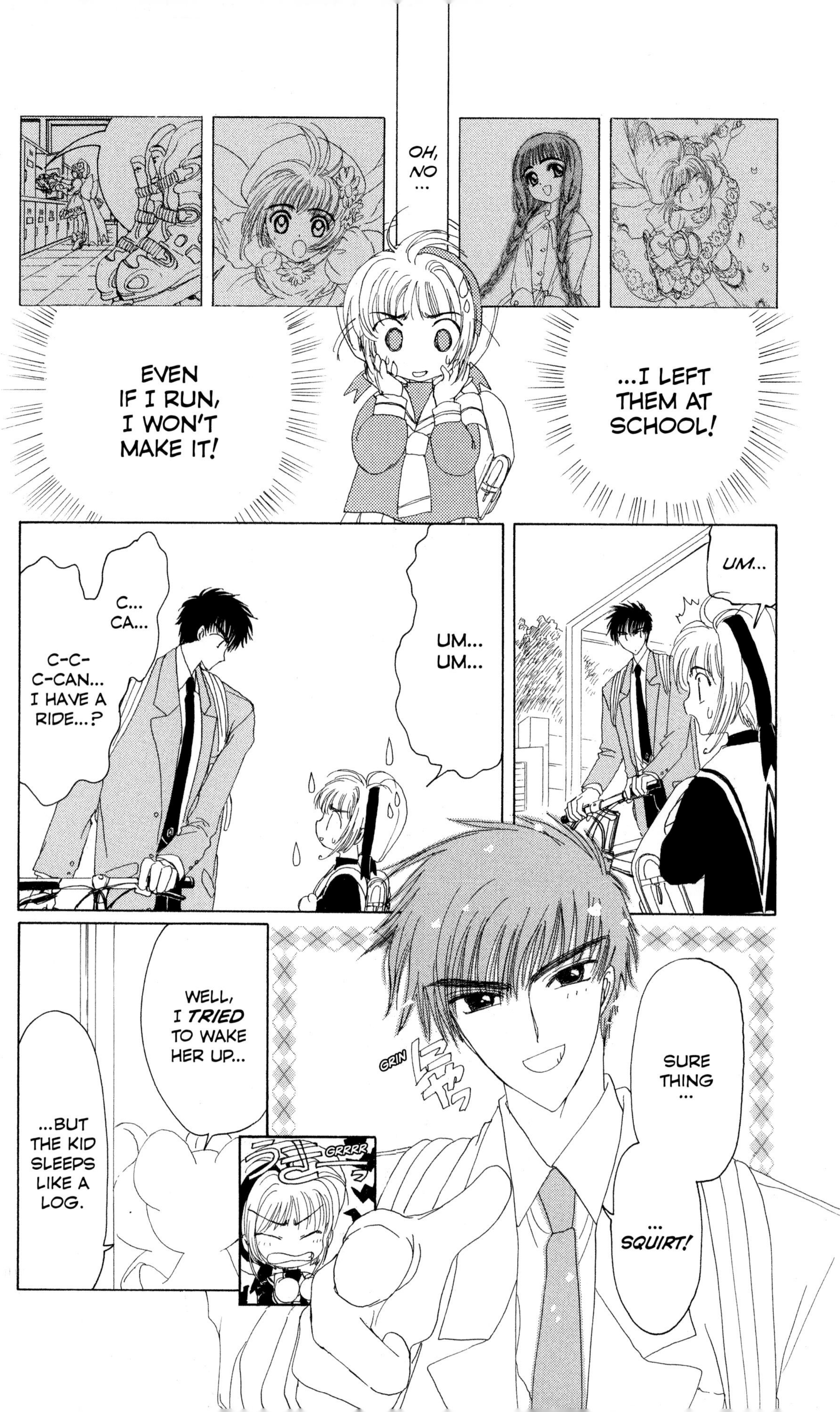
OH, NO ...
...I LEFT THEM AT SCHOOL!
EVEN IF I RUN, I WON'T MAKE IT!
UM...
UM... UM...
C... CA...
C-C-C-CAN... I HAVE A RIDE...?
SURE THING ...
... SQUIRT!
GRIN
GRRRR
WELL, I TRIED TO WAKE HER UP...
...BUT THE KID SLEEPS LIKE A LOG.

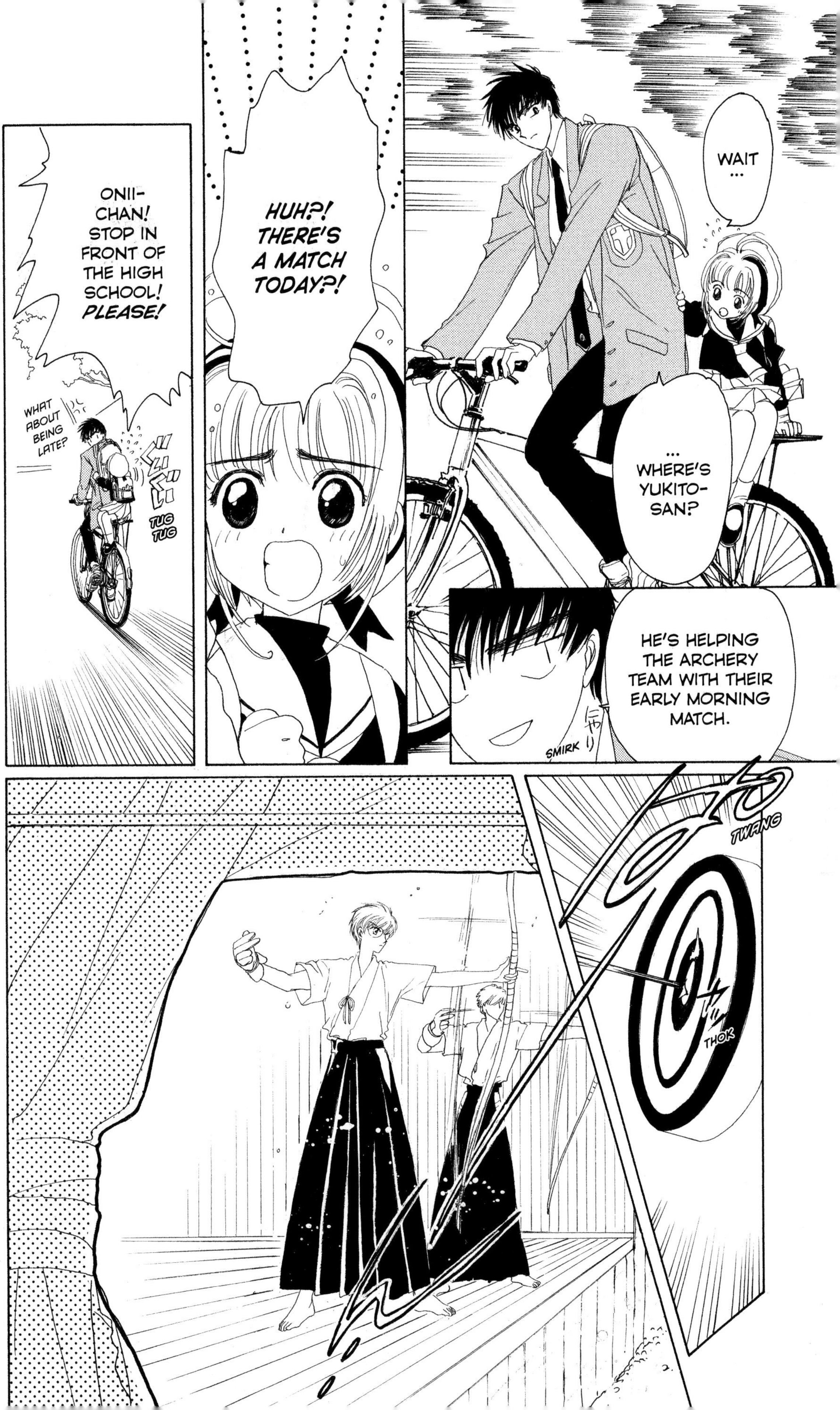
WAIT ...
... WHERE'S YUKITO-SAN?
HE'S HELPING THE ARCHERY TEAM WITH THEIR EARLY MORNING MATCH.
SMIRK
HUH?! THERE'S A MATCH TODAY?!
ONII-CHAN! STOP IN FRONT OF THE HIGH SCHOOL! PLEASE!
WHAT ABOUT BEING LATE?
TUG TUG
TWANG
THOK

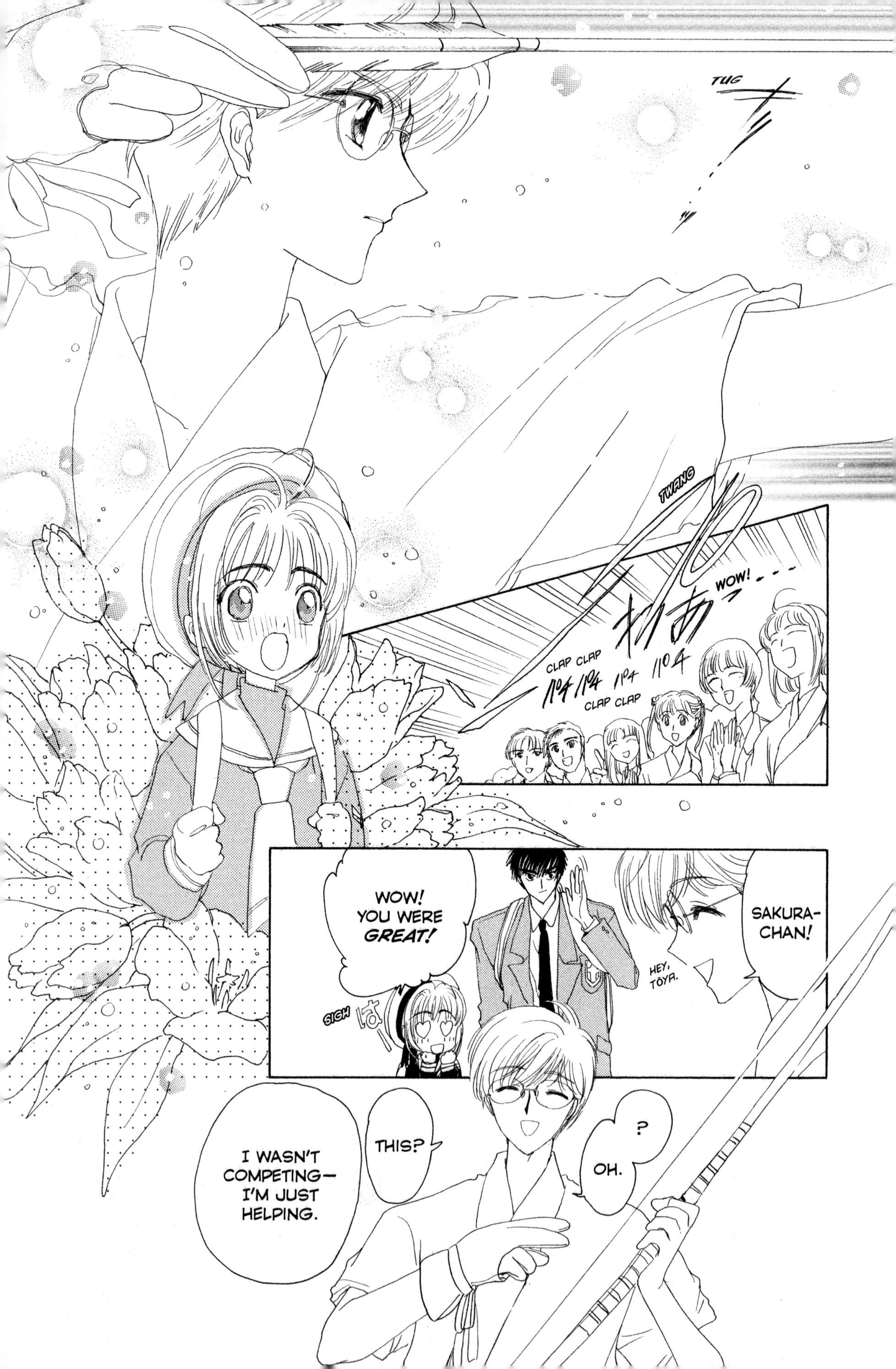
TUG
TWANG
WOW!
CLAP CLAP
CLAP CLAP
SAKURA-CHAN!
HEY, TŌYA.
WOW! YOU WERE GREAT!
SIGH
?
OH.
THIS?
I WASN'T COMPETING— I'M JUST HELPING.

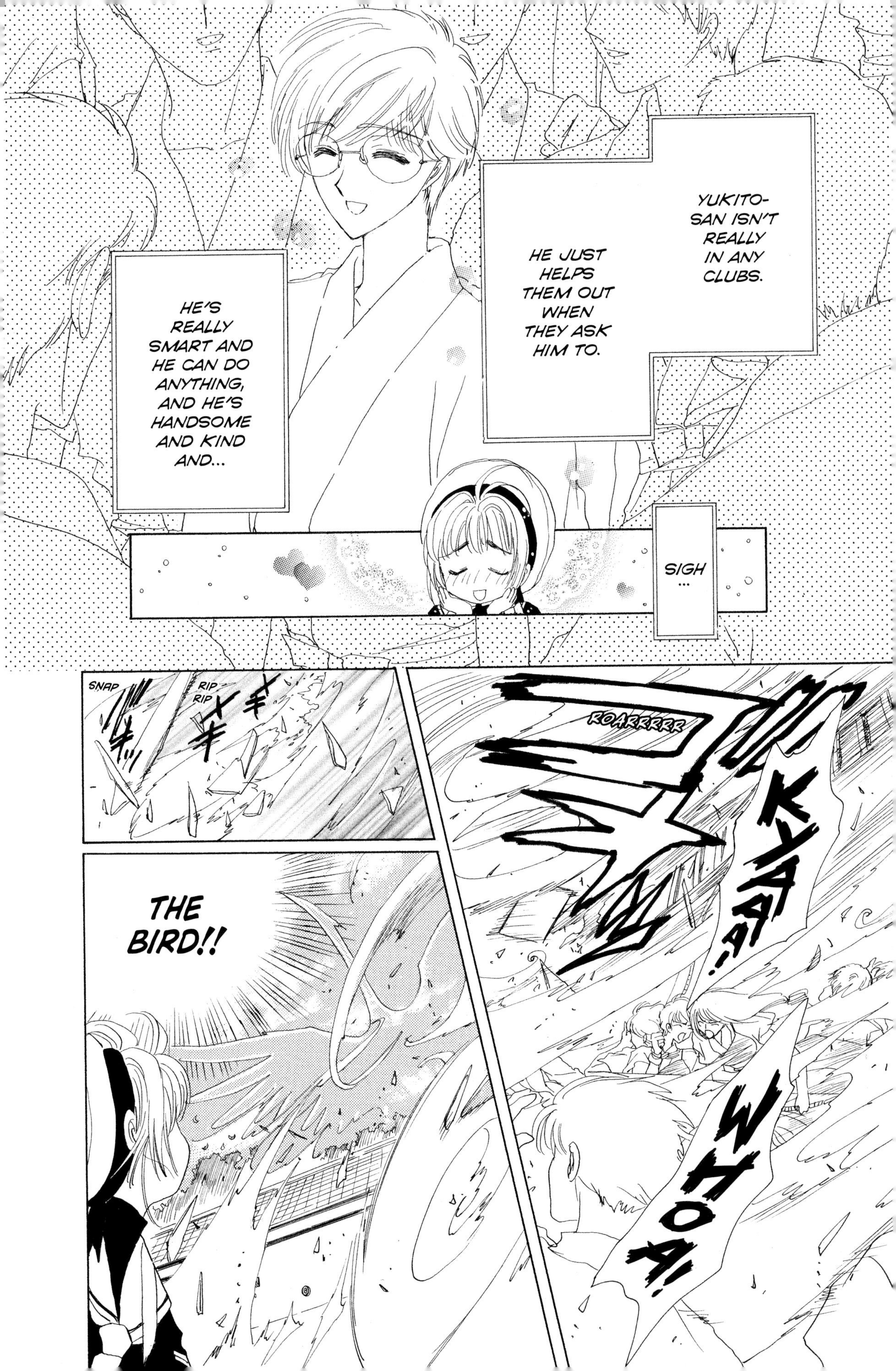
YUKITO-SAN ISN'T REALLY IN ANY CLUBS.
HE JUST HELPS THEM OUT WHEN THEY ASK HIM TO.
HE'S REALLY SMART AND HE CAN DO ANYTHING, AND HE'S HANDSOME AND KIND AND...
SIGH...
ROARRRRR
KYAAA!
WHOA!
SNAP
RIP RIP
THE BIRD!!

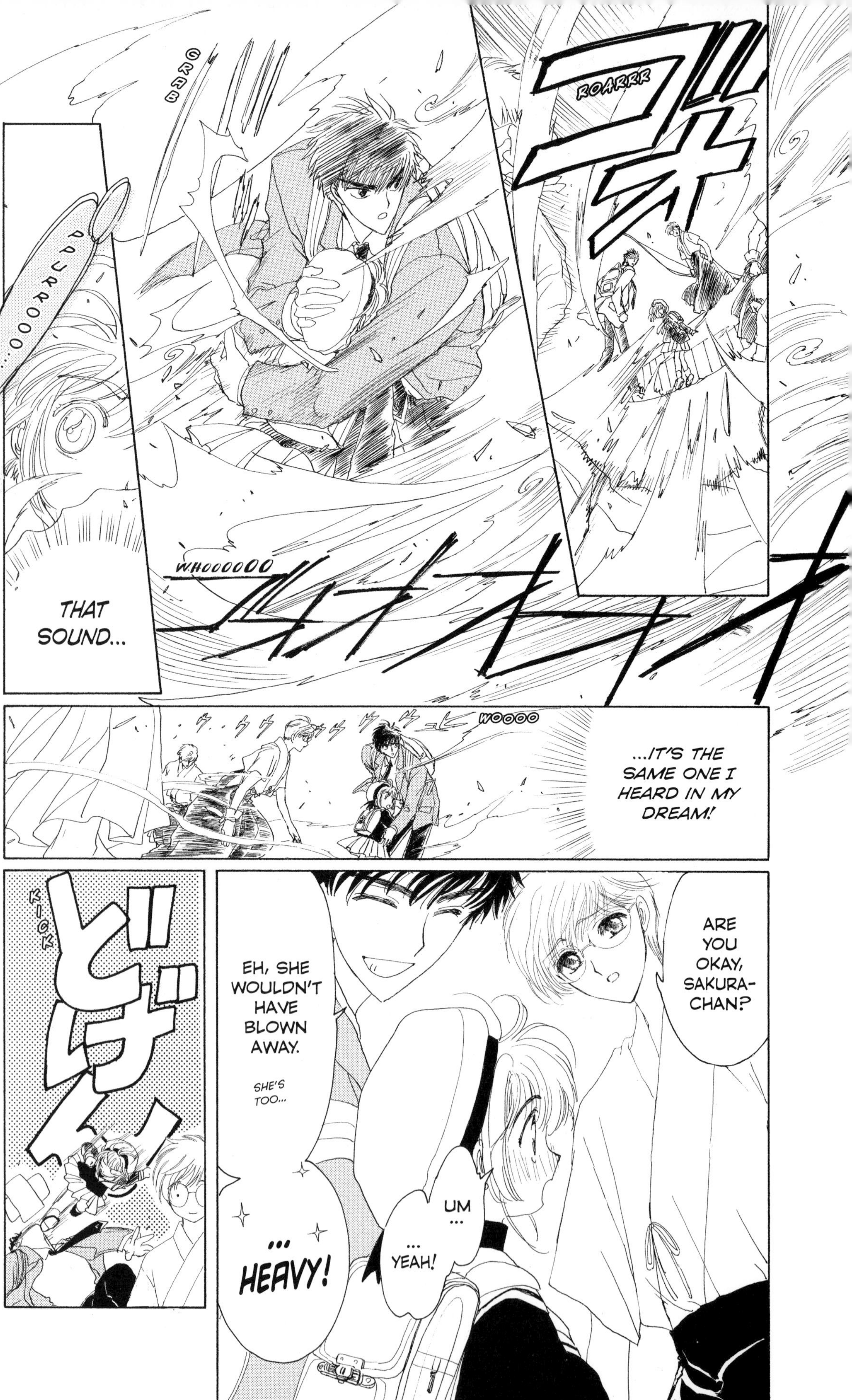
ROARRR
GRRB
WHOOOOOO
PPURROOO...
THAT SOUND...
WOOOO
...IT'S THE SAME ONE I HEARD IN MY DREAM!
ARE YOU OKAY, SAKURA-CHAN?
EH, SHE WOULDN'T HAVE BLOWN AWAY.
SHE'S TOO...
UM...
...YEAH!
...HEAVY!
KICK

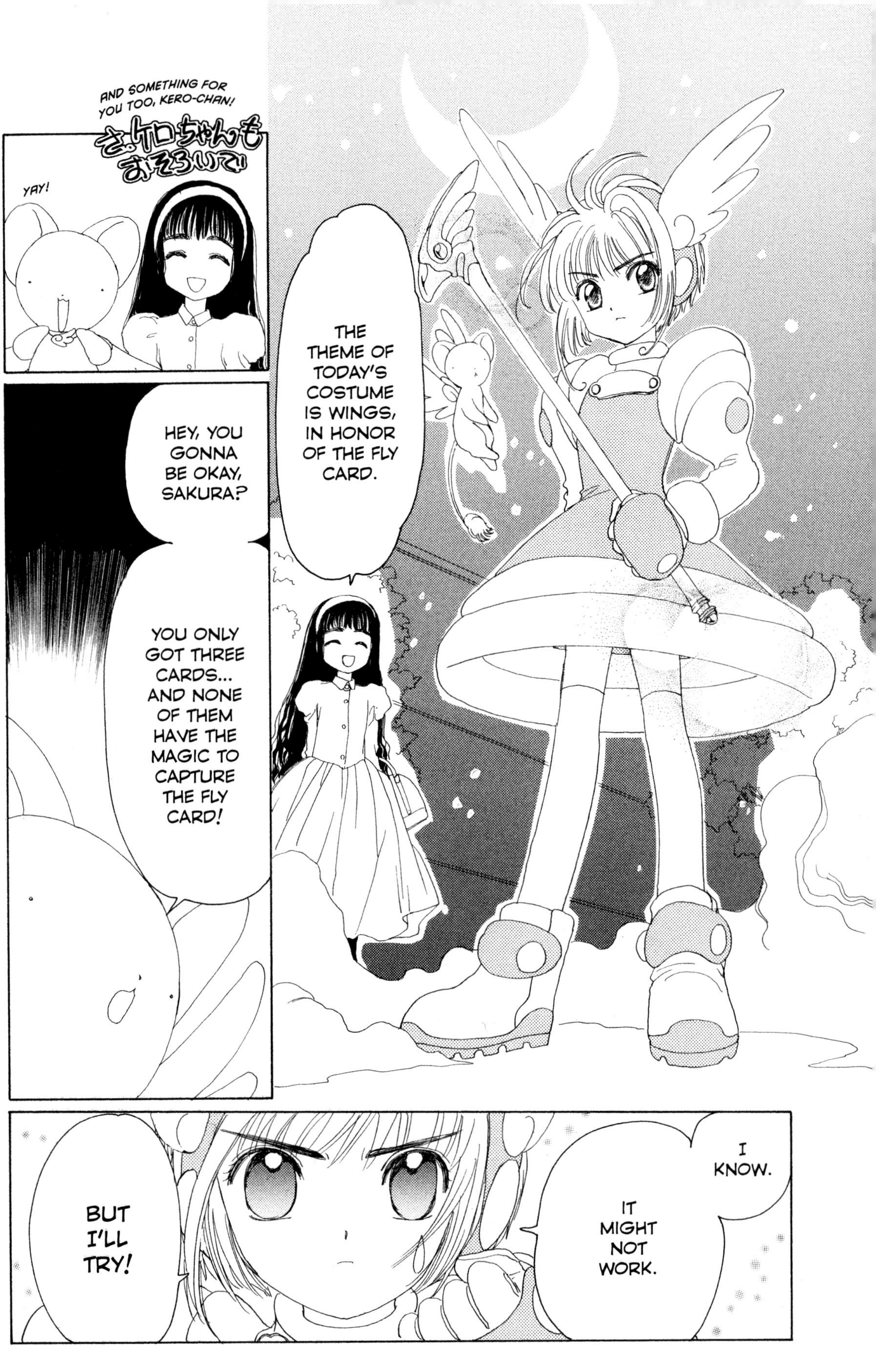
THE THEME OF TODAY'S COSTUME IS WINGS, IN HONOR OF THE FLY CARD.
さ、ケロちゃんもおそろいで
AND SOMETHING FOR YOU TOO, KERO-CHAN!
YAY!
HEY, YOU GONNA BE OKAY, SAKURA?
YOU ONLY GOT THREE CARDS... AND NONE OF THEM HAVE THE MAGIC TO CAPTURE THE FLY CARD!
I KNOW.
IT MIGHT NOT WORK.
BUT I'LL TRY!

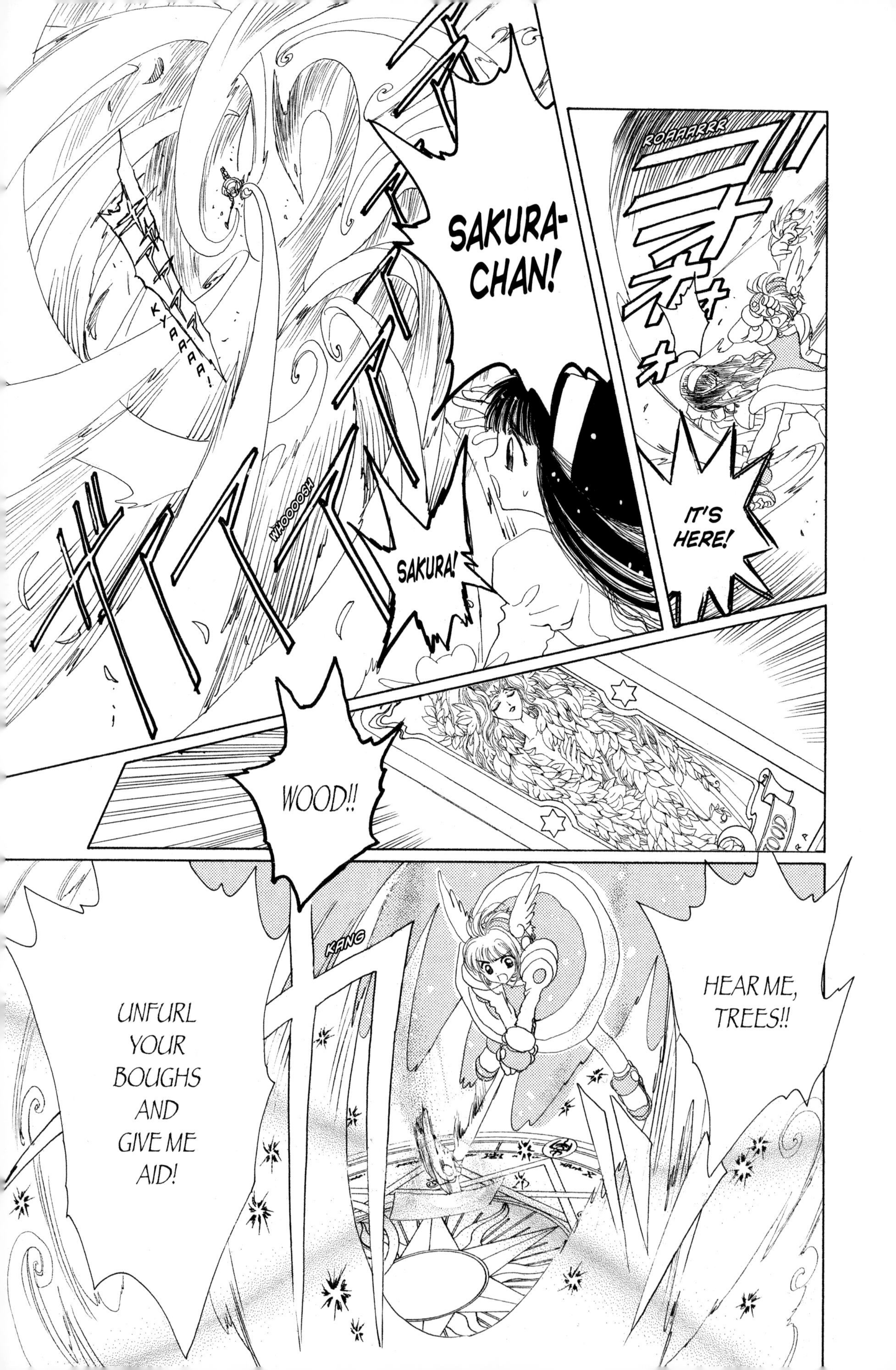
ROARRRRR
IT'S HERE!
SAKURA-CHAN!
SAKURA!
WHOOOOSH
KYAAAAA!
WOOD!!
WOOD
HEAR ME, TREES!!
KANG
UNFURL YOUR BOUGHS AND GIVE ME AID!

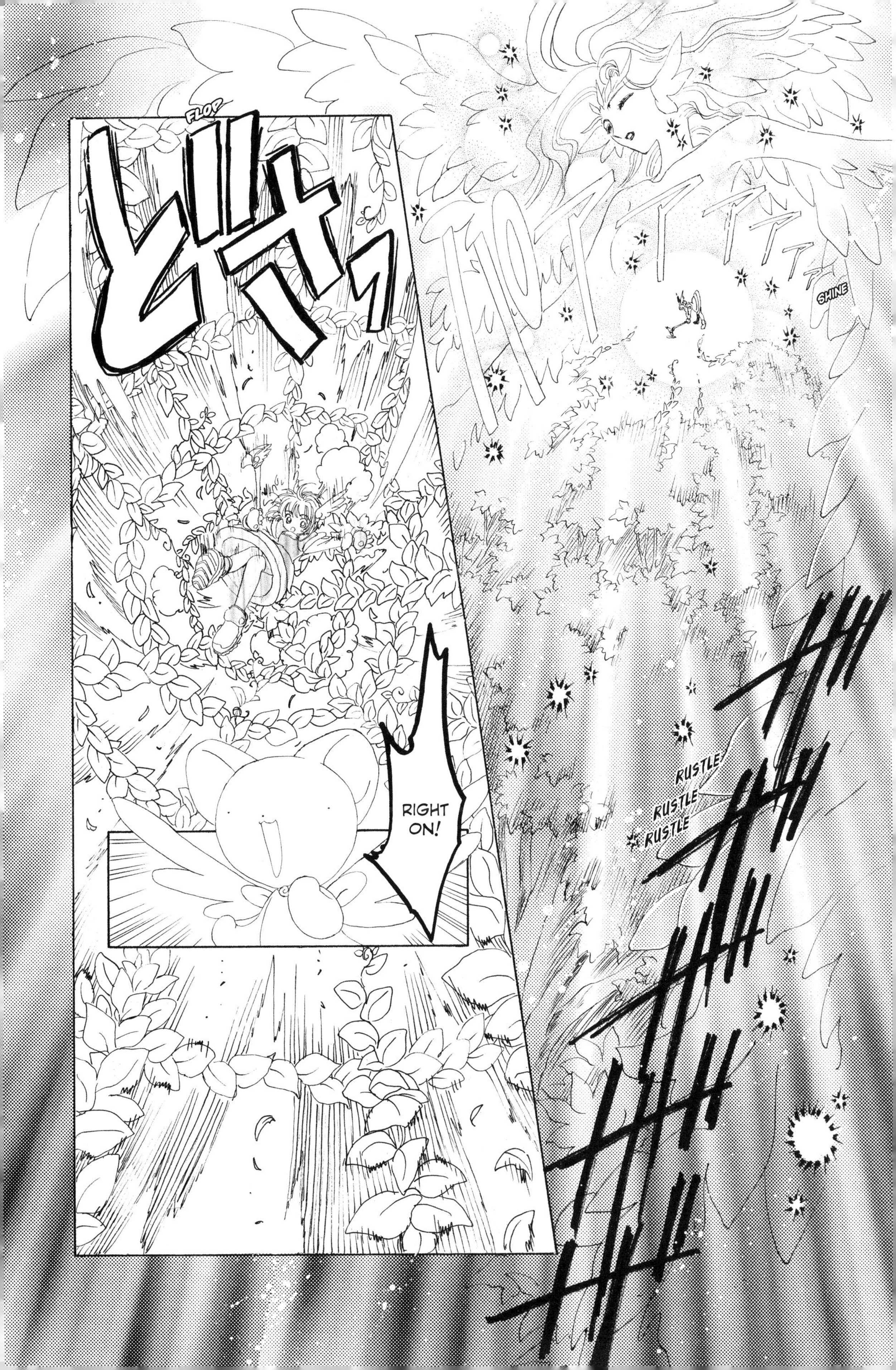
SHINE
RUSTLE
RUSTLE
RUSTLE
FLOP
どサッ
RIGHT ON!

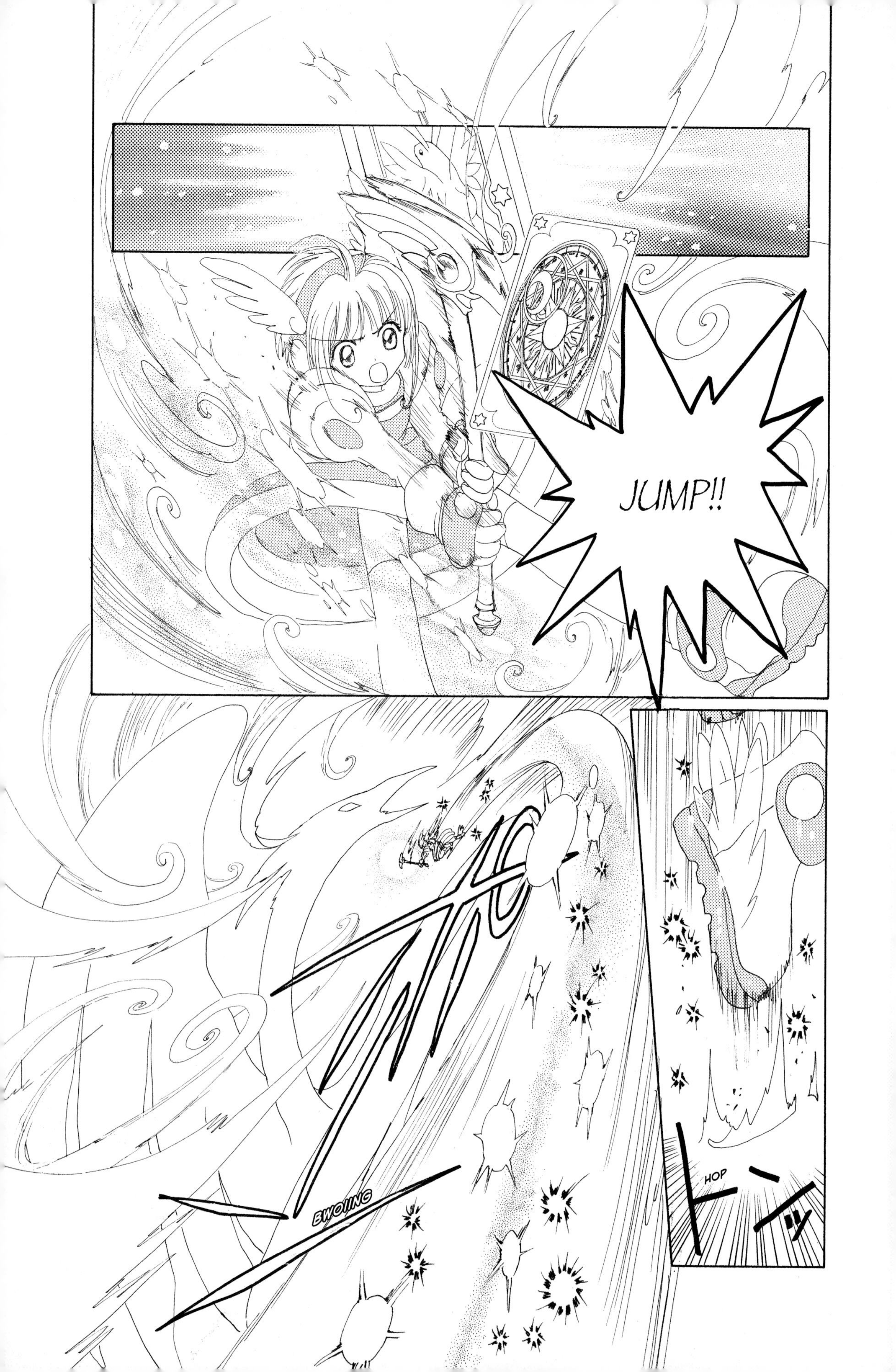
JUMP!!
HOP
BWOIING

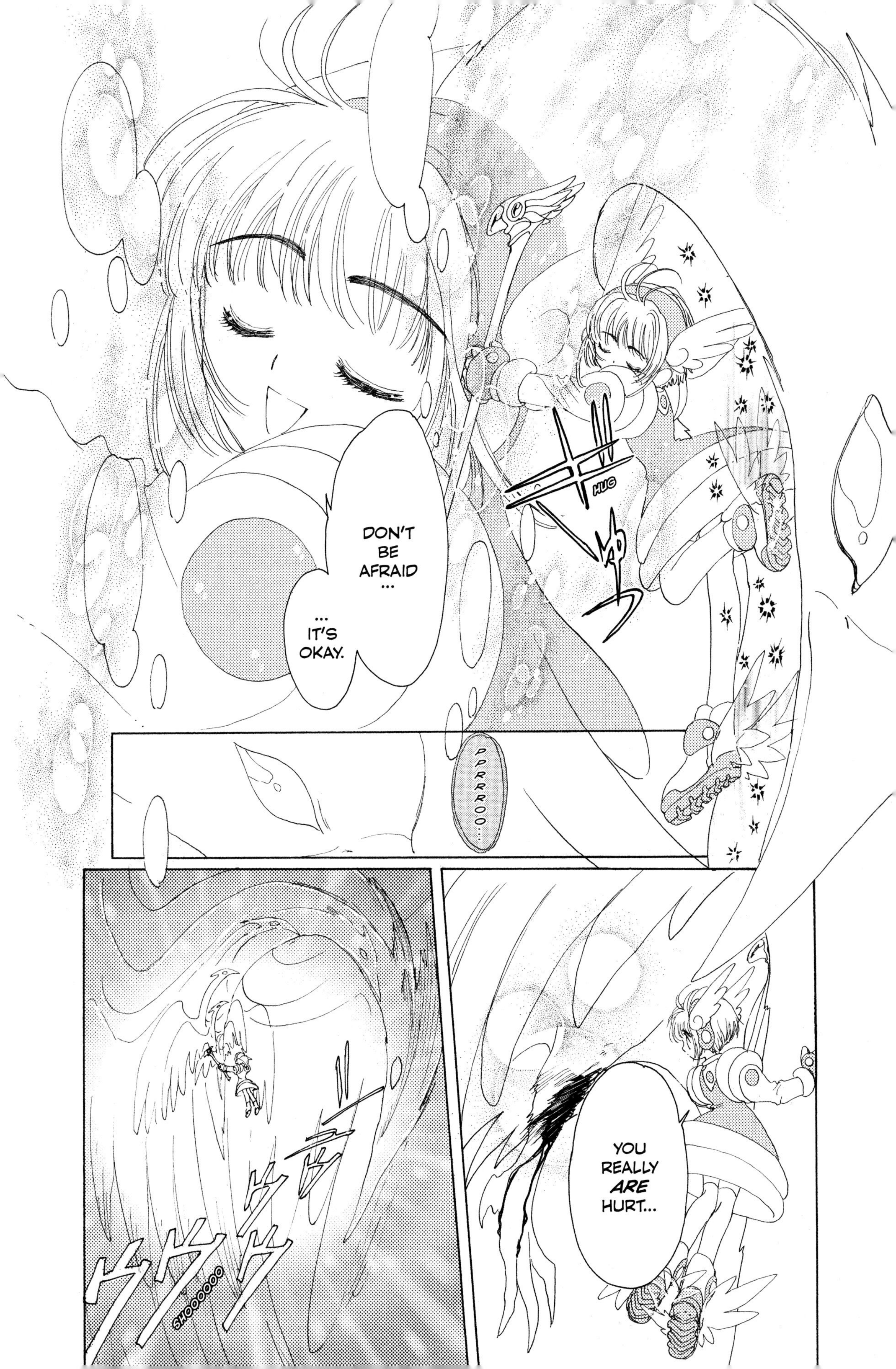
DON'T BE AFRAID...
HUG
...IT'S OKAY.
PRRRROO...
YOU REALLY *ARE* HURT...
SHOOOOOO

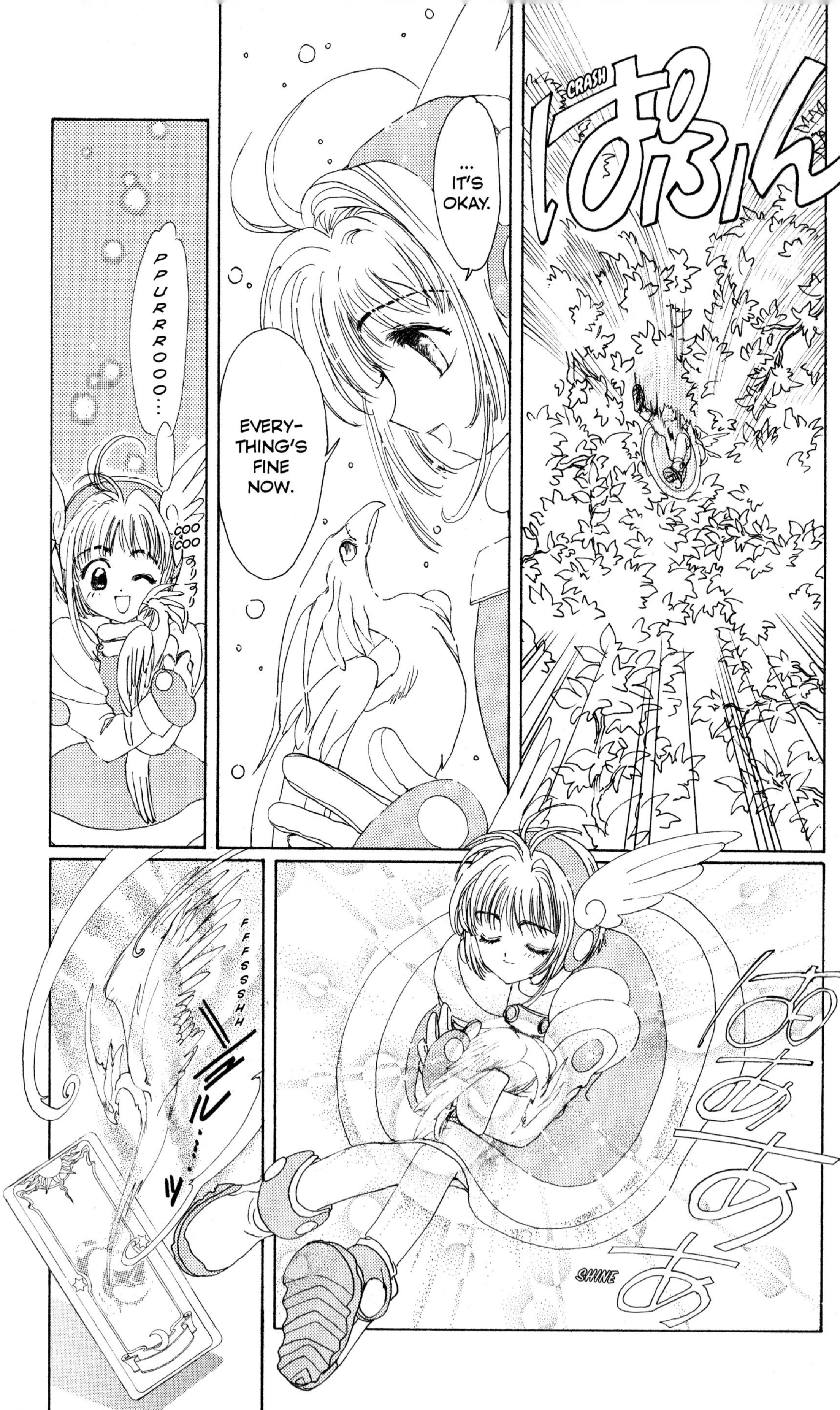
CRASH
ぱふん
... IT'S OKAY.
EVERY-THING'S FINE NOW.
PPURRROOO...
COO COO
すりすり
はあああ
SHINE
FFFSSSHH
シュル…ッ

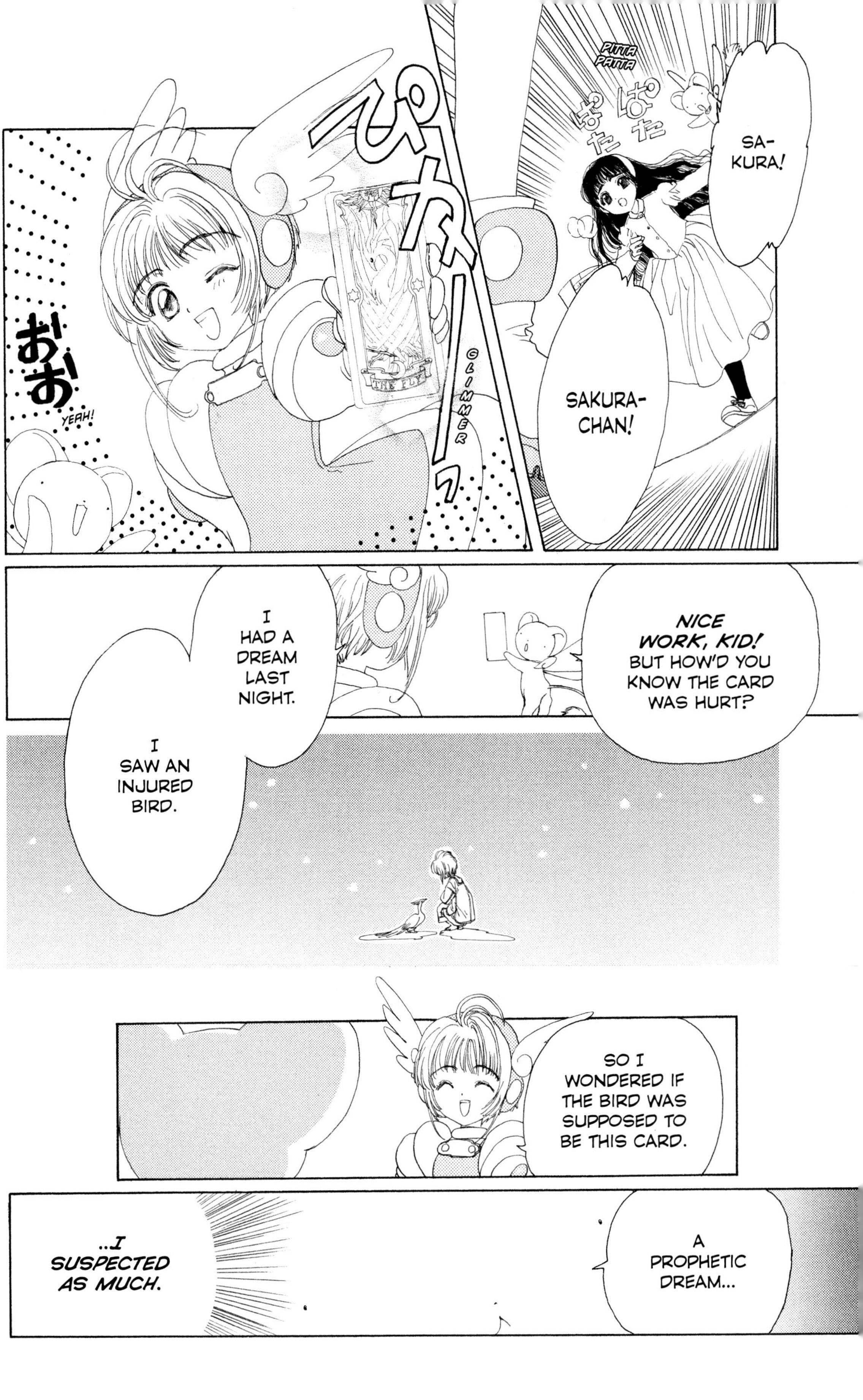
PITTA PATTA
ぱたぱた
SA-KURA!
SAKURA-CHAN!
ぴかーっ
GLIMMER
THE FLY
おお
YEAH!
NICE WORK, KID! BUT HOW'D YOU KNOW THE CARD WAS HURT?
I HAD A DREAM LAST NIGHT.
I SAW AN INJURED BIRD.
SO I WONDERED IF THE BIRD WAS SUPPOSED TO BE THIS CARD.
A PROPHETIC DREAM...
..I SUSPECTED AS MUCH.

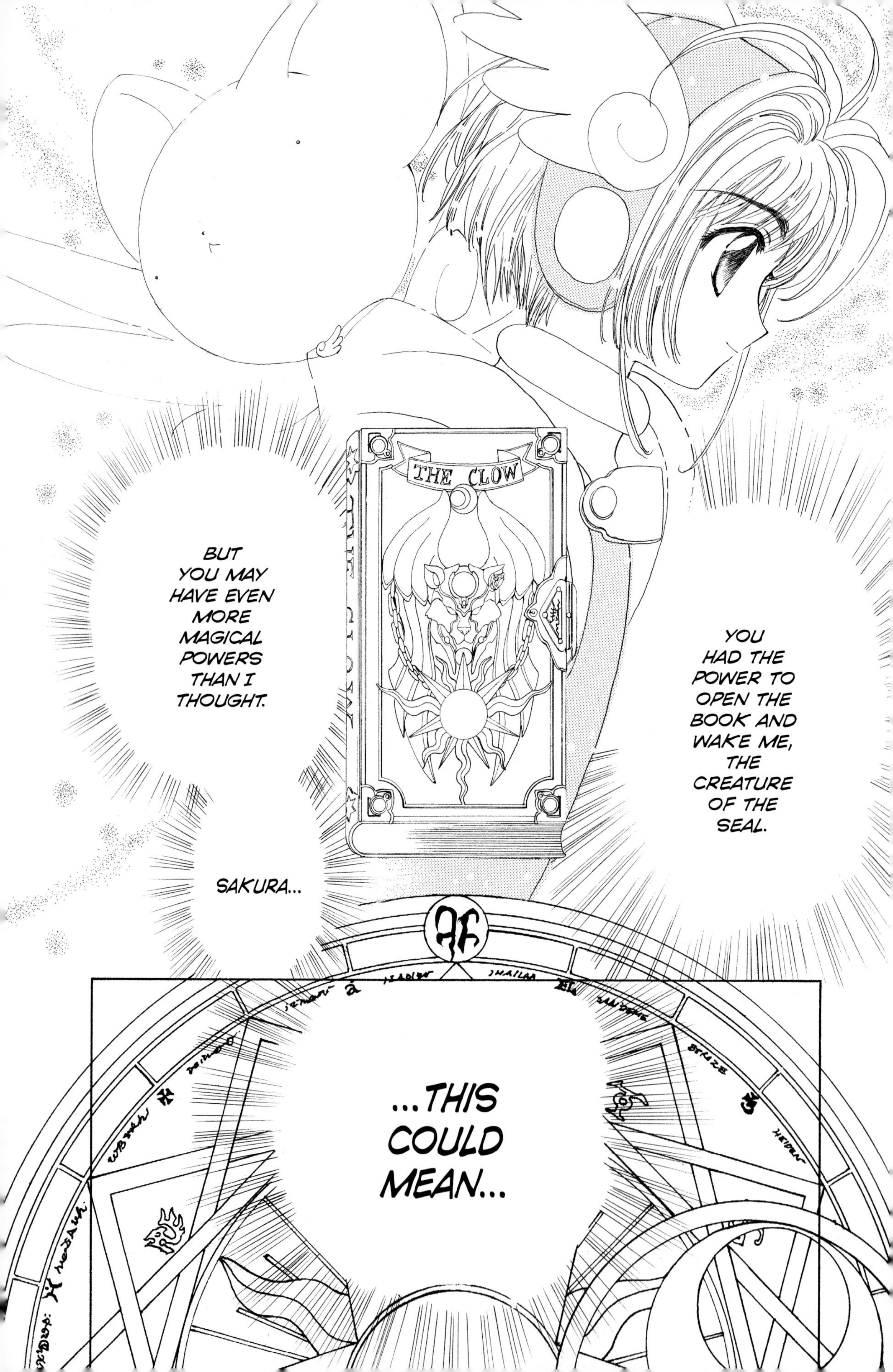

YOU HAD THE POWER TO OPEN THE BOOK AND WAKE ME, THE CREATURE OF THE SEAL.
THE CLOW
BUT YOU MAY HAVE EVEN MORE MAGICAL POWERS THAN I THOUGHT.
SAKURA...
...THIS COULD MEAN...

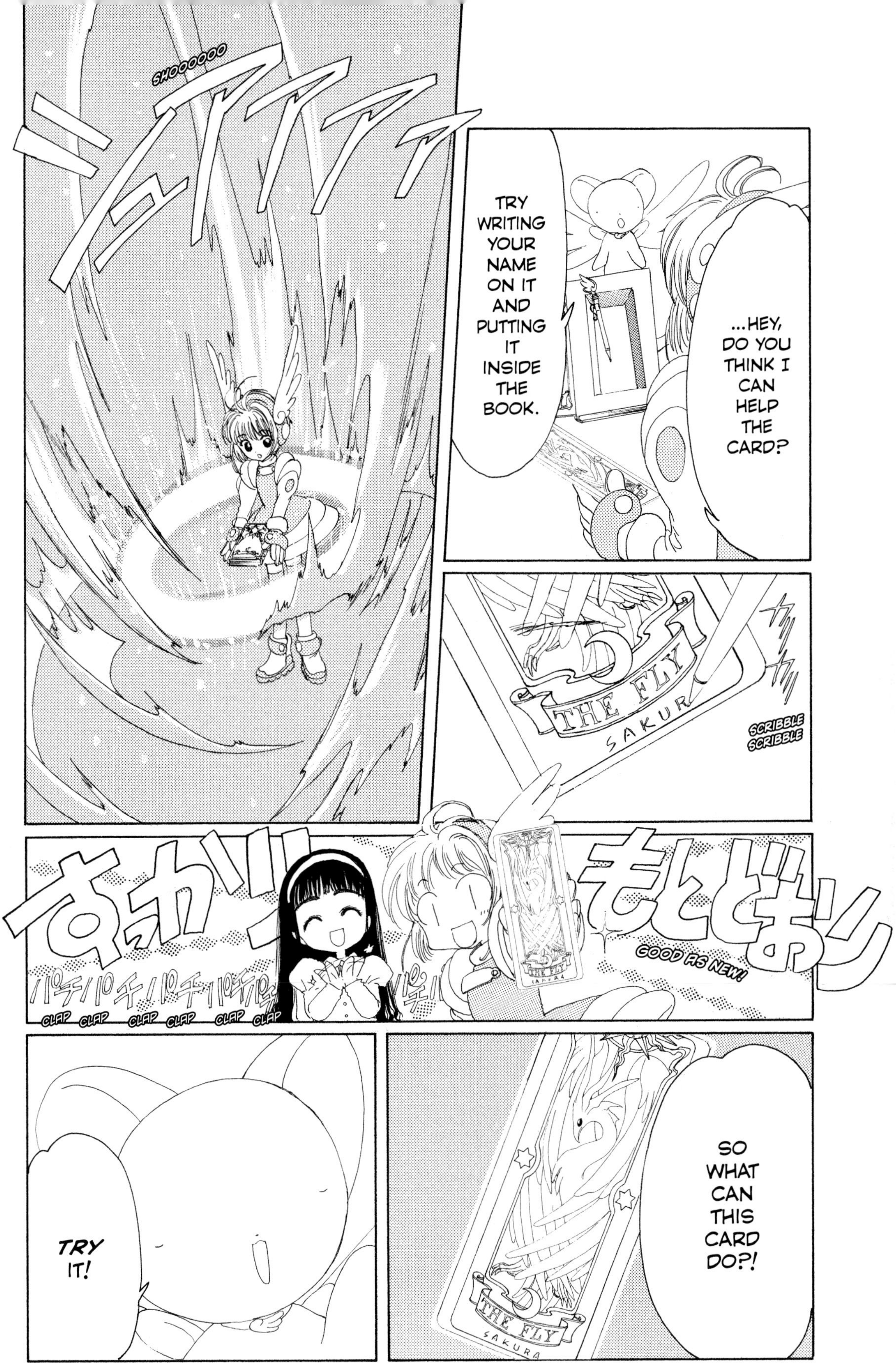
...HEY, DO YOU THINK I CAN HELP THE CARD?
TRY WRITING YOUR NAME ON IT AND PUTTING IT INSIDE THE BOOK.
THE FLY
SAKURA
SCRIBBLE SCRIBBLE
SHOOOOOO
すっかりもとどおり
GOOD AS NEW!
CLAP CLAP CLAP CLAP CLAP CLAP
SO WHAT CAN THIS CARD DO?!
TRY IT!

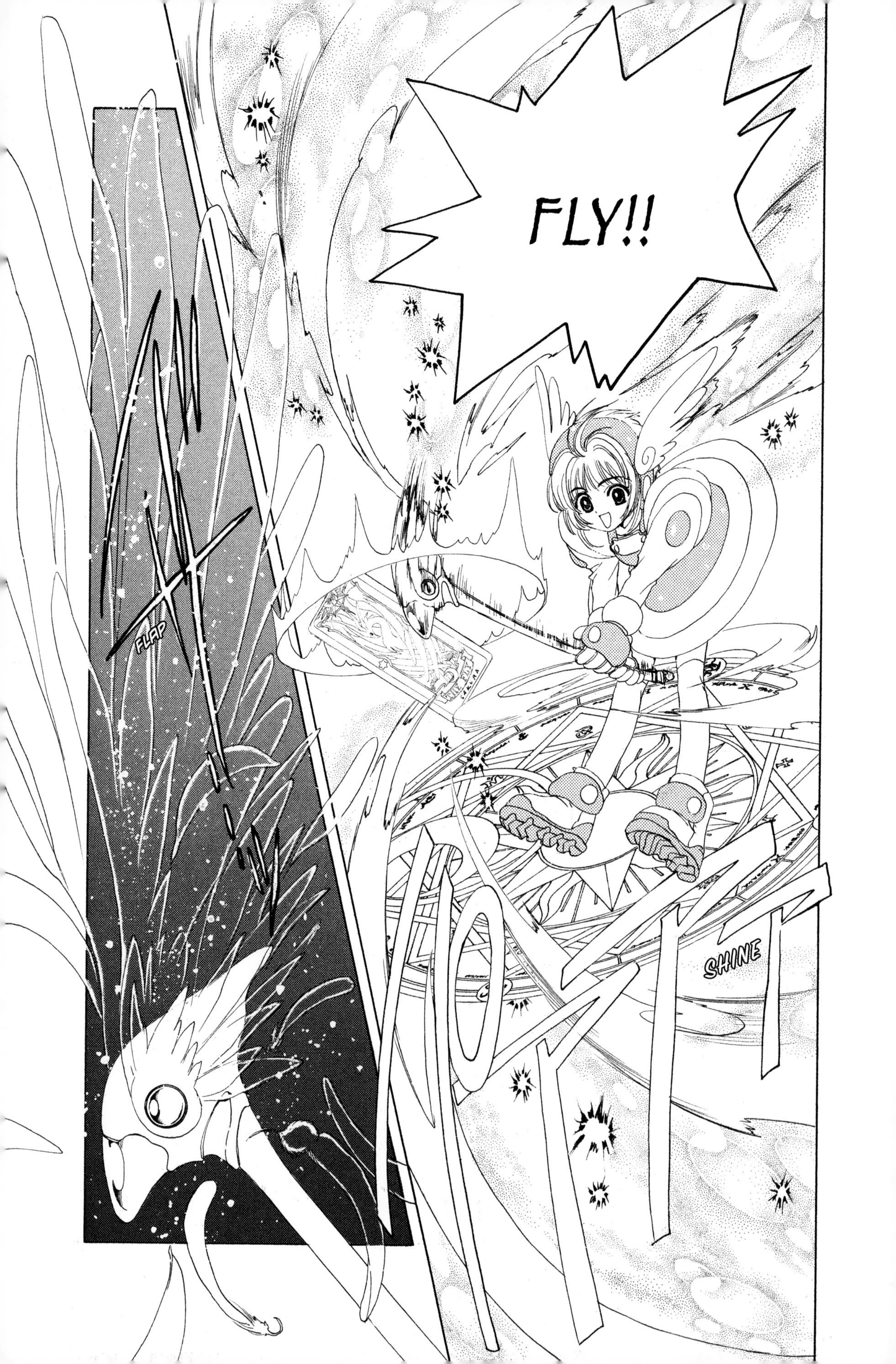
FLY!!
SHINE
FLAP

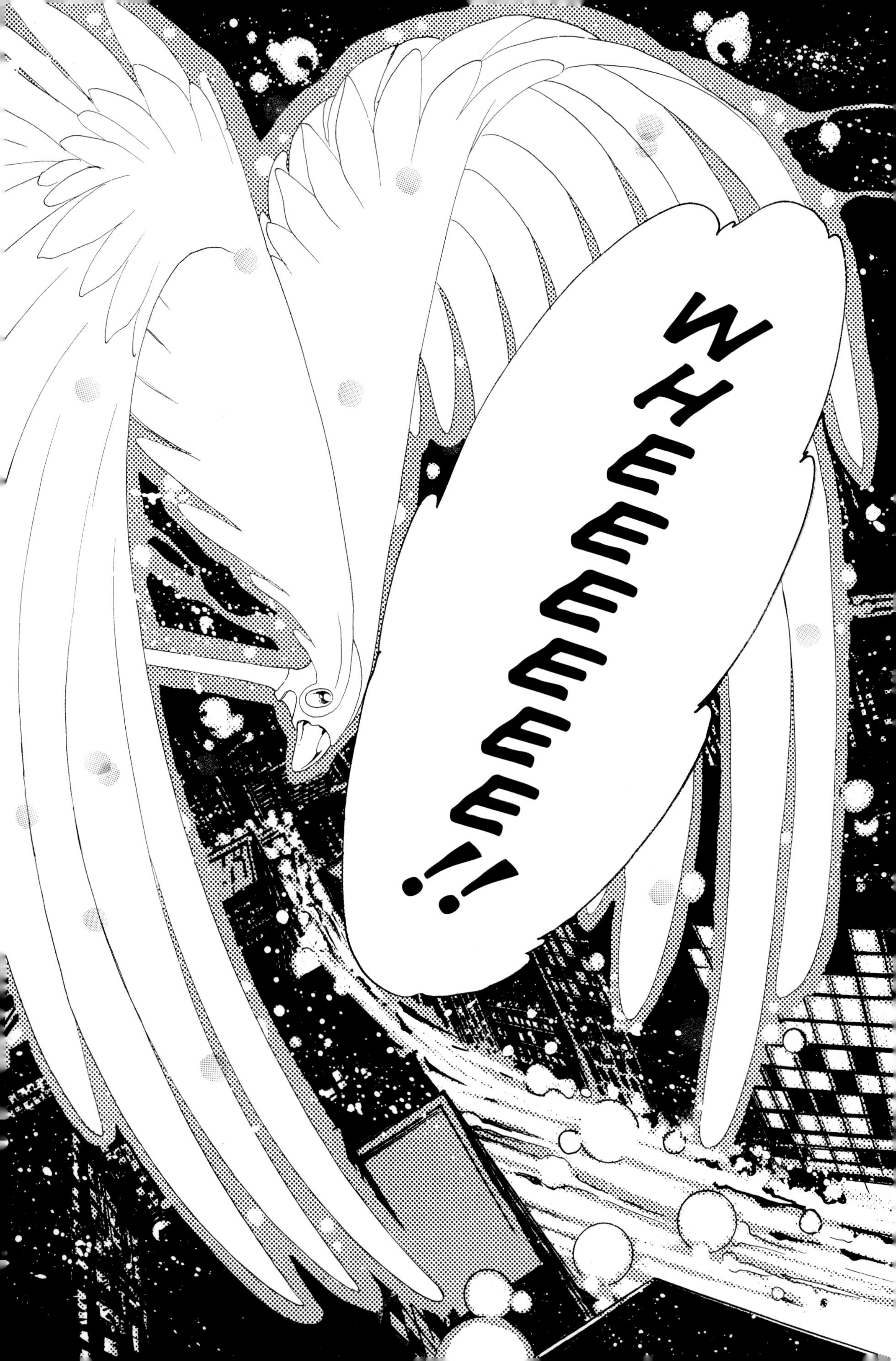
WHEEEEEE!!

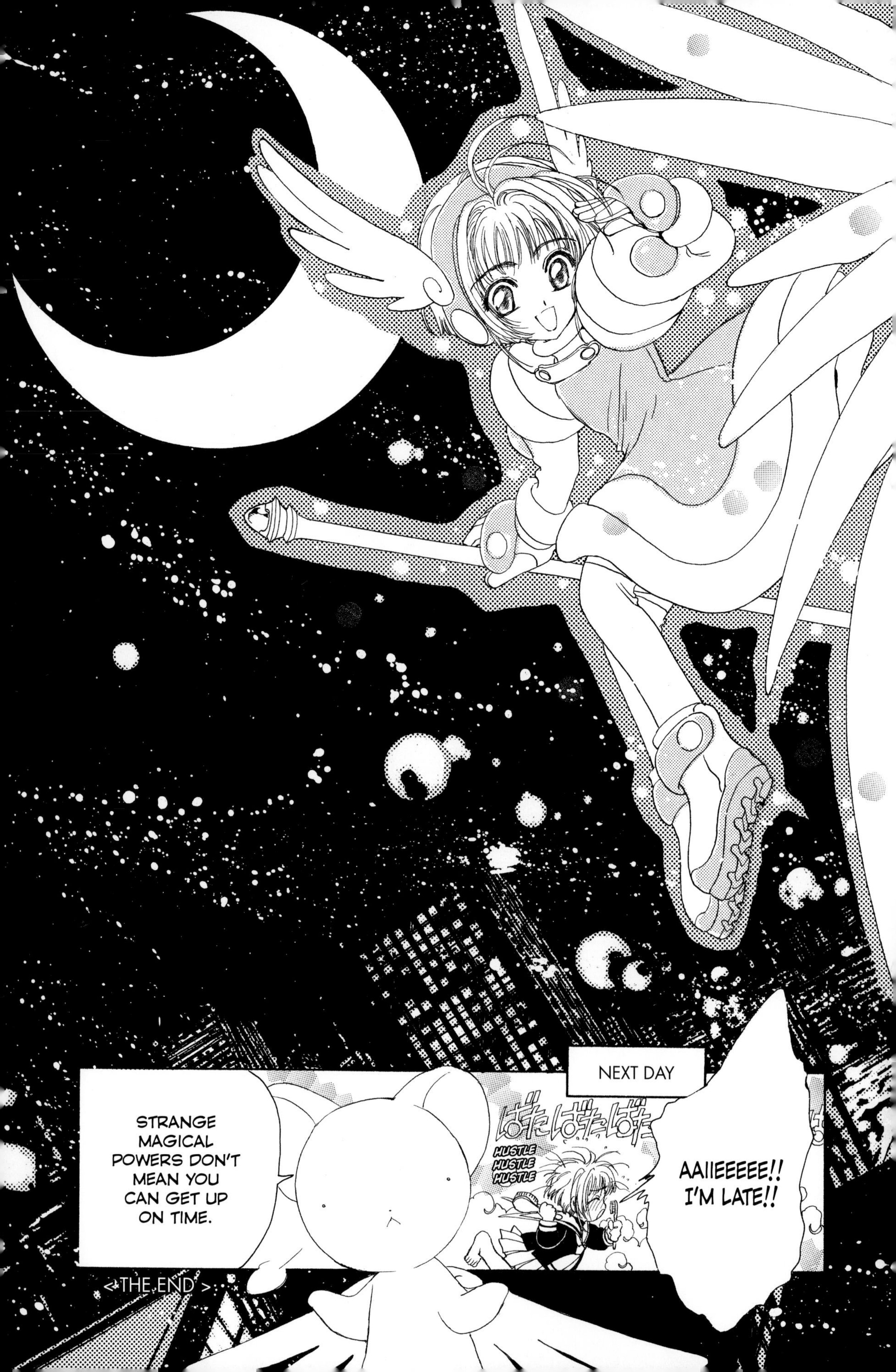
NEXT DAY
AAIIEEEEE!! I'M LATE!!
ばたばたばた
HUSTLE HUSTLE HUSTLE
STRANGE MAGICAL POWERS DON'T MEAN YOU CAN GET UP ON TIME.
< THE END >

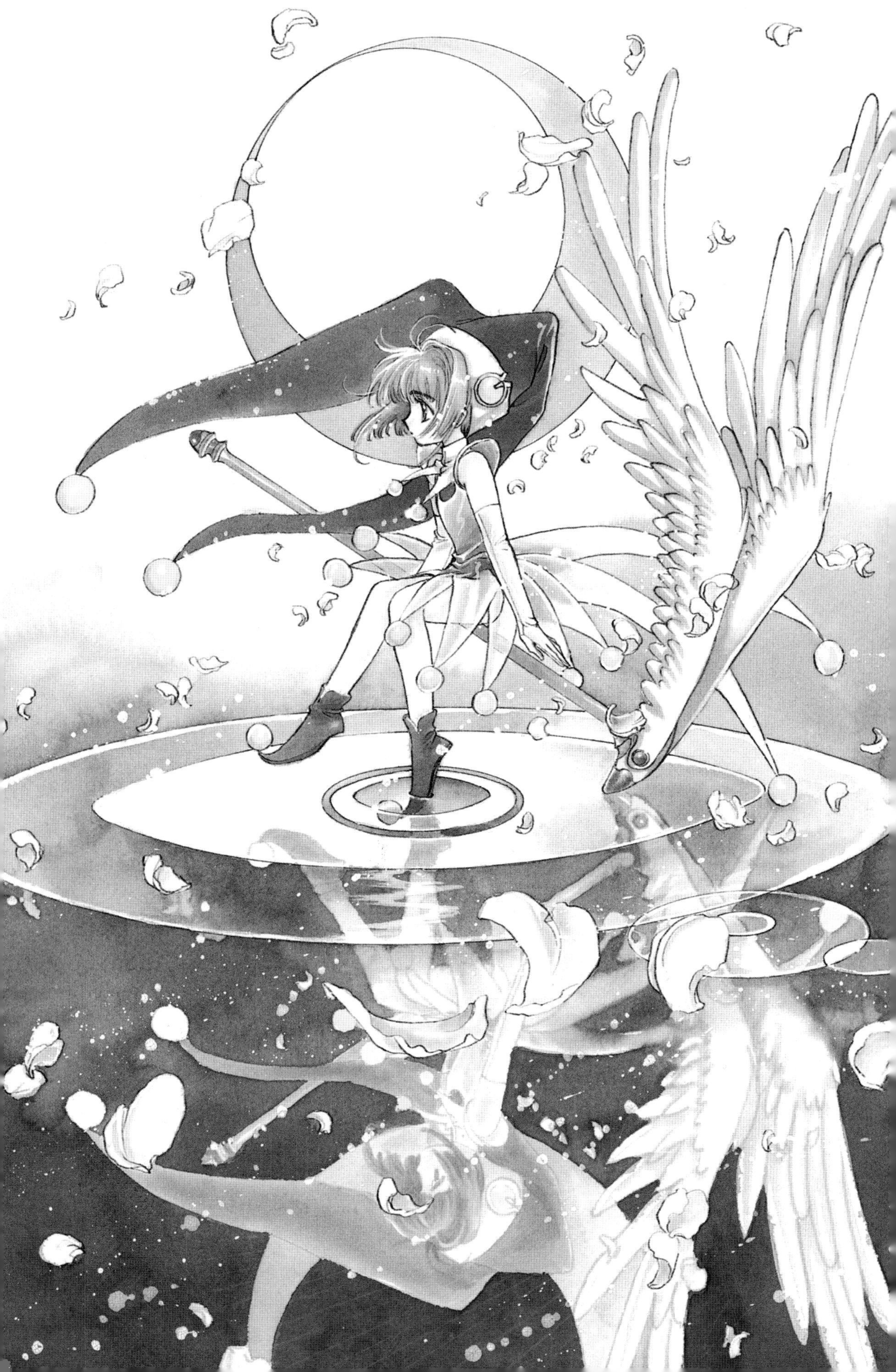

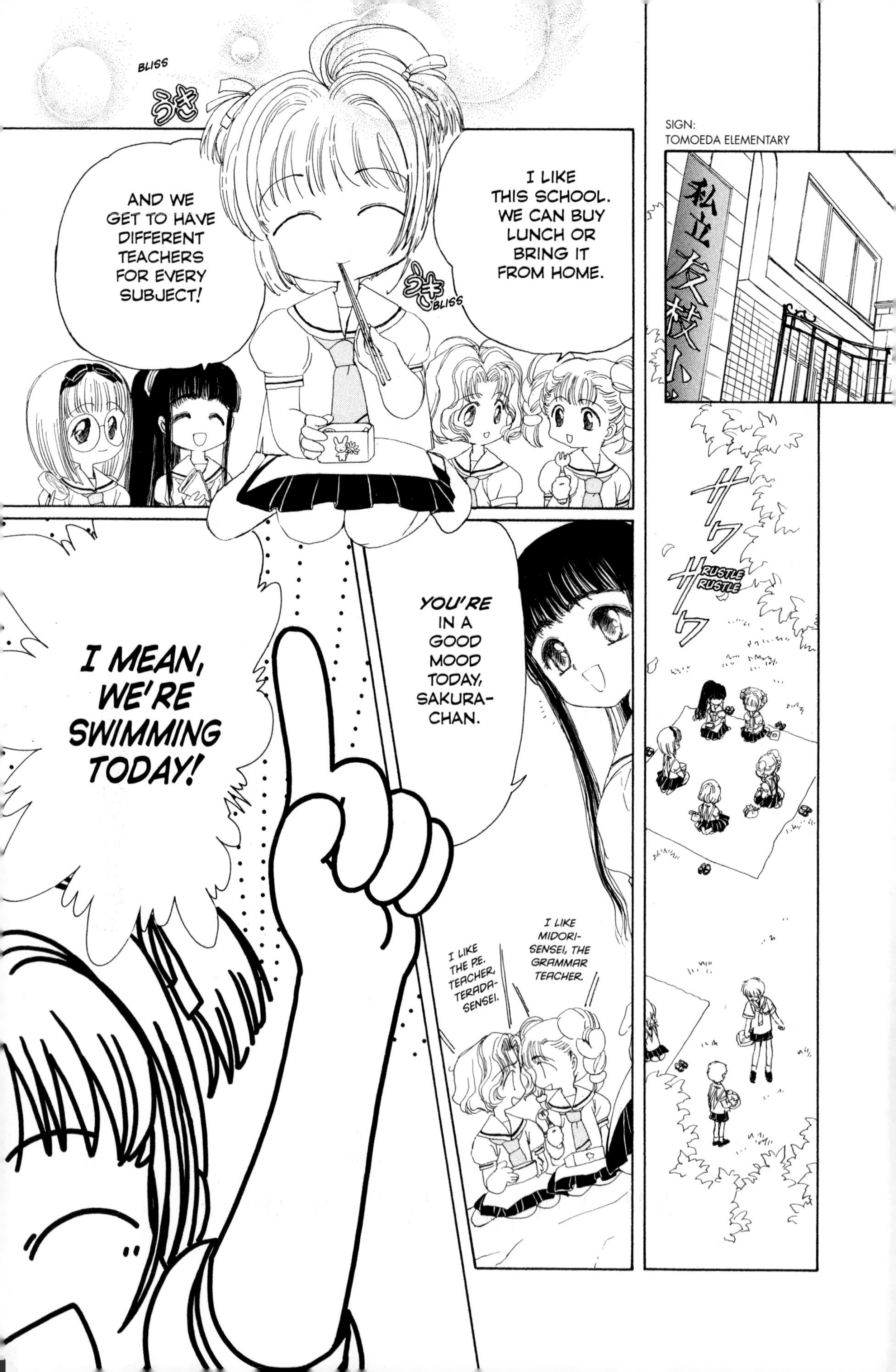
SIGN: TOMOEDA ELEMENTARY
私立友枝小
サワ サワ
RUSTLE RUSTLE
BLISS
うき
I LIKE THIS SCHOOL. WE CAN BUY LUNCH OR BRING IT FROM HOME.
うき BLISS
AND WE GET TO HAVE DIFFERENT TEACHERS FOR EVERY SUBJECT!
YOU'RE IN A GOOD MOOD TODAY, SAKURA-CHAN.
I LIKE MIDORI-SENSEI, THE GRAMMAR TEACHER.
I LIKE THE P.E. TEACHER, TERADA-SENSEI.
I MEAN, WE'RE SWIMMING TODAY!

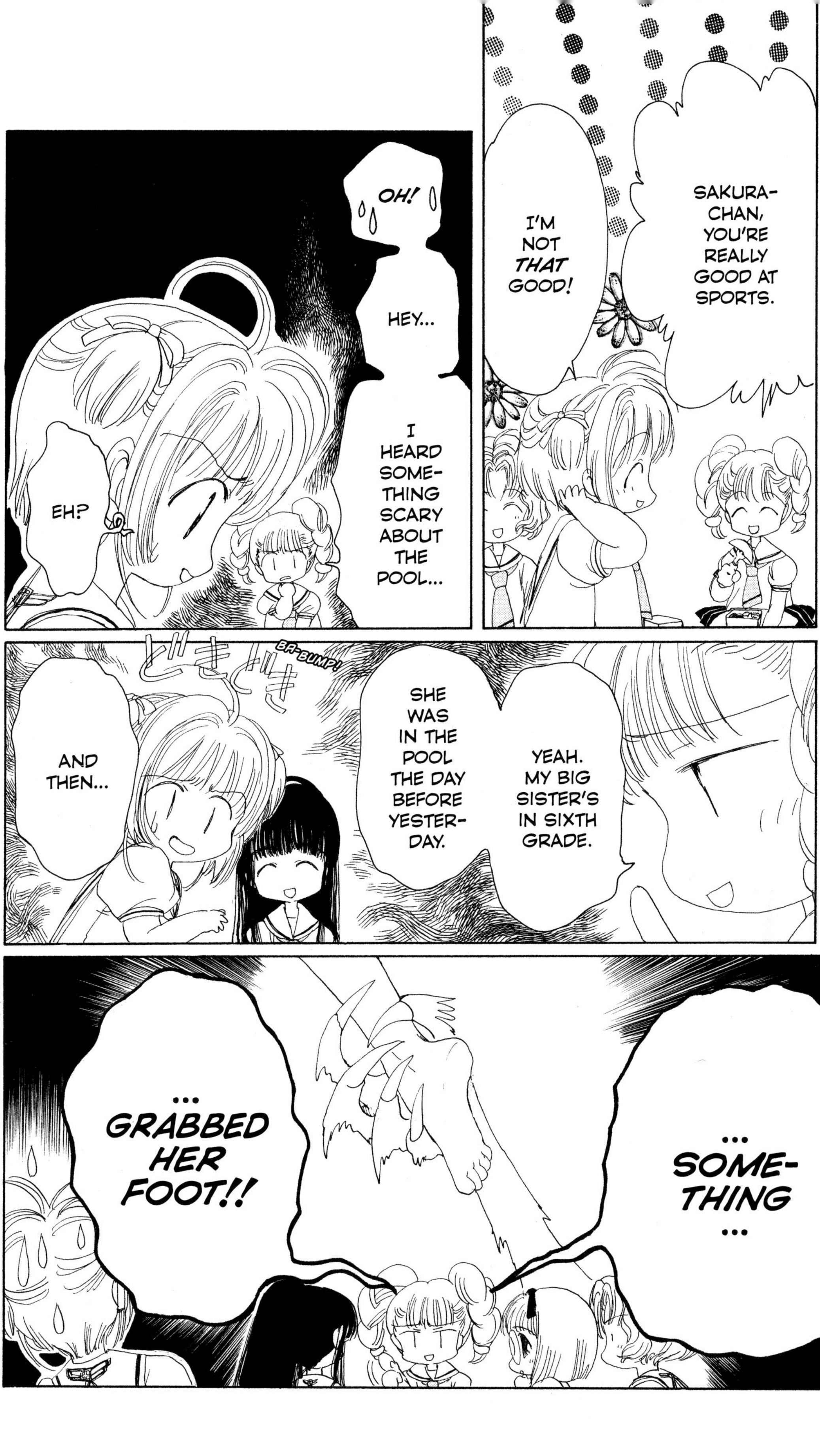
SAKURA-CHAN, YOU'RE REALLY GOOD AT SPORTS.
I'M NOT *THAT* GOOD!
OH!
HEY...
I HEARD SOMETHING SCARY ABOUT THE POOL...
EH?
YEAH. MY BIG SISTER'S IN SIXTH GRADE.
SHE WAS IN THE POOL THE DAY BEFORE YESTERDAY.
BA-BUMP!
AND THEN...
...SOMETHING...
...GRABBED HER FOOT!!

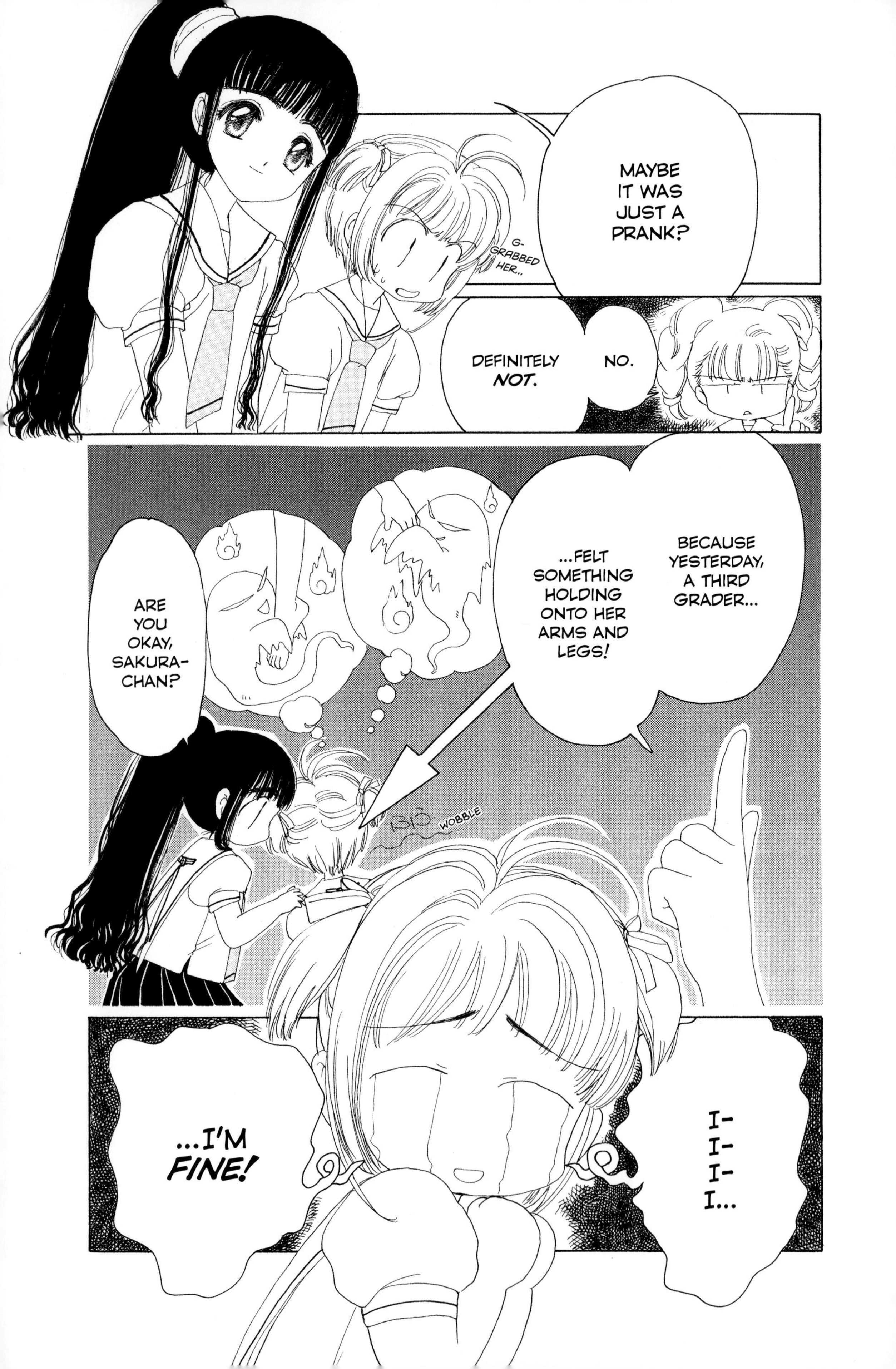
MAYBE IT WAS JUST A PRANK?
G-GRABBED HER...
NO.
DEFINITELY NOT.
BECAUSE YESTERDAY, A THIRD GRADER...
...FELT SOMETHING HOLDING ONTO HER ARMS AND LEGS!
ARE YOU OKAY, SAKURA-CHAN?
WOBBLE
I- I- I- I...
...I'M FINE!

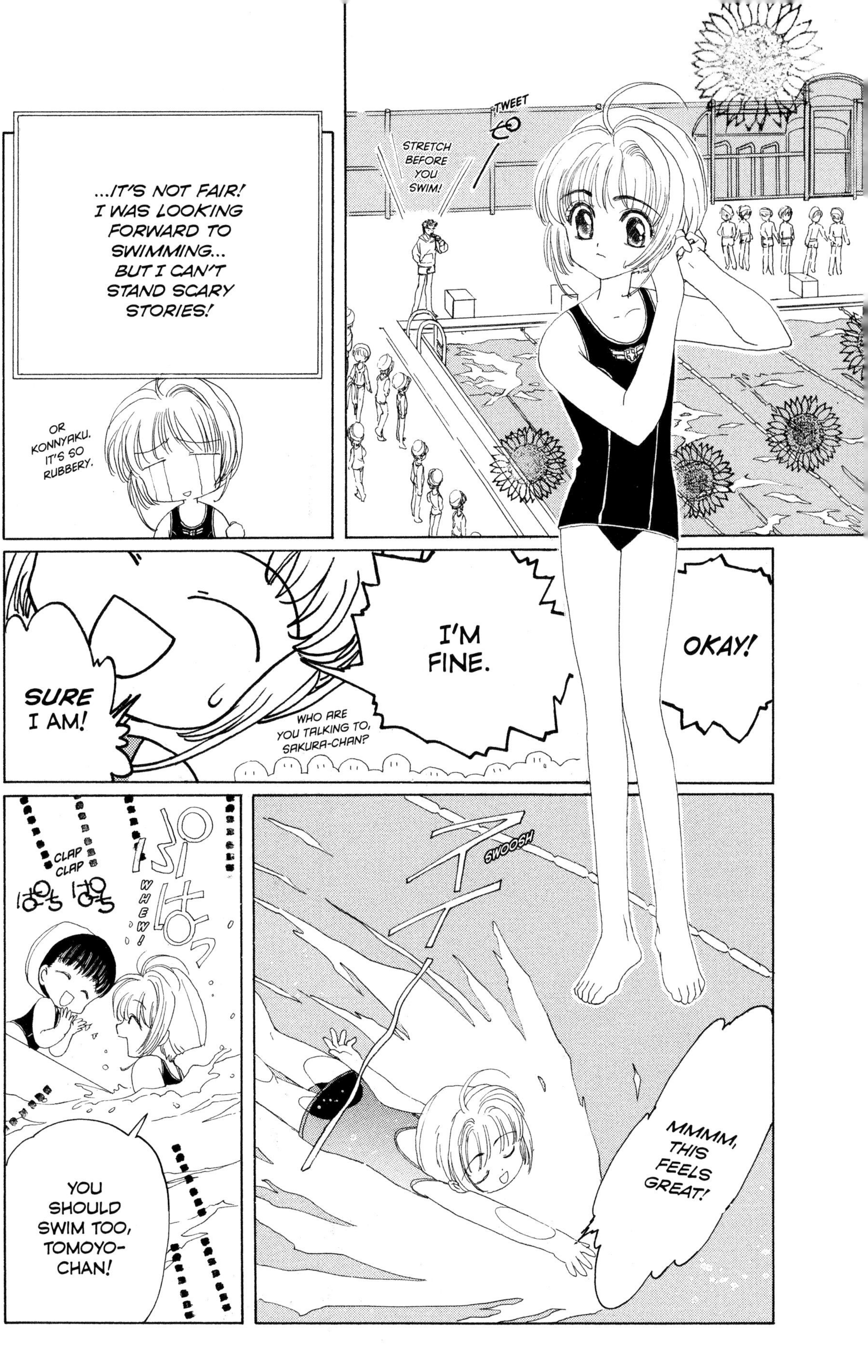
TWEET
STRETCH BEFORE YOU SWIM!
...IT'S NOT FAIR! I WAS LOOKING FORWARD TO SWIMMING... BUT I CAN'T STAND SCARY STORIES!
OR KONNYAKU. IT'S SO RUBBERY.
OKAY!
I'M FINE.
SURE I AM!
WHO ARE YOU TALKING TO, SAKURA-CHAN?
SWOOSH
MMMM, THIS FEELS GREAT!
ぷはっ
WHEW!
CLAP CLAP
ぱちぱち
YOU SHOULD SWIM TOO, TOMOYO-CHAN!

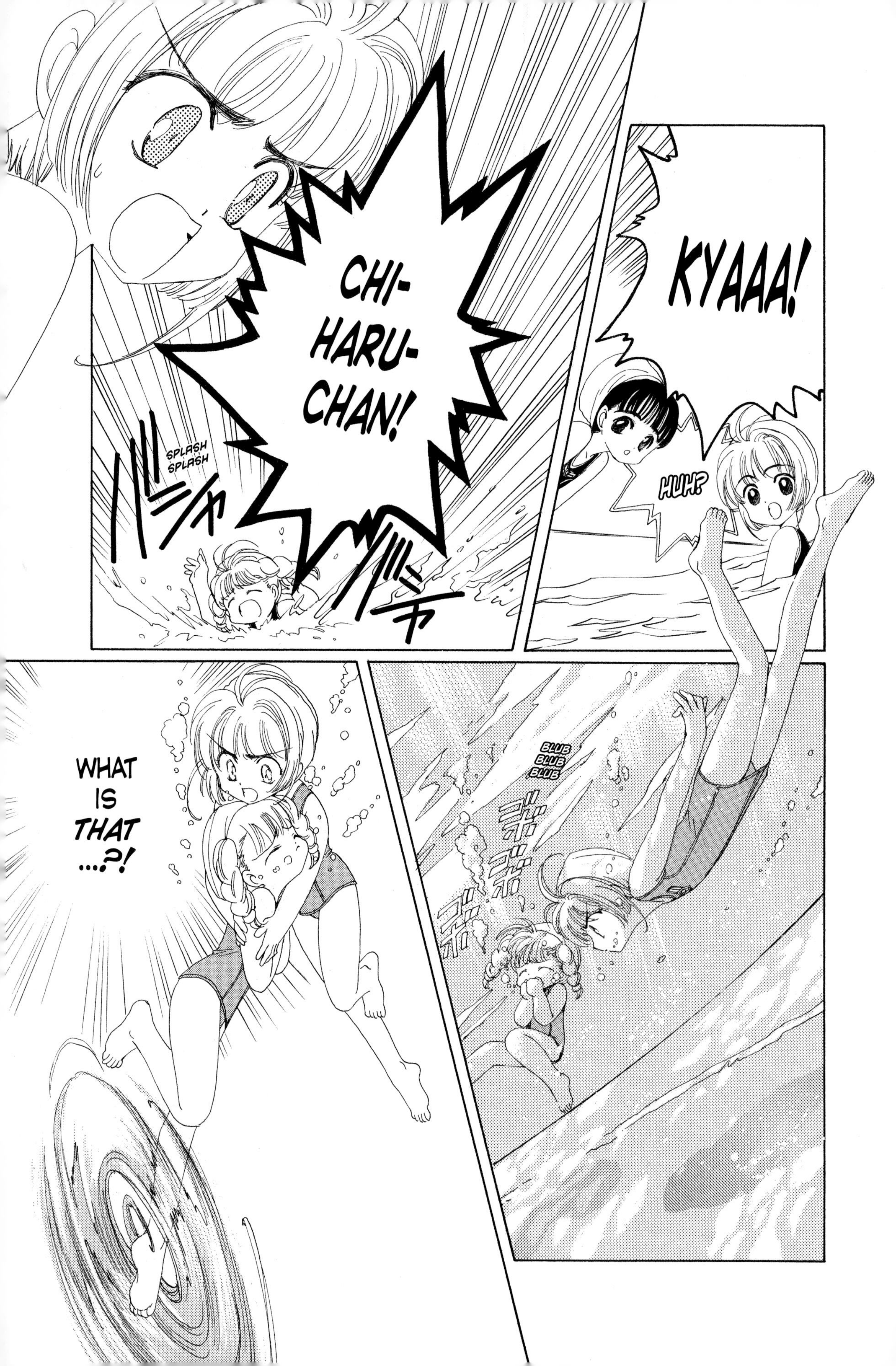
KYAAA!
HUH?
CHI-HARU-CHAN!
SPLASH SPLASH
BLUB BLUB BLUB
WHAT IS THAT ...?!

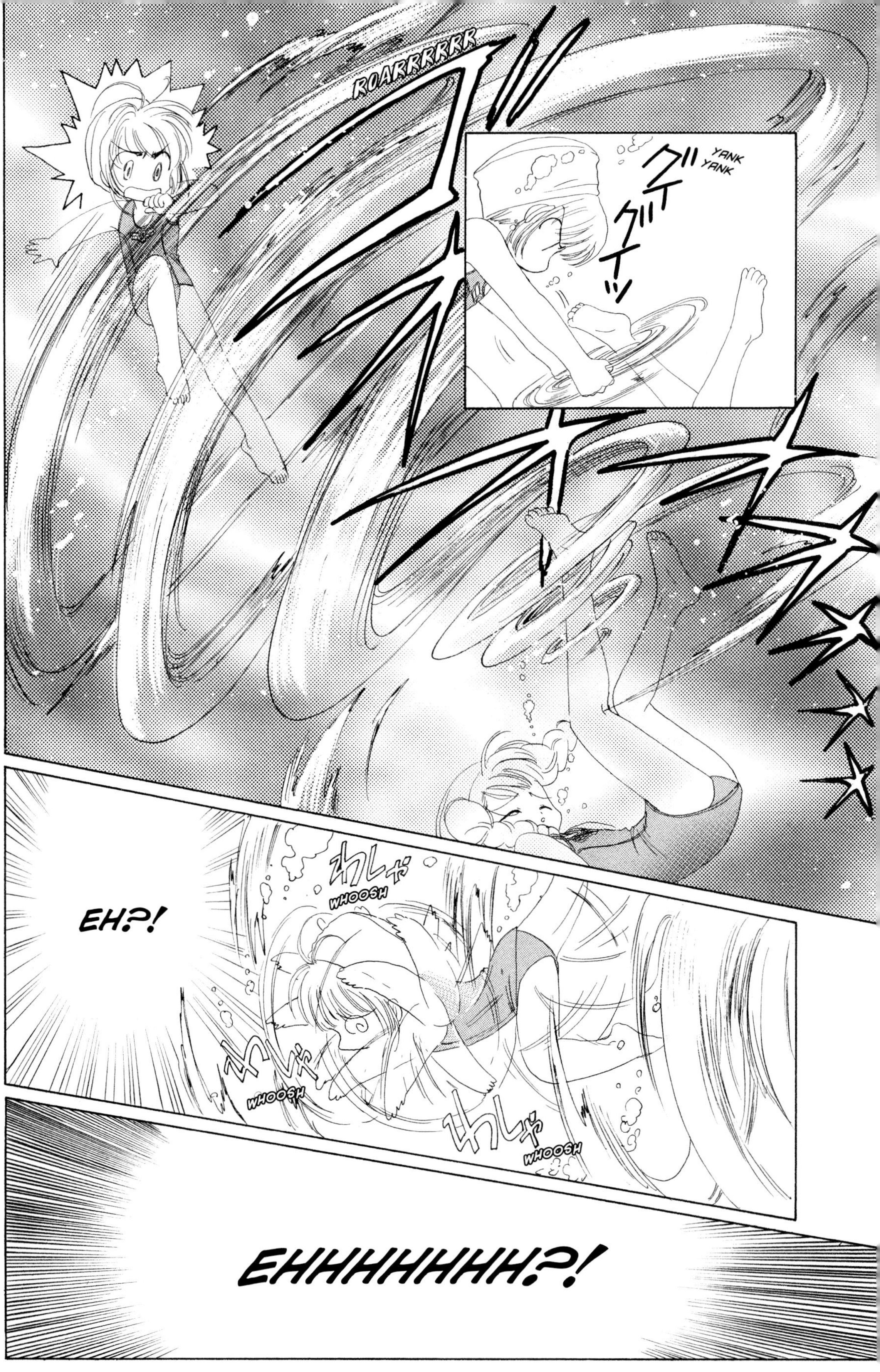
ROARRRRRRR
YANK YANK
WHOOSH
EH?!
WHOOSH
WHOOSH
EHHHHHHHH?!

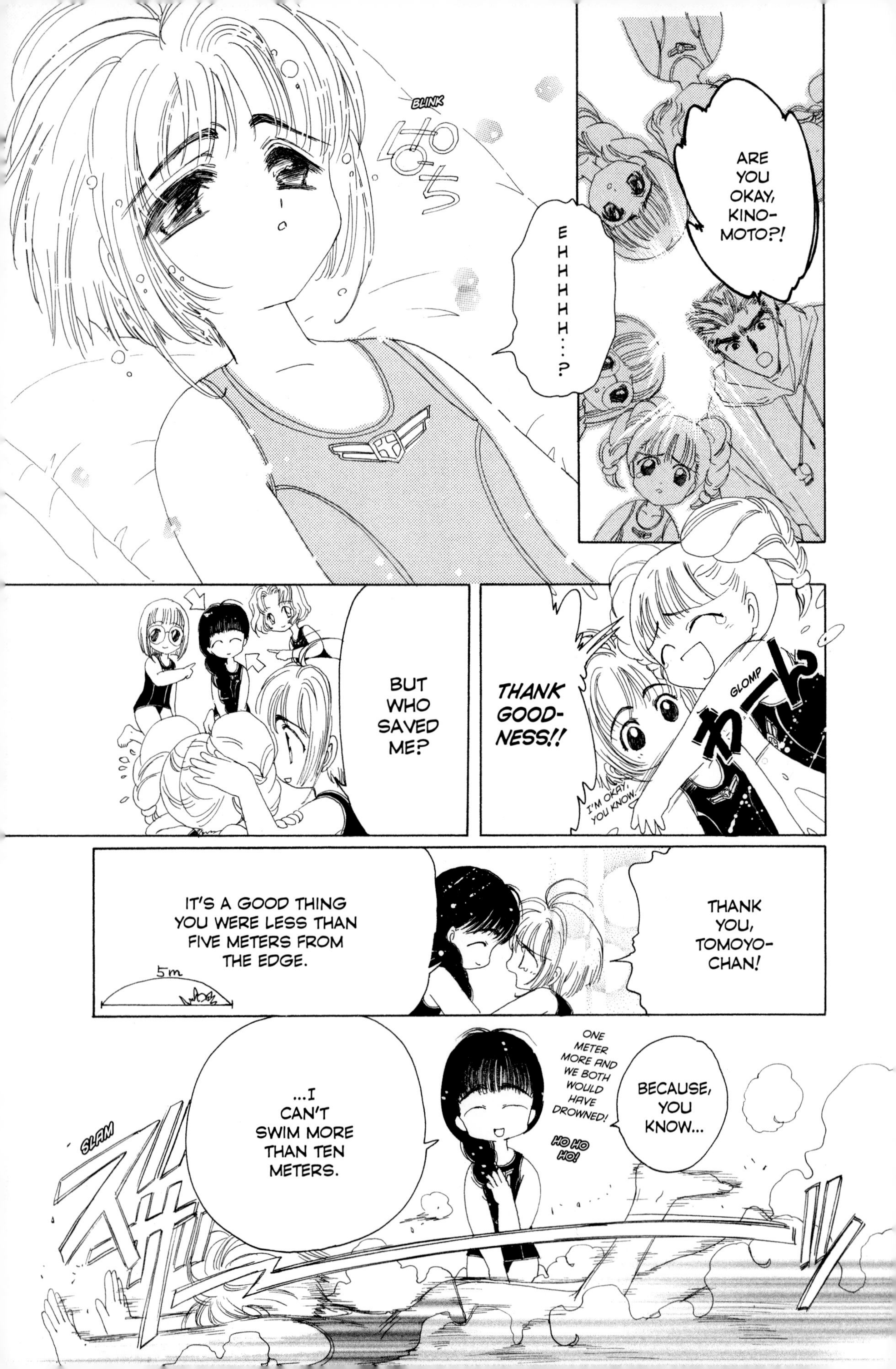
ARE YOU OKAY, KINO-MOTO?!
BLINK
EHHHHH...?
GLOMP
THANK GOOD-NESS!!
I'M OKAY, YOU KNOW.
BUT WHO SAVED ME?
THANK YOU, TOMOYO-CHAN!
IT'S A GOOD THING YOU WERE LESS THAN FIVE METERS FROM THE EDGE.
5m
BECAUSE, YOU KNOW...
ONE METER MORE AND WE BOTH WOULD HAVE DROWNED!
HO HO HO!
...I CAN'T SWIM MORE THAN TEN METERS.
SLAM

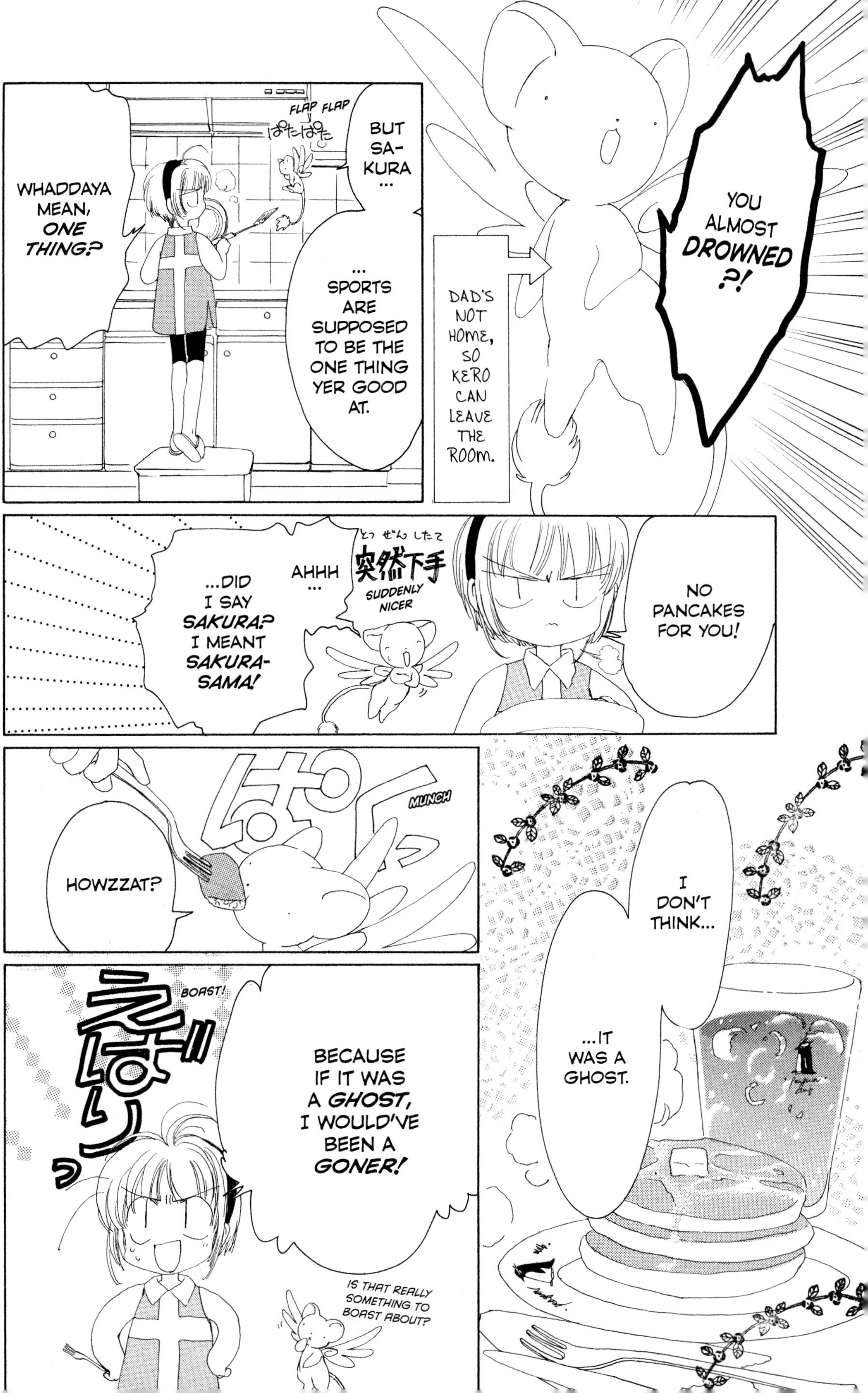
YOU ALMOST DROWNED?!
DAD'S NOT HOME, SO KERO CAN LEAVE THE ROOM.
BUT SAKURA...
...SPORTS ARE SUPPOSED TO BE THE ONE THING YER GOOD AT.
ぱたぱた
FLAP FLAP
WHADDAYA MEAN, ONE THING?
NO PANCAKES FOR YOU!
突然下手
とつぜんしたて
SUDDENLY NICER
AHHH...
...DID I SAY SAKURA? I MEANT SAKURA-SAMA!
I DON'T THINK...
...IT WAS A GHOST.
MUNCH
HOWZZAT?
BECAUSE IF IT WAS A GHOST, I WOULD'VE BEEN A GONER!
えばりっ
BOAST!
IS THAT REALLY SOMETHING TO BOAST ABOUT?

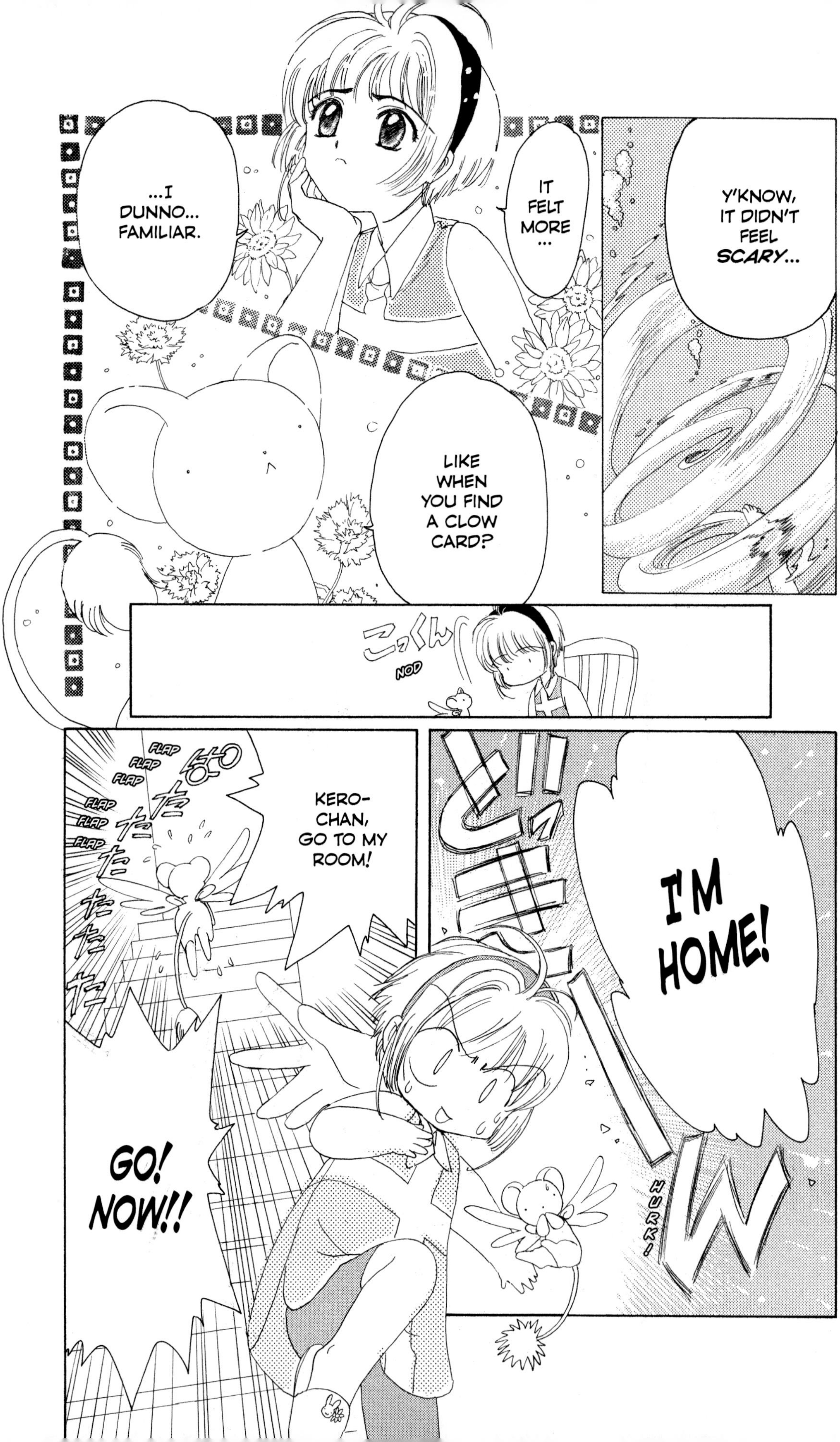
Y'KNOW, IT DIDN'T FEEL SCARY...
IT FELT MORE ...
...I DUNNO... FAMILIAR.
LIKE WHEN YOU FIND A CLOW CARD?
こっくん
NOD
I'M HOME!
HURK!
KERO-CHAN, GO TO MY ROOM!
FLAP
FLAP
FLAP
FLAP
FLAP
FLAP
GO! NOW!!

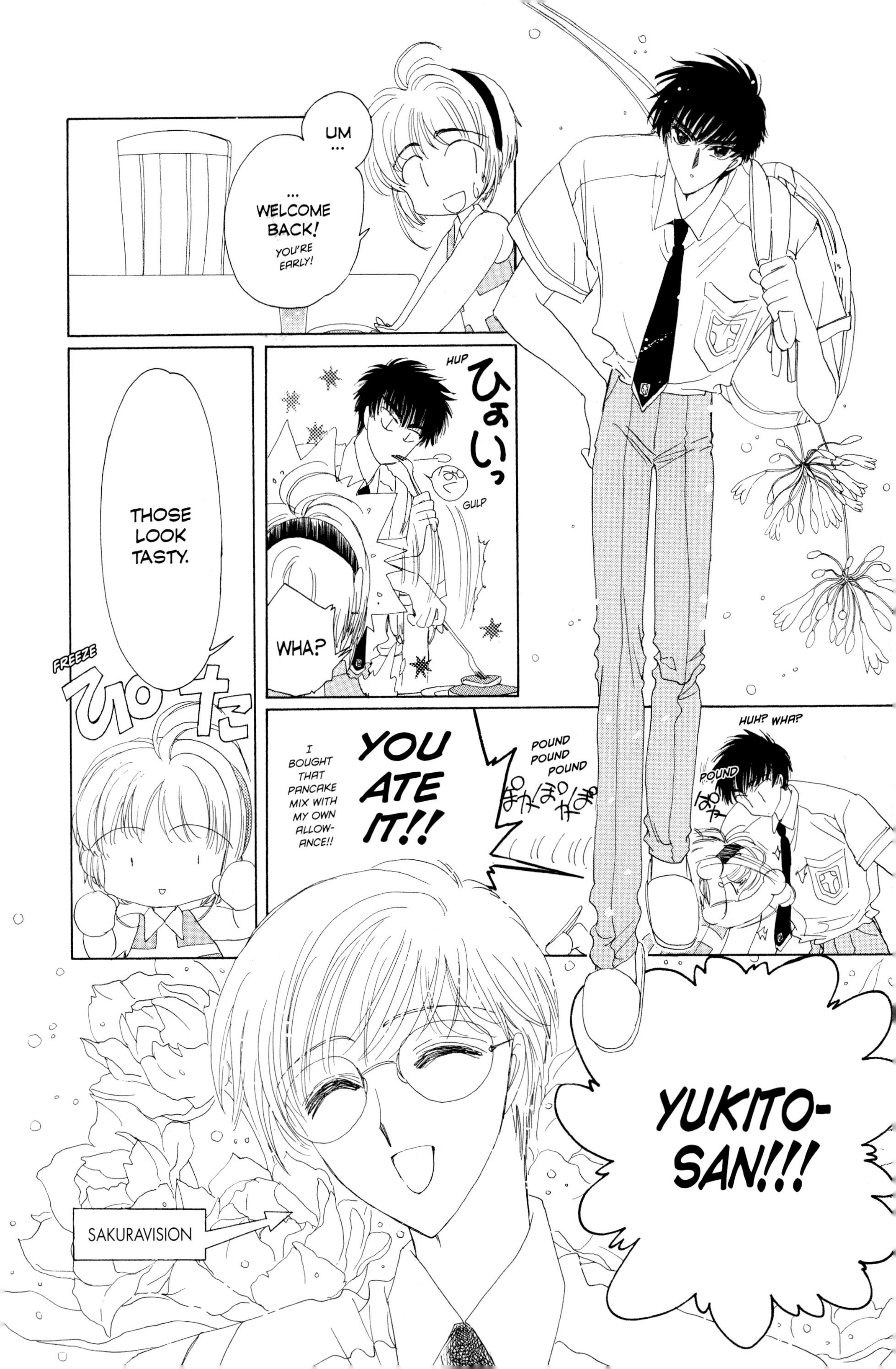
UM ...
... WELCOME BACK! YOU'RE EARLY!
HUP
ひょいっ
GULP
WHA?
HUH? WHA?
POUND
ぽや
POUND POUND POUND
ぽかぽかぽか
YOU ATE IT!!
I BOUGHT THAT PANCAKE MIX WITH MY OWN ALLOW-ANCE!!
THOSE LOOK TASTY.
FREEZE
ぴたっ
YUKITO-SAN!!!
SAKURAVISION

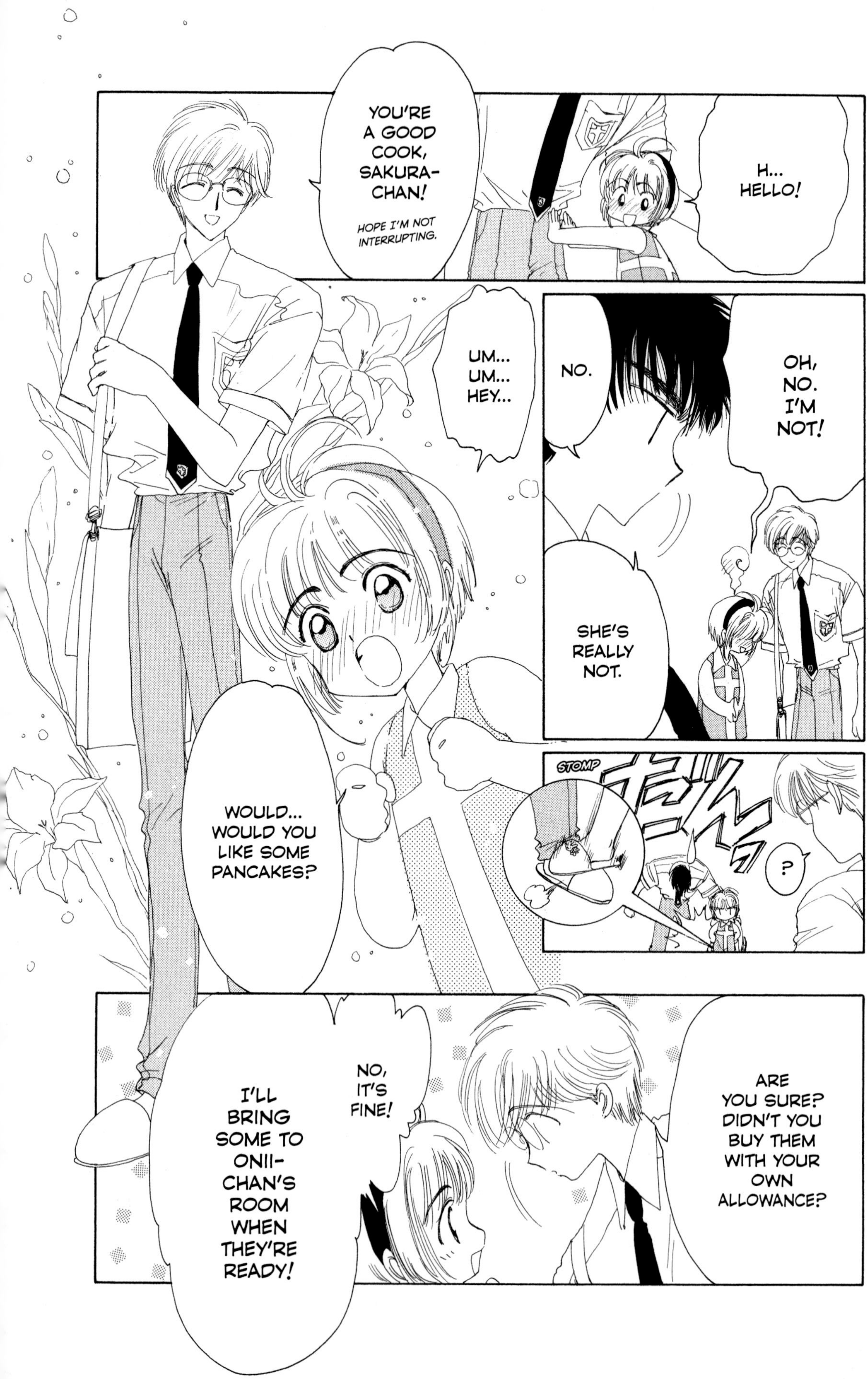
H... HELLO!
YOU'RE A GOOD COOK, SAKURA-CHAN!
HOPE I'M NOT INTERRUPTING.
OH, NO. I'M NOT!
NO.
SHE'S REALLY NOT.
STOMP
?
UM... UM... HEY...
WOULD... WOULD YOU LIKE SOME PANCAKES?
ARE YOU SURE? DIDN'T YOU BUY THEM WITH YOUR OWN ALLOWANCE?
NO, IT'S FINE!
I'LL BRING SOME TO ONII-CHAN'S ROOM WHEN THEY'RE READY!

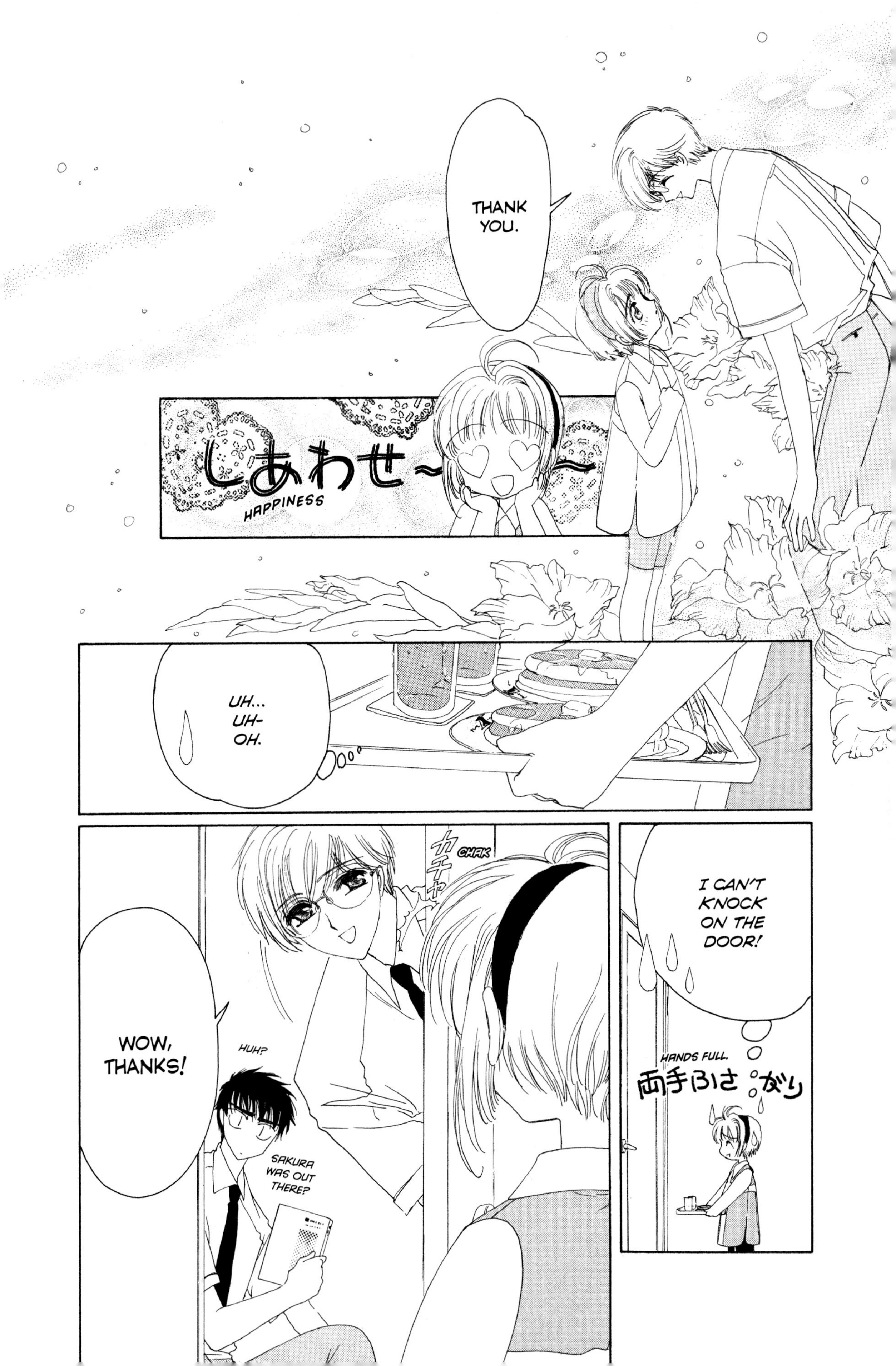
THANK YOU.
しあわせ~
HAPPINESS
UH... UH-OH.
I CAN'T KNOCK ON THE DOOR!
HANDS FULL.
両手ふさがり
カチャ
CHAK
WOW, THANKS!
HUH?
SAKURA WAS OUT THERE?

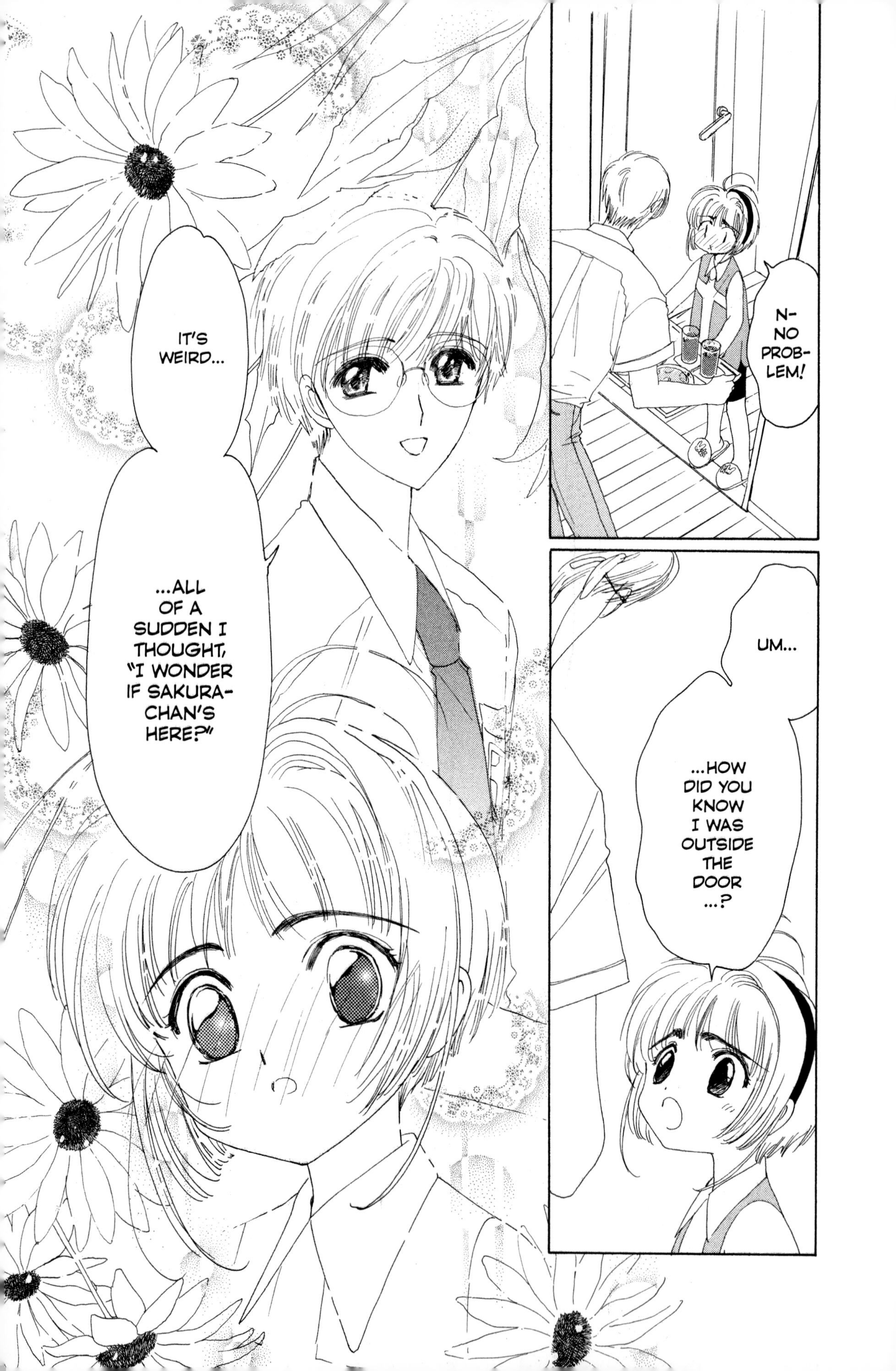
N-NO PROB-LEM!
UM...
...HOW DID YOU KNOW I WAS OUTSIDE THE DOOR ...?
IT'S WEIRD...
...ALL OF A SUDDEN I THOUGHT, "I WONDER IF SAKURA-CHAN'S HERE?"

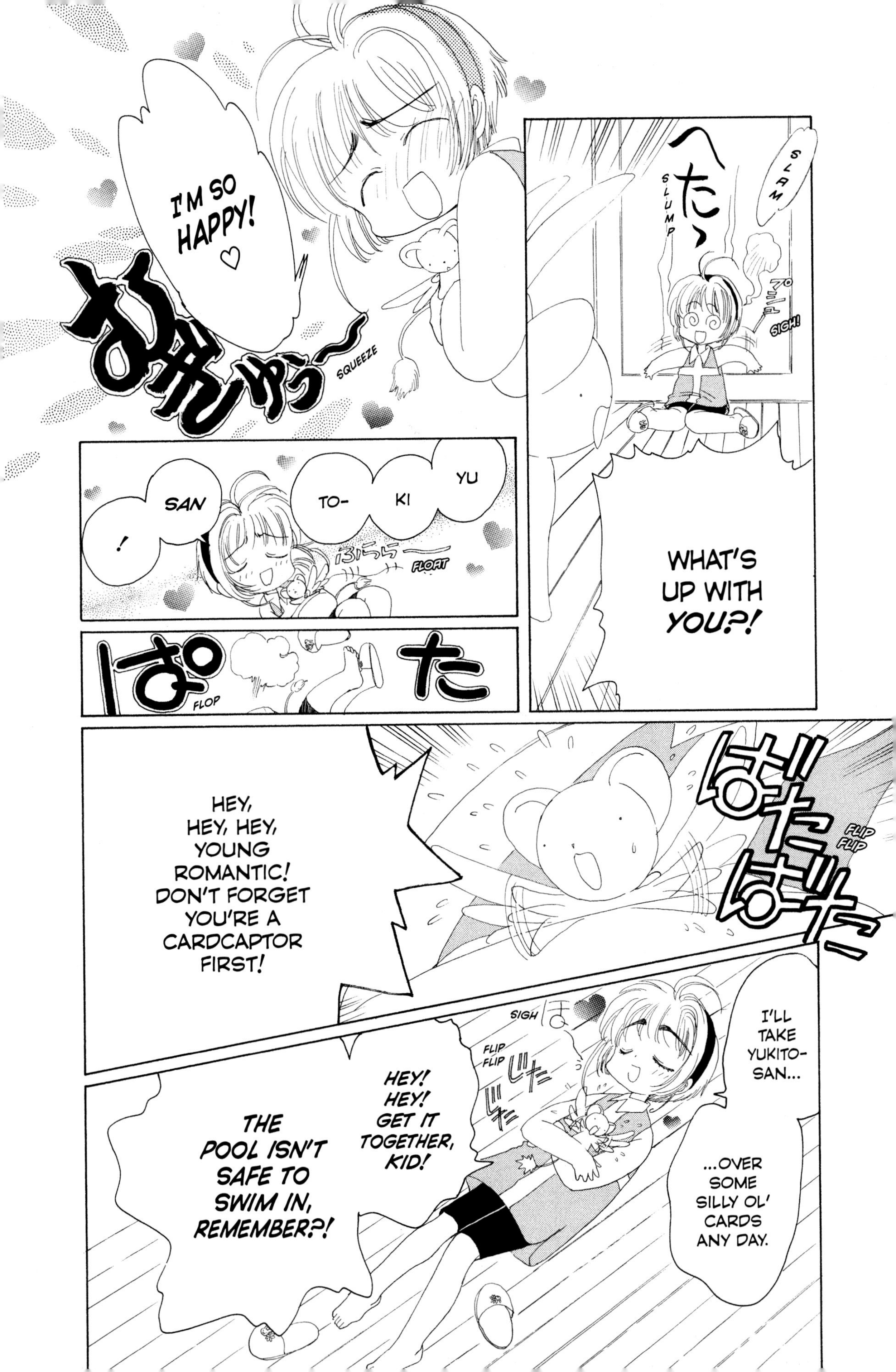

I'M SO HAPPY! ♡
SQUEEZE
YU
KI
TO-
SAN
!
FLOAT
ぱた
FLOP
へた
SLUMP
SLAM
SIGH!
WHAT'S UP WITH YOU?!
はたはた
FLIP FLIP
HEY, HEY, HEY, YOUNG ROMANTIC! DON'T FORGET YOU'RE A CARDCAPTOR FIRST!
SIGH
I'LL TAKE YUKITO-SAN...
...OVER SOME SILLY OL' CARDS ANY DAY.
FLIP FLIP
HEY! HEY! GET IT TOGETHER, KID!
THE POOL ISN'T SAFE TO SWIM IN, REMEMBER?!

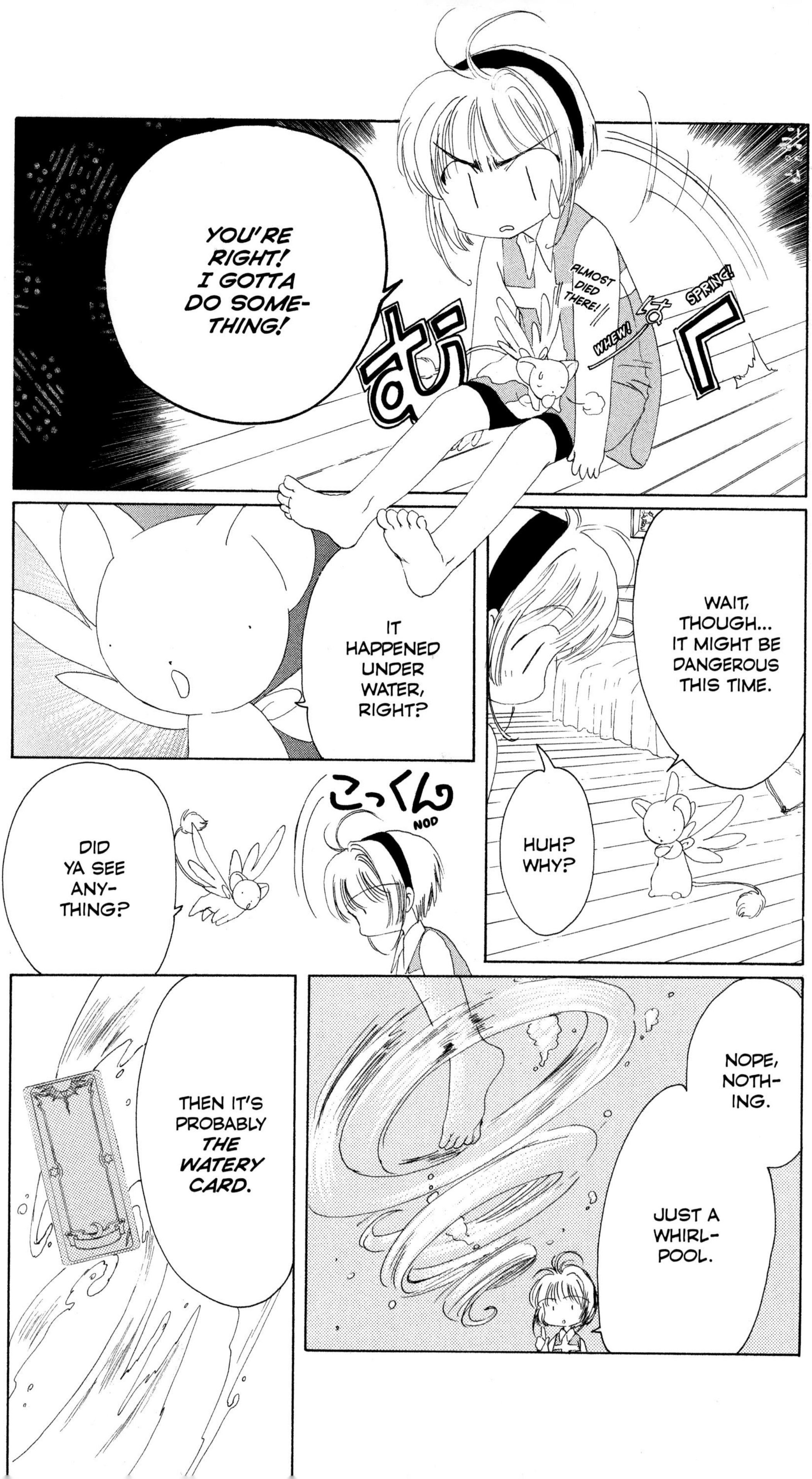
SPRING!
ALMOST DIED THERE!
WHEW!
むっ
YOU'RE RIGHT! I GOTTA DO SOME-THING!
WAIT, THOUGH... IT MIGHT BE DANGEROUS THIS TIME.
HUH? WHY?
IT HAPPENED UNDER WATER, RIGHT?
こっくん
NOD
DID YA SEE ANY-THING?
NOPE, NOTH-ING.
JUST A WHIRL-POOL.
THEN IT'S PROBABLY *THE WATERY CARD*.

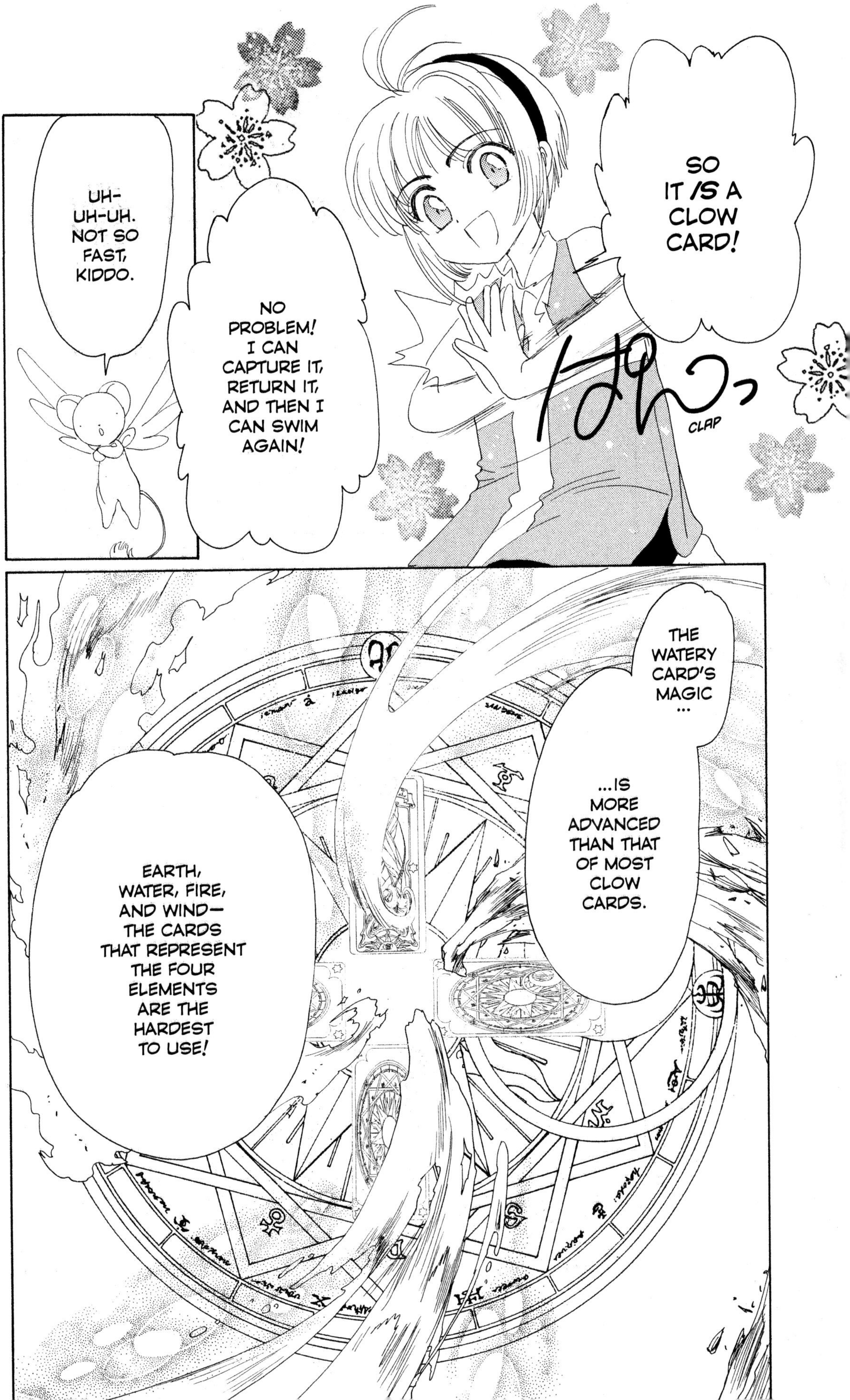
SO IT IS A CLOW CARD!
CLAP
NO PROBLEM! I CAN CAPTURE IT, RETURN IT, AND THEN I CAN SWIM AGAIN!
UH-UH-UH. NOT SO FAST, KIDDO.
THE WATERY CARD'S MAGIC...
...IS MORE ADVANCED THAN THAT OF MOST CLOW CARDS.
EARTH, WATER, FIRE, AND WIND—THE CARDS THAT REPRESENT THE FOUR ELEMENTS ARE THE HARDEST TO USE!

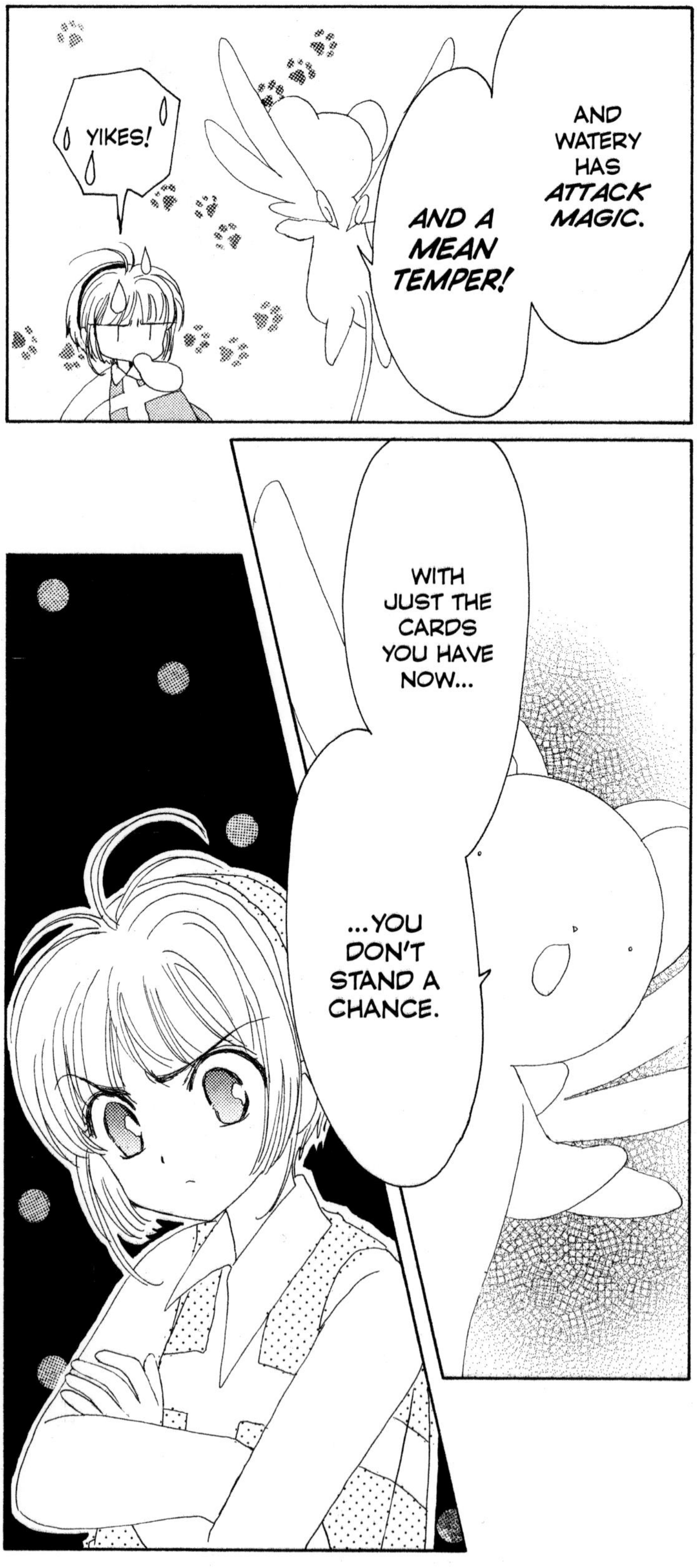
AND WATERY HAS ATTACK MAGIC.
AND A MEAN TEMPER!
YIKES!
WITH JUST THE CARDS YOU HAVE NOW...
...YOU DON'T STAND A CHANCE.

3

TŌYA KINOMOTO

BIRTHDATE:
FEBRUARY 29
BLOOD TYPE:
O
FAVORITE SUBJECT:
CHEMISTRY
LEAST FAVORITE SUBJECT:
NONE
CLUB:
SOCCER
FAVORITE COLOR:
BLUE
FAVORITE FLOWER:
PEACH BLOSSOM
FAVORITE FOOD:
STEAK
LEAST FAVORITE FOOD:
FRIED TOFU
FAVORITE RECIPES:
RICE OMELET, YAKISOBA
WISH LIST:
NEW SNEAKERS

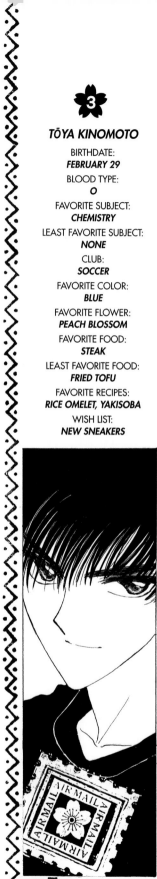

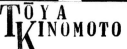

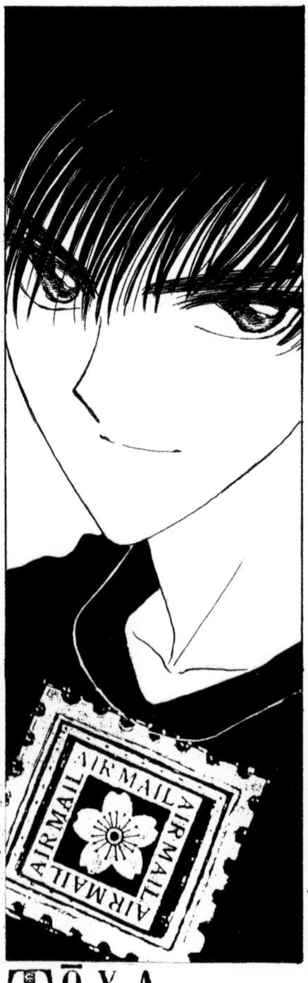
AIR MAIL
AIR MAIL
AIR MAIL
AIR MAIL

TŌYA KINOMOTO

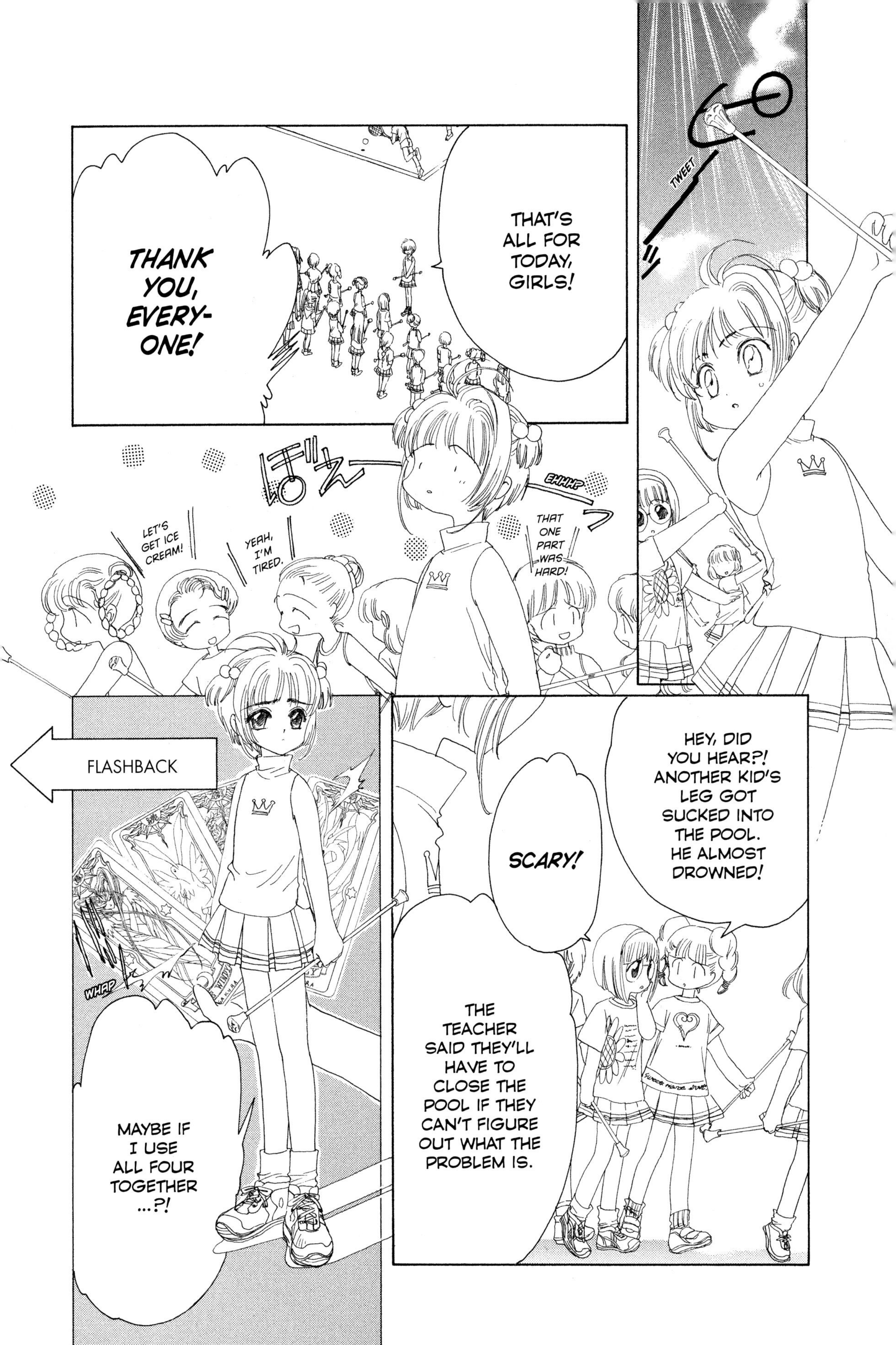
TWEET
THAT'S ALL FOR TODAY, GIRLS!
THANK YOU, EVERY-ONE!
EHHH?
THAT ONE PART WAS HARD!
YEAH, I'M TIRED.
LET'S GET ICE CREAM!
HEY, DID YOU HEAR?! ANOTHER KID'S LEG GOT SUCKED INTO THE POOL. HE ALMOST DROWNED!
SCARY!
THE TEACHER SAID THEY'LL HAVE TO CLOSE THE POOL IF THEY CAN'T FIGURE OUT WHAT THE PROBLEM IS.
FLASHBACK
WHAP
MAYBE IF I USE ALL FOUR TOGETHER ...?!

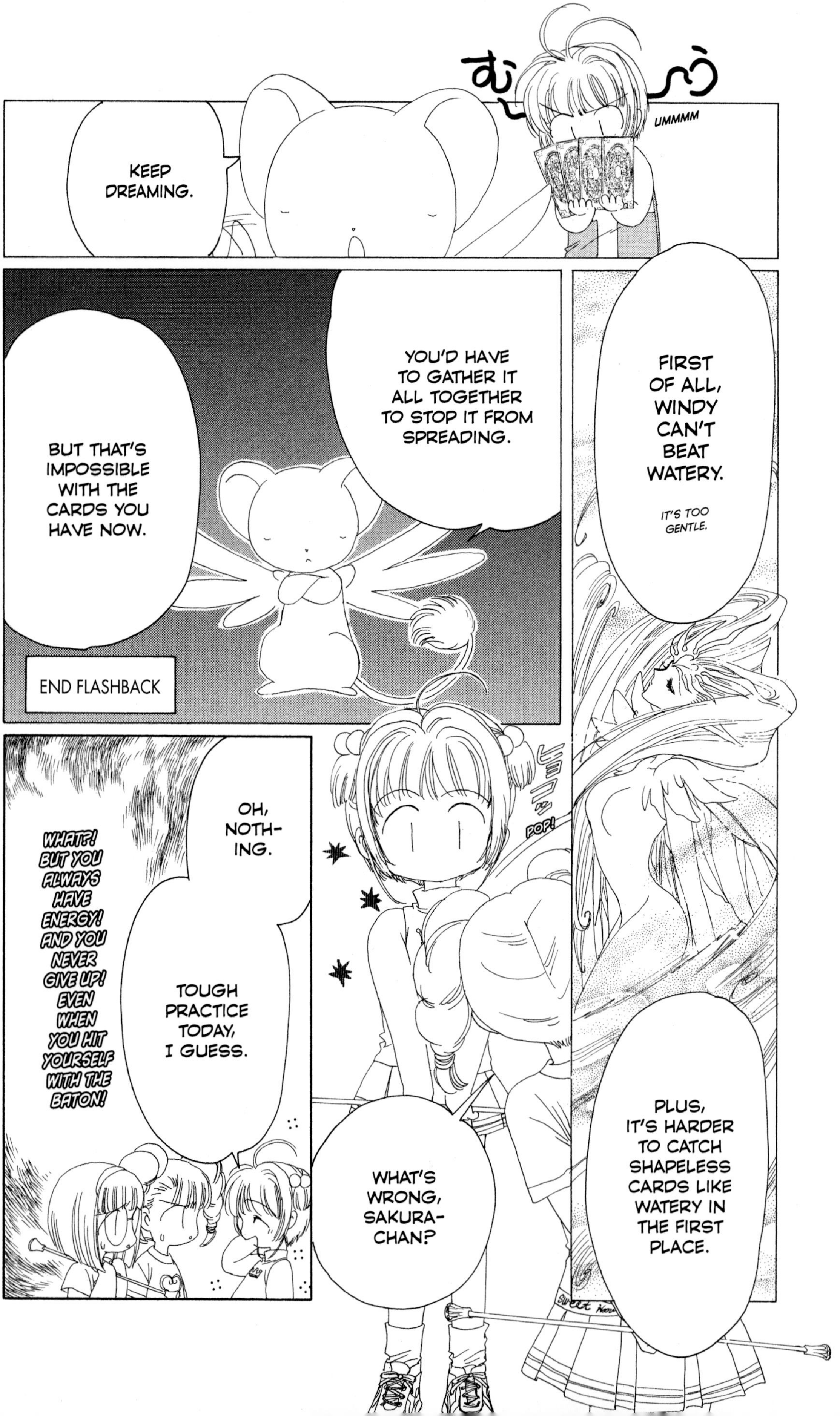
むーう
UMMMM
KEEP DREAMING.
FIRST OF ALL, WINDY CAN'T BEAT WATERY.
IT'S TOO GENTLE.
PLUS, IT'S HARDER TO CATCH SHAPELESS CARDS LIKE WATERY IN THE FIRST PLACE.
YOU'D HAVE TO GATHER IT ALL TOGETHER TO STOP IT FROM SPREADING.
BUT THAT'S IMPOSSIBLE WITH THE CARDS YOU HAVE NOW.
END FLASHBACK
ヒョコッ
POP!
WHAT'S WRONG, SAKURA-CHAN?
OH, NOTH-ING.
TOUGH PRACTICE TODAY, I GUESS.
WHAT?! BUT YOU ALWAYS HAVE ENERGY! AND YOU NEVER GIVE UP! EVEN WHEN YOU HIT YOURSELF WITH THE BATON!

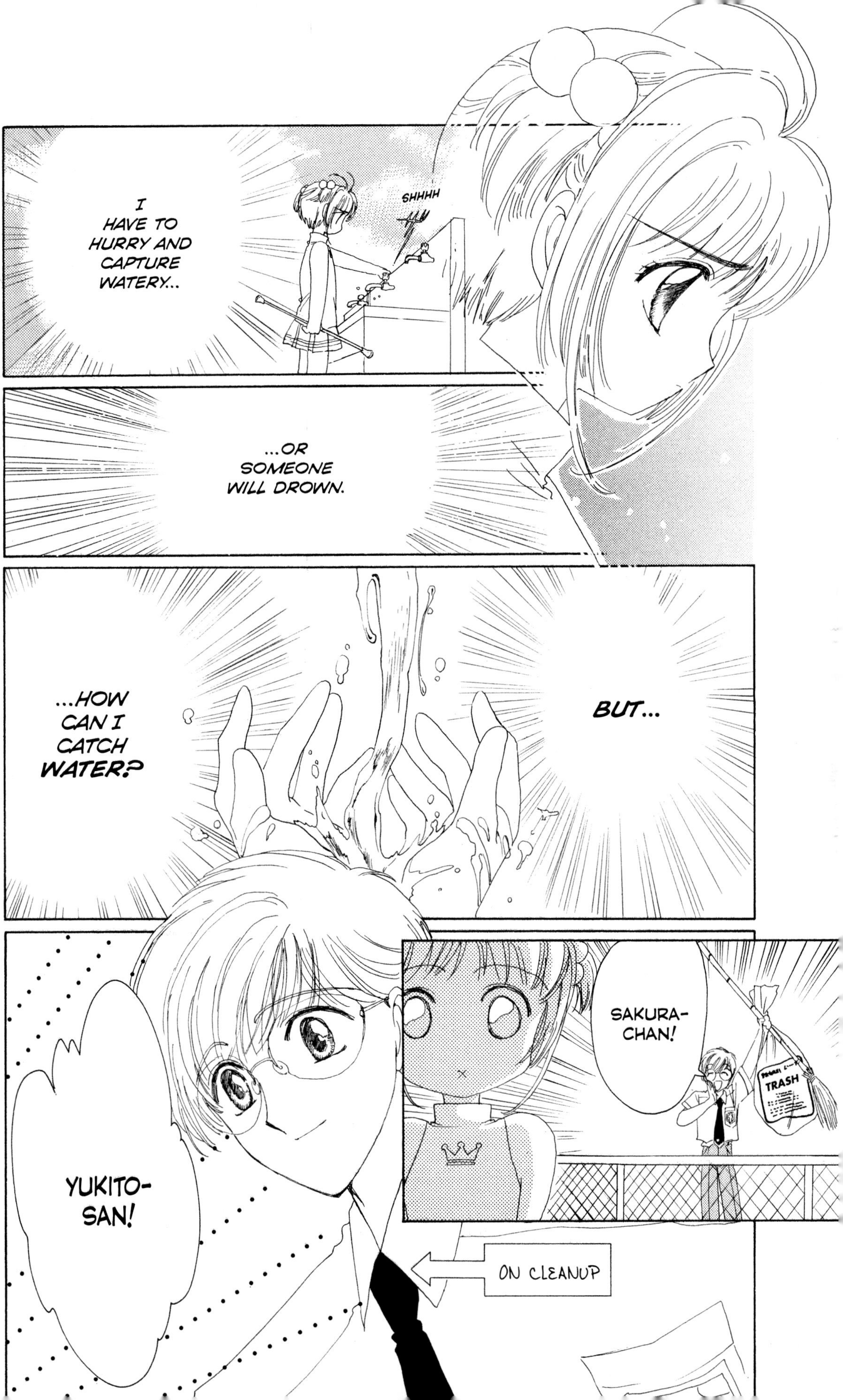
SHHHH
I HAVE TO HURRY AND CAPTURE WATERY...
...OR SOMEONE WILL DROWN.
BUT...
...HOW CAN I CATCH WATER?
SAKURA-CHAN!
TRASH
YUKITO-SAN!
ON CLEANUP

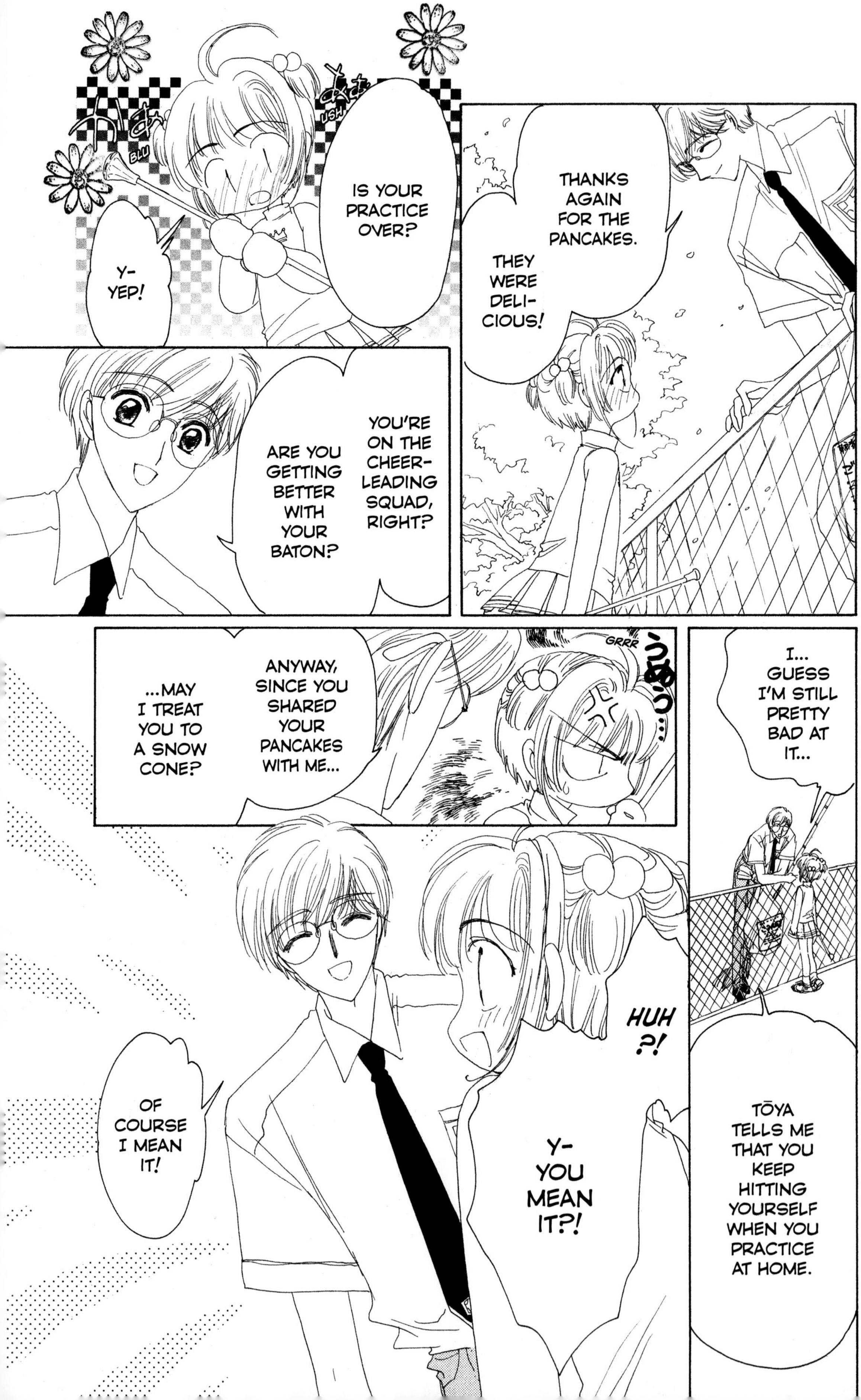
THANKS AGAIN FOR THE PANCAKES.
THEY WERE DELI- CIOUS!
USH
BLU
IS YOUR PRACTICE OVER?
Y- YEP!
YOU'RE ON THE CHEER- LEADING SQUAD, RIGHT?
ARE YOU GETTING BETTER WITH YOUR BATON?
I... GUESS I'M STILL PRETTY BAD AT IT...
TŌYA TELLS ME THAT YOU KEEP HITTING YOURSELF WHEN YOU PRACTICE AT HOME.
GRRR
ANYWAY, SINCE YOU SHARED YOUR PANCAKES WITH ME...
...MAY I TREAT YOU TO A SNOW CONE?
HUH ?!
Y- YOU MEAN IT?!
OF COURSE I MEAN IT!

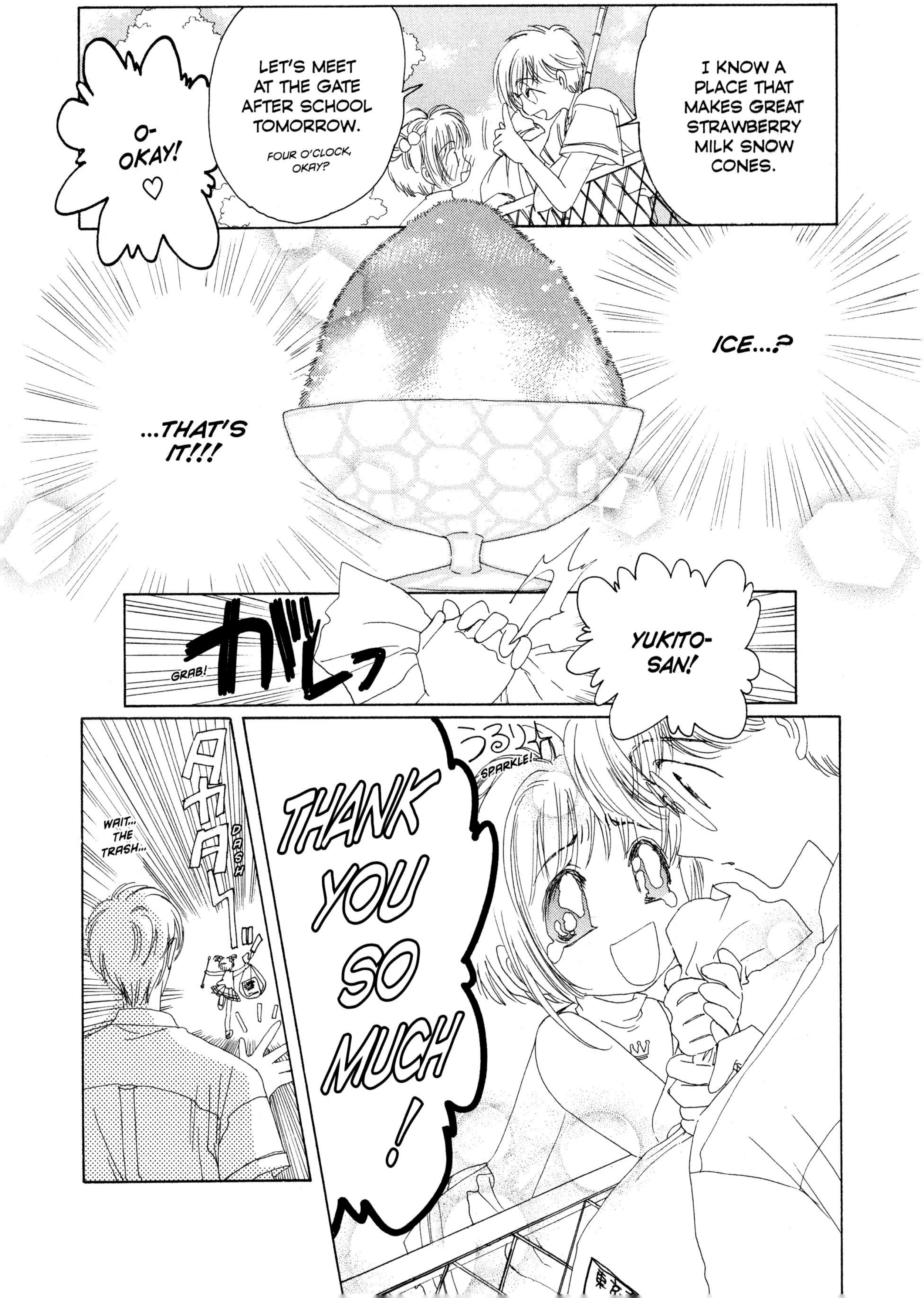
I KNOW A PLACE THAT MAKES GREAT STRAWBERRY MILK SNOW CONES.
LET'S MEET AT THE GATE AFTER SCHOOL TOMORROW.
FOUR O'CLOCK, OKAY?
O-OKAY! ♡
ICE...?
...THAT'S IT!!!
YUKITO-SAN!
GRAB!
SPARKLE!
THANK YOU SO MUCH!
DASH
WAIT... THE TRASH...

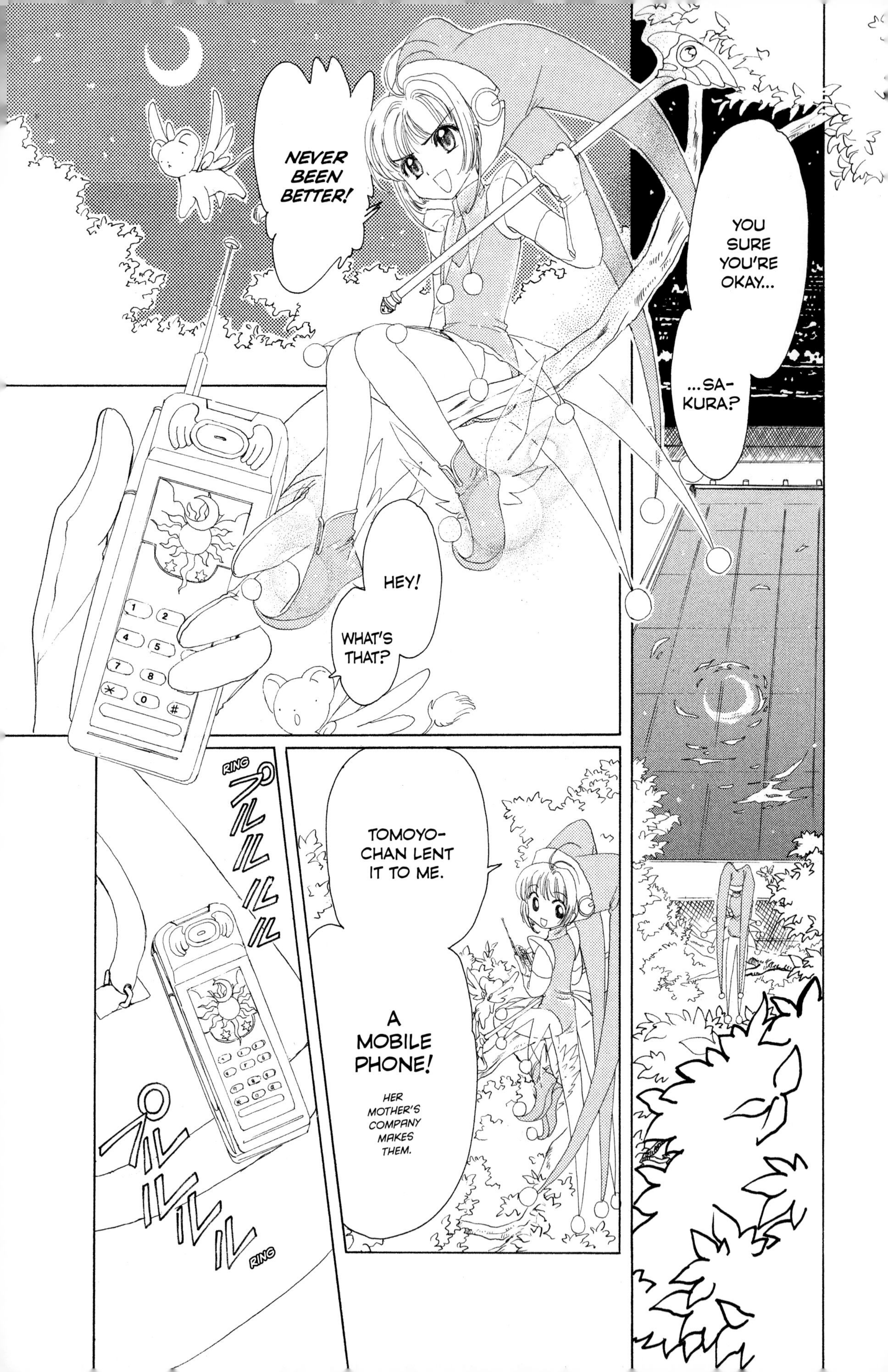
YOU SURE YOU'RE OKAY...
...SA-KURA?
NEVER BEEN BETTER!
HEY!
WHAT'S THAT?
TOMOYO-CHAN LENT IT TO ME.
A MOBILE PHONE!
HER MOTHER'S COMPANY MAKES THEM.
RING
RING

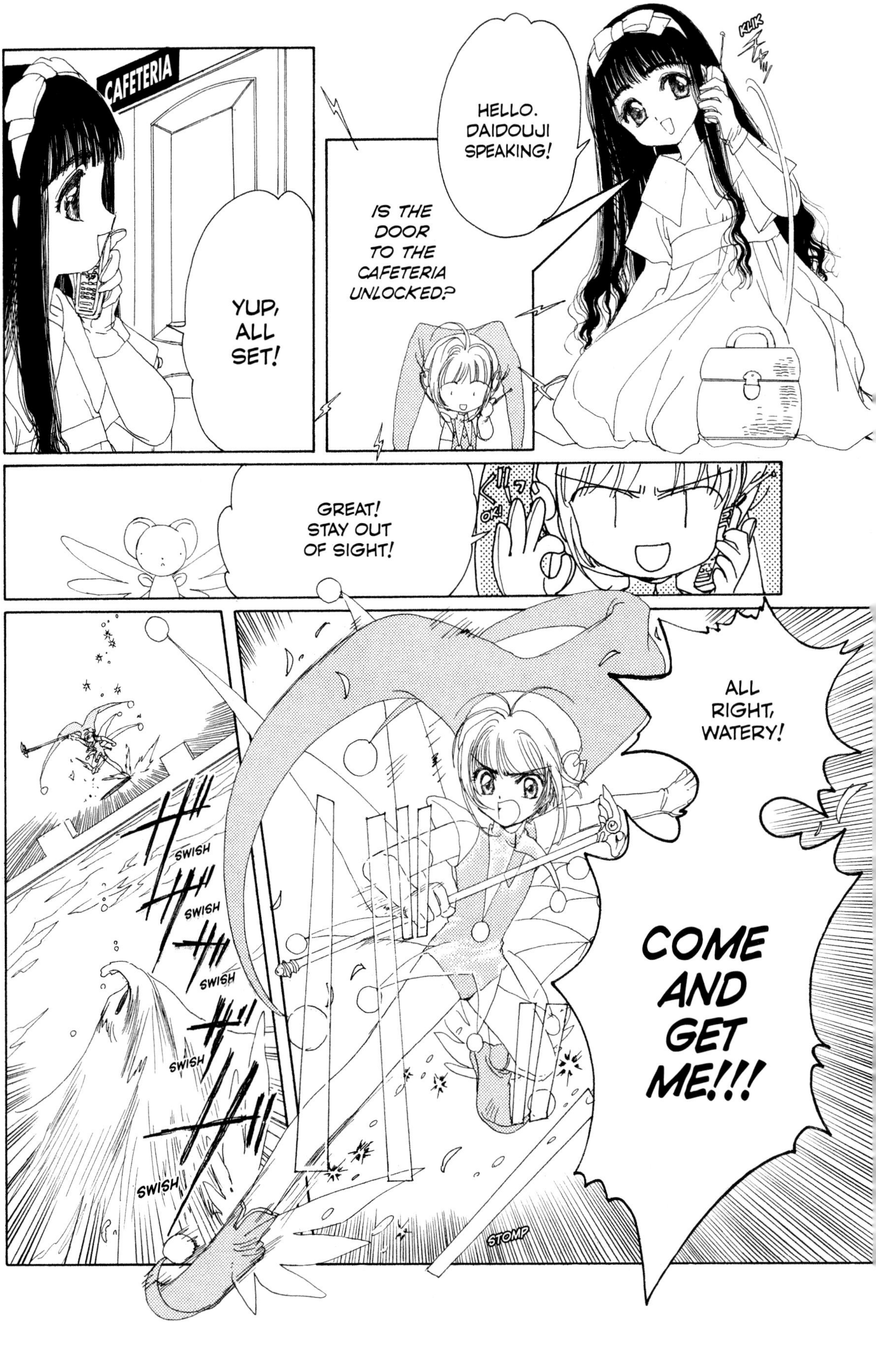
KLIK
HELLO. DAIDOUJI SPEAKING!
IS THE DOOR TO THE CAFETERIA UNLOCKED?
CAFETERIA
YUP, ALL SET!
OK!
GREAT! STAY OUT OF SIGHT!
ALL RIGHT, WATERY!
COME AND GET ME!!!
STOMP
SWISH
SWISH
SWISH
SWISH
SWISH

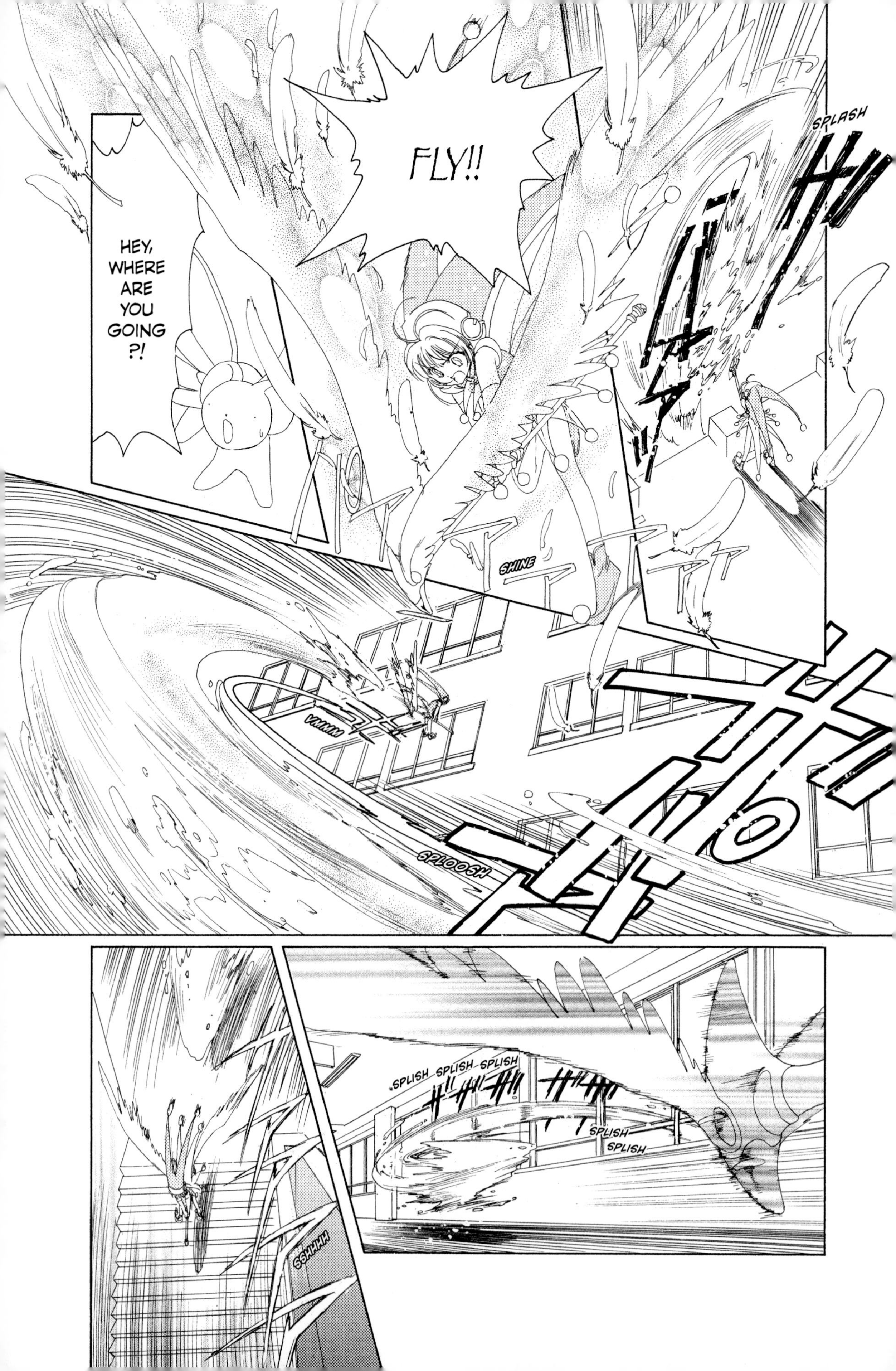
SPLASH
FLY!!
HEY, WHERE ARE YOU GOING ?!
SHINE
VMMMM
SPLOOSH
SPLISH SPLISH SPLISH
SPLISH SPLISH
SSHHHH

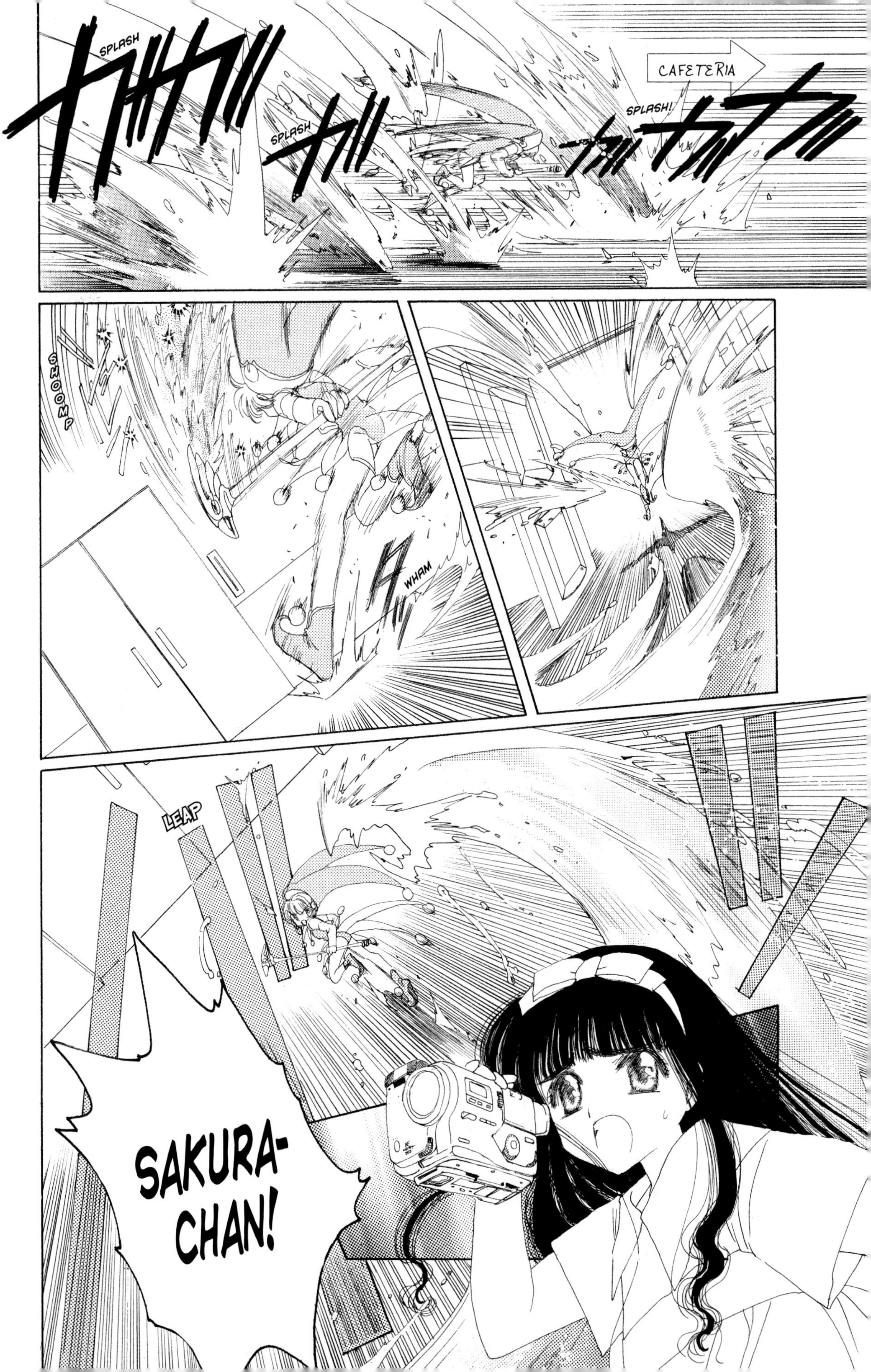
CAFETERIA
SPLASH!
SPLASH
SPLASH
WHAM
SHOOMP
LEAP
SAKURA-CHAN!

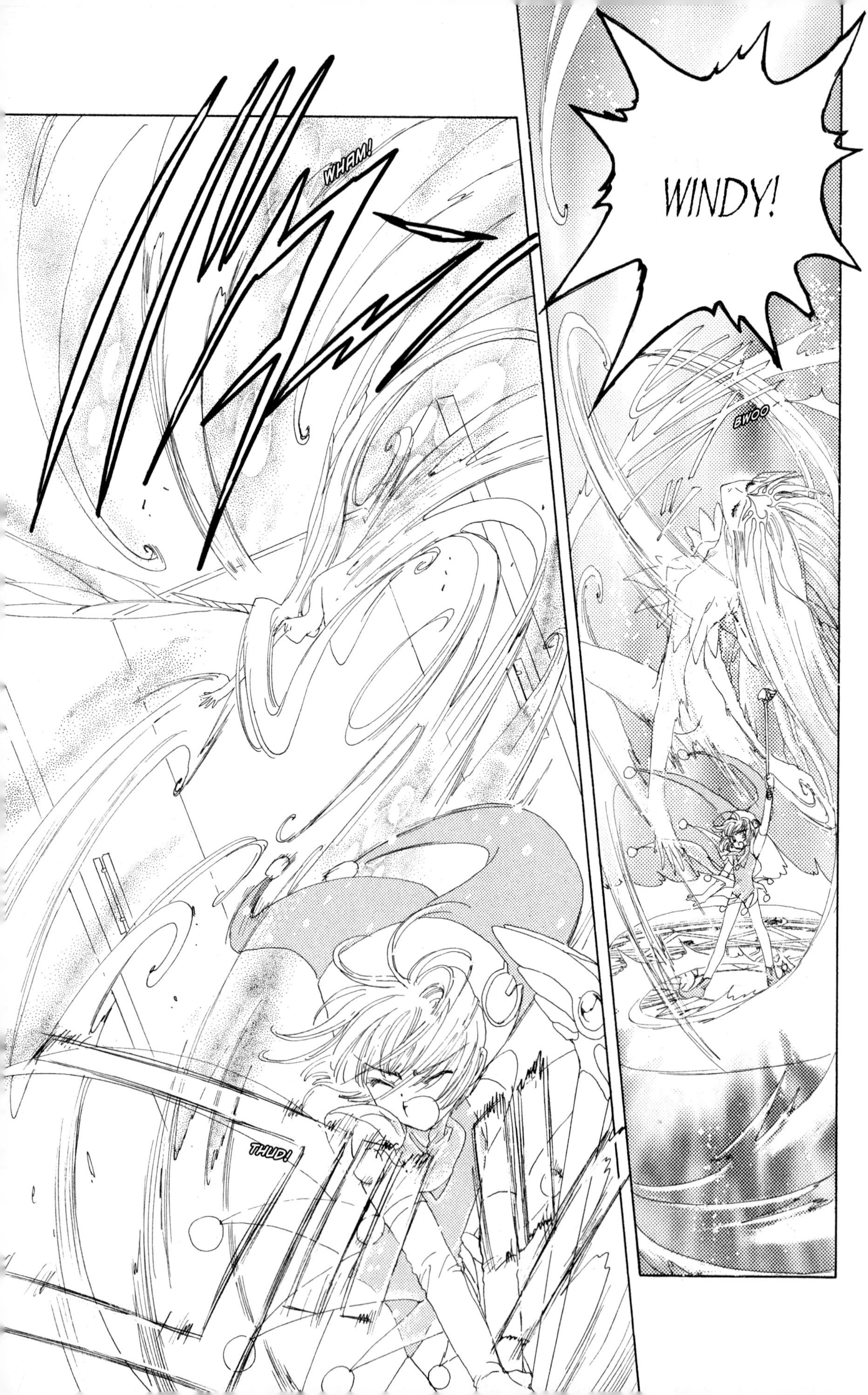
WINDY!
BWOO
WHAM!
THUD!

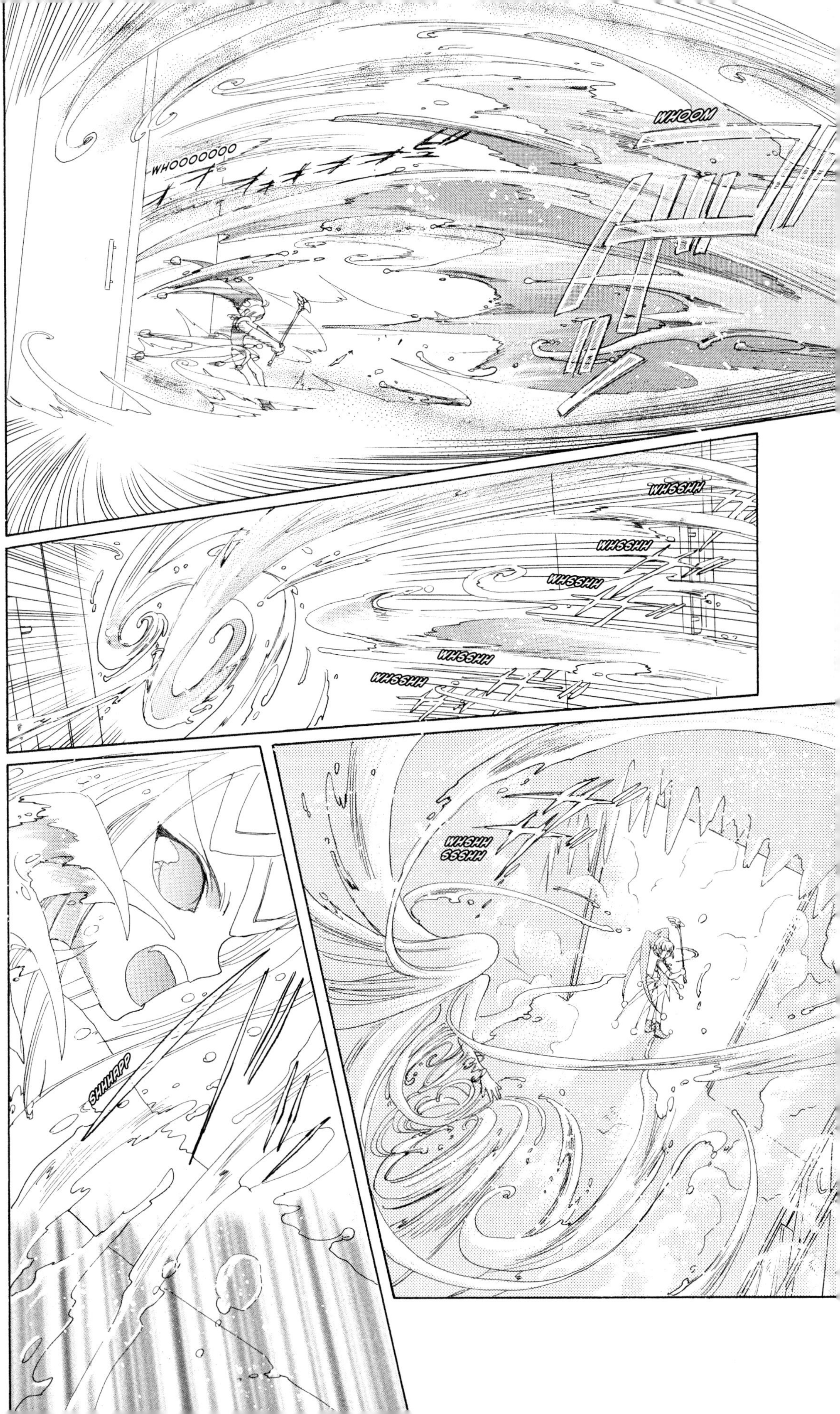
WHOOM
WHOOOOOOO
WHSSHH
WHSSHH
WHSSHH
WHSSHH
WHSSHH
WHSHH SSSHH
SHHHAPP

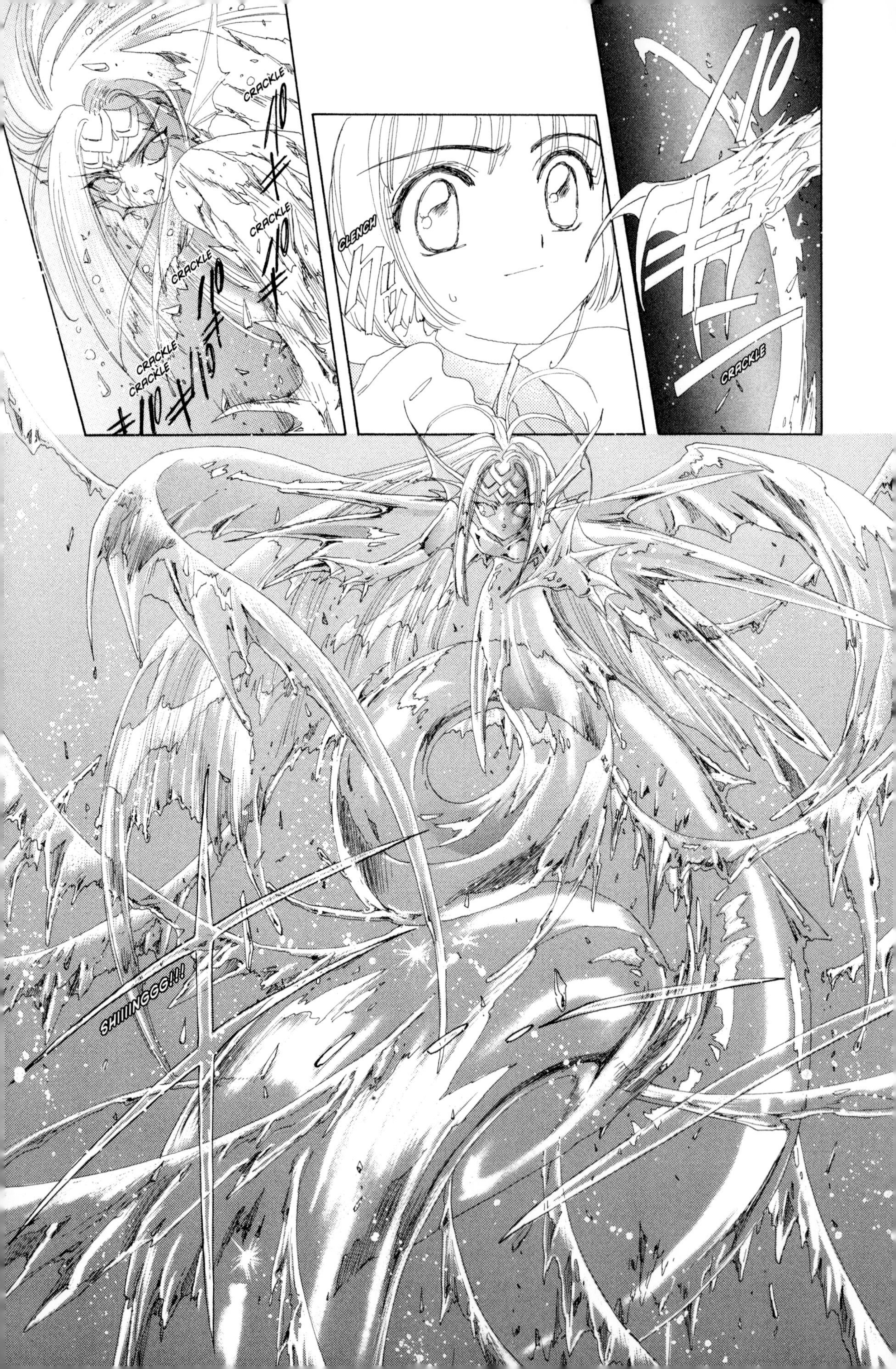
CRACKLE
CLENCH
CRACKLE
CRACKLE
CRACKLE
CRACKLE
CRACKLE
SHIIIINGGG!!!

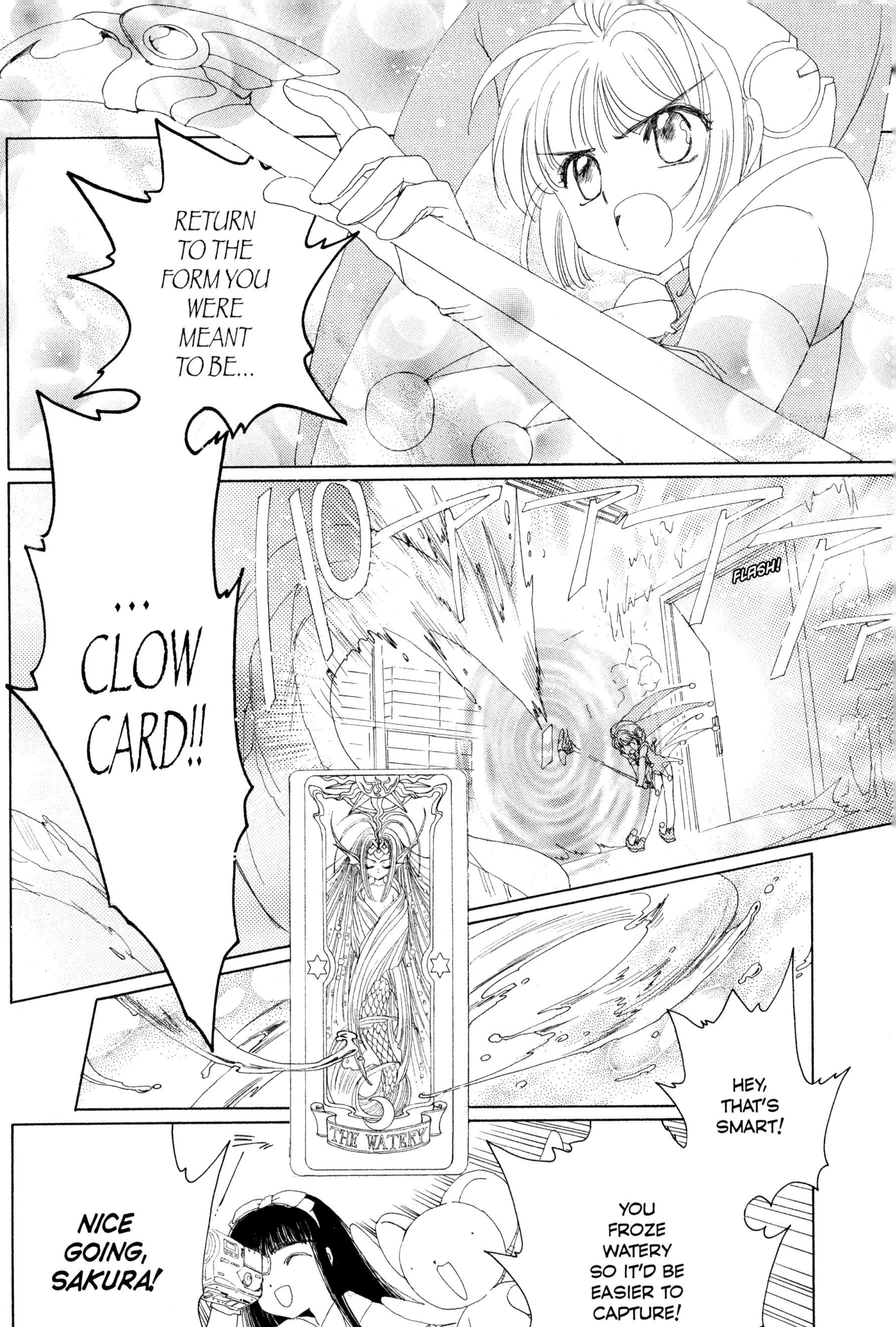
RETURN TO THE FORM YOU WERE MEANT TO BE...
...CLOW CARD!!
FLASH!
THE WATERY
HEY, THAT'S SMART!
YOU FROZE WATERY SO IT'D BE EASIER TO CAPTURE!
NICE GOING, SAKURA!

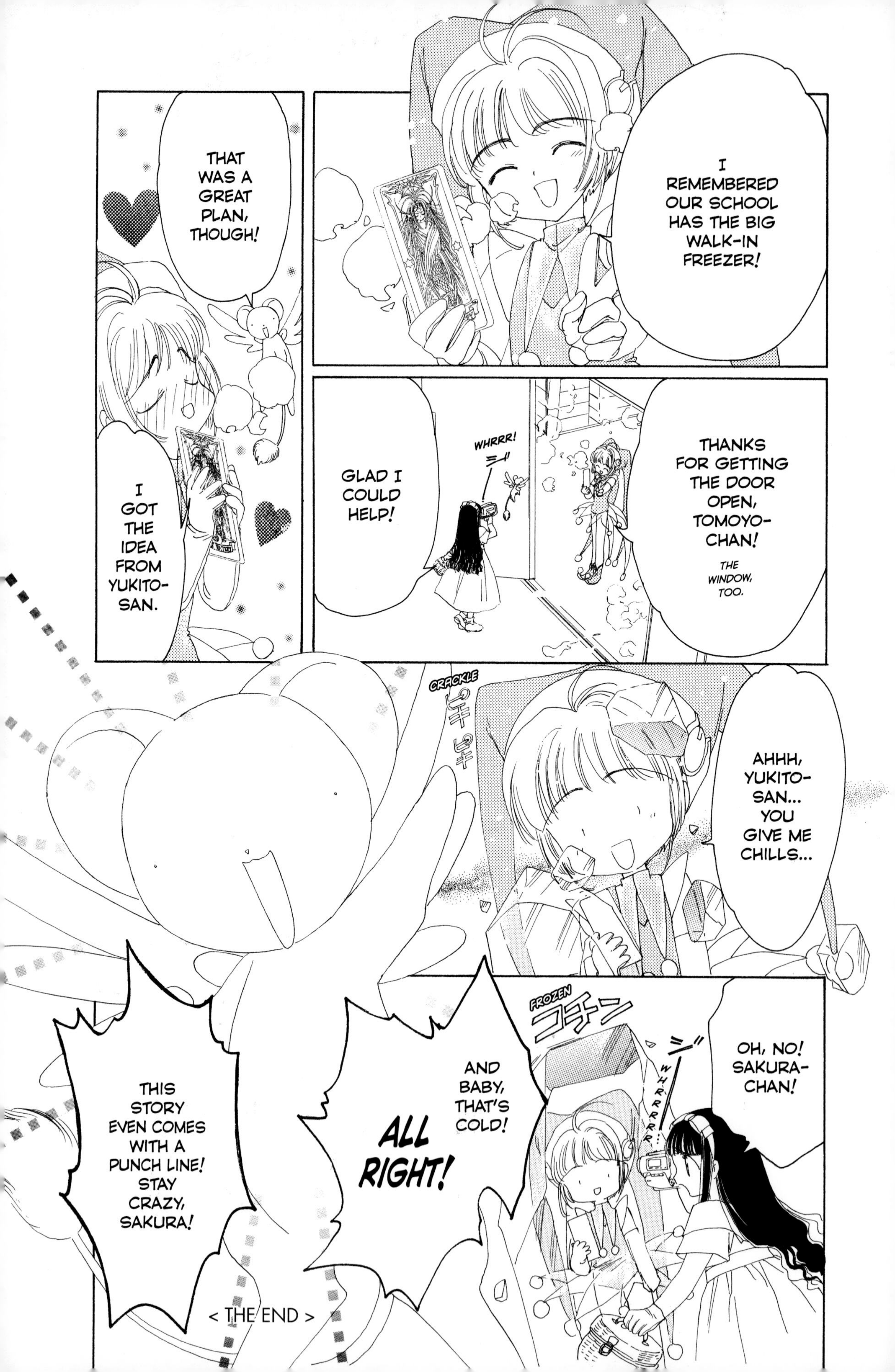
I REMEMBERED OUR SCHOOL HAS THE BIG WALK-IN FREEZER!
THANKS FOR GETTING THE DOOR OPEN, TOMOYO-CHAN!
THE WINDOW, TOO.
WHRRR!
GLAD I COULD HELP!
THAT WAS A GREAT PLAN, THOUGH!
I GOT THE IDEA FROM YUKITO-SAN.
CRACKLE
AHHH, YUKITO-SAN... YOU GIVE ME CHILLS...
FROZEN
OH, NO! SAKURA-CHAN!
WHRRRRR...
AND BABY, THAT'S COLD!
ALL RIGHT!
THIS STORY EVEN COMES WITH A PUNCH LINE! STAY CRAZY, SAKURA!
< THE END >

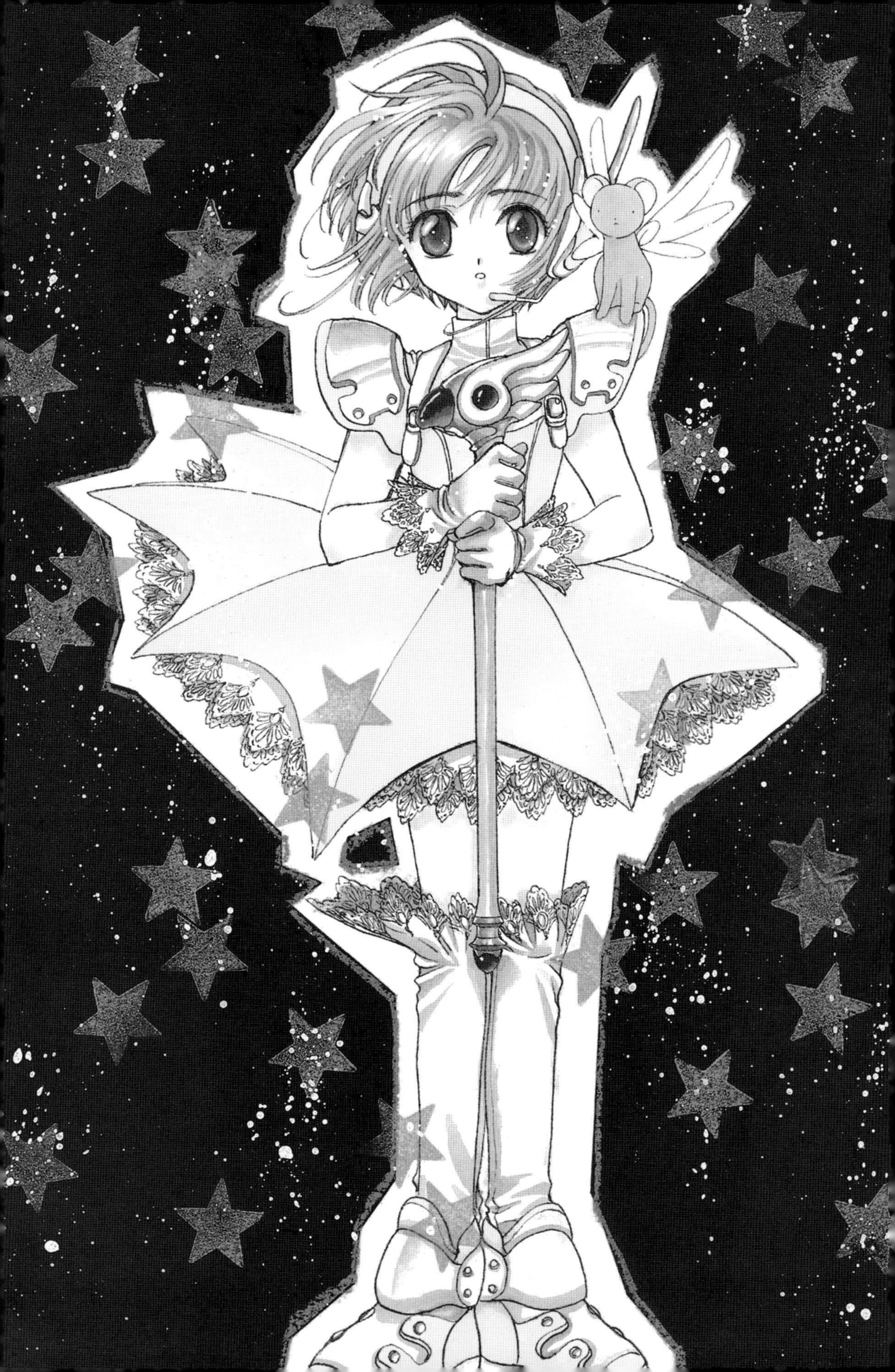

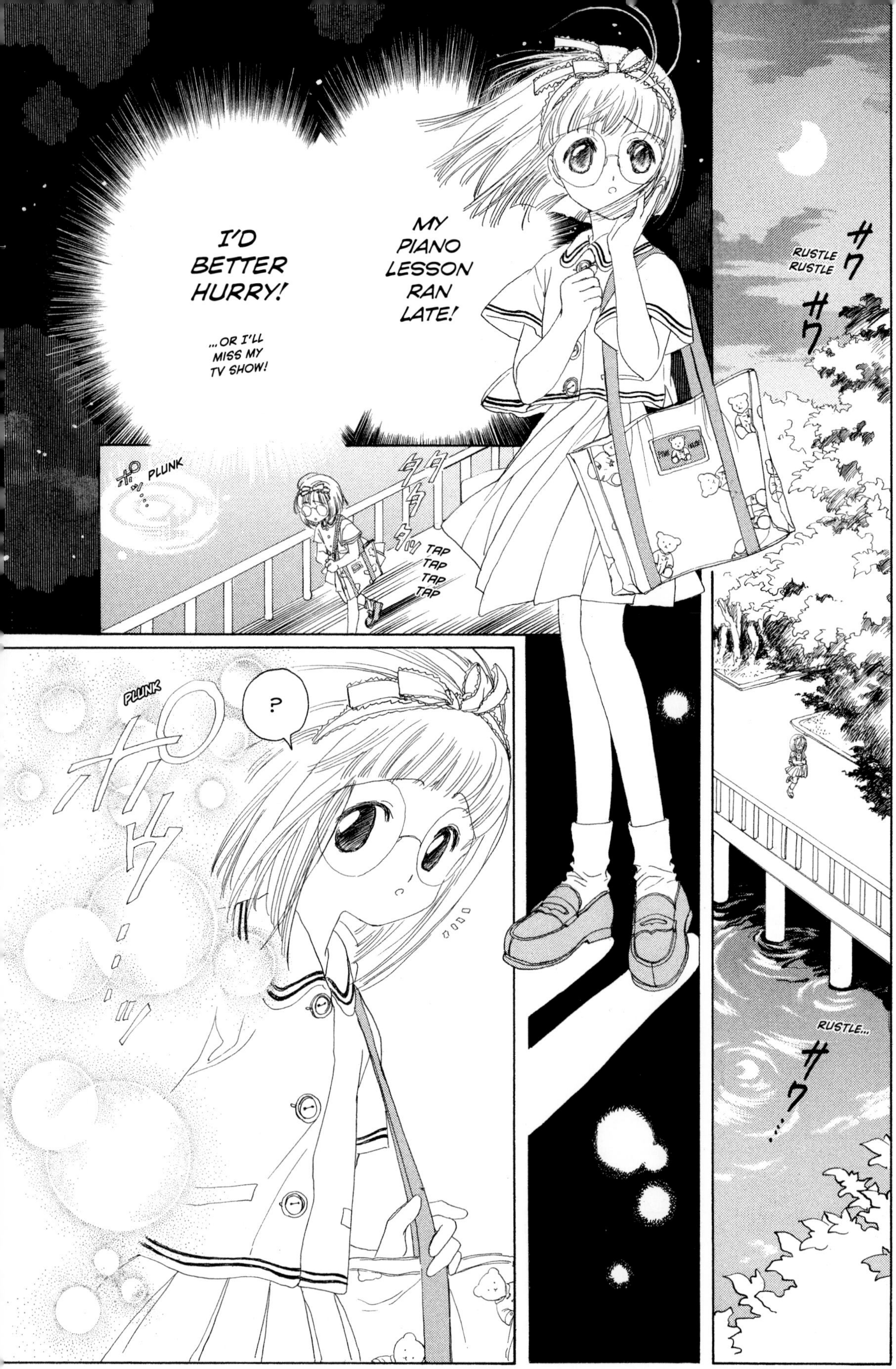

サワ サワ
RUSTLE RUSTLE
サワ…
RUSTLE...
MY PIANO LESSON RAN LATE!
I'D BETTER HURRY!
...OR I'LL MISS MY TV SHOW!
PLUNK
TAP TAP TAP TAP
PLUNK
?

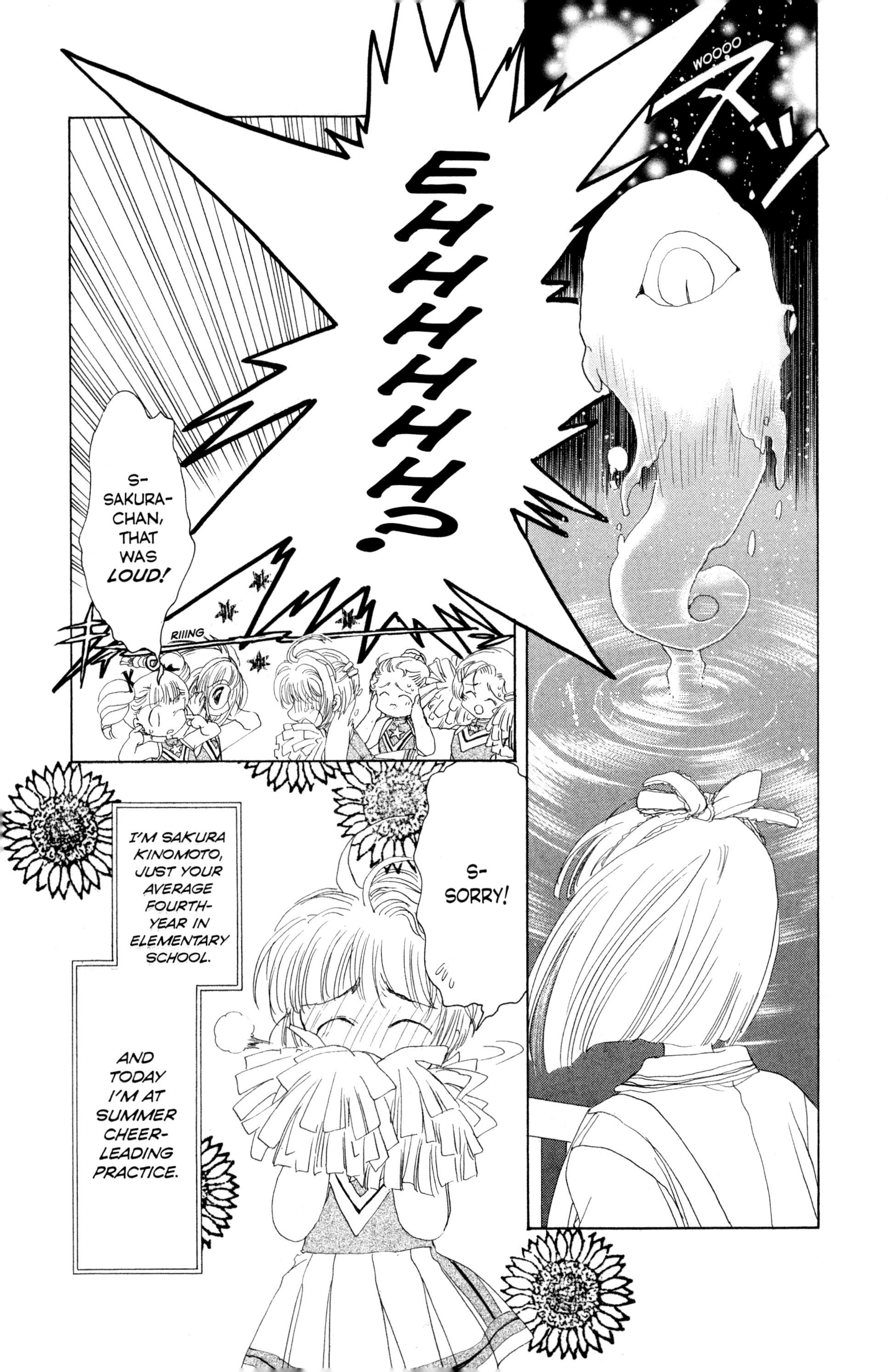

WOOOO
スッ
EHHHHHH?!
S-SAKURA-CHAN, THAT WAS LOUD!
RIIING
S-SORRY!
I'M SAKURA KINOMOTO, JUST YOUR AVERAGE FOURTH-YEAR IN ELEMENTARY SCHOOL.
AND TODAY I'M AT SUMMER CHEER-LEADING PRACTICE.

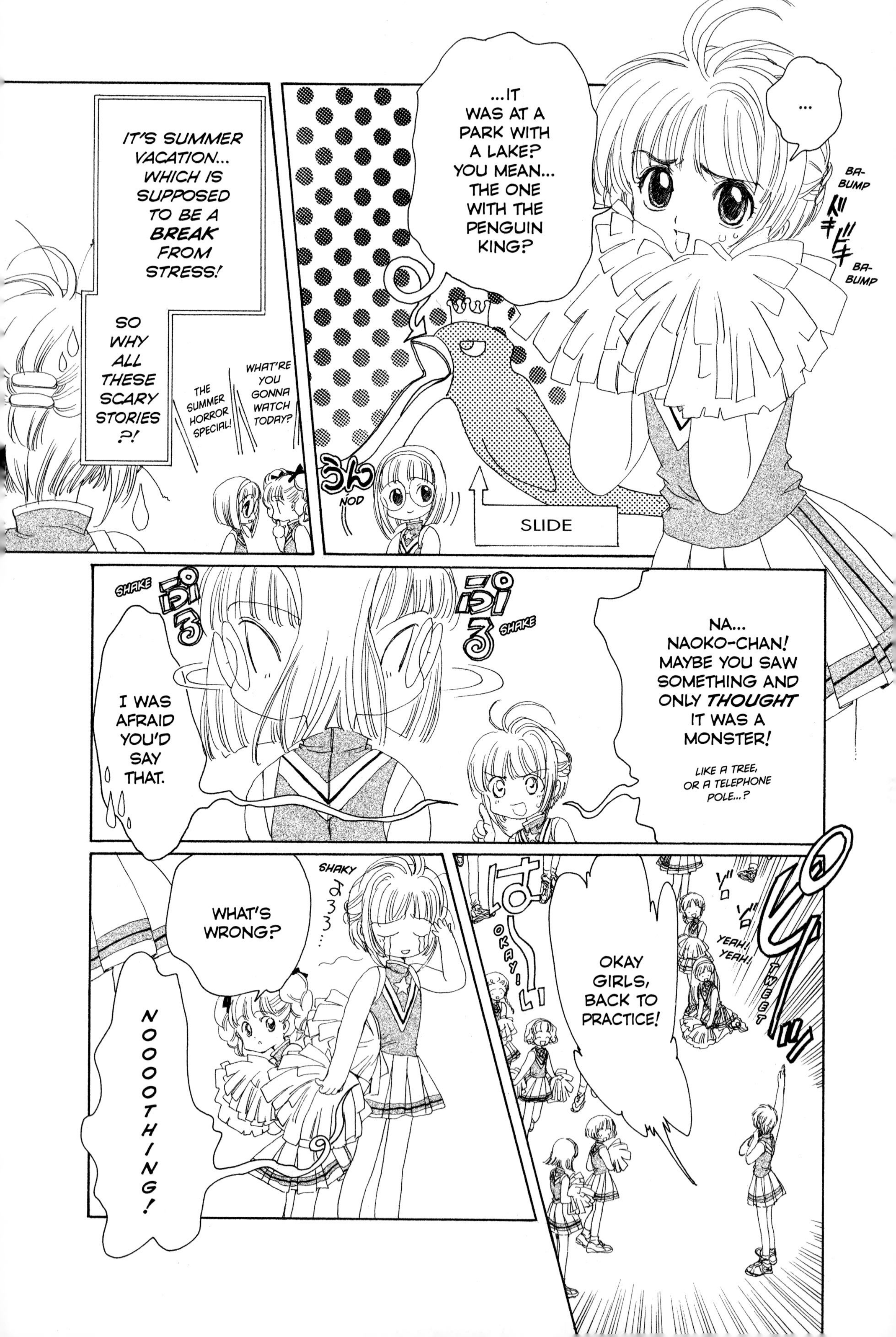

...
BA-BUMP
BA-BUMP
...IT WAS AT A PARK WITH A LAKE? YOU MEAN... THE ONE WITH THE PENGUIN KING?
SLIDE
うん
NOD
IT'S SUMMER VACATION... WHICH IS SUPPOSED TO BE A BREAK FROM STRESS!
SO WHY ALL THESE SCARY STORIES ?!
WHAT'RE YOU GONNA WATCH TODAY?
THE SUMMER HORROR SPECIAL!
NA... NAOKO-CHAN! MAYBE YOU SAW SOMETHING AND ONLY THOUGHT IT WAS A MONSTER!
LIKE A TREE, OR A TELEPHONE POLE...?
ぷる
SHAKE
ぷる
SHAKE
I WAS AFRAID YOU'D SAY THAT.
TWEET
YEAH! YEAH!
OKAY GIRLS, BACK TO PRACTICE!
OKAY!
SHAKY
WHAT'S WRONG?
NOOOOOTHING!

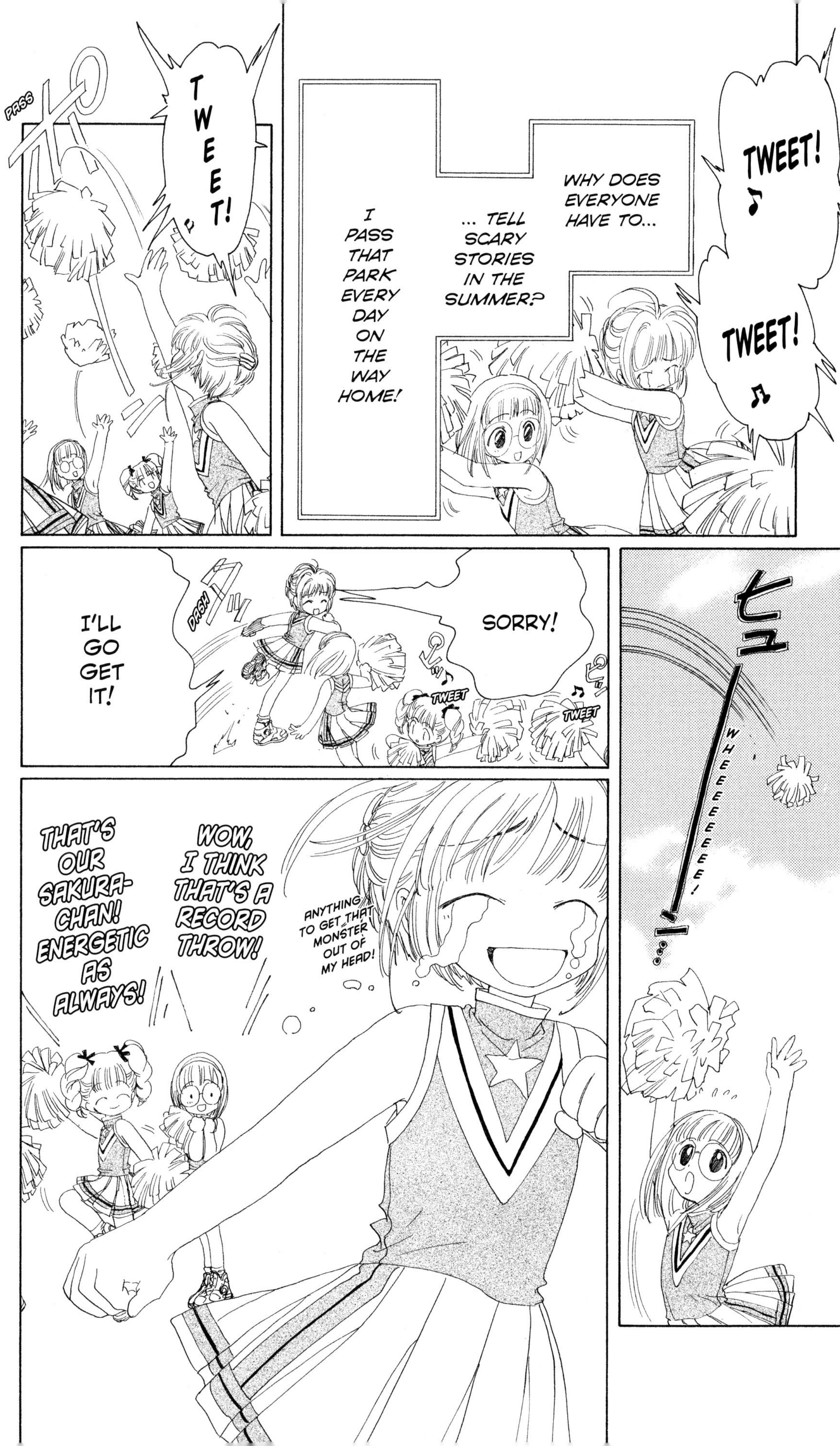

TWEET!
TWEET!
WHY DOES EVERYONE HAVE TO...
... TELL SCARY STORIES IN THE SUMMER?
I PASS THAT PARK EVERY DAY ON THE WAY HOME!
TWEET!
PASS
WHEEEEEEEEEEE!
SORRY!
TWEET
TWEET
DASH
I'LL GO GET IT!
ANYTHING TO GET THAT MONSTER OUT OF MY HEAD!
WOW, I THINK THAT'S A RECORD THROW!
THAT'S OUR SAKURA-CHAN! ENERGETIC AS ALWAYS!

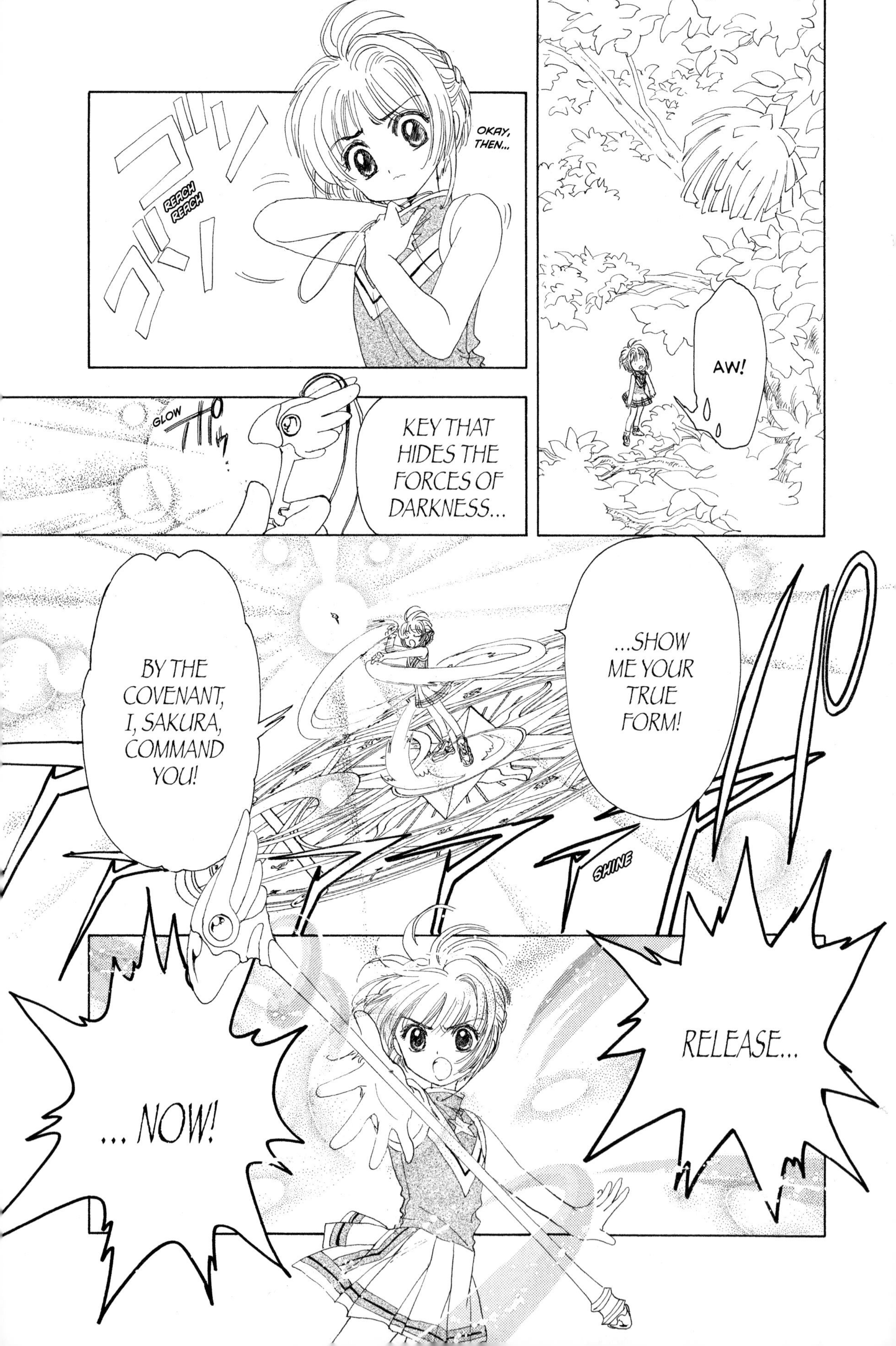
AW!
OKAY, THEN...
REACH REACH
KEY THAT HIDES THE FORCES OF DARKNESS...
GLOW
...SHOW ME YOUR TRUE FORM!
BY THE COVENANT, I, SAKURA, COMMAND YOU!
SHINE
RELEASE...
... NOW!

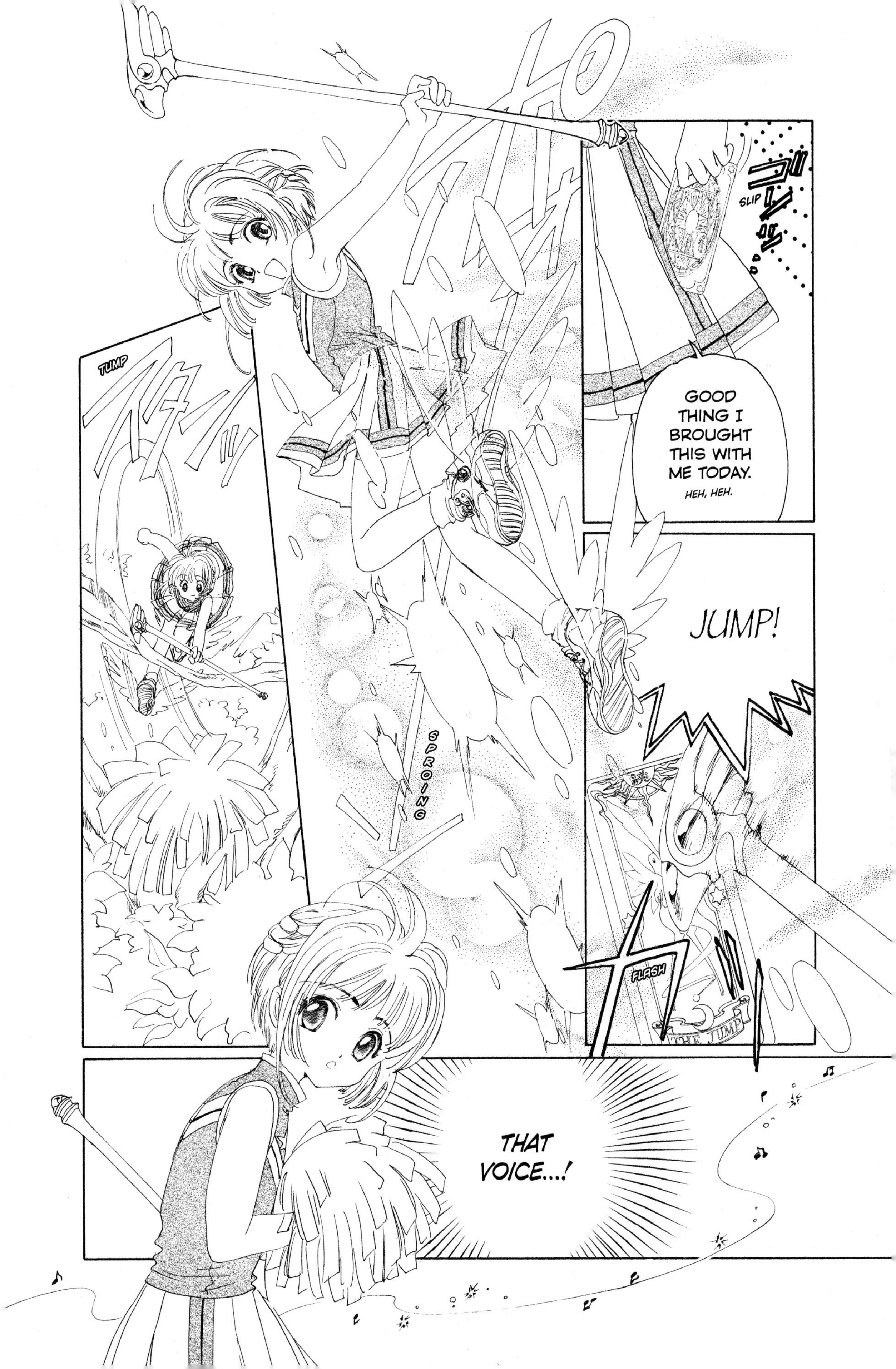
SLIP
GOOD THING I BROUGHT THIS WITH ME TODAY.
HEH, HEH.
JUMP!
FLASH
SPROING
TUMP
THAT VOICE...!

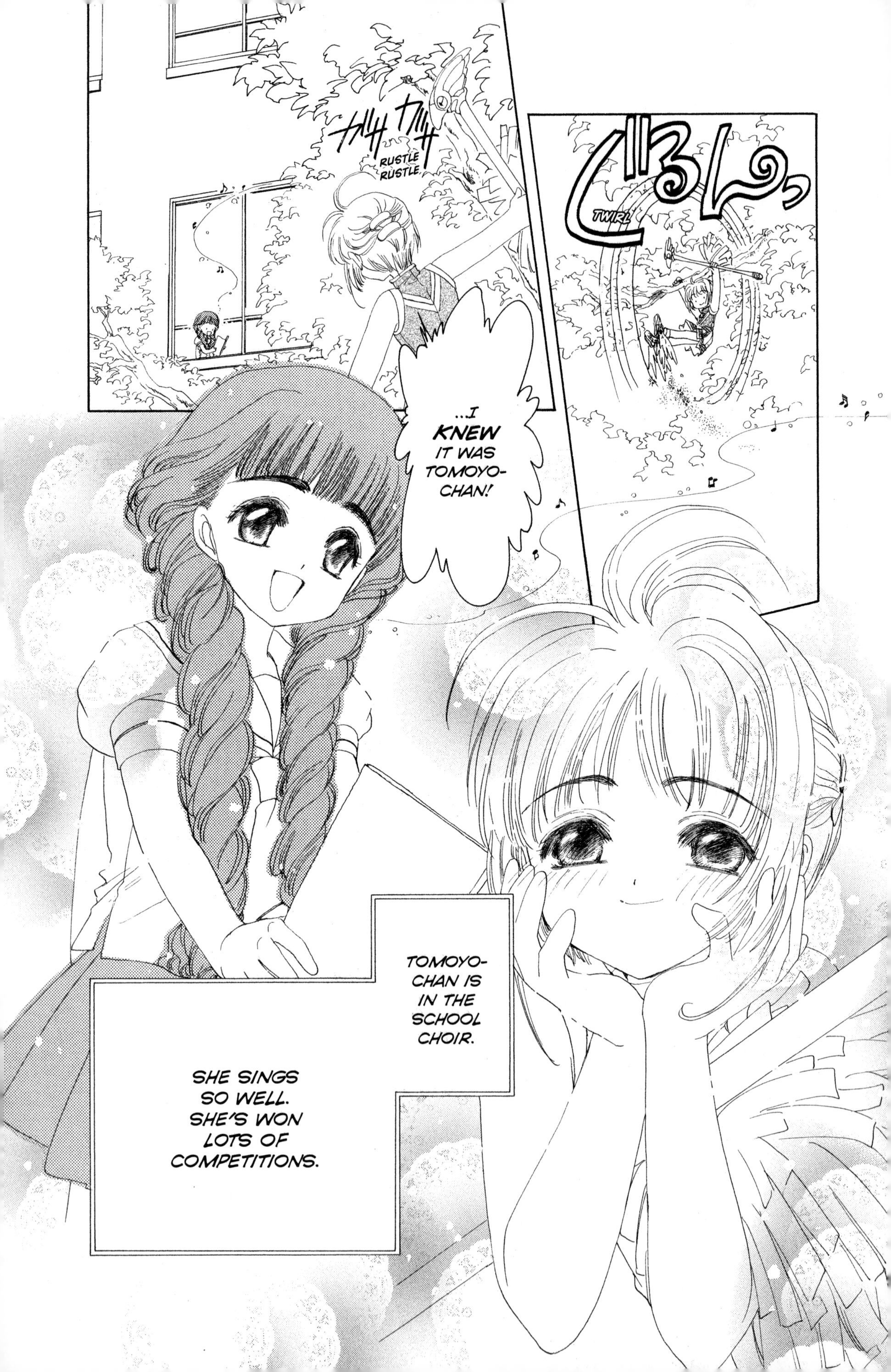
TWIRL
RUSTLE RUSTLE
...I KNEW IT WAS TOMOYO-CHAN!
TOMOYO-CHAN IS IN THE SCHOOL CHOIR.
SHE SINGS SO WELL. SHE'S WON LOTS OF COMPETITIONS.

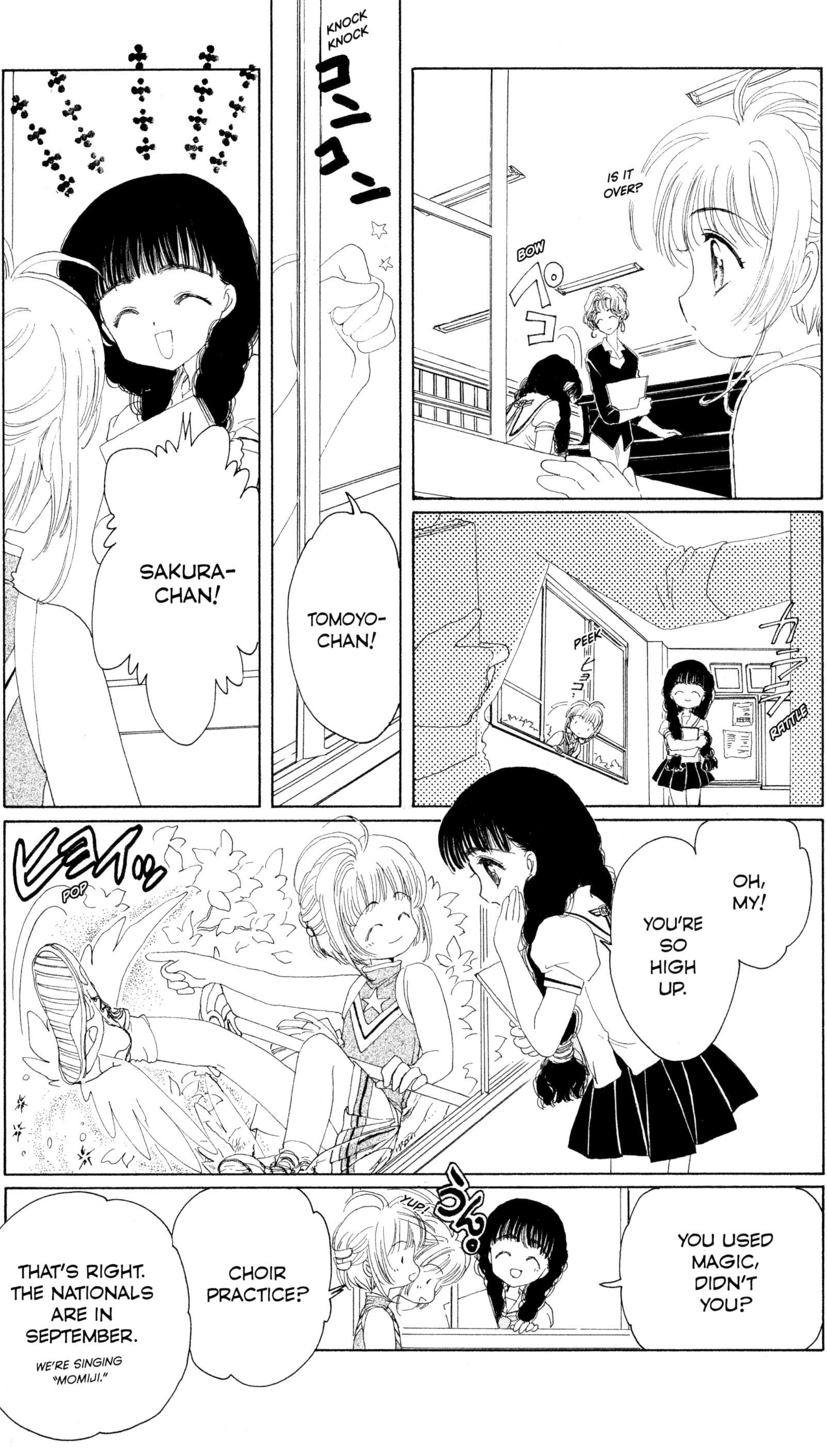
IS IT OVER?
BOW
PEEK
RATTLE
KNOCK KNOCK
TOMOYO-CHAN!
SAKURA-CHAN!
OH, MY!
YOU'RE SO HIGH UP.
POP
YOU USED MAGIC, DIDN'T YOU?
YUP!
CHOIR PRACTICE?
THAT'S RIGHT. THE NATIONALS ARE IN SEPTEMBER.
WE'RE SINGING "MOMIJI."

4

YUKITO TSUKISHIRO

BIRTHDATE:
DECEMBER 25
BLOOD TYPE:
AB
FAVORITE SUBJECT:
MATH
LEAST FAVORITE SUBJECT:
NONE
CLUB:
NONE
FAVORITE COLOR:
WHITE
FAVORITE FLOWER:
HEPATICA
FAVORITE FOOD:
ANYTHING
LEAST FAVORITE FOOD:
NONE
FAVORITE RECIPE:
CURRY STEW
WISH LIST:
NEW LUNCH BOX

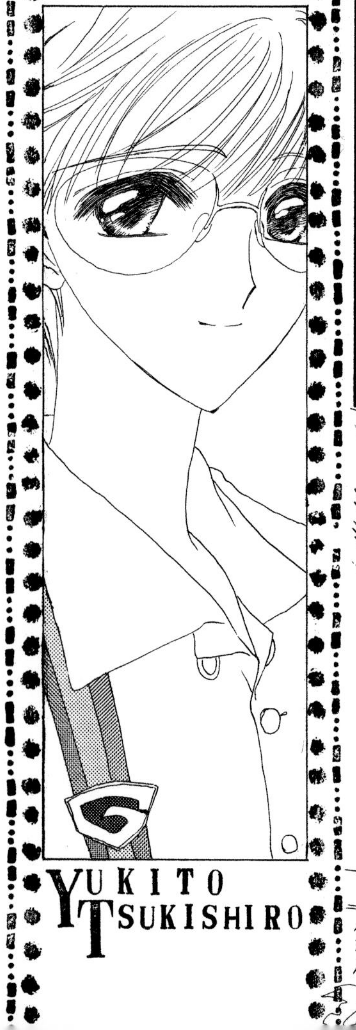

YUKITO TSUKISHIRO

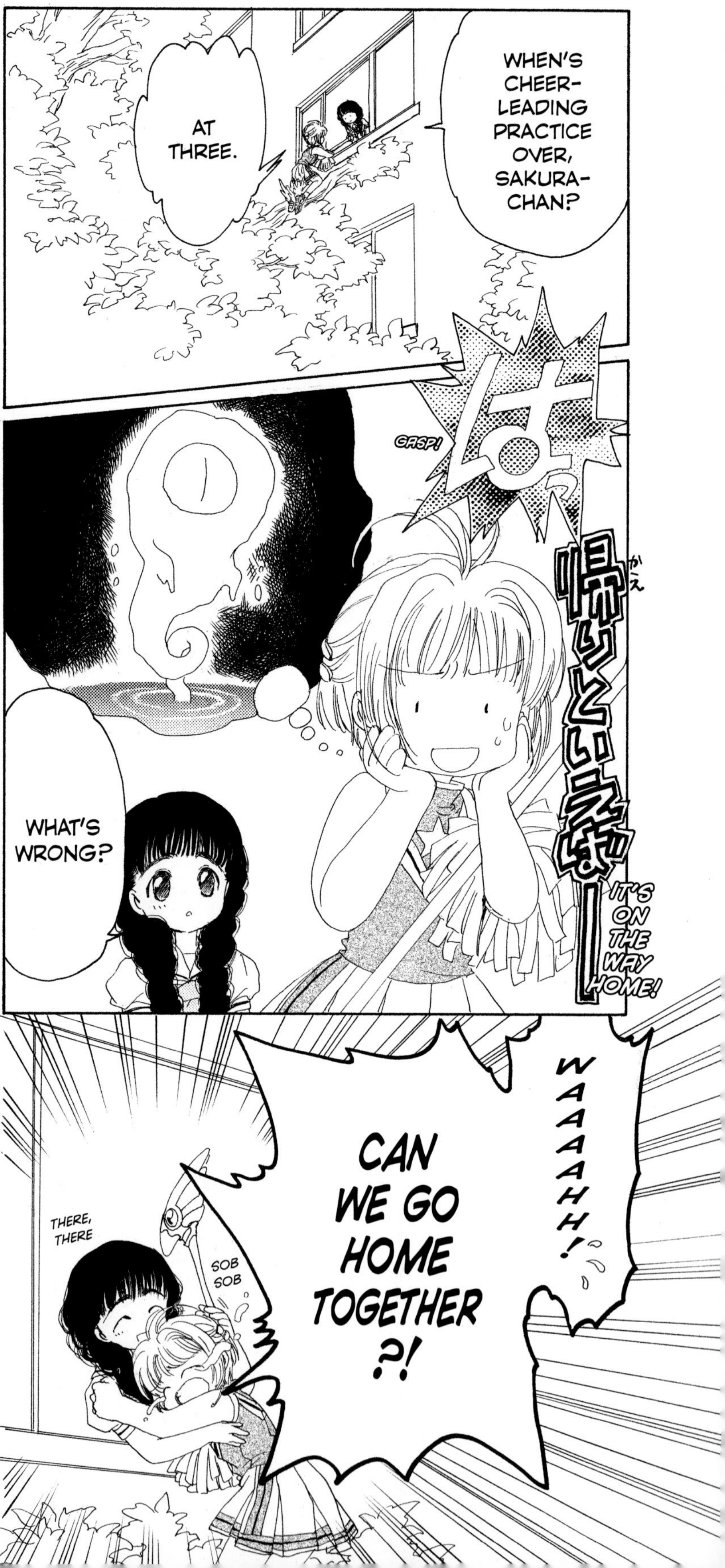
WHEN'S CHEER-LEADING PRACTICE OVER, SAKURA-CHAN?
AT THREE.
GASP!
は
帰りといえば!
IT'S ON THE WAY HOME!
WHAT'S WRONG?
WAAAAAHH!
CAN WE GO HOME TOGETHER?!
SOB SOB
THERE, THERE

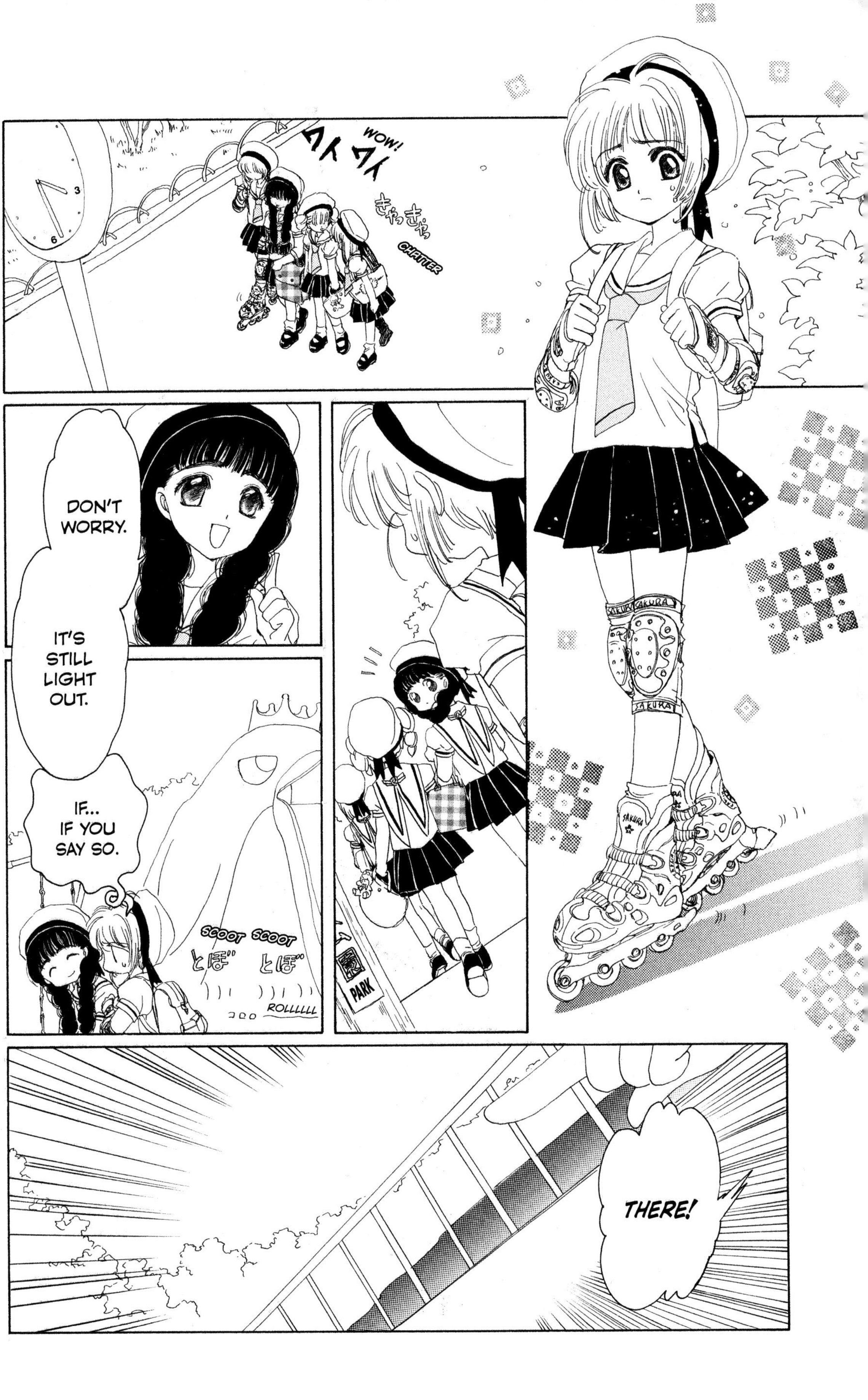

ワイワイ
WOW!
きゃっきゃっ
CHATTER
PARK
DON'T WORRY.
IT'S STILL LIGHT OUT.
IF... IF YOU SAY SO.
とぼ とぼ
SCOOT SCOOT
コロロ
ROLLLLLLL
THERE!

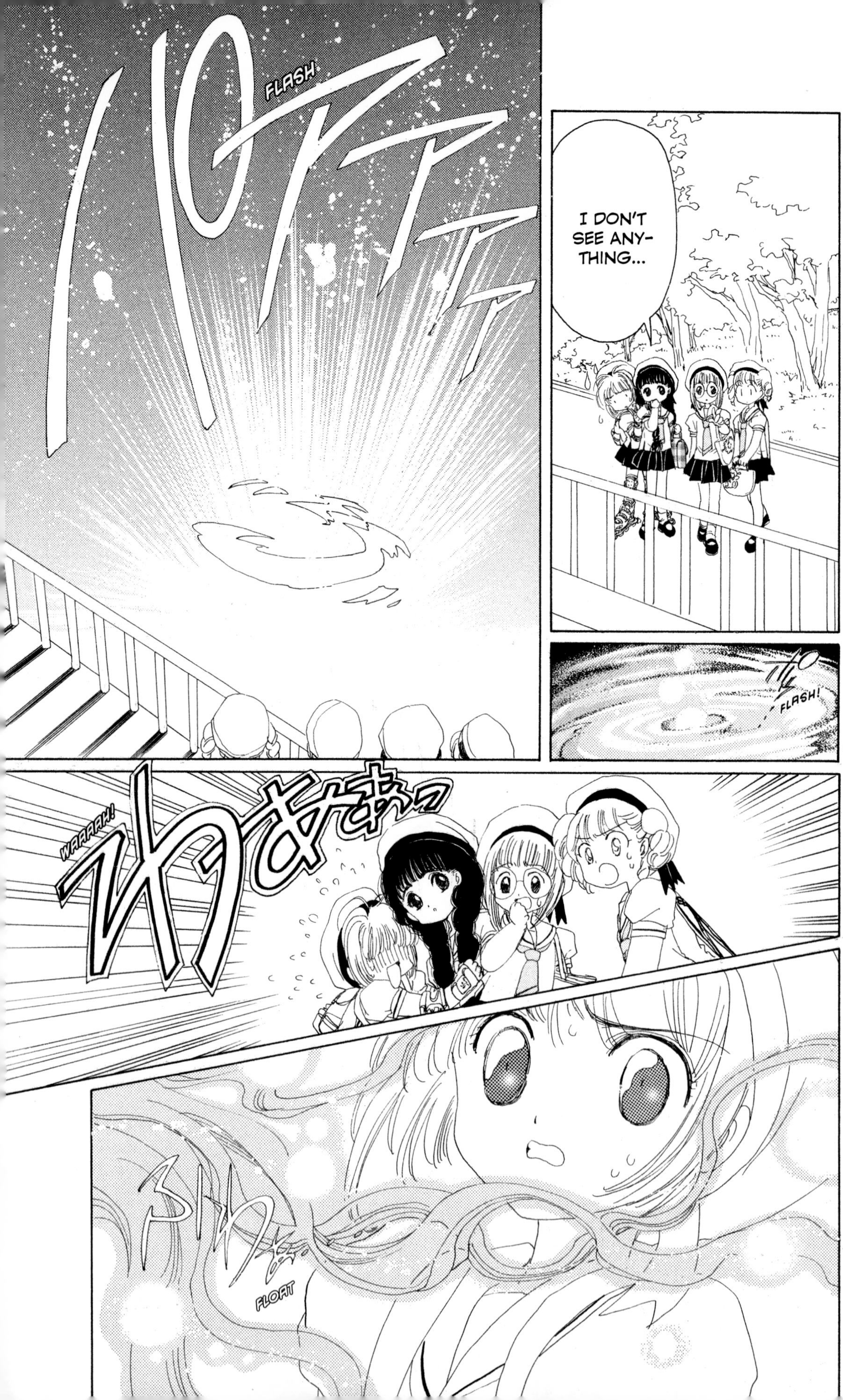
I DON'T SEE ANY-THING...
FLASH!
FLASH
WAAAAH!
FLOAT

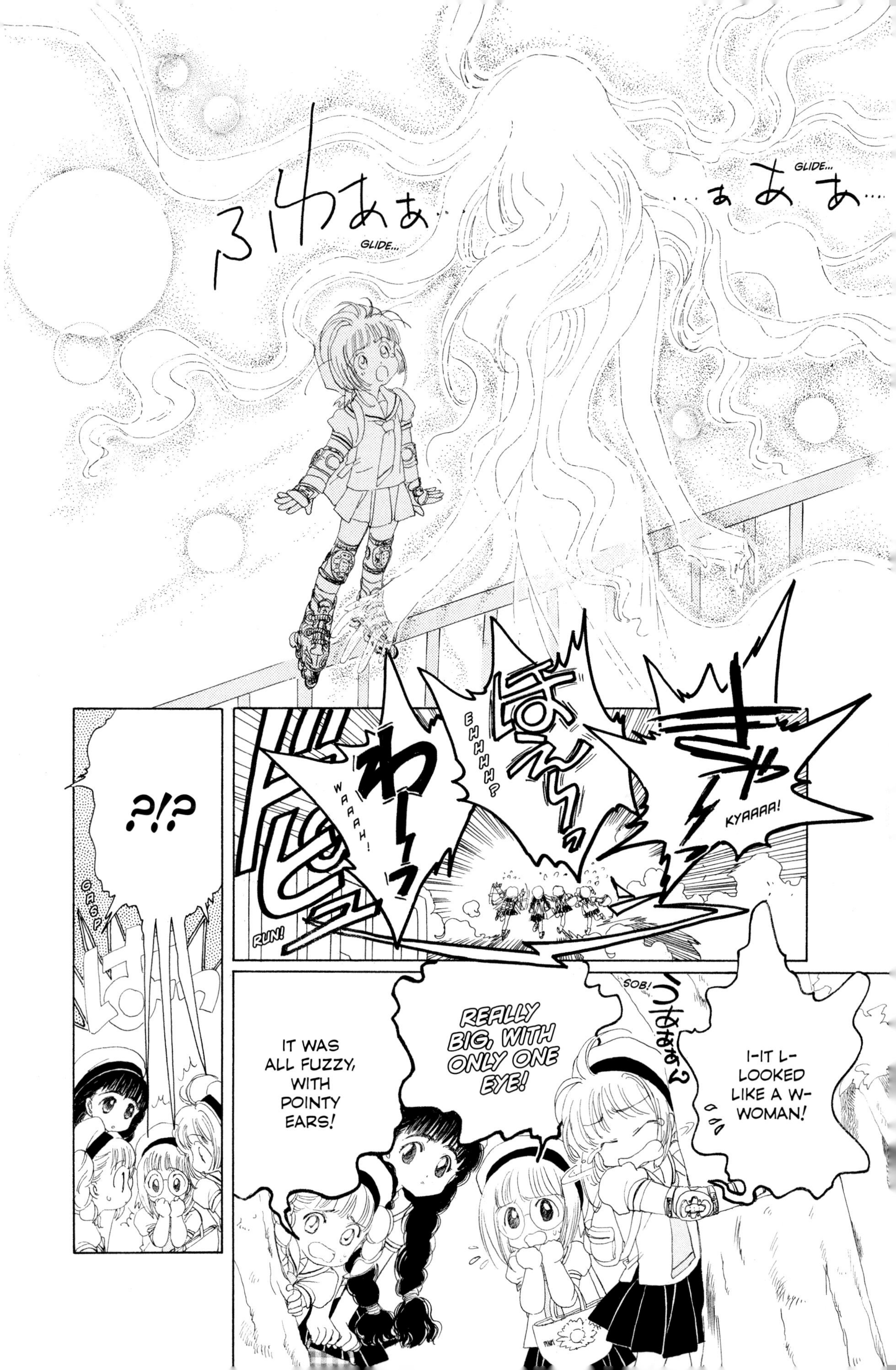
GLIDE...
GLIDE...
KYAAAA!
EHHHHH?
WAAAH!
RUN!
SOB!
I-IT L-LOOKED LIKE A W-WOMAN!
REALLY BIG, WITH ONLY ONE EYE!
IT WAS ALL FUZZY, WITH POINTY EARS!
?!?
GASP

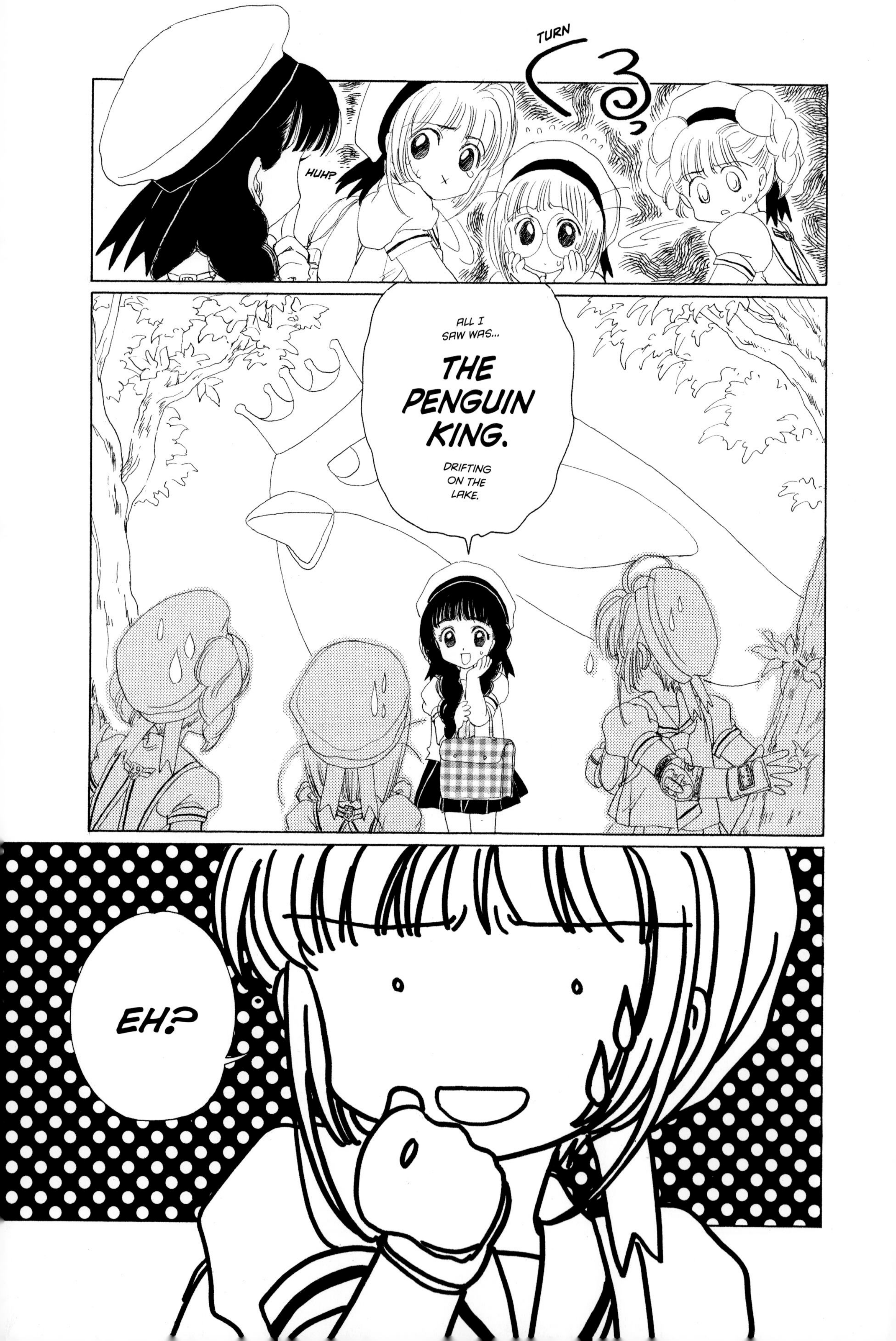
TURN
HUH?
ALL I SAW WAS...
THE PENGUIN KING.
DRIFTING ON THE LAKE.
EH?

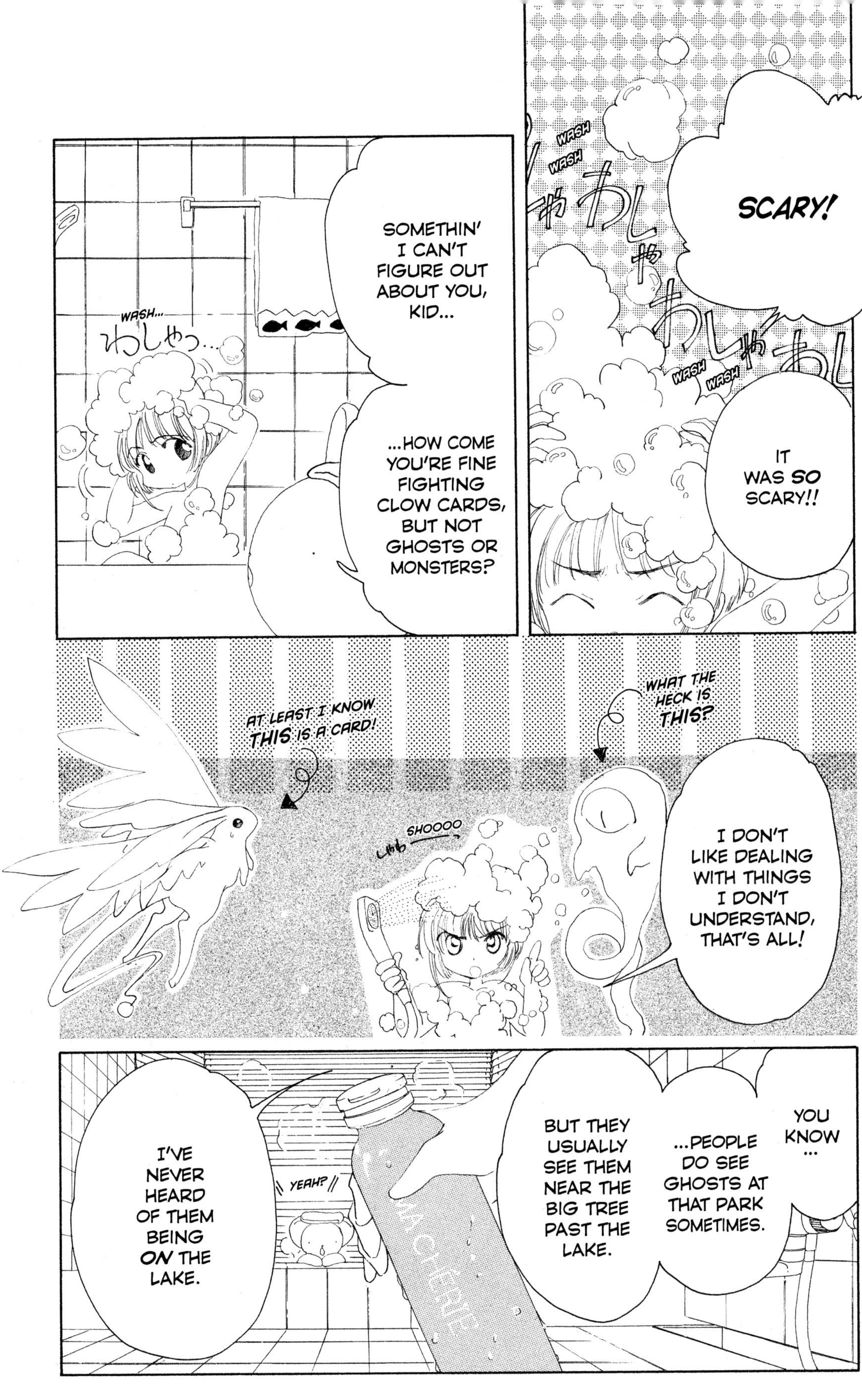
WASH WASH
SCARY!
WASH WASH
IT WAS SO SCARY!!
SOMETHIN' I CAN'T FIGURE OUT ABOUT YOU, KID...
WASH...
わしゃっ…
...HOW COME YOU'RE FINE FIGHTING CLOW CARDS, BUT NOT GHOSTS OR MONSTERS?
WHAT THE HECK IS THIS?
I DON'T LIKE DEALING WITH THINGS I DON'T UNDERSTAND, THAT'S ALL!
SHOOOO
AT LEAST I KNOW THIS IS A CARD!
YOU KNOW...
...PEOPLE DO SEE GHOSTS AT THAT PARK SOMETIMES.
BUT THEY USUALLY SEE THEM NEAR THE BIG TREE PAST THE LAKE.
YEAH?
I'VE NEVER HEARD OF THEM BEING ON THE LAKE.

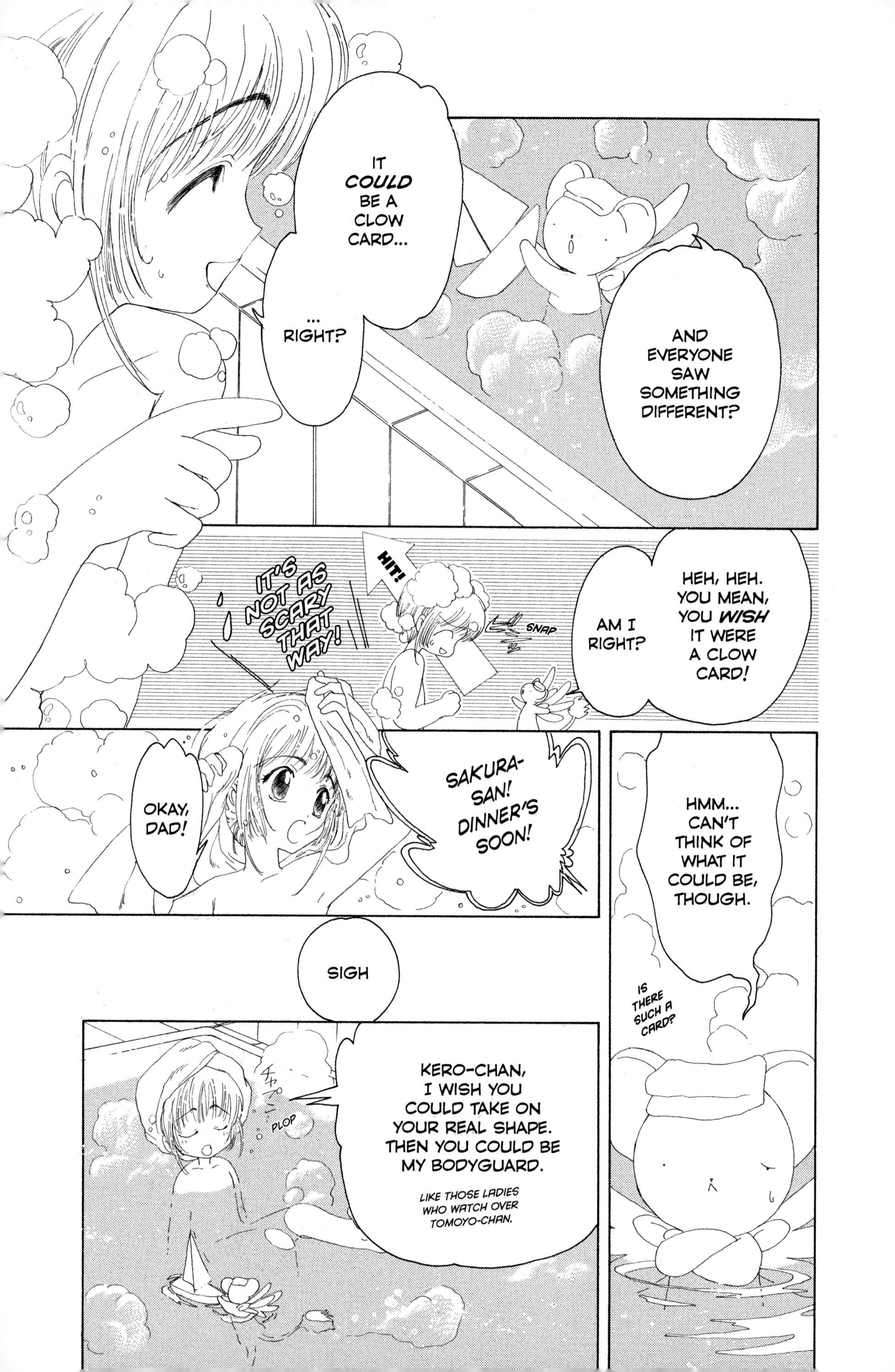
AND EVERYONE SAW SOMETHING DIFFERENT?
IT *COULD* BE A CLOW CARD...
... RIGHT?
HEH, HEH. YOU MEAN, YOU *WISH* IT WERE A CLOW CARD!
AM I RIGHT?
SNAP
HIT!
IT'S NOT AS SCARY THAT WAY!
HMM... CAN'T THINK OF WHAT IT COULD BE, THOUGH.
IS THERE SUCH A CARD?
SAKURA-SAN! DINNER'S SOON!
OKAY, DAD!
SIGH
PLOP
KERO-CHAN, I WISH YOU COULD TAKE ON YOUR REAL SHAPE. THEN YOU COULD BE MY BODYGUARD.
LIKE THOSE LADIES WHO WATCH OVER TOMOYO-CHAN.

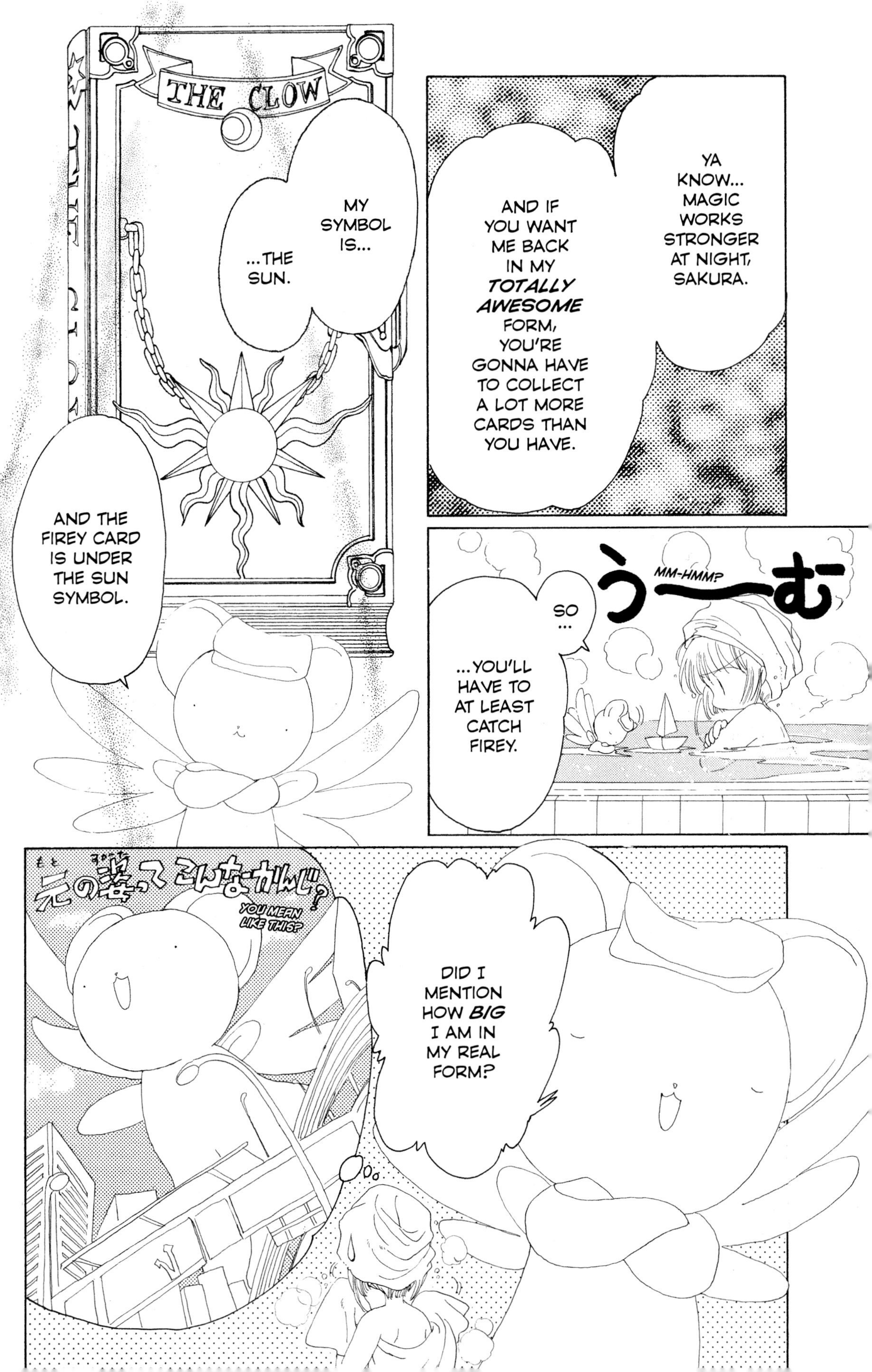
YA KNOW... MAGIC WORKS STRONGER AT NIGHT, SAKURA.
AND IF YOU WANT ME BACK IN MY ***TOTALLY AWESOME*** FORM, YOU'RE GONNA HAVE TO COLLECT A LOT MORE CARDS THAN YOU HAVE.
うーーむ
MM-HMM?
SO...
...YOU'LL HAVE TO AT LEAST CATCH FIREY.
THE CLOW
MY SYMBOL IS...
...THE SUN.
AND THE FIREY CARD IS UNDER THE SUN SYMBOL.
DID I MENTION HOW ***BIG*** I AM IN MY REAL FORM?
元の姿ってこんなかんじ?
YOU MEAN LIKE THIS?

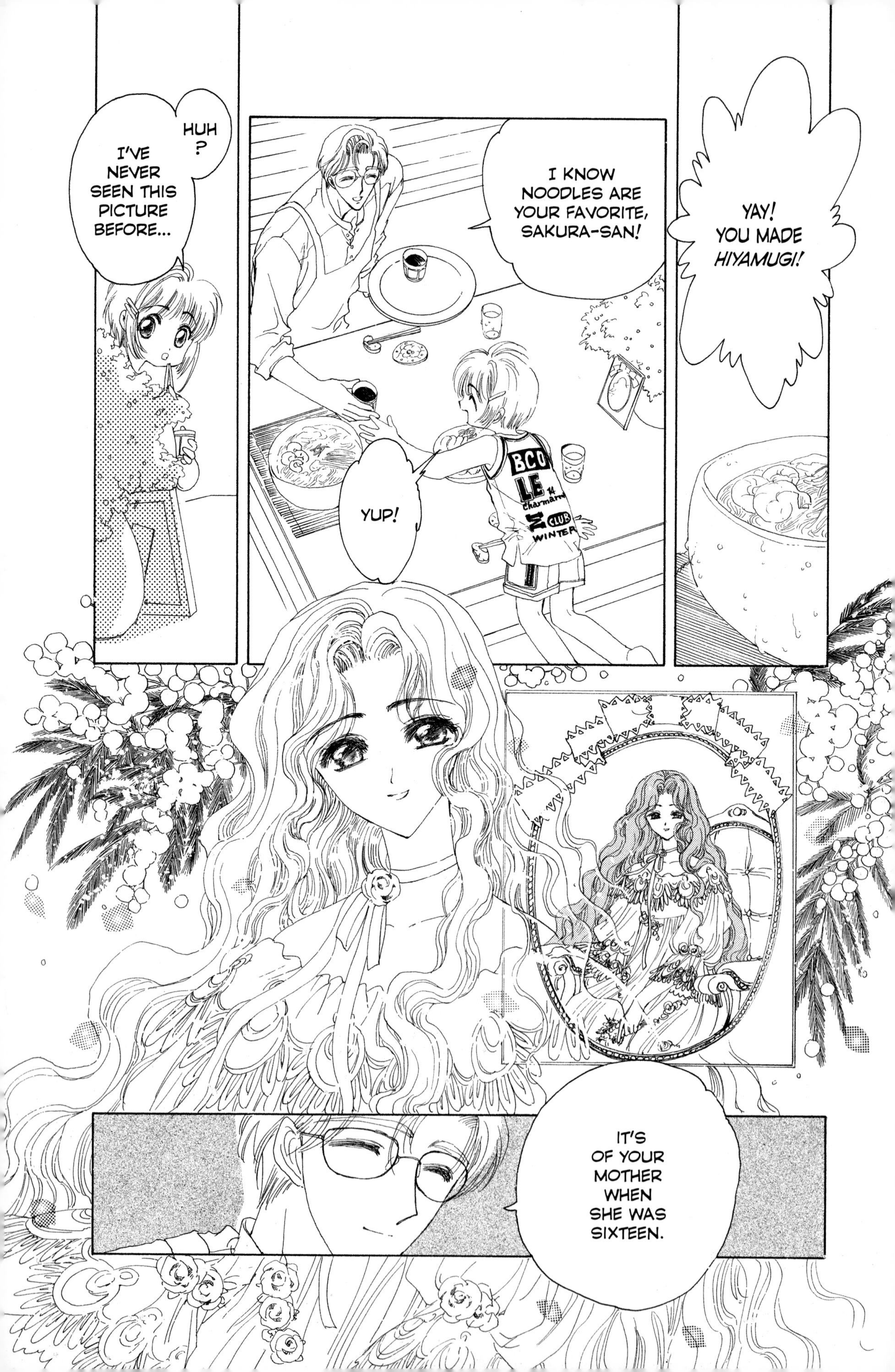
YAY! YOU MADE *HIYAMUGI!*
I KNOW NOODLES ARE YOUR FAVORITE, SAKURA-SAN!
YUP!
HUH?
I'VE NEVER SEEN THIS PICTURE BEFORE...
IT'S OF YOUR MOTHER WHEN SHE WAS SIXTEEN.

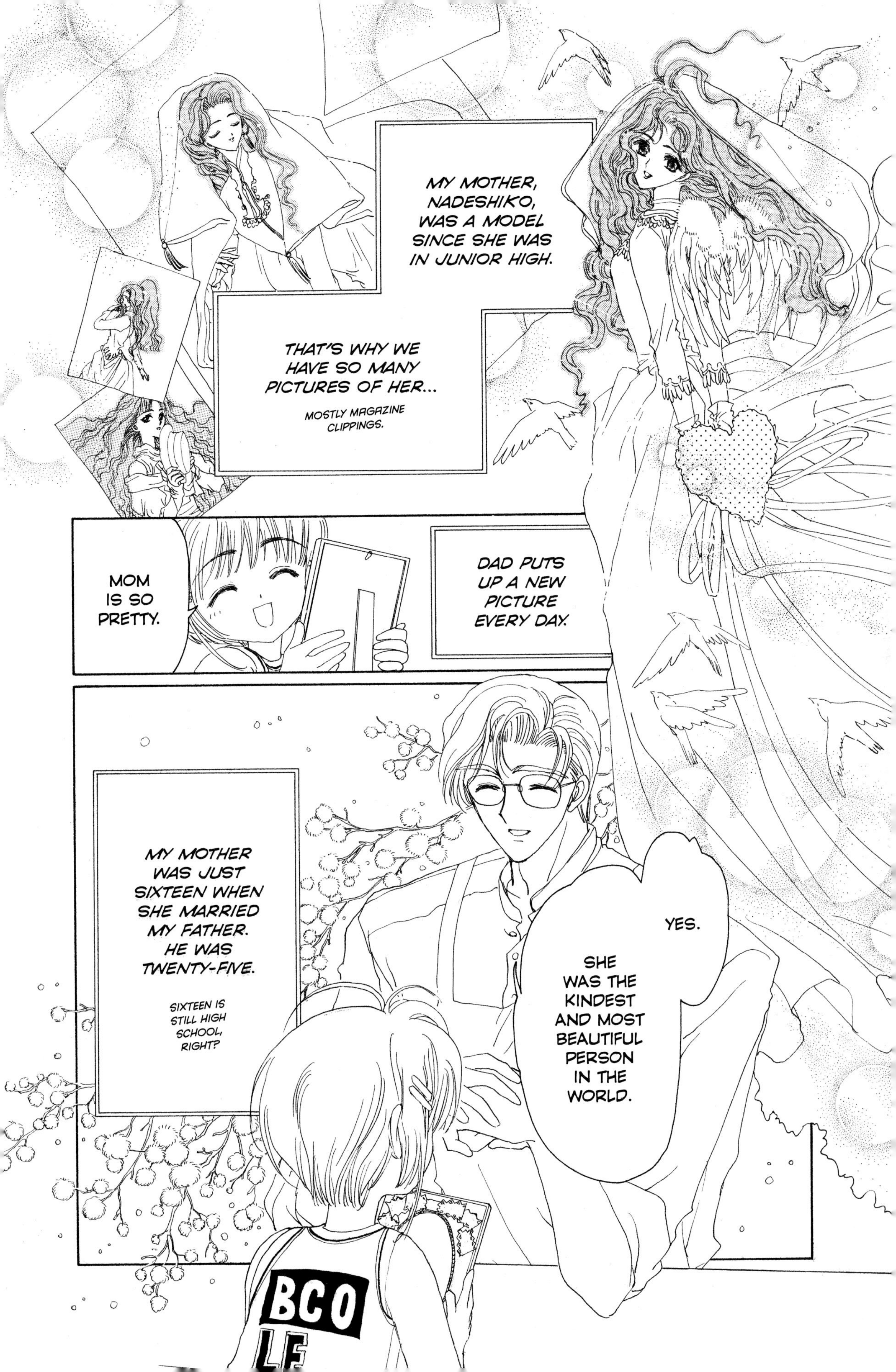
MY MOTHER, NADESHIKO, WAS A MODEL SINCE SHE WAS IN JUNIOR HIGH.
THAT'S WHY WE HAVE SO MANY PICTURES OF HER...
MOSTLY MAGAZINE CLIPPINGS.
DAD PUTS UP A NEW PICTURE EVERY DAY.
MOM IS SO PRETTY.
YES.
SHE WAS THE KINDEST AND MOST BEAUTIFUL PERSON IN THE WORLD.
MY MOTHER WAS JUST SIXTEEN WHEN SHE MARRIED MY FATHER. HE WAS TWENTY-FIVE.
SIXTEEN IS STILL HIGH SCHOOL, RIGHT?
BCO

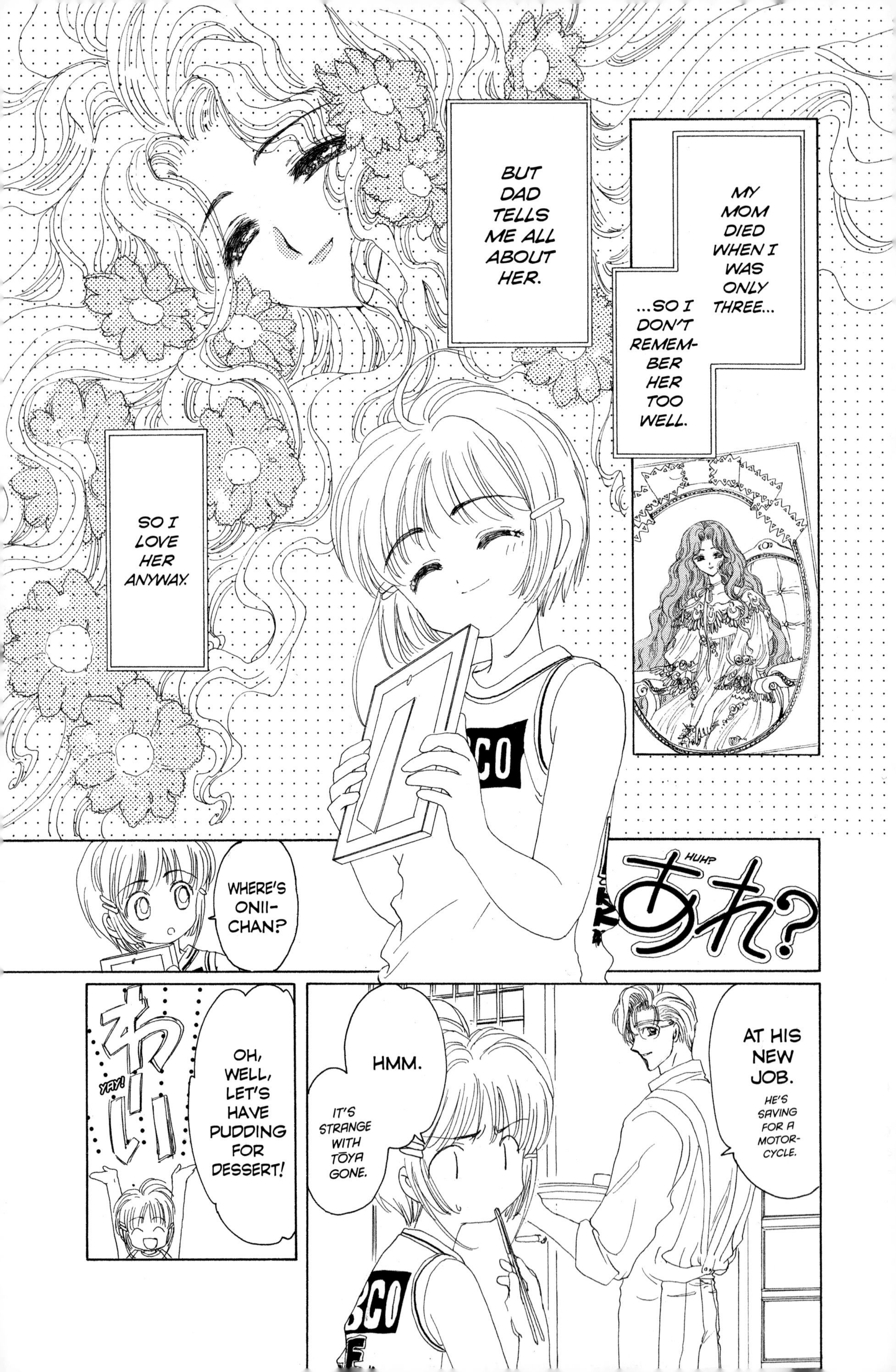
MY MOM DIED WHEN I WAS ONLY THREE...
...SO I DON'T REMEMBER HER TOO WELL.
BUT DAD TELLS ME ALL ABOUT HER.
SO I LOVE HER ANYWAY.
あれ?
HUH?
WHERE'S ONII-CHAN?
AT HIS NEW JOB.
HE'S SAVING FOR A MOTOR-CYCLE.
HMM.
IT'S STRANGE WITH TŌYA GONE.
OH, WELL, LET'S HAVE PUDDING FOR DESSERT!
わーい
YAY!

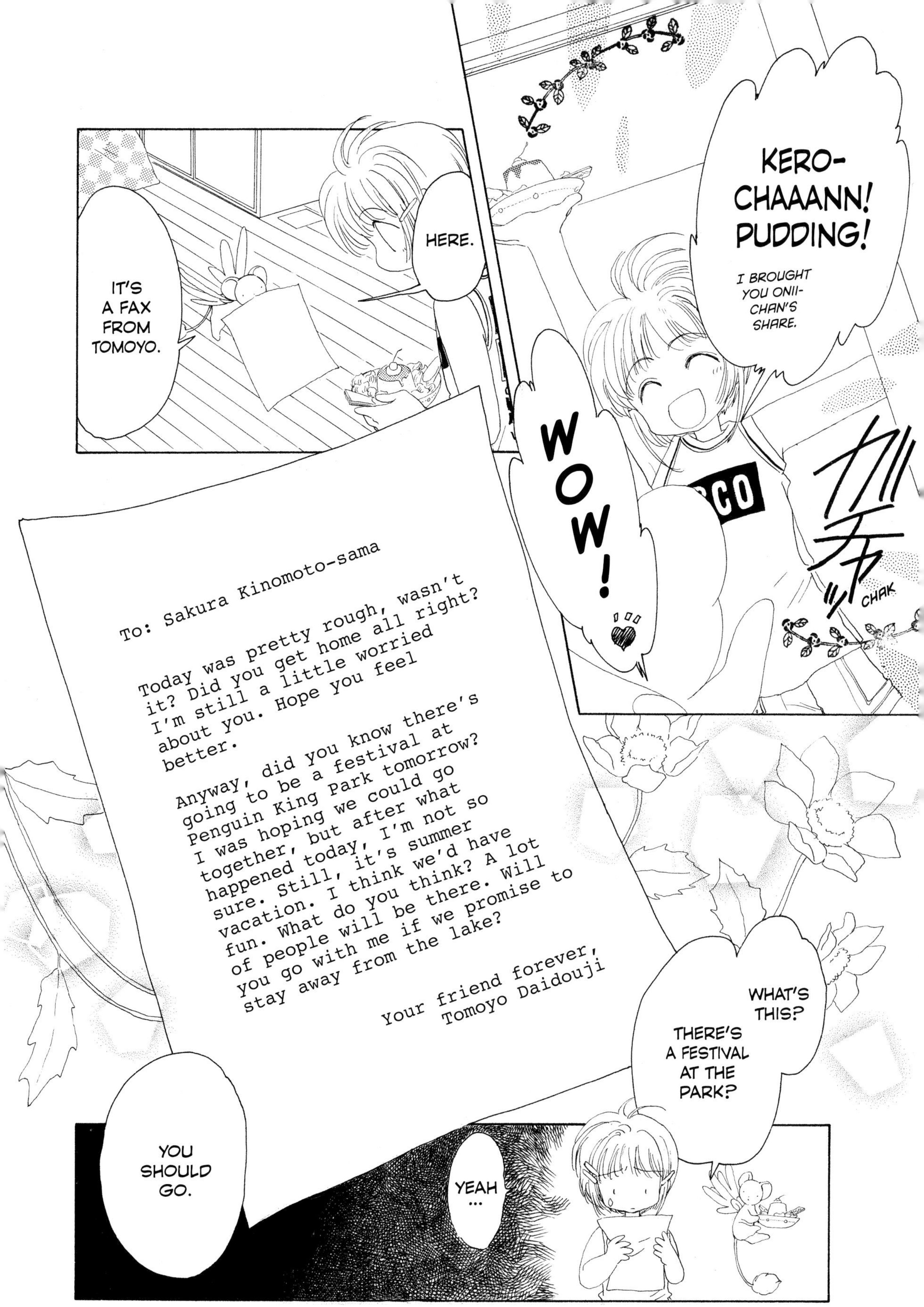
KERO-CHAAANN! PUDDING!
I BROUGHT YOU ONII-CHAN'S SHARE.
WOW!
CHAK
HERE.
IT'S A FAX FROM TOMOYO.
To: Sakura Kinomoto-sama
Today was pretty rough, wasn't it? Did you get home all right? I'm still a little worried about you. Hope you feel better.
Anyway, did you know there's going to be a festival at Penguin King Park tomorrow? I was hoping we could go together, but after what happened today, I'm not so sure. Still, it's summer vacation. I think we'd have fun. What do you think? A lot of people will be there. Will you go with me if we promise to stay away from the lake?
Your friend forever,
Tomoyo Daidouji
WHAT'S THIS?
THERE'S A FESTIVAL AT THE PARK?
YEAH...
YOU SHOULD GO.

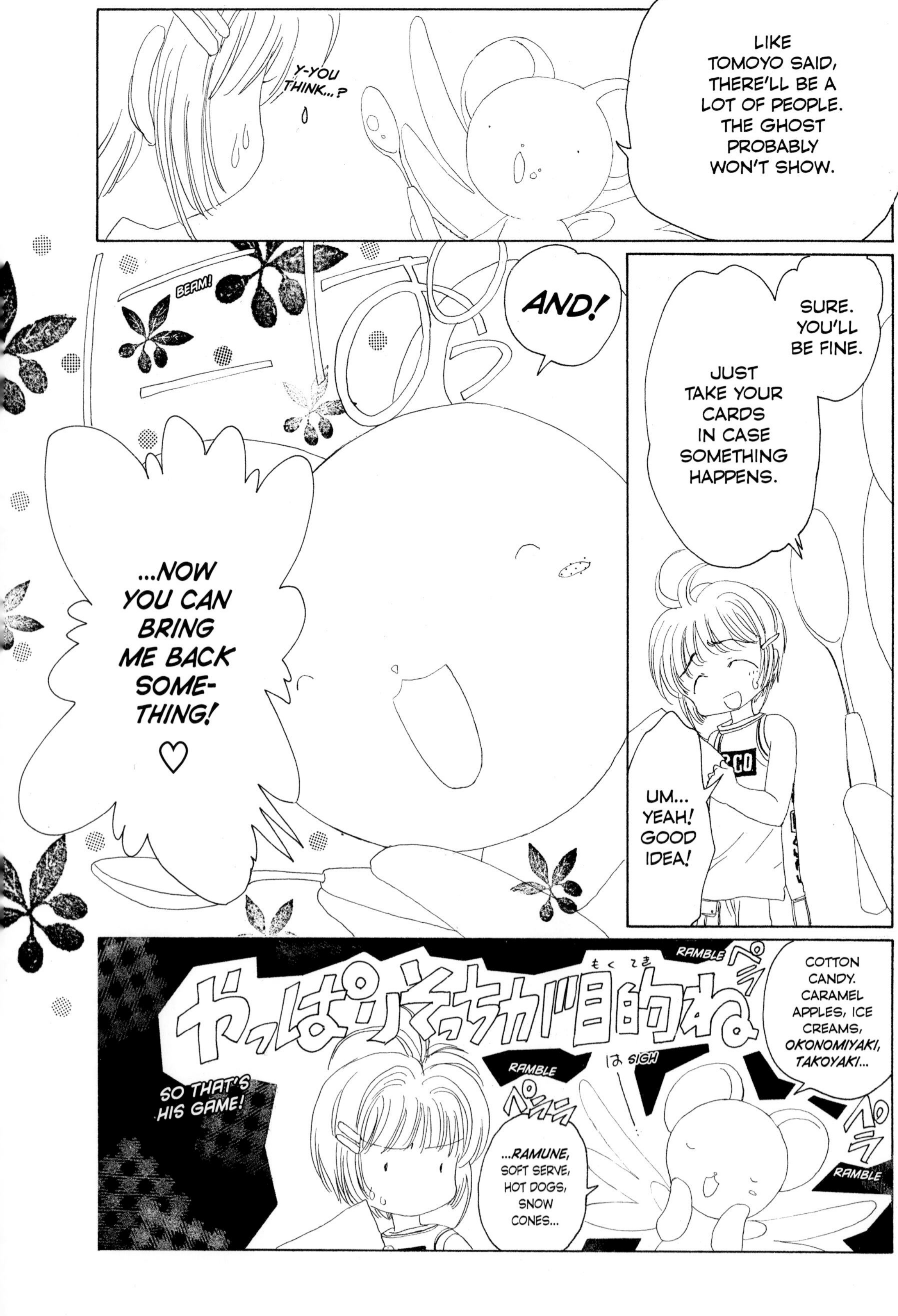
LIKE TOMOYO SAID, THERE'LL BE A LOT OF PEOPLE. THE GHOST PROBABLY WON'T SHOW.
Y-YOU THINK...?
SURE. YOU'LL BE FINE.
JUST TAKE YOUR CARDS IN CASE SOMETHING HAPPENS.
UM... YEAH! GOOD IDEA!
AND!
BEAM!
...NOW YOU CAN BRING ME BACK SOME-THING! ♡
COTTON CANDY. CARAMEL APPLES, ICE CREAMS, OKONOMIYAKI, TAKOYAKI...
RAMBLE
ペラ
RAMBLE
やっぱりそっちが目的ね。
SO THAT'S HIS GAME!
は SIGH
RAMBLE
...RAMUNE, SOFT SERVE, HOT DOGS, SNOW CONES...

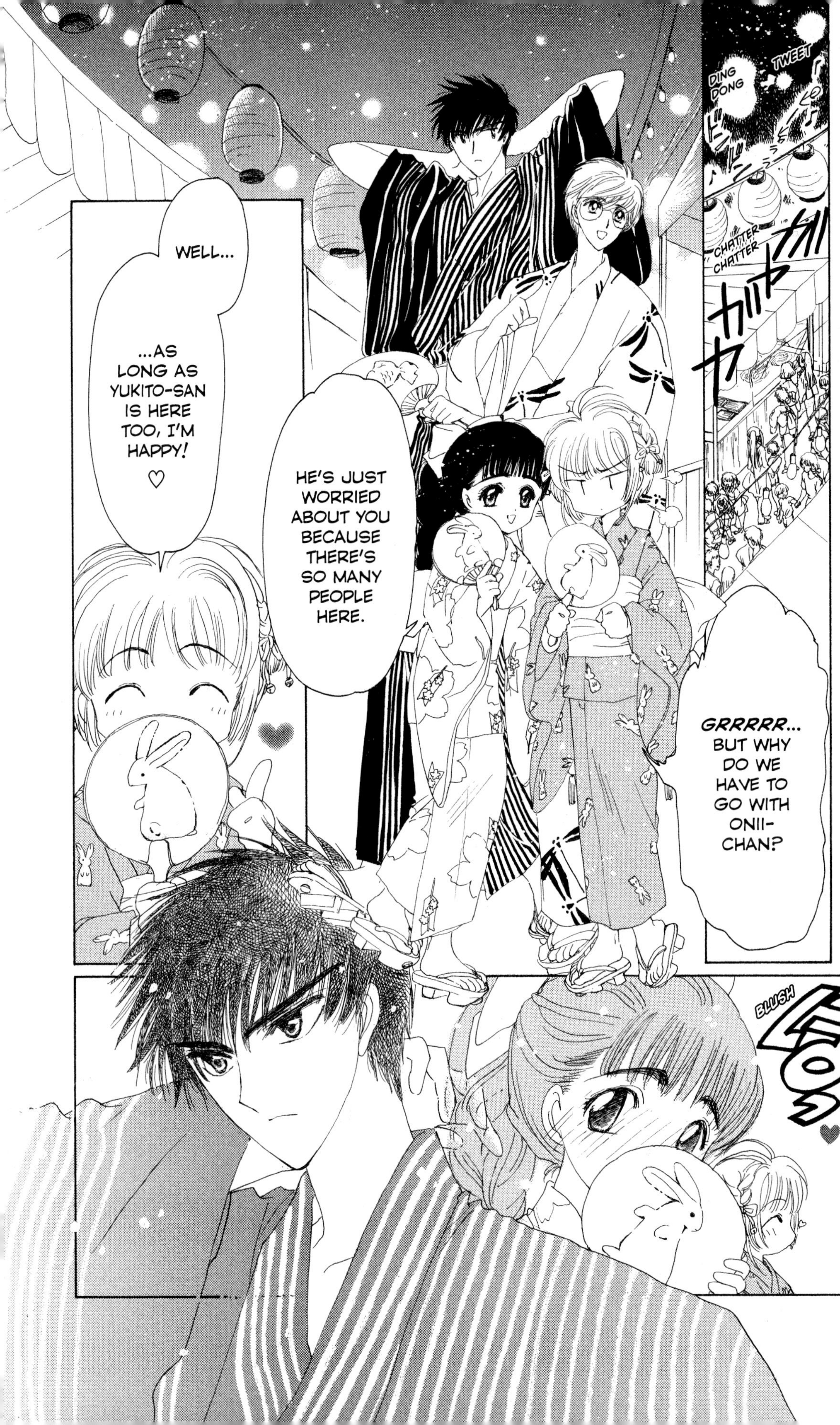
DING DONG
TWEET
CHATTER CHATTER
GRRRRR... BUT WHY DO WE HAVE TO GO WITH ONII-CHAN?
HE'S JUST WORRIED ABOUT YOU BECAUSE THERE'S SO MANY PEOPLE HERE.
WELL...
...AS LONG AS YUKITO-SAN IS HERE TOO, I'M HAPPY! ♡
BLUSH

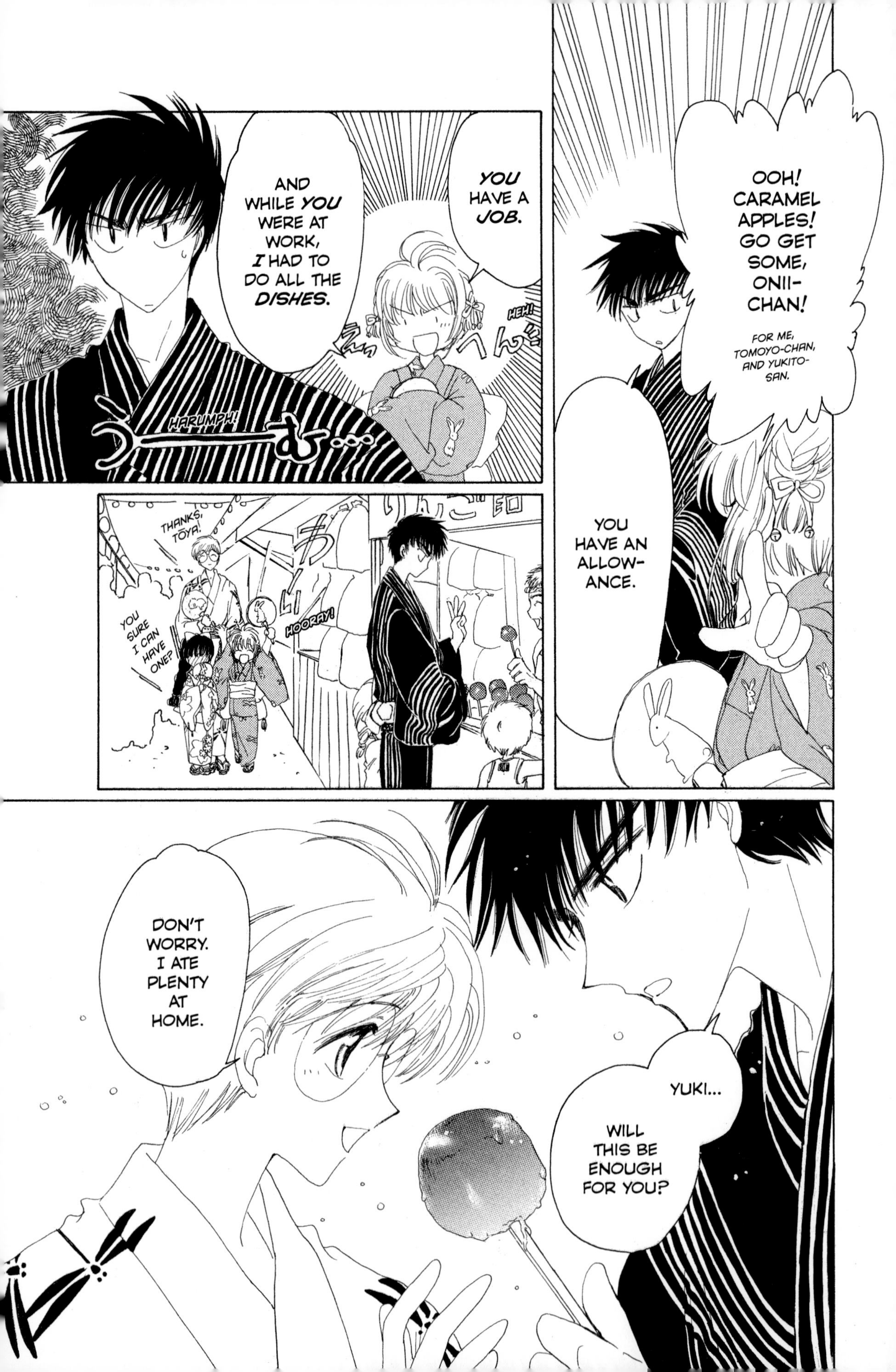
OOH! CARAMEL APPLES! GO GET SOME, ONII-CHAN!
FOR ME, TOMOYO-CHAN, AND YUKITO-SAN.
YOU HAVE AN ALLOWANCE.
YOU HAVE A JOB.
AND WHILE YOU WERE AT WORK, I HAD TO DO ALL THE DISHES.
HEH!
HARUMPH!
HOORAY!
THANKS, TŌYA!
YOU SURE I CAN HAVE ONE?
YUKI...
WILL THIS BE ENOUGH FOR YOU?
DON'T WORRY. I ATE PLENTY AT HOME.

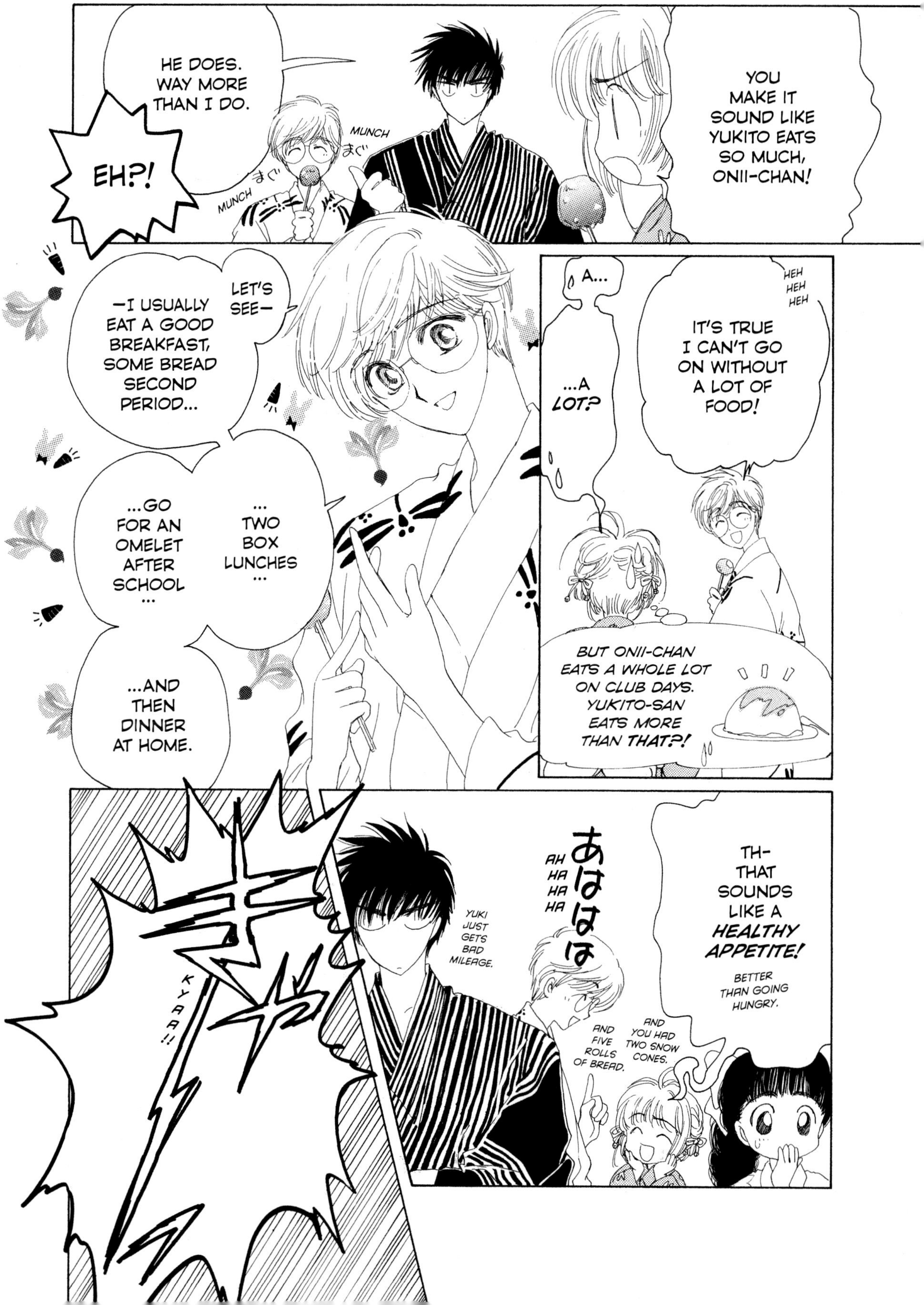
YOU MAKE IT SOUND LIKE YUKITO EATS SO MUCH, ONII-CHAN!
HE DOES. WAY MORE THAN I DO.
MUNCH まぐ
まぐ MUNCH
EH?!
HEH HEH HEH
IT'S TRUE I CAN'T GO ON WITHOUT A LOT OF FOOD!
A...
...A LOT?
BUT ONII-CHAN EATS A WHOLE LOT ON CLUB DAYS. YUKITO-SAN EATS MORE THAN THAT?!
LET'S SEE—
—I USUALLY EAT A GOOD BREAKFAST, SOME BREAD SECOND PERIOD...
... TWO BOX LUNCHES ...
...GO FOR AN OMELET AFTER SCHOOL ...
...AND THEN DINNER AT HOME.
TH-THAT SOUNDS LIKE A HEALTHY APPETITE!
BETTER THAN GOING HUNGRY.
あははは
AH HA HA HA
YUKI JUST GETS BAD MILEAGE.
AND YOU HAD TWO SNOW CONES.
AND FIVE ROLLS OF BREAD.
KYAA!!

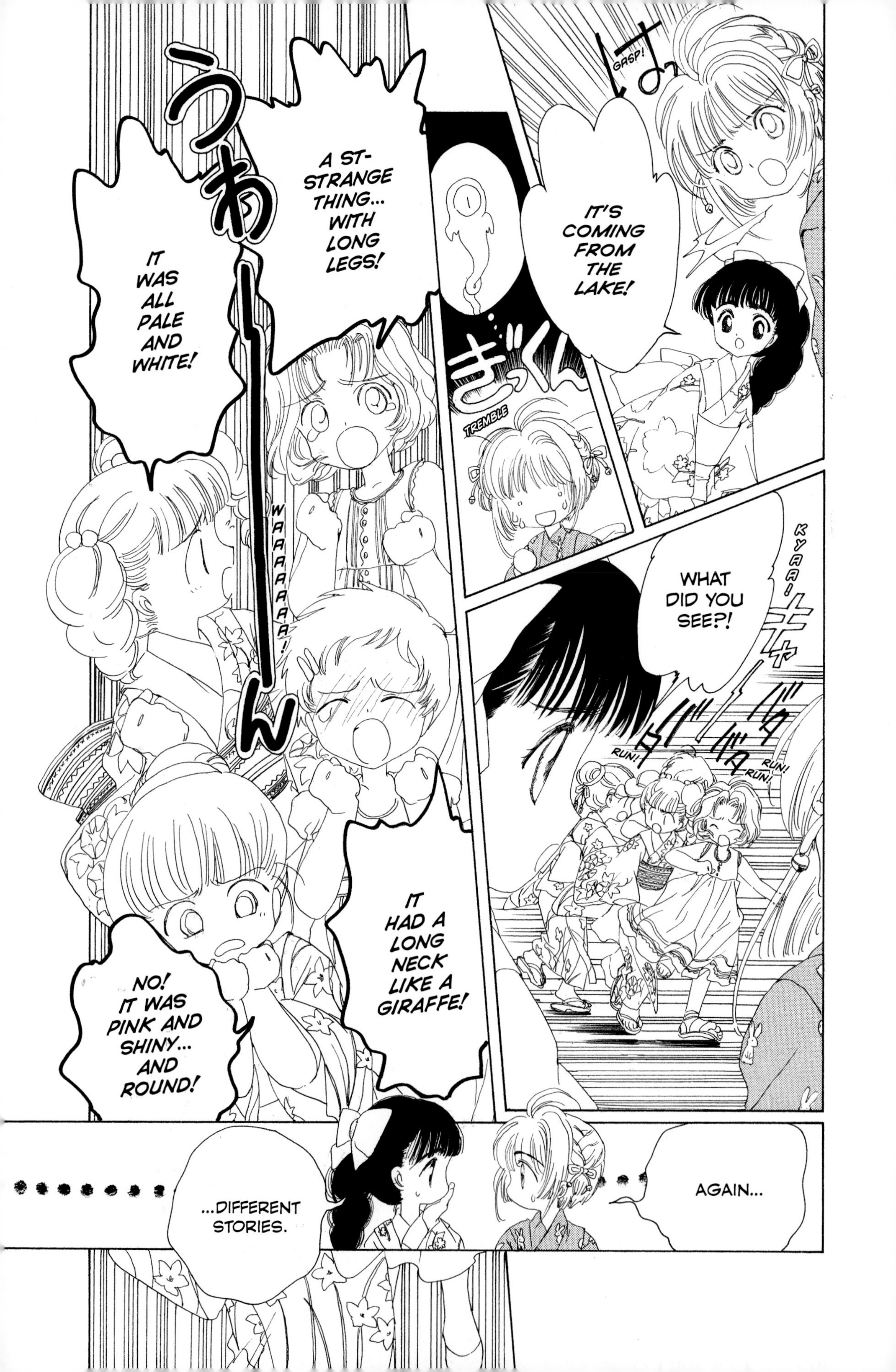
はっ
GASP!
IT'S COMING FROM THE LAKE!
ぎくん
TREMBLE
KYAA!
WHAT DID YOU SEE?!
RUN! RUN!
RUN!
A ST-STRANGE THING... WITH LONG LEGS!
IT WAS ALL PALE AND WHITE!
WAAAAAAAA!
IT HAD A LONG NECK LIKE A GIRAFFE!
NO! IT WAS PINK AND SHINY... AND ROUND!
AGAIN...
...DIFFERENT STORIES.

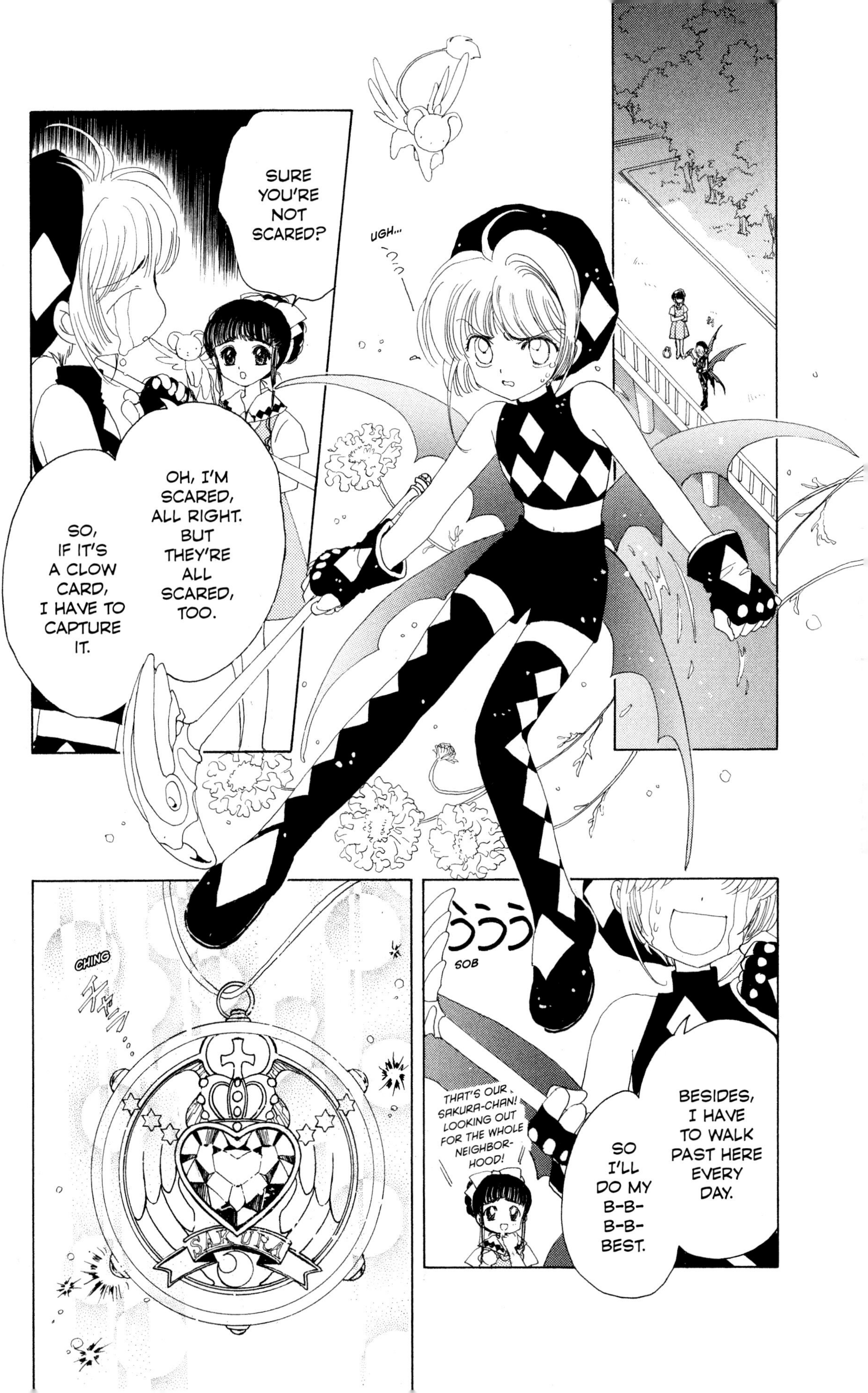
UGH...
SURE YOU'RE NOT SCARED?
OH, I'M SCARED, ALL RIGHT. BUT THEY'RE ALL SCARED, TOO.
SO, IF IT'S A CLOW CARD, I HAVE TO CAPTURE IT.
ううう
SOB
BESIDES, I HAVE TO WALK PAST HERE EVERY DAY.
SO I'LL DO MY B-B-B-B-BEST.
THAT'S OUR SAKURA-CHAN! LOOKING OUT FOR THE WHOLE NEIGHBOR-HOOD!
CHING
チャラ…
SAKURA

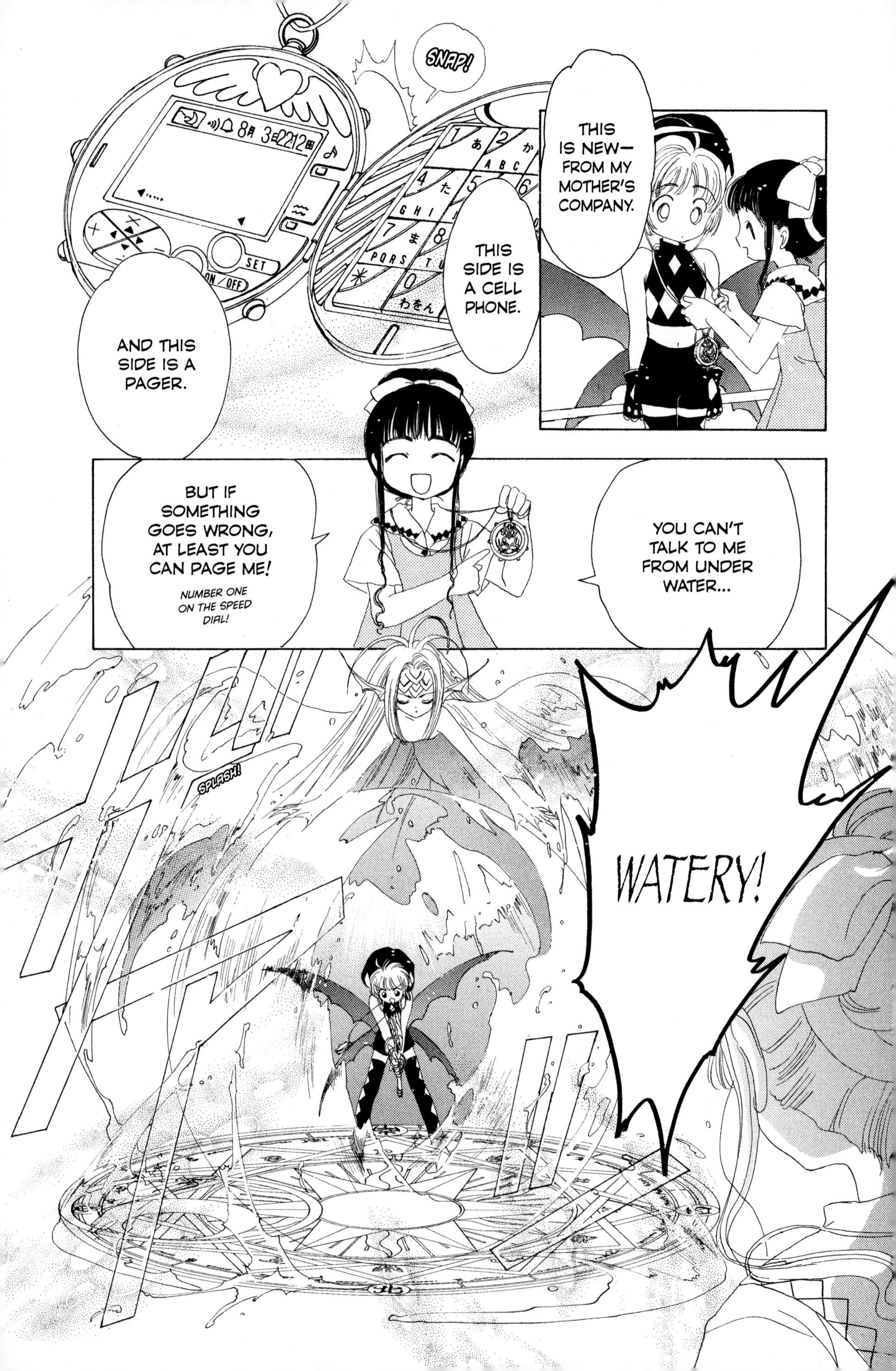
THIS IS NEW— FROM MY MOTHER'S COMPANY.
SNAP!
THIS SIDE IS A CELL PHONE.
AND THIS SIDE IS A PAGER.
YOU CAN'T TALK TO ME FROM UNDER WATER...
BUT IF SOMETHING GOES WRONG, AT LEAST YOU CAN PAGE ME!
NUMBER ONE ON THE SPEED DIAL!
WATERY!
SPLASH!

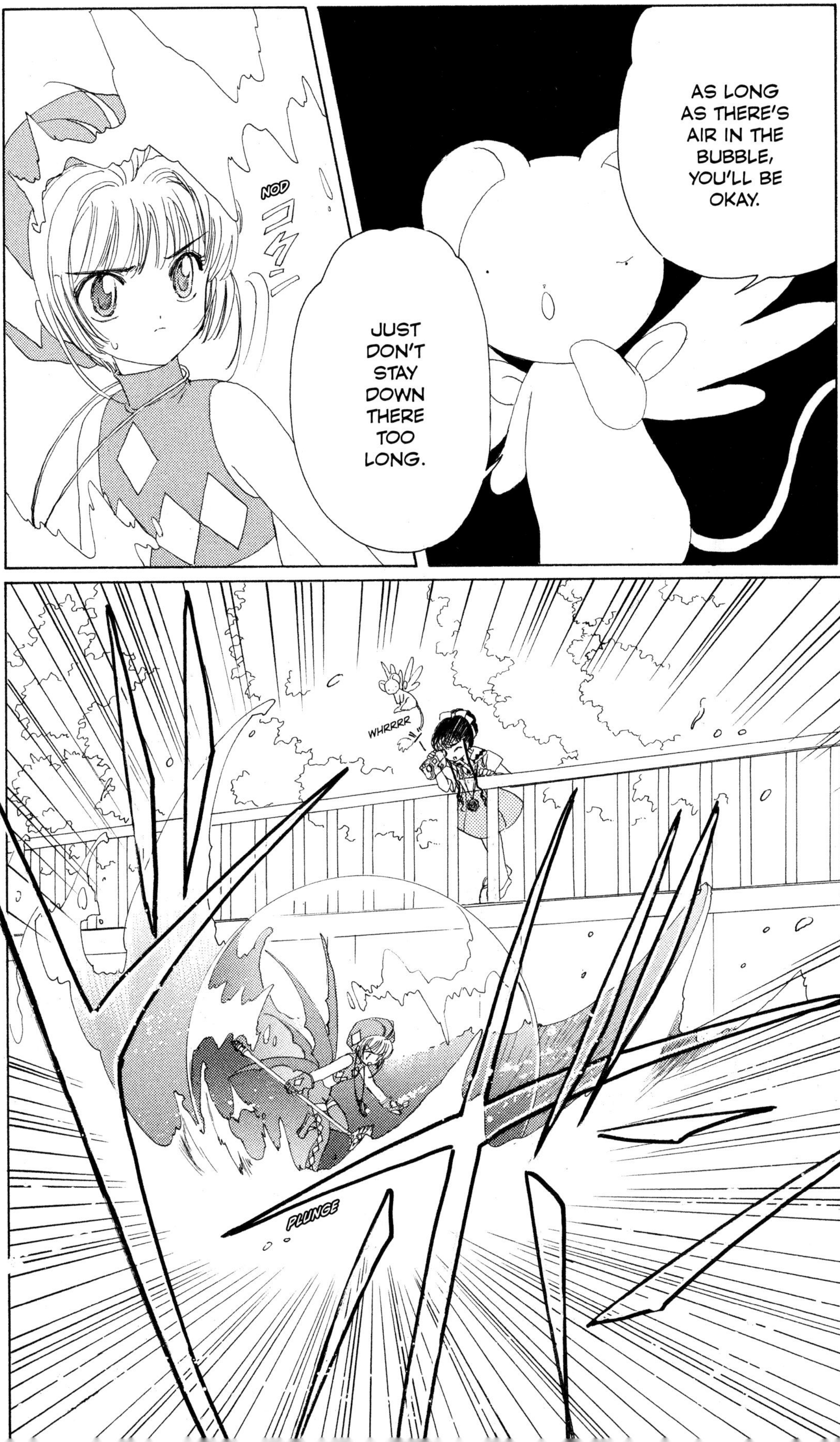
AS LONG AS THERE'S AIR IN THE BUBBLE, YOU'LL BE OKAY.
JUST DON'T STAY DOWN THERE TOO LONG.
NOD
WHRRRR
PLUNGE

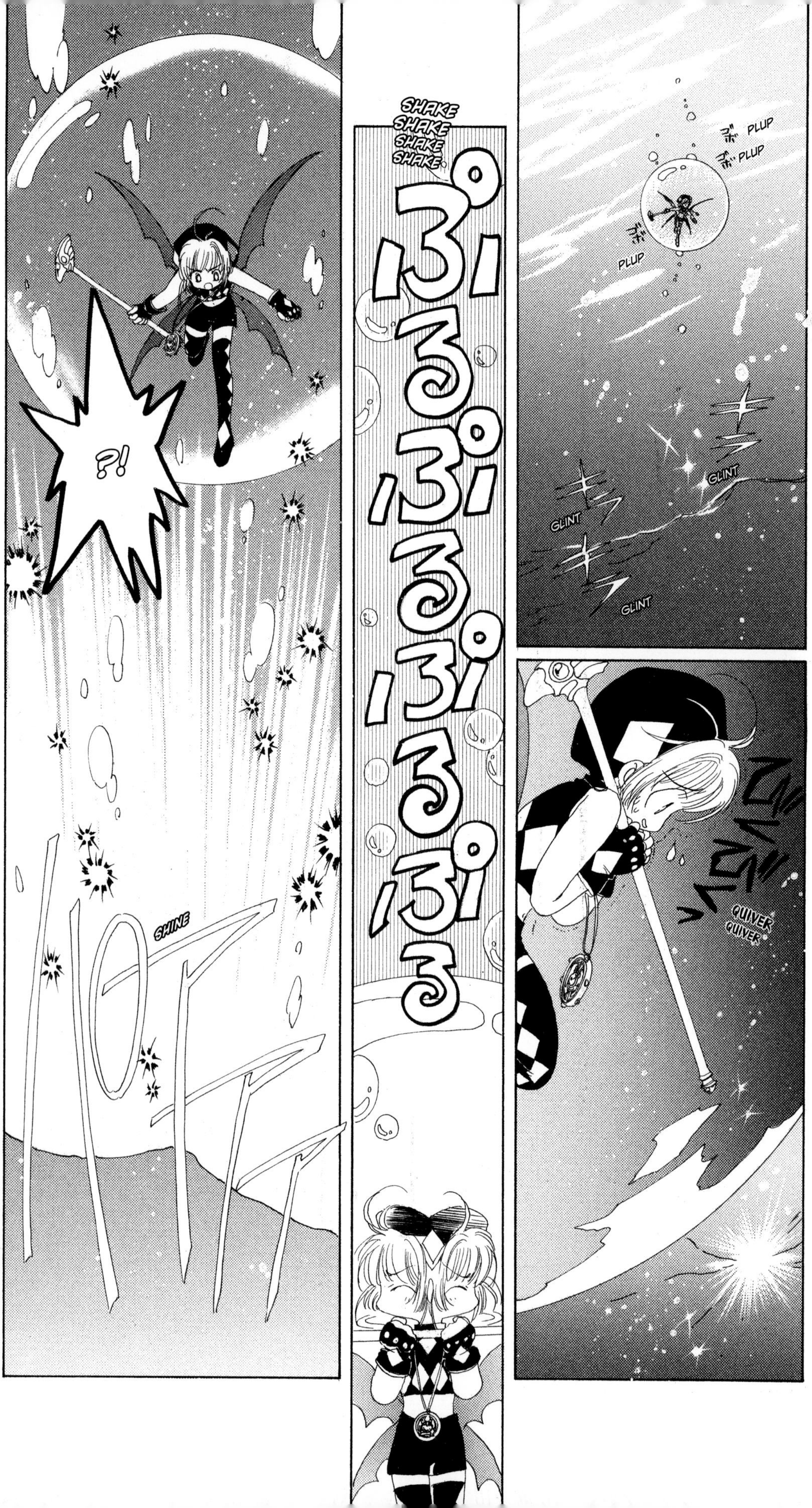
PLUP
PLUP
PLUP
GLINT
GLINT
GLINT
QUIVER QUIVER
SHAKE SHAKE SHAKE SHAKE
?!
SHINE

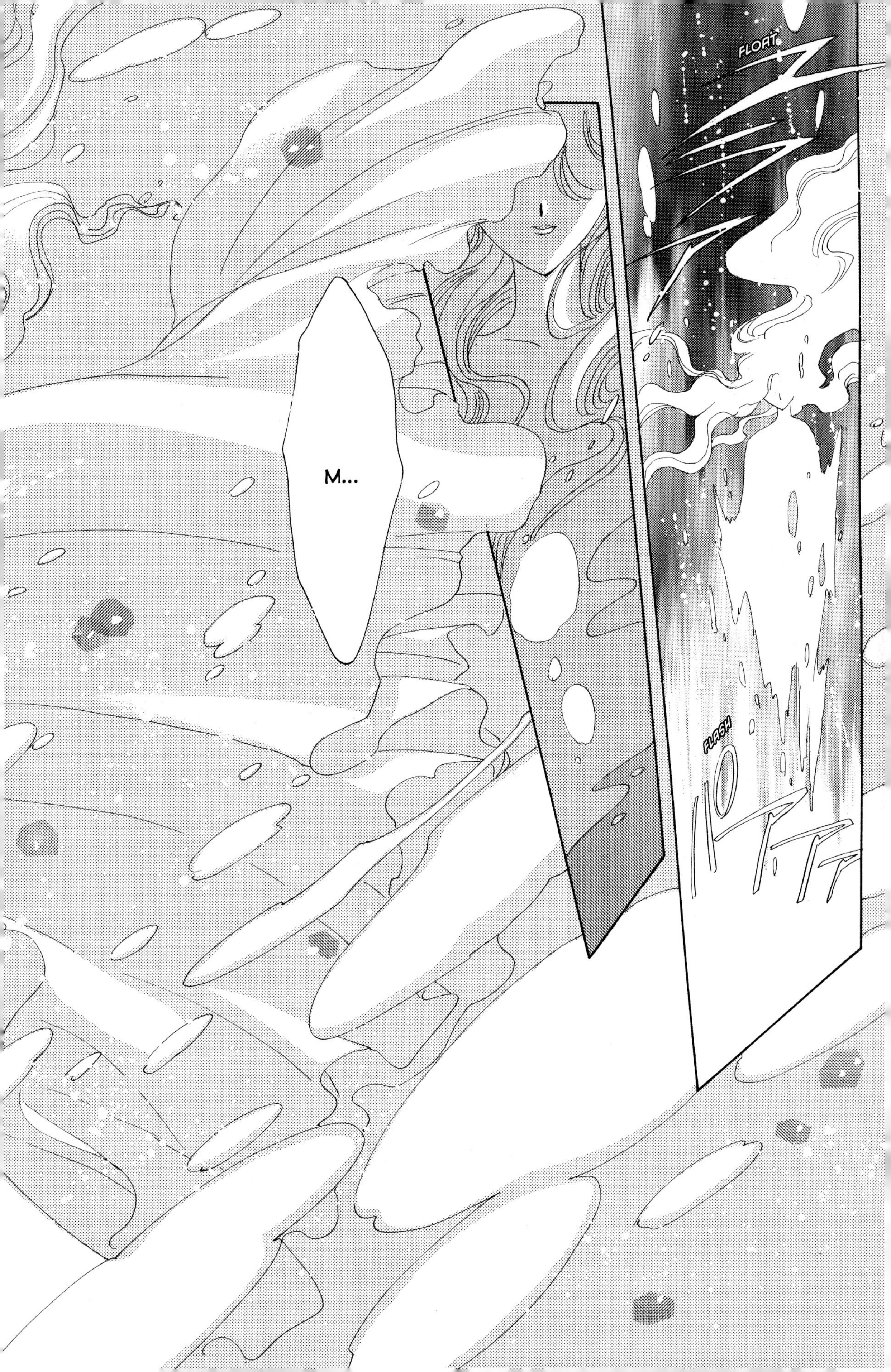
FLOAT
FLASH
M...

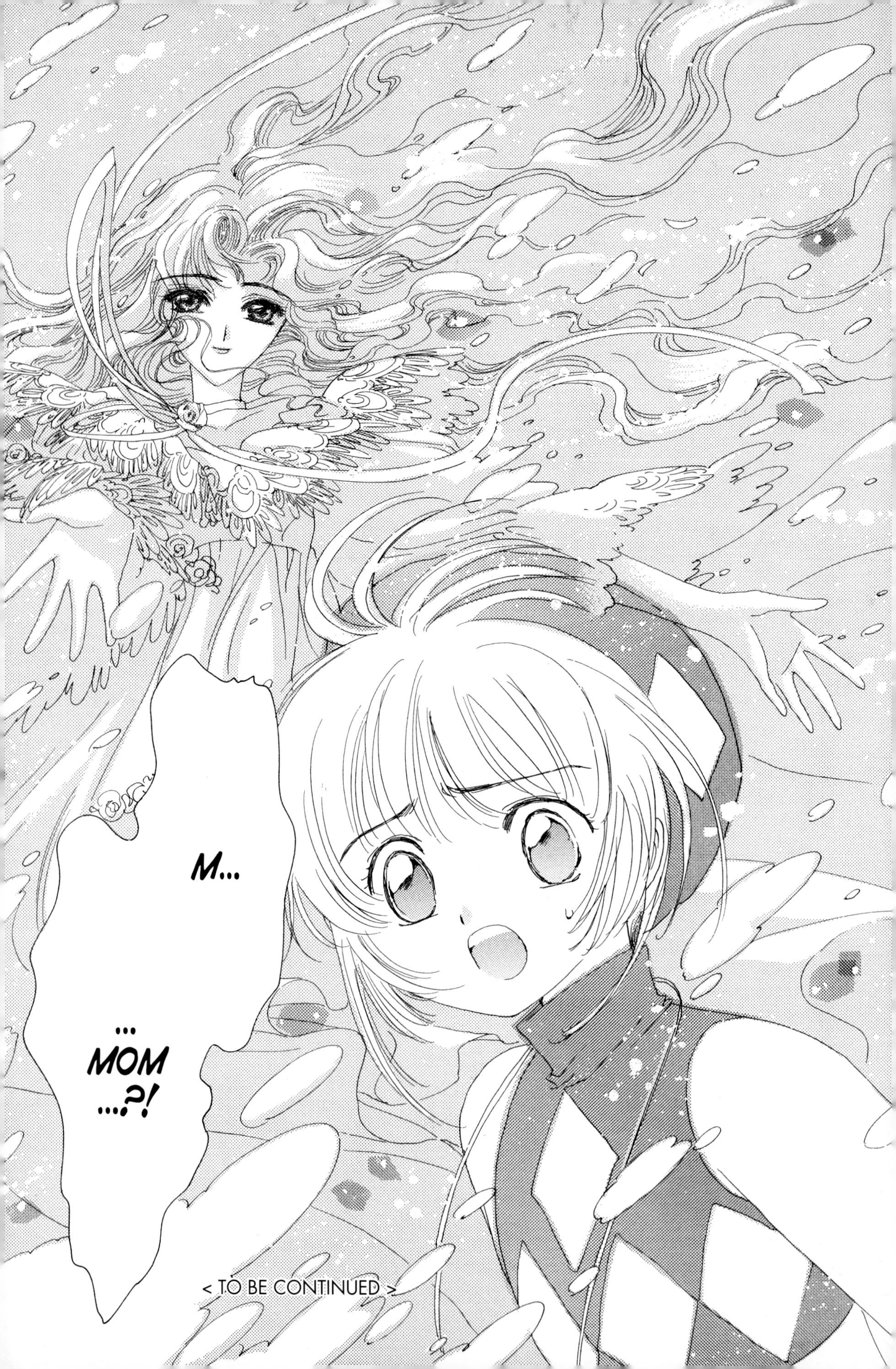
M...
...MOM ...?!
< TO BE CONTINUED >

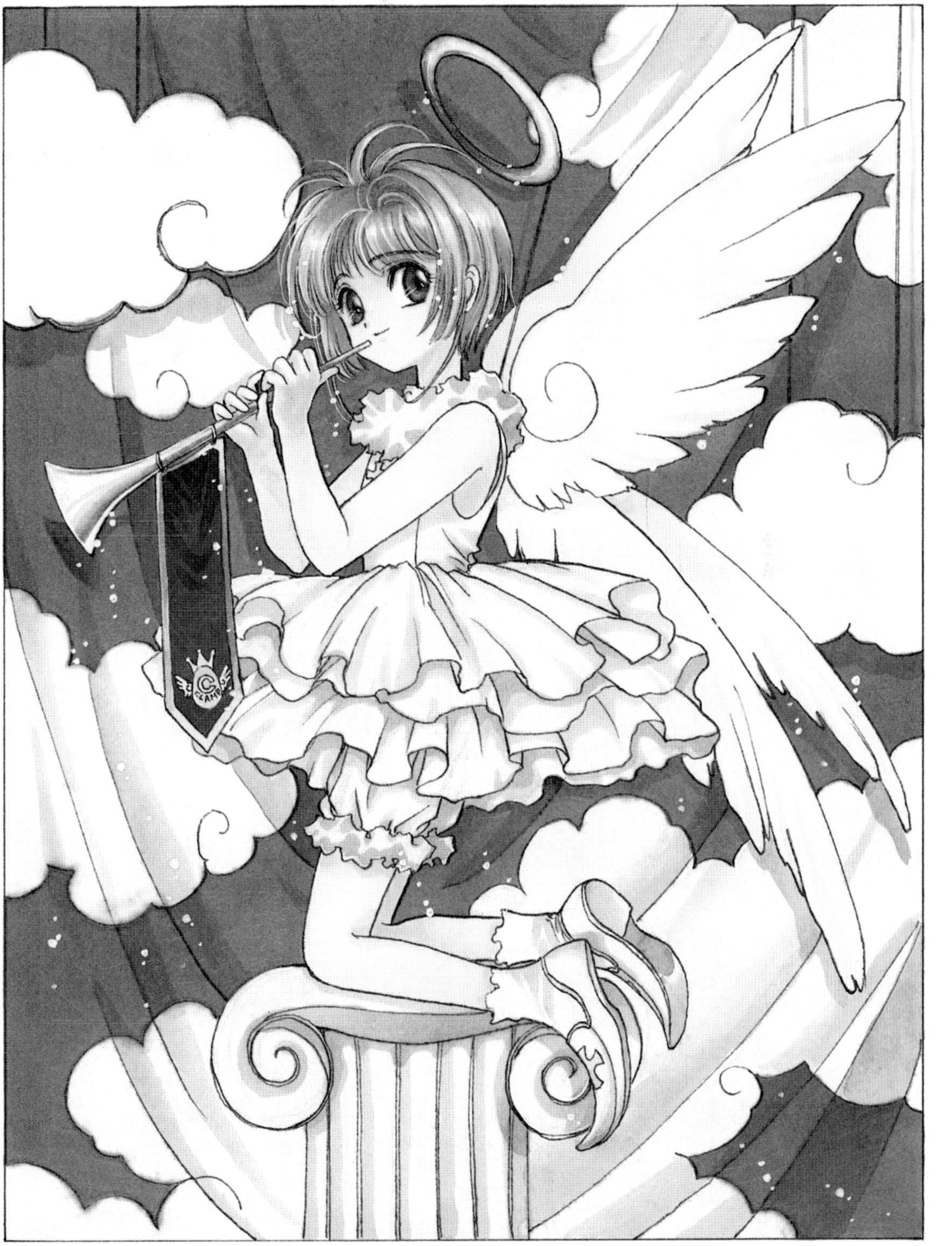

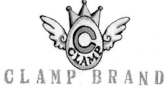

CLAMP BRAND

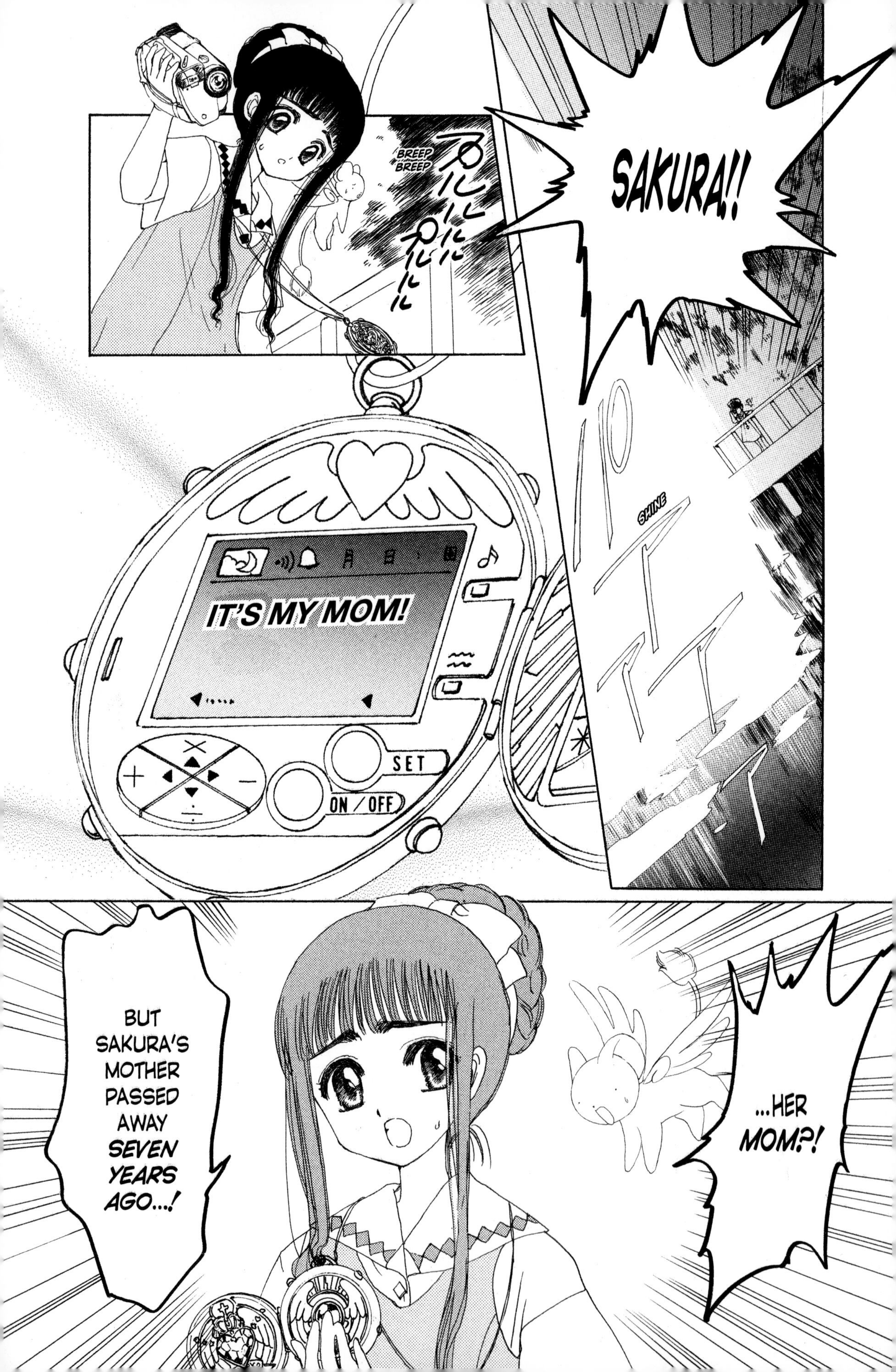

SAKURA!!
BREEP BREEP
SHINE
IT'S MY MOM!
SET
ON / OFF
...HER MOM?!
BUT SAKURA'S MOTHER PASSED AWAY SEVEN YEARS AGO...!

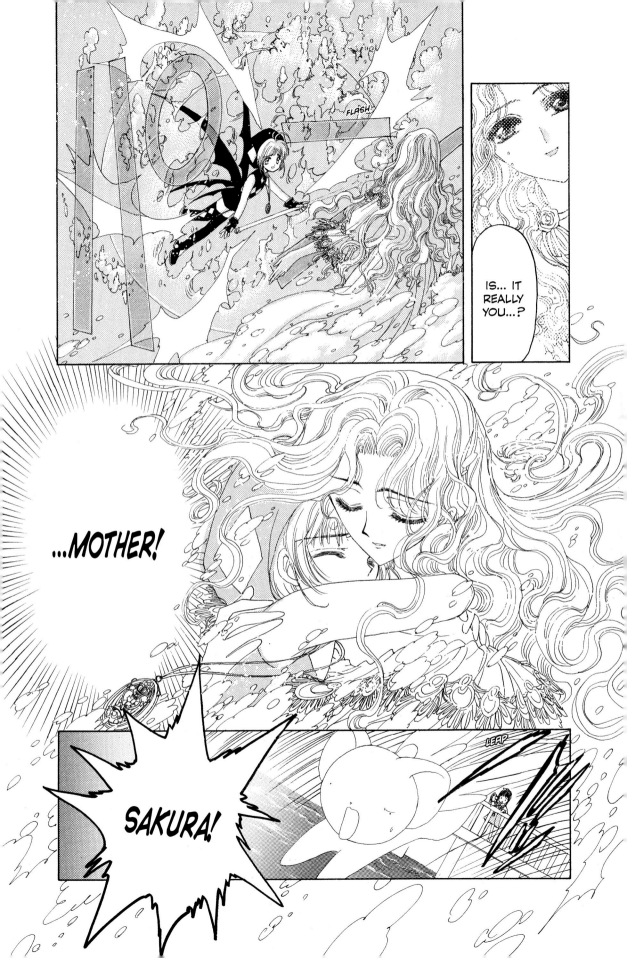

FLASH

IS... IT
REALLY
YOU...?

...MOTHER!

SAKURA!

LEAP

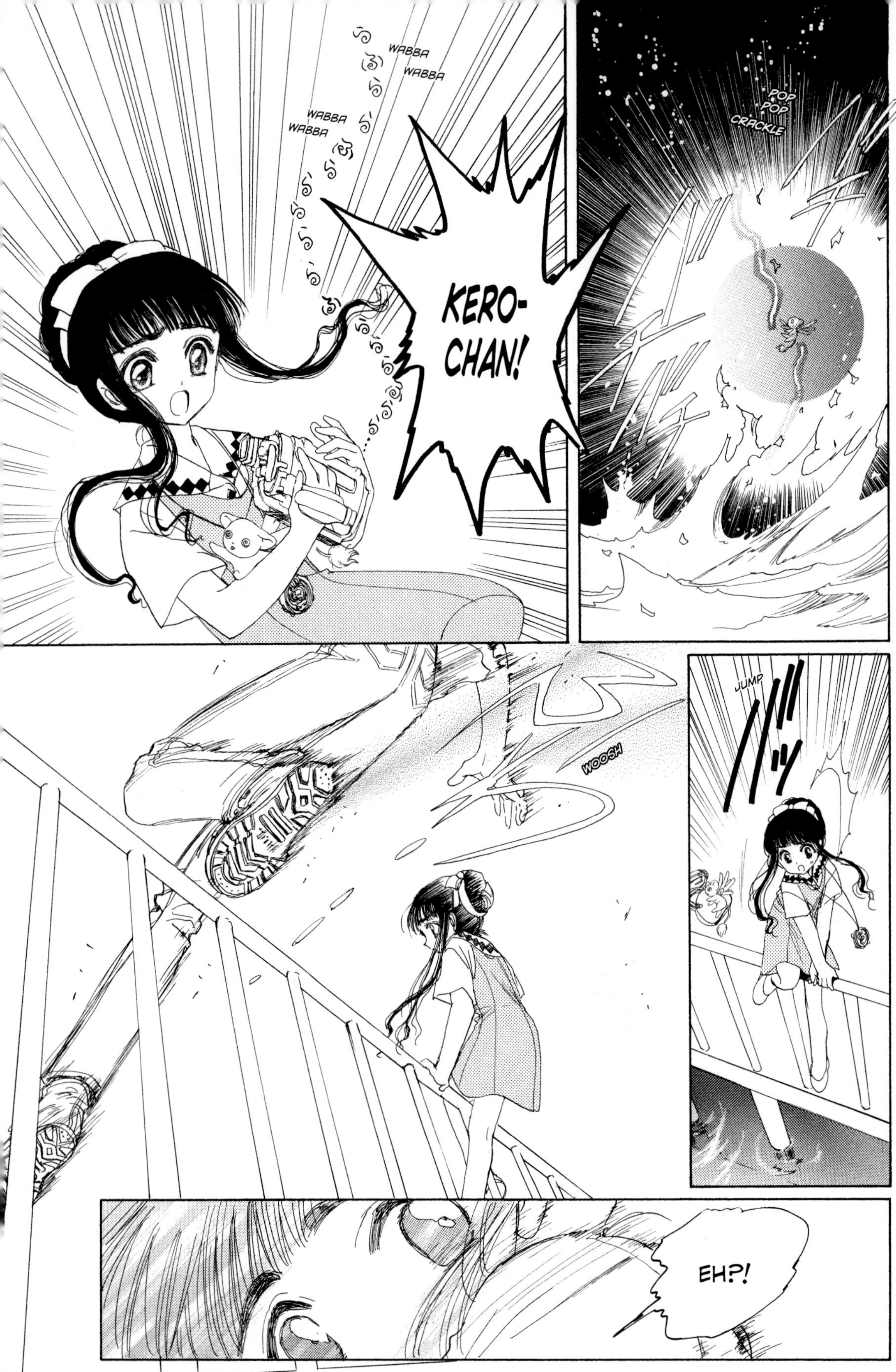
POP
POP
CRACKLE
WABBA
WABBA
WABBA
WABBA
KERO-CHAN!
JUMP
WOOSH
EH?!

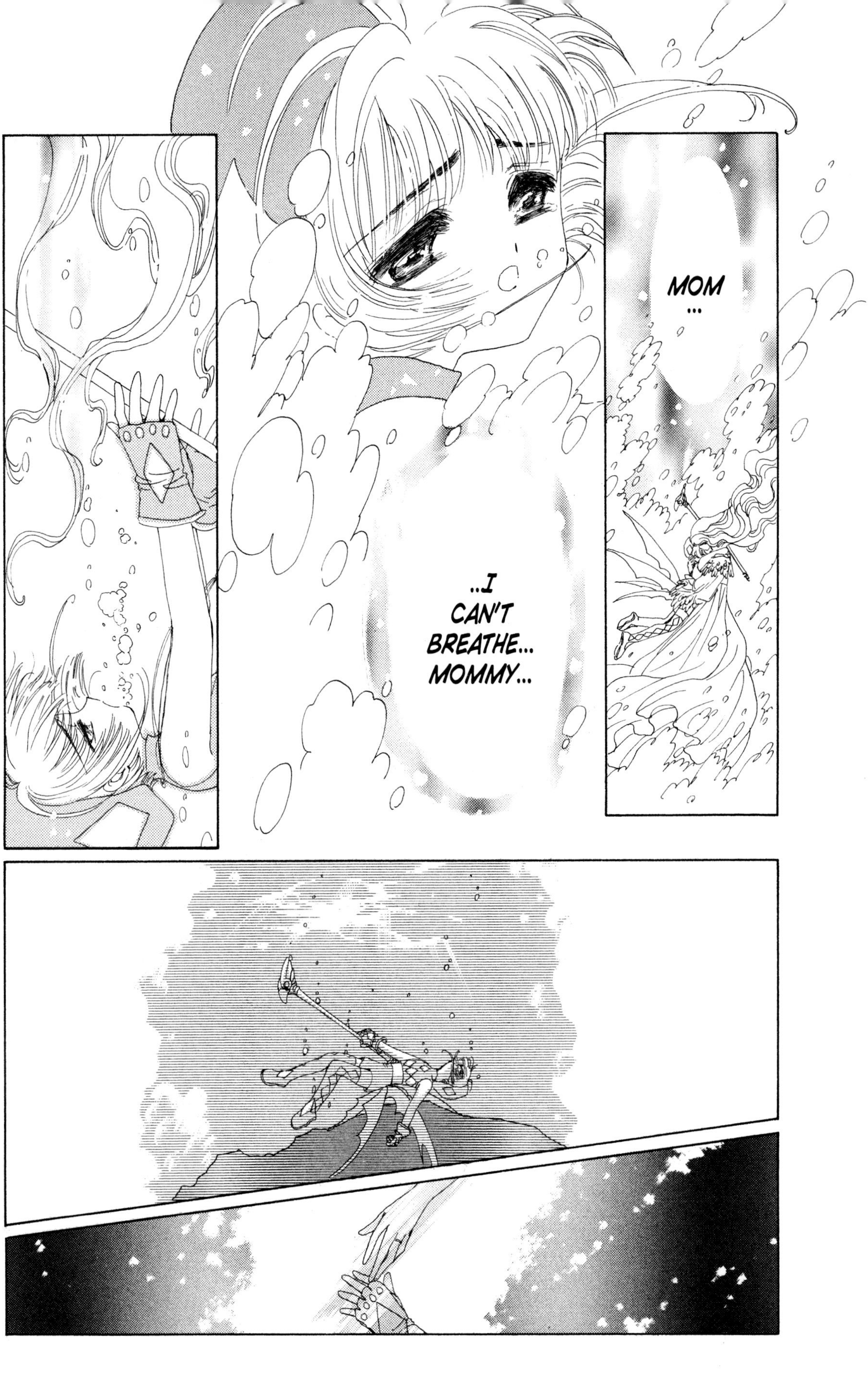
MOM ...
..I CAN'T BREATHE... MOMMY...

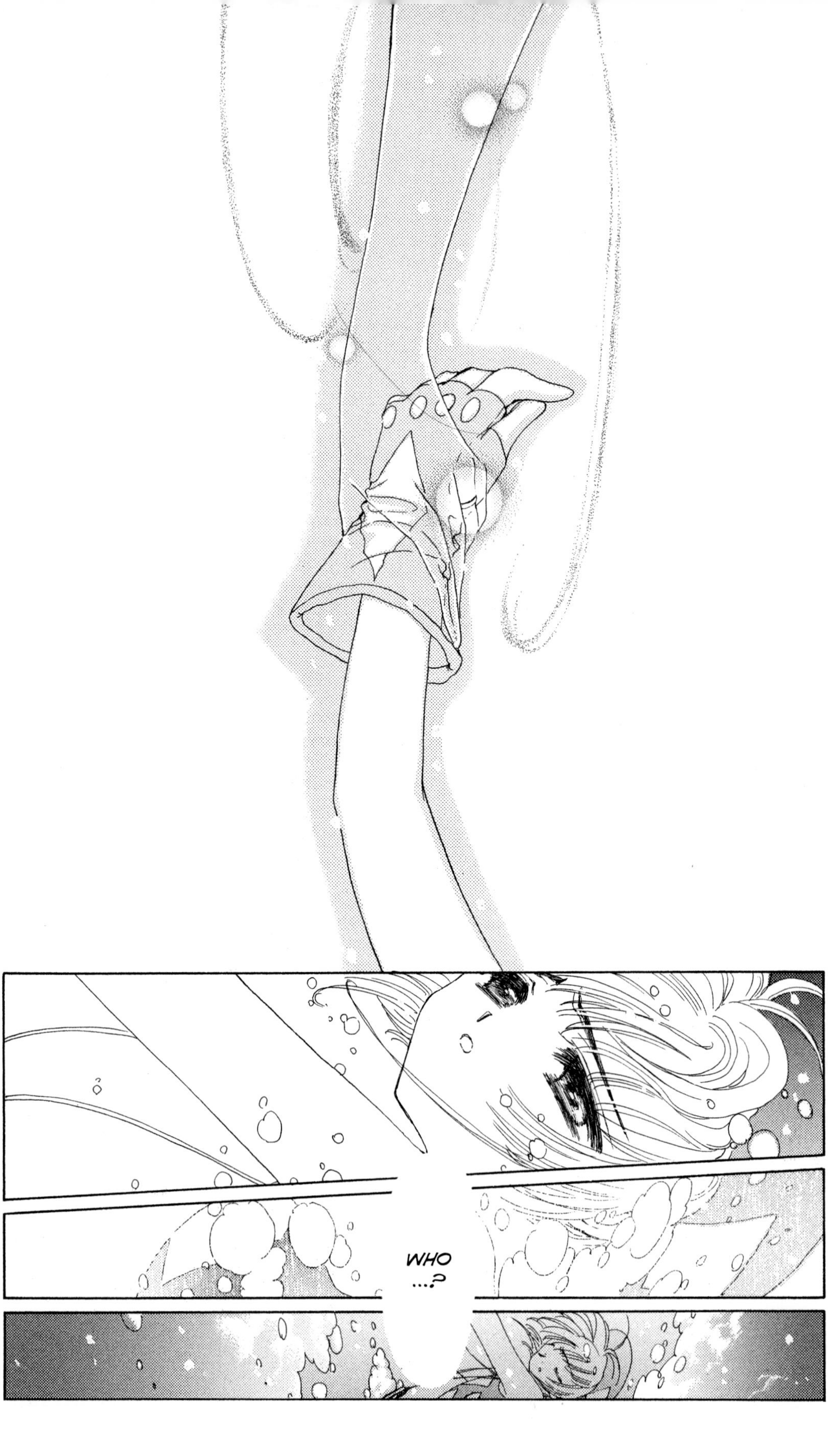
WHO ...?

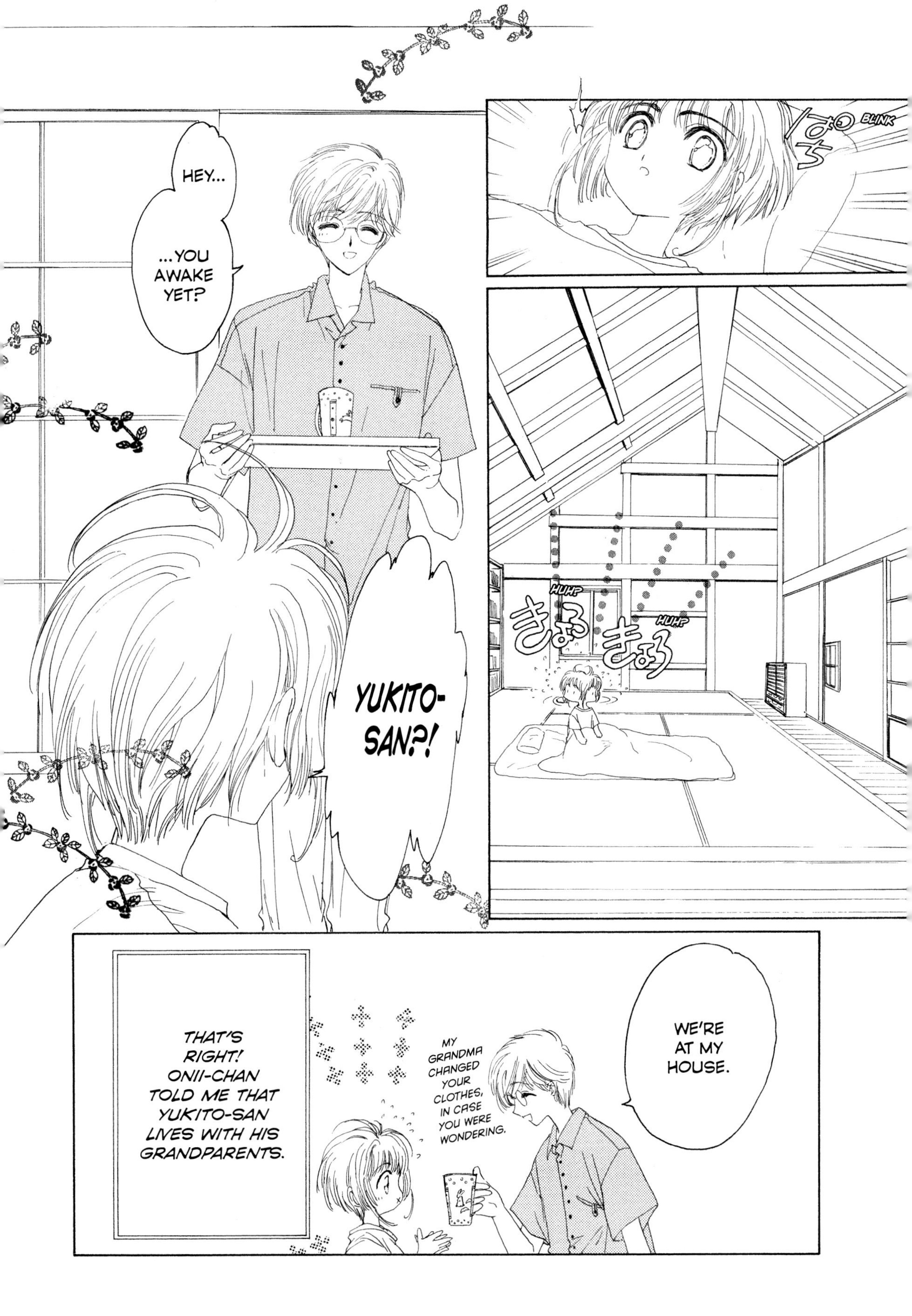
ぱち
BLINK
きょろ
HUH?
きょろ
HUH?
HEY...
...YOU AWAKE YET?
YUKITO-SAN?!
WE'RE AT MY HOUSE.
MY GRANDMA CHANGED YOUR CLOTHES, IN CASE YOU WERE WONDERING.
THAT'S RIGHT! ONII-CHAN TOLD ME THAT YUKITO-SAN LIVES WITH HIS GRANDPARENTS.

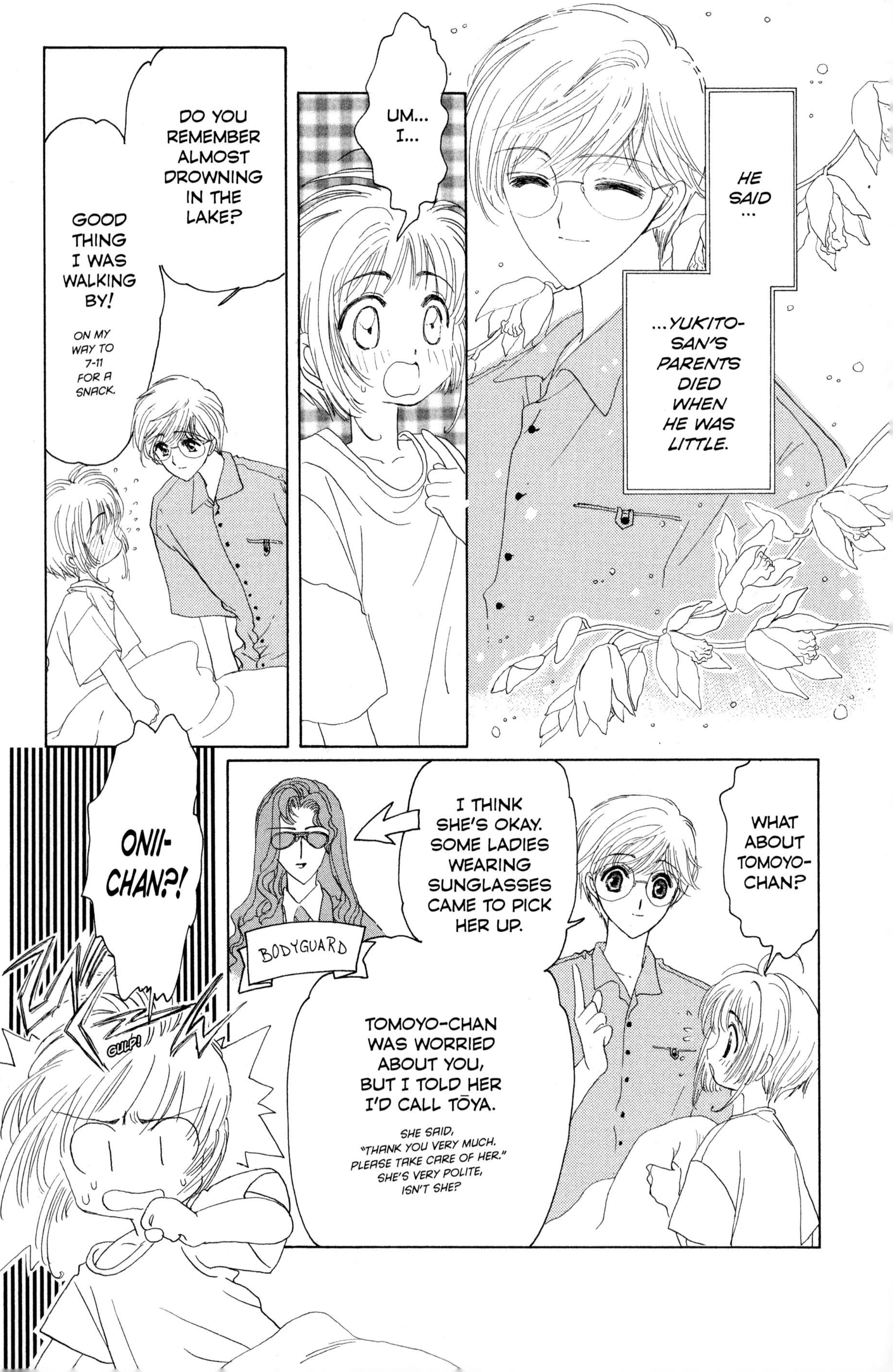
HE SAID ...
...YUKITO-SAN'S PARENTS DIED WHEN HE WAS LITTLE.
UM... I...
DO YOU REMEMBER ALMOST DROWNING IN THE LAKE?
GOOD THING I WAS WALKING BY!
ON MY WAY TO 7-11 FOR A SNACK.
WHAT ABOUT TOMOYO-CHAN?
I THINK SHE'S OKAY. SOME LADIES WEARING SUNGLASSES CAME TO PICK HER UP.
BODYGUARD
TOMOYO-CHAN WAS WORRIED ABOUT YOU, BUT I TOLD HER I'D CALL TŌYA.
SHE SAID, "THANK YOU VERY MUCH. PLEASE TAKE CARE OF HER." SHE'S VERY POLITE, ISN'T SHE?
ONII-CHAN?!
GULP!

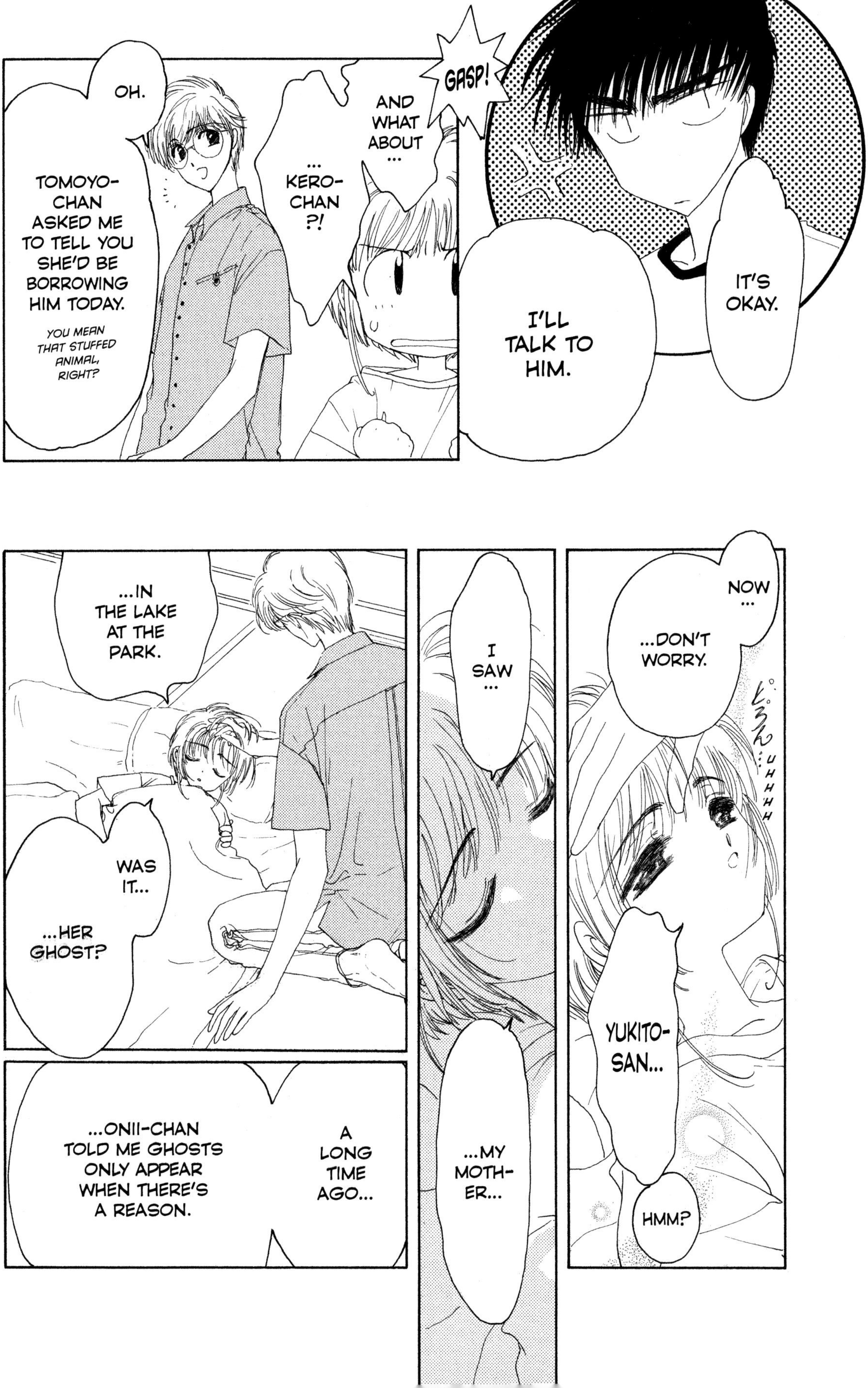
IT'S OKAY.
I'LL TALK TO HIM.
GASP!
AND WHAT ABOUT ...
... KERO-CHAN ?!
OH.
TOMOYO-CHAN ASKED ME TO TELL YOU SHE'D BE BORROWING HIM TODAY.
YOU MEAN THAT STUFFED ANIMAL, RIGHT?
NOW ...
...DON'T WORRY.
UHHHH
YUKITO-SAN...
HMM?
I SAW ...
...MY MOTH-ER...
...IN THE LAKE AT THE PARK.
WAS IT...
...HER GHOST?
A LONG TIME AGO...
...ONII-CHAN TOLD ME GHOSTS ONLY APPEAR WHEN THERE'S A REASON.

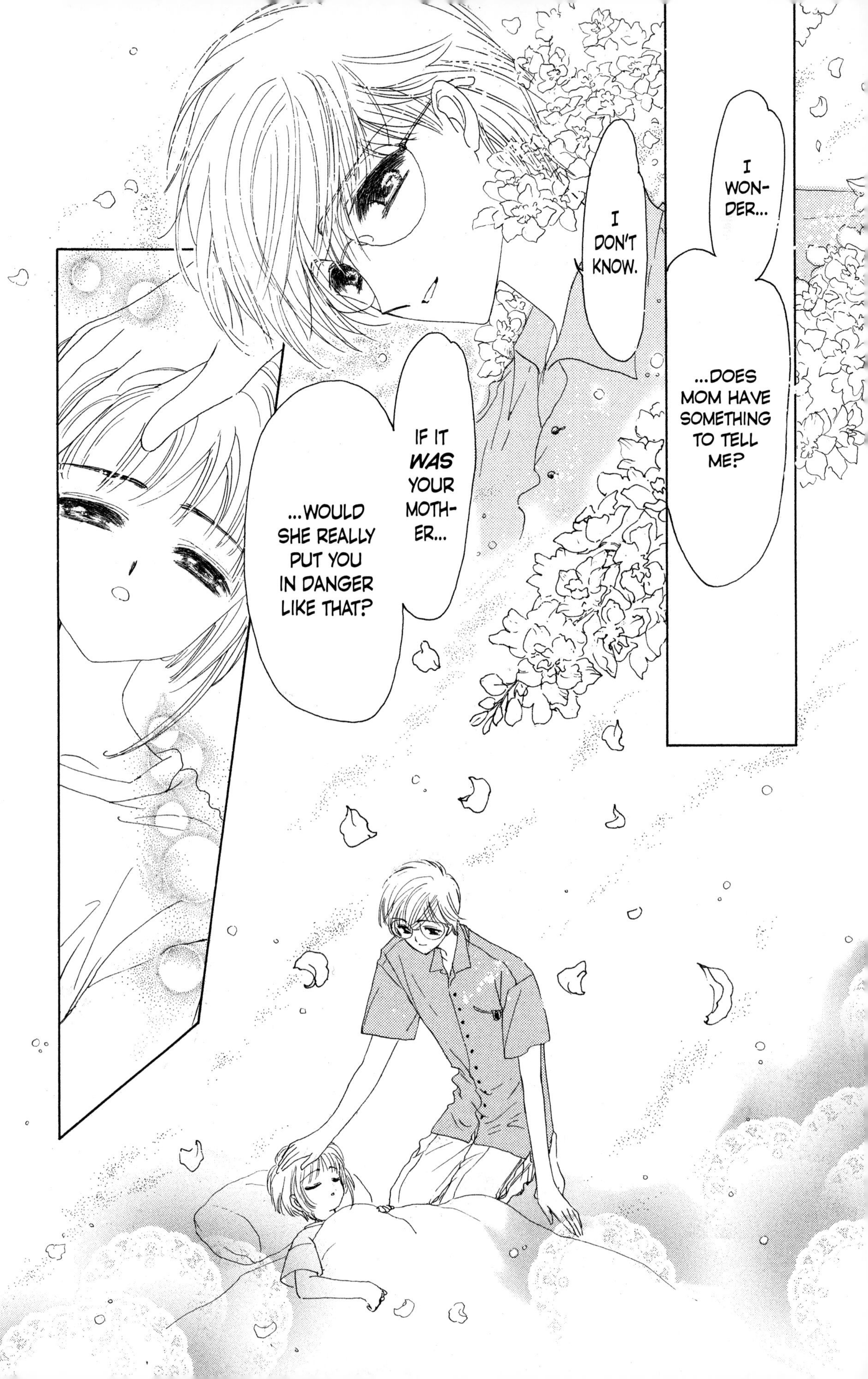
I WONDER...
...DOES MOM HAVE SOMETHING TO TELL ME?
I DON'T KNOW.
IF IT WAS YOUR MOTHER...
...WOULD SHE REALLY PUT YOU IN DANGER LIKE THAT?

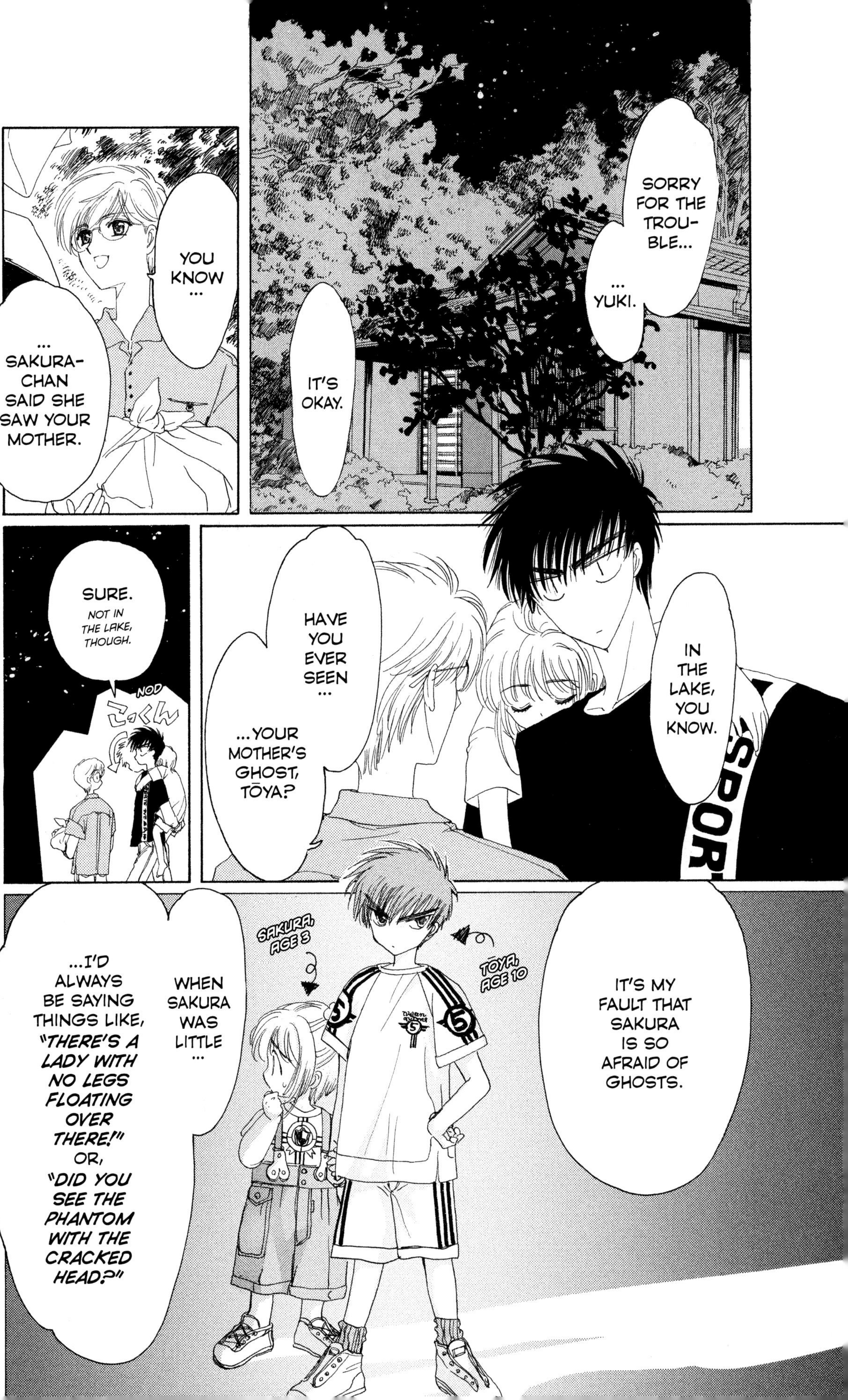
SORRY FOR THE TROUBLE...
... YUKI.
IT'S OKAY.
YOU KNOW ...
... SAKURA-CHAN SAID SHE SAW YOUR MOTHER.
IN THE LAKE, YOU KNOW.
HAVE YOU EVER SEEN ...
...YOUR MOTHER'S GHOST, TŌYA?
SURE. NOT IN THE LAKE, THOUGH.
NOD
こっくん
IT'S MY FAULT THAT SAKURA IS SO AFRAID OF GHOSTS.
TŌYA, AGE 10
SAKURA, AGE 3
WHEN SAKURA WAS LITTLE ...
...I'D ALWAYS BE SAYING THINGS LIKE, "THERE'S A LADY WITH NO LEGS FLOATING OVER THERE!" OR, "DID YOU SEE THE PHANTOM WITH THE CRACKED HEAD?"

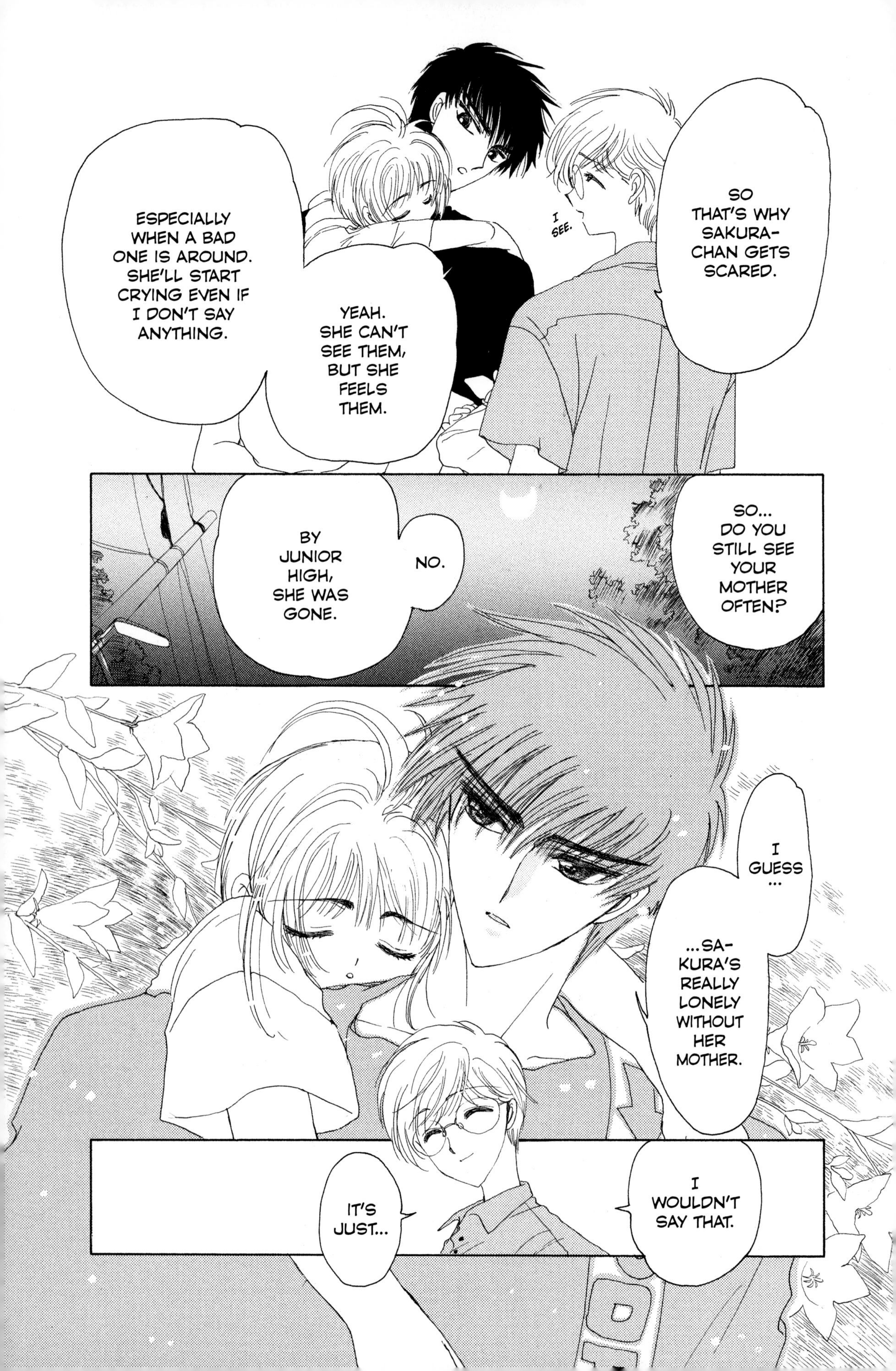
SO THAT'S WHY SAKURA-CHAN GETS SCARED.
I SEE.
YEAH. SHE CAN'T SEE THEM, BUT SHE FEELS THEM.
ESPECIALLY WHEN A BAD ONE IS AROUND. SHE'LL START CRYING EVEN IF I DON'T SAY ANYTHING.
SO... DO YOU STILL SEE YOUR MOTHER OFTEN?
NO.
BY JUNIOR HIGH, SHE WAS GONE.
I GUESS ...
...SA-KURA'S REALLY LONELY WITHOUT HER MOTHER.
I WOULDN'T SAY THAT.
IT'S JUST...

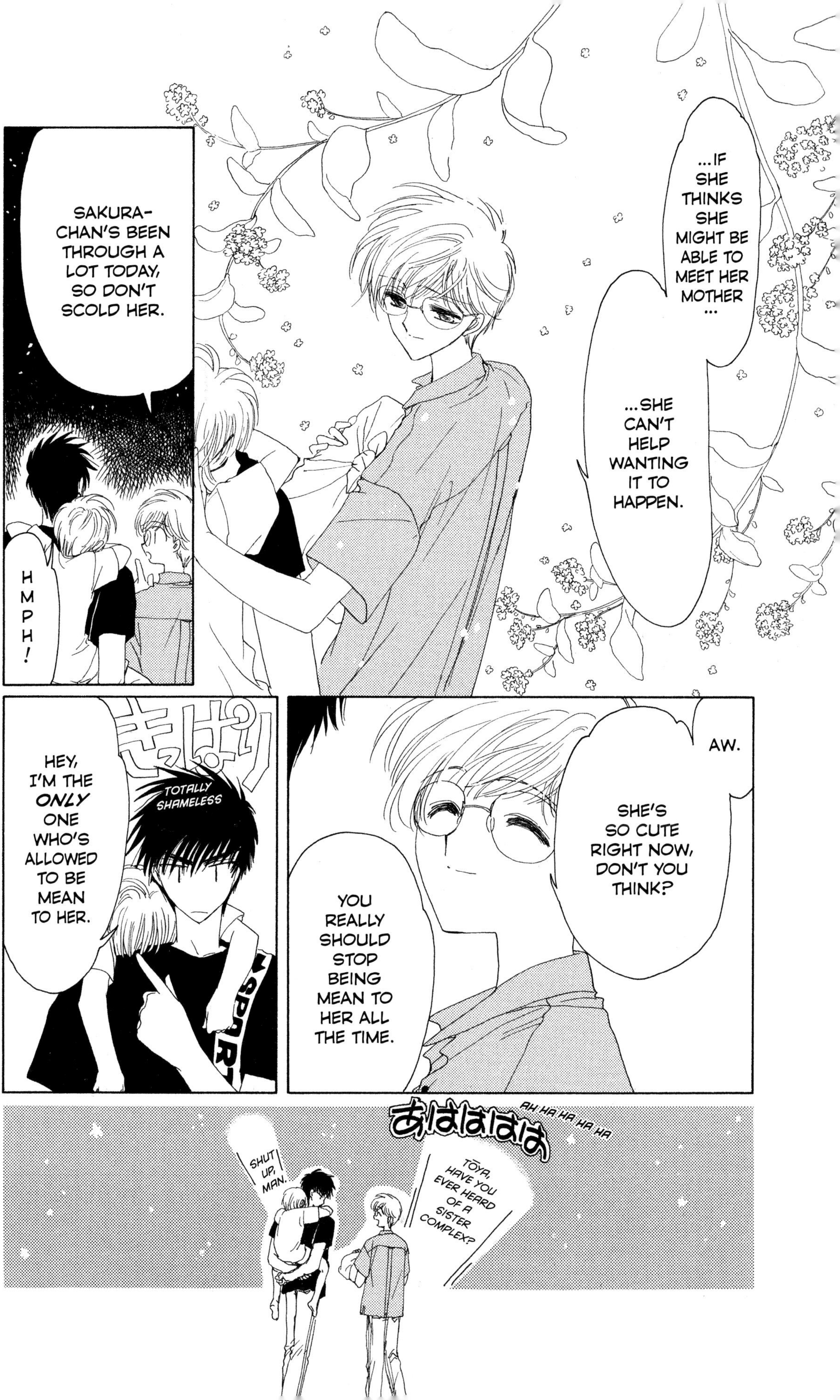
...IF SHE THINKS SHE MIGHT BE ABLE TO MEET HER MOTHER ...
...SHE CAN'T HELP WANTING IT TO HAPPEN.
SAKURA-CHAN'S BEEN THROUGH A LOT TODAY, SO DON'T SCOLD HER.
HMPH!
AW.
SHE'S SO CUTE RIGHT NOW, DON'T YOU THINK?
YOU REALLY SHOULD STOP BEING MEAN TO HER ALL THE TIME.
きっぱり
TOTALLY SHAMELESS
HEY, I'M THE *ONLY* ONE WHO'S ALLOWED TO BE MEAN TO HER.
あはははは
AH HA HA HA HA
TŌYA, HAVE YOU EVER HEARD OF A SISTER COMPLEX?
SHUT UP, MAN.

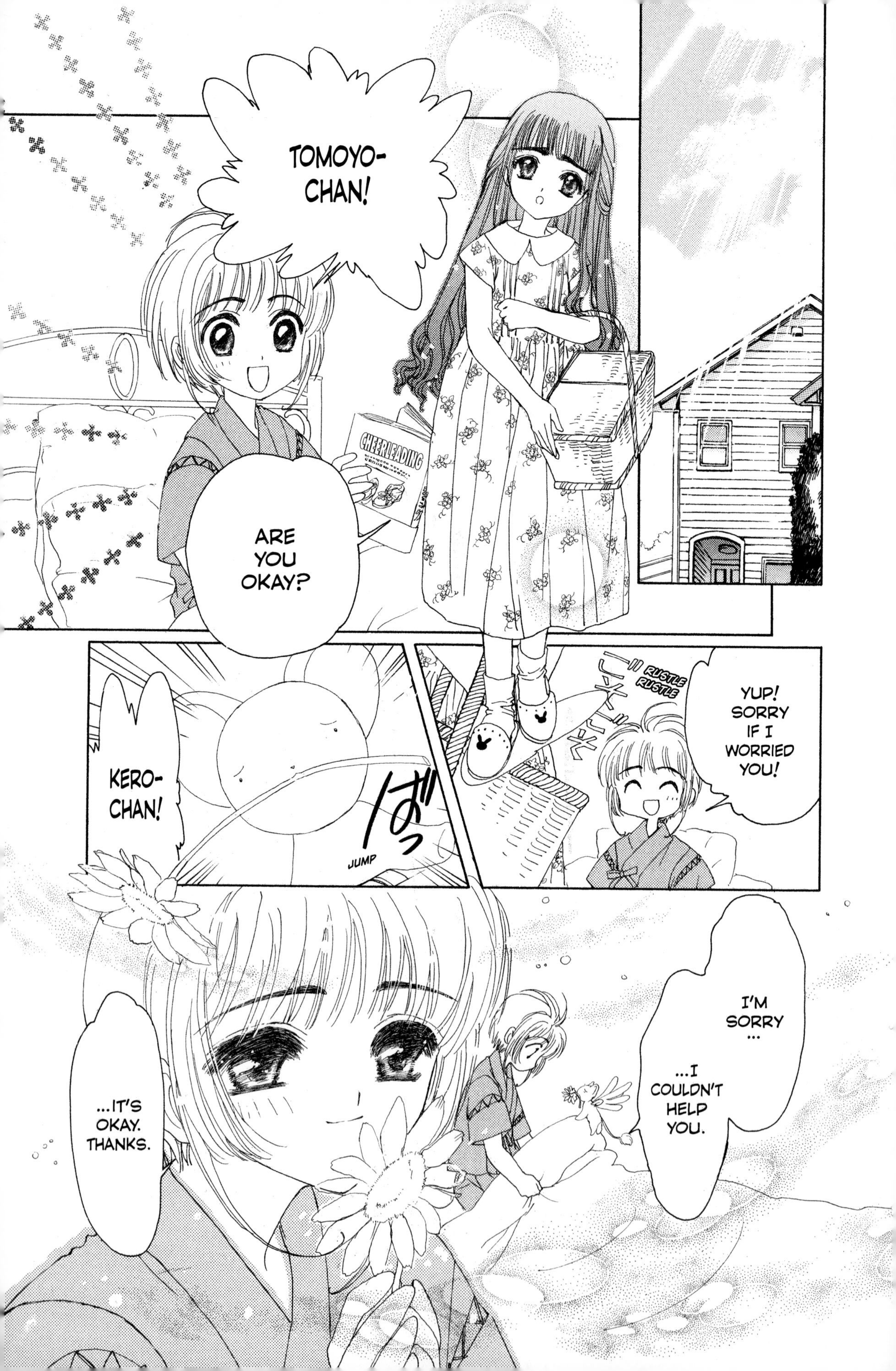
TOMOYO-CHAN!
CHEERLEADING
ARE YOU OKAY?
RUSTLE RUSTLE
YUP! SORRY IF I WORRIED YOU!
KERO-CHAN!
JUMP
I'M SORRY...
...I COULDN'T HELP YOU.
...IT'S OKAY. THANKS.

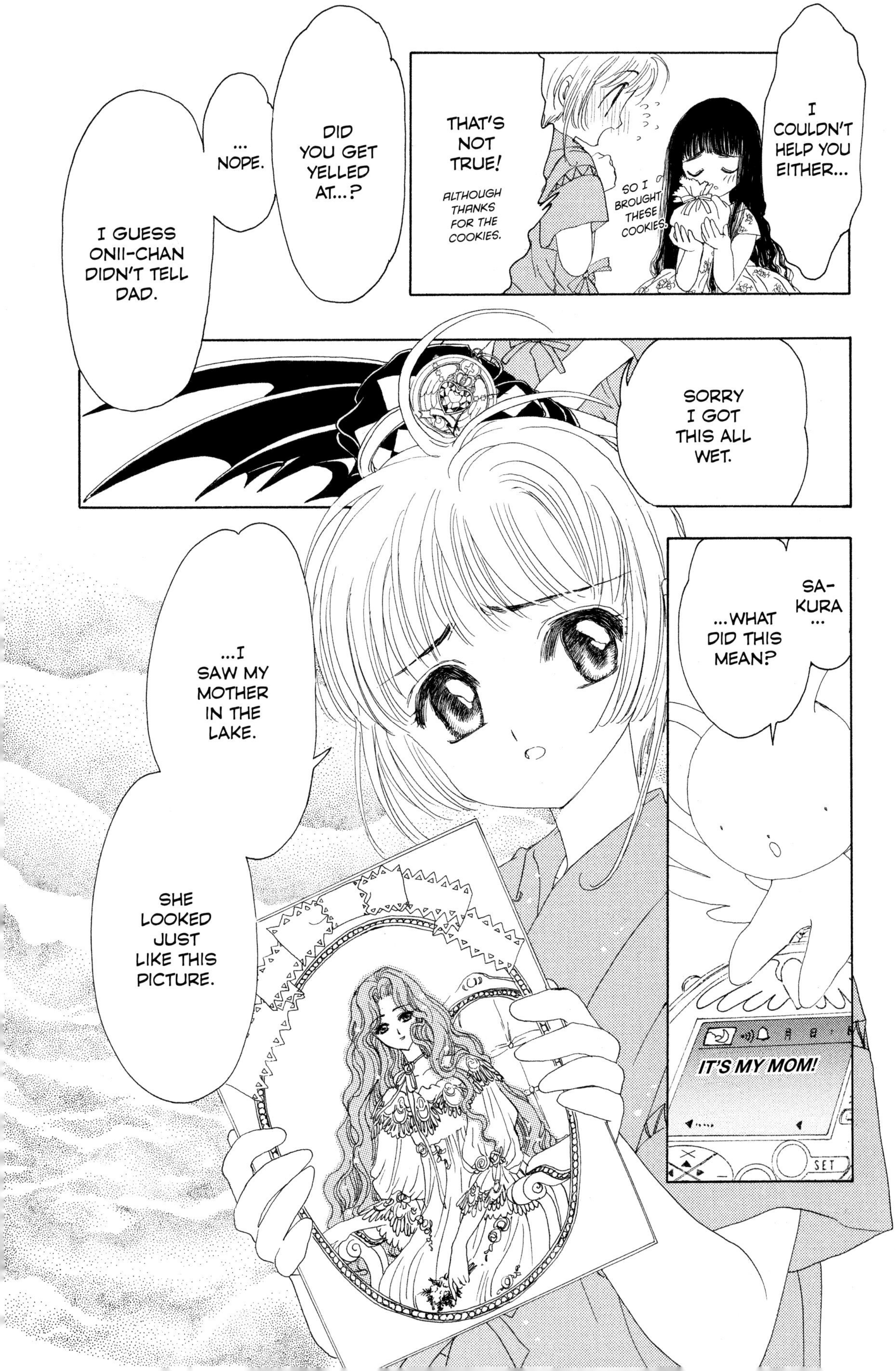
I COULDN'T HELP YOU EITHER...
SO I BROUGHT THESE COOKIES.
THAT'S NOT TRUE!
ALTHOUGH THANKS FOR THE COOKIES.
DID YOU GET YELLED AT...?
...NOPE.
I GUESS ONII-CHAN DIDN'T TELL DAD.
SORRY I GOT THIS ALL WET.
SA-KURA...
...WHAT DID THIS MEAN?
IT'S MY MOM!
...I SAW MY MOTHER IN THE LAKE.
SHE LOOKED JUST LIKE THIS PICTURE.

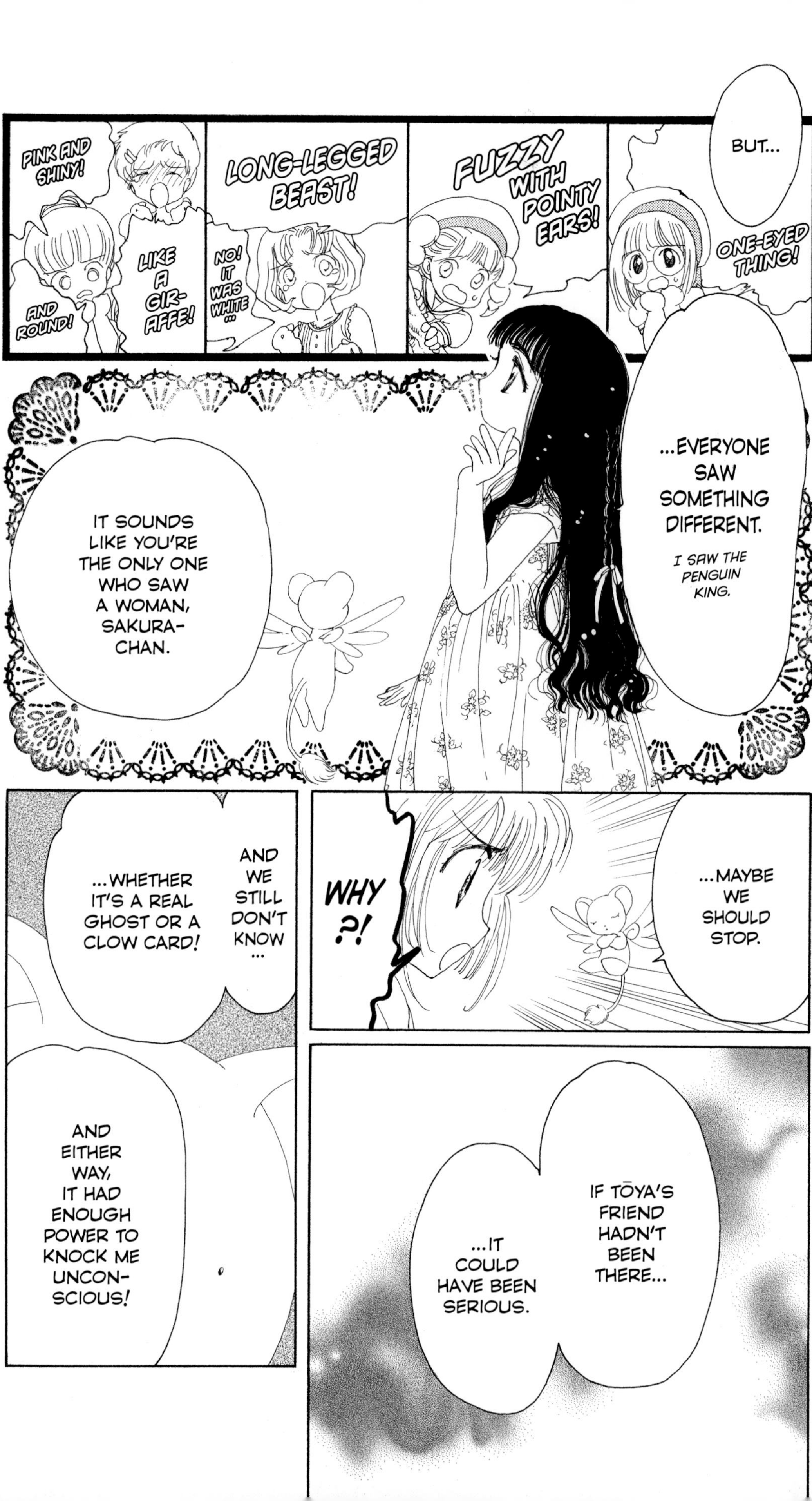
BUT...
ONE-EYED THING!
FUZZY WITH POINTY EARS!
NO! IT WAS WHITE...
LONG-LEGGED BEAST!
PINK AND SHINY!
LIKE A GIRAFFE!
AND ROUND!
...EVERYONE SAW SOMETHING DIFFERENT.
I SAW THE PENGUIN KING.
IT SOUNDS LIKE YOU'RE THE ONLY ONE WHO SAW A WOMAN, SAKURA-CHAN.
...MAYBE WE SHOULD STOP.
WHY?!
AND WE STILL DON'T KNOW...
...WHETHER IT'S A REAL GHOST OR A CLOW CARD!
AND EITHER WAY, IT HAD ENOUGH POWER TO KNOCK ME UNCONSCIOUS!
IF TŌYA'S FRIEND HADN'T BEEN THERE...
...IT COULD HAVE BEEN SERIOUS.

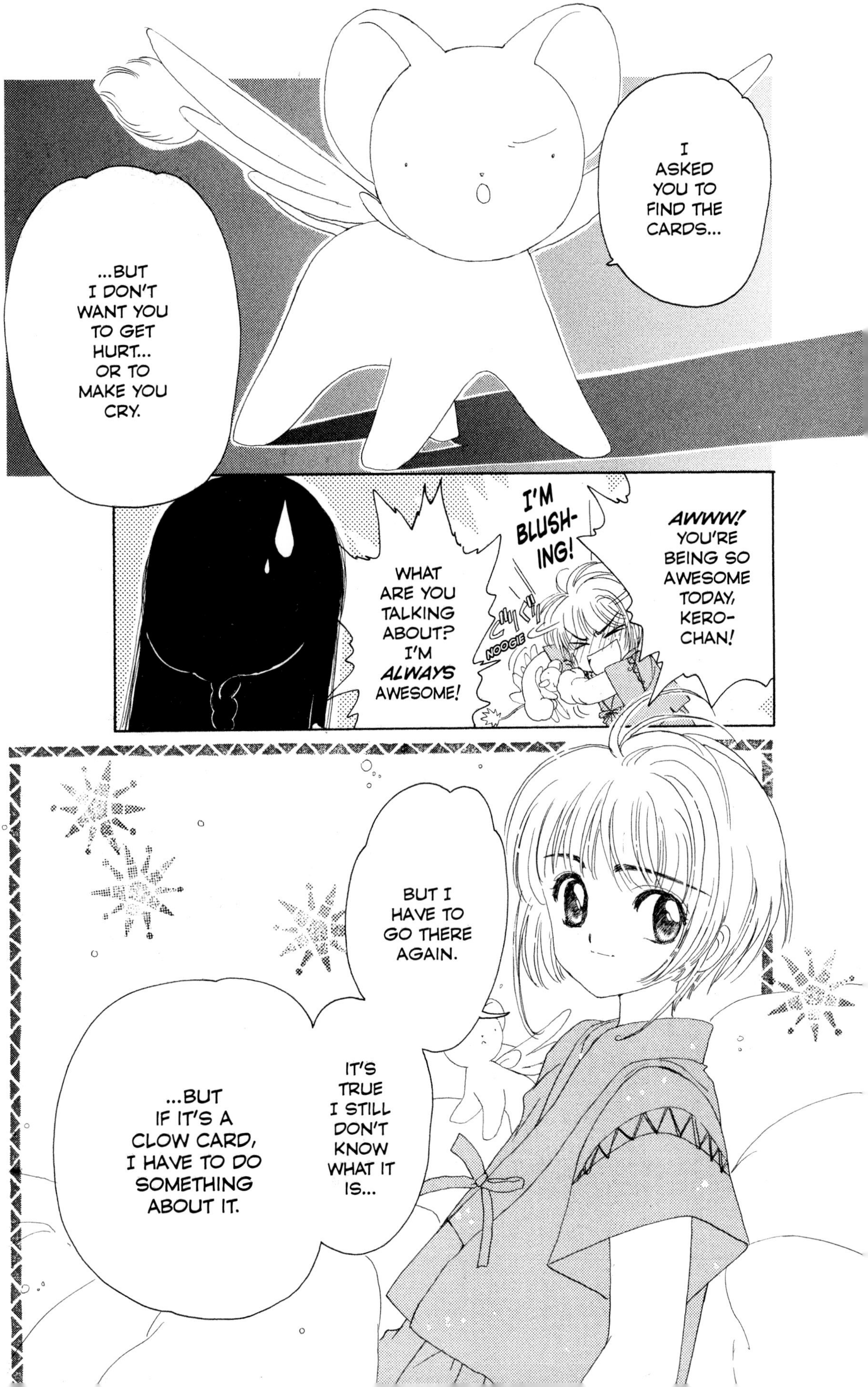
I ASKED YOU TO FIND THE CARDS...
...BUT I DON'T WANT YOU TO GET HURT... OR TO MAKE YOU CRY.
AWWW! YOU'RE BEING SO AWESOME TODAY, KERO-CHAN!
I'M BLUSH-ING!
NOOGIE
WHAT ARE YOU TALKING ABOUT? I'M *ALWAYS* AWESOME!
BUT I HAVE TO GO THERE AGAIN.
IT'S TRUE I STILL DON'T KNOW WHAT IT IS...
...BUT IF IT'S A CLOW CARD, I HAVE TO DO SOMETHING ABOUT IT.

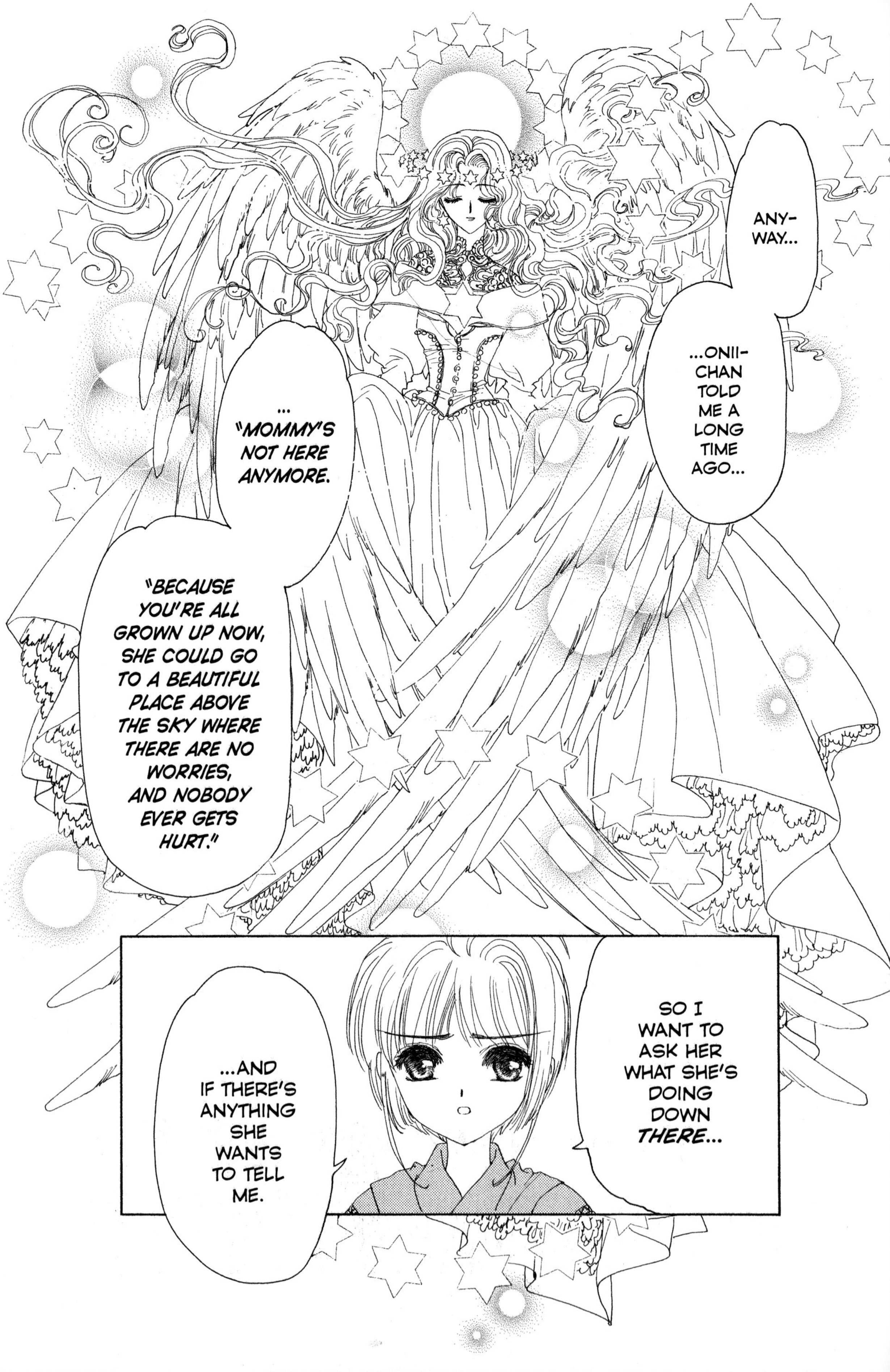
ANY-WAY...
...ONII-CHAN TOLD ME A LONG TIME AGO...
... "MOMMY'S NOT HERE ANYMORE.
"BECAUSE YOU'RE ALL GROWN UP NOW, SHE COULD GO TO A BEAUTIFUL PLACE ABOVE THE SKY WHERE THERE ARE NO WORRIES, AND NOBODY EVER GETS HURT."
SO I WANT TO ASK HER WHAT SHE'S DOING DOWN THERE...
...AND IF THERE'S ANYTHING SHE WANTS TO TELL ME.

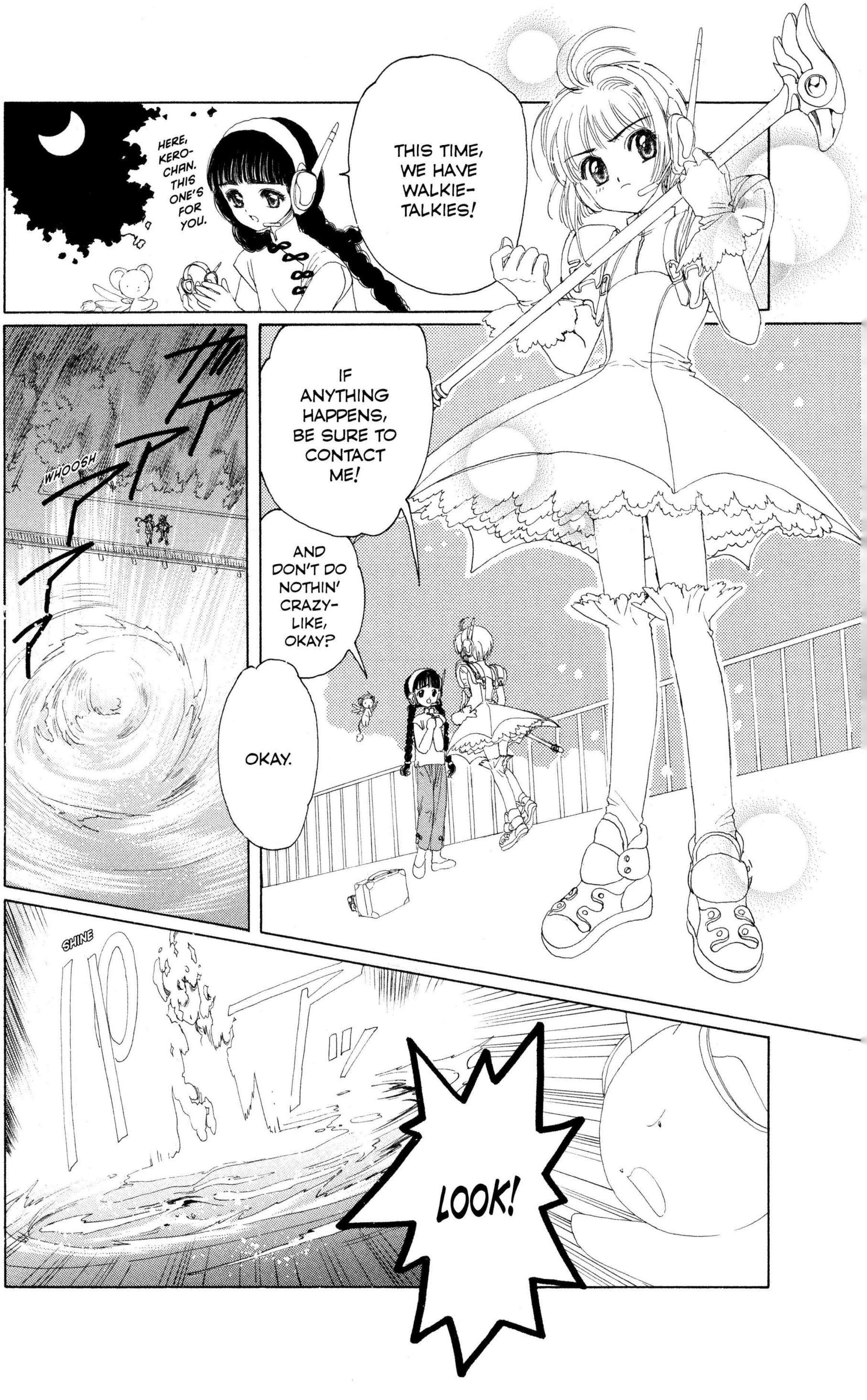
THIS TIME, WE HAVE WALKIE-TALKIES!
HERE, KERO-CHAN. THIS ONE'S FOR YOU.
IF ANYTHING HAPPENS, BE SURE TO CONTACT ME!
AND DON'T DO NOTHIN' CRAZY-LIKE, OKAY?
OKAY.
WHOOSH
LOOK!
SHINE

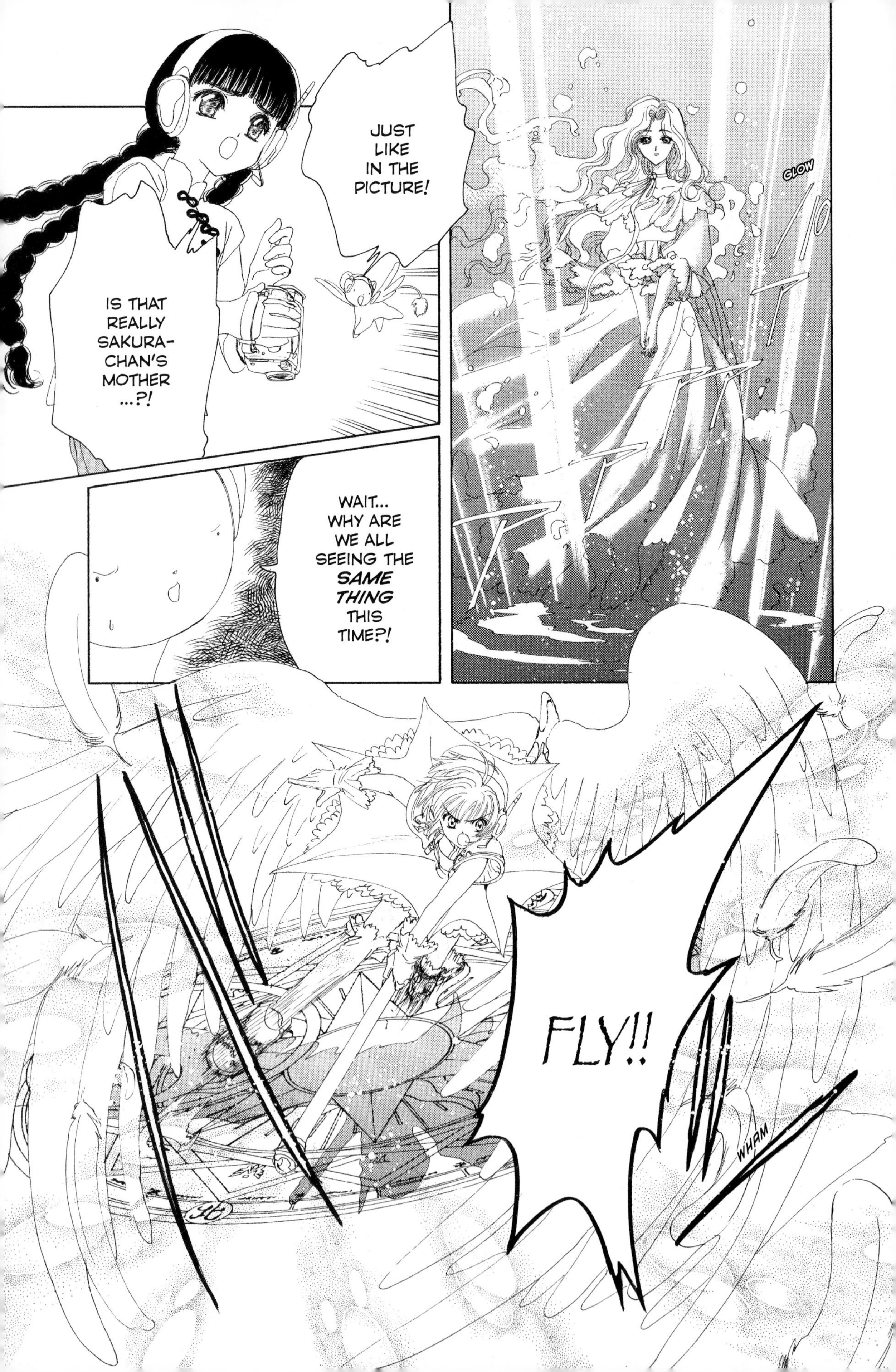
GLOW
JUST LIKE IN THE PICTURE!
IS THAT REALLY SAKURA-CHAN'S MOTHER ...?!
WAIT... WHY ARE WE ALL SEEING THE *SAME THING* THIS TIME?!
FLY!!
WHAM

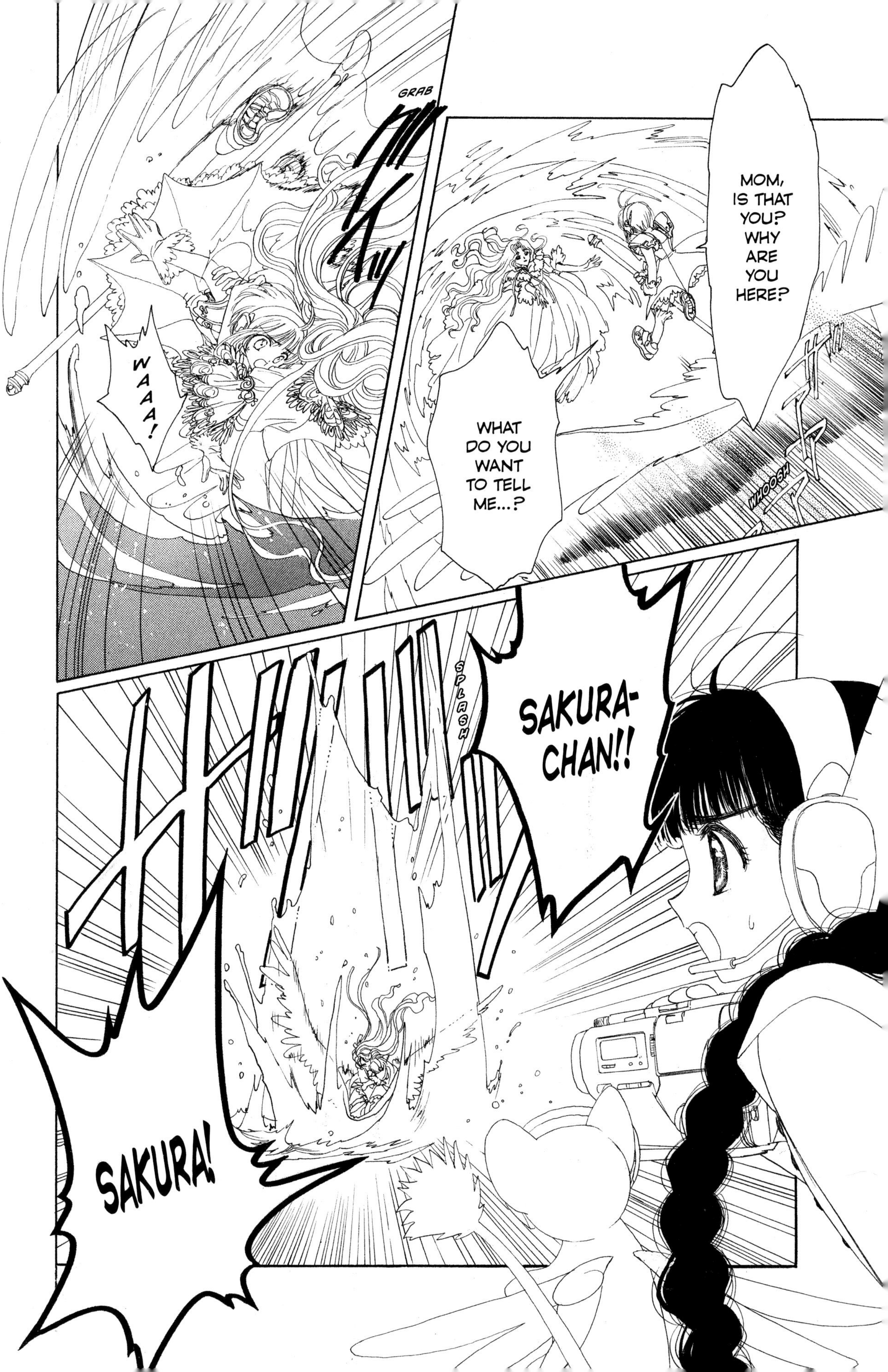
MOM, IS THAT YOU? WHY ARE YOU HERE?
WHAT DO YOU WANT TO TELL ME...?
WHOOSH
GRAB
WAAAA!
SAKURA-CHAN!!
SPLASH
SAKURA!

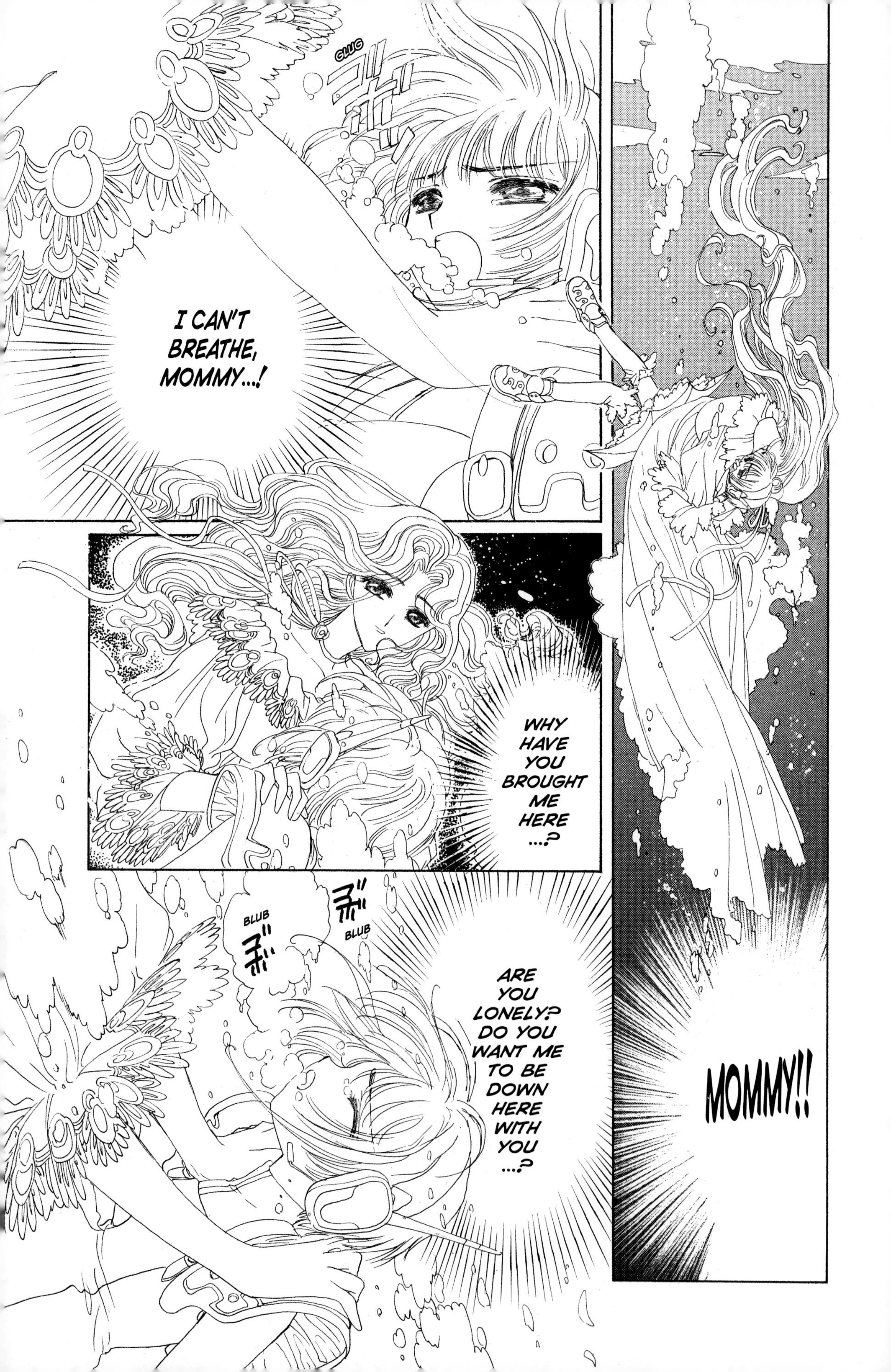
MOMMY!!
GLUG
I CAN'T BREATHE, MOMMY...!
WHY HAVE YOU BROUGHT ME HERE ...?
BLUB
BLUB
ARE YOU LONELY? DO YOU WANT ME TO BE DOWN HERE WITH YOU ...?

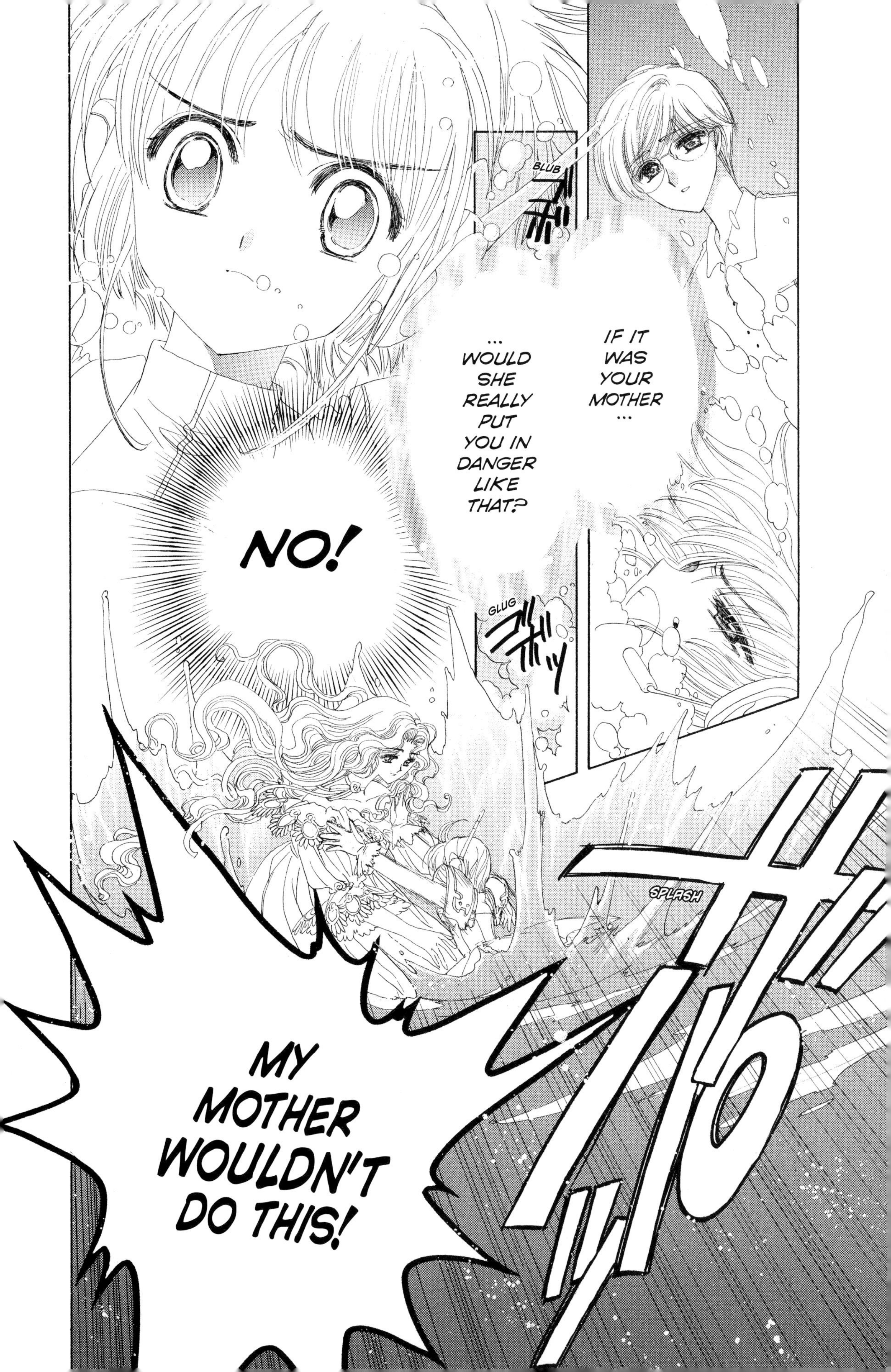
IF IT WAS YOUR MOTHER ...
... WOULD SHE REALLY PUT YOU IN DANGER LIKE THAT?
BLUB
NO!
GLUG
SPLASH
MY MOTHER WOULDN'T DO THIS!

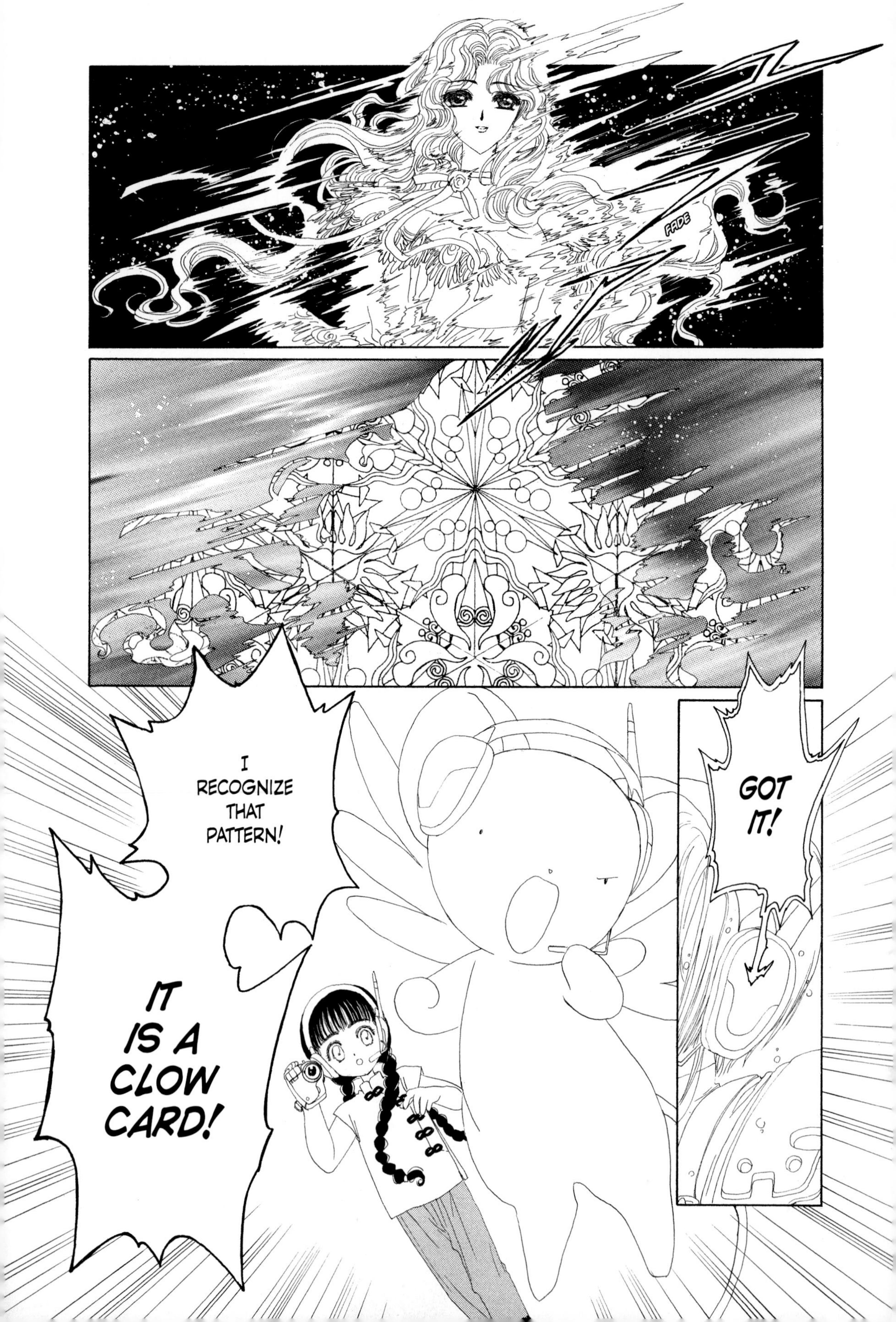
FADE
GOT IT!
I RECOGNIZE THAT PATTERN!
IT IS A CLOW CARD!

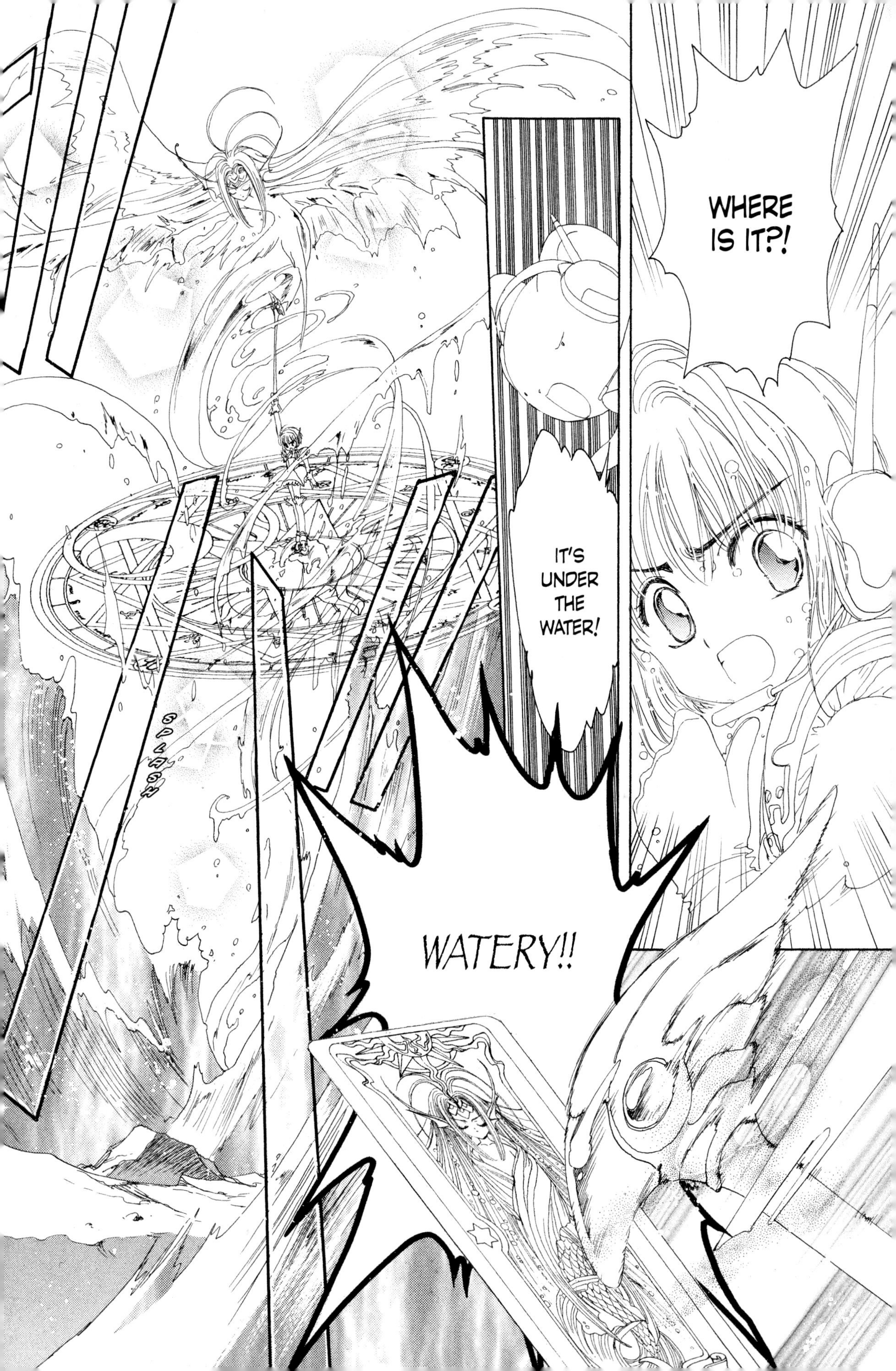
WHERE IS IT?!
IT'S UNDER THE WATER!
WATERY!!
SPLASH

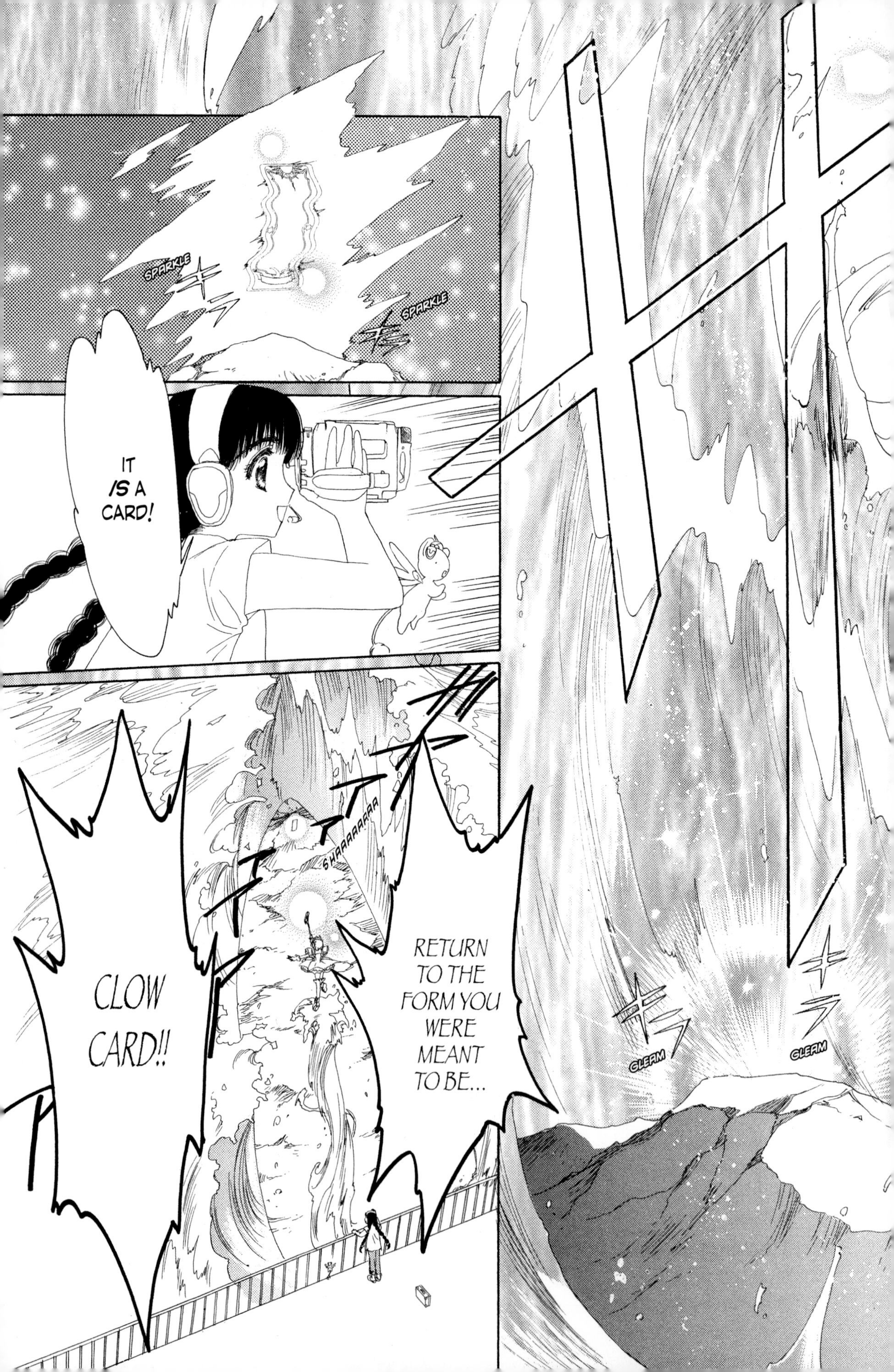
GLEAM
GLEAM
SPARKLE
SPARKLE
IT IS A CARD!
SHAAAAAAAA
RETURN TO THE FORM YOU WERE MEANT TO BE...
CLOW CARD!!

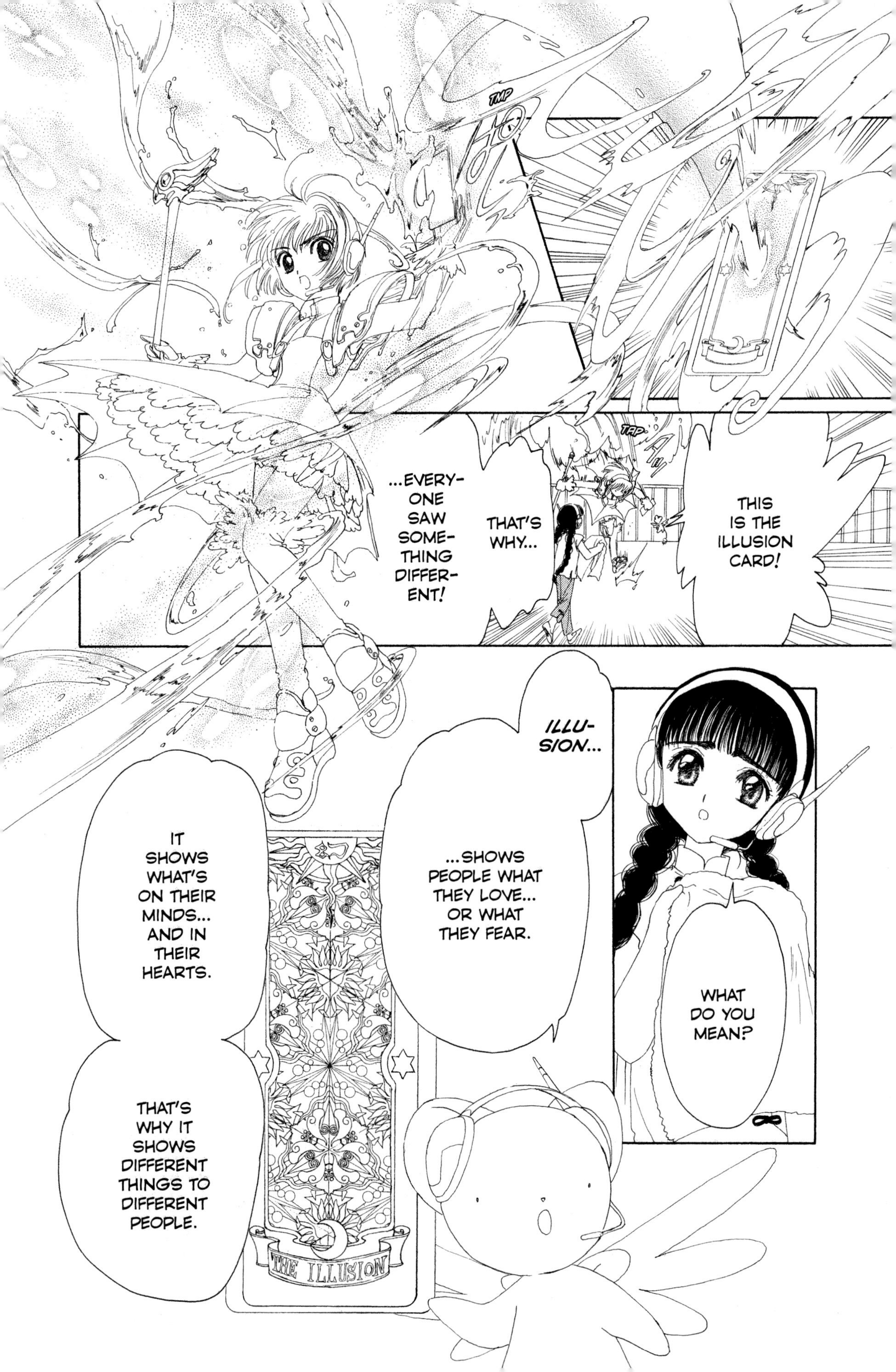
TMP
THIS IS THE ILLUSION CARD!
TAP
THAT'S WHY...
...EVERYONE SAW SOMETHING DIFFERENT!
ILLUSION...
WHAT DO YOU MEAN?
...SHOWS PEOPLE WHAT THEY LOVE... OR WHAT THEY FEAR.
IT SHOWS WHAT'S ON THEIR MINDS... AND IN THEIR HEARTS.
THAT'S WHY IT SHOWS DIFFERENT THINGS TO DIFFERENT PEOPLE.
THE ILLUSION

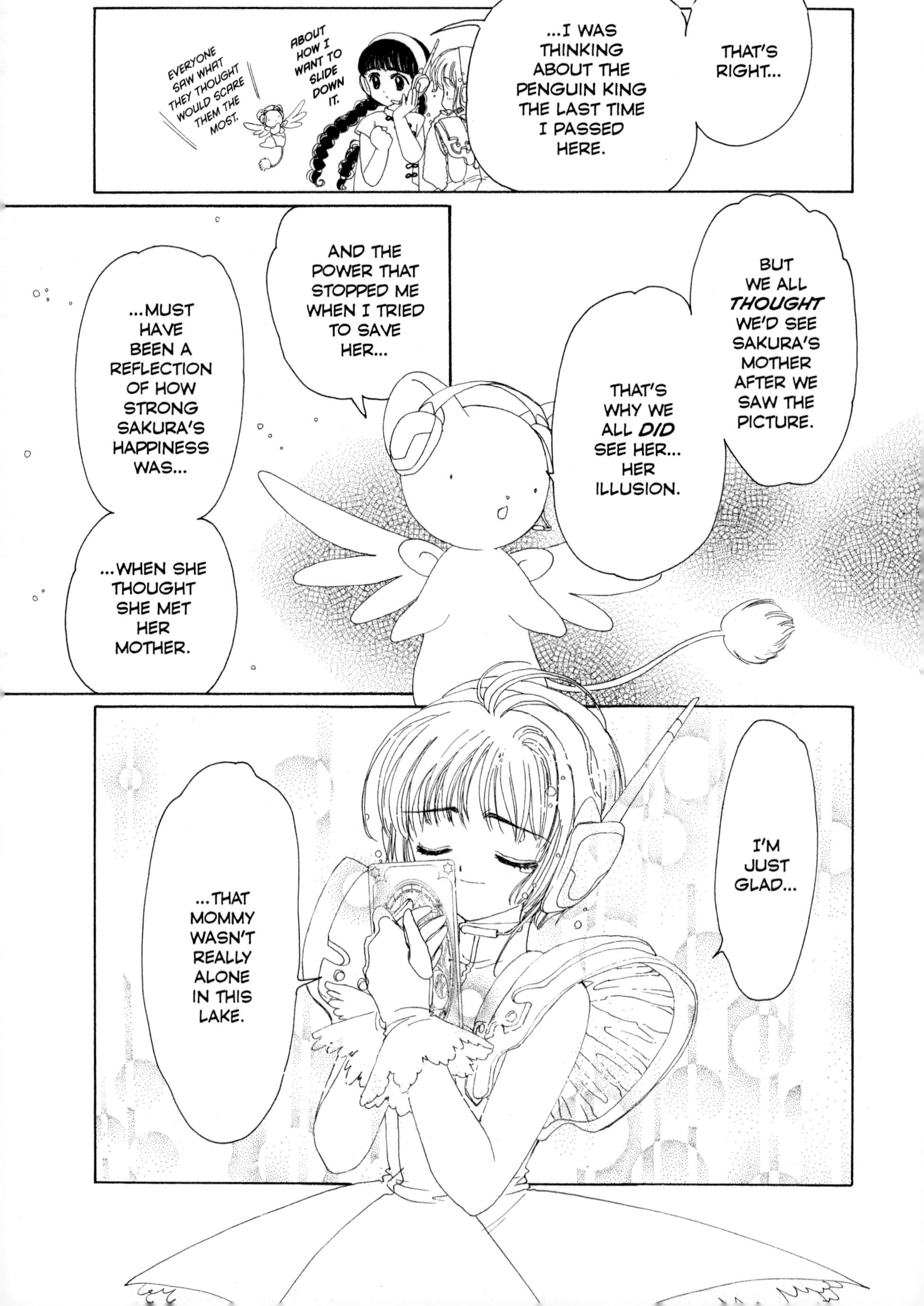
THAT'S RIGHT...
...I WAS THINKING ABOUT THE PENGUIN KING THE LAST TIME I PASSED HERE.
ABOUT HOW I WANT TO SLIDE DOWN IT.
EVERYONE SAW WHAT THEY THOUGHT WOULD SCARE THEM THE MOST.
BUT WE ALL *THOUGHT* WE'D SEE SAKURA'S MOTHER AFTER WE SAW THE PICTURE.
THAT'S WHY WE ALL *DID* SEE HER... HER ILLUSION.
AND THE POWER THAT STOPPED ME WHEN I TRIED TO SAVE HER...
...MUST HAVE BEEN A REFLECTION OF HOW STRONG SAKURA'S HAPPINESS WAS...
...WHEN SHE THOUGHT SHE MET HER MOTHER.
I'M JUST GLAD...
...THAT MOMMY WASN'T REALLY ALONE IN THIS LAKE.

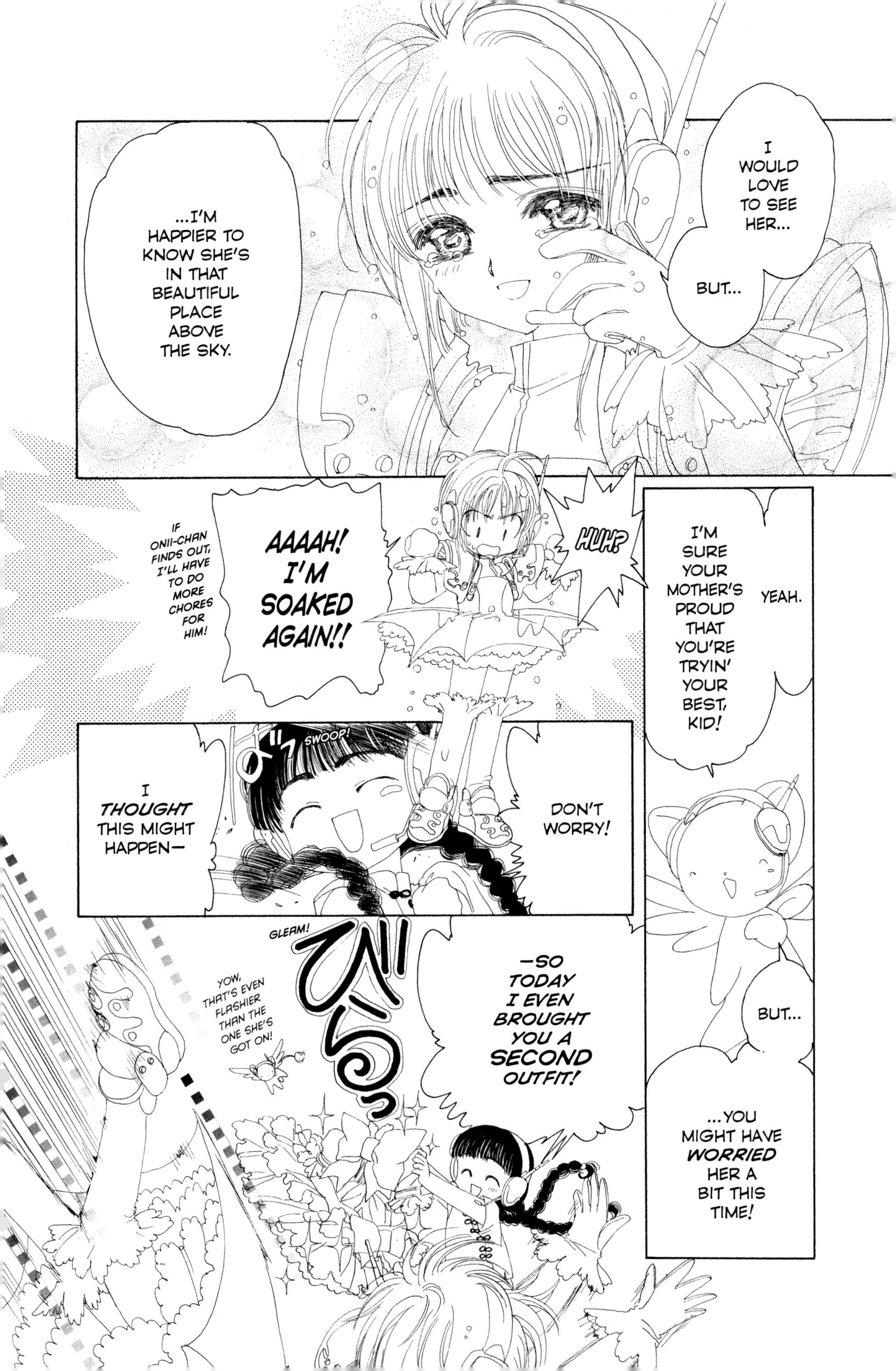
I WOULD LOVE TO SEE HER...
BUT...
...I'M HAPPIER TO KNOW SHE'S IN THAT BEAUTIFUL PLACE ABOVE THE SKY.
I'M SURE YOUR MOTHER'S PROUD THAT YOU'RE TRYIN' YOUR BEST, KID!
YEAH.
BUT...
...YOU MIGHT HAVE *WORRIED* HER A BIT THIS TIME!
HUH?
AAAAH! I'M SOAKED AGAIN!!
IF ONII-CHAN FINDS OUT, I'LL HAVE TO DO MORE CHORES FOR HIM!
SWOOP!
DON'T WORRY!
I *THOUGHT* THIS MIGHT HAPPEN—
—SO TODAY I EVEN BROUGHT YOU A SECOND OUTFIT!
GLEAM!
YOW, THAT'S EVEN FLASHIER THAN THE ONE SHE'S GOT ON!

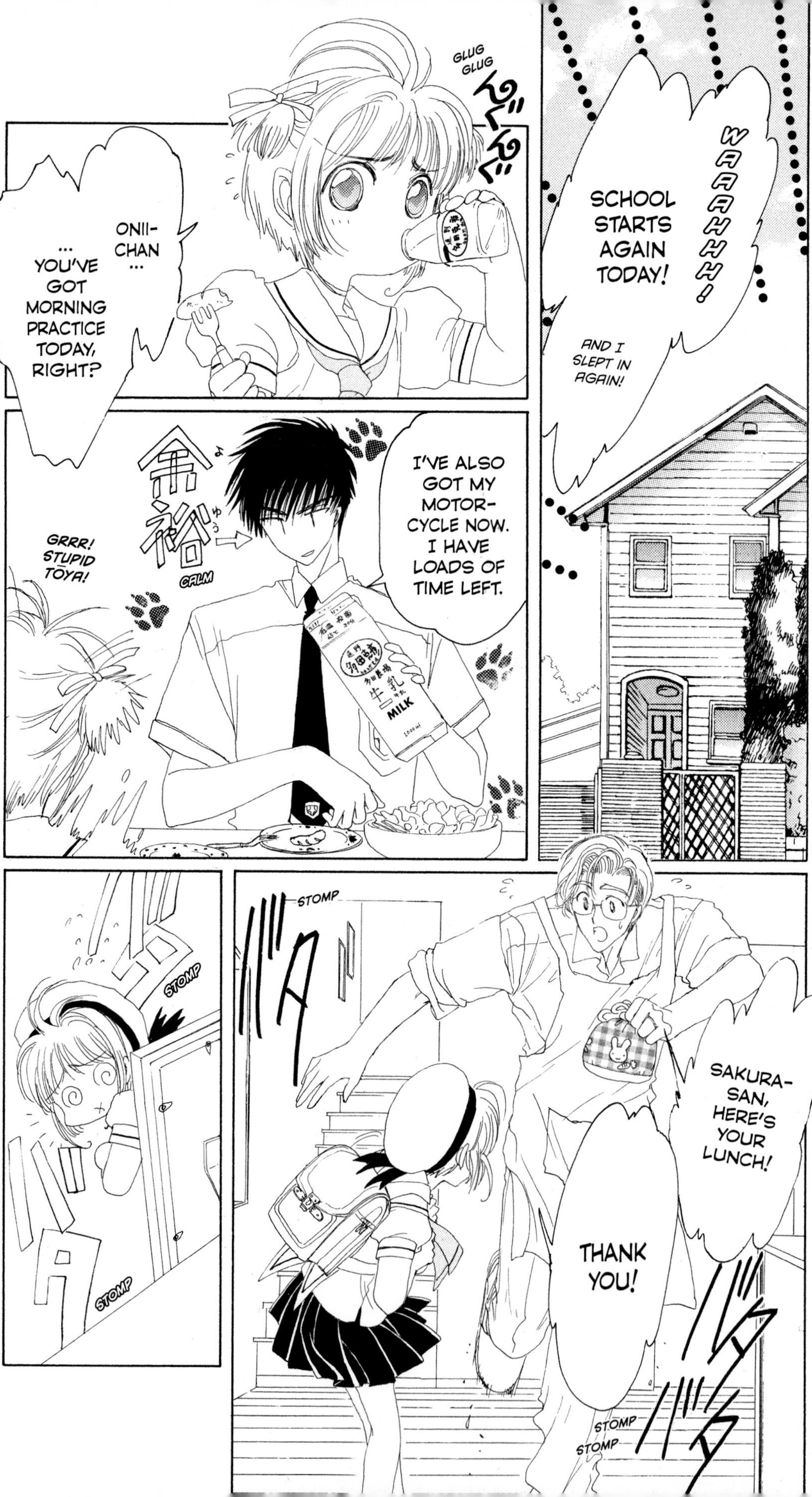
WAAAHHH!
SCHOOL STARTS AGAIN TODAY!
AND I SLEPT IN AGAIN!
GLUG GLUG
ONII-CHAN ...
... YOU'VE GOT MORNING PRACTICE TODAY, RIGHT?
I'VE ALSO GOT MY MOTOR-CYCLE NOW. I HAVE LOADS OF TIME LEFT.
CALM
GRRR! STUPID TŌYA!
MILK
STOMP
SAKURA-SAN, HERE'S YOUR LUNCH!
THANK YOU!
STOMP
STOMP
STOMP
STOMP

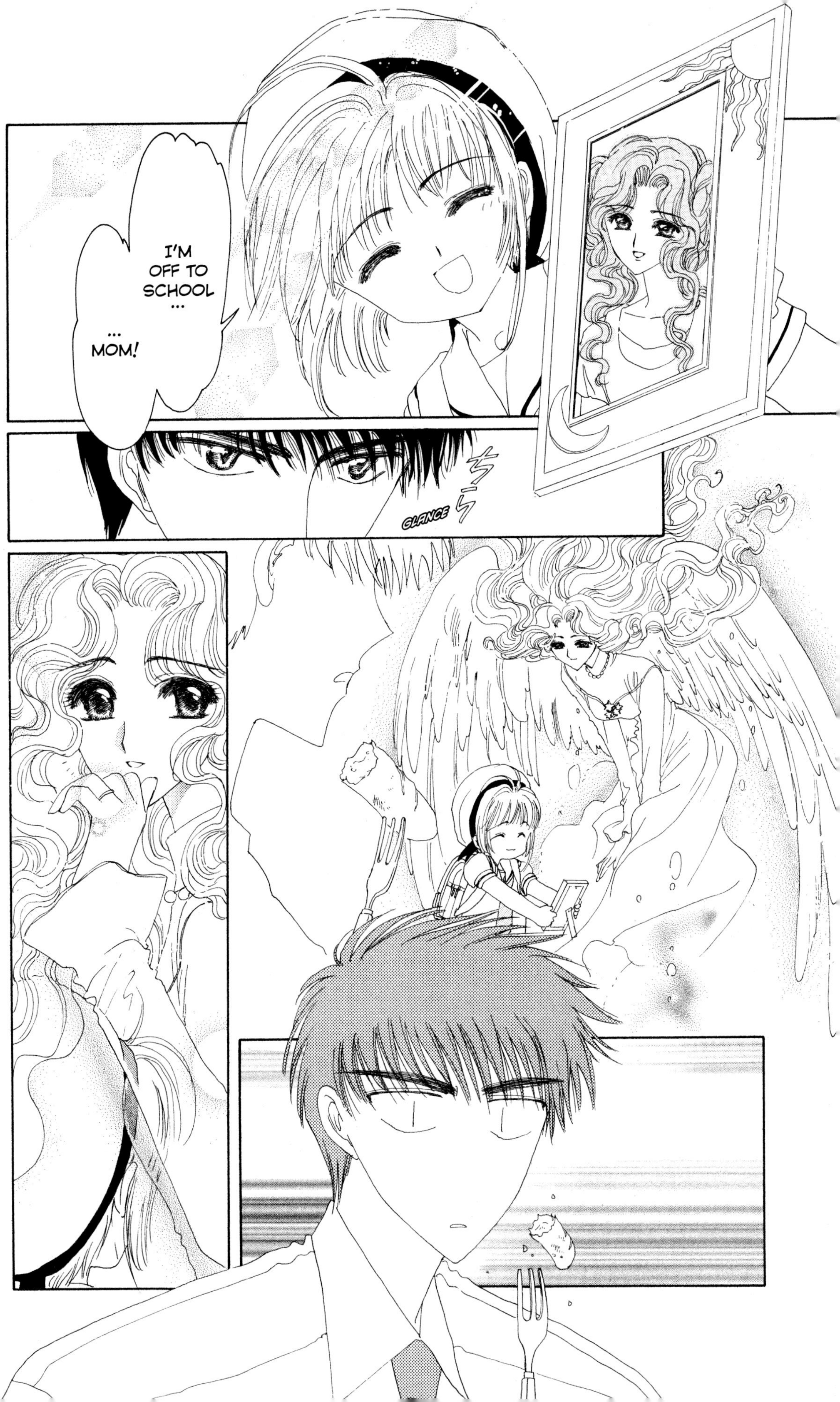
I'M OFF TO SCHOOL ...
... MOM!
GLANCE

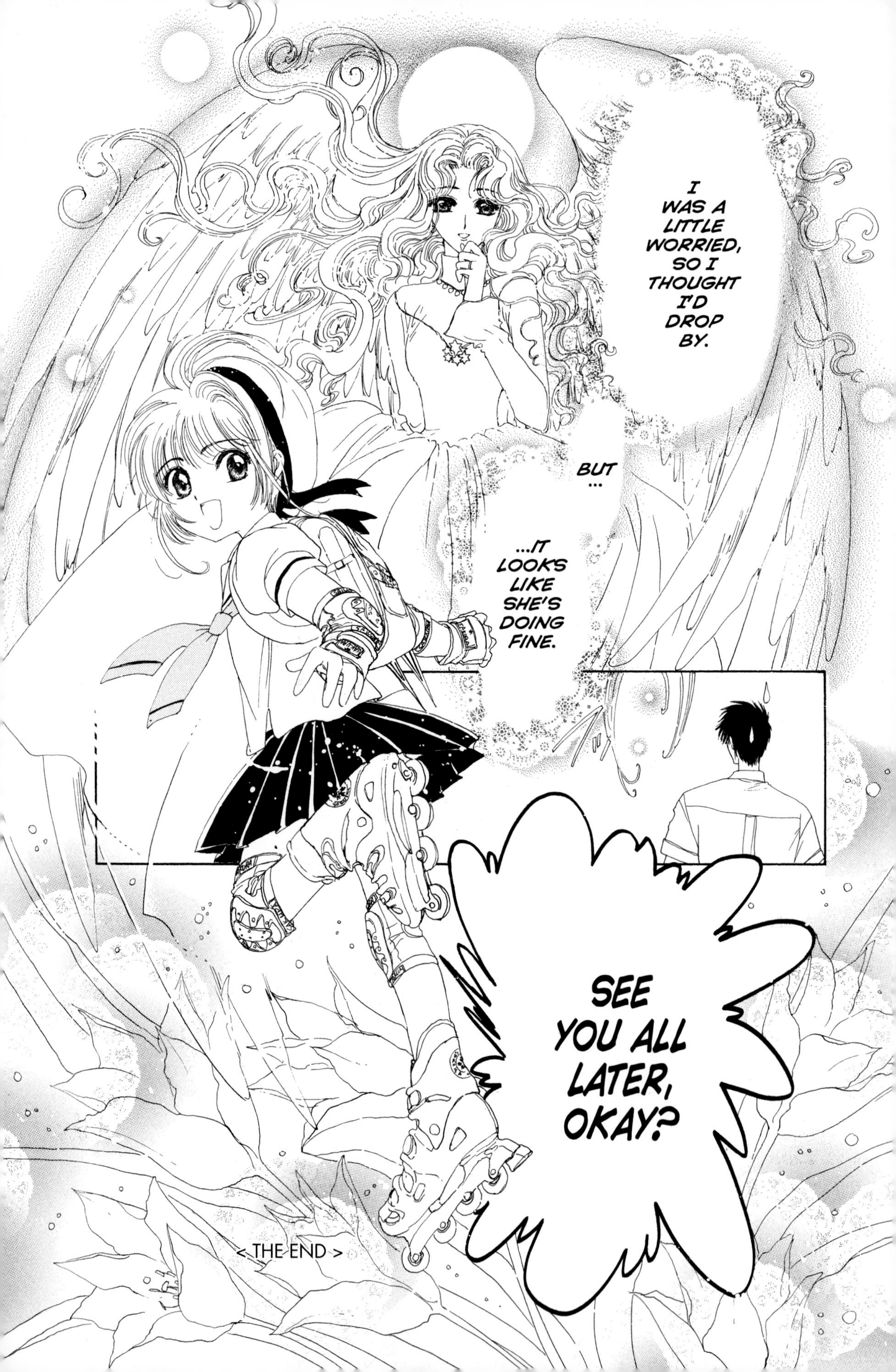
I WAS A LITTLE WORRIED, SO I THOUGHT I'D DROP BY.
BUT ...
...IT LOOKS LIKE SHE'S DOING FINE.
SEE YOU ALL LATER, OKAY?
< THE END >

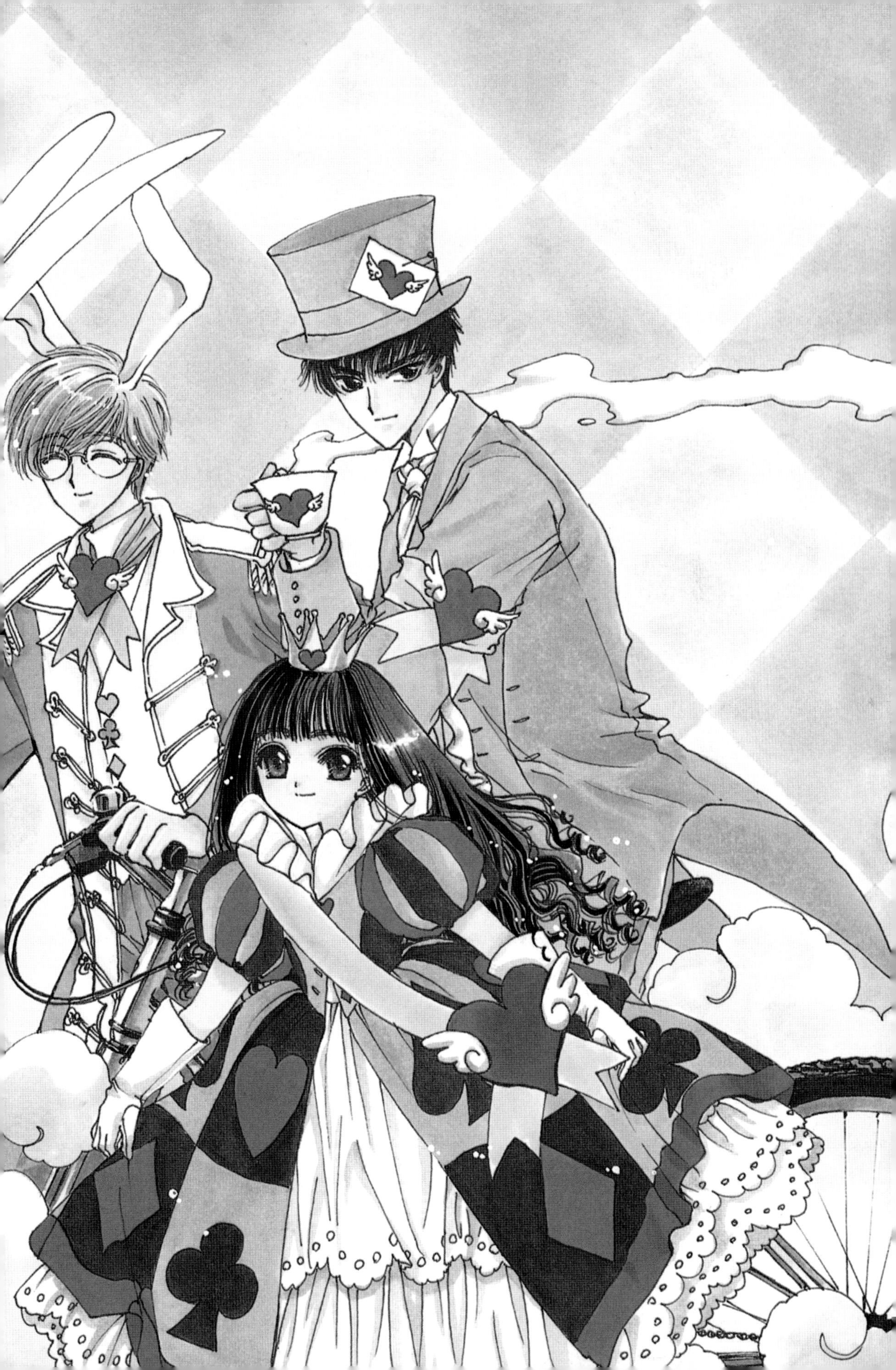

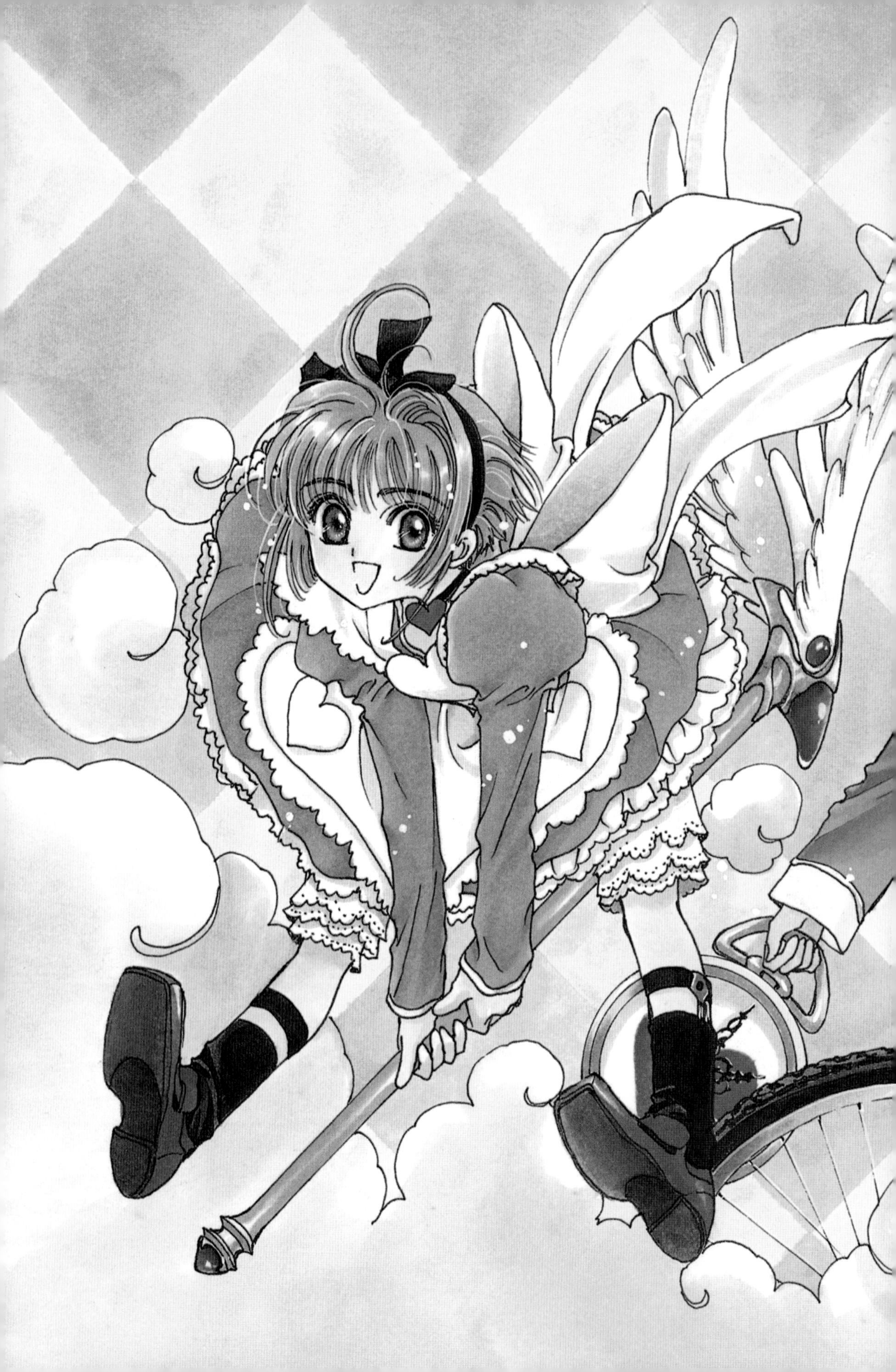

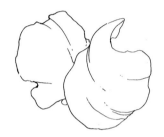
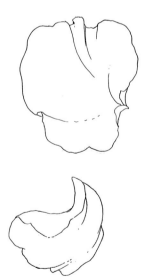

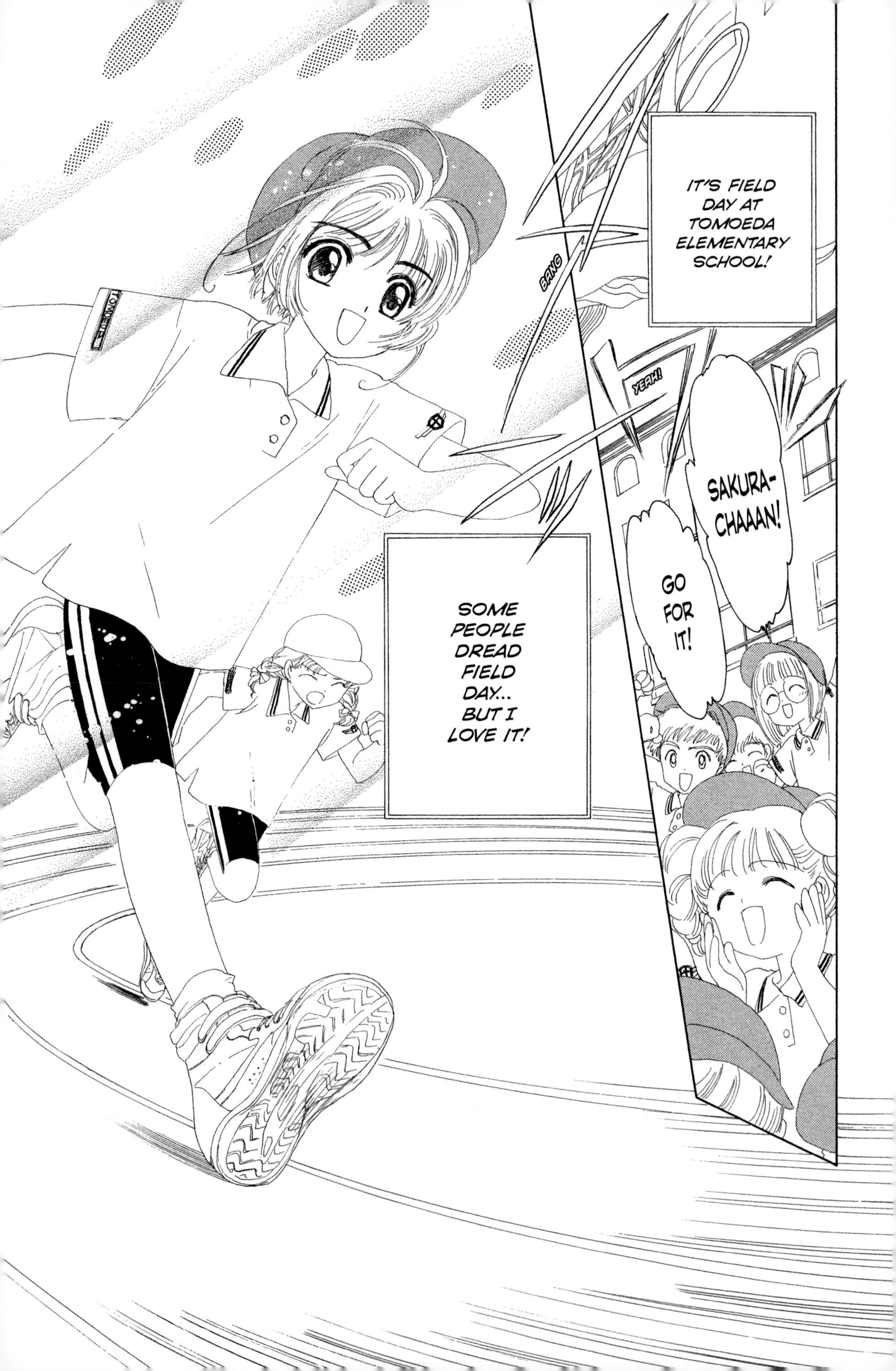
IT'S FIELD DAY AT TOMOEDA ELEMENTARY SCHOOL!
YEAH!
SAKURA-CHAAAN!
GO FOR IT!
BANG
SOME PEOPLE DREAD FIELD DAY... BUT I LOVE IT!

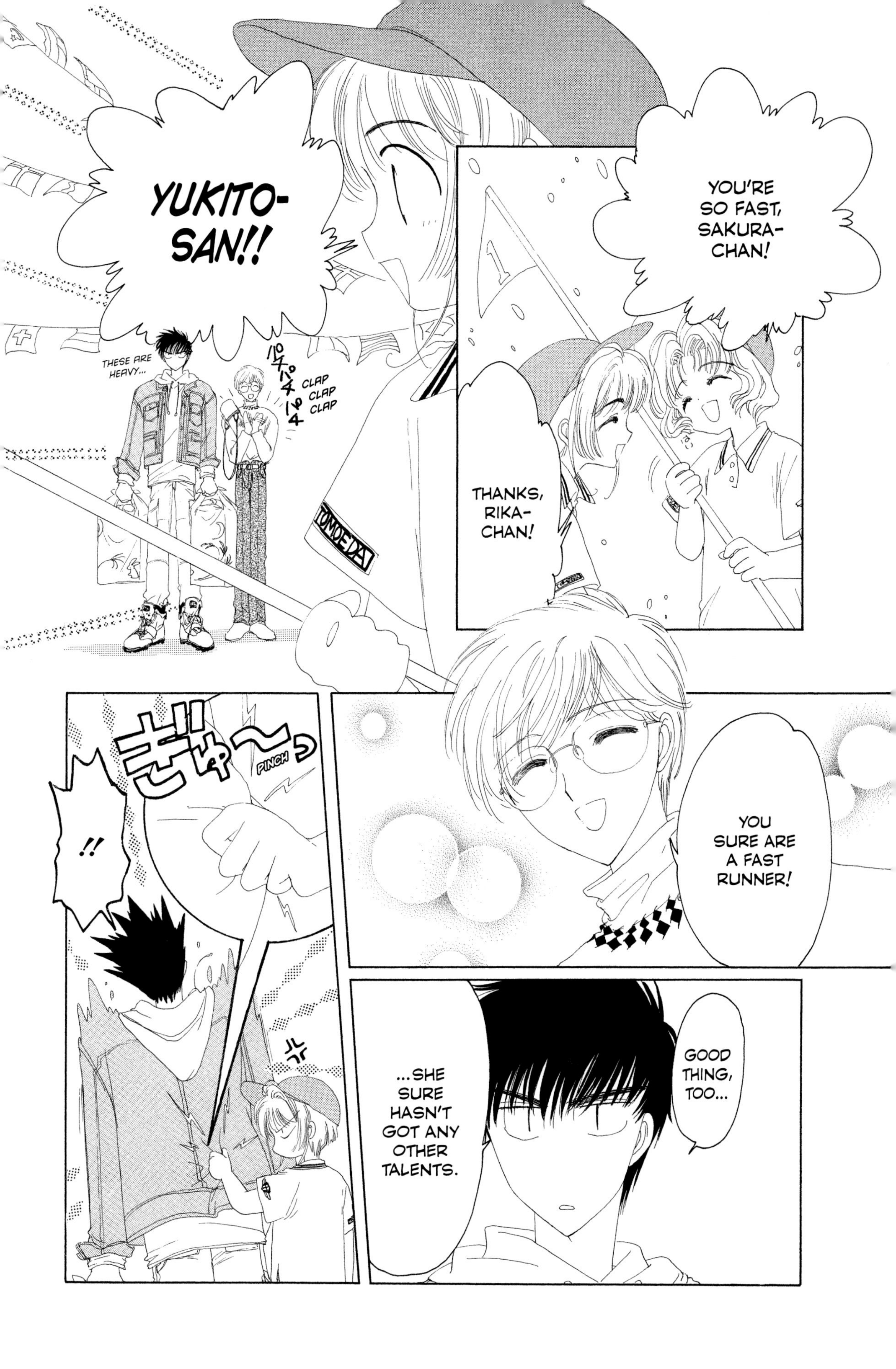

YOU'RE SO FAST, SAKURA-CHAN!
THANKS, RIKA-CHAN!
YUKITO-SAN!!
THESE ARE HEAVY...
CLAP CLAP CLAP
TOMOEDA
YOU SURE ARE A FAST RUNNER!
GOOD THING, TOO...
...SHE SURE HASN'T GOT ANY OTHER TALENTS.
ぎゅ～っ
PINCH
!!

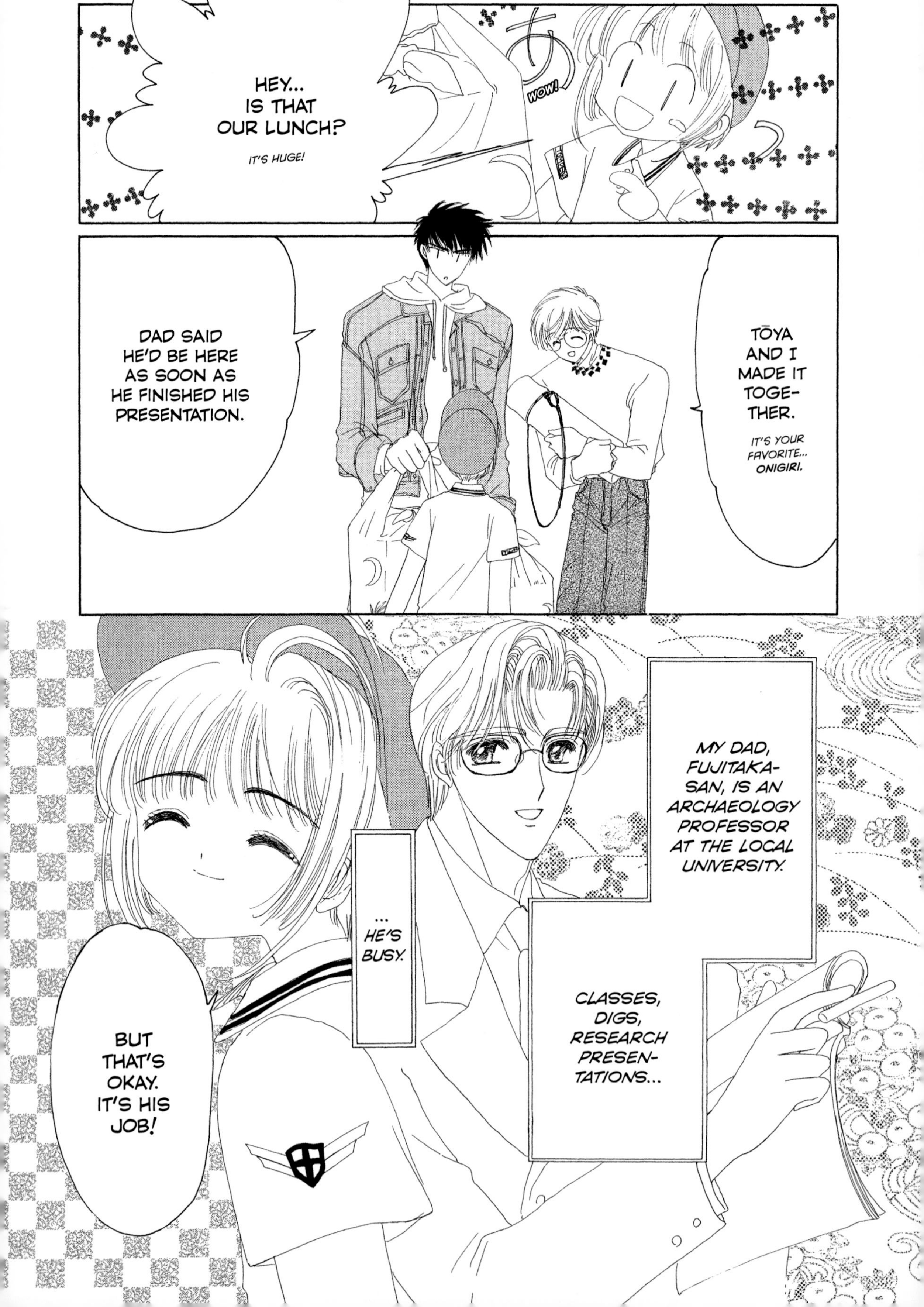
WOW!
HEY... IS THAT OUR LUNCH?
IT'S HUGE!
TŌYA AND I MADE IT TOGE-THER.
IT'S YOUR FAVORITE... ONIGIRI.
DAD SAID HE'D BE HERE AS SOON AS HE FINISHED HIS PRESENTATION.
MY DAD, FUJITAKA-SAN, IS AN ARCHAEOLOGY PROFESSOR AT THE LOCAL UNIVERSITY.
CLASSES, DIGS, RESEARCH PRESEN-TATIONS...
... HE'S BUSY.
BUT THAT'S OKAY. IT'S HIS JOB!

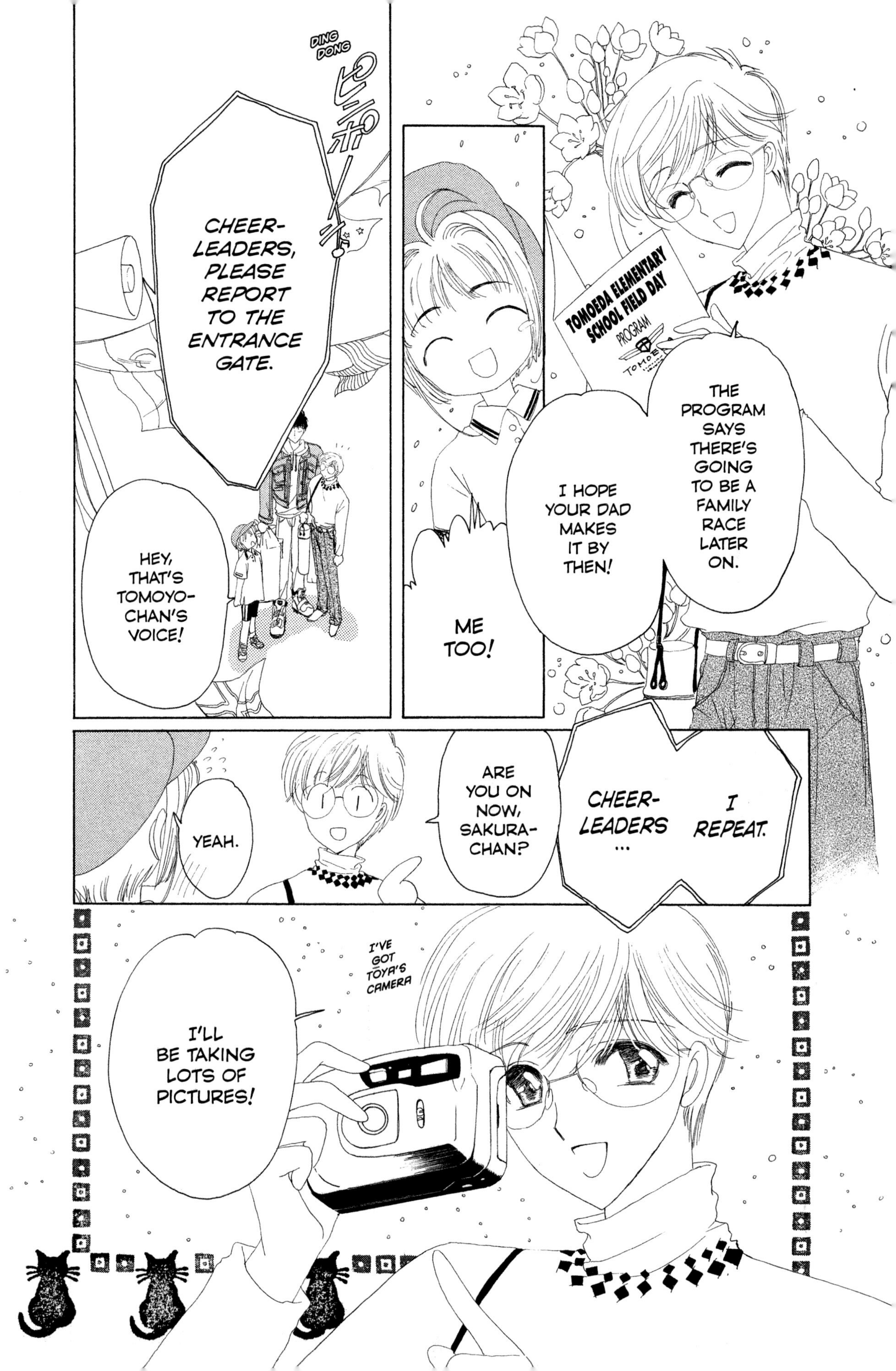
TOMOEDA ELEMENTARY SCHOOL FIELD DAY
PROGRAM
THE PROGRAM SAYS THERE'S GOING TO BE A FAMILY RACE LATER ON.
I HOPE YOUR DAD MAKES IT BY THEN!
ME TOO!
DING DONG
CHEER-LEADERS, PLEASE REPORT TO THE ENTRANCE GATE.
HEY, THAT'S TOMOYO-CHAN'S VOICE!
I REPEAT.
CHEER-LEADERS ...
ARE YOU ON NOW, SAKURA-CHAN?
YEAH.
I'VE GOT TOYA'S CAMERA
I'LL BE TAKING LOTS OF PICTURES!

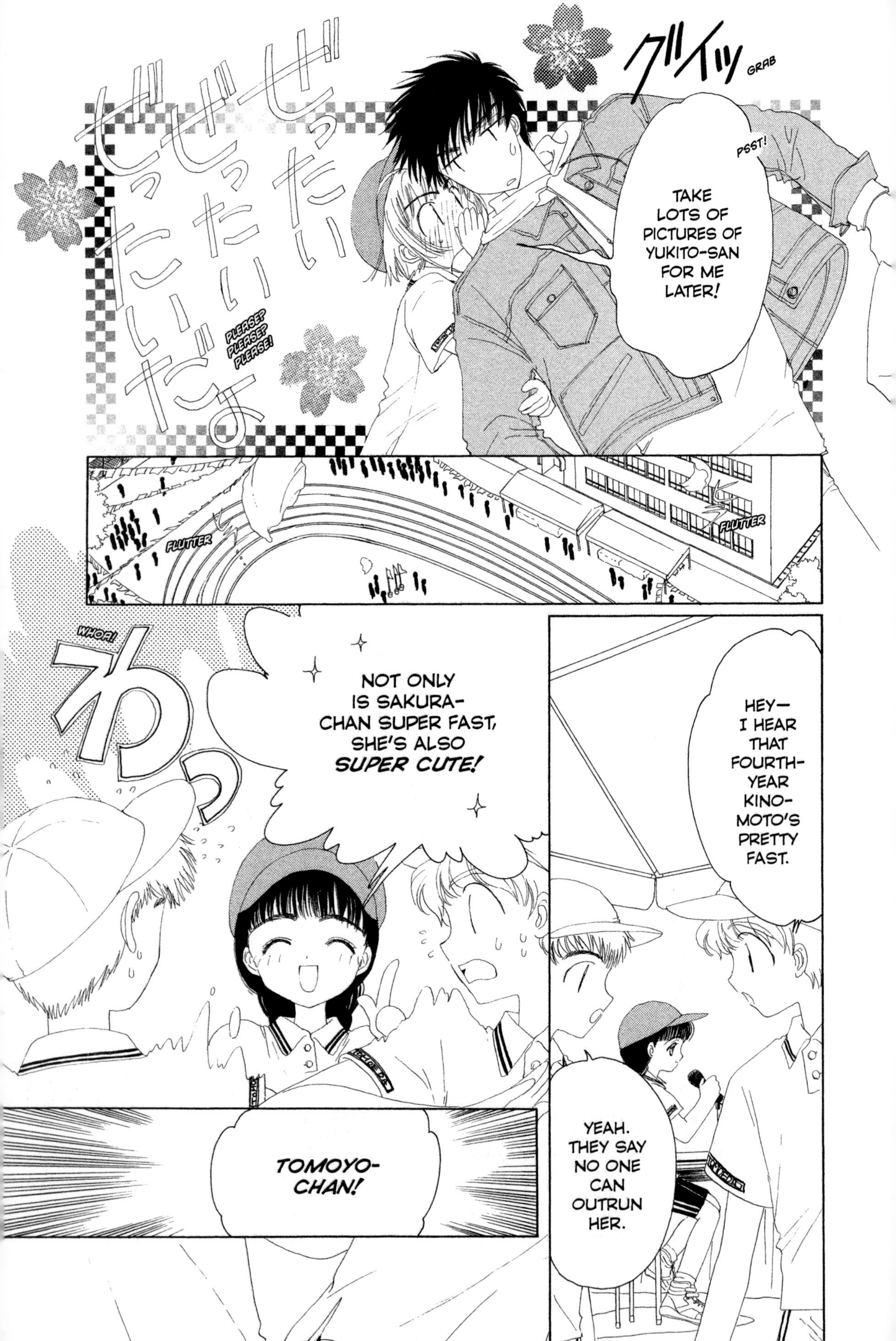
グイッ
GRAB
PSST!
TAKE LOTS OF PICTURES OF YUKITO-SAN FOR ME LATER!
ぜったいぜったいぜったいだよ
PLEASE? PLEASE? PLEASE!
FLUTTER
FLUTTER
HEY— I HEAR THAT FOURTH-YEAR KINOMOTO'S PRETTY FAST.
YEAH. THEY SAY NO ONE CAN OUTRUN HER.
わっ
WHOA!
NOT ONLY IS SAKURA-CHAN SUPER FAST, SHE'S ALSO *SUPER CUTE!*
TOMOYO-CHAN!

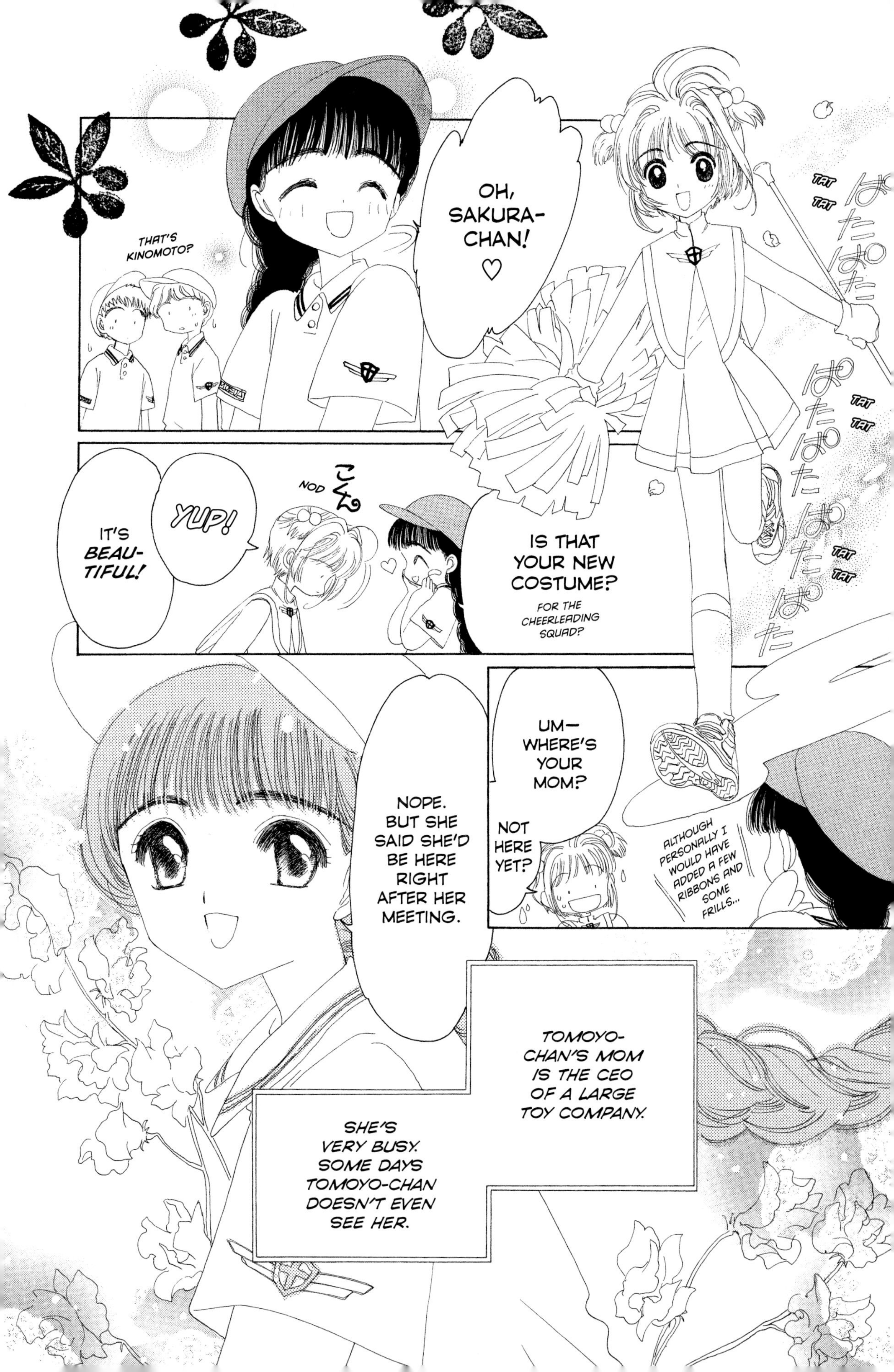
ぱたぱた
TAT TAT
ぱたぱたぱたぱた
TAT TAT
TAT TAT
OH, SAKURA-CHAN! ♡
THAT'S KINOMOTO?
IS THAT YOUR NEW COSTUME?
FOR THE CHEERLEADING SQUAD?
こくん
NOD
YUP!
IT'S BEAUTIFUL!
ALTHOUGH PERSONALLY I WOULD HAVE ADDED A FEW RIBBONS AND SOME FRILLS...
UM— WHERE'S YOUR MOM?
NOT HERE YET?
NOPE. BUT SHE SAID SHE'D BE HERE RIGHT AFTER HER MEETING.
TOMOYO-CHAN'S MOM IS THE CEO OF A LARGE TOY COMPANY.
SHE'S VERY BUSY. SOME DAYS TOMOYO-CHAN DOESN'T EVEN SEE HER.

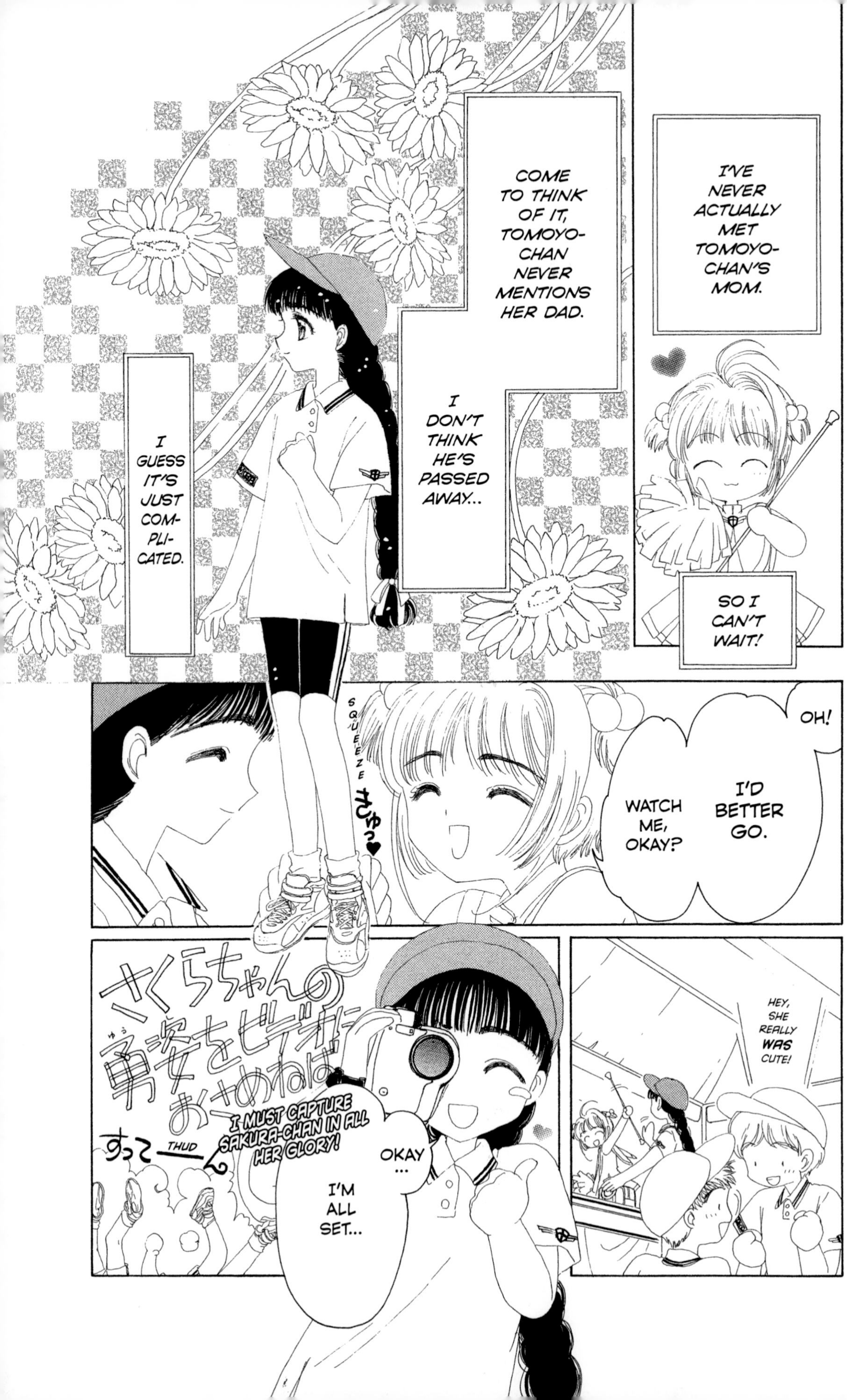
I'VE NEVER ACTUALLY MET TOMOYO-CHAN'S MOM.
SO I CAN'T WAIT!
COME TO THINK OF IT, TOMOYO-CHAN NEVER MENTIONS HER DAD.
I DON'T THINK HE'S PASSED AWAY...
I GUESS IT'S JUST COMPLICATED.
OH!
I'D BETTER GO.
WATCH ME, OKAY?
SQUEEZE
きゅっ♥
HEY, SHE REALLY WAS CUTE!
さくらちゃんの勇姿をビデオにおさめねば
I MUST CAPTURE SAKURA-CHAN IN ALL HER GLORY!
OKAY...
I'M ALL SET...
すってーん
THUD

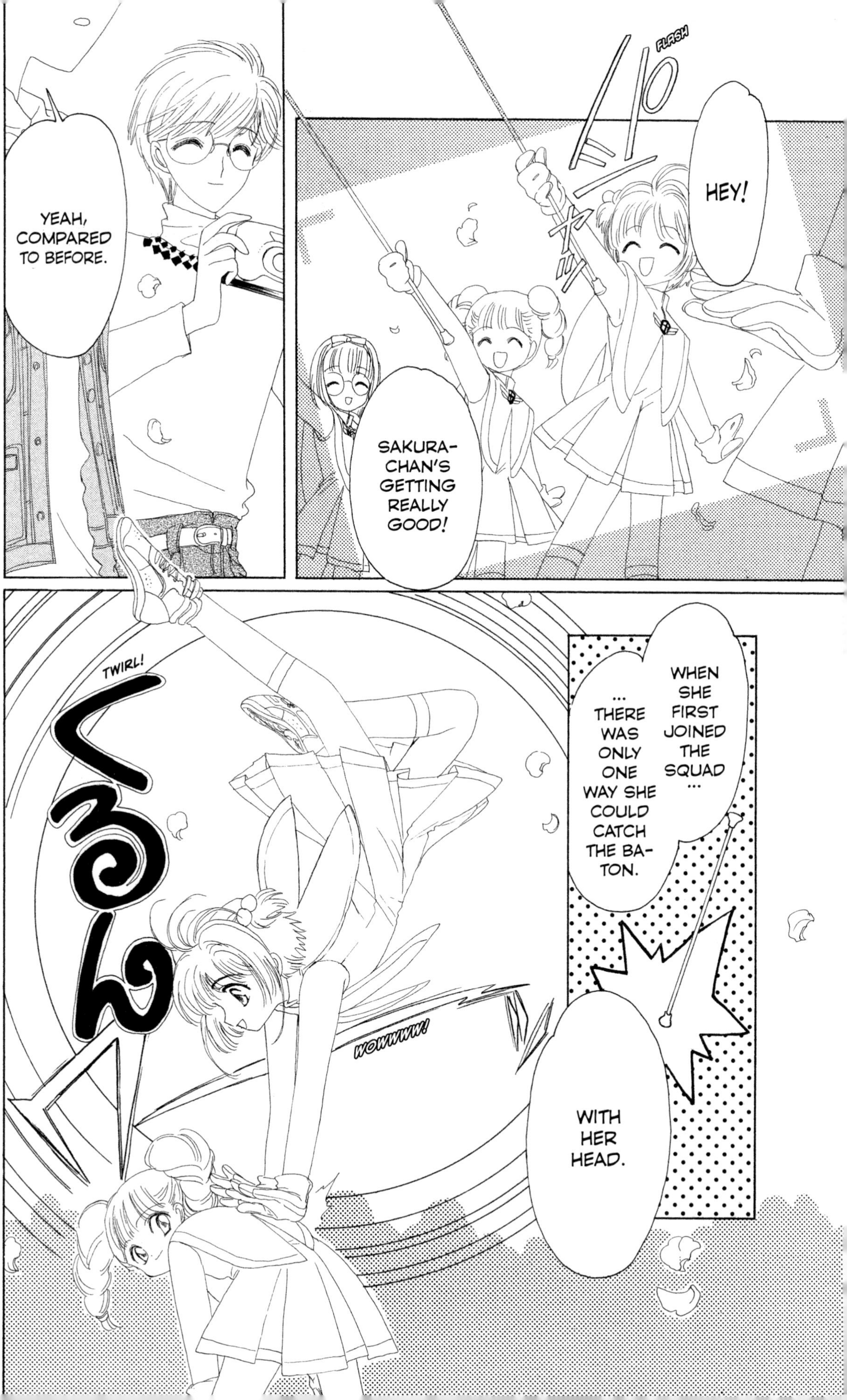
FLASH
HEY!
SAKURA-CHAN'S GETTING REALLY GOOD!
YEAH, COMPARED TO BEFORE.
WHEN SHE FIRST JOINED THE SQUAD...
...THERE WAS ONLY ONE WAY SHE COULD CATCH THE BA-TON.
WITH HER HEAD.
WOWWWW!
TWIRL!

CERBERUS

NICKNAME:
KERO-CHAN
BIRTHDATE:
SECRET
BLOOD TYPE:
AB
FAVORITE FOOD:
SWEETS
LEAST FAVORITE FOOD:
ANYTHING HOT AND SPICY
FAVORITE PASTIME:
VIDEO GAMES
FAVORITE COLORS:
RED, ORANGE
FAVORITE TV SHOWS:
QUIZ SHOWS
FAVORITE FLOWER:
SUNFLOWER
WISH LIST:
A NEW VIDEO GAME
RESIDENCE:
SAKURA'S ROOM, FOR NOW
TRUE FORM:
UNKNOWN

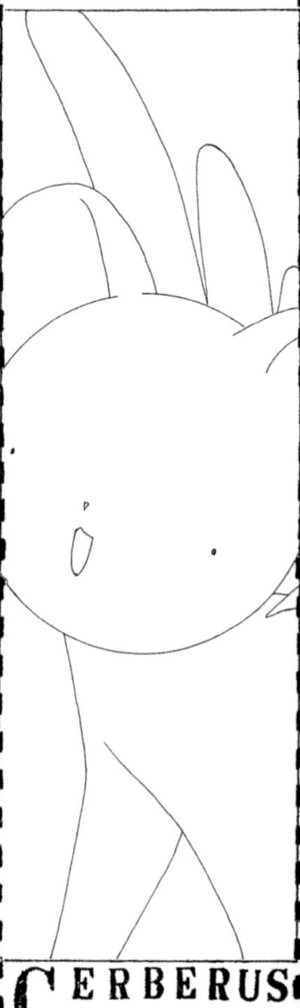

CERBERUS

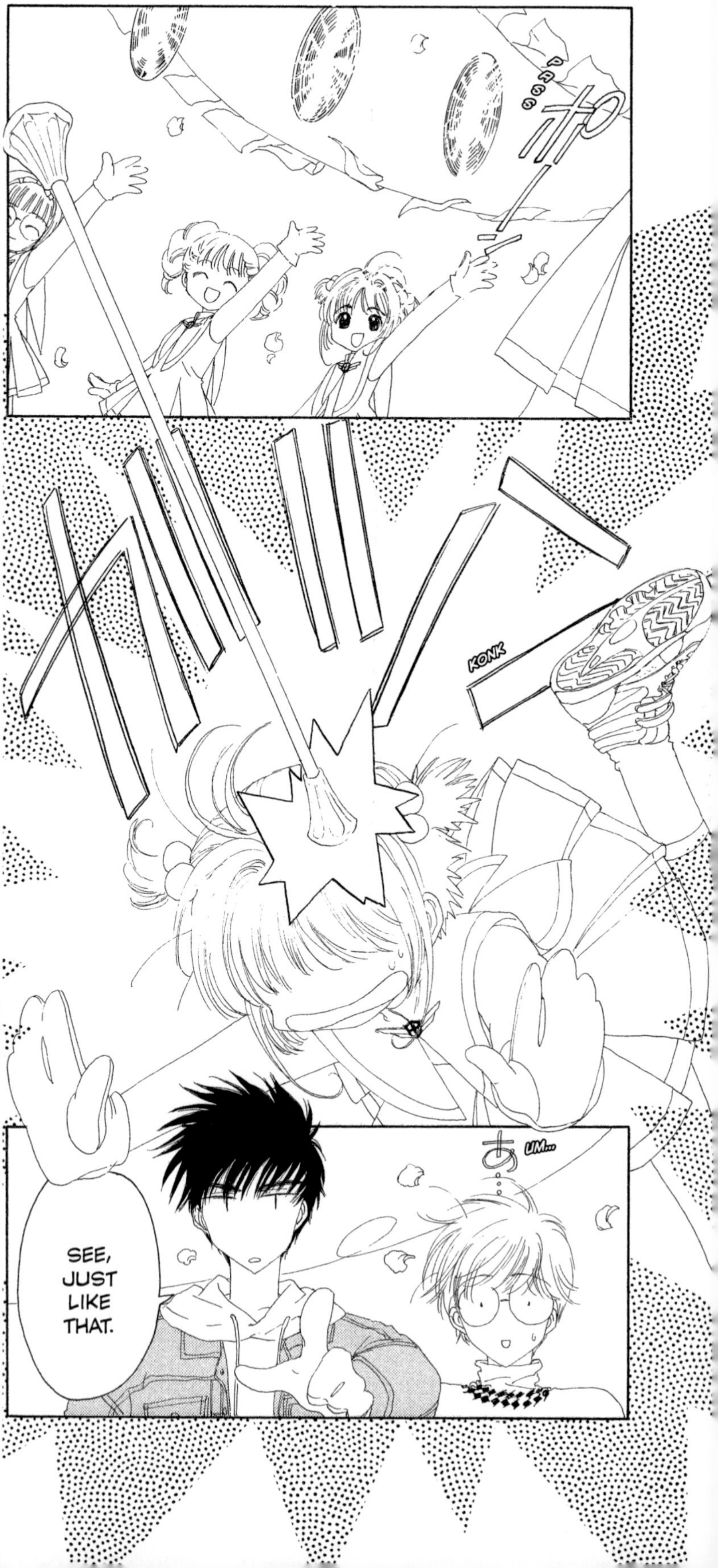
PROG
KONK
UM...
SEE, JUST LIKE THAT.

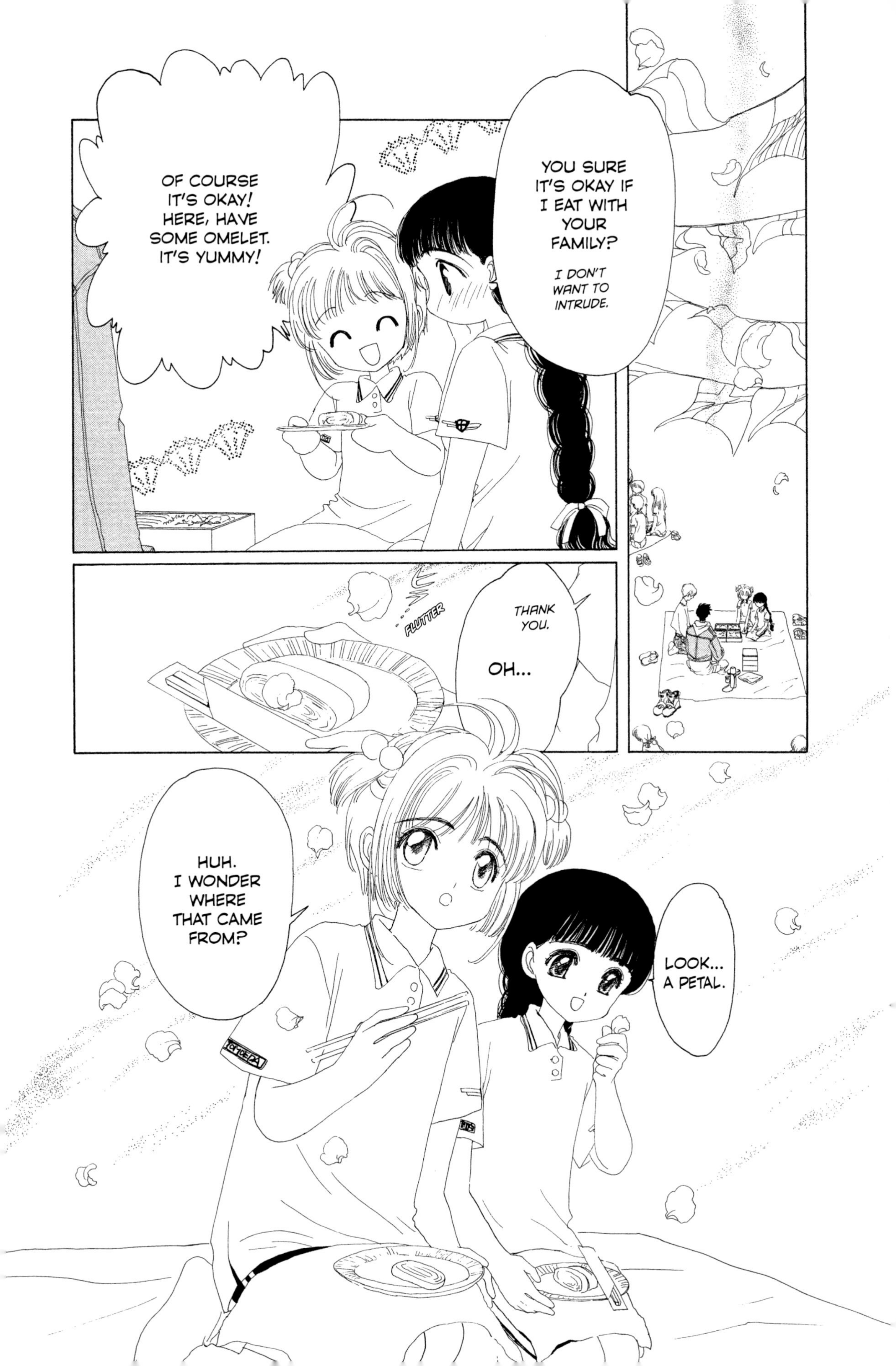
YOU SURE IT'S OKAY IF I EAT WITH YOUR FAMILY?
I DON'T WANT TO INTRUDE.
OF COURSE IT'S OKAY! HERE, HAVE SOME OMELET. IT'S YUMMY!
THANK YOU.
OH...
FLUTTER
LOOK... A PETAL.
HUH. I WONDER WHERE THAT CAME FROM?

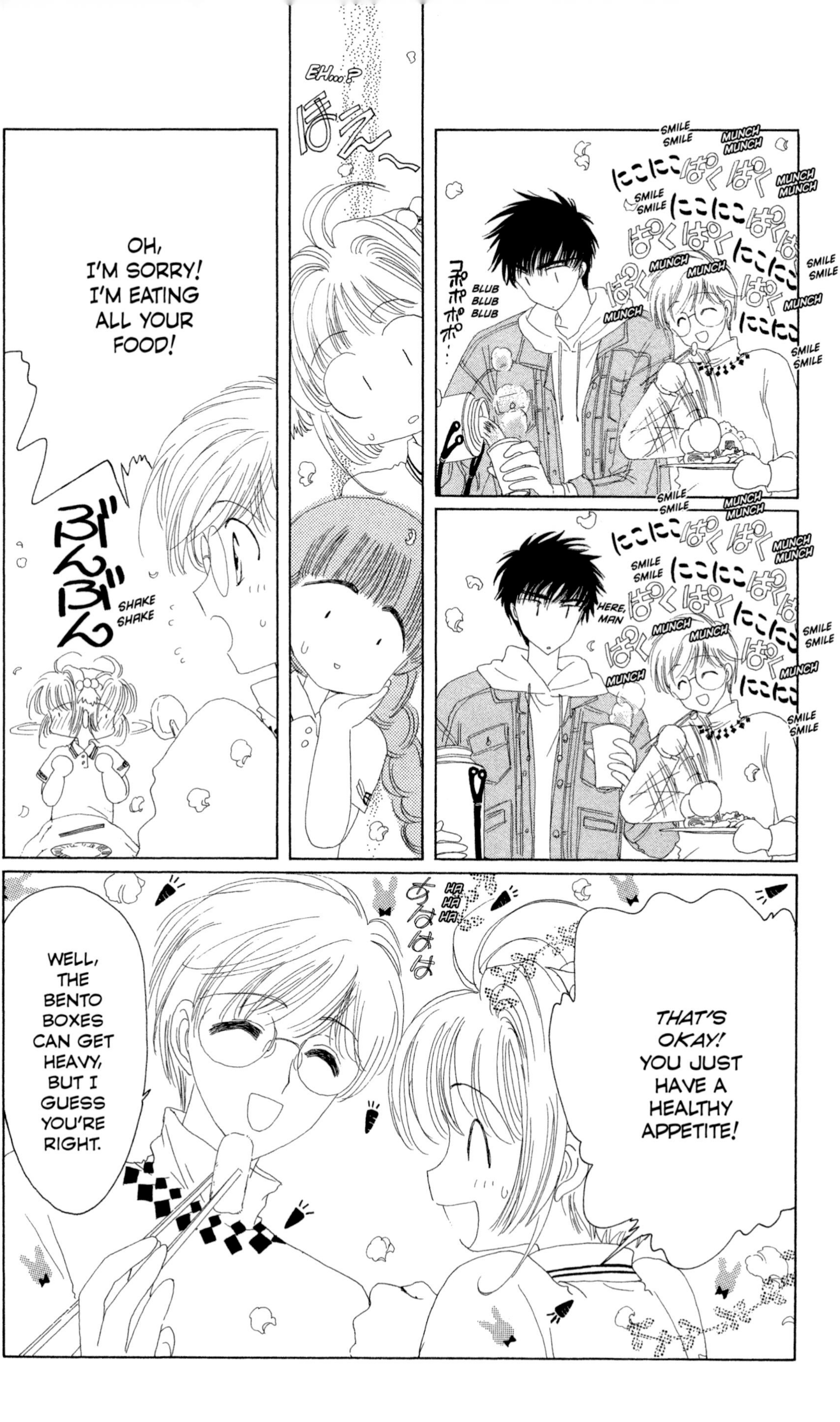
SMILE SMILE
MUNCH MUNCH
BLUB BLUB BLUB
HERE, MAN
EH...?
OH, I'M SORRY! I'M EATING ALL YOUR FOOD!
SHAKE SHAKE
THAT'S OKAY! YOU JUST HAVE A HEALTHY APPETITE!
HA HA HA
WELL, THE BENTO BOXES CAN GET HEAVY, BUT I GUESS YOU'RE RIGHT.

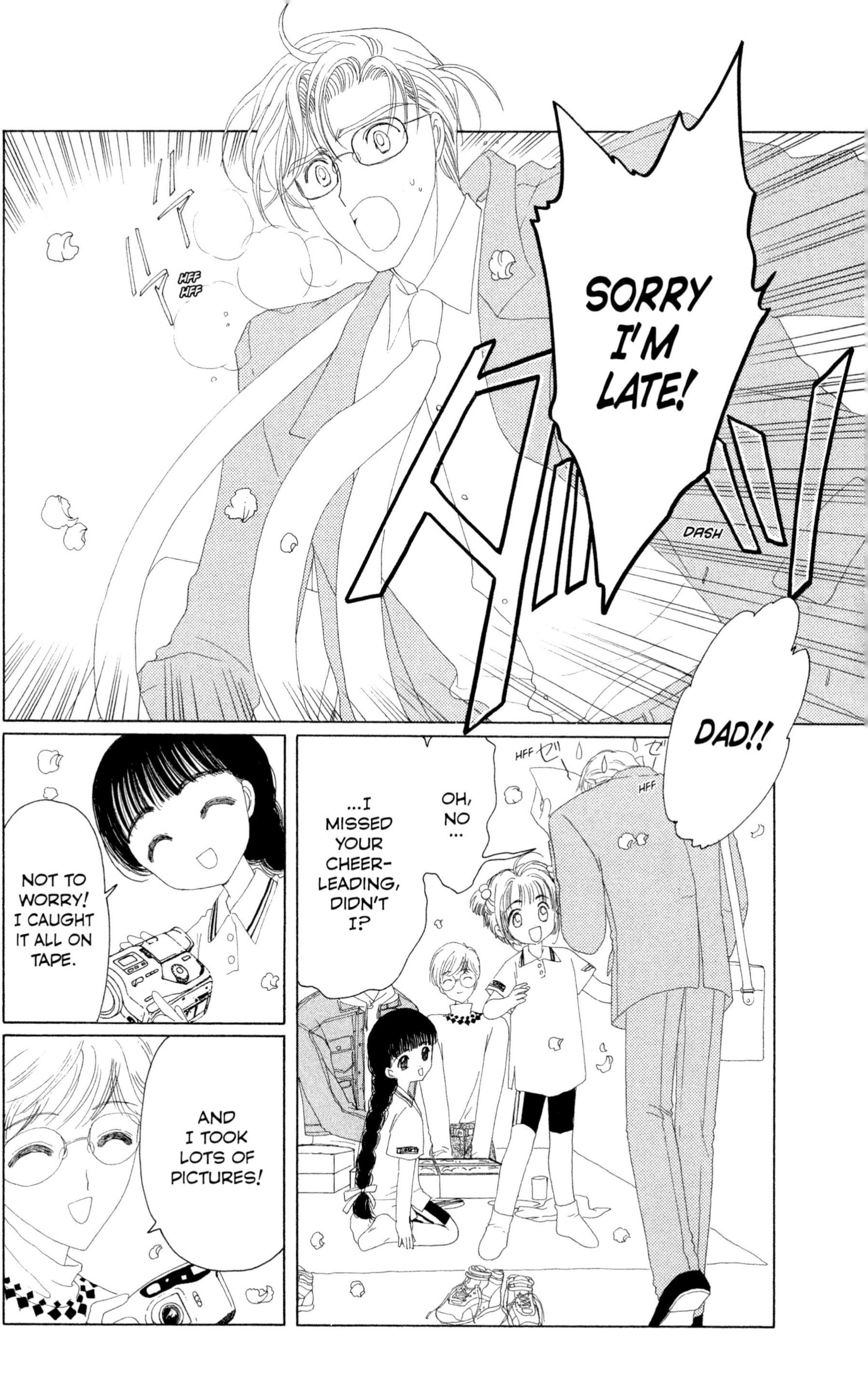
HFF HFF
SORRY I'M LATE!
DASH
DAD!!
HFF
OH, NO ...
...I MISSED YOUR CHEER-LEADING, DIDN'T I?
HFF
NOT TO WORRY! I CAUGHT IT ALL ON TAPE.
AND I TOOK LOTS OF PICTURES!

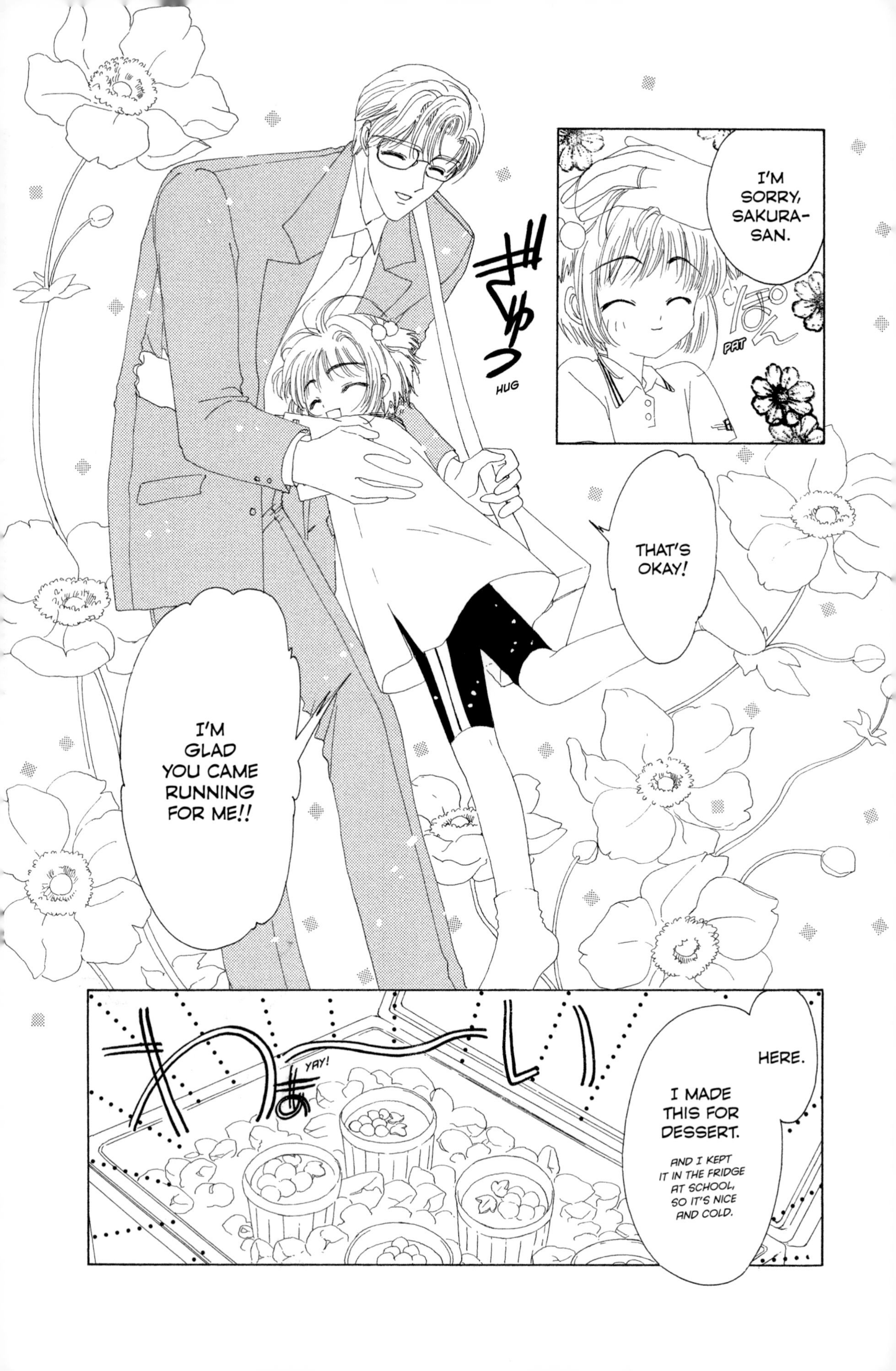
I'M SORRY, SAKURA-SAN.
ぽん
PAT
ぎゅっ
HUG
THAT'S OKAY!
I'M GLAD YOU CAME RUNNING FOR ME!!
HERE.
I MADE THIS FOR DESSERT.
AND I KEPT IT IN THE FRIDGE AT SCHOOL, SO IT'S NICE AND COLD.
わあーい
YAY!

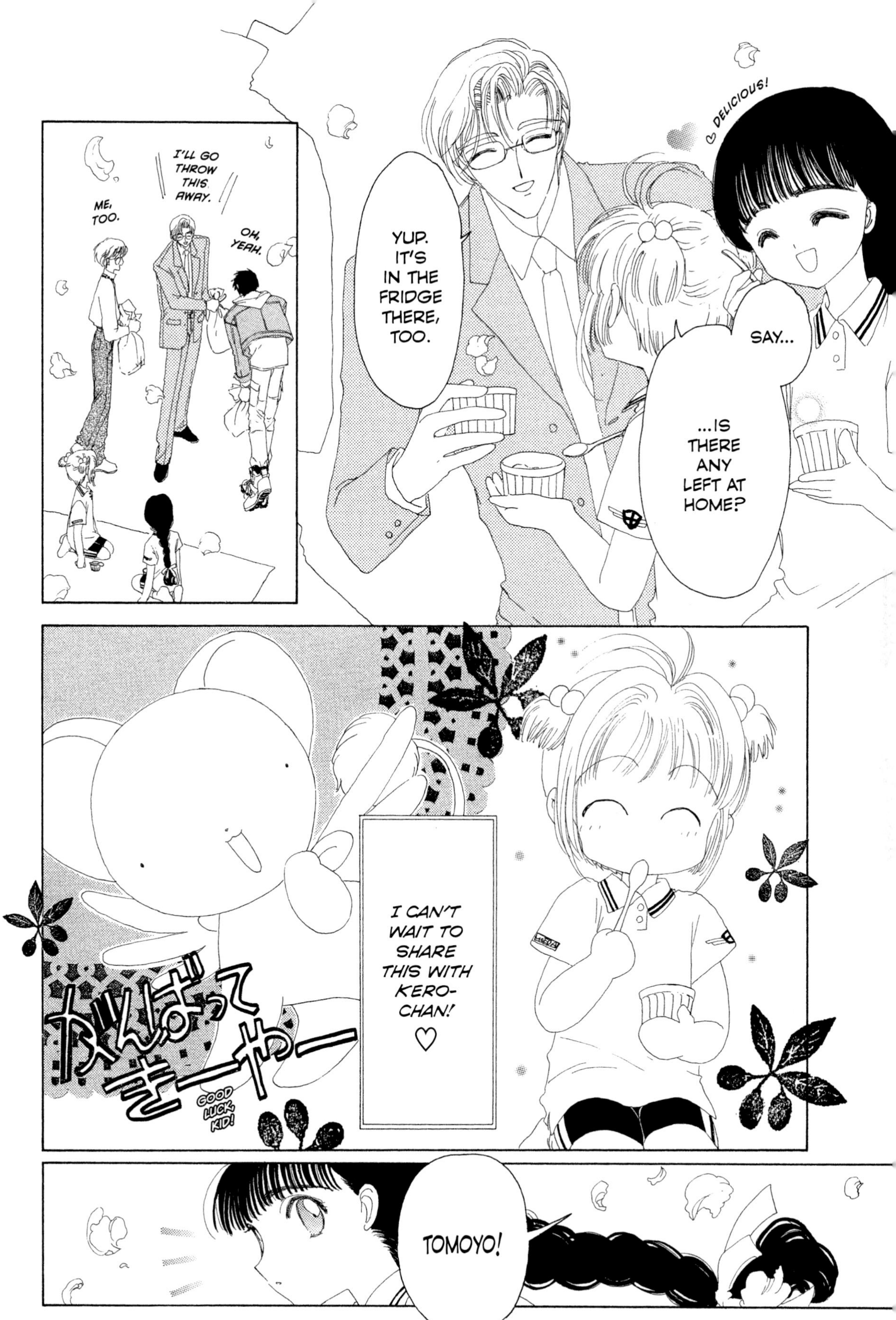
♡ DELICIOUS!
SAY...
...IS THERE ANY LEFT AT HOME?
YUP. IT'S IN THE FRIDGE THERE, TOO.
I'LL GO THROW THIS AWAY.
OH, YEAH.
ME, TOO.
I CAN'T WAIT TO SHARE THIS WITH KERO-CHAN! ♡
がんばってきーやー
GOOD LUCK KID!
TOMOYO!

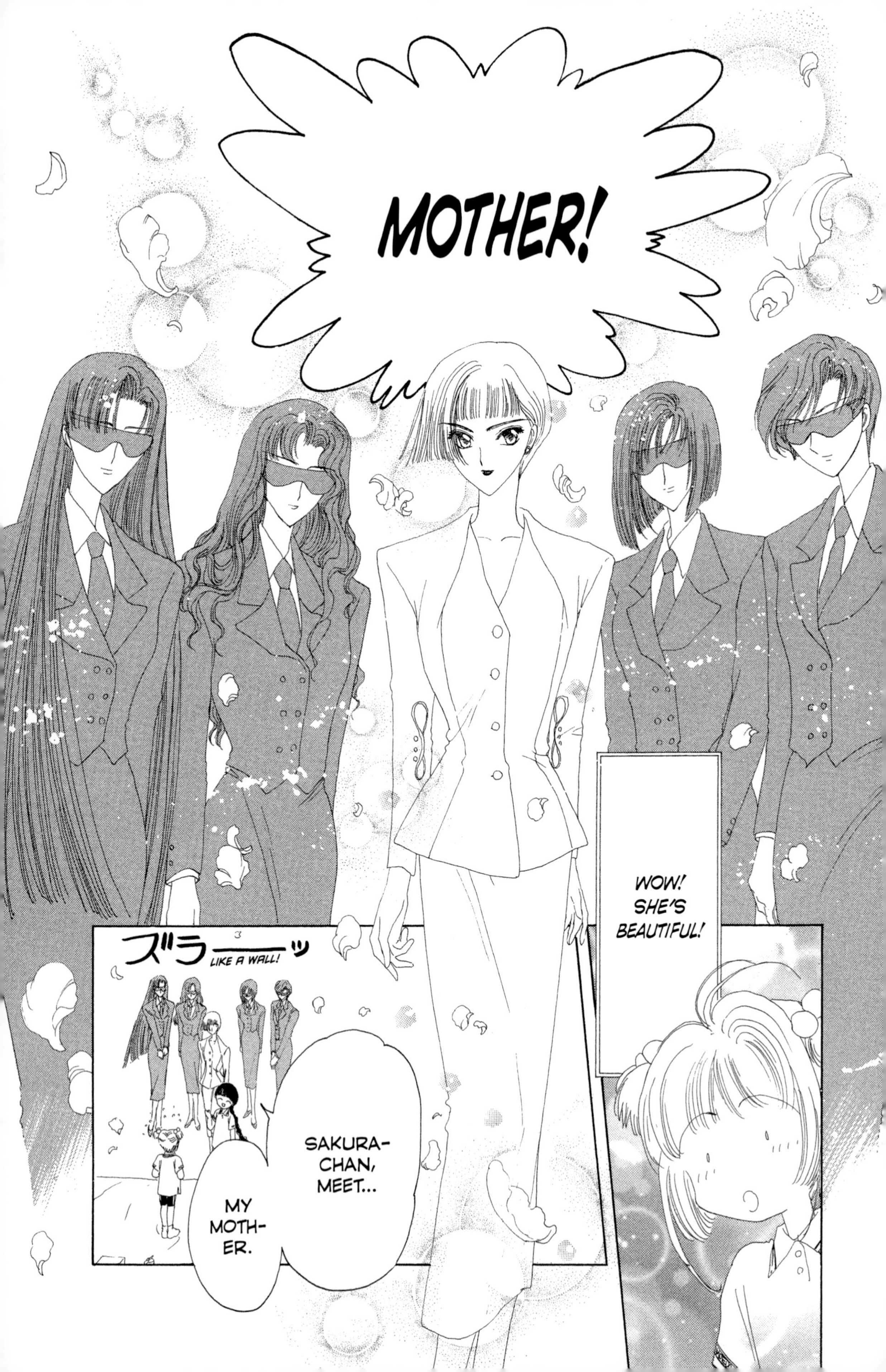
MOTHER!
WOW! SHE'S BEAUTIFUL!
ズラーッ
LIKE A WALL!
SAKURA-CHAN, MEET...
MY MOTH-ER.

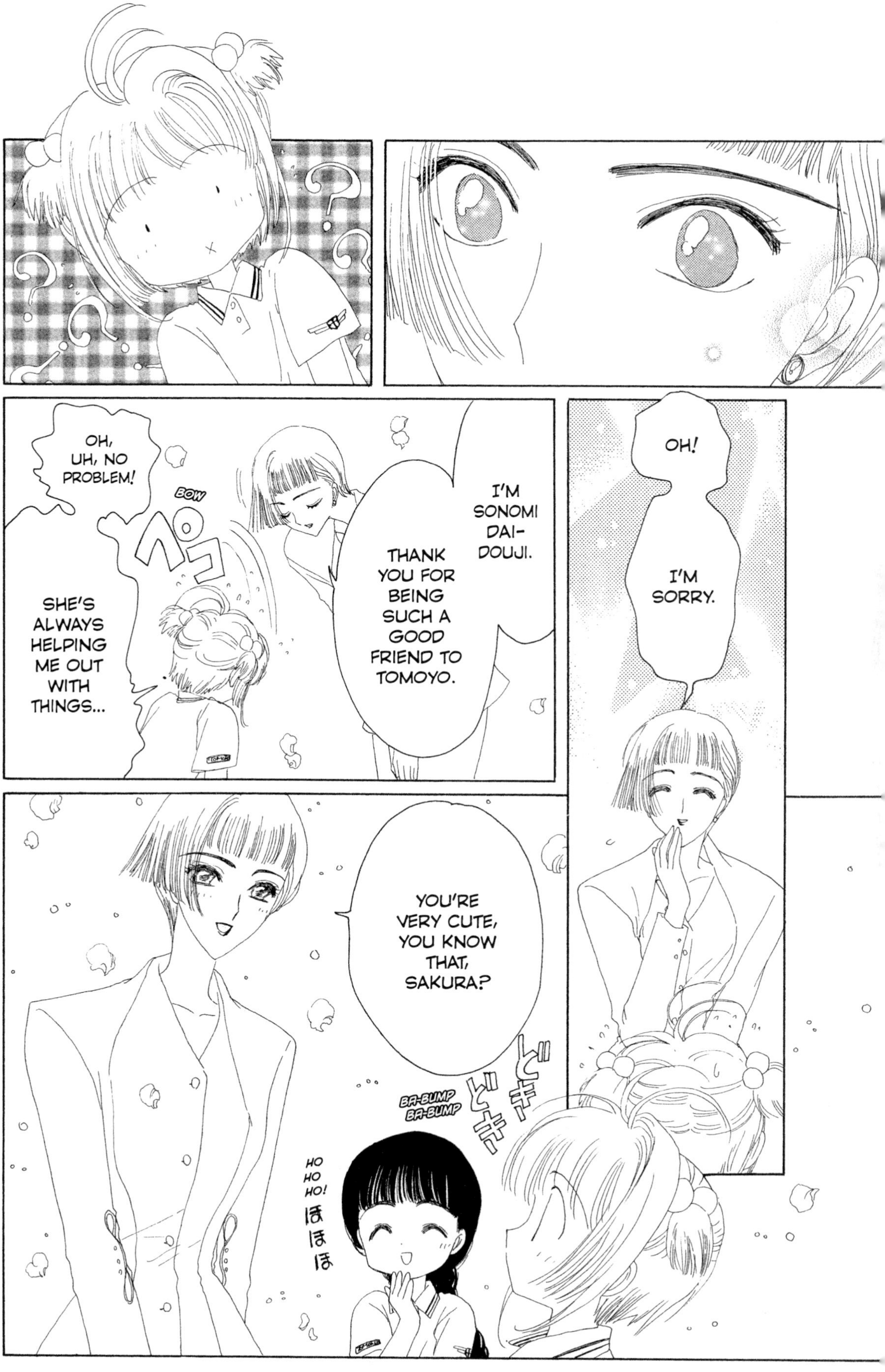
OH!
I'M SORRY.
I'M SONOMI DAI-DOUJI.
THANK YOU FOR BEING SUCH A GOOD FRIEND TO TOMOYO.
BOW
ペコ
OH, UH, NO PROBLEM!
SHE'S ALWAYS HELPING ME OUT WITH THINGS...
YOU'RE VERY CUTE, YOU KNOW THAT, SAKURA?
BA-BUMP BA-BUMP
どきどき
HO HO HO!
ほほほ

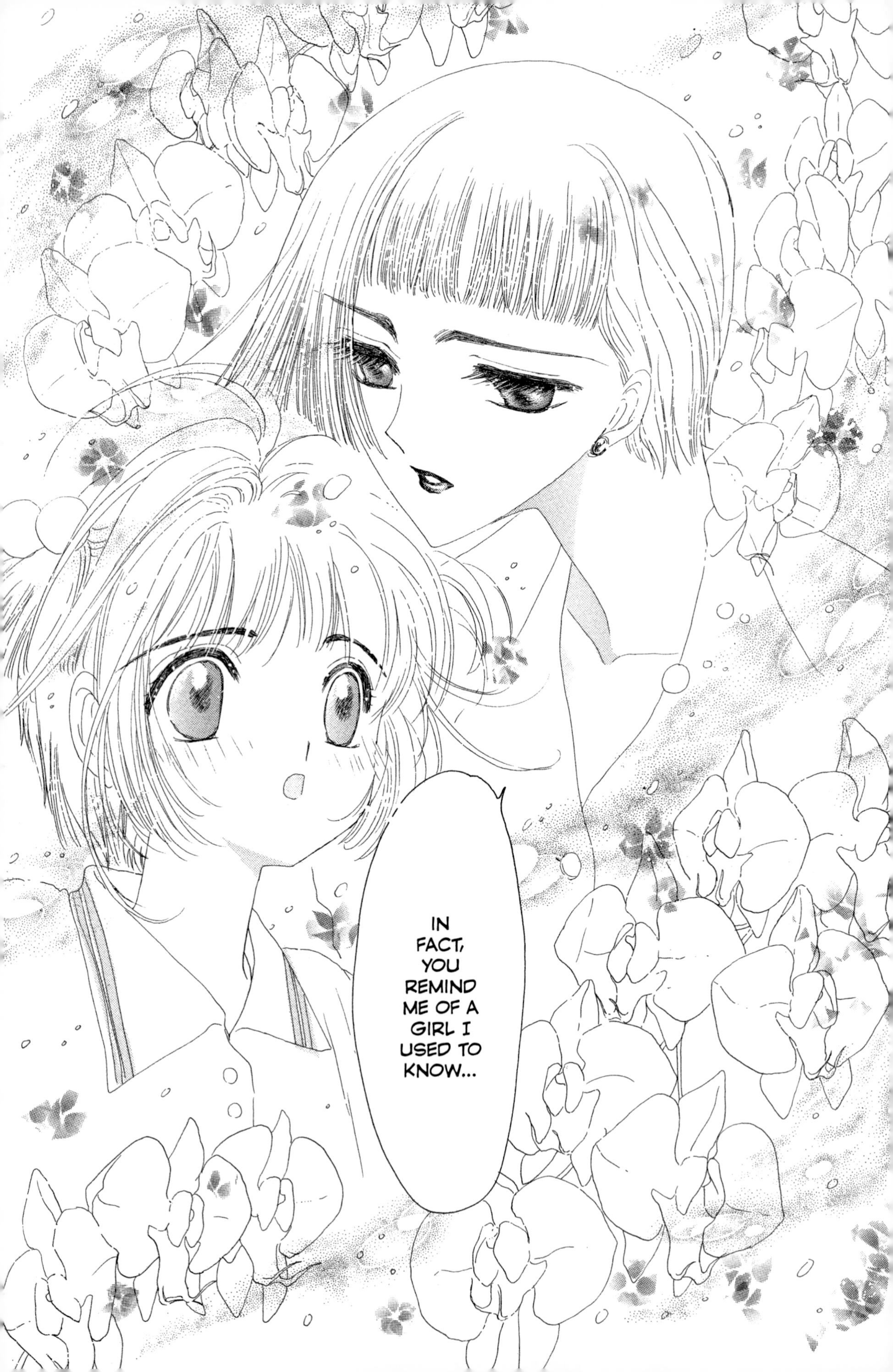
IN FACT, YOU REMIND ME OF A GIRL I USED TO KNOW...

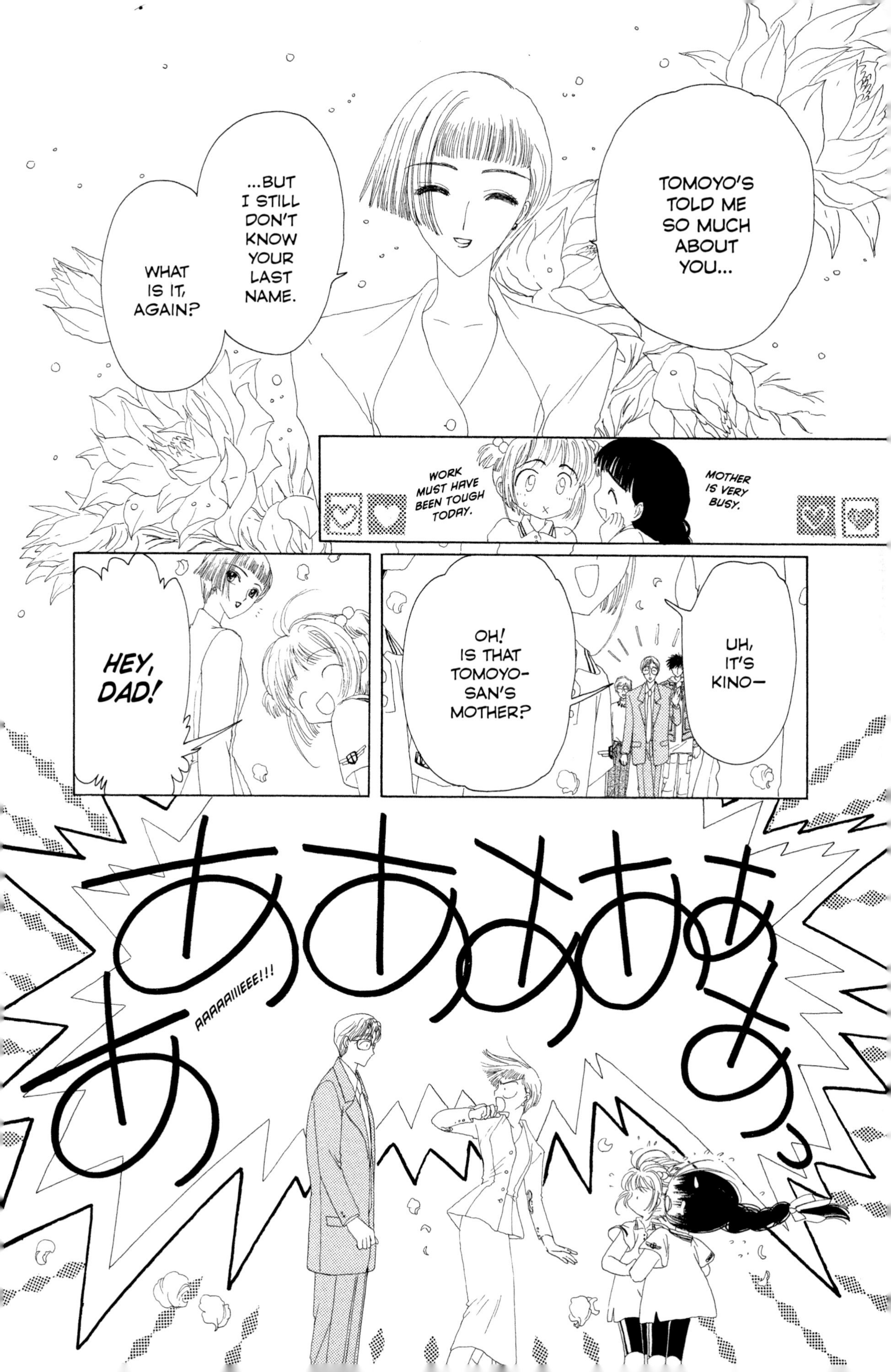
TOMOYO'S TOLD ME SO MUCH ABOUT YOU...
...BUT I STILL DON'T KNOW YOUR LAST NAME.
WHAT IS IT, AGAIN?
MOTHER IS VERY BUSY.
WORK MUST HAVE BEEN TOUGH TODAY.
UH, IT'S KINO—
OH! IS THAT TOMOYO-SAN'S MOTHER?
HEY, DAD!
あああああああ
AAAAAIIIIEEE!!!

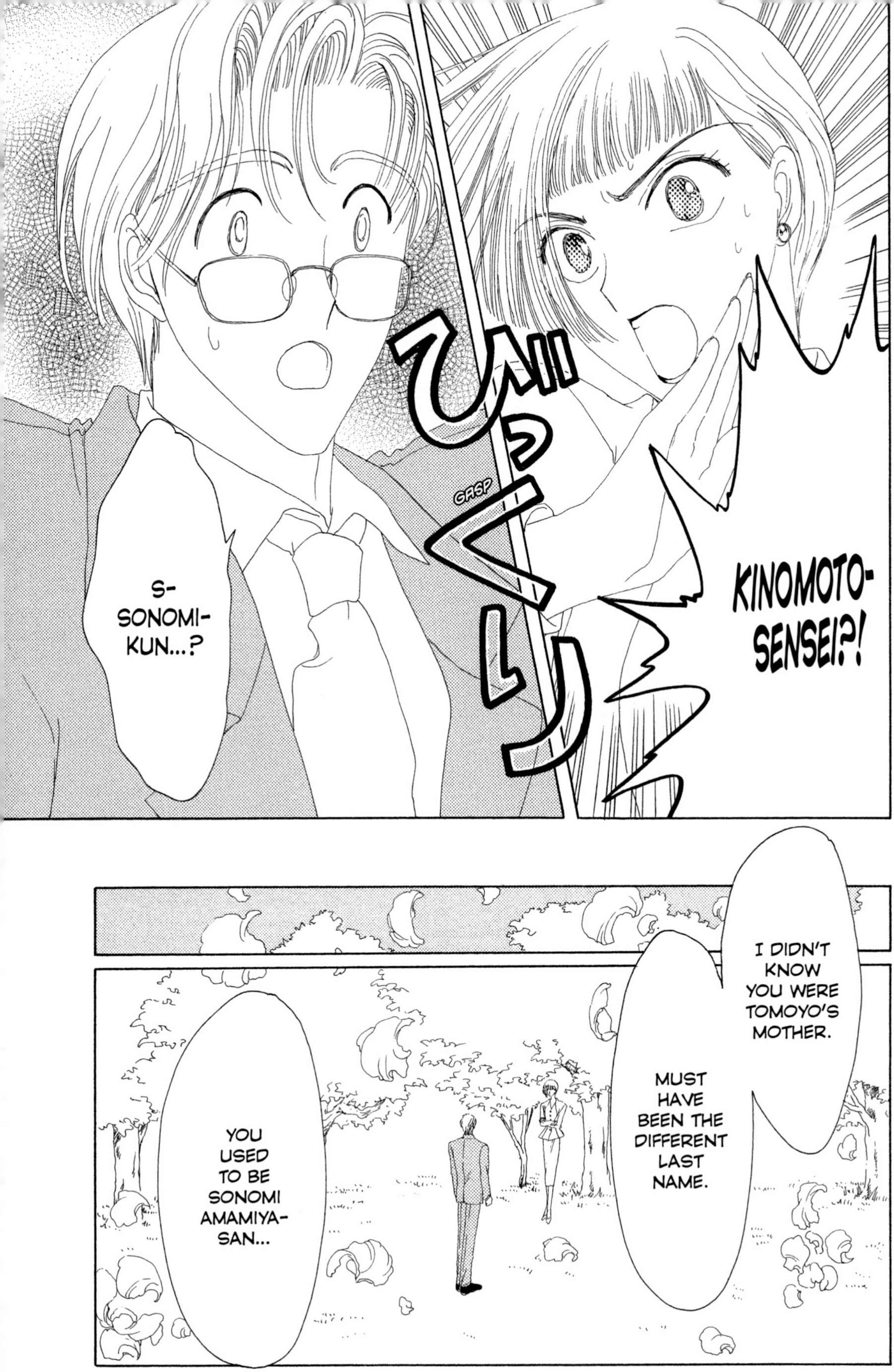
KINOMOTO-SENSEI?!
ひっくり
GASP
S-SONOMI-KUN...?
I DIDN'T KNOW YOU WERE TOMOYO'S MOTHER.
MUST HAVE BEEN THE DIFFERENT LAST NAME.
YOU USED TO BE SONOMI AMAMIYA-SAN...

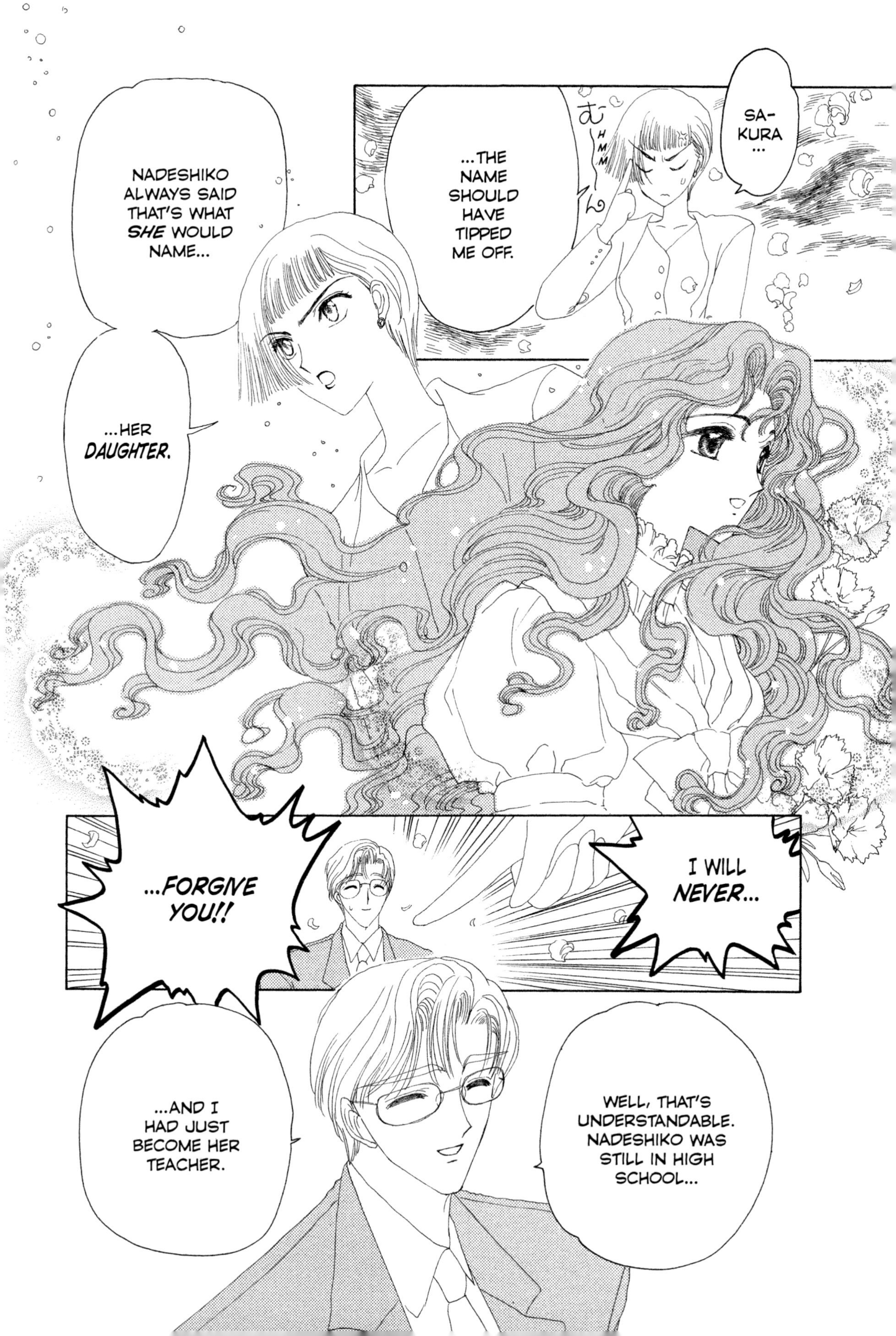
SA-KURA...
HMM
...THE NAME SHOULD HAVE TIPPED ME OFF.
NADESHIKO ALWAYS SAID THAT'S WHAT *SHE* WOULD NAME...
...HER *DAUGHTER.*
I WILL *NEVER...*
...FORGIVE YOU!!
WELL, THAT'S UNDERSTANDABLE. NADESHIKO WAS STILL IN HIGH SCHOOL...
...AND I HAD JUST BECOME HER TEACHER.

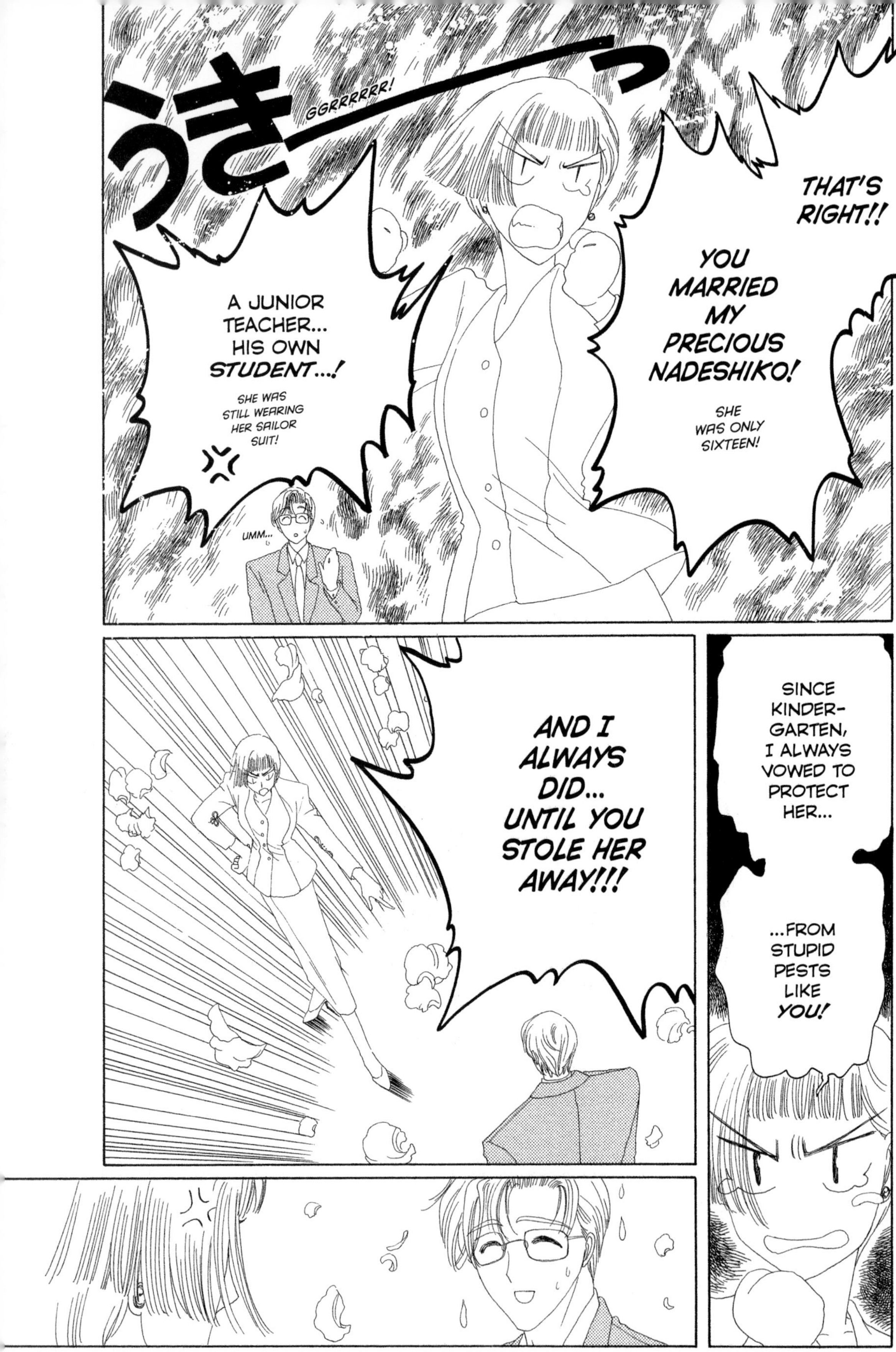
THAT'S RIGHT!!
YOU MARRIED MY PRECIOUS NADESHIKO!
SHE WAS ONLY SIXTEEN!
うきーっ
GGRRRRRR!
A JUNIOR TEACHER... HIS OWN STUDENT...!
SHE WAS STILL WEARING HER SAILOR SUIT!
UMM...
SINCE KINDER-GARTEN, I ALWAYS VOWED TO PROTECT HER...
...FROM STUPID PESTS LIKE YOU!
AND I ALWAYS DID... UNTIL YOU STOLE HER AWAY!!!

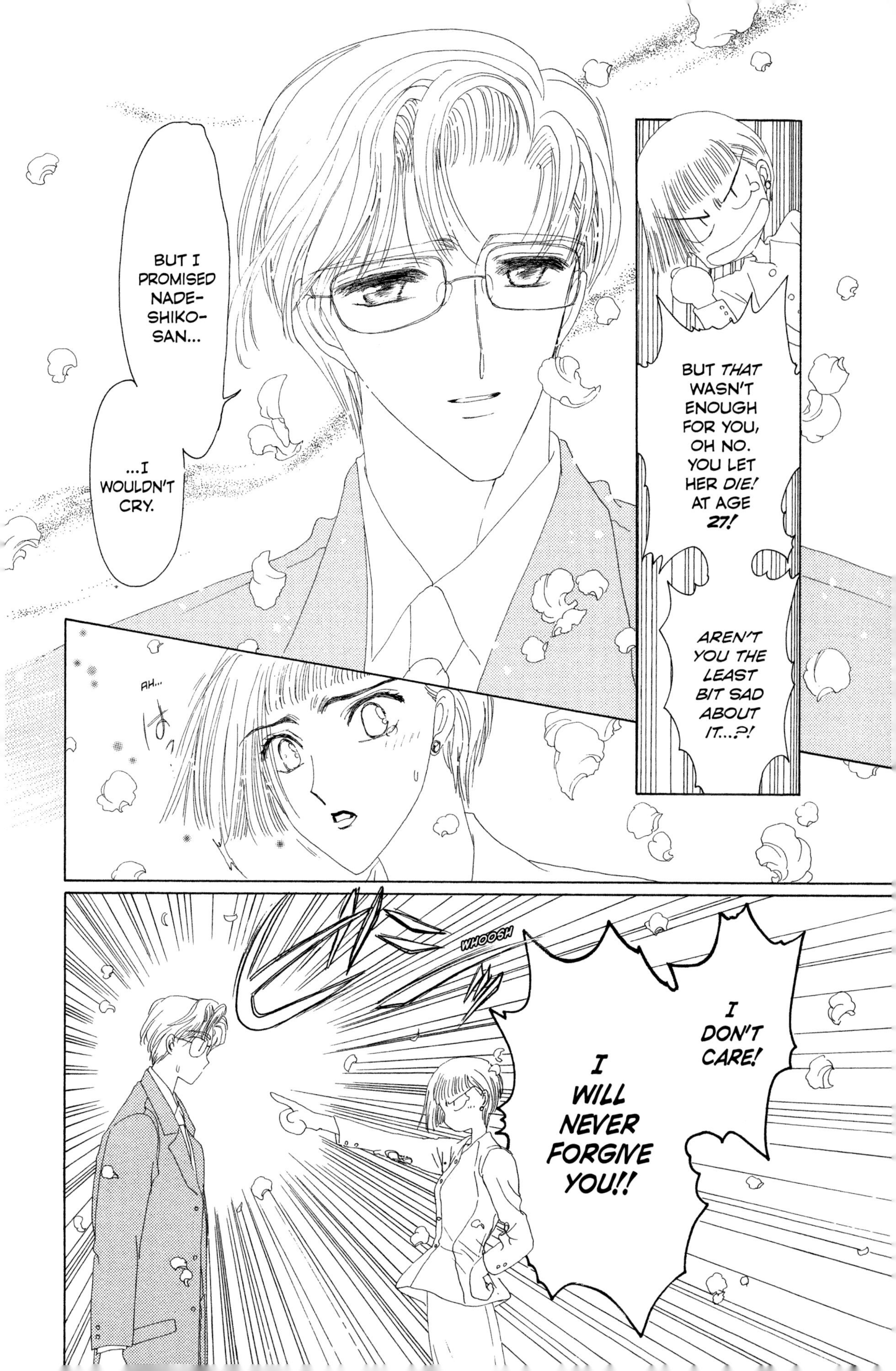
BUT THAT WASN'T ENOUGH FOR YOU, OH NO. YOU LET HER DIE! AT AGE 27!
AREN'T YOU THE LEAST BIT SAD ABOUT IT...?!
BUT I PROMISED NADE-SHIKO-SAN...
...I WOULDN'T CRY.
AH...
WHOOSH
I DON'T CARE!
I WILL NEVER FORGIVE YOU!!

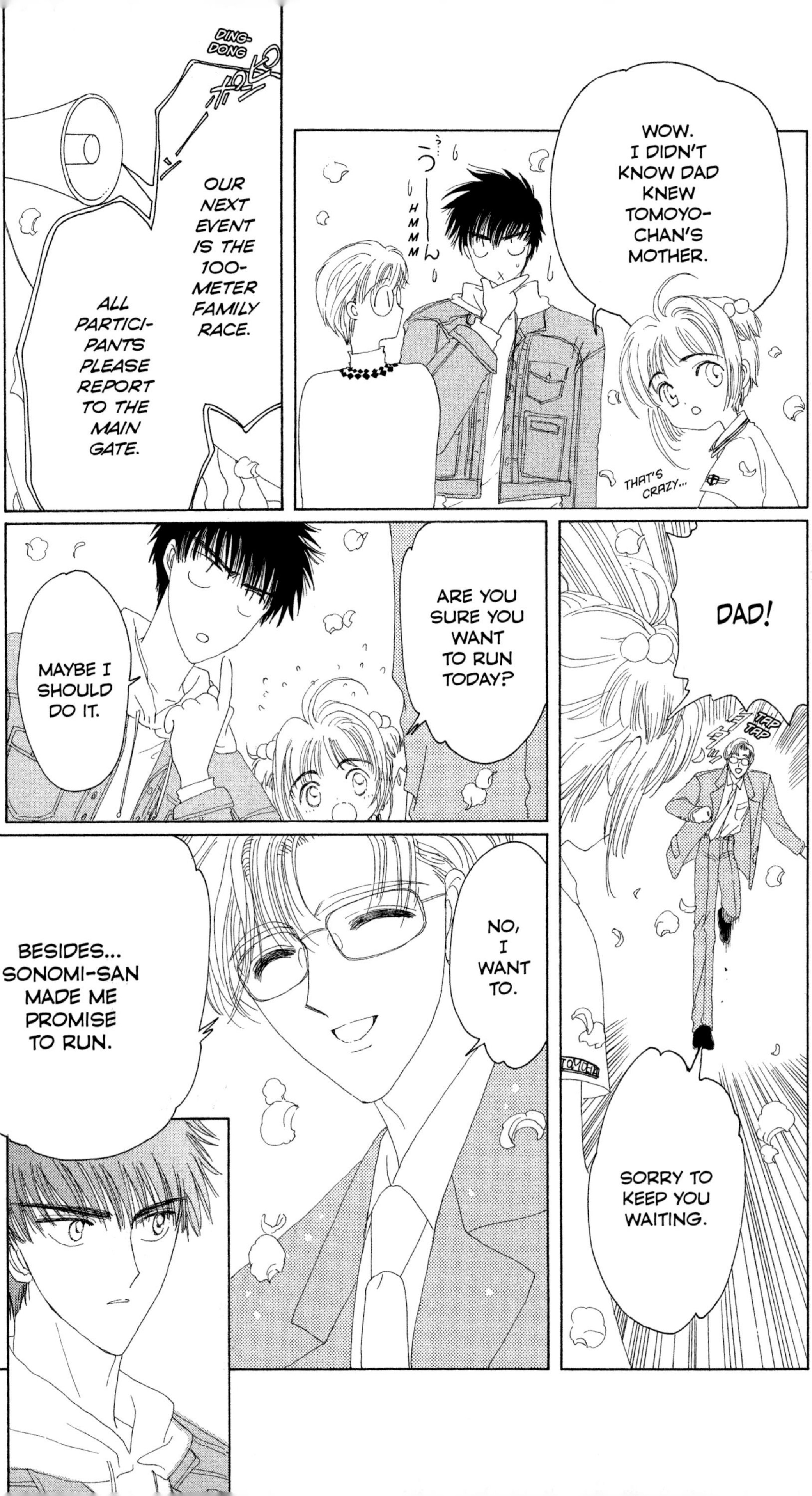
WOW. I DIDN'T KNOW DAD KNEW TOMOYO-CHAN'S MOTHER.
HMMM
THAT'S CRAZY...
DING-DONG
OUR NEXT EVENT IS THE 100-METER FAMILY RACE.
ALL PARTICI-PANTS PLEASE REPORT TO THE MAIN GATE.
DAD!
TAP TAP
SORRY TO KEEP YOU WAITING.
ARE YOU SURE YOU WANT TO RUN TODAY?
MAYBE I SHOULD DO IT.
NO, I WANT TO.
BESIDES... SONOMI-SAN MADE ME PROMISE TO RUN.

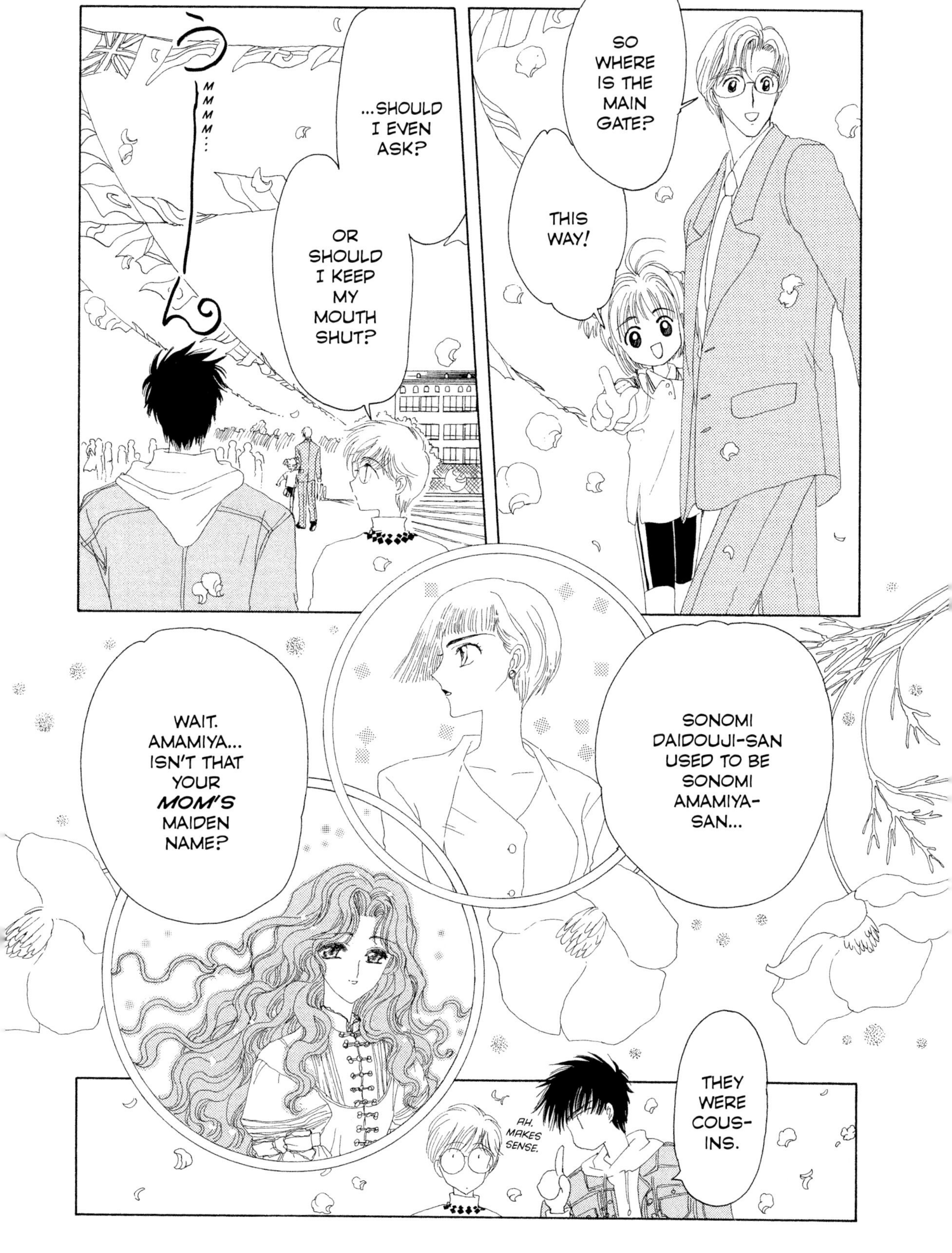
SO WHERE IS THE MAIN GATE?
THIS WAY!
...SHOULD I EVEN ASK?
OR SHOULD I KEEP MY MOUTH SHUT?
MMMM...
SONOMI DAIDOUJI-SAN USED TO BE SONOMI AMAMIYA-SAN...
WAIT. AMAMIYA... ISN'T THAT YOUR *MOM'S* MAIDEN NAME?
THEY WERE COUS-INS.
AH, MAKES SENSE.

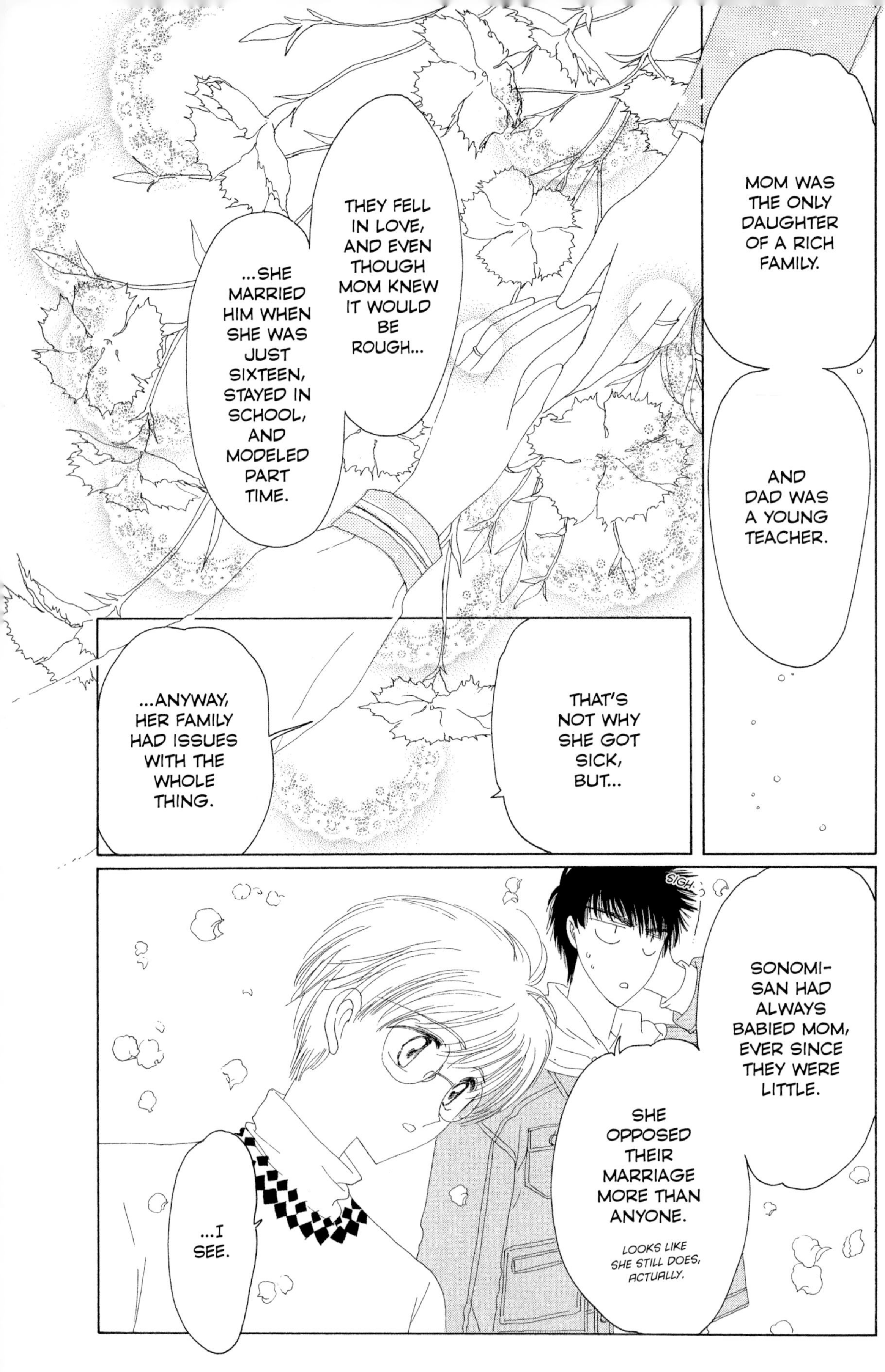
MOM WAS THE ONLY DAUGHTER OF A RICH FAMILY.
AND DAD WAS A YOUNG TEACHER.
THEY FELL IN LOVE, AND EVEN THOUGH MOM KNEW IT WOULD BE ROUGH...
...SHE MARRIED HIM WHEN SHE WAS JUST SIXTEEN, STAYED IN SCHOOL, AND MODELED PART TIME.
THAT'S NOT WHY SHE GOT SICK, BUT...
...ANYWAY, HER FAMILY HAD ISSUES WITH THE WHOLE THING.
SIGH
SONOMI-SAN HAD ALWAYS BABIED MOM, EVER SINCE THEY WERE LITTLE.
SHE OPPOSED THEIR MARRIAGE MORE THAN ANYONE.
LOOKS LIKE SHE STILL DOES, ACTUALLY.
...I SEE.

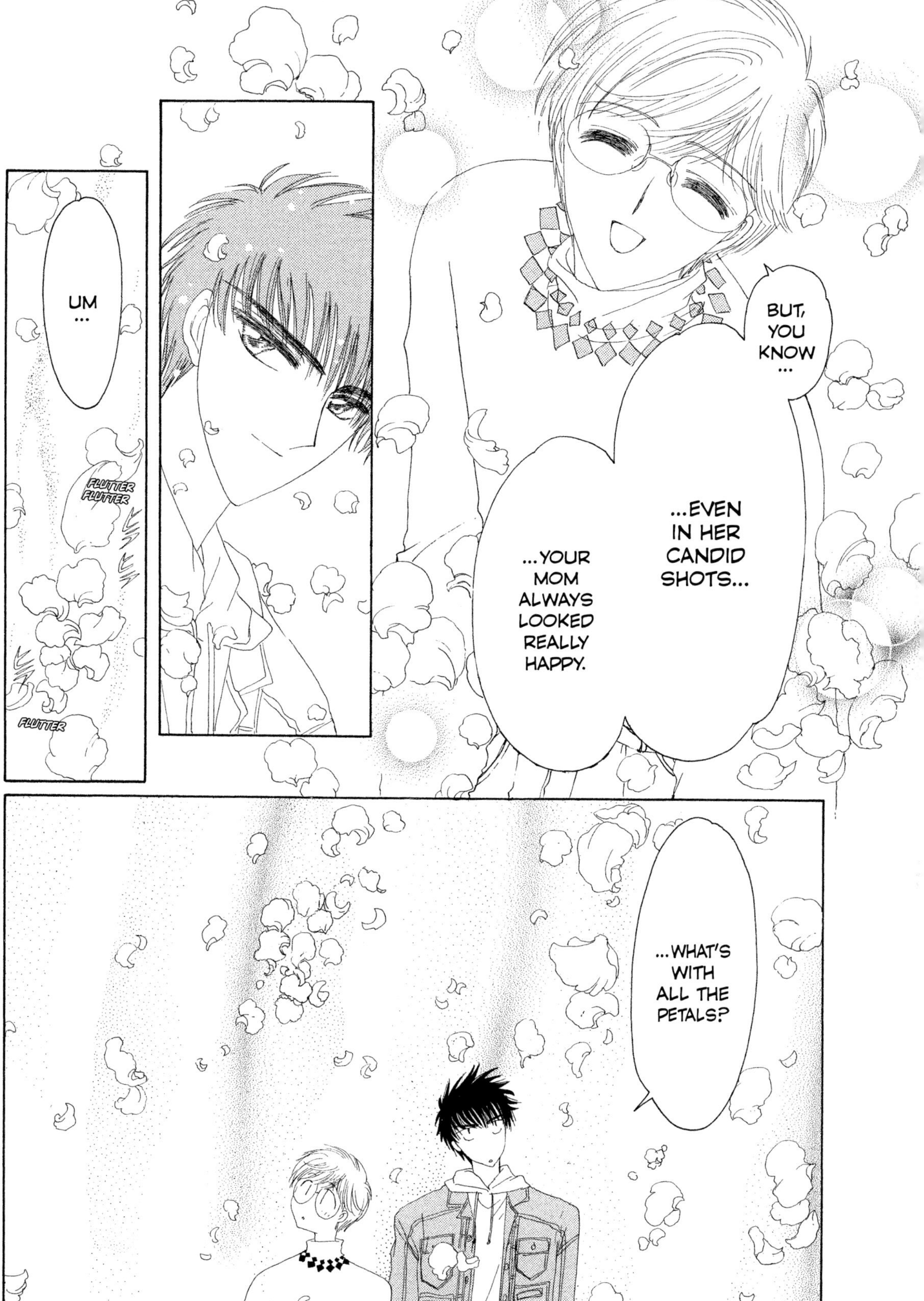
BUT, YOU KNOW...
...EVEN IN HER CANDID SHOTS...
...YOUR MOM ALWAYS LOOKED REALLY HAPPY.
UM...
FLUTTER FLUTTER
FLUTTER
...WHAT'S WITH ALL THE PETALS?

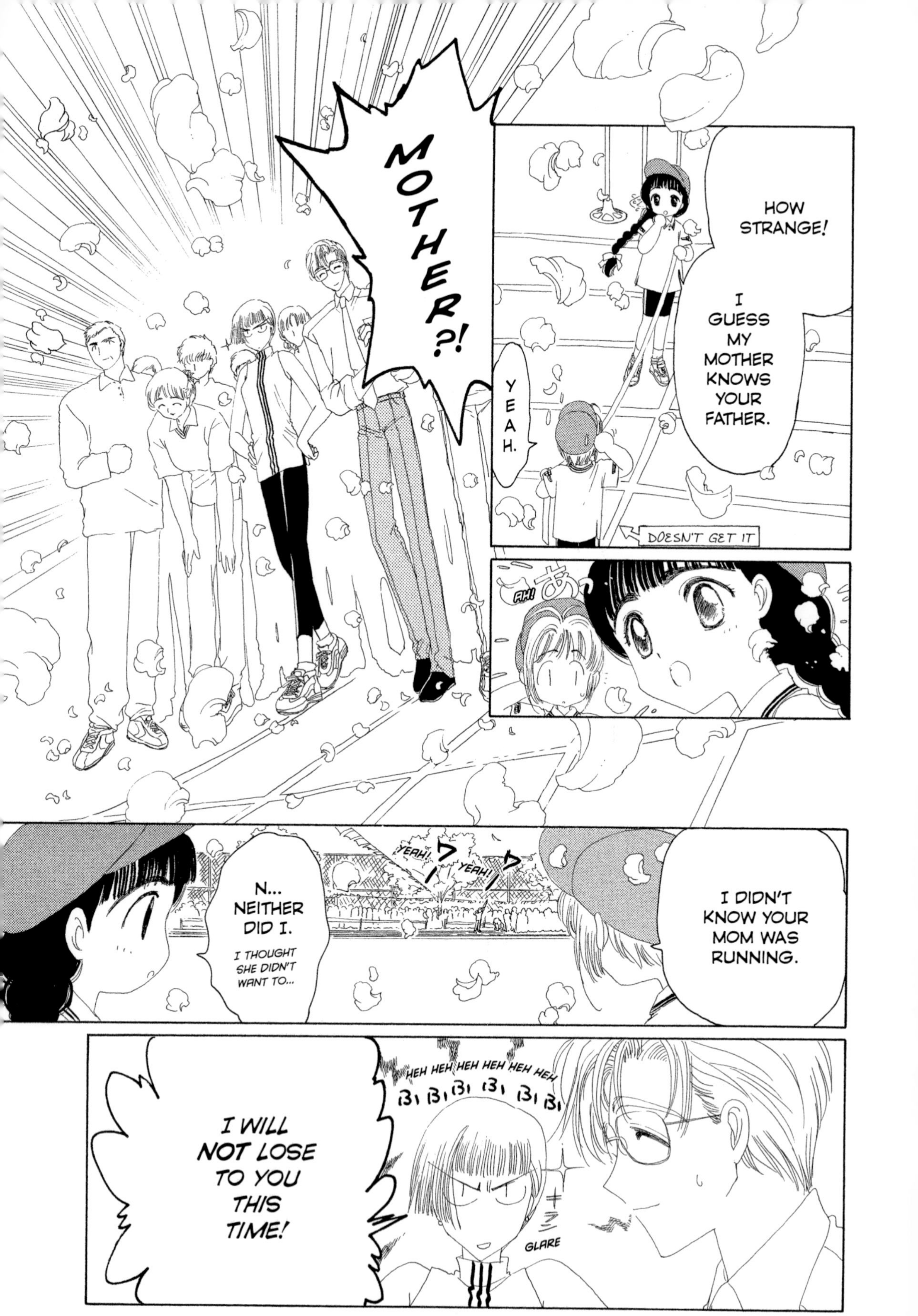
HOW STRANGE!
I GUESS MY MOTHER KNOWS YOUR FATHER.
YEAH.
DOESN'T GET IT
AH!
あっ
MOTHER?!
I DIDN'T KNOW YOUR MOM WAS RUNNING.
YEAH! YEAH!
N... NEITHER DID I.
I THOUGHT SHE DIDN'T WANT TO...
HEH HEH HEH HEH HEH HEH
GLARE
I WILL NOT LOSE TO YOU THIS TIME!

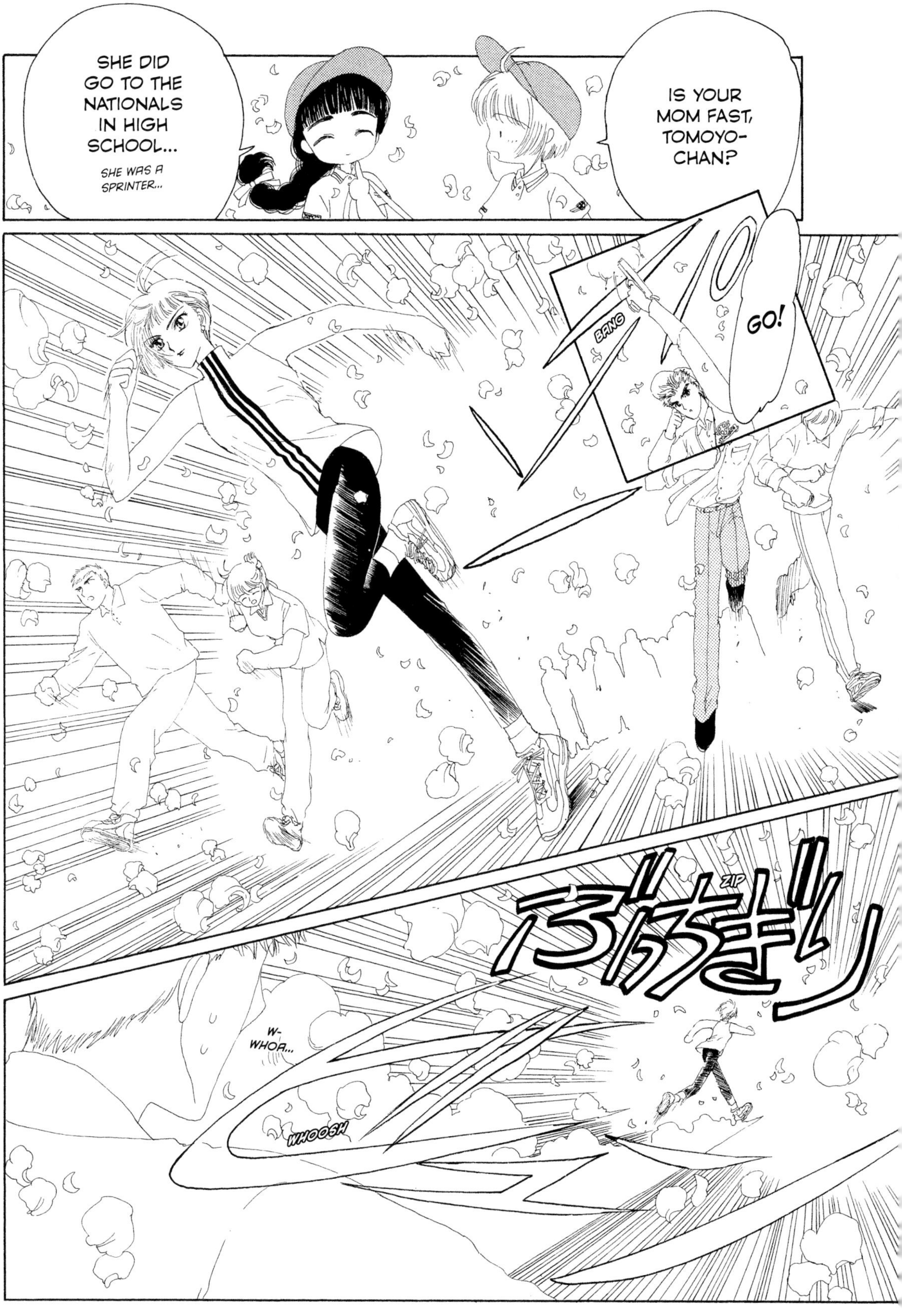
IS YOUR MOM FAST, TOMOYO-CHAN?
SHE DID GO TO THE NATIONALS IN HIGH SCHOOL...
SHE WAS A SPRINTER...
GO!
BANG
ZIP
W-WHOA...
WHOOSH

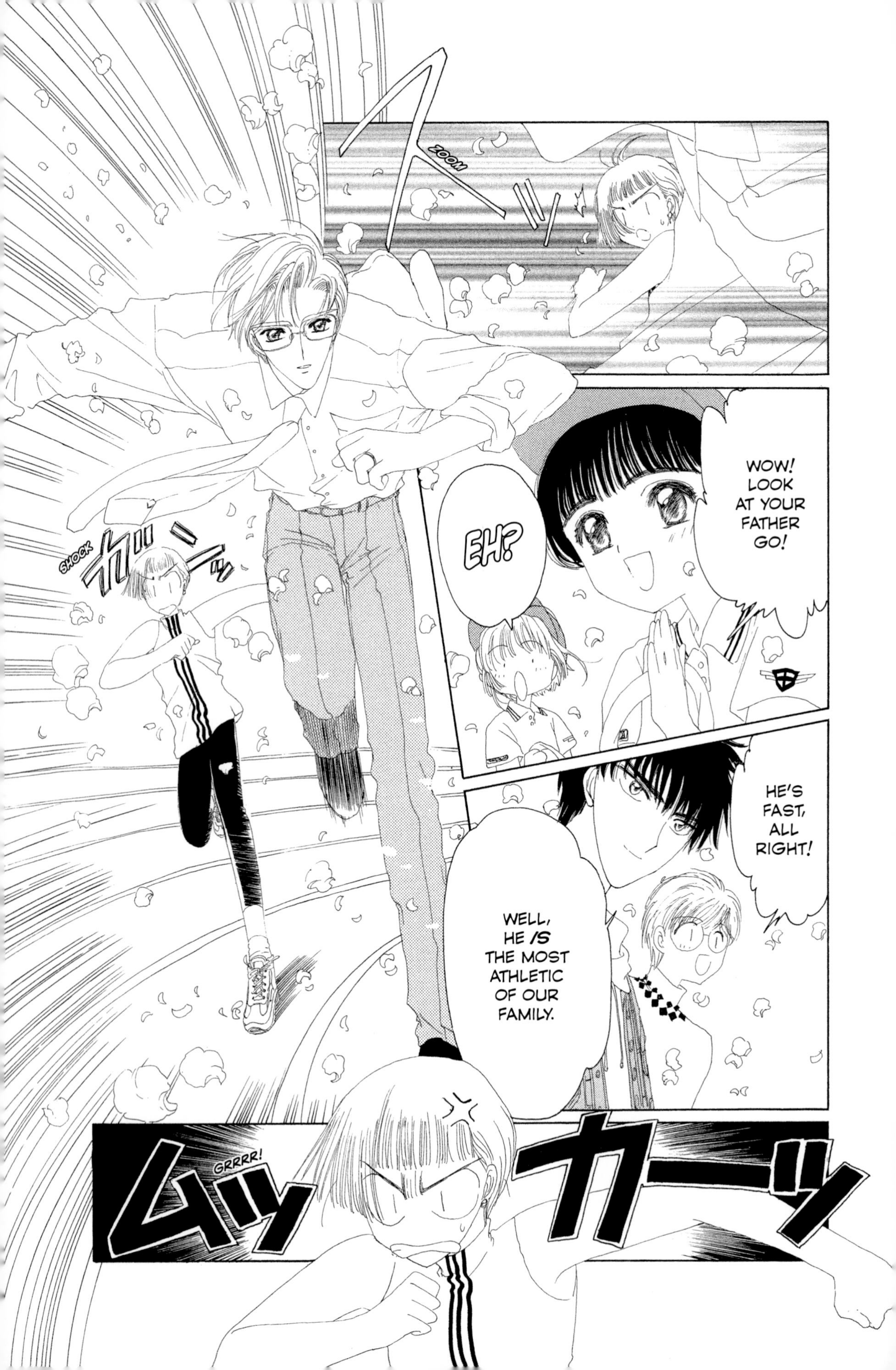
ZOOM
WOW! LOOK AT YOUR FATHER GO!
EH?
HE'S FAST, ALL RIGHT!
WELL, HE IS THE MOST ATHLETIC OF OUR FAMILY.
SHOCK
GRRRR!

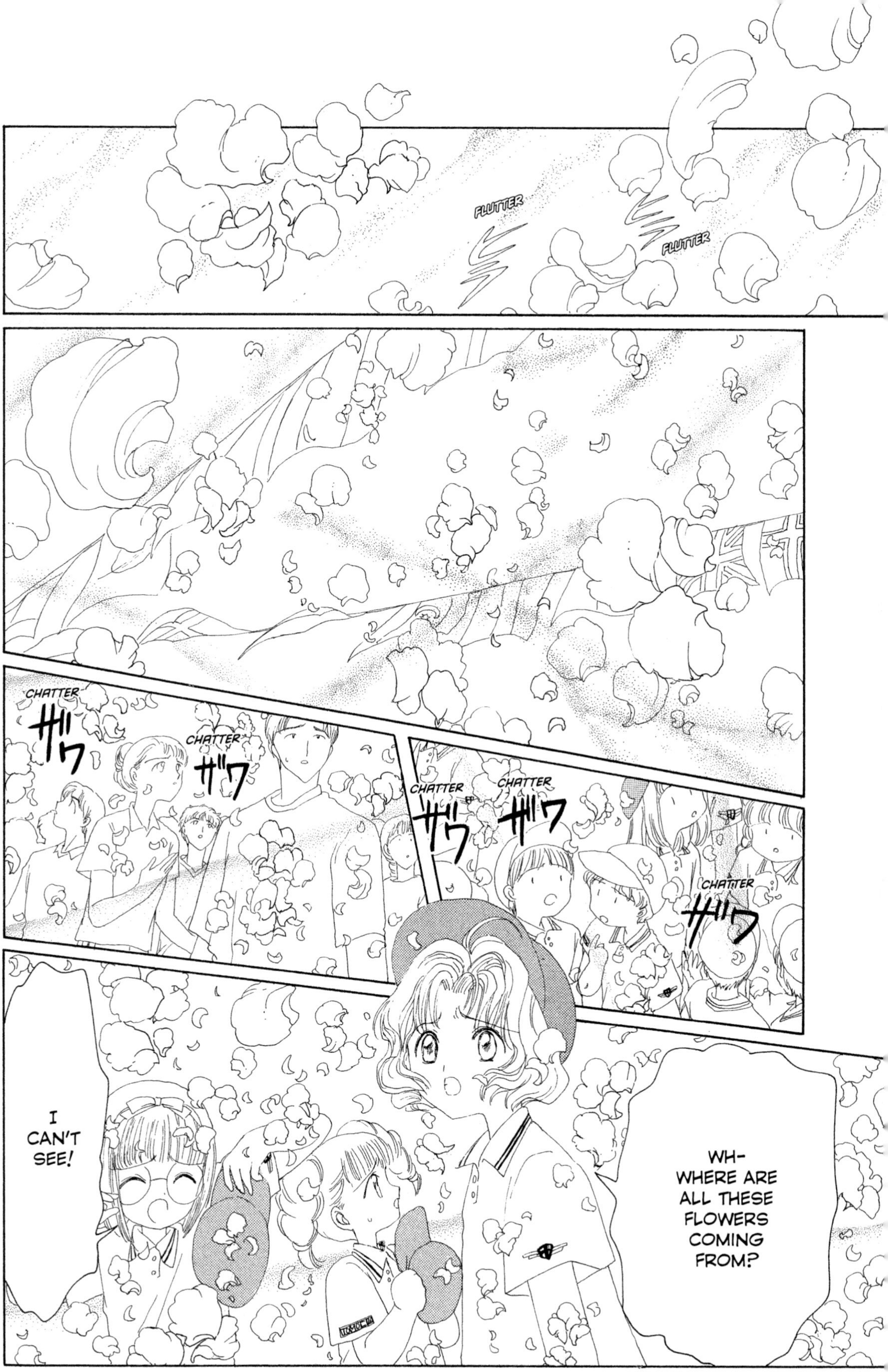
FLUTTER
FLUTTER
CHATTER
ザワ
CHATTER
ザワ
CHATTER
ザワ
CHATTER
ザワ
CHATTER
ザワ
WH-
WHERE ARE
ALL THESE
FLOWERS
COMING
FROM?
I
CAN'T
SEE!

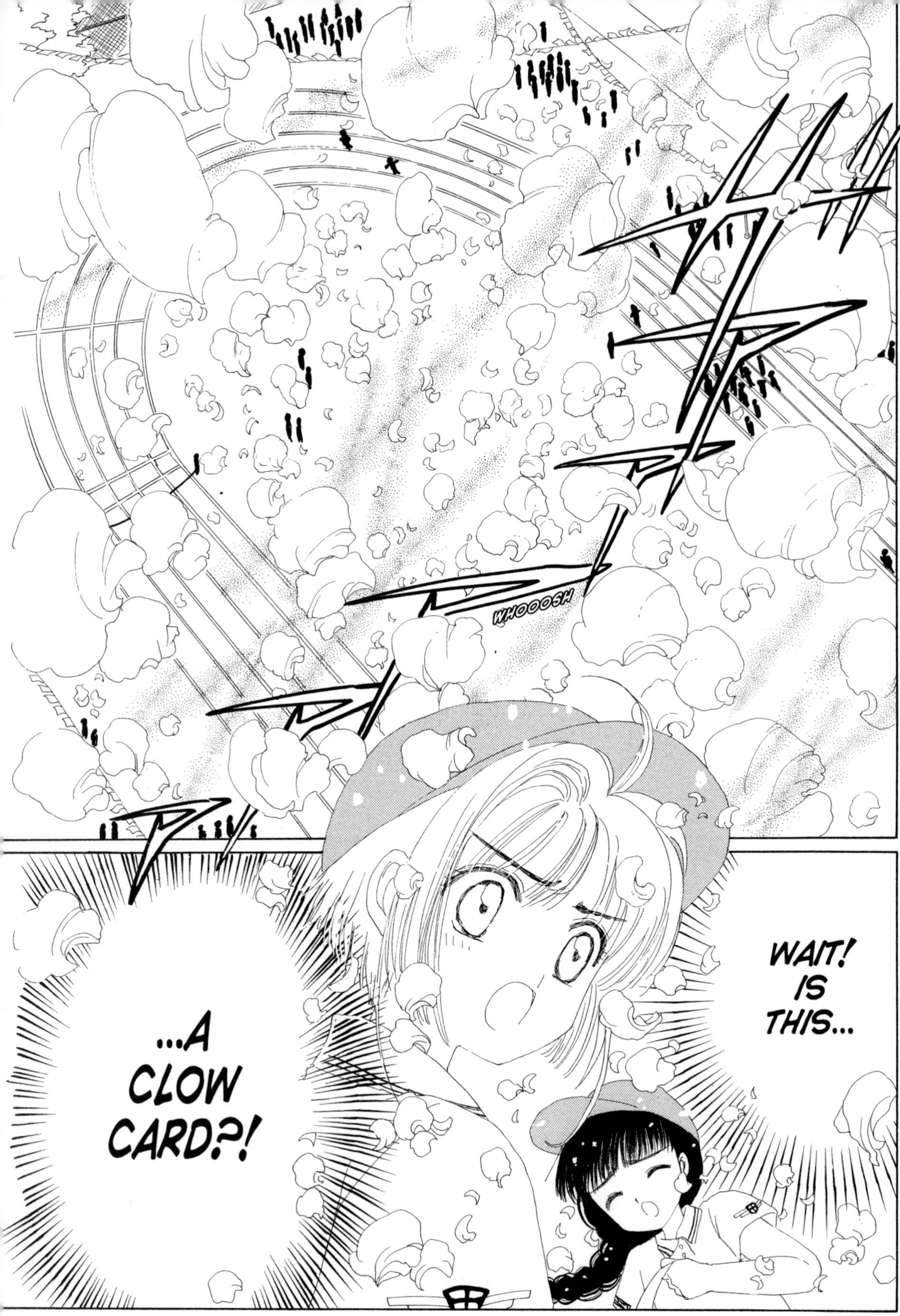
WHOOOSH
WAIT! IS THIS...
...A CLOW CARD?!

< TO BE CONTINUED >

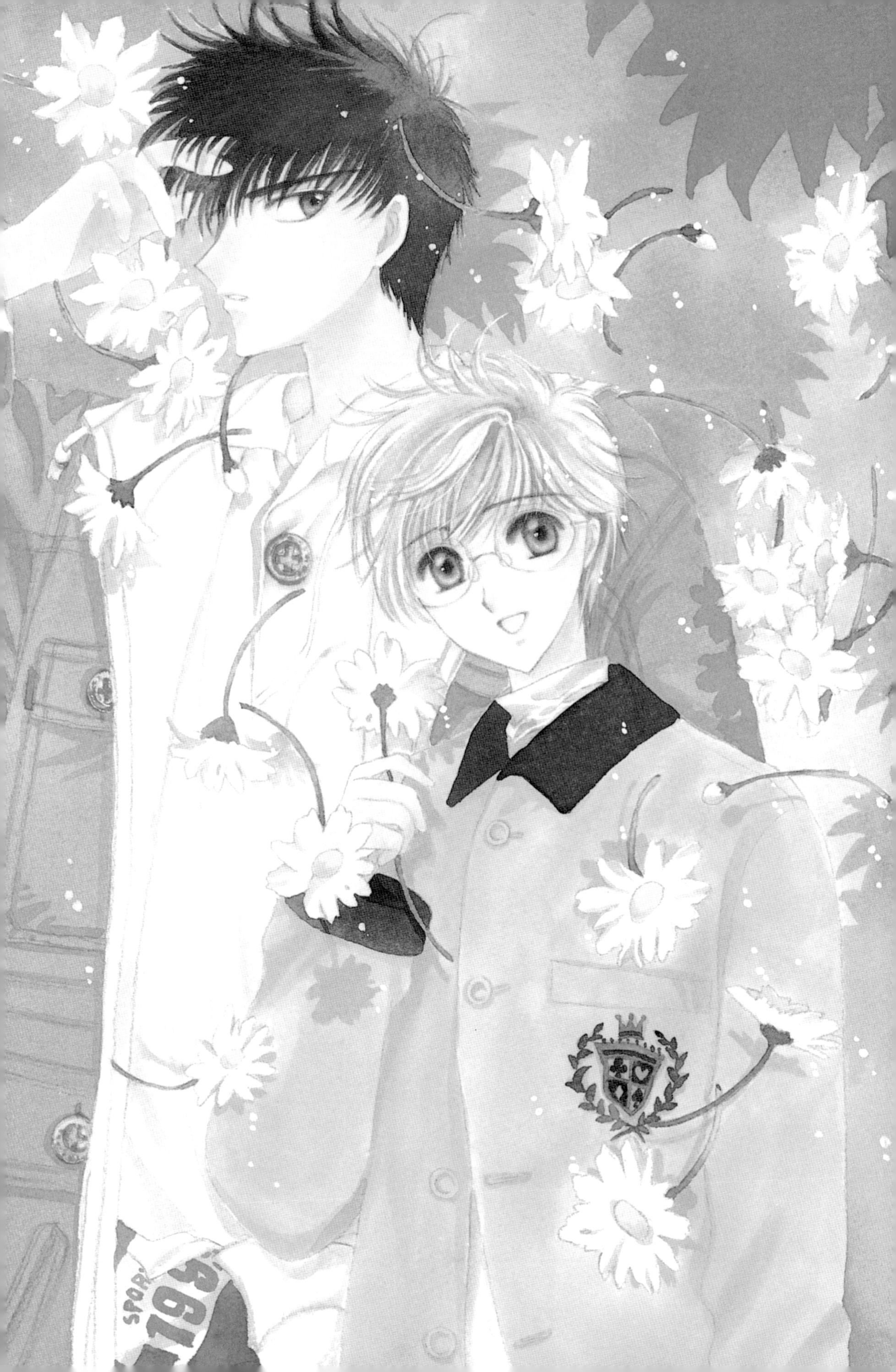

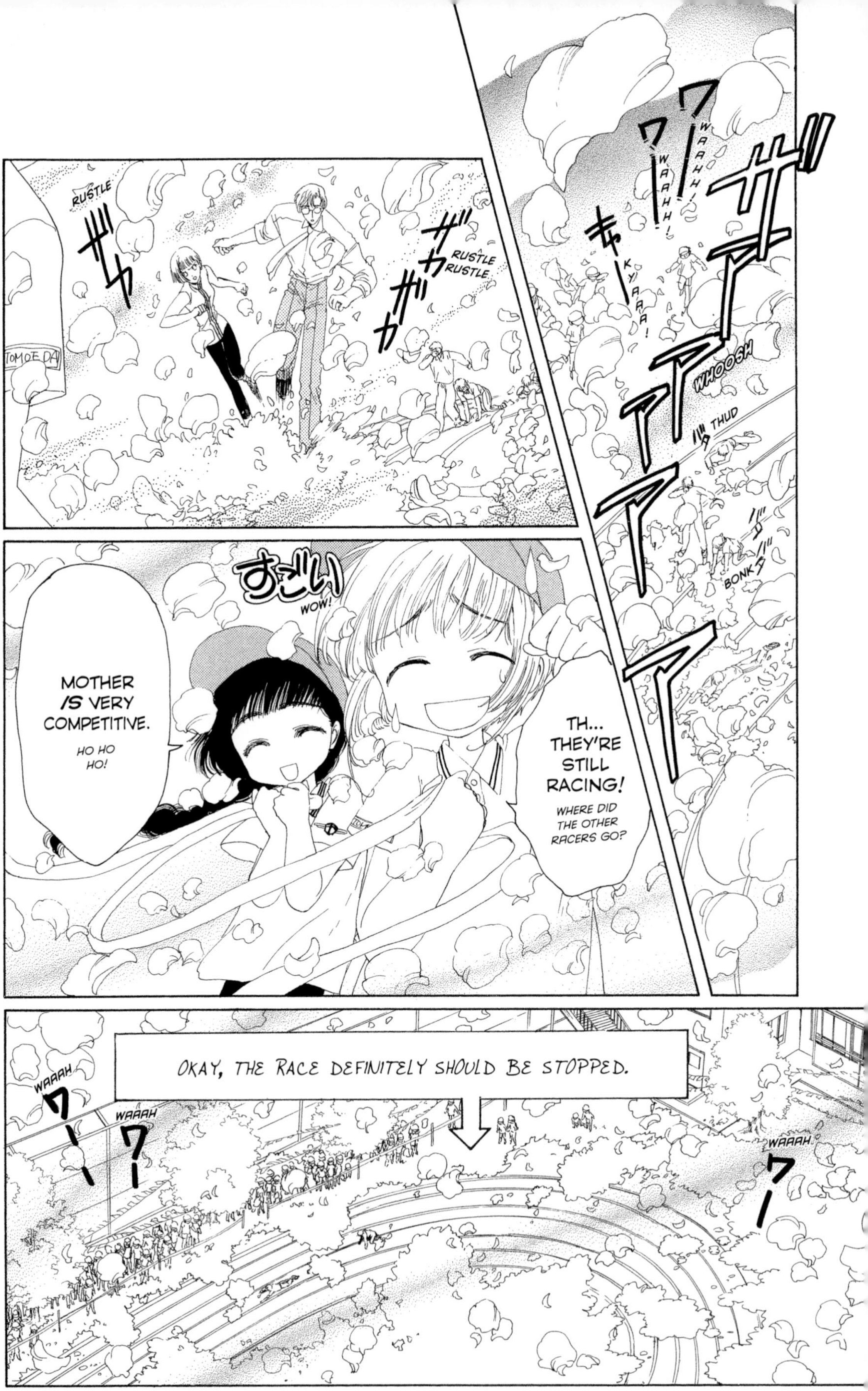
ワー
WAAHH!
ワー
WAAHH!
キャー
KYAAA!
ザザァアアア
WHOOSH
THUD
BONK
RUSTLE
RUSTLE RUSTLE
TOMOEDA
すごい
WOW!
TH... THEY'RE STILL RACING!
WHERE DID THE OTHER RACERS GO?
MOTHER *IS* VERY COMPETITIVE.
HO HO HO!
OKAY, THE RACE DEFINITELY SHOULD BE STOPPED.
WAAAH
ワー
WAAAH
ワー
WAAAH
ワー

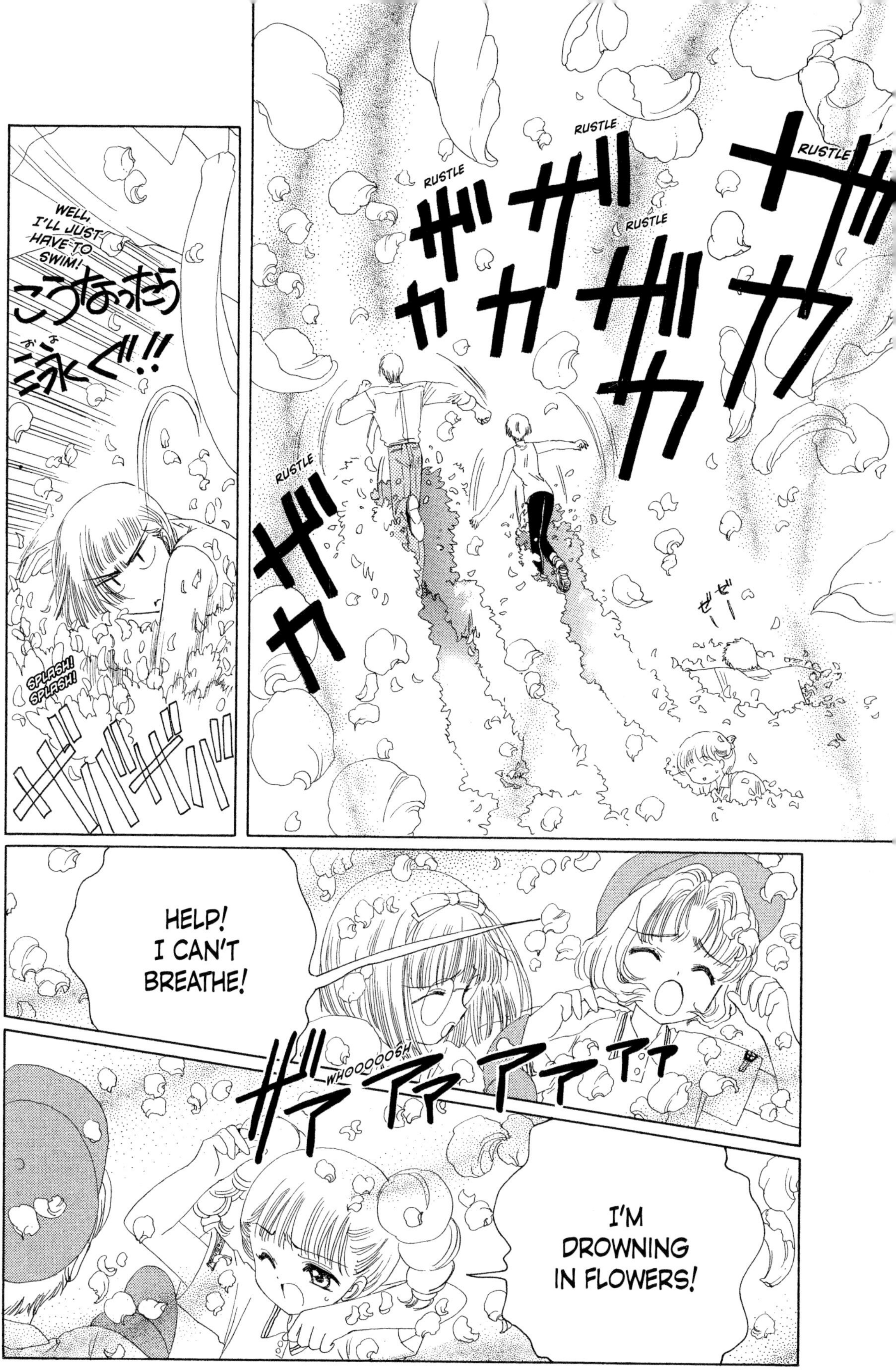
RUSTLE
RUSTLE
RUSTLE
RUSTLE
WELL, I'LL JUST HAVE TO SWIM!
こうなったら泳ぐ!!
SPLASH! SPLASH!
HELP! I CAN'T BREATHE!
WHOOOOOSH
I'M DROWNING IN FLOWERS!

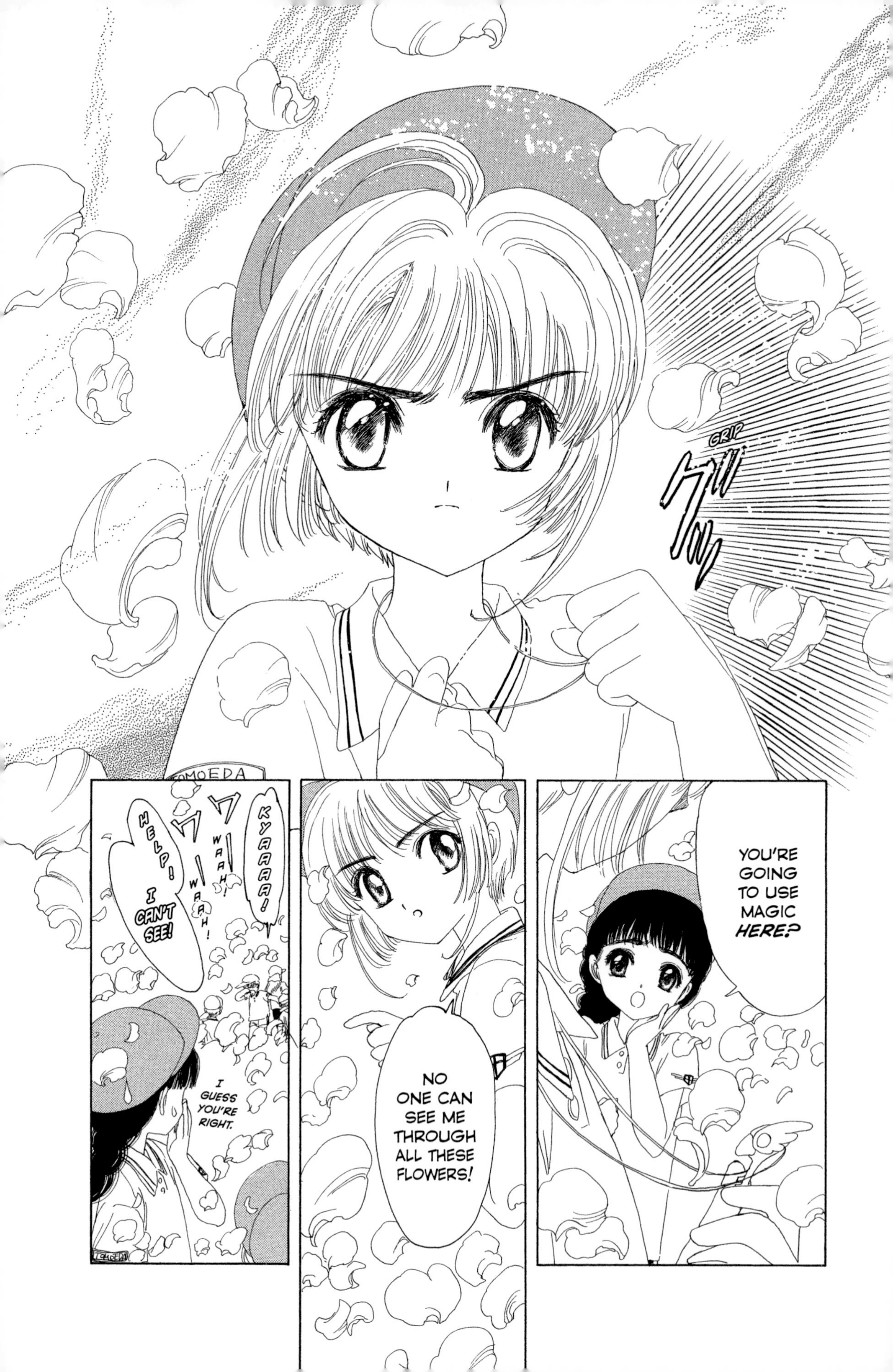
GRIP
YOU'RE GOING TO USE MAGIC *HERE?*
NO ONE CAN SEE ME THROUGH ALL THESE FLOWERS!
KYAAAA!
WAAH! WAAH!
HELP! I CAN'T SEE!
I GUESS YOU'RE RIGHT.
TOMOEDA

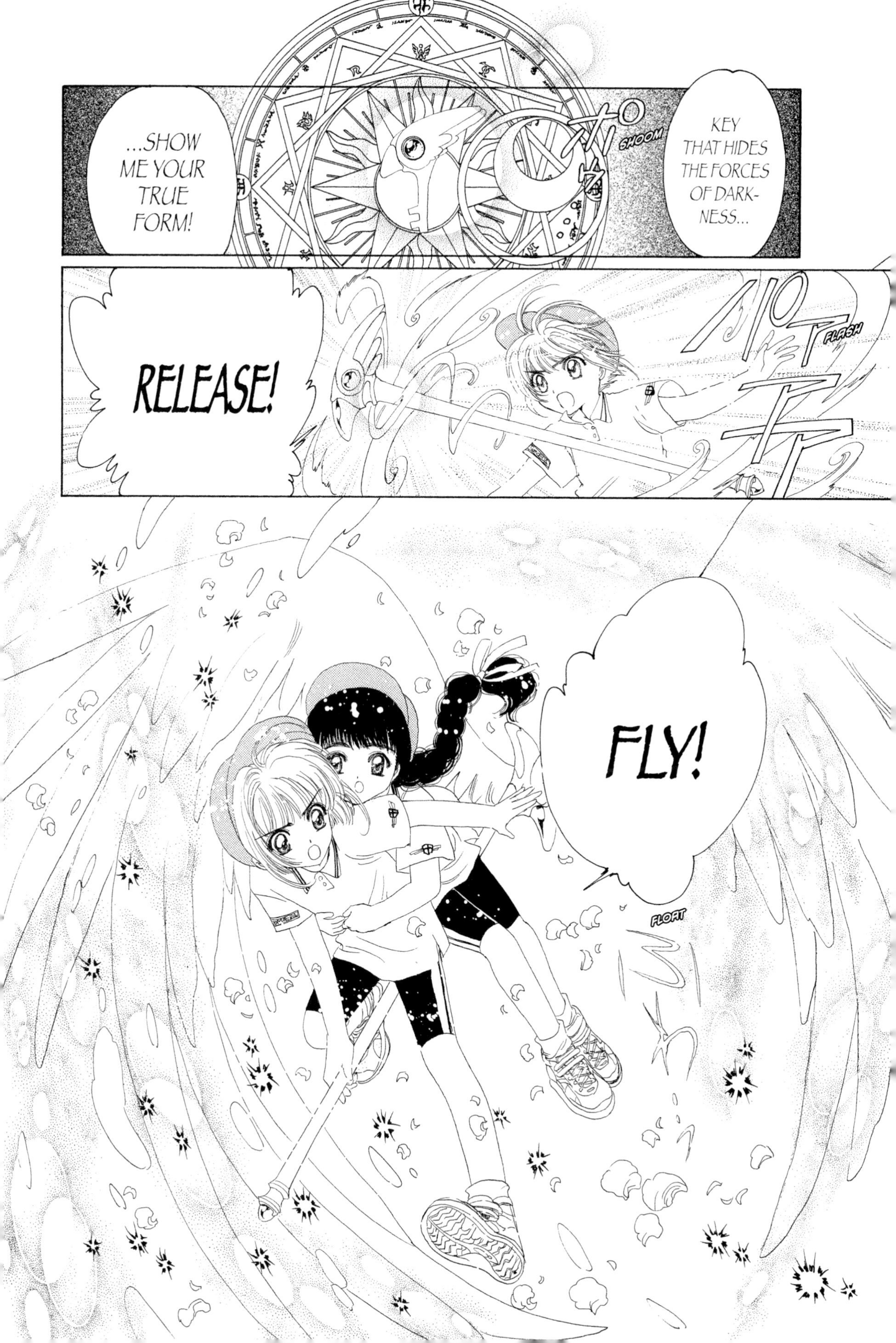
KEY THAT HIDES THE FORCES OF DARKNESS...
SHOOM
...SHOW ME YOUR TRUE FORM!
FLASH
RELEASE!
FLY!
FLOAT

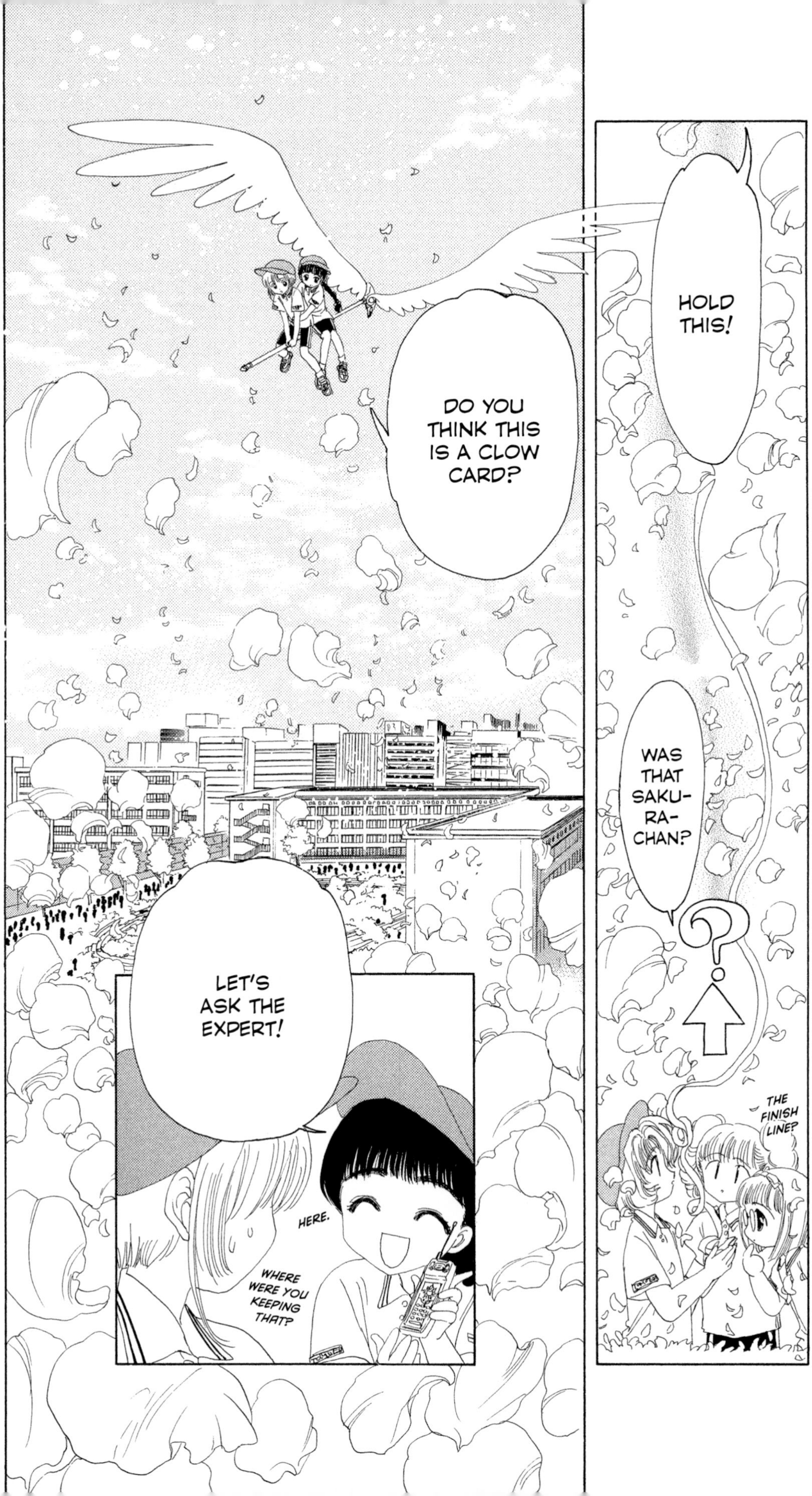
HOLD THIS!
WAS THAT SAKURA-CHAN?
THE FINISH LINE?
DO YOU THINK THIS IS A CLOW CARD?
LET'S ASK THE EXPERT!
HERE.
WHERE WERE YOU KEEPING THAT?

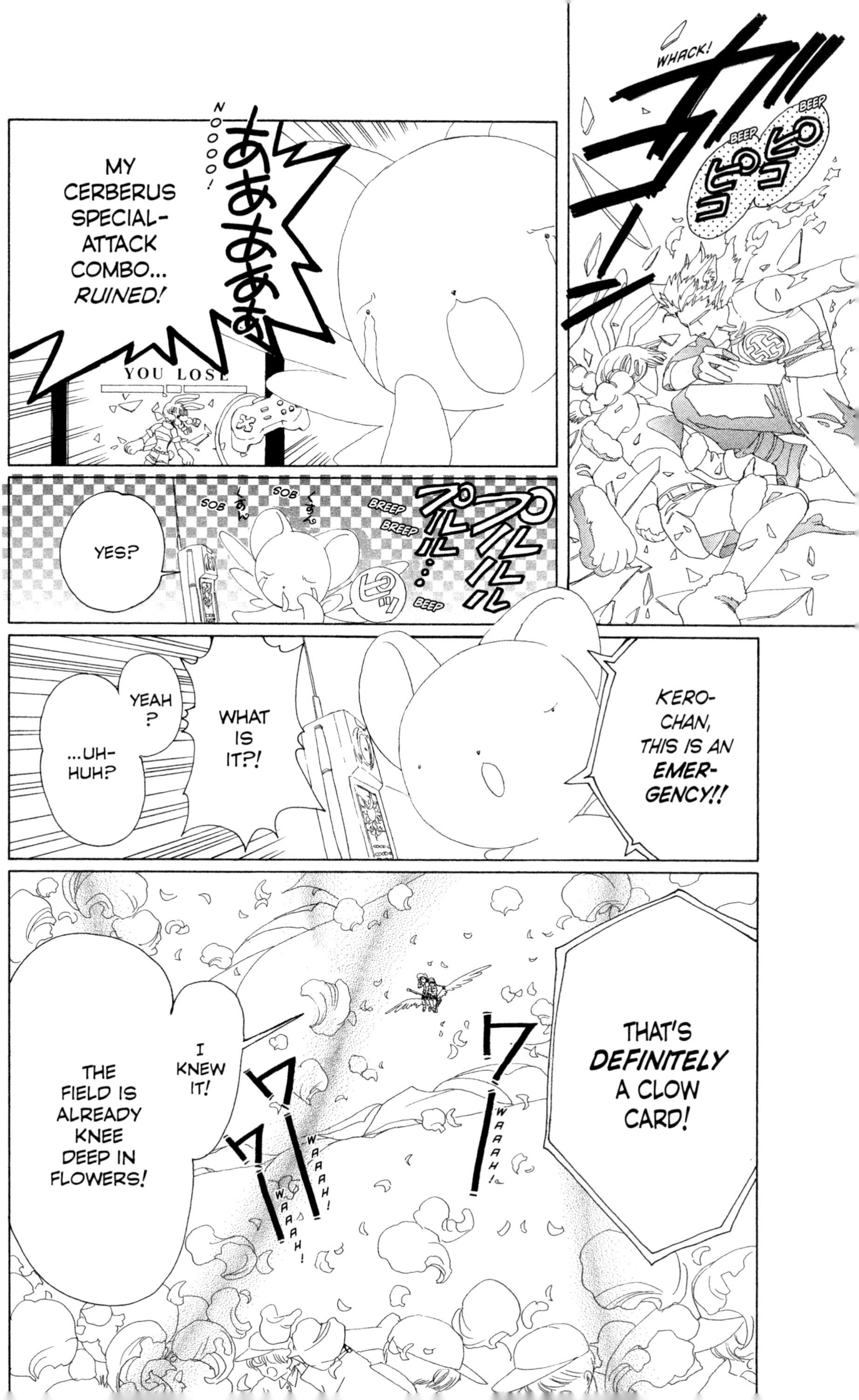
WHACK!
BEEP BEEP
NOOOOO!
MY CERBERUS SPECIAL-ATTACK COMBO... *RUINED!*
YOU LOSE
BREEP BREEP
BEEP
SOB SOB
YES?
KERO-CHAN, THIS IS AN *EMERGENCY!!*
WHAT IS IT?!
YEAH? ...UH-HUH?
THAT'S *DEFINITELY* A CLOW CARD!
WAAAH!
WAAAH!
WAAAH!
I KNEW IT!
THE FIELD IS ALREADY KNEE DEEP IN FLOWERS!

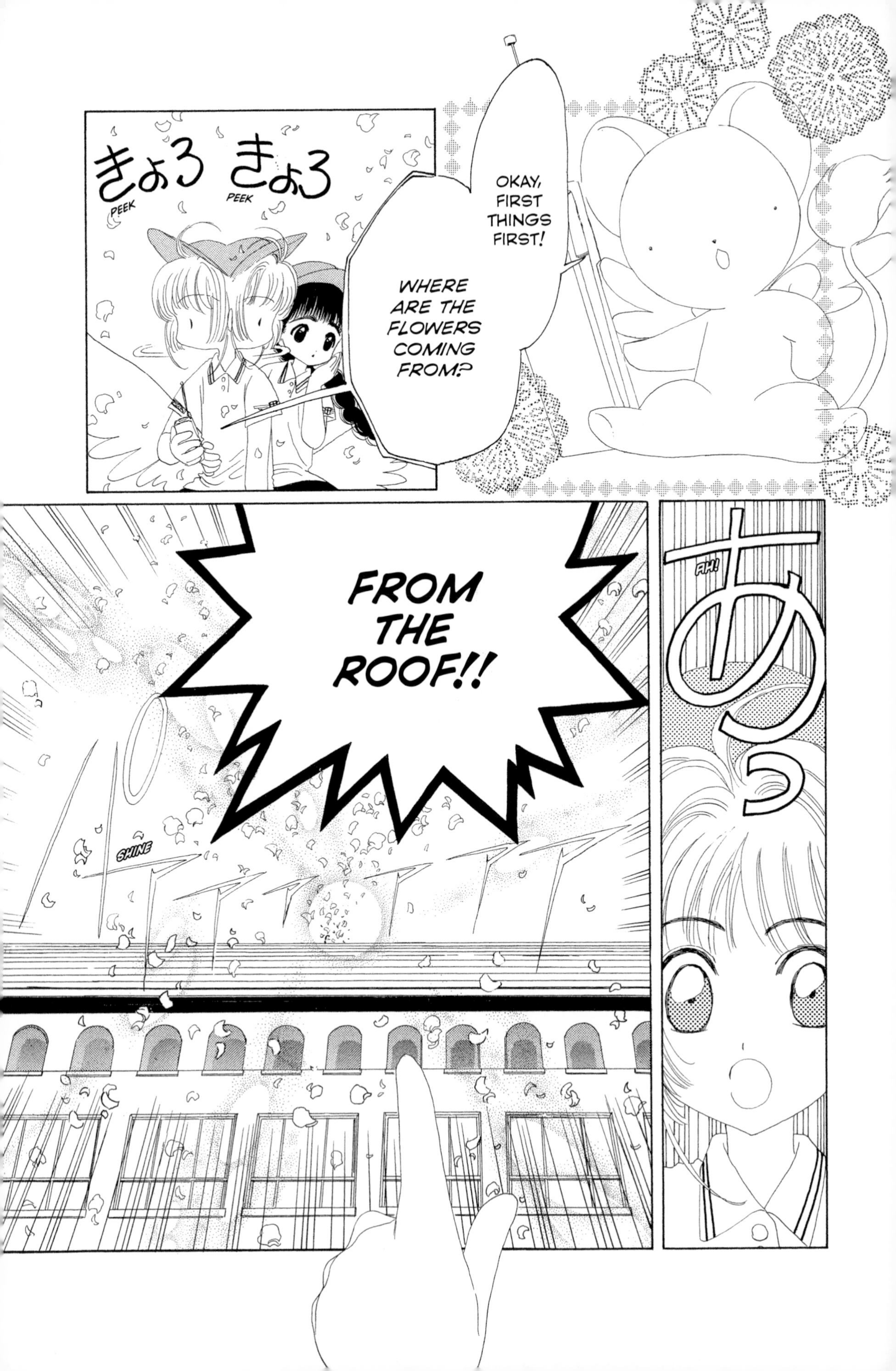
OKAY, FIRST THINGS FIRST!
WHERE ARE THE FLOWERS COMING FROM?
きょろ きょろ
PEEK PEEK
あっ
AH!
FROM THE ROOF!!
SHINE

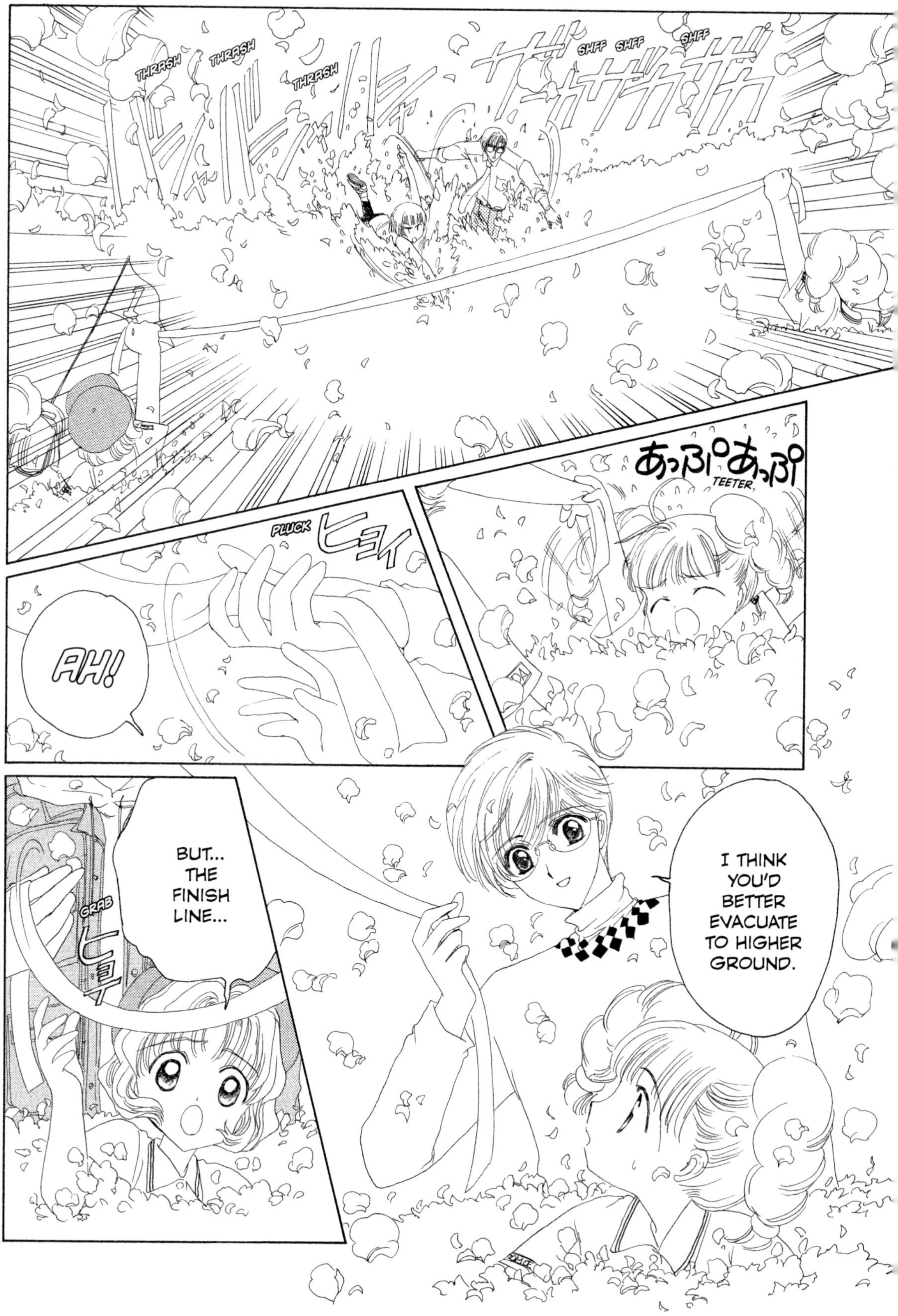
SHFF SHFF SHFF
THRASH THRASH THRASH
あっぷあっぷ
TEETER
PLUCK
ヒョイ
AH!
I THINK YOU'D BETTER EVACUATE TO HIGHER GROUND.
BUT... THE FINISH LINE...
GRAB

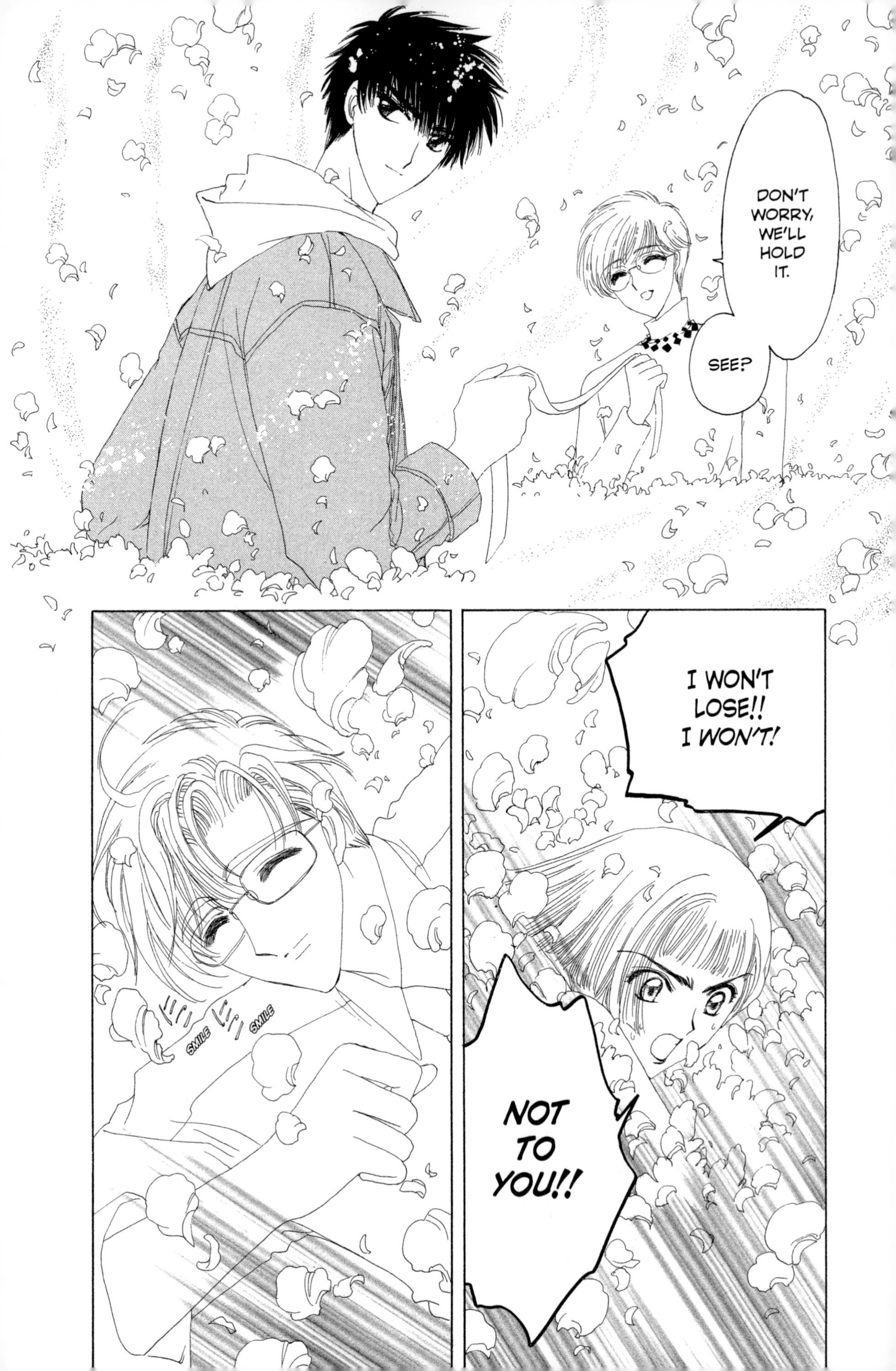
DON'T WORRY, WE'LL HOLD IT.
SEE?
I WON'T LOSE!! I WON'T!
NOT TO YOU!!
SMILE SMILE

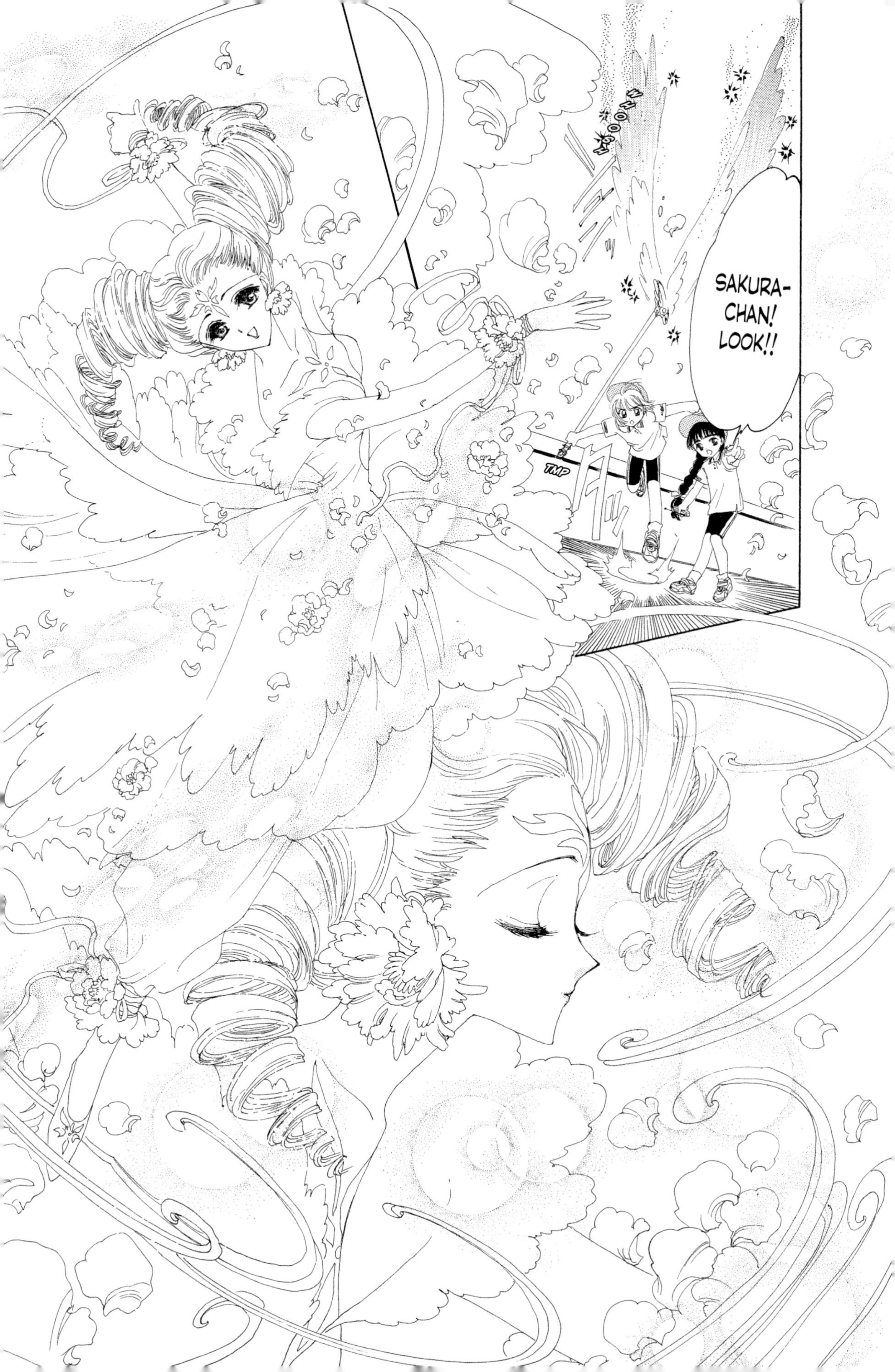
WHOOSH
SAKURA-CHAN! LOOK!!
TMP

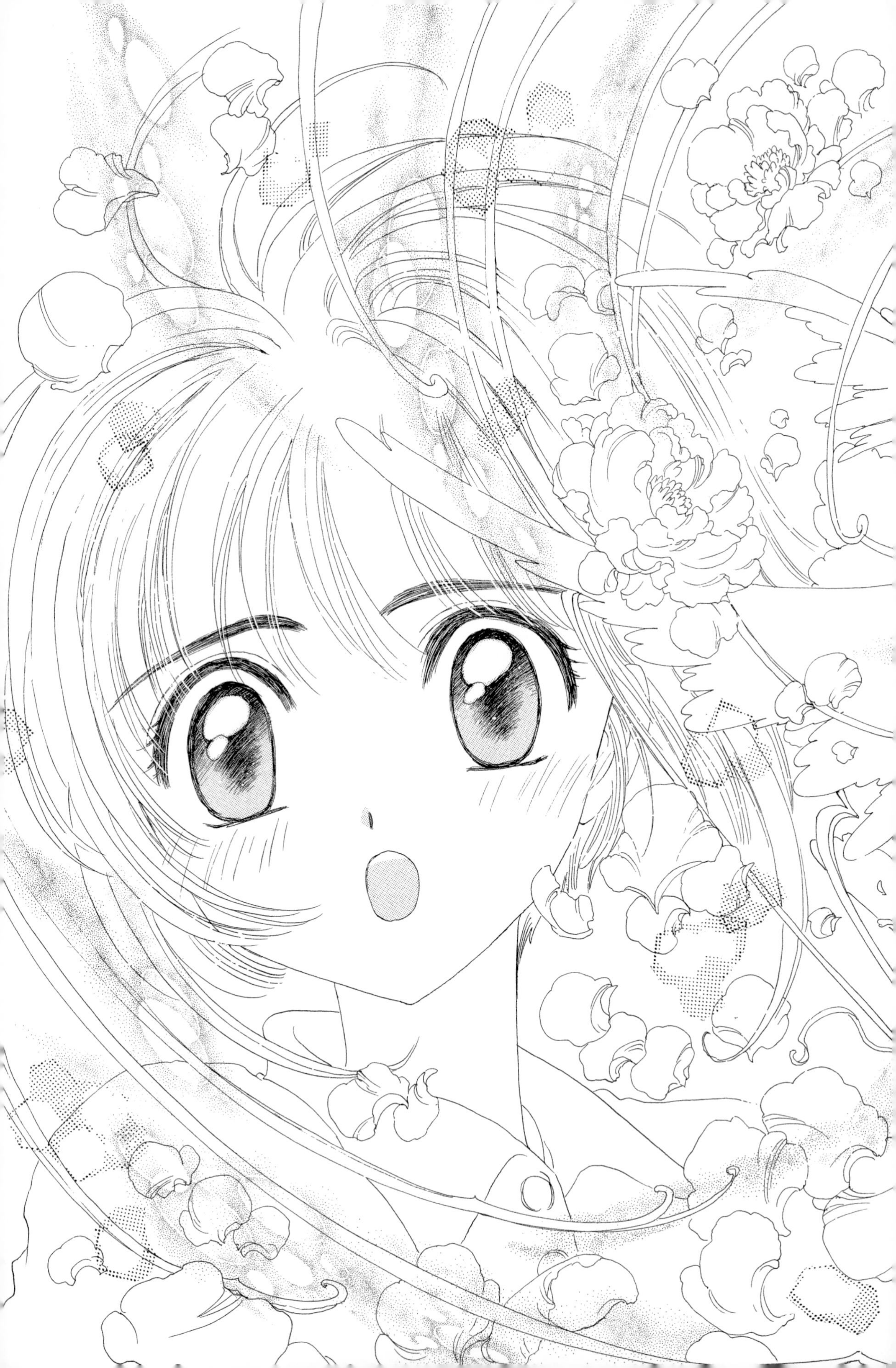

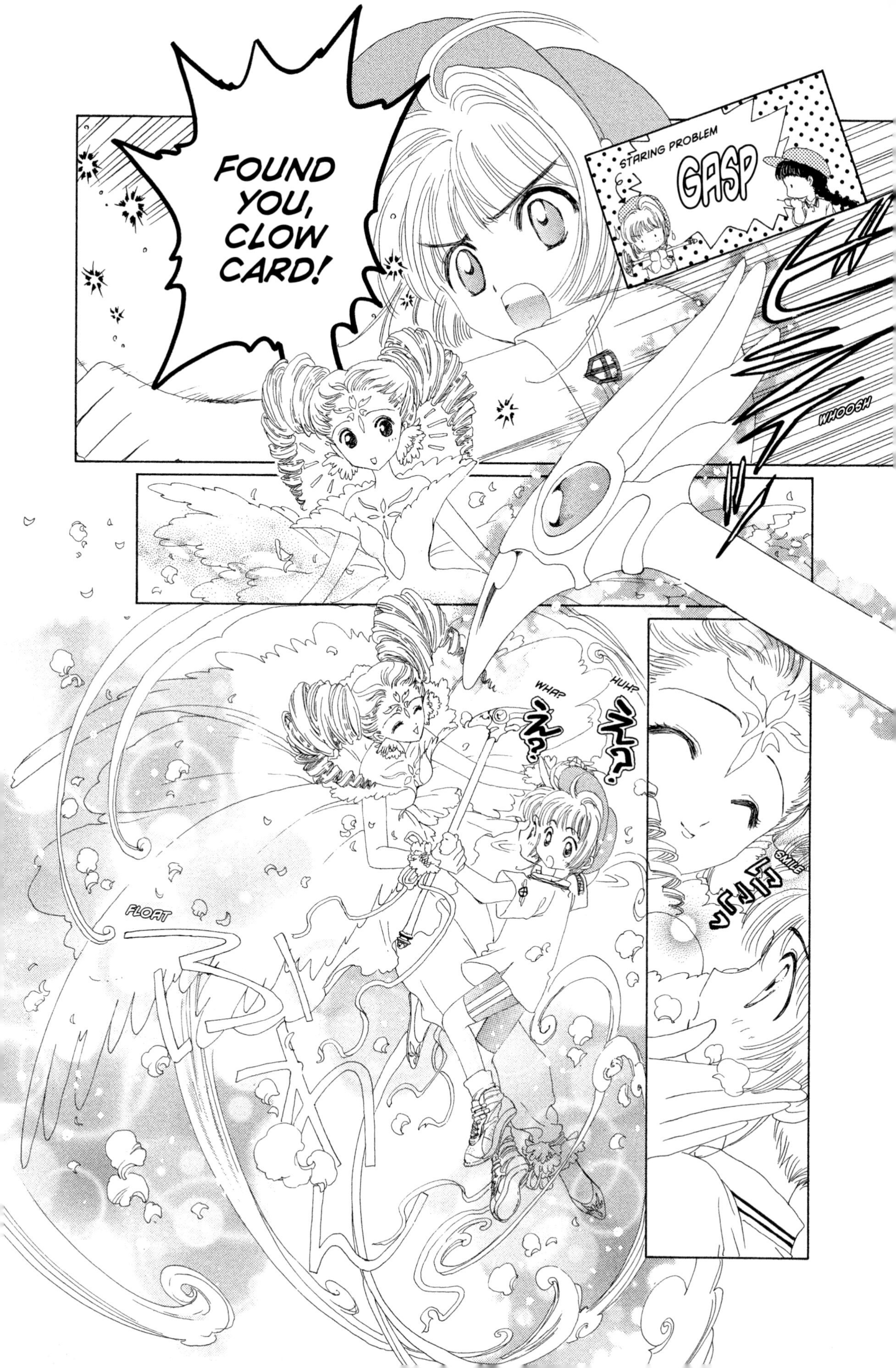
STARING PROBLEM
GASP
FOUND YOU, CLOW CARD!
WHOOSH
SMILE
HUH?
WHA?
FLOAT

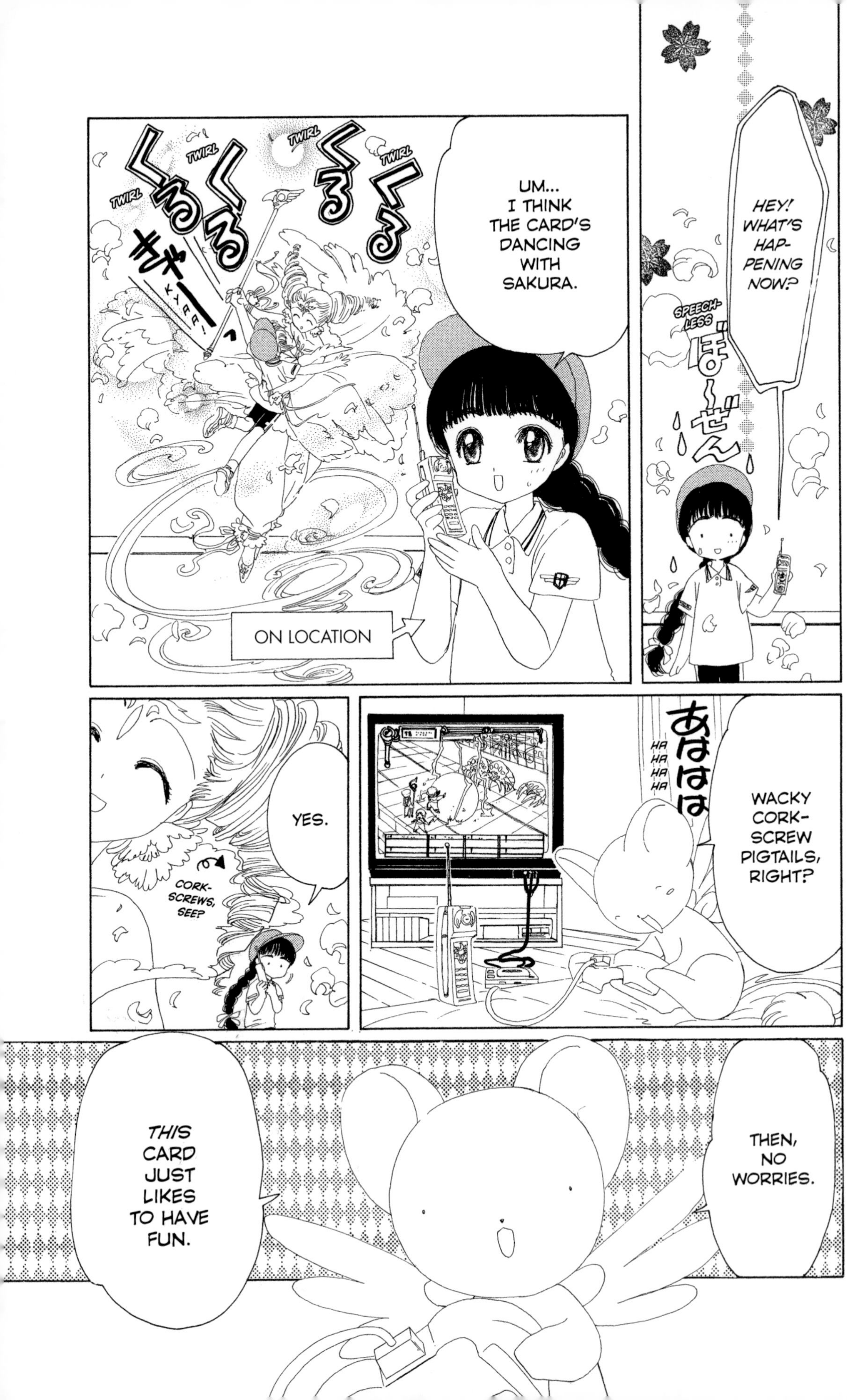

HEY! WHAT'S HAP-PENING NOW?
ぽ～ぜん
SPEECH-LESS
くるくるくるくる
TWIRL TWIRL TWIRL TWIRL
きゃー
KYAA!
UM... I THINK THE CARD'S DANCING WITH SAKURA.
ON LOCATION
あははは
HA HA HA HA
WACKY CORK-SCREW PIGTAILS, RIGHT?
YES.
CORK-SCREWS, SEE?
THEN, NO WORRIES.
THIS CARD JUST LIKES TO HAVE FUN.

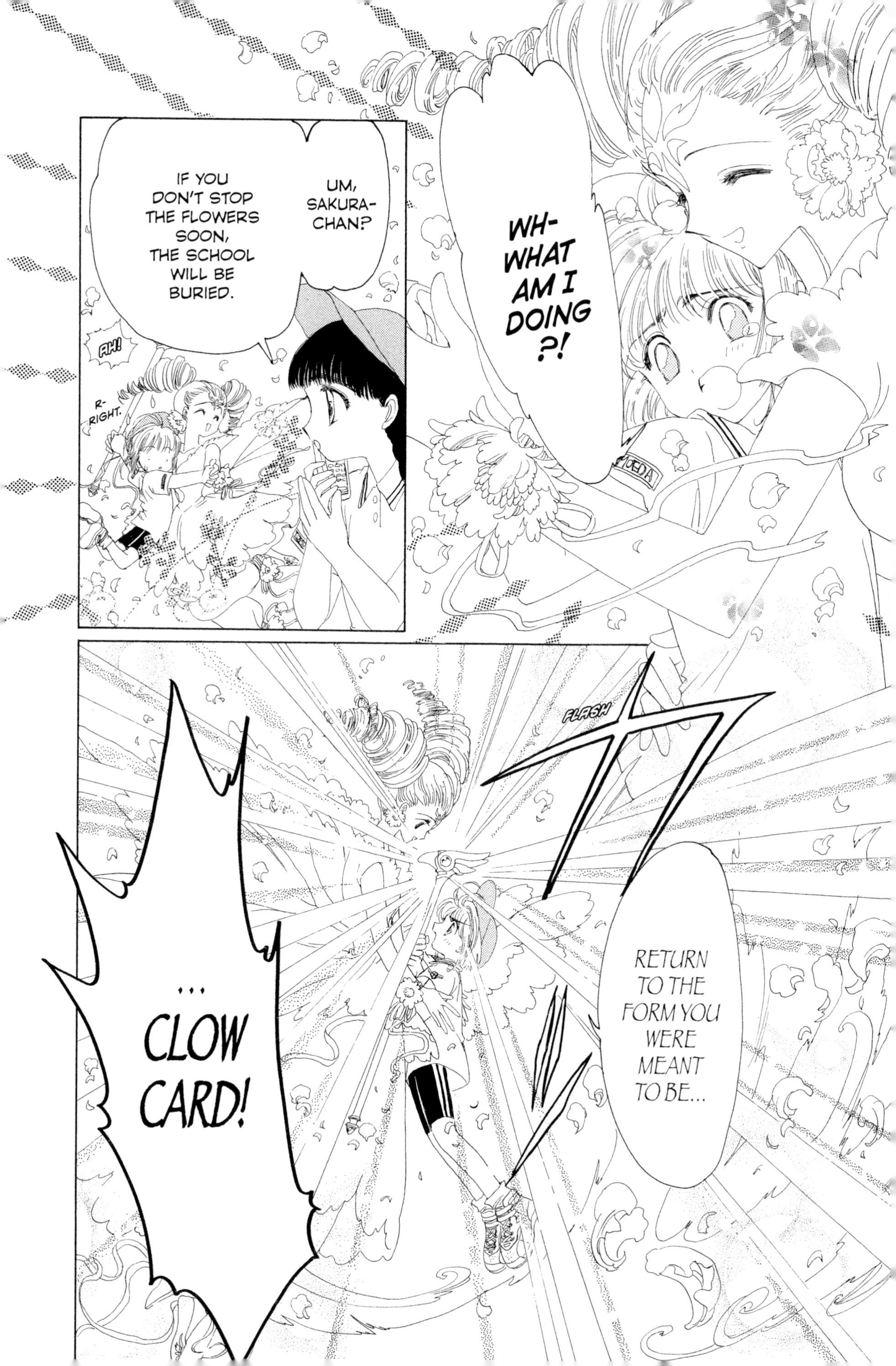
WH-WHAT AM I DOING?!
UM, SAKURA-CHAN?
IF YOU DON'T STOP THE FLOWERS SOON, THE SCHOOL WILL BE BURIED.
AH!
R-RIGHT.
FLASH
RETURN TO THE FORM YOU WERE MEANT TO BE...
... CLOW CARD!

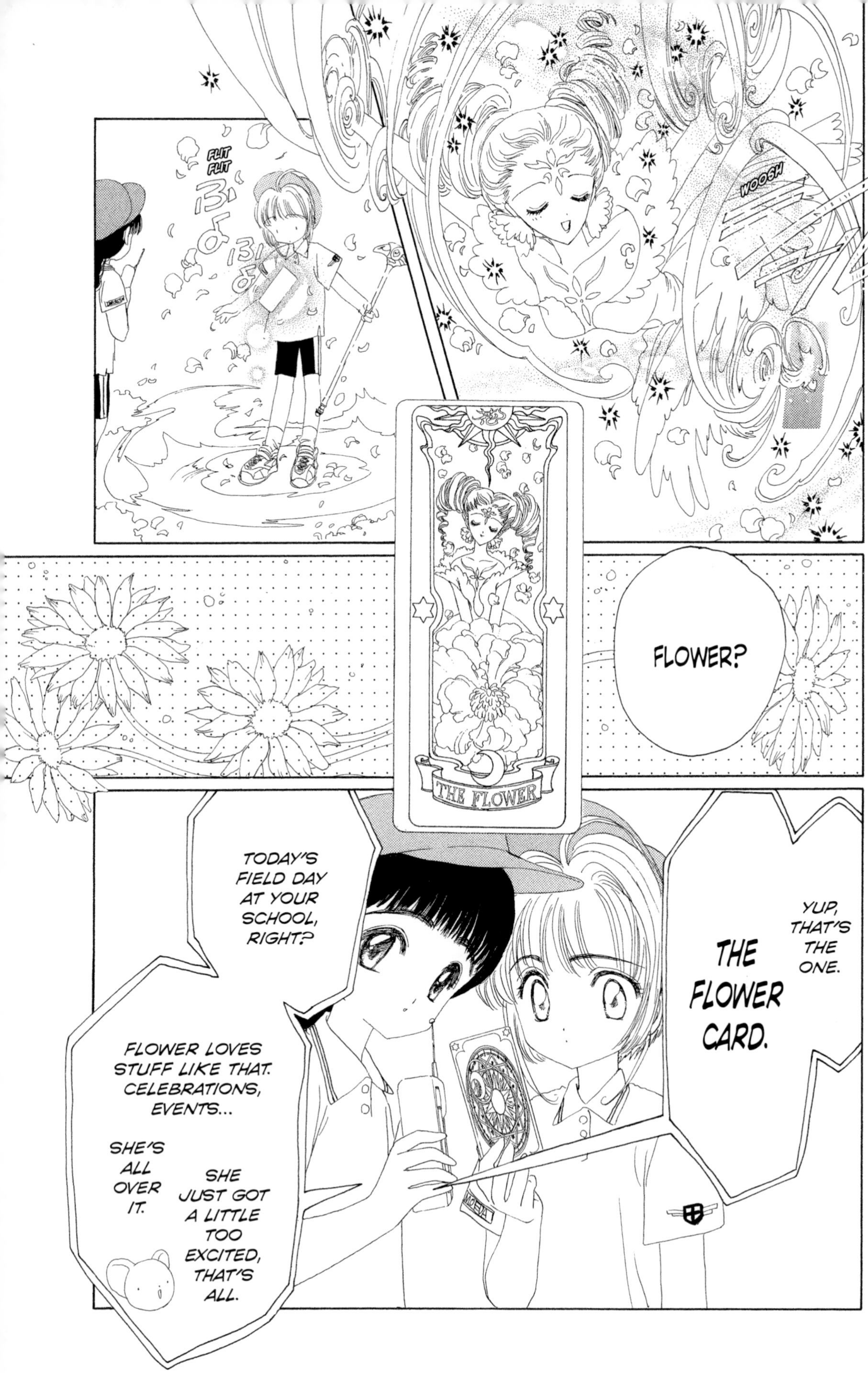
WOOSH
FLIT FLIT
THE FLOWER
FLOWER?
YUP, THAT'S THE ONE.
THE FLOWER CARD.
TODAY'S FIELD DAY AT YOUR SCHOOL, RIGHT?
FLOWER LOVES STUFF LIKE THAT. CELEBRATIONS, EVENTS...
SHE'S ALL OVER IT.
SHE JUST GOT A LITTLE TOO EXCITED, THAT'S ALL.

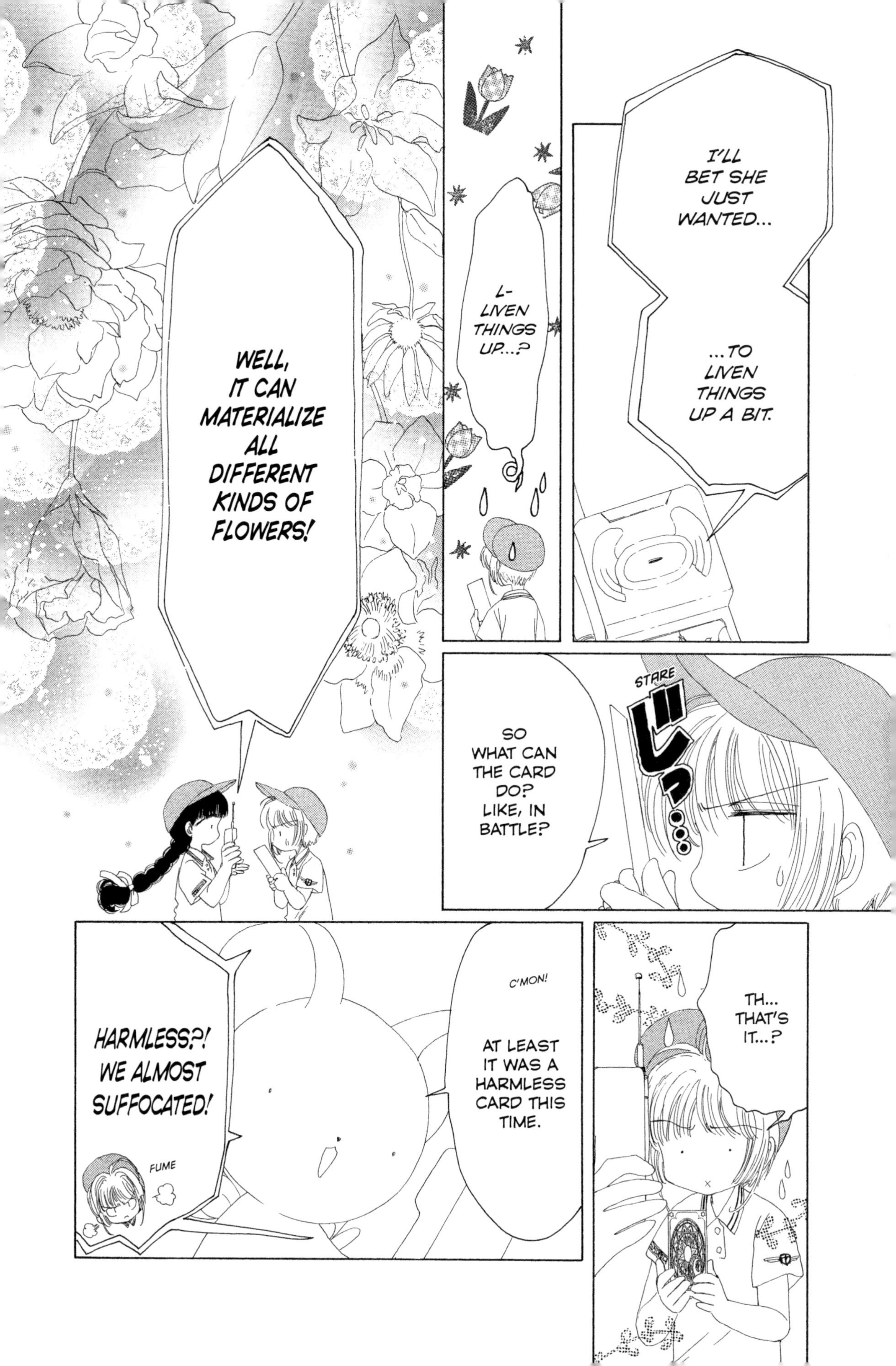
I'LL BET SHE JUST WANTED...
...TO LIVEN THINGS UP A BIT.
L-LIVEN THINGS UP...?
STARE
じっ…
SO WHAT CAN THE CARD DO? LIKE, IN BATTLE?
WELL, IT CAN MATERIALIZE ALL DIFFERENT KINDS OF FLOWERS!
TH... THAT'S IT...?
C'MON!
AT LEAST IT WAS A HARMLESS CARD THIS TIME.
HARMLESS?! WE ALMOST SUFFOCATED!
FUME

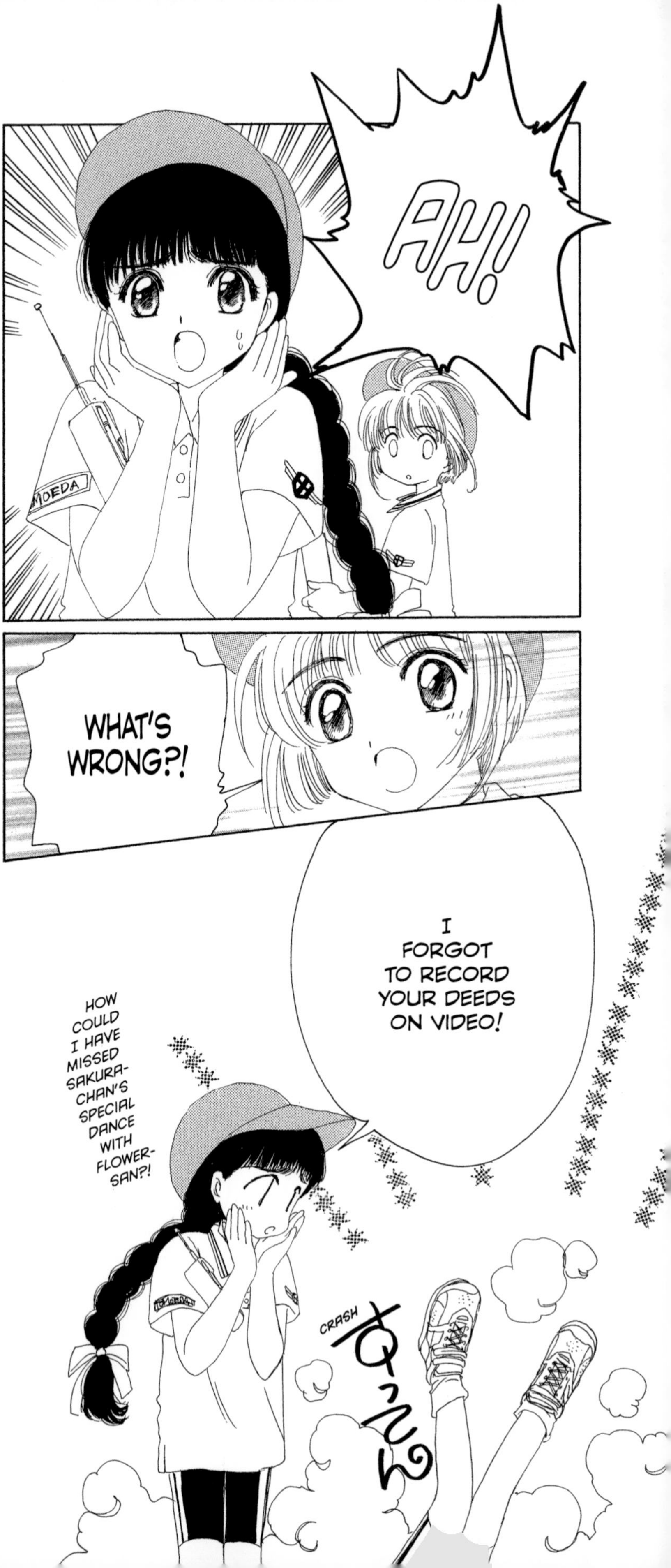
AH!
WHAT'S WRONG?!
I FORGOT TO RECORD YOUR DEEDS ON VIDEO!
HOW COULD I HAVE MISSED SAKURA-CHAN'S SPECIAL DANCE WITH FLOWER-SAN?!
CRASH

6

FUJITAKA KINOMOTO

BIRTHDATE:
JANUARY 3

OCCUPATION:
UNIVERSITY PROFESSOR

FAVORITE FOODS:
SWEETS, NOODLES

FAVORITE PASTIME:
VIDEO GAMES

FAVORITE COLORS:
WHITE, IVORY, BROWN

FAVORITE FLOWERS:
NADESHIKO, PEACH BLOSSOM, CHERRY BLOSSOM

FAVORITE RECIPE:
SWEETS

SPECIAL SKILL:
REMEMBERING PEOPLE'S FACES AND NAMES

HOBBY:
COOKING

WISH LIST:
NOTHING

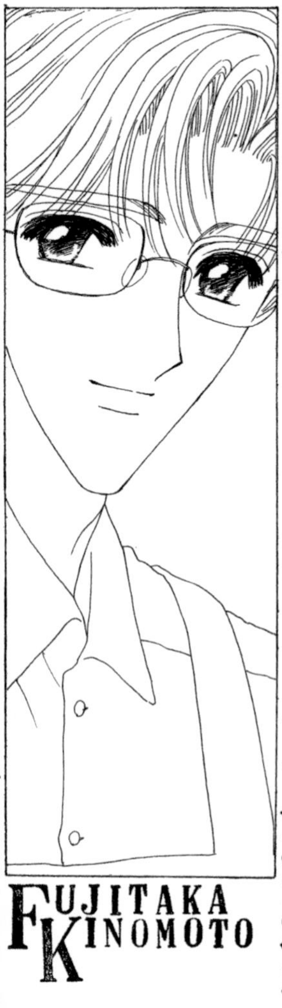

FUJITAKA KINOMOTO

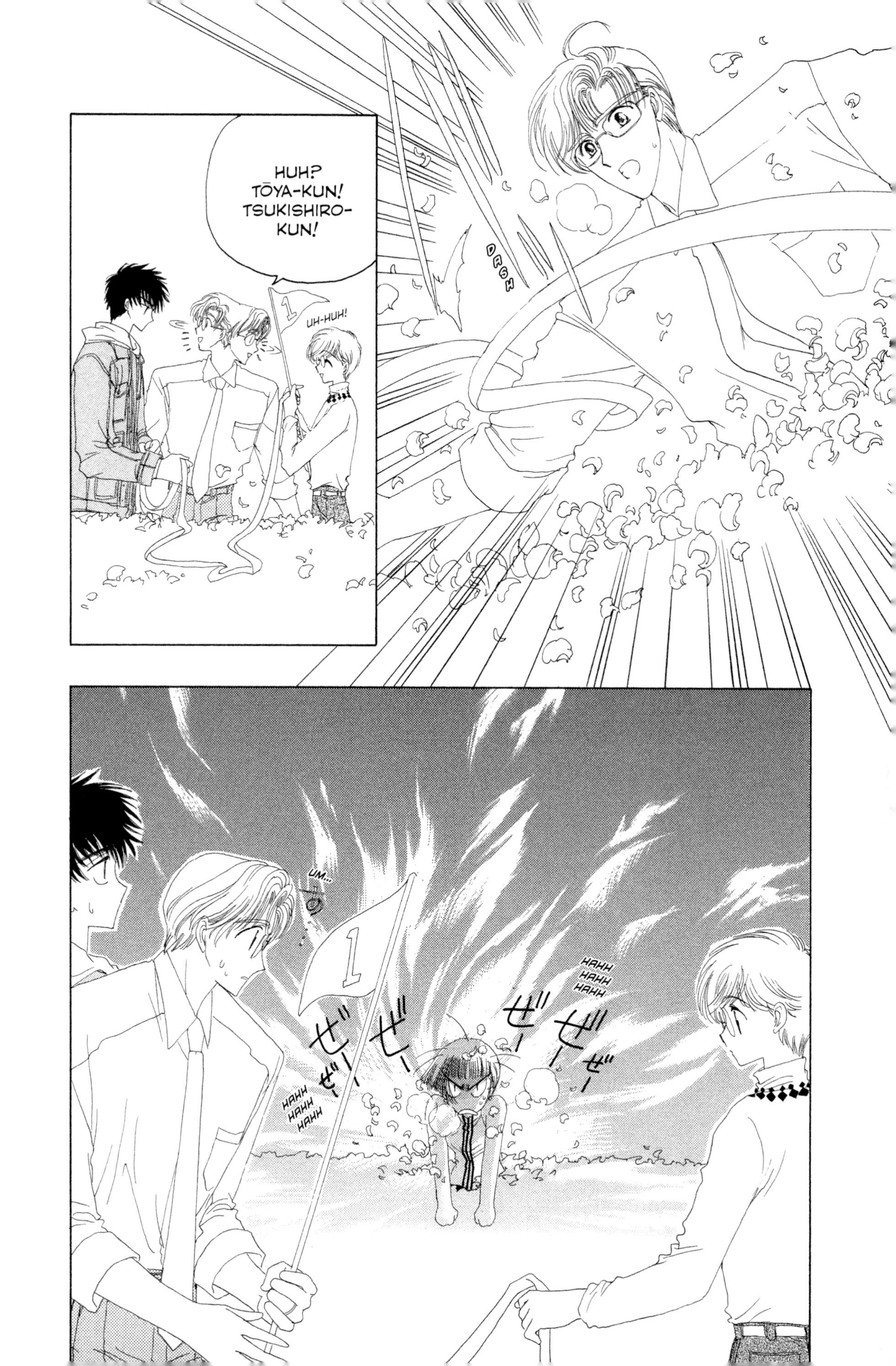
DASH
HUH? TŌYA-KUN! TSUKISHIRO-KUN!
UH-HUH!
UM...
HAHH HAHH HAHH
ぜーぜー
ぜーぜー
HAHH HAHH HAHH

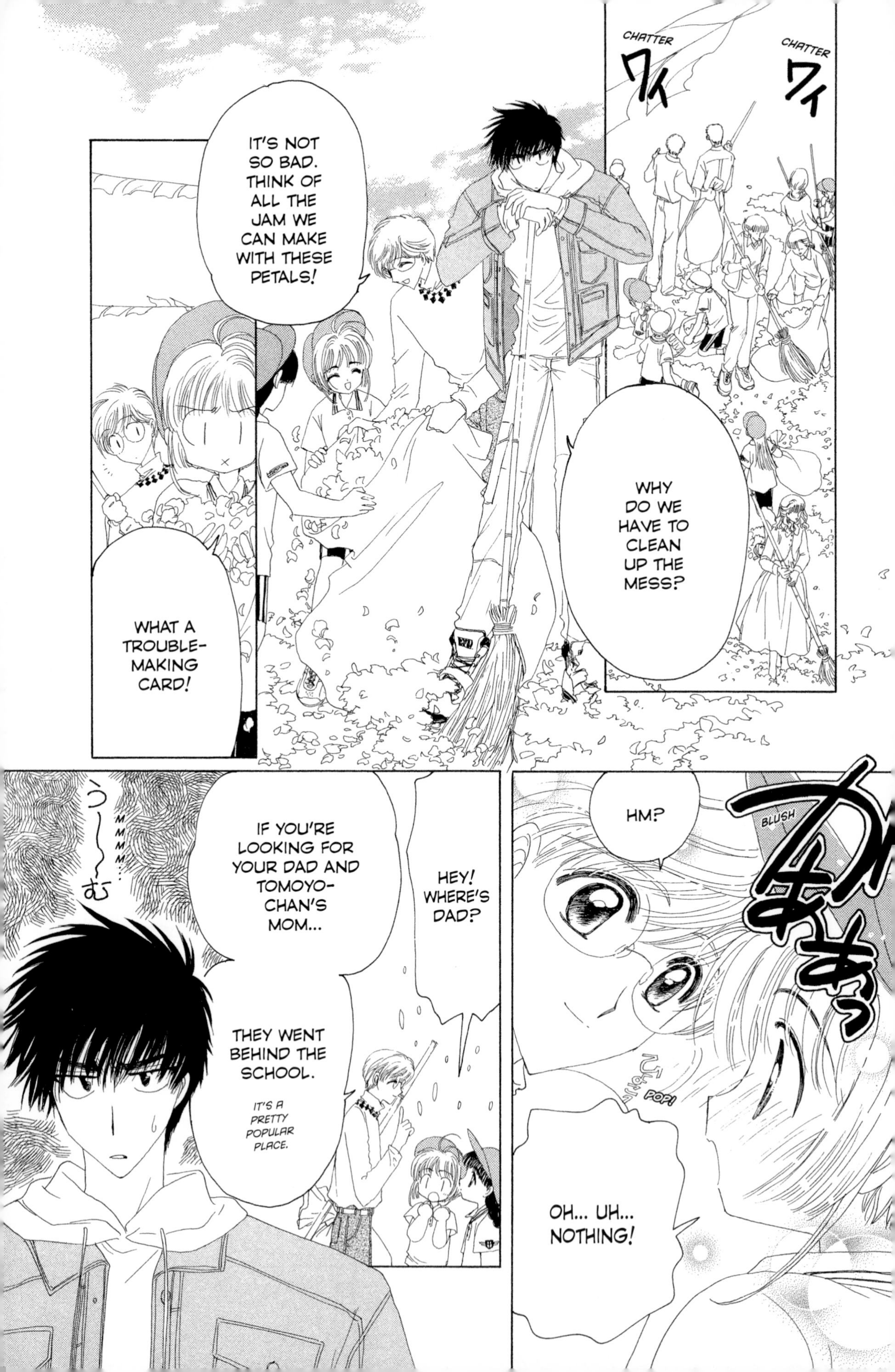
CHATTER
ワイ
CHATTER
ワイ
WHY DO WE HAVE TO CLEAN UP THE MESS?
IT'S NOT SO BAD. THINK OF ALL THE JAM WE CAN MAKE WITH THESE PETALS!
WHAT A TROUBLE-MAKING CARD!
HM?
BLUSH
POP!
OH... UH... NOTHING!
HEY! WHERE'S DAD?
IF YOU'RE LOOKING FOR YOUR DAD AND TOMOYO-CHAN'S MOM...
THEY WENT BEHIND THE SCHOOL.
IT'S A PRETTY POPULAR PLACE.
MMMM...
うーむ

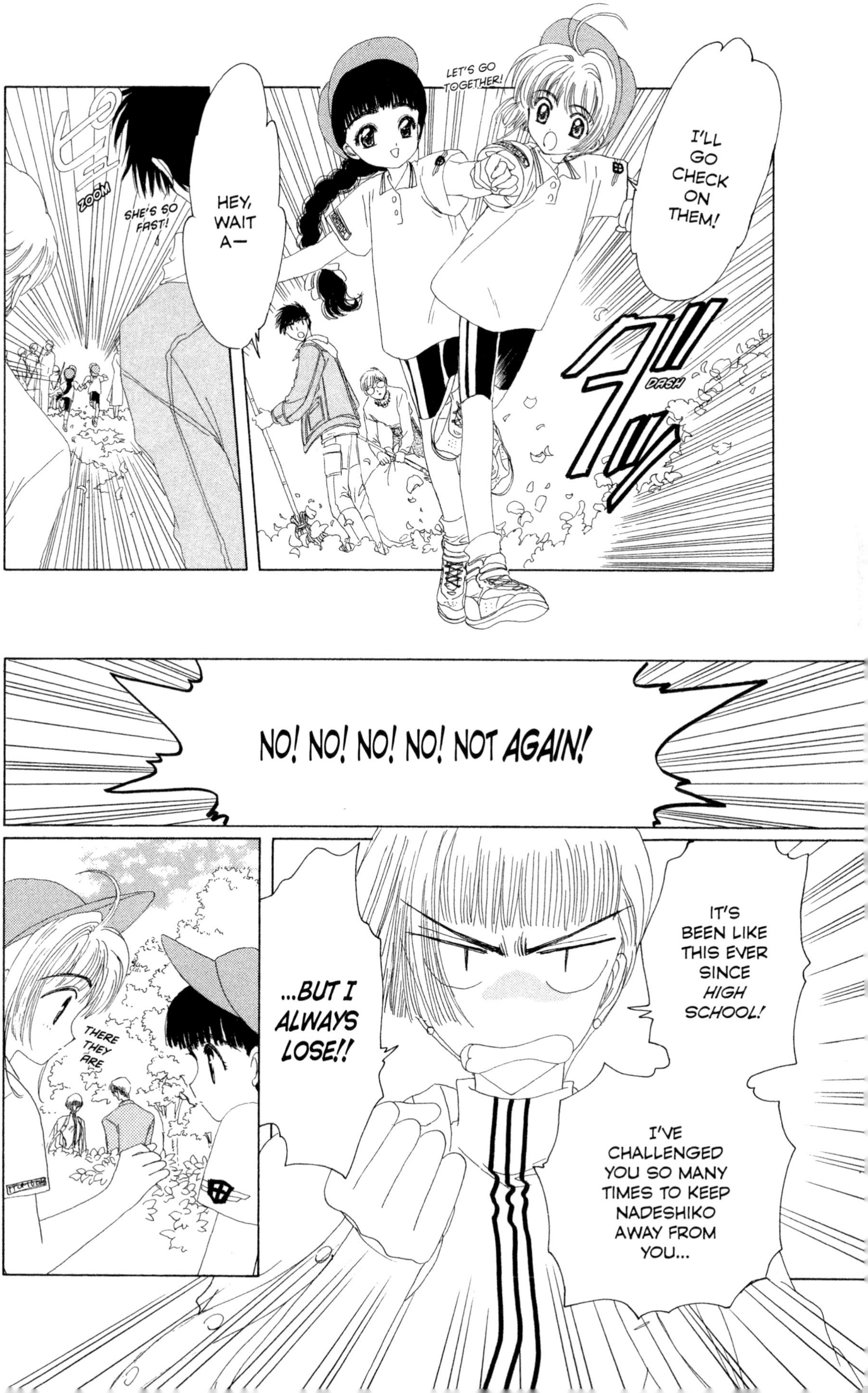
I'LL GO CHECK ON THEM!
LET'S GO TOGETHER!
DASH
HEY, WAIT A—
ZOOM
SHE'S SO FAST!
NO! NO! NO! NO! NOT AGAIN!
IT'S BEEN LIKE THIS EVER SINCE HIGH SCHOOL!
I'VE CHALLENGED YOU SO MANY TIMES TO KEEP NADESHIKO AWAY FROM YOU...
...BUT I ALWAYS LOSE!!
THERE THEY ARE

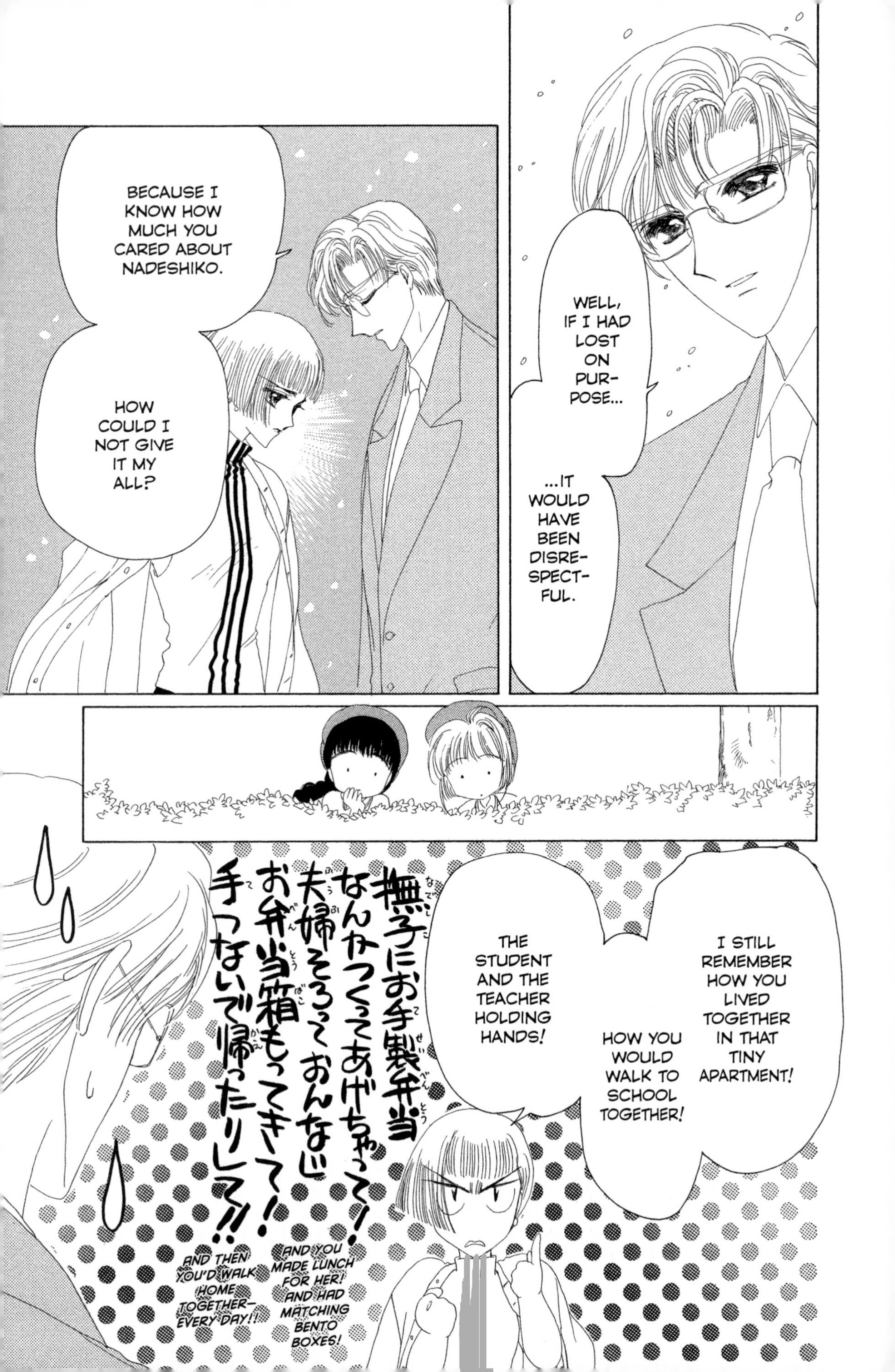
WELL, IF I HAD LOST ON PURPOSE...
...IT WOULD HAVE BEEN DISRESPECTFUL.
BECAUSE I KNOW HOW MUCH YOU CARED ABOUT NADESHIKO.
HOW COULD I NOT GIVE IT MY ALL?
I STILL REMEMBER HOW YOU LIVED TOGETHER IN THAT TINY APARTMENT!
HOW YOU WOULD WALK TO SCHOOL TOGETHER!
THE STUDENT AND THE TEACHER HOLDING HANDS!
撫子にお手製弁当なんかつくってあげちゃって!夫婦そろっておんなじお弁当箱もってきて!!手つないで帰ったりして!!
AND YOU MADE LUNCH FOR HER! AND HAD MATCHING BENTO BOXES!
AND THEN YOU'D WALK HOME TOGETHER–EVERY DAY!!

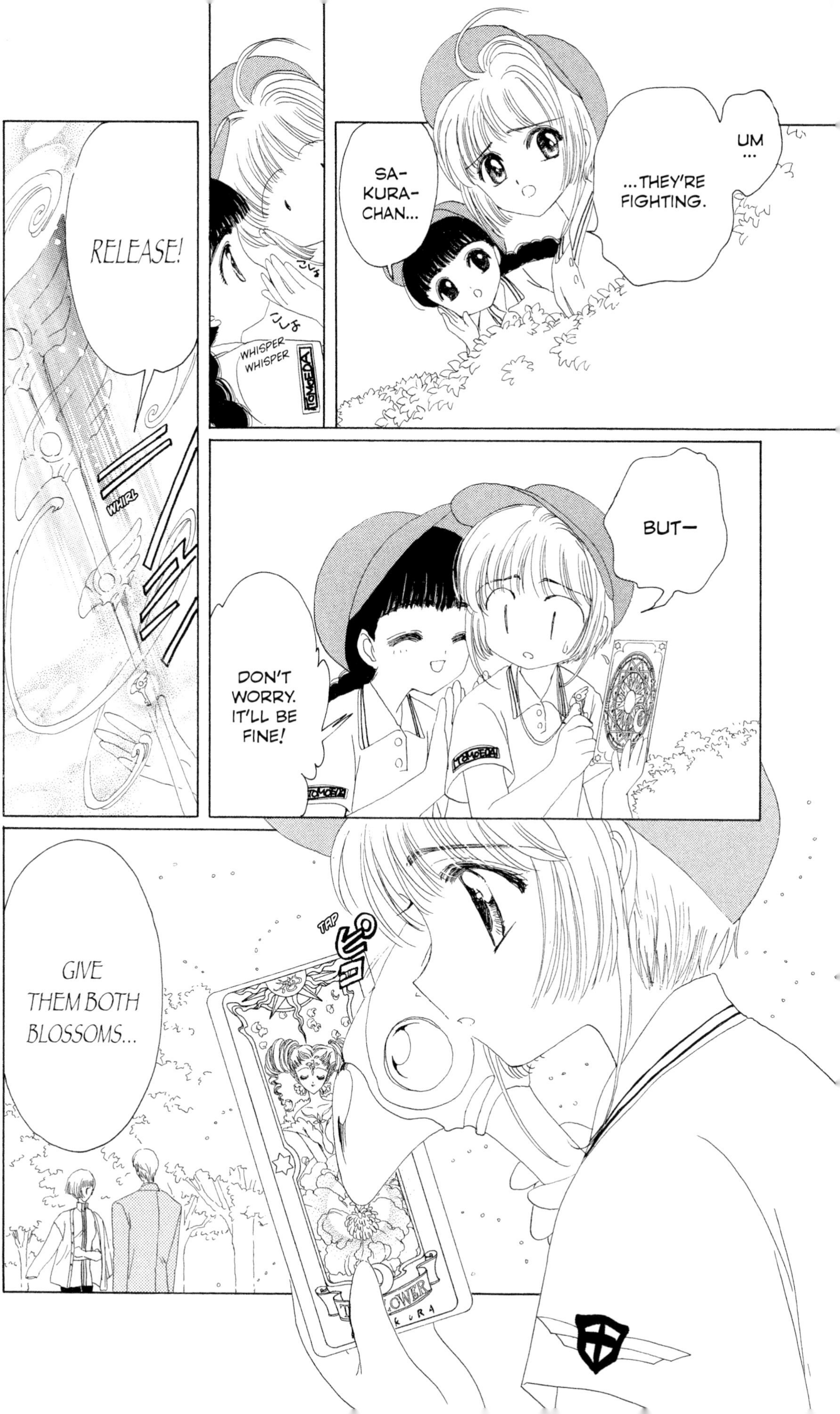
UM ...
...THEY'RE FIGHTING.
SA-KURA-CHAN...
WHISPER WHISPER
BUT—
DON'T WORRY. IT'LL BE FINE!
RELEASE!
WHIRL
TAP
GIVE THEM BOTH BLOSSOMS...

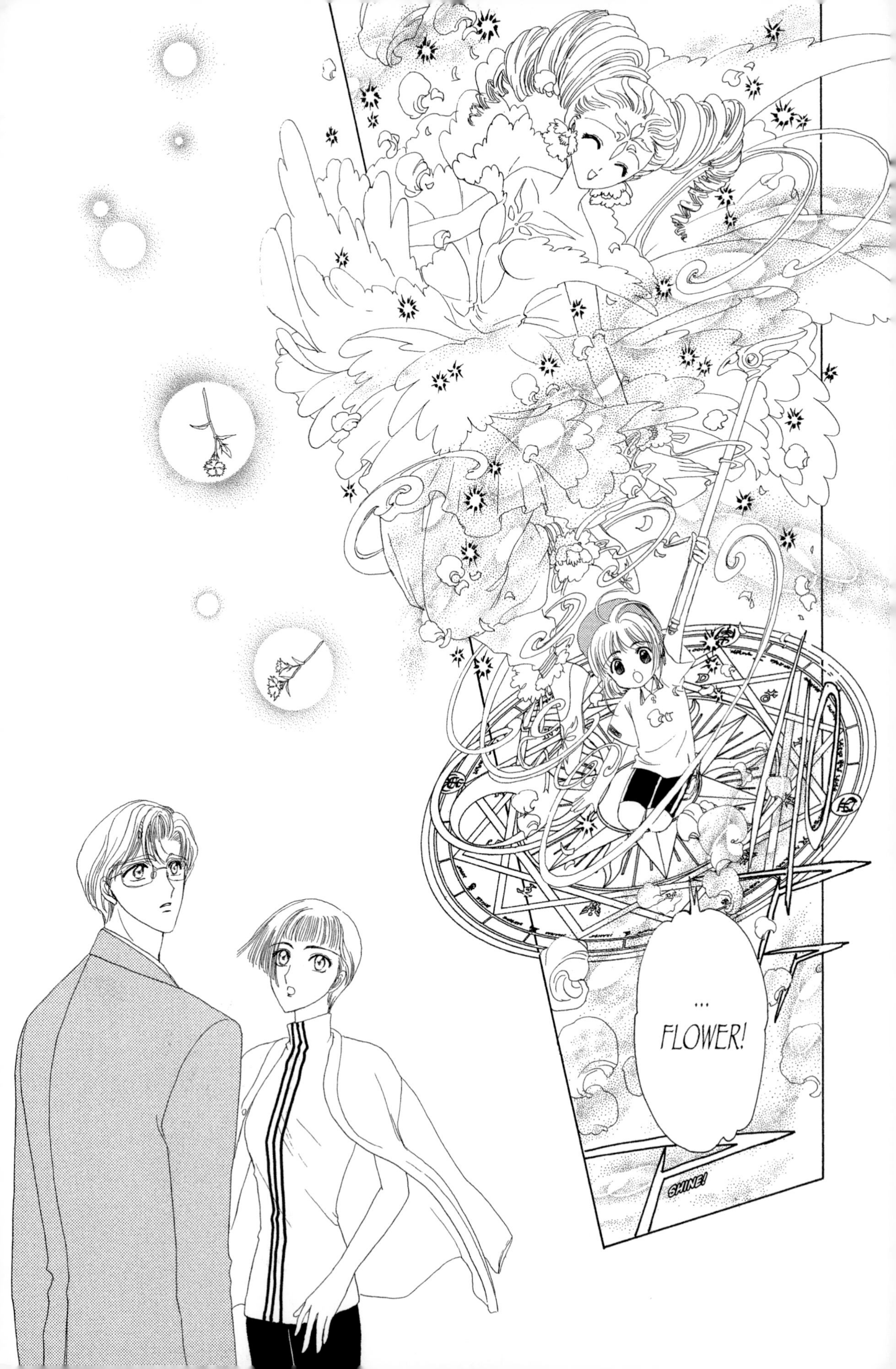
...
FLOWER!
SHINE!

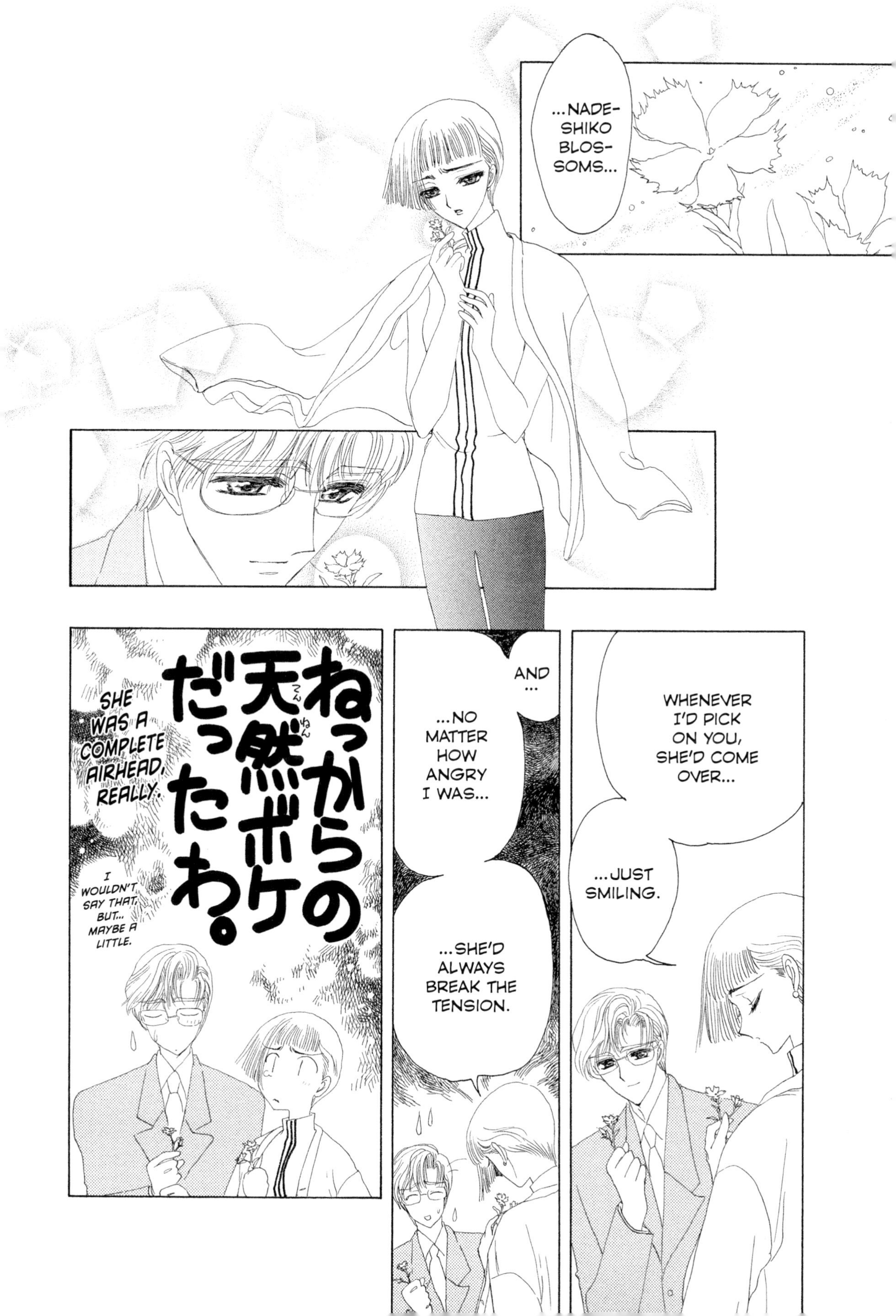

...NADE-SHIKO BLOS-SOMS...
WHENEVER I'D PICK ON YOU, SHE'D COME OVER...
...JUST SMILING.
AND ...
...NO MATTER HOW ANGRY I WAS...
...SHE'D ALWAYS BREAK THE TENSION.
ねっからの天然ボケだったわ。
SHE WAS A COMPLETE AIRHEAD, REALLY.
I WOULDN'T SAY THAT, BUT... MAYBE A LITTLE.

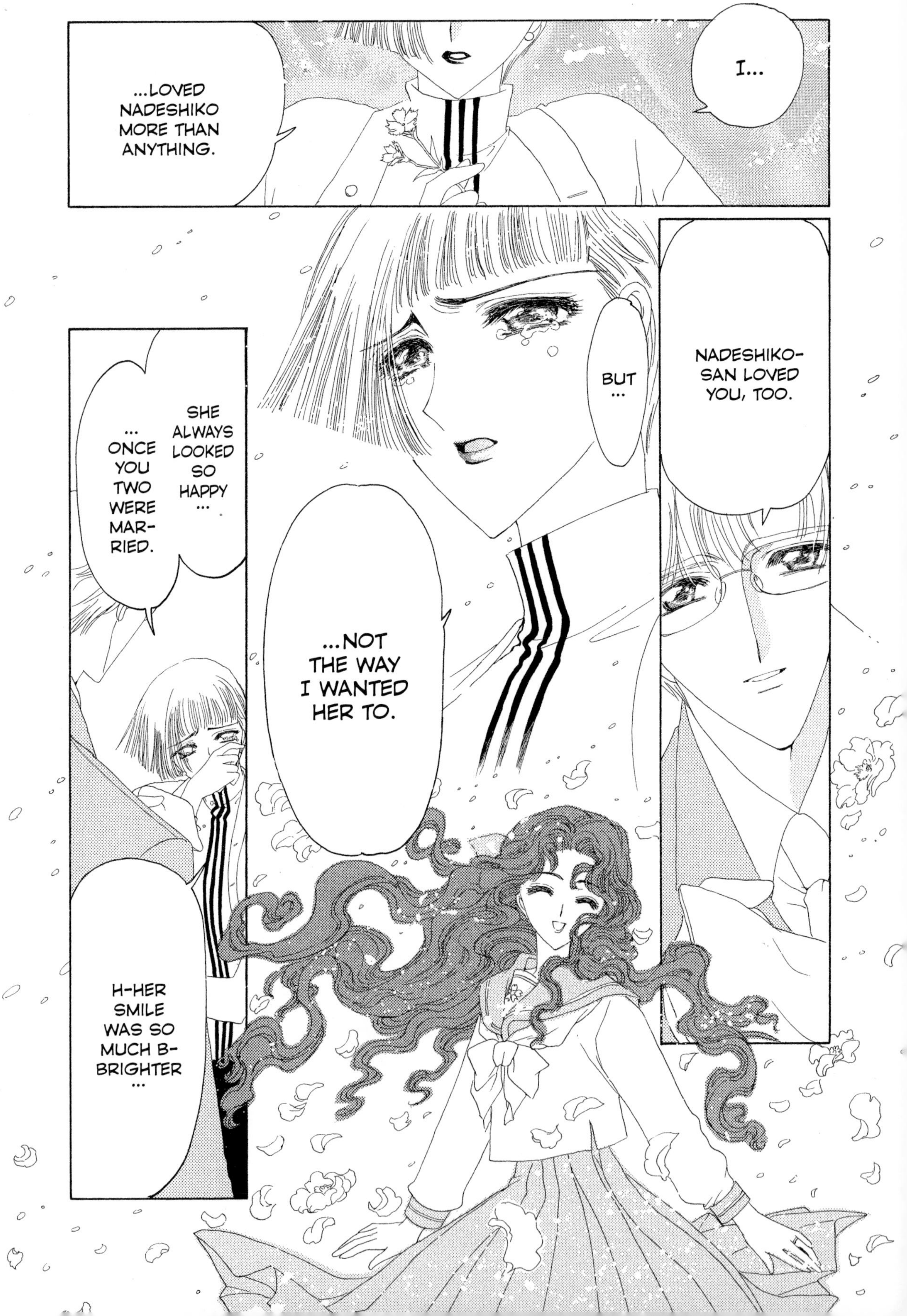
I...
...LOVED NADESHIKO MORE THAN ANYTHING.
NADESHIKO-SAN LOVED YOU, TOO.
BUT ...
...NOT THE WAY I WANTED HER TO.
SHE ALWAYS LOOKED SO HAPPY ...
... ONCE YOU TWO WERE MAR-RIED.
H-HER SMILE WAS SO MUCH B-BRIGHTER ...

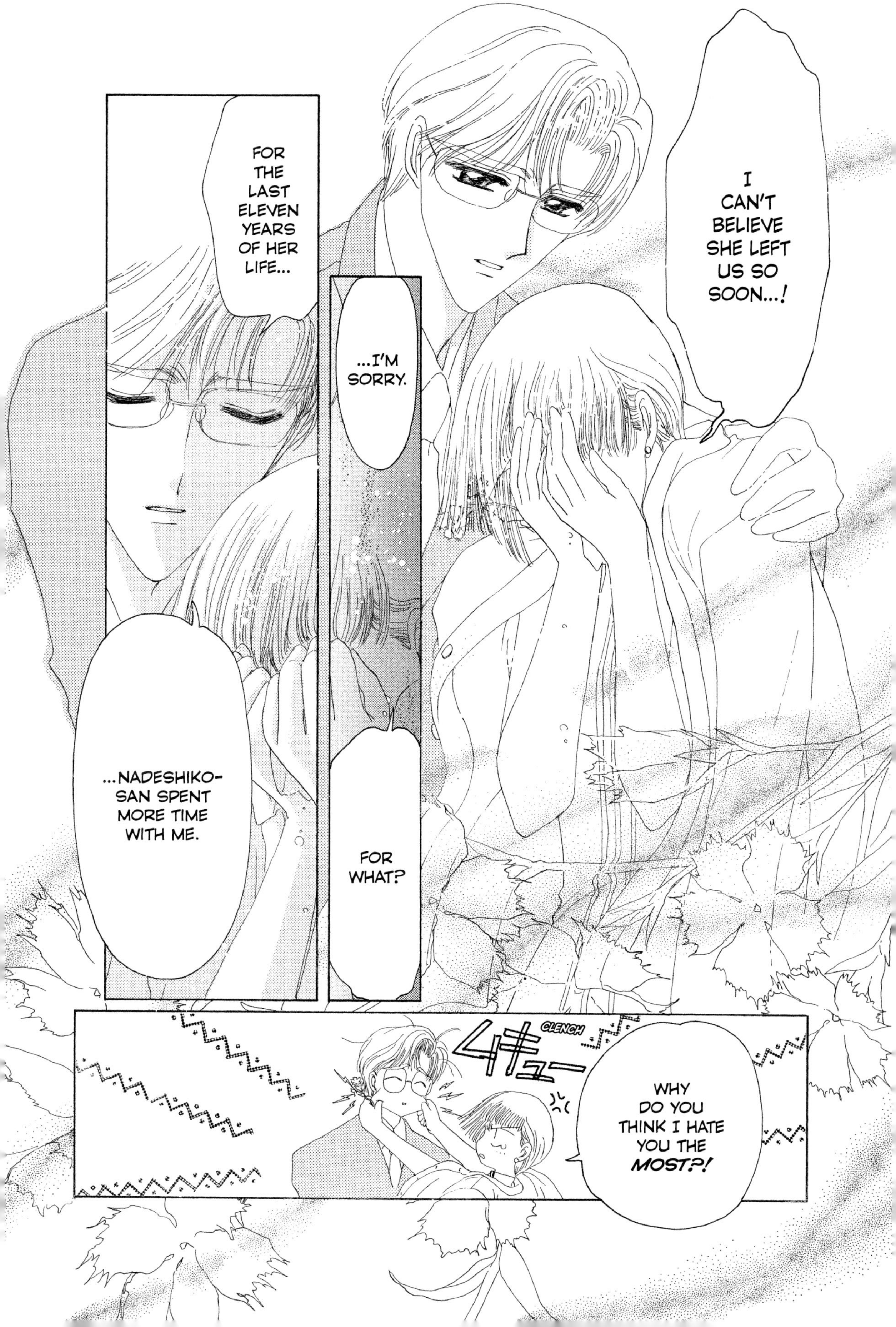
I CAN'T BELIEVE SHE LEFT US SO SOON...!
...I'M SORRY.
FOR WHAT?
FOR THE LAST ELEVEN YEARS OF HER LIFE...
...NADESHIKO-SAN SPENT MORE TIME WITH ME.
ムギュー
CLENCH
WHY DO YOU THINK I HATE YOU THE ***MOST?!***

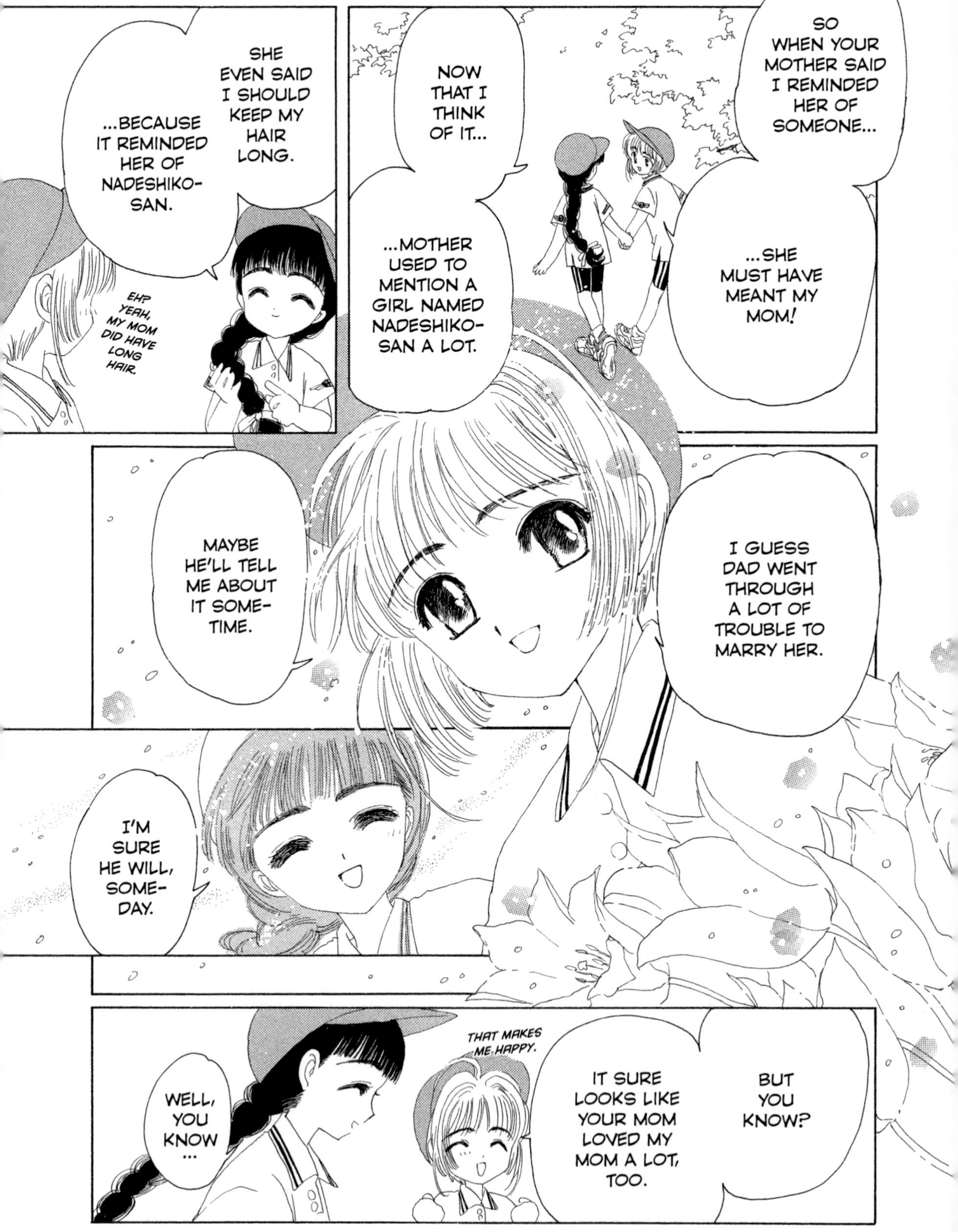
SO WHEN YOUR MOTHER SAID I REMINDED HER OF SOMEONE...
...SHE MUST HAVE MEANT MY MOM!
NOW THAT I THINK OF IT...
...MOTHER USED TO MENTION A GIRL NAMED NADESHIKO-SAN A LOT.
SHE EVEN SAID I SHOULD KEEP MY HAIR LONG.
...BECAUSE IT REMINDED HER OF NADESHIKO-SAN.
EH? YEAH, MY MOM DID HAVE LONG HAIR.
I GUESS DAD WENT THROUGH A LOT OF TROUBLE TO MARRY HER.
MAYBE HE'LL TELL ME ABOUT IT SOME-TIME.
I'M SURE HE WILL, SOME-DAY.
BUT YOU KNOW?
IT SURE LOOKS LIKE YOUR MOM LOVED MY MOM A LOT, TOO.
THAT MAKES ME HAPPY.
WELL, YOU KNOW ...

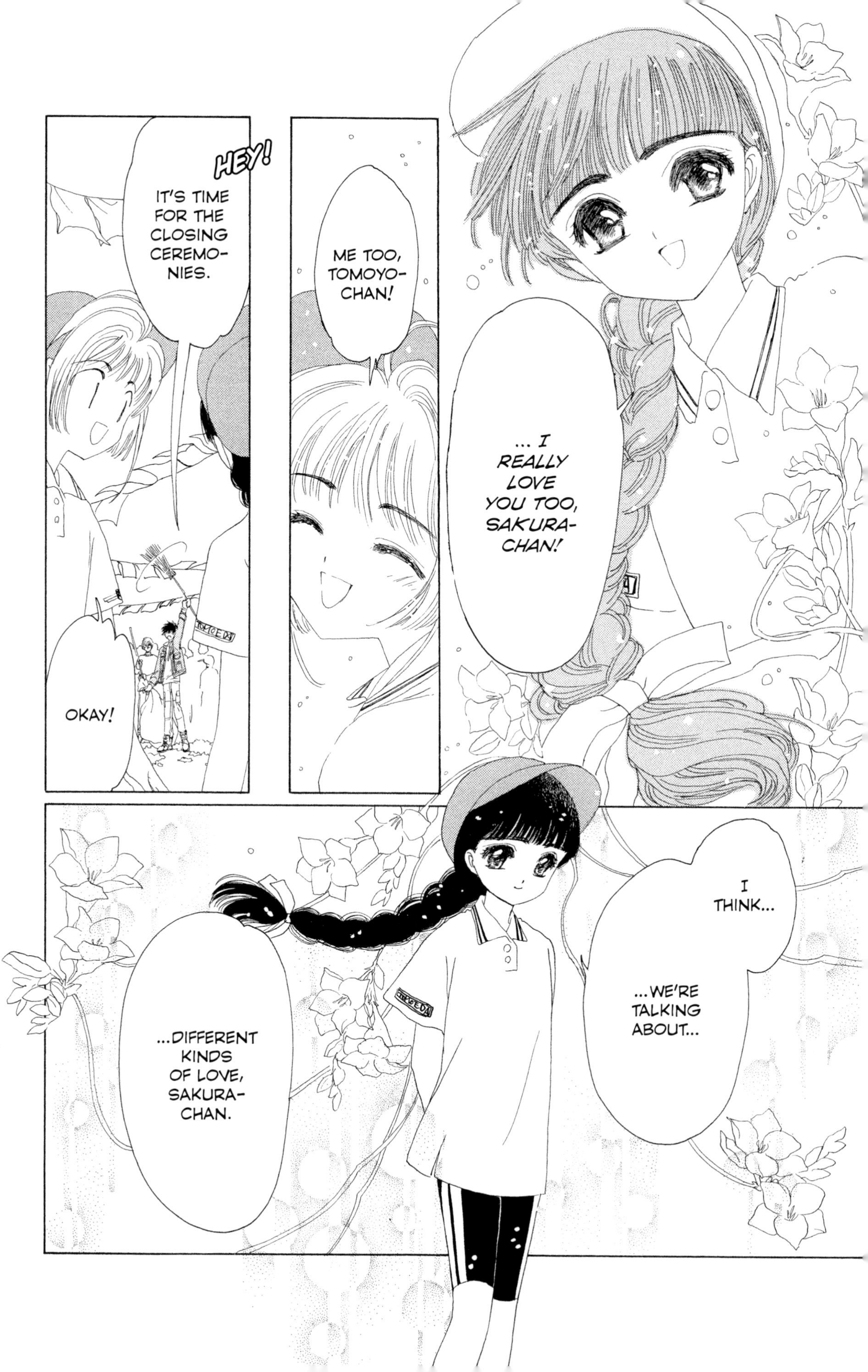
... I REALLY LOVE YOU TOO, SAKURA-CHAN!
ME TOO, TOMOYO-CHAN!
HEY!
IT'S TIME FOR THE CLOSING CEREMONIES.
OKAY!
I THINK...
...WE'RE TALKING ABOUT...
...DIFFERENT KINDS OF LOVE, SAKURA-CHAN.

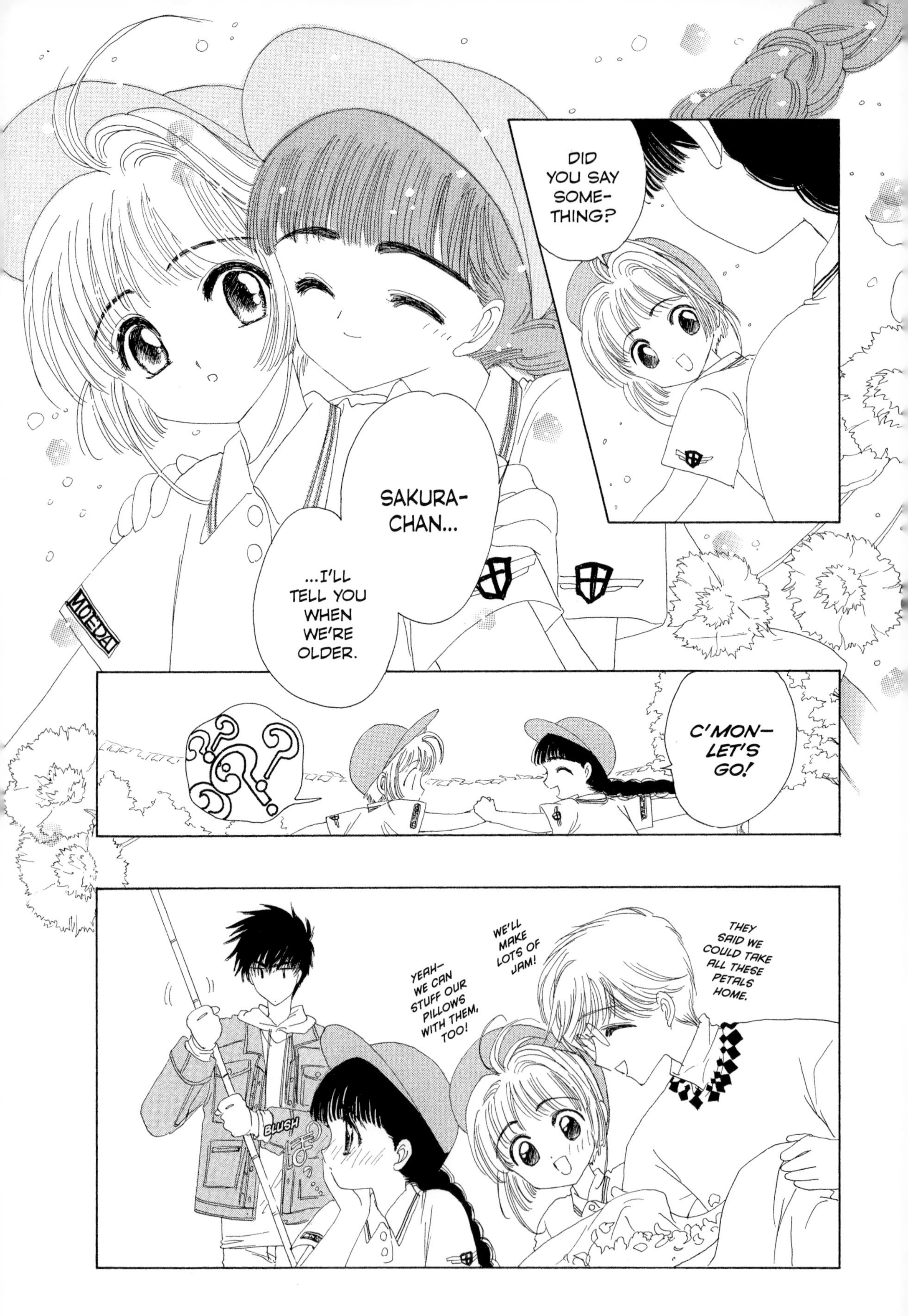
DID YOU SAY SOME-THING?
SAKURA-CHAN...
...I'LL TELL YOU WHEN WE'RE OLDER.
C'MON—LET'S GO!
THEY SAID WE COULD TAKE ALL THESE PETALS HOME.
WE'LL MAKE LOTS OF JAM!
YEAH—WE CAN STUFF OUR PILLOWS WITH THEM, TOO!
BLUSH

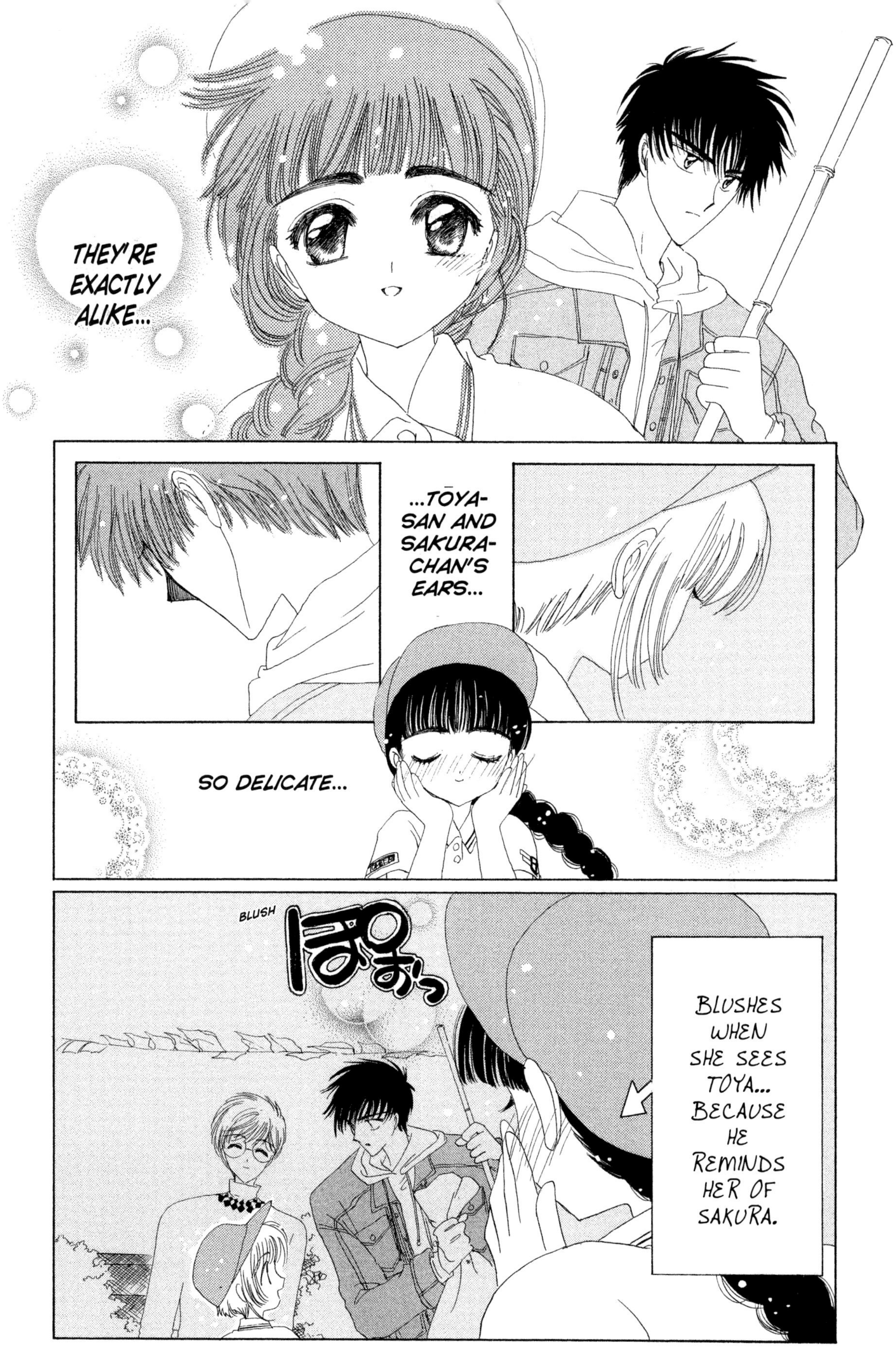
THEY'RE EXACTLY ALIKE...
...TŌYA-SAN AND SAKURA-CHAN'S EARS...
SO DELICATE...
BLUSHES WHEN SHE SEES TOYA... BECAUSE HE REMINDS HER OF SAKURA.
BLUSH
ぽおっ

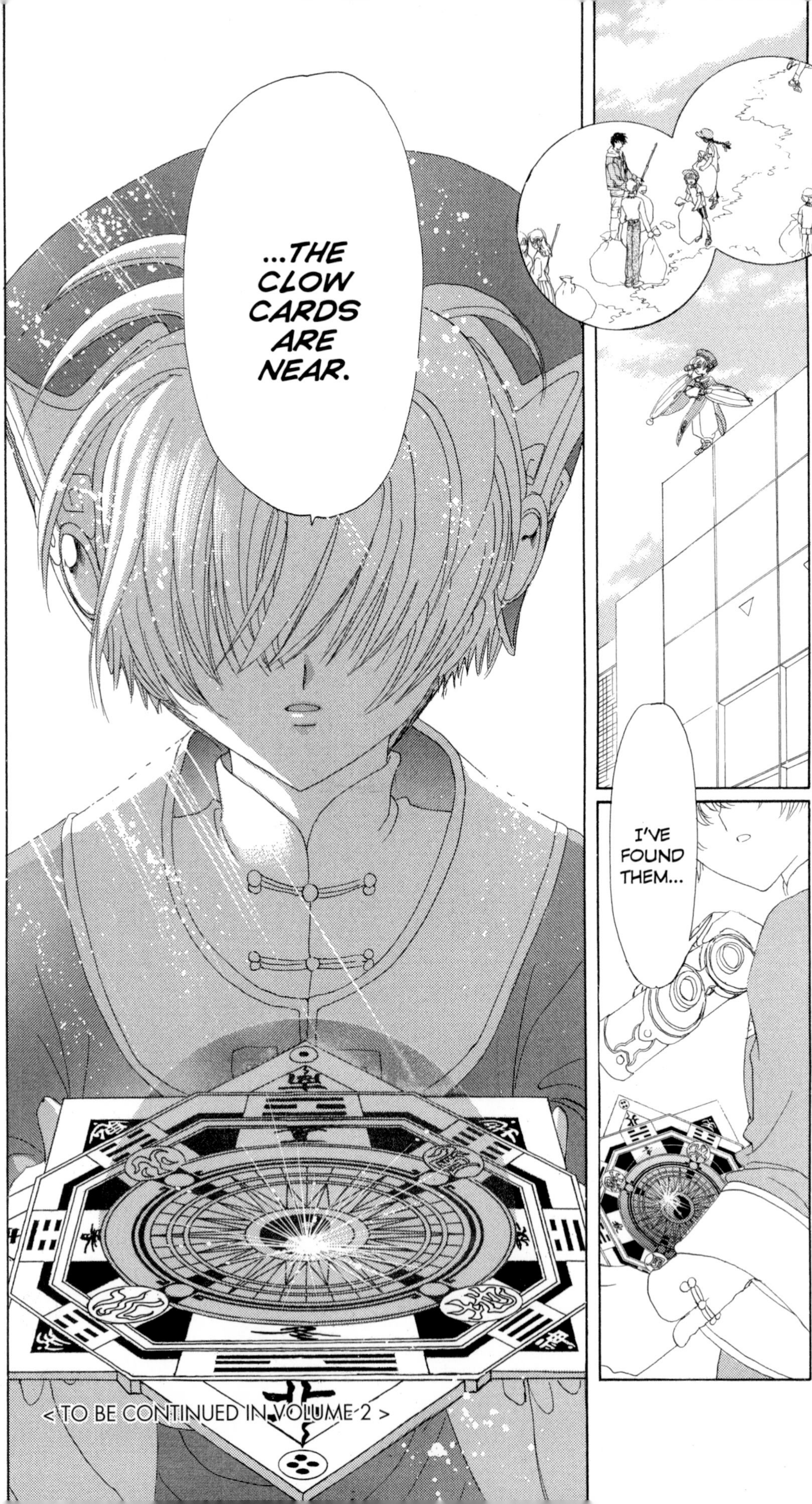
I'VE FOUND THEM...
...THE CLOW CARDS ARE NEAR.
< TO BE CONTINUED IN VOLUME 2 >

Translation Notes

Japanese is a tricky language for most Westerners, and translation is often more art than science. For your edification and reading pleasure, here are notes on some of the places where we could have gone in a different direction with our translation of the work, or where a Japanese cultural reference is used.

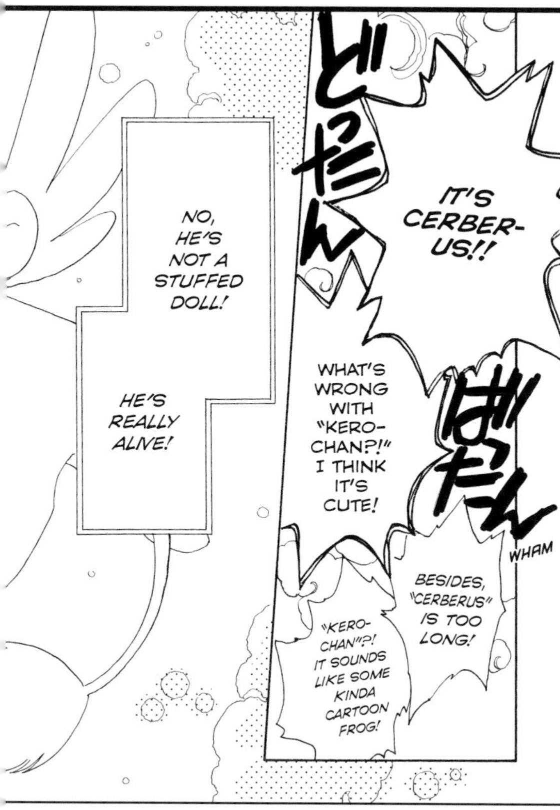
どったん
IT'S CERBERUS!!
WHAT'S WRONG WITH "KERO-CHAN?!" I THINK IT'S CUTE!
ばったん
WHAM
BESIDES, "CERBERUS" IS TOO LONG!
"KERO-CHAN"?! IT SOUNDS LIKE SOME KINDA CARTOON FROG!
NO, HE'S NOT A STUFFED DOLL!
HE'S REALLY ALIVE!

"'Kero-chan'?! It sounds like some kinda cartoon frog!" page 17

He has a legitimate complaint! In Japanese, "Cerberus" is pronounced *keruberos,* which Sakura shortens to "Kero." This happens to also be the Japanese word for "ribbit," the noise a frog makes, and has been made most famous by Sanrio's character Keroppi.

***"Hagure Keiji* is my favorite!" page 52**

Hagure Keiji: Junjouha was a police drama series that ran in Japan from 1988 through 2009. Although the series focuses on crimes, it is generally light-hearted and kid-friendly. The series features a gruff but well-meaning detective somewhat reminiscent of *Colombo,* with a close group of coworkers supporting his mystery-solving efforts in the vein of *Hawaii Five-O.*

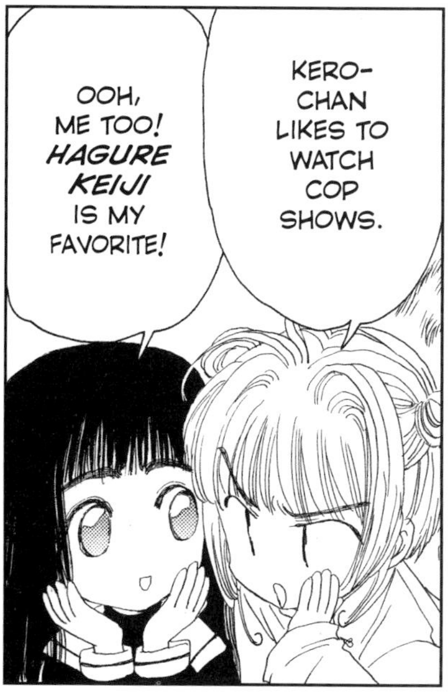
KERO-CHAN LIKES TO WATCH COP SHOWS.
OOH, ME TOO! *HAGURE KEIJI* IS MY FAVORITE!

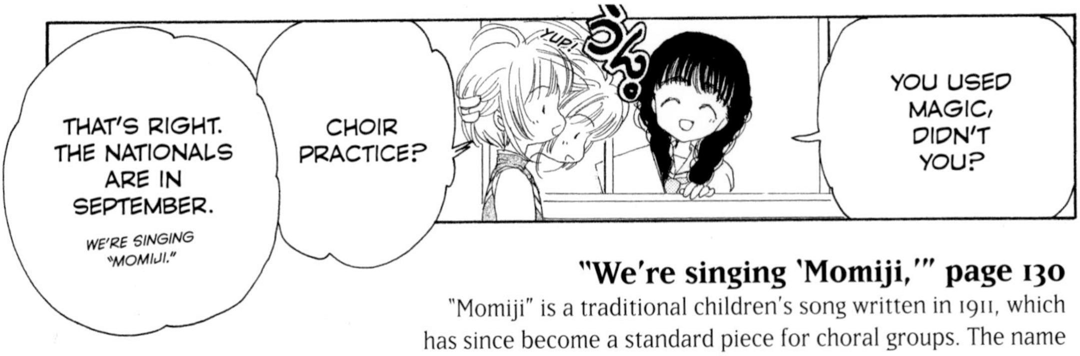
YOU USED MAGIC, DIDN'T YOU?
YUP!
うん
CHOIR PRACTICE?
THAT'S RIGHT. THE NATIONALS ARE IN SEPTEMBER.
WE'RE SINGING "MOMIJI."

"We're singing 'Momiji,'" page 130

"Momiji" is a traditional children's song written in 1911, which has since become a standard piece for choral groups. The name means "Autumn Leaves" (sometimes also translated as "Autumn Colors"). Since it's still summer, apparently Tomoyo's group is taking plenty of time to get ready for nationals!

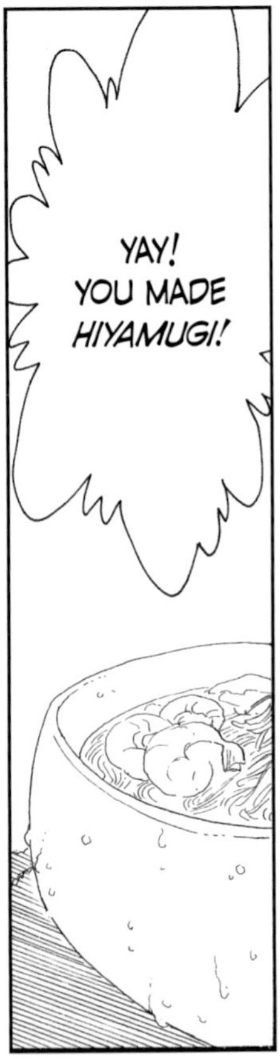
YAY! YOU MADE *HIYAMUGI!*

"Yay! You made *hiyamugi!*" page 139

Hiyamugi are a wheat-based noodle somewhat thinner than udon, and are generally served cold with a mild dipping sauce to provide a refreshing meal on a hot day.

"She was still wearing her sailor suit!" page 209

Sonomi isn't referring to the actual clothes Nadeshiko was wearing the day she married Sakura's father, and she isn't implying that Nadeshiko was in the navy! Rather, "sailor suit" refers to the school uniform Nadeshiko would have been wearing at that age, which students might wear for junior or senior high school (equivalent to grades seven through twelve).

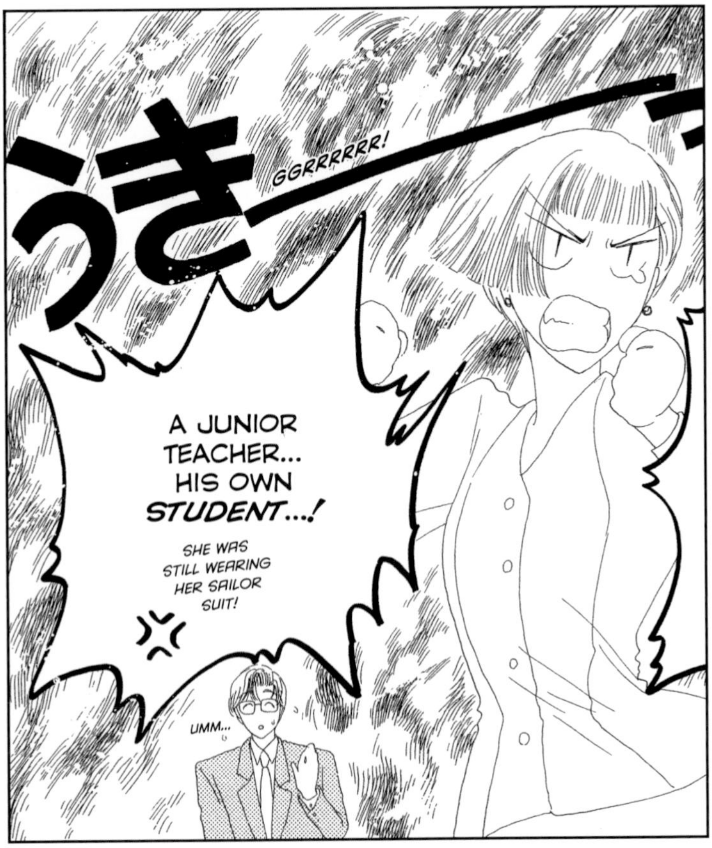
うきーーー
GGRRRRRR!
A JUNIOR TEACHER... HIS OWN *STUDENT*...!
SHE WAS STILL WEARING HER SAILOR SUIT!
UMM...